Forensic Psychology

JOANNA POZZULO
Carleton University

CRAIG BENNELL
Carleton University

ADELLE FORTH
Carleton University

Boston Columbus Indianapolis New York San Francisco Upper Saddle River
Amsterdam Cape Town Dubai London Madrid Milan Munich Paris Montréal Toronto
Delhi Mexico City São Paulo Sydney Hong Kong Seoul Singapore Taipei Tokyo

Editorial Director: Craig Campanella
Editor in Chief: Jessica Mosher
Executive Editor: Susan Hartman
Editorial Assistant: Shivangi Ramachandran
Director of Marketing: Brandy Dawson
Marketing Manager: Wendy Albert
Marketing Assistant: Frank Alarcon
Director of Production: Lisa Iarkowski
Managing Editor: Denise Forlow
Production Project Manager: Annemarie Franklin
Senior Manufacturing and Operations Manager for Arts & Sciences: Mary Fischer

Operations Specialist: Diane Peirano
Art Director, Cover: Jayne Conte
Cover Designer: Bruce Kenselaar
Cover Art: Shutterstock
Senior Digital Media Editor: Peter Sabatini
Digital Media Project Manager: Pam Weldin
Full-Service Project Management: Muralidharan Krishnamurthy
Composition: S4Carlisle Publishing Services
Printer/Binder: Courier/Westford
Cover Printer: Lehigh-Phoenix Color/Hagerstown
Text Font: 10/12 Times LT Std

Credits and acknowledgments borrowed from other sources and reproduced, with permission, in this textbook appear on the appropriate page within text [or on page 418].

Library of Congress Cataloging-in-Publication Data

Pozzulo, Joanna.
  Forensic psychology/Joanna Pozzulo, Craig Bennell, Adelle Forth.—1st ed.
    p. cm.
  ISBN 978-0-205-20927-9—ISBN 0-205-20927-0
  1. Forensic psychology. I. Bennell, Craig. II. Forth, Adelle E. III. Title.
  RA1148.P69 2013
  614′.15—dc23
                       2012029001

10 9 8 7 6 5 4 3 2 1

ISBN 10:   0-205-20927-0
ISBN 13: 978-0-205-20927-9

*This book is dedicated to our many students
who challenge our thinking and inspire us.*

BRIEF CONTENTS

CONTENTS

PREFACE

This is an exciting time in the field of forensic psychology, with many new developments by theorists and researchers. For example, new insights into the biological underpinnings of antisocial behavior, innovative methods for interviewing child witnesses, theories of women offending, and novel methods of assessing violence risk have been developed. *Forensic Psychology* is designed primarily for use in undergraduate courses, although graduate students and practitioners may find the comprehensive and up-to-date summary of key areas a useful resource.

We have taken a broad-based perspective that incorporates both experimental and clinical topics. The text covers topics that might otherwise be discussed in traditional social and cognitive psychology courses—including eyewitness testimony, jury decision making, and police procedures—as well as topics that are clinical in nature and might otherwise be discussed in traditional personality or abnormal psychology courses—such as the meaning of competency to stand trial, mentally disordered offenders, sex offenders, and psychopathy. Our goal is to present the important ideas, issues, and research in a way that students will understand and enjoy, and in some cases find them useful in their professional careers. To provide students with a glimpse into the life of an academic, each chapter includes a profile of a prominent U.S. researcher. We hope that the academic community will find this textbook a valuable teaching tool that provides a comprehensive and current coverage of forensic psychology.

DISTINGUISHING FEATURES

The pedagogical aids are designed to promote student learning and assist instructors in presenting key material. Important features include the following:

- *Learning Objectives and End-of-Chapter Summaries.* Each chapter starts with a list of learning objectives to guide students' learning of the material and closes with a summary linked to the learning objectives.
- *Vignettes.* Chapter-opening vignettes provide students with a context for the key concepts they will encounter in each chapter. These engaging vignettes present real-world scenarios in which students, or people they know, could potentially find themselves.
- *Boxes.* Boxed features within the chapters provide interesting asides to the main text. Some detail current American cases and legal rulings, while others highlight "hot" topics in the news that have not yet been the subject of much psychological research. These boxes will develop students' consciousness of current issues and hopefully spark some research ideas.
- *Case Studies.* With the case studies, students are encouraged to take an active role—putting themselves in the shoes of judges, forensic psychologists, police officers, and so on—in applying material from the chapter to a related scenario.
- *In the Media.* These boxes highlight current issues being portrayed in the media that relate to the chapter topics.
- *Profiles of U.S. Researchers.* To expose students to the varied and excellent research in forensic psychology being conducted by Americans, each chapter includes a profile of a key American researcher whose work is relevant to the chapter topic. These profiles highlight educational background, current position, and research interests, along with a little about the researcher's personal life, so students realize they are people too.
- *Research Methodology.* Research methodology specific to forensic topics is described in the relevant chapters, with the goal of helping students understand how studies in forensic psychology are conducted.

- *Research Studies.* Data reported in original studies is cited throughout the textbook, often in graph or table form for easy interpretation. Diagrams of psychological models and flow charts demonstrate key processes that occur through the criminal justice system.
- *Theoretical Perspectives.* Theories relevant to specific topics areas are described in each of the relevant chapters. The discussion of the various theories emphasizes a multidisciplinary approach, showing the interplay among cognitive, biological, and social factors in understanding the different forensic psychology areas.
- *Law. Forensic Psychology* provides the student with information on current U.S. law relevant to the psychological issues discussed.
- *Discussion Questions.* Several discussion questions are offered at the end of each chapter. Instructors can assign these questions for group discussion, or students can use the questions to examine their comprehension and retention of the chapter material. We hope these questions will inspire critical thought in students.
- *Key Terms and Glossary.* Throughout the chapters, key words with which students in forensic psychology should be familiar with appear in bold type and are defined in marginal notes. These key terms and their definitions are also provided in a glossary at the end of the book for easy reference.

SUPPLEMENTS FOR INSTRUCTORS

Pearson is pleased to offer the following supplements to qualified instructors.

- **Instructor's Manual with Tests** (0-205-94928-2): The instructor's manual is a wonderful tool for classroom preparation and management. Corresponding to the chapters in the text, each of the manual's chapters contains a brief overview of the chapter with suggestions on how to present the material, sample lecture outlines, classroom activities and discussion topics, ideas for in-class and out-of-class projects, and recommended outside readings. The test bank contains multiple-choice, short answer, and essay questions, each referencing the relevant page in the text.
- **MySearchLab** (0-205-94993-2): MySearchLab with eText provides engaging experiences that personalize learning, and comes from a trusted partner with educational expertise and a deep commitment to helping students and instructors achieve their goals.
  - **Survey Tool:** Instructors can survey their students and generate real-time customized reports.
  - **eText:** Just like the printed text, you can highlight and add notes to the eText or download it to your iPad.
  - **Assessment:** Chapter quizzes and flashcards offer immediate feedback and report directly to the gradebook.
  - **Writing and Research:** A wide range of writing, grammar, and research tools and access to a variety of academic journals and Census data help you hone your writing and research skills.

ACKNOWLEDGMENTS

This book would never have come to fruition had we not been mentored by outstanding forensic researchers. Joanna Pozzulo is indebted to Rod Lindsay at Queen's University for his unfailing support, his rich insights, and his commitment to academic excellence that she aspires to achieve. Craig Bennell is grateful to David Canter at the University of Liverpool for providing a stimulating intellectual environment in which to study and for teaching him how to think critically. Adelle Forth wishes to express her admiration, respect, and gratitude to Robert Hare at the University of British Columbia, who nurtured her interest in the area of psychopathy and who has provided consistent support and guidance. These researchers continue to be a source of inspiration to us.

We would like to acknowledge that the forensic program at Carleton University, of which we are part, would not exist without our colleagues Shelley Brown, Kevin Nunes, and Ralph Serin who have contributed to our program and our thinking of forensic issues.

We are thankful to the exceptional researchers we profiled in this textbook for giving us their time and insight into their life. Specifically, Curt Bartol, Linda Teplin, Saul Kassin, Richard Rogers, Elizabeth Loftus, Stephen Ceci, Bette Bottoms, Hank Steadman, Francis Cullen, John Monahan, Joseph Newman, Rolf Loeber, Murray Strauss, and Raymond Knight. All have made significant contributions to the field of forensic psychology.

We would like to thank the reviewers who provided us with exceptional feedback that allowed us to make the textbook stronger. Reviewers include the following:

Robert Morgan
Texas Tech University

Mohammad Khalid Hamza
Lamar University

Éva Szeli
Arizona State University

Kathleen Hart
Xavier University

Zeiven Beitchman
Nova Southeastern University

Jennifer Beaudry
University of South Carolina Beaufort

Andy Young
Lubbock Christian University

Russell Espinoza
California State University

Dan Murrie
University of Virginia

Jessica Langley
University of New Haven

Michael Vitacco
Medical College of Georgia

We have tried to incorporate as many of the suggestions as possible, but of course we were restricted in terms of page length. In the end, we feel this textbook provides excellent breadth and good depth.

We thank our many undergraduate and graduate students who over the years have challenged our thinking and who have influenced the ideas expressed in this book. We also would like to thank the great staff at Pearson. Susan Hartman, Jessica Mosher, Shivangi Ramachandran, and Muralidharan Krishnamurthy at S4Carlisle Publishing Services deserve special mention—this book would not exist without their enthusiasm, expertise, and dedication. Tara Tovell (copy editor), Amanda Wesson (production editor), and Sandy Cooke (photo researcher) also played important roles in making *Forensic Psychology* become a reality.

Finally on a personal note, Joanna Pozzulo would like to thank her nieces, Jessica and Emma, for making her feel like the coolest aunt ever. She also would like to thank Craig and Adelle for being great collaborators, dear friends, and putting up with her idiosyncrasies. Craig Bennell would like to thank his wife Cindy for her love, patience, and support during the long hours of writing, and his sons Noah and Elijah for making him always remember what is most important. Adelle Forth would like to thank her partner, colleague, and friend, John Logan, for his insights, suggestions, and feedback that improved the book, as well as his understanding and support while preparing the book. She would also like to acknowledge the contribution of her numerous four-legged furry friends for keeping her sane.

ABOUT THE AUTHORS

Dr. Joanna Pozzulo is a Professor in the Department of Psychology at Carleton University in Canada. Dr. Pozzulo's research and teaching falls under the domain of Forensic Psychology (borrowing from developmental, social, and cognitive psychology). Dr. Pozzulo is focused on understanding the development of face memory and the procedures that police can use to increase the reliability of face identification from lineups wth an emphasis on children's identification evidence. Dr. Pozzulo also is a child clinical psychologist registered with the Ontario College of Psychologists.

Dr. Craig Bennell is an Associate Professor in the Department of Psychology at Carleton University in Canada where he also serves as Director of the Police Research Lab. Research in Dr. Bennell's lab is focused on assessing the reliability and validity of procedures used within criminal investigations, such as offender profiling, and in understanding the factors that influence police decision making, particularly in use of force encounters. Dr. Bennell is currently the co-editor of the Journal of Police and Criminal Psychology and the incoming President of the Society for Police and Criminal Psychology. He teaches classes in forensic psychology and police psychology.

Dr. Adelle Forth is an Associate Professor in the Department of Psychology at Carleton University in Canada where she also serves as Director of the Psychopathy Research Lab. She conducts research on the validity of the construct of psychopathy in different populations, the emotional and cognitive processes that underlie psychopathy, evaluating the impact psychopaths have on victims, and violence risk assessment. Dr. Forth is currently on the board of directors for the Society for the Scientific Study of Psychopathy. She teaches forensic psychology classes both at the undergraduate and graduate level.

An Introduction to Forensic Psychology

LEARNING OBJECTIVES

- Provide a narrow and a broad definition of forensic psychology.

- Describe the differences between clinical and experimental forensic psychology.

- List the three ways in which psychology and the law can interact.

- Identify some of the major milestones in the history of forensic psychology.

- List criteria used in the United States to decide when expert testimony is admissible.

Jennifer Chen is a university student who wants to become a forensic psychologist. She has just finished watching her favorite movie, *The Silence of the Lambs*. In fact, Jennifer always seems to be watching movies like this. If she's not watching movies, Jennifer's watching television shows like *CSI* and *Criminal Minds*, or reading the latest true crime book. Fortunately, Jennifer's neighbor works as a probation officer and she has come into regular contact with forensic psychologists. This neighbor has repeatedly told Jennifer that forensic psychology isn't necessarily what you see in the movies. Jennifer finally decides to find out for herself what forensic psychology is all about and enrolls in a course, much like the one you are currently taking.

Although you may not appreciate it yet, **forensic psychology** is all around you. Every time you turn on the television or pick up the newspaper, there are stories that relate directly to the field of forensic psychology. Hollywood has also gotten in on the act. More and more often, blockbuster movies focus on issues that are related directly to the field of forensic psychology—whether it is profiling serial killers, selecting jury members, or determining someone's sanity. Unfortunately, the way in

Forensic psychology

A field of psychology that deals with all aspects of human behavior as it relates to the law or legal system

Gene Hackman's role as a jury consultant in John Grisham's *Runaway Jury* relates to a task that some forensic psychologists are involved in. However, much of what is seen in this Hollywood movie is an exaggeration of what actually occurs in jury selection.

which the media portray forensic psychology is usually inaccurate. Although forensic psychologists often carry out the sorts of tasks you see depicted in the movies, the way in which they carry them out is typically very different from (and certainly less glamorous than) the typical Hollywood image. One of our primary goals throughout this book is to provide you with a more accurate picture of what forensic psychology is and to encourage you to think more critically about the things you see and hear in the media. See the In the Media box on the next page for further discussion about this issue.

WHAT IS FORENSIC PSYCHOLOGY?

So, if Hollywood hasn't gotten it right, what exactly is forensic psychology? On the surface, this seems like a relatively simple question to answer, and it is undoubtedly an important question to ask. When being introduced to a new field of psychology, as you are now, one of the first questions you probably ask yourself is "What am I going to be studying?" Although providing a clear and comprehensive definition of the discipline is obviously a logical way to begin a textbook on forensic psychology, this task is far more difficult than it seems because there is no generally accepted definition of the field (Brigham, 1999). Indeed, experts in this area don't even agree on what the field should be called, let alone how it should be defined (Ogloff, 2002). For example, you will often see forensic psychology being referred to as legal psychology or criminological psychology.

Much of the ongoing debate about how forensic psychology should be defined centers on whether the definition should be narrow or broad (Brigham, 1999). A narrow definition of forensic psychology would focus on certain aspects of the field while ignoring other, potentially important aspects. For example, a narrow definition of forensic psychology might focus on clinical aspects of the field while ignoring the experimental research that many psychologists (who refer to themselves as forensic psychologists) conduct.

IN THE MEDIA   The Reality of Reality TV

Crime has always been a popular topic for TV shows and researchers are interested in understanding the role that TV plays in shaping the perceptions and attitudes of viewers toward crime-related matters. Recently, this line of research has taken on a new twist due largely to the introduction of crime-based reality TV. And no crime-based reality show has been more popular than the U.S.-based *Cops*, originally introduced by Fox network in 1989.

If shows like *Cops* are influencing the perceptions and attitudes of viewers (e.g., toward the police and their response to crime), one obvious question to ask is whether this is problematic. Of course, asking this question leads to a range of other questions, such as whether these shows present an accurate portrayal of crime and the legal system's response to it. These types of issues have recently been explored by researchers and some of the results might surprise you.

For example, despite the fact that its producers refer to the show as "unfiltered television," an analysis of *Cops* indicates quite the opposite. In contrast to how the show is pitched to viewers, some researchers have argued that *Cops* "offers a very particular and select vision of policing" (Doyle, 2003, p. 34). Indeed, rather than referring to *Cops* as reality TV, Doyle suggests it is probably best seen as *reality fiction*, a "constructed version of reality with its own biases, rather than a neutral record" (p. 35). Once one understands how shows like *Cops* are actually produced, this argument probably becomes more convincing.

Consider the following examples, highlighted by Doyle (2003):

- While the producers of *Cops* state that the show allows viewers to share a cop's point of view in "real time," this is not actually true. As Doyle shows, while each of the seven- to eight-minute vignettes that make up a *Cops* episode does tend to unfold in a linear fashion, the sequence of events is not typically presented in real time. Instead, the various parts of the vignette that are ultimately aired have often taken place over many hours, only to be edited together later. In fact, according to Doyle, each hour of *Cops* airtime is typically edited down from between 50 and 60 hours of actual footage.
- Clever techniques for giving the illusion of real-time flow are also regularly used by the editors of *Cops*. For example, as Doyle reveals, although it appears as if the visual and sound elements of *Cops* were both captured simultaneously, this is often not the case. Rather, "sound is edited to overlap cuts in the visuals . . . [with the continuing sound suggesting] continuity in time, as if the viewer has simply looked in a different direction during continuous action . . . although in fact an hour's worth of action and dialogue could have been omitted between the cuts" (p. 36).
- *Cops* is also made more realistic by ensuring that the camera crew is never seen, even during those segments of the episode when police officers are driving the camera crew to and from incidents. This involves considerable editing (e.g., of civilians reacting to the cameras). It also ensures that viewers are never left with the impression that what they are watching could ever have been impacted by the presence of TV cameras.
- Unsurprisingly, the stories selected for ultimate airing on a *Cops* episode are also delivered in a way that ensures certain audience reactions. As pointed out by Doyle, a range of story-telling techniques are used to encourage viewers to identify with the police, but not with suspects. For example, most *Cops* vignettes are hosted by a particular officer who we get to know throughout the vignette. Suspects in all vignettes remain nameless; they are criminals who have given their consent to be shown, but who otherwise remain anonymous and detached from the viewer.

So, as you proceed through this course, take some time to think about the shows that you watch. Think also about how these shows may be impacting your perceptions and attitudes toward the topics we cover and whether this is a good thing or not. Of course, reality fiction can make for great TV, but perhaps it should not shape our perceptions and attitudes about crime-related matters as much as it sometimes does.

This appears to be how many leading psychologists, and the professional associations to which they belong, prefer to define the discipline. For example, reflecting on the petition made to the American Psychological Association in 2001 to recognize forensic psychology as a specialization, Otto and Heilbrun (2002) state that "it was ultimately decided that the petition . . . should define forensic psychology narrowly, to include the primarily clinical aspects of forensic assessment, treatment, and consultation" (p. 8).

According to this definition, the only individuals who should call themselves forensic psychologists are those individuals engaged in clinical practice (i.e., assessing, treating, or consulting) within the legal system. Any psychologist who spends all of his or her time conducting forensic-related research—for example, studying the memory of eyewitnesses, examining the decision-making processes of jurors, or evaluating the effectiveness of offender treatment programs—would not technically be considered a forensic psychologist using the narrow definition of forensic psychology just presented. For reasons such as these, many psychologists have problems with using narrow definitions to define the field of forensic psychology.

By their very nature, broad definitions of forensic psychology are less restrictive than narrow definitions. One of the most commonly cited examples of a broad definition of forensic psychology is the one proposed by Dr. Curt Bartol, who is profiled in Box 1.1. Dr. Bartol and his wife, Anne, define the discipline as "(a) the research endeavor that examines aspects of human behavior directly related to the legal process . . . and (b) the professional practice of psychology within, or in consultation with, a legal system that embraces both civil and criminal law" (Bartol & Bartol, 2006, p. 3). Thus, unlike the narrow definition of forensic psychology provided above, which focuses solely on the *application* of psychology, this definition does not restrict forensic psychology to applied issues. It also focuses on the *research* that is required to inform applied practice in the field of forensic psychology.

Throughout this textbook, we adopt a broad definition of forensic psychology. Although we will often focus on the application of psychological knowledge to various aspects of the U.S. legal system, our primary goal is to demonstrate that this application of knowledge must always be based on a solid grounding of psychological research. In line with a broad definition of forensic psychology, this research frequently originates in areas of psychology that are often not obviously connected with the forensic area, such as social, cognitive, personality, and developmental psychology. The fact that forensic psychology is such an eclectic field is just one of the reasons why it is such an exciting area of study.

THE ROLES OF A FORENSIC PSYCHOLOGIST

What is consistent across the various definitions of forensic psychology that currently exist is that individuals who call themselves forensic psychologists are always interested in issues that arise at the intersection between psychology and the law. What typically differs across the definitions is the particular focus the forensic psychologist takes. For example, by looking at the definitions provided above, it is clear that forensic psychologists can take on the role of clinician or researcher. In reality, however, these roles are not mutually exclusive and one individual can take on more than one role. Indeed, some of the best-known forensic psychologists, many of whom will be profiled in this book, are both clinicians *and* researchers, while others are clinicians, researchers, *and* legal

BOX 1.1   Researcher Profile: Dr. Curt Bartol

Undecided about what he was going to do with his life, Dr. Curt Bartol's undergraduate major at the University of Maine changed almost weekly, beginning with engineering but quickly shifting to premed, business, forestry, wildlife management, and finally to psychology. His professional career followed a similar shifting, fortuitous odyssey. After a stint in the military, he became a social caseworker, attended graduate school in social work, and became a casework supervisor in child welfare. Although social work was a rewarding personal experience, it did not satisfy the strong interest in research that Dr. Bartol had discovered while majoring in psychology.

Dr. Curt Bartol

In 1968, Dr. Bartol enrolled in a graduate program in clinical psychology at Northern Illinois University. Still fascinated with well-executed research, he changed his Ph.D. concentration to personality/social psychology and worked with Professors Randall B. Martin and Martin F. Kaplan. His research interests and doctoral dissertation focused on the personality theory of Hans J. Eysenck, a theory that moved him in the direction of studying criminal behavior.

Four years later, Ph.D. in hand, Dr. Bartol began teaching at Castleton State College in Vermont. Vermont provided him with his first opportunity to consult with the law enforcement community, something he continues to do today. He also taught at the police academy and served on executive boards, including one offering several years of consultation services to the Behavioral Science Unit of the FBI.

Dr. Bartol's serious involvement in police psychology began shortly after receiving his Ph.D. when he was asked to teach a course in abnormal psychology at a state police academy. Shortly thereafter, law enforcement agencies began seeking his help in dealing with various psychological issues, such as job stress, interactions with people with mental disorders, screening and selection, profiling, and fitness-for-duty evaluations. In addition to a heavy teaching load, he soon found himself sliding into longer and longer hours of consulting and training. He became a certified police academy instructor in crisis intervention, interviewing and interrogation, hostage and crisis negotiations, and criminal psychology, and he helped establish standards for psychological evaluation procedures and methods.

These experiences rapidly expanded into providing psychological services to virtually every law enforcement agency in Vermont. Soon, other state and federal agencies requested clinical and research services from Dr. Bartol and it dawned on him that the workload was getting out of hand. However, this experience also emphasized to him that psychologists interested in providing services to law enforcement have many opportunities. This service is especially appreciated by police agencies if it is research based and has considerable validity in its application.

The informality of a small college setting also helped Dr. Bartol launch his incredible writing career. He wrote his first book, *Criminal Behavior: A Psychosocial Approach*, in 1980 with his wife, Dr. Anne Bartol. This was followed shortly by another book written with Anne, entitled *Psychology and Law,* and many others, including *Introduction to Forensic Psychology* and *Current Perspectives in Forensic Psychology and Criminal Behavior.* Other recent books that Dr. Bartol has coauthored include *Juvenile Delinquency and Antisocial Behavior: A Developmental Perspective* and *Juvenile Delinquency: A Systems Approach.* Currently, he and Anne are working on a text on offender profiling.

In 1986, Dr. Bartol became book review editor of the prestigious journal, *Criminal Justice and Behavior.* Ten years later, he became editor of the journal, a position which he has held for

(continued)

BOX 1.1   *Continued*

15 years. Editing this journal is extremely time consuming, but also very satisfying. Dr. Bartol says that it helps him stay current with cutting-edge research and allows him to help young scholars get their work published.

After 32 years of college teaching, Dr. Bartol decided that he wanted to spend more time writing, editing, and in his private practice in forensic psychology. Although retired from teaching, Dr. Bartol has fond memories of the college classroom. Over the years he says he has always been invigorated, pleasantly surprised, and touched by interactions with students, and he strongly believes that, while students expect competence and expertise from their professors, they also appreciate compassion, a sense of humor, honesty, and flexibility. Reflecting back on his time as a professor, one of the things he says he has learned is that students interested in becoming forensic psychologists should focus on receiving a broad, research-based education, and it does not necessarily have to be a degree or concentration in forensic psychology.

Dr. Bartol now lives in New York with his wife, Anne, and his loyal Vizsla, J.D. (abbreviation for Juvenile Delinquent). His positive days in forestry continue to influence him and he enjoys planting and identifying trees on their acres of land. In addition to finding aquatic plants and flowers for their fish pond, Dr. Bartol most enjoys romping with his four grandkids and decorating a wooded trail for them with ornaments, lights, and surprises pertinent to the season.

---

scholars. Since we will continually touch upon these various roles throughout the upcoming chapters, we will briefly clarify what each role entails.

The Forensic Psychologist as Clinician

Clinical forensic psychologists

Psychologists who are broadly concerned with the assessment and treatment of mental health issues as they pertain to the law or legal system

Clinical forensic psychologists are broadly concerned with mental health issues as they pertain to the legal system (Otto & Heilbrun, 2002). This can include both research and practice in a wide variety of settings, such as schools, prisons, and hospitals. For example, clinical forensic psychologists are often concerned with the assessment and treatment of people with mental disorders within the context of the law. On the research side, a frequent task for the clinical forensic psychologist might involve the validation of an assessment tool that has been developed to predict the risk of an offender being violent (e.g., Kropp & Hart, 2000). On the practical side, a frequent task might involve the assessment of an offender to assist in making an accurate determination of whether that offender is likely to pose a risk to the community if released. Other issues that clinical forensic psychologists are interested in may include, but are certainly not limited to, the following:

- Divorce and child custody mediation
- Determinations of insanity and fitness to stand trial/plead guilty
- Providing expert testimony in court on questions of a psychological nature
- Personnel selection (e.g., for law enforcement agencies)
- Conducting critical incident stress debriefings with police officers
- Designing and conducting treatment programs for offenders

Clinical forensic psychologists in the United States must be licensed psychologists. The educational requirements to obtain a license vary across states, but most require a doctoral degree in psychology or a related discipline (Ph.D., Psy.D., or Ed.D.) (De Vaney Olvey, Hogg, & Counts, 2002). The licensing process also requires that applicants write a standardized exam that tests the applicant's knowledge of psychology, with many states also requiring additional exams, such as an ethics examination (De Vaney Olvey et al., 2002). Finally, to successfully obtain a license, applicants must undergo supervised practice in an appropriate setting under the watchful eye of an experienced clinical supervisor, though the number of required hours varies from state to state (De Vaney Olvey et al., 2002).

One of the most common questions that undergraduate students ask us is "What is the difference between forensic psychology and **forensic psychiatry**?" In fact, many people, including those in the media, often confuse these two fields. To some extent in the United States, clinical forensic psychology and forensic psychiatry are more similar than they are different and, as a result, it is often difficult to separate them clearly. For example, both clinical forensic psychologists and forensic psychiatrists in this country are trained to assess and treat individuals experiencing mental health problems who come into contact with the law, and you will see psychologists and psychiatrists involved in nearly every component of the criminal justice system. In addition, clinical forensic psychologists and forensic psychiatrists often engage in similar sorts of research (e.g., trying to understand the origins of violent behavior).

However, there are also important differences between the two fields. Probably the most obvious difference is that psychiatrists, including forensic psychiatrists, are medical doctors. Therefore, forensic psychiatrists undergo training that is quite different from the training clinical forensic psychologists receive, and this leads to several other distinctions between the fields. For example, in contrast to a psychiatrist's general (but not sole) reliance on a medical model of mental illness, psychologists tend to view mental illness more as a product of an individual's physiology, personality, and environment. See Box 1.2, which looks at some other important forensic-related disciplines practiced in the United States that are often confused with the field of forensic psychology.

Forensic psychiatry
A field of medicine that deals with all aspects of human behavior as it relates to the law or legal system

The Forensic Psychologist as Researcher

A second role for the forensic psychologist is that of experimenter, or researcher. As mentioned above, although this role does not necessarily have to be separate from the clinical role, it often is. As with clinical forensic psychologists, **experimental forensic psychologists** are concerned with mental health issues as they pertain to the legal system, and they can be found in a variety of criminal justice settings. However, researchers in the forensic area are usually concerned with much more than just mental health issues. Indeed, they can be interested in any research issue that relates to the law or legal system. The list of research issues that are of interest to this type of forensic psychologist is far too long to present here, but they include the following:

Experimental forensic psychologists
Psychologists who are broadly concerned with the study of human behavior as it relates to the law or legal system

- Examining the effectiveness of risk assessment strategies
- Determining what factors influence jury decision making
- Developing and testing better ways to conduct eyewitness line-ups
- Evaluating offender and victim treatment programs
- Studying the impact of questioning style on eyewitness memory recall
- Examining the effect of stress management interventions on police officers

Not only do clinical forensic psychologists differ from experimental forensic psychologists in terms of what they do, but they also differ in terms of their training. The forensic psychologist who is interested primarily in research will have typically undergone Ph.D.-level graduate training in one of many different types of experimental

BOX 1.2	Other Forensic Disciplines

Nowadays, people are being bombarded by media portrayals of various forensic disciplines, beyond just forensic psychology and forensic psychiatry. Although this does much to promote the respective specialties, it can also be the source of a lot of confusion. Listed below are brief descriptions of just a few forensic specialty areas.

- *Forensic anthropology.* Forensic anthropologists examine the remains of deceased individuals to determine how they might have died and to establish facts about them, such as their gender, age, appearance, and so forth.
- *Forensic art.* Often working in conjunction with other forensic scientists, forensic artists use art to aid in the identification, apprehension, and conviction of offenders. Forensic artists might accomplish this by drawing sketches of suspects, reconstructing faces of deceased victims, or determining how missing children might look as they age.
- *Forensic entomology.* Forensic entomologists are concerned with how insects can assist with criminal investigations. For example, forensic entomologists can help determine when someone died based on an analysis of insect presence/development on a decomposing body.
- *Forensic odontology.* Forensic odontologists study the dental aspects of criminal activity. For example, forensic odontologists might assist the police in identifying deceased individuals through an examination of dental records or they might help determine whether bite marks found on an individual were made by an adult or child.
- *Forensic pathology.* Referred to as coroners in some states, forensic pathologists are medical doctors who examine the remains of dead bodies in an attempt to determine the time and cause of death through physical autopsy.
- *Forensic podiatry.* Forensic podiatrists use their knowledge of how the feet and lower limbs function to assist with police investigations and court proceedings. Advice provided by these individuals might relate to the degree of match between footprints found at crime scenes and the footwear of potential suspects. Forensic podiatrists can also assist in determining whether gait patterns caught on security cameras match those of a particular suspect.

Sources: "Forensic entomology: The use of insects in death investigations" by G. Anderson from *Forensic Disciplines*, International Association for Identification (2012).

graduate programs (and no internship is typically required). Only some of these graduate programs will be devoted solely to the study of forensic psychology. Others will be programs in social, cognitive, personality, organizational, or developmental psychology, although the program will typically have a faculty member associated with it who is conducting research in a forensic area.

Regardless of the type of graduate program chosen, the individual's graduate research will be focused primarily on a topic related to forensic psychology (e.g., the malleability of child eyewitness memory). As can be seen in the short list of topics provided above, research in forensic psychology is eclectic and requires expertise in areas such as memory processing, decision making, and organizational issues. This is one of the reasons why the training for experimental forensic psychology is more varied than the training for clinical forensic psychology.

The Forensic Psychologist as Legal Scholar

A third role for the forensic psychologist, which is far less common than the previous two, but no less important, is that of legal scholar. According to Brigham (1999), forensic psychologists in their role as legal scholars "would most likely engage in scholarly analyses of mental health law and psychologically oriented legal movements," whereas their applied work "would most likely center around policy analysis and legislative consultation" (p. 281). Because this role is less common than the role of clinician or researcher, we will not deal with it as much throughout this textbook. However, it is important to briefly mention the impact that academic institutions in the United States have had on the development of this role. Most importantly perhaps is the role played by the University of Nebraska, the first institution to develop a joint program in psychology and law (Melton, 1990; University of Nebraska, 2010). Developed in 1974, this program still "specializes in training scholars who will be able to apply psychology and other behavioral sciences to analyses of empirical questions in law and policy." The program at the University of Nebraska has also served as a model for subsequent programs (in the United States and further afield) that are now helping to train psychologically informed legal scholars.

THE RELATIONSHIP BETWEEN PSYCHOLOGY AND LAW

Not only is forensic psychology a challenging field to be in because of the diversity of roles that a forensic psychologist can play, it is also challenging because forensic psychology can be approached from many different angles. One way of thinking about these various angles, although not the only way, has been proposed by Craig Haney, a professor of psychology at the University of California, Santa Cruz. Haney (1980) suggests there are three primary ways in which psychology and the law can relate to each other. He calls these relationships **psychology *and* the law**, **psychology *in* the law**, and **psychology *of* the law**. Throughout this textbook, we will focus on the first two relationships, psychology and the law and psychology in the law. Clinical and experimental forensic psychologists are typically involved in these areas much more often than the third area. Psychology of the law is largely the domain of the legal scholar role and, therefore, we will only touch on it very briefly.

Psychology and the law

The use of psychology to examine the operation of the legal system

Psychology in the law

The use of psychology in the legal system as that system operates

Psychology of the law

The use of psychology to examine the law itself

Psychology and the Law

In this relationship, "psychology is viewed as a separate discipline [to the law], examining and analyzing various components of the law [and the legal system] from a psychological perspective" (Bartol & Bartol, 1994, p. 2). Frequently, research that falls under the category of psychology *and* the law examines assumptions made by the law or the legal system, asking questions such as these: Are eyewitnesses accurate? Do certain interrogation techniques cause people to make false confessions? Are judges fair in the way they hand down sentences? Is it possible to accurately predict whether an offender will be violent when released from prison? When working within the area of psychology *and* the law, forensic psychologists attempt to answer these sorts of questions so that the answers can be communicated to the legal community. Much of forensic psychology deals with this particular relationship. Therefore, research issues that fall under the general heading of "psychology and the law" will be thoroughly discussed throughout this textbook.

Psychology in the Law

Once a body of psychological knowledge exists in any of the above-mentioned areas of study, that knowledge can be used in the legal system by psychologists, police officers, lawyers, judges, and others. As the label indicates, psychology *in* the law involves the use of psychological knowledge in the legal system (Haney, 1980). As with psychology and the law, psychology in the law can take many different forms. It might consist of a psychologist in court providing expert testimony concerning some issue of relevance to a particular case. For example, the psychologist might testify that, based on his or her understanding of the psychological research, the eyewitness on the stand may have incorrectly identified the defendant from a police line-up. Alternatively, psychology in the law might consist of a police officer using his or her knowledge of psychology in an investigation. For example, the officer may base his questioning strategy during an interrogation on his knowledge of various psychological principles that are known to be useful for extracting confessions. Many of the research applications that we focus on in this textbook fit nicely with the label "psychology in the law."

Psychology of the Law

Psychology *of* the law involves the use of psychology to study the law itself (Haney, 1980), and it addresses questions such as these: What role should the police play in domestic disputes? Does the law reduce the amount of crime in our society? Why is it important to allow for discretionary decision making in the criminal justice system? Although often not considered a core topic in forensic psychology, there does appear to be a growing interest in the area of psychology of the law. The challenge in this case is that to address the sorts of questions posed above, a set of skills from multiple disciplines (e.g., criminology, sociology, law) is often important and sometimes crucial. The new focus in North America and elsewhere on the role of the forensic psychologist as legal scholar will no doubt do much to assist in this endeavor, and we are confident that in the future more research in the area of forensic psychology will focus on issues surrounding psychology of the law.

THE HISTORY OF FORENSIC PSYCHOLOGY

Now that we have defined the field of forensic psychology and discussed the various roles that forensic psychologists can play, we will turn to a discussion of where the field came from and where it is currently headed. Compared to other areas of psychology, forensic psychology has a relatively short history, dating back roughly to the late nineteenth century. In the early days, this type of psychology was actually not referred to as forensic psychology, and most of the psychologists conducting research in the area did not formally identify themselves as forensic psychologists. However, their research formed the building blocks of an emerging field of psychology that continues to be strong today. See Figure 1.1 for a timeline of some significant dates in the history of forensic psychology.

Early Research: Eyewitness Testimony and Suggestibility

In the late nineteenth century, research in the area of forensic psychology was taking place in both North America and Europe, though as indicated above, it wasn't being referred to as forensic psychology at the time. Some of the first experiments were those of James McKeen Cattell (who is perhaps better known for his research in the area of intelligence testing) at Columbia University in New York (Bartol & Bartol, 2006). Cattell, a previous student of Wilhelm Wundt, who developed the first psychology laboratory in

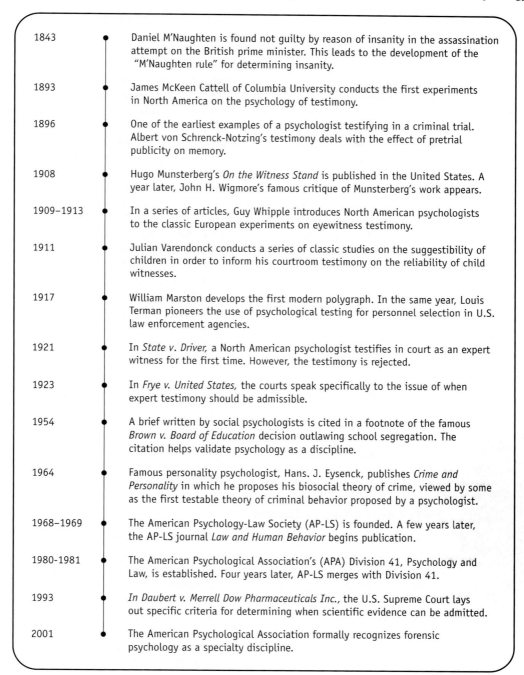

1843	Daniel M'Naughten is found not guilty by reason of insanity in the assassination attempt on the British prime minister. This leads to the development of the "M'Naughten rule" for determining insanity.
1893	James McKeen Cattell of Columbia University conducts the first experiments in North America on the psychology of testimony.
1896	One of the earliest examples of a psychologist testifying in a criminal trial. Albert von Schrenck-Notzing's testimony deals with the effect of pretrial publicity on memory.
1908	Hugo Munsterberg's *On the Witness Stand* is published in the United States. A year later, John H. Wigmore's famous critique of Munsterberg's work appears.
1909–1913	In a series of articles, Guy Whipple introduces North American psychologists to the classic European experiments on eyewitness testimony.
1911	Julian Varendonck conducts a series of classic studies on the suggestibility of children in order to inform his courtroom testimony on the reliability of child witnesses.
1917	William Marston develops the first modern polygraph. In the same year, Louis Terman pioneers the use of psychological testing for personnel selection in U.S. law enforcement agencies.
1921	In *State v. Driver,* a North American psychologist testifies in court as an expert witness for the first time. However, the testimony is rejected.
1923	In *Frye v. United States,* the courts speak specifically to the issue of when expert testimony should be admissible.
1954	A brief written by social psychologists is cited in a footnote of the famous *Brown v. Board of Education* decision outlawing school segregation. The citation helps validate psychology as a discipline.
1964	Famous personality psychologist, Hans. J. Eysenck, publishes *Crime and Personality* in which he proposes his biosocial theory of crime, viewed by some as the first testable theory of criminal behavior proposed by a psychologist.
1968–1969	The American Psychology-Law Society (AP-LS) is founded. A few years later, the AP-LS journal *Law and Human Behavior* begins publication.
1980-1981	The American Psychological Association's (APA) Division 41, Psychology and Law, is established. Four years later, AP-LS merges with Division 41.
1993	*In Daubert v. Merrell Dow Pharmaceuticals Inc.,* the U.S. Supreme Court lays out specific criteria for determining when scientific evidence can be admitted.
2001	The American Psychological Association formally recognizes forensic psychology as a specialty discipline.

FIGURE 1.1

Some Important European and North American Developments in the History of Forensic Psychology

Sources: "Some Important European and North American Developments in the History of Forensic Psychology", based on Bartol & Bartol, 2004; Brigham,1999.

Leipzig, Germany, was one of the major powerhouses of psychology in North America. After developing an expertise in the study of human cognitive processes while in Leipzig, Cattell conducted some of the first North American experiments looking at what would later be called the psychology of eyewitness testimony (e.g., Cattell, 1895). Cattell would ask people to recall things they had witnessed in their everyday life (e.g., "In which direction do apple seeds point?"), and he found that their answers were often inaccurate.

At around the same time, a number of other psychologists began studying eyewitness testimony and suggestibility (see Ceci & Bruck, 1993, for a review). For example, the famous French psychologist Alfred Binet conducted numerous studies in which he showed that the testimony provided by children was highly susceptible to suggestive questioning techniques. In a study discussed by Ceci and Bruck (1993), Binet (1900) presented children with a series of objects for a short period of time (e.g., a button glued to poster board). After viewing an object, some of the children were told to write down everything that they saw while others were asked questions. Some of these questions were direct (e.g., "How was the button attached to the board?"), others were mildly leading (e.g., "Wasn't the button attached by a thread?"), and still others were highly misleading (e.g., "What was the color of the thread that attached the button to the board?"). As found in numerous studies since this experiment, Binet demonstrated that asking children to report everything they saw (i.e., free recall) resulted in the most accurate answers and that highly misleading questions resulted in the least accurate answers.

Shortly after Binet's study, a German psychologist named William Stern also began conducting studies examining the suggestibility of witnesses (Bartol & Bartol, 2006; Ceci & Bruck, 1993). The "reality experiment" that is now commonly used by eyewitness researchers to study eyewitness recall and recognition can, in fact, be attributed to Stern. Using this research paradigm, participants are exposed to staged events and are then asked to recall information about the event. In one of Stern's experiments, participants were exposed to a scenario that involved two students arguing in a classroom setting until one of the students drew a revolver (Stern, 1910). As was the case with Binet, Stern found that eyewitness testimony can often be incorrect, and he was perhaps the first researcher to demonstrate that an observer's level of emotional arousal can have an impact on the accuracy of that person's testimony.

Early Court Cases in Europe

Around the time that this research was being conducted, psychologists in Europe also started to appear as expert witnesses in court. Unsurprisingly, given the research being conducted at the time, much of the testimony that they were providing dealt with issues surrounding the accuracy of eyewitness testimony. For example, in 1896, Albert von Schrenck-Notzing was probably the first expert witness to provide testimony in court on the effect of pretrial publicity on memory (Bartol & Bartol, 2006). The case took place in Munich, Germany, and involved a series of three sexual murders. The court case attracted a great deal of attention from the press of the time, and Schrenck-Notzing testified that this extensive pretrial press coverage could influence the testimony of witnesses by causing what he called "retroactive memory falsification" (Bartol & Bartol, 2006). This referred to a process whereby witnesses confuse actual memories of events with the events described by the media. Schrenck-Notzing supported his expert testimony with laboratory research, and this research is in line with more recent studies that have examined the effects of pretrial publicity (e.g., Ruva, McEvoy, & Bryant, 2007).

Following this case, Julian Varendonck, a Belgian psychologist, was called on to be an expert witness in a 1911 case involving the murder of a young girl, Cecile. Ceci and Bruck (1993) describe the case:

> Two of Cecile's friends who had played with her on the day of her murder were awakened that night by Cecile's mother to ask of her whereabouts. One of the children replied that she did not know. Later that night, she led the police to the spot where the children had played, not far from where Cecile's body was found. In the next month, the two children were repeatedly interviewed by authorities who asked many suggestive questions. The children quickly changed their original testimony of not knowing about Cecile's actions on the day of her murder. They provided details of the appearance of the murderer as well as his name. Because of an anonymous letter, the police arrested the father of one of the playmates for the murder of Cecile. On the basis of the details of the case, Varendonck was convinced of the defendant's innocence. He quickly conducted a series of studies with the specific intent of demonstrating the unreliability of children's testimony. (p. 406)

According to Ceci and Bruck (1993), in one of his studies, Varendonck (1911) asked a group of children to describe a person who had supposedly approached him in front of the children earlier that morning. Although this person did not exist, Varendonck was able to demonstrate, in line with more recent studies, that many of the children were easily led by suggestive questioning. Based on these findings, Varendonck concluded to the court that the testimony provided by the children in this case was likely to be inaccurate and that, as a group, children are prone to suggestion.

Advocates of Forensic Psychology in North America

Although it was not until years later that psychologists began testifying on similar issues in North America, psychology in North America was making great strides in other areas of the criminal justice system. Perhaps one of the most important landmarks was the publication in 1908 of Hugo Munsterberg's *On the Witness Stand* (Munsterberg, 1908). Another student of Wilhelm Wundt, Munsterberg is considered by many to be the father of applied psychology (Bartol & Bartol, 2006). Coming from Germany to Harvard University in 1892, he quickly established a name for himself (Brigham, 1999). In his book, Munsterberg argued that psychology had much to offer the legal system. Through a collection of his essays, he discussed how psychology could assist with issues involving eyewitness testimony, crime detection, false confessions, suggestibility, hypnotism, and even crime prevention.

Unfortunately, Munsterberg presented his ideas in a way that led to heavy criticism from the legal profession (Bartol & Bartol, 2006). This is unsurprising given the way in which he wrote. Consider the following quotation from the introduction to his book:

> The lawyer and the judge and the juryman are sure that they do not need the experimental psychologist. They do not wish to see that in this field pre-eminently applied experimental psychology has made strong strides. . . . They go on thinking that their legal instinct and their common sense supplies them with all that is needed and somewhat more . . . if the time is ever to come when even the jurist is to

show some concession to the spirit of modern psychology, public opinion will have to exert some pressure. (Munsterberg, 1908, pp. 10–11)

Munsterberg's biggest critic was John Henry Wigmore, a well-respected law professor at Northwestern University in Chicago. Wigmore is known for many things, most notably his *Treatise on Evidence*, which is a critical examination of the laws of evidence. In the field of forensic psychology, however, what Wigmore is most commonly known for is his ruthless critique of Munsterberg's book. Through a series of fabricated "transcripts," Wigmore (1909) put Munsterberg on "trial," where he was sued, and found guilty of "claiming more than he could offer" (Brigham, 1999, p. 276). Wigmore criticized Munsterberg for the lack of relevant research publications to back up his claims and, more generally, for the lack of applied research in the field of forensic psychology as a whole.

Due perhaps in large part to Wigmore's comprehensive attack on Munsterberg's work, North American psychologists working in areas that we would now define as forensic psychology were largely ignored by the legal profession for a period of time. However, according to some, Munsterberg was still instrumental in pushing North American psychologists into the legal arena (Bartol & Bartol, 2006).

Forensic Psychology in Other Areas of the Criminal Justice System

After the publication of Munsterberg's controversial book, forensic psychology in North America gradually caught up to what was happening in Europe. Not only were theories of crime being proposed at a rapid rate (see Box 1.3), these theories were informing

---

BOX 1.3   Biological, Sociological, and Psychological Theories of Crime

While an in-depth discussion of crime theories is beyond the scope of this book, efforts to develop such theories are clearly an important part of the history of forensic psychology. During the past century, a variety of biological, sociological, and psychological theories of crime have been proposed and tested. Below are brief descriptions of some of these theories.

Biological Theories of Crime

- *Sheldon's (1949) constitutional theory.* Sheldon proposed that crime is largely a product of an individual's body build, or somatotype, which is assumed to be linked to an individual's temperament. According to Sheldon, endomorphs (obese) are jolly, ectomorphs (thin) are introverted, and mesomorphs (muscular) are bold. Sheldon's studies indicated that, due to their aggressive nature, mesomorphs were more likely to become involved with crime.
- *Jacobs, Brunton, Melville, Brittain, and McClemont's (1965) chromosomal theory.* Jacobs and her colleagues proposed that chromosomal irregularity is linked to criminal behavior. A normal female has two X chromosomes, whereas a normal male has one X and one Y chromosome. However, it was discovered that some men possess two Y chromosomes, which, it was proposed, made them more masculine and, therefore, more aggressive. According to Jacobs and her colleagues, this enhanced aggressiveness would result in an increased chance that these men would commit violent crimes.

- *Mark and Ervin's (1970) dyscontrol theory.* Mark and Ervin proposed that lesions in the temporal lobe and limbic system result in electrical disorganization within the brain, which can lead to a "dyscontrol syndrome." According to Mark and Ervin, symptoms of this dyscontrol syndrome can include outbursts of sudden physical violence, impulsive sexual behavior, and serious traffic violations.

Sociological Theories of Crime

- *Merton's (1938) strain theory.* Merton proposed that crime is largely a product of the strain felt by certain individuals in society (typically from the lower class) who have limited access to legitimate means (e.g., education) for achieving valued goals of success (e.g., money). Merton argued that while some of these individuals will be happy with lesser goals that are achievable, others will turn to illegitimate means (e.g., crime) in an attempt to achieve the valued goals.
- *Sutherland's (1939) differential association theory.* Sutherland proposed that criminal behavior is learned through social interactions in which people are exposed to values that are favorable to violations of the law. More specifically, Sutherland maintained that a person is likely to become a criminal when he or she learns more values (i.e., attitudes) that are favorable to violations of the law than values that are unfavorable to it.
- *Becker's (1963) labelling theory.* Unlike most other theories of crime, Becker proposed that deviance is not inherent to an act, but a label attached to an act by society. Thus, a "criminal" results from a process of society labelling an individual a criminal. This labelling process is thought to promote the individual's deviant behavior through a self-fulfilling prophecy, defined by Becker as a prediction, which is originally false, but made true by the person's actions.

Psychological Theories of Crime

- *Bowlby's (1944) theory of maternal deprivation.* Bowlby argued that the early separation of a child from his mother prevents effective social development from taking place. Without effective social development, Bowlby hypothesized that children will experience long-term problems in developing positive social relationships and will instead develop antisocial behavior patterns.
- *Eysenck's (1964) biosocial theory of crime.* Eysenck believed that some individuals (e.g., extraverts and neurotics) are born with cortical and autonomic nervous systems that influence their ability to learn from the consequences of their behavior, especially the negative consequences experienced in childhood as part of the socialization and conscience-building process. Due to their poor conditionability, it is assumed that individuals who exhibit high levels of extraversion and neuroticism will have strong antisocial inclinations.
- *Gottfredson and Hirschi's (1990) general theory of crime.* Gottfredson and Hirschi argue that low self control, internalized early in life, in the presence of criminal opportunities explains an individual's propensity to commit crimes.

research conducting by North American psychologists. This research was also being practically applied in a wide range of criminal justice settings. For example, as Bartol and Bartol (2004) highlight, forensic psychologists were instrumental in establishing the first clinic for juvenile delinquents in 1909, psychologists began using psychological testing for law enforcement selection purposes in 1917, and 1919 saw the first forensic assessment laboratory (to conduct pretrial assessments) set up in a U.S. police agency. After these events, psychologists in the United States began to be more heavily involved in the judicial system as well, starting with the case of *State v. Driver* in 1921.

Landmark Court Cases in the United States

Unlike their European counterparts who had provided expert testimony in courts as early as the late nineteenth century, the first time this happened in the United States was 1921 (*State v. Driver*, 1921). However, according to Bartol and Bartol (2006), the *Driver* trial was only a partial victory for forensic psychology. This West Virginia case involved the attempted rape of a young girl. The court accepted expert evidence from a psychologist in the area of juvenile delinquency. However, the court rejected the psychologist's testimony that the young girl was a "moron" and, therefore, could not be believed. In its ruling the court stated, "It is yet to be demonstrated that psychological and medical tests are practical, and will detect the lie on the witness stand" (quoted in Bartol & Bartol, 2006, pp. 11–12).

A number of more recent U.S. court cases are also enormously important in the history of forensic psychology. Perhaps the best-known case is that of *Brown v. Board of Education* (1954). This case challenged the constitutionality of segregated public schools (Benjamin & Crouse, 2002). Opponents of school segregation argued that separating children based on their race creates feelings of inferiority, especially among African American children. On May 17, 1954, the U.S. Supreme Court agreed. In the Court's ruling, Chief Justice Earl Warren stated,

> Segregation of White and colored children in public school has a detrimental effect upon the colored children. The impact is greater when it has the sanction of the law, for the policy of separating the races is usually interpreted as denoting the inferiority of the Negro group. A sense of inferiority affects the motivation of the child to learn. Segregation with the sanction of law, therefore, has a tendency to retard the educational and mental development of Negro children and to deprive them of some of the benefits they would receive in a racially integrated school system. Whatever may have been the extent of psychological knowledge [in previous court cases] this finding is amply supported by modern authority. (Benjamin & Crouse, 2002, p. 39)

Beyond the obvious social importance of this ruling, it is important in the field of forensic psychology because of a footnote that was attached to the last sentence of the ruling—the famous footnote 11. The "modern authority" that the U.S. Supreme Court was referring to in this ruling was research in the social sciences demonstrating the detrimental effect of segregation. At the top of the list of seven references included in footnote 11 was the work of Kenneth Clark, an African American psychologist who taught psychology at City College in New York City and studied how prejudice and discrimination affected personality development. This was the first time that psychological research was cited in a U.S. Supreme Court decision and some have argued that this validated psychology as a science (e.g., Benjamin & Crouse, 2002).

The last court case that we will discuss here is *Jenkins v. United States* (1962). The trial involved charges of breaking and entering, assault, and intent to rape, with the defendant, Jenkins, pleading not guilty by reason of insanity. Three clinical psychologists were presented by the defendant, each of them supporting an insanity defense on the basis that the defendant was suffering from schizophrenia at the time of the crimes. At the conclusion of the trial, the judge instructed the jury to disregard the testimony from the psychologists because "psychologists were not qualified to give expert testimony on the issue of mental disease" (American Psychological Association [APA], 2007). The case was appealed. As part of the appeal, the American Psychological Association provided a report to the court stating their view that clinical psychologists are competent to provide opinions concerning the existence of mental illness. On appeal, the court reversed the conviction and ordered a new trial, stating that "some psychologists are qualified to render expert testimony on mental disorders . . . the determination of a psychologist's competence to render an expert opinion . . . must depend upon the nature and extent of his knowledge and not simply on the claim to the title 'psychologist'" (APA, 2007). This decision helped to increase the extent to which psychologists could contribute directly to the legal system as expert witnesses.

Despite the fact that he wasn't a forensic psychologist, Kenneth Clark made an extremely important contribution to this field. The citation of his work by the U.S. Supreme court in *Brown v. Board of Education* showed that psychological research could play a role in the courtroom.

Although the landmark U.S. court cases we have discussed so far have been fundamental in shaping forensic psychology, many other court cases have also been influential. A brief discussion of some of these cases is provided in Box 1.4. We will provide a more detailed discussion of some of the cases in the relevant chapters when we focus on research relating to these rulings.

Signs of a Legitimate Field of Psychology

Although the field of forensic psychology has perhaps not come as far as many forensic psychologists would have hoped in its relatively short history, it has now become a recognized and legitimate field of study within psychology. Indeed, forensic psychology now appears to have many of the markings of an established discipline. This is reflected in numerous ways, as highlighted by Schuller and Ogloff (2001). First, a growing number of high-quality textbooks have been published that provide the opportunity to teach students about forensic psychology. This is particularly so in the United States. Second, a large number of academic journals are now dedicated to various aspects of the field, and more mainstream psychology journals are beginning to publish research from the forensic domain at a regular rate. Third, a number of professional associations have now been developed to represent the interests of forensic psychologists and to promote research and practice in the area. The largest of these associations in North America is the American Psychology-Law Society (AP-LS). Fourth, new training opportunities in forensic psychology, at both the undergraduate and graduate level, are being established in North America, and existing training opportunities are being improved. Finally, and perhaps most importantly, in 2001 the American Psychological Association formally recognized forensic psychology as a specialty discipline.

MODERN-DAY DEBATES: PSYCHOLOGICAL EXPERTS IN COURT

Since the field of forensic psychology has become more widely accepted, forensic psychologists have increasingly been asked to provide expert testimony in court. The variety of topics that forensic psychologists testify about is very broad indeed, including, but not limited to, competency to stand trial, custody issues, malingering and deception, the accuracy of eyewitness identification, the effects of crime on victims, and the assessment of dangerousness. In order for forensic psychologists to increase the extent to which they can contribute to the judicial system in this way, it is important for them to become more knowledgeable about the law and the legal system. This includes becoming more

BOX 1.4	Influential U.S. Court Cases in the History of Forensic Psychology

While it is obviously not possible to provide an exhaustive review of influential U.S. court cases that relate to the field of forensic psychology, the small sample of cases provided below illustrates the wide variety of issues that impact the field:

- *Dusky v. United States (1960).* The U.S. Supreme court outlines the standard for determining competency to stand trial, which includes an ability to consult with counsel and possessing a reasonable understanding of the court proceedings.
- *Miranda v. Arizona (1966).* The U.S. Supreme Court rules that statements made in police interrogations will be admissible only if the defendant was informed of and understood his or her right to consult an attorney and the right against self-incrimination.
- *United States v. Wade (1967).* In recognizing the important role that eyewitness testimony can play in legal proceedings, the U.S. Supreme Court rules that a defendant has the right to have his or her attorney present during pretrial police line-ups.
- *In re Gault (1967).* The U.S. Supreme Court rules that juveniles involved in criminal proceedings must be accorded the same rights as adults (e.g., the right to counsel).
- *Griggs v. Duke Power Co. (1971).* Emphasizing the importance of job analyses in personnel selection (e.g., in law enforcement), the U.S. Supreme Court finds that selection tests must target criteria that are directly related to the job for which the test is required.
- *Neil v. Biggers (1972).* The U.S. Supreme Court concludes that eyewitness evidence resulting from suggestive police procedures should not necessarily be viewed as inadmissible if certain criteria are met (e.g., the eyewitness displays a high level of confidence in his or her identification).
- *Tarasoff v. Regents of the University of California (1976).* The Supreme Court of California rules that mental health professionals have a duty to warn a third party if they have reasonable grounds to believe that their client intends to harm that individual.
- *Batson v. Kentucky (1986).* Confirming the importance of an impartial and representative jury, the U.S. Supreme Court rules that a prosecutor's use of peremptory challenges cannot be used to exclude jurors based solely on their race.
- *Foucha v. Louisiana (1992).* The U.S. Supreme Court rules that a person who is found not guilty by reason of insanity cannot be held indefinitely in a psychiatric facility if the person no longer suffers from the mental illness that served as the basis for the original commitment.
- *Daubert v. Merrell Dow Pharmaceuticals (1993).* The U.S. Supreme Court establishes criteria for determining when expert testimony should be admitted into court.
- *State v. Michaels (1994).* The Supreme Court of New Jersey rules that highly suggestive or coercive interviewing techniques used on children can lead to unreliable testimony and, thus, such tactics require a pretrial hearing to determine the appropriateness of the procedures employed.
- *Roper v. Simmons (2005).* The U.S. Supreme Court rules that it is unconstitutional to impose the death penalty on juvenile offenders.
- *United States v. Binion (2005).* The U.S. Court of Appeals for the 8th Circuit rules that malingering (feigning mental illness) during a competency evaluation can be considered an obstruction of justice and can lead to an enhanced sentence.

aware of what the role of an expert witness is, the various ways in which psychology and the law differ from one another, and the criteria that courts consider when determining whether psychological testimony should be admitted.

The Functions of the Expert Witness

According to Ogloff and Cronshaw (2001), an expert witness generally serves one of two functions. One is to provide the court with information that assists them in understanding a particular issue, and the other is to provide the court with an opinion. Understanding these functions is important because they are what separate the **expert witness** from other witnesses who regularly appear in court (e.g., eyewitnesses). To be clear on this issue, in contrast to other witnesses in court, who can testify only about what they have directly observed, expert witnesses can provide the court with their personal opinion on matters relevant to the case and they are often allowed to draw inferences based on their observations (Ogloff & Cronshaw, 2001). However, these opinions and inferences must always fall within the limits of expert witnesses' areas of expertise, which they typically get through specialized training and experience, and the testimony must be deemed reliable and helpful to the court.

Expert witness
A witness who provides the court with information (often an opinion on a particular matter) that assists the court in understanding an issue of relevance to a case

The Challenges of Providing Expert Testimony

Providing expert testimony to the courts in an effective way is not a simple task. This probably explains why in the past few years numerous manuals have been published for the purpose of assisting expert witnesses with the task of preparing for court (e.g., Brodsky, 1991, 1999). In large part, these difficulties arise because of the inherent differences (often conflicts) that exist between the fields of psychology and law. Numerous individuals have discussed these differences, but we will focus on one particular attempt to describe them.

According to Hess (1987, 1999), psychology and law differ along at least seven different dimensions:

1. *Knowledge.* Knowledge gain in psychology is accomplished through cumulative research. In the law, knowledge comes through legal precedent, logical thinking, and case law.
2. *Methodology.* Methodological approaches in psychology are predominantly nomothetic. In other words, the goal is to uncover broad patterns and general trends through the use of controlled experiments and statistical methods. In contrast, the law is idiographic in that it operates on a case-by-case basis.
3. *Epistemology.* Psychologists assume that it is possible to uncover hidden truths if the appropriate experiments are conducted. Truth in the law is defined subjectively and is based on who can provide the most convincing story of what really happened.
4. *Criteria.* In terms of a willingness to accept something as true, psychologists are cautious. To accept a hypothesis, results must be replicated, and conservative statistical criteria are used. The law decides what is true based on a single case and criteria that are often more lenient.
5. *Nature of law.* The goal in psychology is to describe how people behave. Law, however, is prescriptive. It tells people how they should behave.
6. *Principles.* Good psychologists always consider alternative explanations for their findings. Good lawyers always convince the judge and jury that their explanation of the findings is the only correct explanation.

7. *Latitude.* The behavior of the psychologist when acting as an expert witness is severely limited by the court. The law imposes fewer restrictions on the behavior of lawyers (though they are also restricted in numerous ways).

Understanding these differences is important because they help us to appreciate why the courts are often so reluctant to admit testimony provided by psychological experts. For example, after considering how psychology and the law differ with respect to their methodological approach, it may not be surprising that judges often have difficulty seeing how psychologists can assist in court proceedings. Indeed, numerous legal scholars have questioned whether the general patterns and trends that result from a nomothetic psychological approach should ever be used in court. As Sheldon and Macleod (1991) state:

> The findings derived from empirical research are used by psychologists to formulate norms of human behavior. From observations and experiments, psychologists may conclude that in circumstance X there is a likelihood that an individual . . . will behave in manner Y. . . . [N]ormative data of this sort are of little use to the courts. The courts are concerned to determine the past behavior of accused *individuals*, and in carrying out that function, information about the past behavior of *other individuals* is wholly irrelevant. (emphasis added, p. 815)

Currently, little attempt has been made to understand these differences between psychology and law, or their implications for the field of forensic psychology. Once we gain such an understanding perhaps forensic psychologists will be in a better position to assist the courts with the decisions they are required to make. We believe that research conducted by forensic psychologists will greatly assist in this endeavor. This research will also increase our understanding of the criteria the courts use for determining the conditions under which they will accept expert testimony from psychologists.

Criteria for Accepting Expert Testimony

General acceptance test

A standard for accepting expert testimony, which states that expert testimony will be admissible in court if the basis of the testimony is generally accepted within the relevant scientific community

In order for a forensic psychologist to provide expert testimony in court, he or she must meet certain criteria. In the United States, criteria of one sort or another have been in place since the early twentieth century. In fact, until relatively recently, the admissibility of expert testimony in the United States was based on a decision handed down by the courts in *Frye v. United States* (1923). Frye was being tried for murder and the court rejected his request to admit the results from a polygraph exam he had passed. On appeal, the court also rejected requests to allow the polygraph expert to present evidence on Frye's behalf (Bartol & Bartol, 1994). In the ruling, the court spoke specifically to the issue of when expert testimony should be admitted into court. The court indicated that, for novel scientific evidence to be admissible in court, it must be established that the procedure(s) used to arrive at the testimony is/are generally accepted in the scientific community. More specifically, the court stated, "while courts will go a long way in admitting expert testimony deduced from a well-recognized scientific principle or discovery, the thing from which the deduction is made must be sufficiently established to have gained general acceptance in the particular field in which it belongs" (*Frye v. United States*, 1923, p. 1).

This criterion came to be called the "**general acceptance test**," and although it formed the basis of admissibility decisions in the United States for a long time, it has been heavily criticized. The major criticism centers on the vagueness of terms such as "general acceptance" and "the particular field in which it belongs" and whether trial judges are able to make appropriate determinations of what these terms mean. As just one example of where problems might emerge, consider a defense lawyer who would like to have a criminal profiler provide expert testimony in court (as you will see in Chapter 3, a profiler is someone who attempts to predict the personality and demographic characteristics of an unknown offender based on how that offender's crimes were committed). How should the trial judge decide whether the profiler used generally accepted profiling techniques? If the courts turned to the profiling community (typically consisting of specially trained law enforcement personnel) to make this determination, the answer would most likely be far more favorable than if they had asked forensic psychologists who conduct research in the area of criminal profiling (e.g., Alison, Bennell, Mokros, & Ormerod, 2002). So, whom should the judge turn to and believe? In what "particular field" does criminal profiling belong?

THE *Daubert* CRITERIA   This issue of vagueness was addressed more recently in the U.S. Supreme Court decision handed down in *Daubert v. Merrell Dow Pharmaceuticals, Inc.* (1993), when more specific admissibility criteria were set. Daubert sued Merrell Dow because he believed a morning sickness drug his mother ingested while pregnant, which was produced by the company, led to his birth defects. At trial, Merrell Dow presented experts who provided evidence that the use of the drug Bendectin does not result in birth defects. In turn, Daubert provided evidence from experts who claimed that Bendectin could lead to birth defects. The state court and the appeal court both rejected the testimony provided by Daubert's experts on the basis that the methods they used to arrive at their results were not generally accepted by the scientific community. On appeal before the U.S. Supreme Court, Daubert's lawyers challenged the state and appeal courts' interpretation of "general acceptance."

> *Daubert* **criteria**
> A standard for accepting expert testimony, which states that scientific evidence is valid if the research upon which it is based has been peer reviewed, is testable, has a recognized rate of error, and adheres to professional standards

In addressing this issue, the U.S. Supreme Court stated that, for scientific evidence to be admitted into court, it must (1) be provided by a qualified expert, (2) be relevant, and (3) be reliable (meaning scientifically valid). To assist judges in making the decision as to whether evidence is in fact valid, the U.S. Supreme Court laid out four specific criteria, now commonly referred to as the ***Daubert* criteria**. These criteria suggest that scientific evidence is valid if:

1. The research has been peer reviewed.
2. The research is testable (i.e., falsifiable through experimentation).
3. The research has a recognized rate of error.
4. The research adheres to professional standards.

Using this information read the scenario described in the Case Study box and see what challenges you might encounter as a judge when trying to apply the *Daubert* criteria.

Despite being a positive step in the right direction, what remains unclear with respect to the *Daubert* case is whether the criteria that were identified for assessing an individual's testimony have had their intended impact—to increase the quality threshold that needs to be met in order for expert evidence to be admitted into court. Currently, it appears that the criteria have increased the extent to which the courts scrutinize the qualifications of experts, but it does not seem to have had the same impact on assessments of reliability, or validity (Groscup, Penrod, Studebaker, Huss, & O'Neil, 2002). Indeed,

CASE STUDY

YOU BE THE JUDGE

Pretend for a second that you are a judge. The case before you attracted a great deal of media attention and involved a black defendant who allegedly committed a very violent armed robbery at a grocery store. During the investigation, two eyewitnesses came forward, both of whom were white. The defense attorney is trying to introduce testimony from a psychologist that suggests various factors in the case would impair the witnesses' ability to make an accurate identification. The testimony relates to problems with cross-racial identifications and the influence of post-event information on memory.

Your Turn . . .

Your decision as the judge in this case is to determine whether the witness should be allowed to present his testimony in court. Using the information contained in this chapter as a guide, what are the major issues that you would consider when making this decision? How would you go about determining if the witness is an expert and whether the evidence that the witness plans to introduce is necessary for assisting the court? How would you go about determining whether the evidence is valid? What challenges might you face in answering these questions and what sorts of things might assist you with your task?

while there are certainly exceptions (e.g., see Box 1.5), a review of court cases occurring before and after the *Daubert* ruling was handed down indicate that other factors (e.g., the potential for assisting the trier of fact) are often weighted more heavily than the *Daubert* criteria when determining the admissibility of expert evidence (Groscup et al., 2002).

BOX 1.5   *Daubert* in Action: *New Jersey vs. Fortin* (1999–2000)

On April 3, 1995, Vicki Gardner, a Maine state trooper, was sexually assaulted and killed by Steven Fortin, who pled guilty to the crime and was sentenced to 20 years in prison. In August 1994, Melissa Padilla was also sexually assaulted and killed in the city of Avenel, New Jersey. At the request of the state of New Jersey, retired FBI agent Roy Hazelwood conducted a linkage analysis on these cases, which involved an evaluation of the crime scene behaviors to determine if the two offenses were committed by the same offender (*New Jersey v. Fortin*, 1999a).

Based on his review of the cases, Hazelwood was prepared to present testimony that Fortin was responsible for the two crimes in question (*New Jersey v. Fortin*, 1999a). According to Hazelwood, the two crimes were highly similar, both in terms of behavior and motivation. Specifically, Hazelwood concluded that "in my 35 years of experience with a variety of violent crimes . . . I have never observed this combination of behaviors. . . . The likelihood of different offenders committing two such extremely unique crimes is highly improbable" (Turvey, 2008, p. 335).

Despite objections from the defense, the trial court judge admitted Hazelwood's testimony and Fortin was convicted for the murder of Melissa Padilla. In reaching its decision, the court used previous admissibility standards applied in *New Jersey v. Kelly* (1994), which focused on the general acceptance of an expert's testimony and whether the testimony provides information that goes beyond the common understanding of the court.

On appeal, the decision to admit Hazelwood's testimony was reversed. The appellate court reasoned that because linkage analysis involves the application of behavioral science, Hazelwood's testimony should be evaluated using admission criteria established for scientific evidence (*New Jersey v. Fortin*, 1999b). Based on an evaluation of *Daubert* criteria, the appellate court concluded that Hazelwood's linkage analysis was not sufficiently reliable (i.e., valid) to warrant its admission in court. In 2000, the Supreme Court of New Jersey agreed with this decision and upheld the ruling of the appellate court (*New Jersey v. Fortin*, 2000). They also pointed out additional *Daubert* criteria that were problematic in this case (e.g., a lack of peer-reviewed research in the area of linkage analysis).

Summary

1. Forensic psychology can be defined in a narrow or broad fashion. Narrow definitions tend to focus only on the clinical *or* experimental aspects of the field, whereas broad definitions are less restrictive and encompass both aspects.

2. Forensic psychologists can play different roles. Clinical forensic psychologists are primarily interested in mental health issues as they pertain to the law. Experimental forensic psychologists are interested in studying any aspect of human behavior that relates to the law (e.g., eyewitness memory, jury decision making, risk assessment, etc.).

3. Psychology can relate to the field of law in three ways. The phrase *psychology and the law* refers to the use of psychology to study the operation of the legal system. *Psychology in the law* refers to the use of psychology within the legal system as it operates. *Psychology of the law* refers to the use of psychology to study the legal system itself.

4. The history of forensic psychology is marked by many important milestones, both in the research laboratory and in the courtroom. Early research consisted of studies of eyewitness testimony and suggestibility, and many of the early court cases in Europe where psychologists appeared as experts dealt with similar issues. Hugo Munsterberg played a significant role in establishing the field of forensic psychology in North America and by the early 1900s, forensic psychologists were active in many different parts of the criminal justice system. Currently, forensic psychology is viewed as a distinct and specialized discipline, with its own textbooks, journals, and professional associations.

5. Expert witnesses differ from regular witnesses in that expert witnesses can testify about their opinions, whereas other witnesses can only testify as to what they know to be fact. In many jurisdictions in the United States, for an expert's testimony to be accepted, it must (1) be provided by a qualified expert, (2) be relevant, and (3) be reliable (meaning scientifically valid).

Key Concepts

clinical forensic
   psychologists *6*

Daubert criteria *21*

experimental forensic
   psychologists *7*

expert witness *19*

forensic psychiatry *7*

forensic
   psychology *1*

general acceptance
   test *20*

psychology and the
   law *9*

psychology
   in the law *9*

psychology
   of the law *9*

Discussion Questions

1. You are sitting on a panel of experts that has been charged with the task of redefining the field of forensic psychology. In your role as a panel member, you have to consider whether forensic psychology should be defined in a narrow or broad fashion. What are some of the advantages and disadvantages of adopting a narrow definition? What are some of the advantages and disadvantages of adopting a broad definition? Decide what type of definition you prefer and explain why.

2. The majority of forensic psychologists have no formal training in law. Do you think this is appropriate given the extent to which many of these psychologists are involved in the judicial system?

3. You have just been hired as a summer intern at a law office. One of your tasks is to assist in preparing for a high-profile murder case that has attracted a great deal of media attention. One of the lawyers has found out that you've taken this course and she wants to know whether the extensive pretrial press coverage the crime has received will make it difficult to find impartial jurors. Design a study to determine whether this is likely to be the case.

4. Put yourself in the shoes of an expert witness. You are supposed to act as an educator to the judge and jury, not as an advocate for the defense or for the prosecution. To what extent do you think you could do this? Why or why not?

Police Psychology

LEARNING OBJECTIVES

- Outline the major steps in developing a valid police selection procedure.

- Describe the various instruments that are used to select police officers.

- Define what is meant by the term *police discretion*.

- List some key decisions in policing that require the use of discretion.

- Outline some of the major sources and consequences of stress in policing.

- Describe various strategies for dealing with police stress.

It's Wednesday night, just after 2 a.m., and Constable Vincent Kwan is performing a routine patrol in a rough area of town. It's an area known for prostitution, drug dealing, and a large homeless population. Just when he is about to head back to the station, he receives a call from dispatch that gunshots have been heard coming from a nearby apartment. Being closest to the scene, Constable Kwan responds to the call. He pulls his cruiser in front of the apartment building and makes his way up the stairs. Outside the apartment door, he can hear a man yelling. The door is slightly ajar so he can see inside. It doesn't look like there's anyone else in the apartment so he knocks on the door. The man inside continues to yell as Constable Kwan enters the apartment. The man is only partially dressed and is yelling out his window. Constable Kwan can't under-stand what he saying, but as the man turns around Constable Kwan sees that he's holding a large knife in his hands and is bleeding from the arm. He tells the man to put down the knife, but the man runs to his balcony. He backs up to the railing and threatens to jump. He keeps swinging the knife in front of him and says he has a gun in his pocket. By his speech and demeanor, Constable Kwan can tell that there is something seriously wrong with the man, but he doesn't know what. Constable Kwan now has to decide how to protect this man, while also protecting himself.

T he scenario described above raises many questions about police officers and the nature of the work they do. For example, we might ask whether Constable Kwan is well suited to deal with this sort of situation. Is he the type of person who can think clearly under pressure? If not, why was he able to successfully graduate from the police academy? Alternatively, we might be curious about what Constable Kwan should do in this case. What options are available to him? How much force, if any, should he use to subdue the individual? Finally, we might be interested in how Constable Kwan is reacting to the events that are unfolding. Is he experiencing serious stress reactions? If so, what are they, how might they impact his decisions, and are they likely to cause any long-term negative effects?

This chapter will provide some of the answers to these questions by examining a number of issues that are currently being investigated in the area of police psychology. First, we will look at how police officers are selected and examine whether it is possible to identify individuals who are likely to become good police officers. We will then turn our attention to police discretion where we will focus on why discretion is important and how we might control the inappropriate use of police discretion. Finally, we will explore what we know about police stress, including the causes and consequences of stress in policing, and potential ways to prevent or manage this stress.

POLICE SELECTION

As part of ongoing recruitment efforts, many police departments in the United States post information about the policing profession on their recruitment websites (see the In the Media box on the next page for other innovative recruitment strategies being used by police agencies). Consider the following excerpt from the website of the New York City Police Department:

> Police officers perform general police duties and related work in the New York City Police Department. They patrol an assigned area on foot or in a vehicle; apprehend crime suspects; intervene in various situations involving crimes in progress, aided cases, complaints, emotionally disturbed persons, etc.; respond to and investigate vehicular accidents; investigate specific offenses; interact with prisoners; operate and maintain patrol vehicles; issue summonses; obtain information regarding incidents by interviewing witnesses, victims, and/or complainants; safeguard and voucher found, seized or recovered property; provide information to the public; handle situations involving maltreated, abused or missing children; interact with juveniles; prepare forms and reports; testify in court; and perform related work. (New York Police Department, 2011)

As this excerpt clearly indicates, police work is a multifaceted, complex, demanding, stressful, and potentially dangerous occupation. It requires intelligent, creative, patient, ethical, caring, and hard-working individuals. The job may not be for everyone and, therefore, it is important for all those involved to ensure that the individuals who are accepted for the job have the highest potential for success. The purpose of police selection is to ensure that this happens (Ash, Slora, & Britton, 1990; Sanders, 2008). This requires the use of valid **police selection procedures** that allow police agencies to effectively screen out applicants who possess undesirable characteristics and select in applicants who possess desirable characteristics (Fabricatore, 1979; Sanders, 2008). These characteristics may relate to a variety of personal features, including but not limited to an applicant's physical fitness, cognitive abilities, personality, and performance on various job-related tasks.

Police selection procedures

A set of procedures used by the police to either screen out undesirable candidates or select in desirable candidates

IN THE MEDIA   Using Social Media to Recruit Police Officers

Many police agencies in the United States are experiencing a substantial shortage of police officers. To fill this gap, young people will need to apply for policing jobs more frequently than is currently the case. In an attempt to address this issue, some police agencies are using innovative advertising strategies, including the use of social media. For example, agencies in Oregon, Texas, and Virginia, to name just a few, are capitalizing on young peoples' use of electronic social media to provide them with information about employment opportunities in policing and the hiring process (International Association of Chiefs of Police [IACP], 2010). Rather than waiting for young people to come to them, police forces are taking their message to the computer screens of young people.

The recruitment methods being used by these agencies vary (IACP, 2010). Recruitment websites have been around for some time. However, some agencies are now using more innovative social media strategies. For example, blogs are now frequently used for recruitment purposes, allowing for a more personal and interactive touch than recruitment websites. The use of Facebook pages is also becoming common practice in some police agencies for the purpose of having one-on-one discussions, and Twitter is proving to be an ideal format to quickly update potential recruits on the hiring process or to provide brief messages to new recruits. Some police forces even post recruitment videos to sites such as YouTube, which might show viewers what a typical police officer's day looks like.

While the impact of these social media strategies on recruitment success has yet to be formally evaluated in most agencies, some obvious advantages are associated with these approaches (IACP, 2010). For example, compared to other forms of advertising, the use of social media is relatively inexpensive. In addition, social media are an effective way of getting one's message out to a high volume of potential applicants, particularly young people. Finally, social media provide a useful platform for interacting with interested parties at a personal level, while also sharing the information with the broader public.

A Brief History of Police Selection

The task of selecting appropriate police officers is not a new one for police agencies. Indeed, psychologists have been involved in police selection since the early twentieth century. In what is considered one of the earliest examples, Lewis Terman, in 1917, used the Stanford-Binet intelligence test to assist with police selection in California. Terman (1917) tested the intelligence of 30 police and firefighter applicants, which led him to recommend a minimum IQ score of 80 for future applicants. Following this, attempts were made to use personality tests to predict police performance in the mid-twentieth century (e.g., Humm & Humm, 1950), and by the mid-1950s, psychological and psychiatric screening procedures of police applicants became a standard part of the selection procedure in several major police forces (Reiser, 1982).

In the 1960s and 1970s, major changes to police selection procedures took place in the United States, primarily as a result of two major events. As described by Ho (1999), in 1967, the President's Commission on Law Enforcement and Administration of Justice recommended that police forces adopt a higher educational requirement for police officers, obviously implying that intelligence is a core characteristic of successful officers. In 1973, the National Advisory Commission on Criminal Justice Standards and Goals in the United States recommended that police agencies establish formal selection processes, which would include the use of tests to measure the cognitive abilities and personality

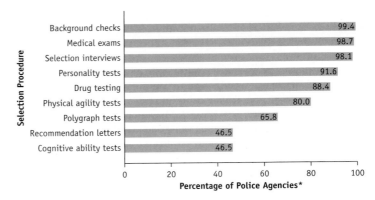

FIGURE 2.1   **U.S. Police Agency Selection Procedures**
*These data represent responses from 155 U.S. police agencies that responded to a survey sent out by Cochrane et al., 2003.
Source: Based on data from "Psychological Testing and the Selection of Police Officers: A National Survey" by Robert E. Cochrane, Robert P. Tett, Leon Vandecreek, from *Criminal Justice and Behavior*, vol. 30, Sage Publications (2003).

features of applicants. Since that time, police selection has indeed become more formalized, with police forces using a wide range of selection procedures, as indicated in Figure 2.1 (Cochrane, Tett, & Vandecreek, 2003).

The Police Selection Process

Regardless of whether a police agency decides to adopt a screening-out approach or a selecting-in approach, the general stages a force must go through to develop a valid selection process are the same (Gowan & Gatewood, 1995). In general terms, there are two separate stages to this process. Stage 1 is referred to as the job analysis stage. Here, the agency must define the knowledge, skills, and abilities (KSAs) of a "good" police officer. Stage 2 is referred to as the construction and validation stage. In this stage, the agency must develop an instrument for measuring the extent to which police applicants possess these KSAs. A crucial part of this stage also requires that the agency determine the instrument's validity, or the extent to which the scores on the instrument actually relate to measures of actual, on-the-job police performance.

Job analysis

A procedure for identifying the knowledge, skills, and abilities that describe a good police officer

CONDUCTING A JOB ANALYSIS   As indicated above, a **job analysis** involves a procedure to identify and define the KSAs that describe a good police officer. An organizational psychologist, working in conjunction with a police agency, frequently conducts the job analysis. These psychologists can use a range of techniques for identifying relevant KSAs, including survey methods and observational techniques. At other times, a job analysis can be conducted more informally, simply by asking members of a police agency to list the range of qualities they feel are essential for their job. Each of these approaches has certain advantages and disadvantages. However, for the moment, we will focus on some common problems that emerge when conducting any sort of job analysis in the policing context.

One of the major problems that can be encountered in a job analysis is that the KSAs of a good police officer may not be stable over time, making it difficult to determine what the selection procedures should actually be testing for. For example, Pugh (1985a, 1985b) found that, at two years of service, police officers who were enthusiastic and fit in well were rated as the best officers, while at four years of service officers who were stable and responsible were given the highest performance ratings.

Another problem with conducting a job analysis is that individuals may disagree over which KSAs are important. For example, if you were to ask a group of patrol officers and a group of senior police managers to define the characteristics of a good police officer, the answers could be quite different (though some similarities might also be expected). To illustrate this point, consider a survey in which Ainsworth (1993) asked patrol officers to list the qualities they thought were essential for effective policing. Topping their list was a sense of humor. In contrast, this personal quality is rarely identified as being important when senior police managers are asked to list the essential qualities for effective policing. When this is done, the most important KSAs typically relate to cognitive skills (Sanders, 2003).

Despite these problems, there does appear to be some agreement, even across police officers of varying ranks, on what type of person is "right for the job" (Sanders, 2003). For example, regardless of how the job analysis is conducted, the following KSAs are typically viewed as important: honesty, reliability, sensitivity to others, good communication skills, high motivation, problem-solving skills, and being a team player.

CONSTRUCTING AND VALIDATING SELECTION INSTRUMENTS   Recall that the goals in stage 2 of the police selection process are (1) to develop a selection instrument for measuring the extent to which police applicants possess relevant KSAs (construction) and (2) to ensure that this instrument relates to measures of police performance (validation). The measure of validation that we are most interested in is referred to as *predictive validity*, which refers to our ability to use a selection instrument to predict how applicants will perform in the future. Box 2.1 presents a more thorough discussion of predictive validity.

BOX 2.1   Validation and Police Selection

Many different types of validation measures have been devised, and each refers to something slightly different. The most common validation measure used in police selection focuses on predictive validity, in which the goal is to determine if there is a relationship between scores obtained from a selection instrument and measures of actual job performance (Gowan & Gatewood, 1995). In the policing context, predictive validity involves collecting data from police applicants using a selection instrument, such as scores on a test of decision making under stress. Then, the results on this test are compared with a measure of job performance, such as performance scores provided by supervisors. If the selection data accurately predict job performance, then the selection instrument is said to have *predictive validity*.

A selection instrument's predictive validity can be determined by calculating validity coefficients, which range from +1.00 to –1.00. These coefficients indicate the strength and direction of the relationship between the scores from a selection instrument and ratings of job performance. If a selection instrument is shown to have a validity coefficient near +1.00, then a very strong positive relationship exists, indicating that, as performance on the selection instrument increases, ratings of job performance also increase (see Figure 2.2). Conversely, if a selection instrument is shown to

(continued)

BOX 2.1   *Continued*

have a validity coefficient near –1.00, a very strong negative relationship exists: as performance on the selection instrument increases, ratings of job performance decrease (see Figure 2.3). Any value between these two extreme values represents an intermediate level of predictive validity.

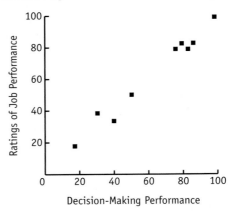

FIGURE 2.2   A Positive Relationship between Scores on a Selection Instrument and Job Performance Ratings

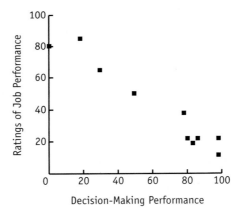

FIGURE 2.3   A Negative Relationship between Scores on a Selection Instrument and Job Performance Ratings

Note that validity coefficients of +1.00 and –1.00 both represent high levels of predictive validity, even if the values are not what we would expect. For example, it seems unlikely that a measure of decision-making performance under stress would relate negatively to the job performance of police officers, but if it did, we could still use those measures to predict job performance. We would simply predict that people who make poor decisions under stress make great police officers!

Researchers have identified a number of major problems with validation research in the area of police selection. Arguably, one of the most serious problems relates to how we measure the performance of police officers (Hargrave & Hiatt, 1987). This is a crucial question to address, since it will have a direct impact on the validity of any selection instrument. Unfortunately, no answer currently exists (Sanders, 2008). This is not to say that a variety of performance measures do not exist. Indeed, researchers have used several measures as indicators of job performance, including the number of times an officer is tardy, the number of complaints against an officer, the number of commendations received by an officer, graduation from a training academy, academy exam scores, performance ratings by supervisors, performance ratings by peers, and so forth. The problem is that there is no evidence to suggest that one of these measures is any better than another, and even police agencies do not agree on how to define good performance (Falkenberg, Gaines, & Cordner, 1991). Furthermore, research suggests that a different picture of performance can emerge depending on what measure is used. For example, measures of performance during training often do not generalize to on-the-job performance (Kleinman & Gordon, 1986) and ratings by different individuals (e.g., peers versus supervisors) can be contradictory (Gardner, Scogin, Vipperman, & Varela, 1998).

The Validity of Police Selection Instruments

Now that we have discussed some of the problems with constructing and validating police selection instruments, we will describe some of the instruments that are currently in use and present some research on their validity. Although some of these instruments might be new to you, there are many others, such as the selection interview, that you will be familiar with. We will focus our attention here on three specific selection instruments: the selection interview, psychological tests, and situational tests.

THE SELECTION INTERVIEW The **selection interview** is one of the most common selection instruments used by the police. Typically, a selection interview is a semistructured interview. In a semistructured interview, the interviewer has a preset list of questions that are asked of each applicant, thus ensuring a more objective basis for comparing applicants (Gowan & Gatewood, 1995). One of the main goals of the selection interview is to determine the extent to which the applicant possesses the KSAs that have been deemed important in a job analysis. These qualities may differ from agency to agency and they may depend on the specific job being applied for.

Surprisingly, given its frequent use as a selection instrument, there is relatively little research examining the predictive validity of the selection interview in the policing context (Aamodt, 2004). Based on the research that does exist, the results are somewhat mixed — that is, some research indicates that selection interviews can be used in a relatively accurate fashion to predict job performance (e.g., Hargrave & Hiatt, 1987), whereas other research suggests that basing police selection decisions on interviews can be potentially problematic (e.g., Doerner, 1997). These findings accord well with the general research literature from the field of organizational psychology, where mixed results regarding the predictive validity of the selection interview are also reported (McDaniel, Whetzel, Schmidt, & Maurer, 1994).

Despite the fact that some research suggests that interviews might provide information that is predictive of job performance, many police researchers remain cautious about their use. To understand why, consider Doerner's (1997) study, where he examined the degree to which different interviewers agreed on their ratings of various attributes when interviewing the same applicant (where agreement could vary from +1.00, indicating total agreement between interviewers, to –1.00, indicating total disagreement). As illustrated in Table 2.1, Doerner found that the majority of inter-rater

Selection interview

In recruiting police officers, an interview used by the police to determine the extent to which an applicant possesses the knowledge, skills, and abilities deemed important for the job

TABLE 2.1	Measures of Inter-Rater Reliability					
Attribute of Interviewee	**Interviewers**					
	1 and 2	**1 and 3**	**1 and 4**	**1 and 5**	**1 and 6**	**1 and 7**
Appearance	0.55*	0.14	0.58*	−0.25	0.50*	0.18
Self-confidence	0.06	0.30	0.43*	0.55	0.45*	0.63
Self-expression	0.27	0.42	0.27	0.26	0.15	0.69*
Understanding	0.85*	0.03	0.67*	0.46	0.35*	0.47
Comprehension	0.47	0.56	0.24	0.14	0.42*	0.59
Background	0.38	0.72*	0.38*	−0.28	0.26	0.70*
Overall impression	0.45	0.38	0.37*	0.00	0.30	0.52
N (number of interviews)	15	10	22	10	28	10

*Denotes a significant finding.

Source: "The Utility of the Oral Interview Board in Selecting Police Academy Admissions" by William G. Doerner from *Policing: An International Journal of Police Strategies & Management,* vol. 20, National Criminal Justice Reference Service (NCJRS), 1997.

reliability measures were relatively low. This was the case across a number of different interviewer pairs, who were assessing a range of personal attributes. Indeed, out of the 42 comparisons Doerner examined, only 14 were found to be statistically significant, and most of these came from only one pair of interviewers.

Given such findings, the validity of the interview technique as a method for selecting police officers must be carefully considered and it should continue to be used with caution. Also remember, however, that changing the way in which an interview is constructed and conducted can have a large impact on its validity (e.g., Campion, Palmer, & Campion, 1997). For example, the more structured an interview is, the more likely that it can be used to predict future job performance with some degree of success (Cortina, Goldstein, Payne, Davison, & Gilliland, 2000). Therefore, police psychologists should continue to examine how selection interviews in the policing context can be improved and the predictive accuracy of new interview procedures should be established.

PSYCHOLOGICAL TESTS   In addition to the selection interview, psychological tests are also commonly used by police agencies to select suitable officers (Cochrane et al., 2003). Some of these tests have been developed to measure cognitive abilities, whereas others have been designed to assess an applicant's personality. In addition, some of these tests have been developed with police selection in mind, whereas others have been developed in other contexts, such as the mental health field. Many questions remain unanswered when it comes to the use of psychological tests for police selection. However, there seems to be general agreement among police researchers that psychological tests are useful in deciding whether a person possesses certain attributes, and it is believed that this knowledge can be helpful, to some extent at least, in selecting applicants to become police officers.

Cognitive Ability Tests   A wide variety of **cognitive ability tests** are available for police use. Although each test may emphasize something slightly different, they are

Cognitive ability tests

Procedure for measuring verbal, mathematical, memory, and reasoning abilities typically used to measure verbal, mathematical, memory, and reasoning abilities. For example, the cognitive abilities exam used by the Cincinnati Police Department consists of approximately 150 multiple-choice and true/false questions. The exam measures a number of core KSAs that are considered essential in performing the duties of a police officer in Cincinnati: human relations, dealing effectively with a diverse group of people, oral and written communication, reading comprehension, basic math, evaluating situations and decision making, following directions, reasoning, and observation and memory (City of Cincinnati Police Department, 2010).

In general, the reliance on cognitive ability tests for police selection purposes is supported by empirical research. However, these tests appear to be more useful for predicting performance during police academy training compared with performance on the job (Gowan & Gatewood, 1995). For example, Hirsh, Northrop, and Schmidt (1986) conducted a meta-analysis of 40 validation studies involving cognitive ability tests. They found average validity coefficients of 0.36 and 0.13 for predicting training success and on-the-job performance, respectively. A more recent meta-analytic study reports similar results. Specifically, Aamodt (2004) found validity coefficients of 0.41 and 0.16 when examining the use of cognitive ability tests for predicting academy performance and on-the-job performance, respectively, where on-the-job performance was assessed via supervisor ratings.

Various explanations have been suggested for why higher scores are found when cognitive ability tests are used to predict academy performance versus on-the-job performance, but one interesting possibility is that personality variables also play a large role in determining job success, above and beyond one's cognitive abilities (e.g., Forero, Gallardo-Pujol, Maydeu-Olivares, & Andres-Pueyo, 2009). Thus, it is worthwhile describing some of the personality tests used for police selection and the degree of validity associated with each.

Personality Tests   A number of different personality tests are used for police selection, but one of the most common tests is an assessment instrument known as the **Minnesota Multiphasic Personality Inventory** (MMPI), now in its second version. According to Cochrane et al. (2003), of the 155 U.S. police agencies that responded to their survey, 71.9% of them indicated that the MMPI-2 was the personality test they used most often for selection purposes. Interestingly, the MMPI, originally designed in the 1940s, was not developed for selecting police officers. Neither was the MMPI-2. Rather, this instrument was developed as a general inventory for identifying people with psychopathological problems. Currently, the MMPI-2 consists of 567 true/false questions that attempt to identify psychopathological problems including depression, paranoia, and schizophrenia.

Although Aamodt's (2004) meta-analysis of the MMPI revealed that it possesses little power in predicting academy performance or on-the-job behavior, some research does suggest that the MMPI and MMPI-2 can be associated with significant, but relatively low validity coefficients. This may be especially true when the tests are used to predict problematic police behaviors (e.g., disciplinary suspensions; Chibnall & Detrick, 2003; Sanders, 2003). In part, the relatively low levels of predictive validity associated with the MMPI tests may be due to the fact that they were never developed as selection instruments. If this is the case, it may be that personality tests developed for police selection purposes will be associated with higher levels of predictive validity. In fact, this does appear to be the case, as indicated by studies examining the **Inwald Personality Inventory** (IPI).

Minnesota Multiphasic Personality Inventory

An assessment instrument for identifying people with psychopathological problems

Inwald Personality Inventory

An assessment instrument used to identify police applicants who are suitable for police work by measuring their personality attributes and behavior patterns

Unlike the MMPI tests, the IPI was developed specifically for the law enforcement community. According to Inwald (1992), the creator of the IPI, the purpose of this selection instrument is to identify police applicants who are most suitable for police work by measuring their personality attributes and behavior patterns. The instrument consists of 310 true/false questions that measure factors such as stress reactions, interpersonal difficulties, and alcohol and other drug use.

According to several researchers, the IPI appears to be more predictive of police officer performance than the MMPI (e.g., Inwald & Shusman, 1984; Scogin, Schumacher, Gardner, & Chaplin, 1995). For example, in one study, Scogin et al. (1995) compared the MMPI, the IPI, and the Shipley Institute of Living Scale (SILS), a brief intellectual screening device, on their ability to predict seven different job performance indicators: supervisor ratings, verbal reprimands, written reprimands, vehicular reprimands, citizen complaints, an overall composite of negative indicators, and an overall composite of positive recognitions. The participants in the study were 82 trainees at the University of Alabama Law Enforcement Academy. Each participant completed the three selection instruments during the first week of academy training. One year following their graduation from the academy, each participant's police agency was contacted to obtain job performance indicators.

The results found that the IPI was a slightly better predictor of on-the-job performance in the one-year follow-up period than both the MMPI and SILS. More specifically, the MMPI and the SILS could accurately predict only one of the seven performance indicators (supervisor ratings). The IPI, on the other hand, was able to predict three of the seven indicators (supervisor ratings, citizen complaints, and the overall composite of negative indicators). In addition, combining the MMPI and IPI scores did not appreciably improve predictive power over that observed with the IPI alone. As the authors of this study indicate, the one-year follow-up used in this study might not have been long enough for sufficient positive and negative on-the-job behavior to occur. However, the results of this study do provide some preliminary evidence that the IPI performs slightly better than the MMPI under certain conditions, something that is confirmed in more recent meta-analytic studies (e.g., Aamodt, 2004).

Assessment center

A facility in which the behavior of police applicants can be observed in a number of situations by multiple observers

Situational test

A simulation of a real-world policing task

ASSESSMENT CENTERS **Assessment centers** appear to be growing in popularity in Europe and North America (Lowry, 1996). An assessment center is a facility at which the behavior of police applicants can be observed in a number of different ways by multiple observers (Pynes & Bernardin, 1992). The primary selection instrument used within an assessment center is the **situational test**, which involves simulations of real-world policing tasks. Trained observers evaluate how applicants perform during these tasks, and the performance appraisals are sometimes used for the purpose of police selection.

The situational tests used in assessment centers attempt to tap into the KSAs identified as part of a job analysis. For example, the situational tests evaluated by Pynes and Bernardin (1992) were based on a job analysis that identified eight core skill sets deemed crucial for effective policing: directing others, interpersonal skills, perception, decision making, decisiveness, adaptability, oral communication, and written communication. Based on these skill sets, four assessment exercises were developed, which allowed the applicants to be evaluated across the range of relevant KSAs. For example, one of the scenarios was a simulated domestic disturbance. Each applicant was given 15 minutes of the 35-minute exercise to meet with two people involved in a dispute. The applicant was expected to intervene in the dispute as a police officer and resolve it. At the end of the 15 minutes, the applicant was given 20 minutes to complete an incident report. This exercise requires excellent interpersonal skills in order to excel, in addition to good decision-making and written communication skills.

Although there is not a great deal of research examining the validity of situational tests for police selection, some research does suggest that situational tests have moderate levels of predictive validity. For example, Pynes and Bernardin (1992) examined the scores given to each applicant across four simulation exercises. These scores were then compared with training academy performance and future on-the-job performance. Overall, the correlations were 0.14 and 0.20 for training academy performance and future on-the-job performance, respectively. Each of these validity coefficients was statistically significant. Similar results were presented by Aamodt (2004) in his meta-analysis of six studies where the predictive validity of assessment centers was examined.

POLICE DISCRETION

As indicated by job analyses, many of the qualities deemed necessary for success as a police officer have to do with the applicant being adaptable, having common sense, possessing effective decision-making skills, and being a good problem solver (Sanders, 2003). In large part, these qualities are necessary because police officers are required to use discretion in much of their daily work. **Police discretion** can be defined in numerous ways, but McKenna (2002) has perhaps stated it best:

> Police discretion is the term that represents the critical faculty that individual officers must possess that will allow them to differentiate and discriminate between those circumstances that require absolute adherence to the letter of the law and those occasions when a degree of latitude is justified, based on the officer's knowledge, experience, or instinct. (p. 118)

Police discretion

A policing task that involves discriminating between circumstances that require absolute adherence to the law and circumstances where a degree of latitude is justified

To appreciate the extent to which the police use discretion, consider the following decisions that need to be made routinely by police officers:

- What street should I patrol tonight?
- Should I stop that vehicle for a traffic violation?
- What level of force is required to achieve my objective?
- Should I run after that suspect or wait for backup?
- Should I call an end to this investigation?
- Should I take this person to a psychiatric hospital or the police station?
- Should I arrest this person, or let them off with a warning?

The list of scenarios requiring some degree of police discretion is endless and, therefore, police discretion is a topic of major concern to researchers in the field of police psychology. More specifically, researchers are interested in whether police discretion is really necessary, the sorts of situations in which discretion is used, and ways of controlling the inappropriate use of police discretion. Each of these issues will be examined in this section.

Why Is Police Discretion Necessary?

Although some individuals and interest groups believe that police officers should always enforce the law, police officers clearly do not (and perhaps cannot) do this all the time. Indeed, police officers often have great latitude in how they apply the law (McKenna, 2002). But is this discretion necessary? What good are laws if they are only applied under certain conditions? The typical answers that researchers (and police agencies) offer for such questions are based on the fact that it is impossible to establish laws that adequately encompass all the possible situations an officer can encounter and, therefore, a degree of discretion is inevitable. However, in addition to this explanation, there are many other arguments for why police discretion is a necessary part of modern-day policing.

For example, Sheehan and Cordner (1989) have provided the following important reasons for police discretion:

- A police officer who attempts to enforce all the laws all the time would be in the police station and in court all the time and, thus, of little use when serious problems arise in the community.
- Legislatures pass some laws that they clearly do not intend to have strictly enforced all the time.
- Legislatures pass some laws that are vague, making it necessary for the police to interpret them and decide when to apply them.
- Most law violations are minor in nature, such as driving slightly over the posted speed limit, and do not require full enforcement of the law.
- Full enforcement of all the laws all the time would alienate the public and undermine support for the police.
- Full enforcement of all the laws all the time would overwhelm the criminal justice system, including the prisons.
- The police have many duties to perform with limited resources. Good judgment must therefore be used in establishing enforcement priorities.

However, it should be stressed that, if we accept police discretion as an inevitable part of policing, we as a society must be prepared to deal with the consequences. Although the arguments put forward by researchers like Sheehan and Cordner (1989) highlight some obvious advantages of police discretion, there are also potential disadvantages. For example, for police discretion to be advantageous, officers must exercise discretion in a non-discriminatory manner. Unfortunately, this does not always happen, as seen in Box 2.2.

Areas Where Police Discretion Is Used

Having established the various rationales for the use of police discretion, we now consider some of the situations in which it is used. As indicated above, police officers make relatively few decisions that do not require at least some degree of discretion. However, several domains are worthy of a more in-depth discussion, including encounters with youths, individuals with mental illnesses, domestic violence, and use-of-force situations.

YOUTH CRIME According to Siegal and Senna (1994), as the "initial gatekeepers" to the juvenile justice system, police officers have a great deal of discretion when dealing with young offenders. Common police responses to youth crime include formal arrests, police cautions, community referrals, and family conferences. Since at least the early 1960s, research has demonstrated that youth crime is often dealt with by the police in an informal manner. For

BOX 2.2	Inappropriate Police Discretion: The Case of Racial Profiling

Police officers routinely have to decide whether to pull over vehicles for traffic stops and most of us would agree that a degree of police discretion is warranted when making such decisions. When a decision is made to pull over a vehicle, we expect that the police will have based their decision on evidence of wrongdoing and in the vast majority of cases this is how decisions are made. Relatively recently, however, it has come to light that some police officers may decide to pull over vehicles based on a consideration of other factors, such as the race of the individual who is driving the vehicle, presumably because they assume that race is a reliable predictor of wrongdoing. This practice is commonly referred to as *racial profiling*.

Racial profiling refers to any police-initiated action that relies on the race or ethnicity of an individual, rather than the individual's criminal behavior. According to Harris (1999a), one of the most common forms of racial profiling is the police practice of stopping and searching vehicles (for drugs and weapons usually) because the driver does not "match" the vehicle he or she is driving. In the United States, this usually means pulling over black men who are driving expensive vehicles. For example, consider the case of Shawn Lee, a football player with the San Diego Chargers who, while driving his Jeep Cherokee in 1997, was pulled over and handcuffed because he was thought to be driving a vehicle that matched the description of a stolen car (Muffler, 2006). It later turned out that the stolen car was nothing like Lee's vehicle, but was in fact a Honda sedan.

So, is racial profiling actually used by the police in the United States? If so, is it a valid practice or is it a case of inappropriate police discretion?

Certainly, U.S. citizens believe the police actively engage in racial profiling. For example, a 1999 Gallup Poll indicated that 56% of whites and 77% of blacks believed that racial profiling is pervasive (Gallup Poll, 1999). What appears to differ by race, however, is the percentage of people who believe they have been the target of racial profiling. For example, results from the same Gallup Poll indicated that only 6% of white men believed they had been stopped by the police based on their race alone, versus 42% of black men, and this percentage increased further for black men between the ages of 18 and 34.

Empirical research also confirms that racial profiling is practiced by some U.S. police agencies (Ramirez et al., 2000). For example, Lamberth (1999) conducted an analysis of police stop-and-search practices in Maryland. Using data from the Maryland State Police, he compared the drivers who were stopped and searched along a major highway in Maryland with those who were actually violating traffic laws. According to Harris (1999b), who discussed Lamberth's study in some detail, approximately 74% of Lamberth's "law violator" sample consisted of white individuals while only 17.5% were black individuals. More importantly, a staggering 79.2% of the drivers who were stopped and searched were black.

Of course, the possibility exists that such behavior simply reflects an accurate perception on the part of the police that members of some minority groups are more likely to be involved in illegal activity. Existing research, however, does not support this assumption. In Lamberth's (1999) study, for example, he found that a similar percentage of black and white drivers who were stopped and searched were actually found with drugs in their possession (28.4% and 28.8%, respectively; cited by Harris, 1999b).

It appears, therefore, that racial profiling is not a valid police procedure for determining who should be stopped and searched, at least in the police jurisdictions where it has been studied. Instead, racial profiling is an inappropriate use of police discretion that discriminates against minority groups.

example, Goldman's (1963) analysis of arrest records in Pennsylvania showed that the majority of police contacts with juveniles resulted in informal dispositions. Similar findings emerge from more recent studies. For example, Worden and Meyers' (2001) study of youth crime in Indiana and Florida demonstrated that only a small percentage of encounters with youth end in an arrest (13%), with the most common disposition being a threat of arrest (38%).

INDIVIDUALS WITH MENTAL ILLNESSES   As is the case with young offenders, police officers frequently come into contact with offenders suffering from mental illnesses. According to Teplin (2000), several factors have increased the likelihood of these encounters. Primary among these factors is the movement toward de-institutionalizing individuals who have a mental illness. In an attempt to ensure these encounters are dealt with effectively, formal policies are often put in place, which specify how police officers should deal with offenders who have a mental illness. These policies typically instruct police officers to apprehend the individual whenever he or she poses a danger to self or others, or is causing some other kind of serious disturbance (Teplin, 2000). However, although these policies provide the police with the legal power to intervene, police officers must still rely on their discretion to choose the most appropriate course of action.

When police officers encounter an individual with a mental illness who is creating a disturbance, they generally have three options available to them: (1) they can transport that person to a psychiatric institution of some kind, (2) they can arrest the person and take him or her to jail, or (3) they can resolve the matter informally (Teplin, 2000). Although this decision may not seem difficult, in practice it often is. For example, as Teplin states, "emergency hospitalization often is fraught with bureaucratic obstacles and the legal difficulties of obtaining commitment for treatment . . . many psychiatric programs will not accept everyone, particularly those considered dangerous, those who also have substance abuse disorders, or those with numerous previous hospitalizations" (p. 9). As a result, police officers may be forced to take actions that are not in the best interest of the offender, such as taking the individual to jail.

The limited options that are often available to the police when they are dealing with offenders who have a mental illness can mean that these offenders become criminalized (Teplin, 1984). In other words, individuals who would have typically been treated within the mental health system are now dealt with by the criminal justice system. This criminalization process appears to be at work in a study reported by Teplin (2000), which involved 506 police–offender encounters, 147 of which resulted in an arrest. As you can see in Table 2.2, the probability of being arrested if you are an offender in Teplin's study is much greater if the suspect shows signs of being mentally ill. More specifically, 14 of the 30 suspects with a mental illness (47%) in this study were arrested, compared with only 133 of the 476 other suspects (28%).

TABLE 2.2	**Mental Illness and the Likelihood of Being Arrested**		
		Presence of a Mental Illness		
		No	Yes	Total
	No	343 (72%)	16 (53%)	359 (71%)
Arrest	**Yes**	133 (28%)	14 (47%)	147 (29%)
	Total	476 (97%)	30 (6%)	506 (100%)

Source: "Keeping the peace: Police discretion and mentally ill persons" by Linda A. Teplin from *National Institute of Justice Journal*, National Criminal Justice Reference Service (2000).

These figures raise many difficult questions. For example, do these figures reflect the discriminatory use of discretion on the part of the police or do they reflect the fact that offenders who have a mental illness commit more serious crimes? Alternatively, could it be that these figures simply reflect the fact that the hands of the police are often tied, with arrests being one of the few options available to ensure that individuals with mental illness remain free from harm? To know what these figures actually mean, more systematic research clearly needs to be conducted. Thankfully, researchers are currently carrying out such research. Leading the charge is Dr. Linda Teplin, who is profiled in Box 2.3.

BOX 2.3   Researcher Profile: Dr. Linda Teplin

Dr. Linda Teplin

Perhaps no one has contributed more to our understanding of how the police interact with individuals with mental illness as Dr. Linda Teplin. But this research might never have happened if Dr. Teplin had followed her original dream of becoming a pianist. Fortunately for us, Dr. Teplin's interest in the human condition won her over and instead of specializing in music at Roosevelt University she decided to major in psychology and sociology.

After graduating from Roosevelt University, Dr. Teplin applied and was accepted into the graduate program at Northwestern University. While at Northwestern, Dr. Teplin was exposed to courses in psychology, sociology, and anthropology. It was in this interdisciplinary climate that she learned to appreciate how the research methods used in different social science disciplines could complement one another and this appreciation has influenced how she has conducted her research ever since.

After completing her Ph.D. dissertation, which examined young children's racial prejudice, Dr. Teplin began her long and distinguished career in the Department of Psychiatry at Northwestern University Medical School. Having no training in psychiatry, this posting caused her some initial fear, but she soon found her footing and began her first studies of individuals with mental illness who come into contact with the police.

One of the things that Dr. Teplin noticed when she first started examining the data on police encounters with individuals with mental illness was that only rarely would these individuals be seen in emergency psychiatric facilities. Curious to understand why this was not happening, she began to dig deeper.

Dr. Teplin's early research in this area led to a surprising finding—despite the fact that the individuals with mental illness in her studies were not committing more crime than individuals without a mental illness, they were more likely to be arrested by the police. Rather than reflecting biased decisions on the part of the police, her investigation led to an equally distressing conclusion—most police officers knew that arresting individuals with mental illness was not the best option, but mental health options were often blocked.

Since these early studies, Dr. Teplin has dedicated her career to finding out what happens to individuals with mental illness when they come into contact with the law. Some of this research has involved observational studies where Dr. Teplin and her students have gone on ride-alongs with police officers. Dr. Teplin's research has led to countless articles and many well-deserved awards, including the Award for Distinguished Contribution to Research in Public Policy from the American Psychological Association. These awards highlight the significant impact that Dr. Teplin's work has had on the well-being of individuals with mental illness and the police officers who are sometimes tasked with ensuring their safety.

Source: "Award for Distinguished Contribution to Research in Psychology: Linda A. Teplin" from *American Psychologist*, vol. 48. Copyright © 1993 by American Psychological Association.

DOMESTIC VIOLENCE   Another area in which police officers have a great deal of discretion is in their response to domestic disputes. Historically, domestic violence by a husband against his wife was often ignored by the police. However, in the 1960s and 1970s people became more aware of victim needs in domestic violence situations, and numerous individuals and interest groups began pushing for a more aggressive policy of arrest (Melton, 1999).

According to Melton (1999), this push was helped along by a number of factors. First, several lawsuits were successfully brought against U.S. police departments that had failed to arrest offenders of domestic violence. Second, domestic violence research began being conducted, with some of this research suggesting that arrests had a deterrent effect on offenders of domestic violence. Eventually, pro-arrest policies were put in place in many police agencies and new government legislation was enacted. However, even with new policies and legislation in place, there are still a range of responses available to police officers when faced with domestic disputes. In addition to making arrests, these include mediation (e.g., talking to the victim), community referrals (e.g., recommending the couple seek professional help), and separation (e.g., asking one of the participants to leave).

Currently, it appears that police agencies in the United States are taking the issue of domestic violence very seriously. For example, a relatively recent study conducted by Townsend, Hunt, Kuck, and Baxter (2006) indicated that the vast majority of police agencies in the United States now have written policies in place that describe how their officers should respond in cases of domestic violence and most agencies require that their officers receive specialized domestic violence training. However, a lot of variation remains across policies with respect to the definition of domestic relationships (e.g., with regard to same-sex partners) and how police officers are to respond to calls for service (e.g., with regard to taking custody of children).

If you were a police officer, how would you make decisions in cases of domestic disputes? To experience some of the challenges you might face when making a decision, see the Case Study box below.

CASE STUDY

YOU BE THE POLICE OFFICER

You are a police officer who has just received a call over your radio about a domestic disturbance. You arrive at the scene to find a woman and a man arguing. The woman has a bloody nose and a black eye and it is clear the man is the person who hit her. The woman pleads with you not to arrest the man. She states that she has a serious drinking problem, that she started the argument with her husband, and that it was totally her fault that she ended up getting hit. While crying, she also says that she can't take care of her fours kids by herself because she doesn't work and she depends on her husband to take care of the house and pay the bills. If you arrest the husband, he may go to jail.

Your Turn . . .

As the police officer on the scene, what would you do and why? What factors would influence your decision?

USE-OF-FORCE SITUATIONS   Perhaps the topic that has received the most attention when it comes to police discretion is the use of force, particularly lethal force, by law enforcement officers. Highly publicized cases of police use of force, such as the 1991 Rodney King incident that is described in Box 2.4, have done much to fuel this debate. Police officers are granted the right to use force to protect the general public and themselves. However, police officers can only use force when it is necessary to suppress a situation, and only to the extent that is necessary to accomplish this goal. When a police officer uses force for any other purpose, or in excess of what is needed, that officer has made inappropriate use of his or her discretionary power. When this happens, the result can be deadly. It can also be very costly for the police, who may have to deal with potential lawsuits.

BOX 2.4   Police Brutality in the Rodney King Incident

On the night of March 2, 1991, a speeding Hyundai driven by Rodney King was spotted by two officers of the California Highway Patrol. The officers pursued King's vehicle, which resulted in a high-speed chase along a freeway in the San Fernando Valley area of Los Angeles and into residential streets. Eventually, with the help of a helicopter and several cruisers, the police were able to stop King's car and they ordered King and his two passengers to exit the vehicle.

King's passengers complied with the officer's orders and were taken into custody. King, however, remained in his car. When he did get out of his car, he reportedly started acting in a strange manner. At one point, one of the officers at the scene believed that King was reaching for a weapon and she unholstered her firearm and pointed it at King. The ranking officer at the scene ordered her to holster the weapon and instructed four other officers to restrain King.

As the officers attempted to restrain King he physically resisted them and they fell back. The ranking officer then used his Taser on King, which temporarily stunned him. A video recording made by a bystander then shows one of the officers at the scene striking King in the head with his baton. King continually tried to get up, resulting in many more baton blows from the officers and several kicks. After finally putting King in cuffs, he was dragged to a waiting ambulance and taken to the hospital.

At the hospital, tests revealed that King was under the influence of alcohol and had been smoking marijuana. King was also found to be suffering from several broken bones, bruises, and lacerations. Believing he was the victim of police brutality, King sued the city, and four of the officers at the scene were charged with the use of excessive force.

After the initial trial judge was replaced and the original venue and jury pool were changed in an attempt to reduce biases resulting from media coverage of the case, the trial of the officers took place. On April 29, 1992, the jury acquitted three of the officers and could not agree on the charges for the fourth officer. Immediately following news of the acquittals, widespread riots erupted in Los Angeles, which resulted in deaths and injuries, and an incredible amount of destruction.

After the riots, the U.S. Department of Justice reopened the investigation against the four police officers and they were charged with violating King's civil rights. A federal trial took place and the jury ultimately found two of the officers guilty (the other two were acquitted on all charges). The guilty officers were each subsequently sentenced to 30 months in prison.

Sources: Cannon (1999); Independent Commission on the Los Angeles Police Department (1991); *Koon v. United States* 518 U.S. 81 (1996); Whitman (1993).

Fortunately, police use of force is a relatively rare phenomenon. As MacDonald, Manz, Alpert, and Dunham (2003) stated, "Whether measured by use-of-force reports, citizen complaints, victim surveys, or observational methods, the data consistently indicate that only a small percentage of police–public interactions involve use of force" (p. 120). Recently, for example, the Police Public Contact Survey developed by the U.S. Bureau of Justice Statistics found that only 1.5% of people who come into contact with police in the United States either experience force firsthand or are threatened by the use of force (U.S. Bureau of Justice Statistics, 2005). Furthermore, when police do decide to use force, it is often the minimal amount of force necessary (Adams, 1999), and it is typically in response to a resistant suspect (Alpert & Dunham, 1999).

Controlling Police Discretion

In an attempt to ensure that police officers exercise their discretion appropriately, most organizations have established guidelines that allow police discretion to be controlled. In addition, specific codes of conduct for police officers have been developed that help control the use of discretion.

In this section, we will deal specifically with methods for controlling inappropriate police discretion in use-of-force situations. One reason for focusing on such situations is the public's widespread interest in this area. The other reason is that numerous attempts have been made to develop innovative approaches for controlling the abuse of force by the police. One approach is the development of administrative policies within police agencies that are specifically meant to control the use of force by police officers. A related approach is the development of models (the most common being the **use-of-force continuum**) to help guide a police officer's decision-making process in use-of-force situations.

DEPARTMENTAL POLICIES   Departmental policies for restricting use of force by police officers are not new. Research on the effectiveness of these policies is also not new. For example, Fyfe (1979) examined the impact of use-of-force policies put in place by the New York Police Department (NYPD) in 1972. These policies were meant to decrease the use of lethal force by NYPD officers and Fyfe's study indicated just that. Not only did the frequency of police shootings decrease in New York from 1971 to 1975, but the numbers of officers injured and killed during the same period also decreased. Similar findings have been reported in several other U.S. cities, indicating that departmental policies can effectively restrict the use of inappropriate force (e.g., Geller & Scott, 1992). However, White (2001) draws attention to the fact that restrictive use-of-force policies do not always have the desired impact, and that other factors can minimize their effect. For instance, he has argued that the philosophies of senior police officers can often outweigh departmental polices. As White puts it, if the police leadership has a "bust their heads" philosophy, departmental policies will likely not have their intended effect (p. 135).

THE USE-OF-FORCE CONTINUUM   Although use-of-force continuum models may not directly restrict the use of force by police officers in the same way that departmental policies try to, they may indirectly control force by ensuring that officers carefully assess and evaluate potential use-of-force situations when deciding what course of action to take. In the words of Walma and West (2002):

Use-of-force continuum

A model that is supposed to guide police officer decision making in use-of-force situations by providing the officer with some guidance as to what level of force is appropriate given the suspect's behavior and other environmental conditions

The theory behind the continuum is that, in order to subdue a suspect, the officer must be prepared to use a level of force that is one step higher than that used by the suspect in resisting the officer. There is no need for the officer to move up the continuum of force step by step since it is certainly unlikely that the suspect will do so. Once the suspect displays his or her level of resistance, the officer must react with subduing force. If, however, the officer moves to a level of force that is disproportionate to the force offered by the suspect, the officer is open to the accusation of using excessive force. (p. 67)

Thus, use-of-force continuums help to control police officer actions in the sense that they encourage them to use only that amount of force necessary to deal adequately with a situation.

Unlike some countries where attempts have been made to develop a single use-of-force model for use by all police agencies, in the United States use-of-force continuums tend to vary from agency to agency. One such model is described more fully in Box 2.5. Like all use-of-force continuums, it is hoped that this model will have its intended effect

BOX 2.5   Use-of-Force Continuums

To provide guidelines to police officers with regard to what level of force is reasonable under various circumstances, police agencies often incorporate a use-of-force continuum into their training of officers. Many such continuums exist, but all represent the process by which a police officer assesses, plans, and responds to use-of-force situations.

As indicated in Figure 2.4, which represents what a standard use-of-force continuum might look like, the process for the officer involved in a use-of-force encounter begins with an

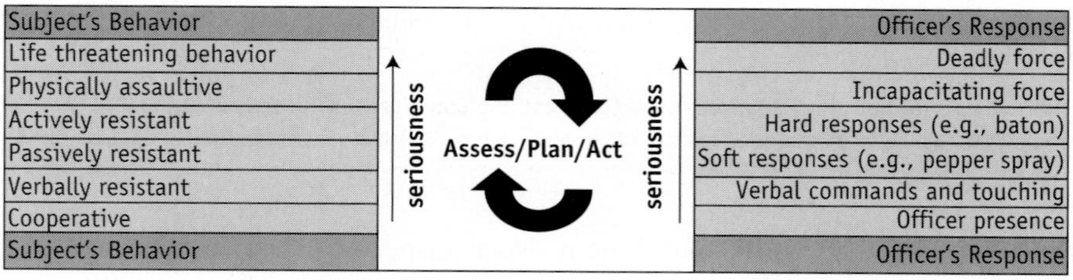

Subject's Behavior		Officer's Response
Life threatening behavior		Deadly force
Physically assaultive		Incapacitating force
Actively resistant		Hard responses (e.g., baton)
Passively resistant	seriousness ↑ Assess/Plan/Act seriousness ↑	Soft responses (e.g., pepper spray)
Verbally resistant		Verbal commands and touching
Cooperative		Officer presence
Subject's Behavior		Officer's Response

FIGURE 2.4 A Use-of-Force Continuum

Source: Based on Wolf, Mesloh, Henych, & Thompson, 2009

(continued)

BOX 2.5   *Continued*

assessment of the situation confronting the officer. Officers are usually instructed to consider a range of factors, such as subject characteristics, officer capabilities, environmental conditions, and tactical issues.

In addition to these factors, the officer must also assess the subject's behavior. Different levels of subject resistance are depicted on the left-hand side of the model in Figure 2.4. At the lower end of this continuum are behaviors representing compliance with officer demands and low levels of resistance. At the upper end of the continuum are assaultive behaviors, which have the potential to cause serious injury or death.

Based on the officer's assessment of the situation, and particularly the subject's behavior, he or she can select from the use-of-force options contained on the right-hand side of the model. At the lower end of this continuum are interventions that are unlikely to lead to injury (e.g., simply being present), while the upper end of the continuum culminates in deadly force.

Generally speaking, there is an approximate correspondence between the graphic's depiction of a subject's behavior and the use-of-force options available to the officer (Wolf, Mesloh, Henych, & Thompson, 2009). For example, if a subject is acting in an extremely assaultive manner that is putting the officer's life at risk, it may be necessary and justifiable for the police officer to use deadly force.

After the officer comes up with a plan and chooses an appropriate response option, the officer must continue to assess the entire situation to determine if his or her initial response was appropriate and effective, or if a new use-of-force option should be selected. This reassessment will consider all of the various factors included in the original assessment.

When deciding on a new response it is important to realize that officers are not required to move up or down the use-of-force continuum in step-by-step fashion. Indeed, the next appropriate response from an officer may be multiple steps away from their initial response (e.g., moving from verbal commands to deadly force very quickly as a result of a rapidly changing situation).

Although a use-of-force continuum like the one depicted in Figure 2.4 may be a useful heuristic for determining an appropriate course of action, the decisions that a police officer has to make when deciding whether to use force (and what type of force) are still not easy. The whole process may take only a few seconds. The process is also dynamic and constantly evolving, and requires that the officer be able to consider many factors simultaneously while developing an appropriate plan of action.

Source: Based on data from "Police use of force and the cumulative force factor" from *Policing: An International Journal of Police Strategies & Management*, vol. 32, Emerald Group Publishing, Ltd. (2009).

of assisting police officers in controlling resistant suspects while also ensuring that the officer does not use excessive force (thus minimizing the chance of injury to the suspect and officer and reducing the chance of legal liability).

POLICE STRESS

Many police psychologists, as well as police officers and their families, consider policing to be one of the most stressful occupations (Anshel, 2000). After our discussion of some of the dangerous situations police officers encounter, you have probably come to a similar conclusion yourself. Even if policing is not considered one of the most stressful occupations, we can all probably agree that police officers are exposed to many stressful events. Not only has research demonstrated that this is the case, but it has also indicated that these stressful events can have a negative impact on police officers and their families, as well as the organizations they work for (Brown & Campbell, 1994). In this section, we will discuss some of the sources of police stress and examine the potential consequences that result when exposed to police stressors. In addition, we will briefly focus on what can be done to prevent and manage police stress.

Sources of Police Stress

As Finn and Tomz (1996) make clear, "different officers are likely to perceive different events as stressful, depending on their individual background, personalities, expectations, law enforcement experience, years on the job, type of law enforcement work they perform, and access to coping resources" (p. 6). However, research suggests that there are a number of common sources of police stress (Abdollahi, 2002). Although the labeling of these categories may differ depending on what article or book you read, the major sources of police stress tend to include organizational stressors, occupational stressors, criminal justice stressors, and public stressors. Finn and Tomz (1996) have provided a reasonably comprehensive list of specific stressors that fall into each of these categories, a partial listing of which is presented in Table 2.3.

     Although the majority of people assume that **occupational stressors** are the most stressful for police officers, officers sometimes indicate that they experience a degree of stress for each of the stressors described in Table 2.3. In fact, some police researchers believe they have evidence to show that **organizational stressors** can sometimes affect officers more strongly than occupational stressors. For example, in their survey of 154 full-time police officers, Taylor and Bennell (2006) found that organizational stressors

Occupational stressors

In policing, stressors relating to the job itself

Organizational stressors

In policing, stressors relating to organizational issues

TABLE 2.3	Sources of Police Stress

1. Organizational Stressors

- *Lack of career development.* In most police agencies, there is little room for advancement, regardless of the performance of the officer.
- *Excessive paperwork.* The need for duplicate forms of every police transaction is often questioned.

2. Occupational Stressors

- *Irregular work schedule.* Shift work is disruptive to the personal lives of most police officers.
- *Human suffering.* Officers are constantly exposed to the inequities and brutalities of life.

3. Criminal Justice Stressors

- *Ineffectiveness of the corrections system.* Officers are alarmed by the recidivism rate of criminals who seem to be perpetually "on the street" rather than incarcerated.
- *Unfavorable court decisions.* Many court decisions are viewed by officers as unfairly increasing the difficulty of police work.

4. Public Stressors

- *Distorted press accounts.* Reports of incidents are often inaccurate and perceived as derogatory by officers, whether or not the inaccuracy is intentional.
- *Ineffectiveness of referral agencies.* The ineffectiveness of social service agencies frustrates officers who view these agencies as their only source of assistance.

Source: Developing a law enforcement stress program for officers and their families by Peter Finn and Julie E. Tomz, 1996.

Although occupational stressors, such as police shootings, can cause a great deal of stress for many police officers, organizational stressors, such as perceptions of inadequate departmental support, can also result in harmful levels of stress.

such as "inconsistent leadership style" were rated as more stressful than occupational stressors such as "risk of being injured on the job." Such claims are backed up by anecdotal evidence. Consider the words of a wife interviewed in Finn and Tomz's (1996) study, for example, whose husband ended up resigning as a police officer due to stress: "My husband came home more screwed up with department problems than with anything he ever encountered on the streets" (p. 7).

Consequences of Police Stress

When a police officer experiences a potentially life-threatening situation, the acute stress reactions that the officer experiences can have serious repercussions that last long after the actual event. Likewise, constant exposure to other police stressors, particularly organizational stressors, can affect police officers on a more chronic basis (McCraty, Tomasino, Atkinson, & Sundram, 1999). Without an effective prevention or management strategy (at both the individual and the organizational level) to deal with police stressors, police officers, their families, and the organizations they work for will suffer in numerous ways. The general consequences of police stress have been categorized by Brown and Campbell (1994) into physical health problems, psychological and personal problems, and job performance problems, and large-scale research projects are starting to systematically examine these effects (see Box 2.6). See Table 2.4 on page 47 for a summary of possible consequences of police stress that fall into each of these categories.

During the past several years, the largest, most comprehensive study of police stress ever conducted has been taking place in Buffalo, New York, under the lead of Dr. John Violanti, a long-serving (now retired) member of the New York State Police and a leader in the field of police stress research at the University of Buffalo.

The primary purpose of the research is to study the effects of police stress on adverse metabolic and cardiovascular outcomes with the goal being to prevent stress-related disorders. To date, hundreds of police officers have participated in the study, which involves the collection of a huge amount of data, including:

- The completion of questionnaires, which measure demographic, lifestyle, and psychological factors (e.g., depression)
- Measurements of bone density and body composition
- Ultrasounds of arteries
- Eighteen salivary cortisol samples throughout the day, and in response to a series of challenges
- Blood samples
- The quantity and quality of sleep that the officers are getting, as measured by a watch-like device called an actigraph
- Work history records

The plan is to sample the *entire* Buffalo Police Department, which would make this the first ever population-based study of police stress that examines both psychological and physiological measures of stress. Already the data that have emerged from this study are revealing important information. For example, it appears that female officers may suffer more from certain post-traumatic stress symptoms and depressive symptoms than male officers.

For years to come, this study will provide valuable information about the consequences of police stress that will benefit police officers and the people they serve.

Source: National Institute for Occupational Safety and Health, 2010.

TABLE 2.4   Possible Consequences of Police Stress

Physical Health Problems	Psychological and Personal Problems	Job Performance Problems
High blood pressure	Depression and anxiety	Low morale
Cardiovascular disease	Aggression	Tardiness
High cholesterol	Post-traumatic stress disorder	Absenteeism
Stomach ulcers	Drug and alcohol abuse	Early retirement
Respiratory problems	Suicide	Reduced productivity
Skin problems	Domestic violence	Reduced efficiency
Weight gain	Separation and divorce	Citizen complaints
Diabetes	Extramarital affairs	Turnover
Death	Burnout	Hostile interactions

Source: Table from "Possible consequences of police stress" adapted from *Stress and Policing: Sources and Strategies* by Jennifer M. Brown and Elizabeth A. Campbell. Copyright © 1994 by Jennifer M. Brown and Elizabeth A. Campbell. Published by John Wiley & Sons. Reprinted with permission of the author.

PHYSICAL HEALTH PROBLEMS One of the major consequences of police stress is the impact it can have on an officer's physical health. As McCraty et al. (1999) explain, constant exposure to acutely stressful events can result in the chronic activation of the body's stress response systems to a point where physiological breakdown occurs. The result of such a breakdown can take many different forms. For example, Kroes, Margolis, and Hurrell (1974) reported that more than 32% of the Cincinnati police officers they examined experienced digestive disorders, which is significantly higher than the prevalence rate in the civilian population. In addition, research by Franke, Collins, and Hinz (1998) has suggested that Iowa police officers are more than twice as likely as people in other occupations to develop cardiovascular disease. Furthermore, in a large-scale study of 2,376 police officers from the United States, Violanti, Vena, and Marshall (1986) found that rates of death due to cancer were significantly higher among police officers than among the general population. However, the limited amount of research in the area makes it difficult to determine how many of these health problems are due to the stressful events that police officers are exposed to and how many of them are due to the lifestyle habits adopted by police officers (Abdollahi, 2002).

PSYCHOLOGICAL AND PERSONAL PROBLEMS Psychological and personal problems, including depression, post-traumatic stress disorder, drug and alcohol abuse, marriage breakups, and suicide, can also emerge when police officers are exposed to stressful situations. Note, however, that the research in this area can often be contradictory and, therefore, caution must be used when interpreting the results of any single study. For example, although numerous studies have suggested that alcohol use may be particularly problematic among police officers (e.g., Violanti, Marshall, & Howe, 1985), Alexander, Innes, Irving, Sinclair, and Walker (1991) found that alcohol consumption by police officers was not statistically greater than consumption rates found for firefighters, prison officers, or nurses. Similarly, although some researchers have found indications of burnout among police officers (e.g., Anson & Bloom, 1988), other researchers have failed to find significant levels of burnout (Loo, 1994).

Police-related suicide rates and divorce rates have also recently been examined, and here as well there are many contradictory findings. For example, in contrast to popular belief (Loh, 1994), studies of suicide in North American police agencies demonstrate that the rates are not significantly different from the suicide rates found in comparable male populations (Aamodt & Stalnaker, 2006). Likewise, despite the view voiced by some that the divorce rate is very high in the police population (Territo & Sewell, 2007), recent research suggests that the divorce rate for law enforcement personnel in the United States is actually lower than that of the general population, even when controlling for demographic and various job-related variables (McCoy & Aamodt, 2010).

JOB PERFORMANCE PROBLEMS Job performance problems are the third major category of stress consequences. Often as a direct result of the physical and psychological problems discussed above, the way a police officer performs on the job can suffer greatly. As with other stress reactions, impaired job performance can take many forms, including a decrease in work efficiency and productivity, increased absenteeism and tardiness, and early retirement. Although these consequences may not seem as serious as the physical and psychological problems caused by police stress, from an organizational perspective they certainly are significant. For example, consider the problem of absenteeism due to illness. According to one newspaper article from the late 1980s, it was estimated that each year in England and Wales the police service lost approximately 1.6 million working days through sickness, some of which can undoubtedly be attributed to stress (*The Guardian*, 1988). While we know of no comparable estimates for police organizations in the United States, the cost of worker stress on the American economy is staggering, with some putting the figure at around $300 billion annually (e.g., Leiter & Maslach, 2005).

Preventing and Managing Police Stress

Most police officers and police agencies have now recognized the need to prevent and manage negative reactions to stressful events. Indeed, during the past 20 years, formal stress programs have been set up in most agencies to combat the effects of police stress. A variety of strategies are included in these programs, including informal support networks, physical fitness programs, professional counseling services, family assistance programs, and special assessments following exposure to critical events such as shootings or accidents (Brown & Campbell, 1994). A thorough discussion of each of these strategies is beyond the scope of this chapter. Here, we will simply focus on two particular strategies—one preventive strategy and one management strategy.

EFFECTIVE COPING SKILLS   Police stress is not only a result of being exposed to stressful events, it is also a result of the poor coping skills that some police officers use when faced with these events (Anshel, 2000). Many coping strategies are maladaptive and can lead to further, more serious problems for the police officer. For example, Burke (1993) found that officers who coped with stress by using alcohol, other drugs, anger, or withdrawal were more likely to suffer from health problems and further stress than were officers who used more adaptive coping strategies. Thus, one potentially useful method for preventing stress at the level of the individual police officer is to teach officers how to use adaptive coping strategies.

Many of these adaptive coping strategies are fairly basic, such as teaching police officers how to communicate with others more effectively (given that ineffective communication is a primary cause of stress). Other strategies are more specific stress-relieving techniques, such as the use of Freeze-Frame®, which forms part of the Heart-Math Stress Management Program (McCraty et al., 1999). This is a technique in which officers are taught to "consciously disengage from negative mental and emotional reactions as they occur by shifting their attention to the area of the heart, then self-generating a positive or neutral feeling" (McCraty et al., 1999, p. 6).

As Anshel (2000) points out, training police officers how to use adaptive coping strategies proactively may be a particularly useful approach because "although police officers often cannot control the sources of job-related stress, their effective use of coping strategies following unpleasant events is controllable" (p. 377). Furthermore, this intervention has been shown to have a significant and positive impact, not only on job-related performance, but also on the health and general well-being of police officers in their everyday lives (McCraty et al., 1999).

PSYCHOLOGICAL DEBRIEFINGS   One of the most commonly used methods for managing police stress is the **psychological debriefing** (e.g., Mitchell, 1983), which often consists of a brief psychologically oriented intervention delivered to officers following exposure to an event that has resulted in psychological distress. Typically forming one part of a larger crisis intervention program, psychological debriefings revolve around a

Psychological debriefing

A psychologically oriented intervention delivered to police officers following exposure to an event that resulted in psychological distress

group or individual meeting aimed at mitigating emotional distress and preventing long-term psychopathology. Its key elements frequently involve social support and the ventilation of emotions through discussion, while facilitators educate participants about stress responses and coping mechanisms in an attempt to restore adaptive functioning (Everly, Flannery, & Mitchell, 2000; Raphael & Wilson, 2000).

Although numerous studies have examined the effectiveness of psychological debriefings, confusion still remains as to whether this stress management strategy actually works. For example, early meta-analytic research suggested that Mitchell's group-based Critical Incident Stress Debriefing (Mitchell, 1983) was effective (Everly & Boyle, 1999). A subsequent meta-analysis by Everly, Boyle, and Lating (1999), which examined a wider array of debriefing procedures, reported similar (although slightly more modest) results. However, two more recent meta-analytic studies concluded that psychological debriefings only have a small effect on reducing symptoms of post-traumatic stress disorder (PTSD) (van Emmerik, Kamphuis, Hulsbosch, & Emmelkamp, 2002) or no effect at all (Mitte, Steil, & Nachtigall, 2005).

To some extent, these contrasting results can likely be attributed to the various forms of psychological debriefings that have been examined in these studies. For example, some of the debriefings were presented in a single session, whereas others took place over multiple sessions. The types of incidents encountered by the people being debriefed also varied from study to study, ranging from natural disasters to victims of crime. Furthermore, the person facilitating the debriefing is not constant across studies, and includes both peers (e.g., fellow police officers) and mental health professionals. Whether these (and other) factors are important is a hotly debated topic and more research is clearly needed before we can determine conclusively whether psychological debriefings are an effective stress management tool (and how they should be delivered).

Summary

1. The development of a useful police selection process requires two major steps: (1) identify the knowledge, skills, and abilities that are required for the job and (2) construct and validate selection instruments that measure these qualities and compare them with job performance.

2. Some of the most common police selection procedures are semistructured interviews, psychological tests, and the use of situational tests in assessment centers.

3. Police discretion refers to the power that police officers have to decide which laws apply to a given situation and whether or not to apply them. Many view police discretion as an inevitable part of police work and, as long as it is used in an unbiased manner, police discretion can be very useful.

4. Nearly every decision that a police officer has to make requires some degree of discretion. However, four of the most commonly studied areas of police discretion deal with youth crime, offenders with mental illnesses, domestic violence, and use-of-force situations.

5. Policing is considered by many to be one of the most stressful occupations. Sources of stress include organizational stressors, occupational stressors, criminal justice stressors, and public stressors. These stressors can lead to serious physical health problems, psychological and personal problems, and job performance problems if they are not dealt with appropriately.

6. To combat the negative effects of stress, police forces are developing and using a variety of prevention and management strategies. One prevention strategy that looks particularly promising involves teaching police officers how to use adaptive coping skills when faced with stressful events. A common management strategy is the use of psychological debriefings. Currently, there is disagreement as to whether this strategy is effective at reducing stress symptoms.

Key Concepts

assessment center *34*
cognitive ability tests *32*
Inwald Personality
   Inventory *33*
job analysis *28*

Minnesota Multiphasic
   Personality
   Inventory *33*
occupational
   stressors *45*

organizational
   stressors *45*
police discretion *35*
police selection
   procedures *26*

psychological
   debriefing *49*
selection interview *31*
situational test *34*
use-of-force continuum *42*

Discussion Questions

1. You are a member of a community group that has been put together to provide your local police agency with recommendations regarding police selection criteria. What do you, as a community citizen, feel are the most important characteristics of a good police officer? Do you think these characteristics should be considered when police forces select police officers? Why or why not?

2. Members of police forces have rated sense of humor as an important characteristic of an effective police officer. As a researcher in the area of police psychology, what problems might you encounter when developing a situational test to determine whether police applicants have a good sense of humor?

3. Imagine you are a police officer who encounters a well-dressed woman walking down the street who is obviously intoxicated. Public drunkenness is a crime in your town. What would you do? Would you arrest her and take her to jail, or would you drive her home? What factors would you consider when making your decision? Would your decision have been different if you encountered an older man who was drunk and dressed in dirty clothes? Why or why not?

4. Your friend has been a police officer for five years. He constantly talks to you about the stress he feels, but rarely does he raise any issues about occupational stressors. Instead, he seems most upset with the organization he works for. Why do you think organizational stressors have such a big impact on police officers?

3

The Psychology of Police Investigations

LEARNING OBJECTIVES

- Describe the Reid model of interrogation and summarize the rationale for its use.

- Outline three potential problems with the Reid model of interrogation.

- Define the three major types of false confessions.

- Describe the vulnerability factors associated with each type of false confession.

- Explain why the police use criminal profiling and outline three potential problems with its use.

- Explain what geographic profiling is and how it can be used in police investigations.

Mark Jackson was arrested for shooting a man inside a convenience store. After his arrest, he was taken to the police station for questioning. Over the course of a 24-hour period, Mark was interrogated three times. The last interrogation took place at 2:00 a.m. Although Mark stated he was exhausted, he was told the interrogation would not take long and that it was best to "get it over with." In reality, the interrogation lasted for more than three hours.

Initially, Mark maintained that although he was at the store on the day of the shooting, he had nothing to do with the crime. However, throughout the interrogations the police challenged him, stating they had hard evidence proving he was the killer. This evidence included statements from several eyewitnesses. None of this evidence actually existed. In addition, the police minimized the seriousness of the crime, stating that the victim was a known drug dealer who "had it coming" and that Mark "did everyone a favor."

Over the course of his interrogations, the police continually pressured Mark to stop denying his involvement in the crime and said that if he told the truth "all of this would end." Finally, during his last interrogation, Mark admitted to the shooting. The case went to court, and Mark was convicted, largely on the basis of his confession. Months later, it was discovered that he had not committed the crime. Mark had confessed to a crime he had nothing to do with.

A s seen in Chapter 2, forensic psychology plays an important role in many aspects of police work. One element we have yet to discuss, however, is psychology's role in criminal investigations, such as the Mark Jackson investigation described above. Many people are aware that psychology is used in criminal investigations, and recent movies and television shows have done much to promote this fact. However, as you will see throughout this chapter, psychology played an important role in the investigative process long before Hollywood became interested in the topic, and it continues to do so today.

Psychologists have identified a number of key investigative tasks where psychology is particularly relevant. One of these tasks relates to the collection and evaluation of investigative information—information that is often obtained from suspects. Another task relates to investigative decision making, especially decisions that require an in-depth understanding of criminal behavior. This chapter will focus on how psychology contributes to these tasks by looking first at how the police interrogate suspects, and some possible consequences of their interrogation practices, and then by examining the practice of profiling the characteristics of criminals based on the way they commit their crimes.

POLICE INTERROGATIONS

Confession evidence is often viewed as "a prosecutor's most potent weapon" (Kassin, 1997, p. 221). In some countries, people may be convicted solely on the basis of their confession, although in North America, a confession usually has to be backed up by some other form of evidence (Gudjonsson, 2003). Regardless of whether corroborative evidence is required, it is likely that people who confess to a crime are more likely to be prosecuted and convicted than those who do not. Indeed, some legal scholars have gone so far as to claim that a confession makes other aspects of a trial unnecessary, because "the real trial, for all practical purposes, occurs when the confession is obtained" (McCormick, 1972, p. 316). Given the importance of confession evidence, it should come as no surprise that one of the major goals of a **police interrogation** is to obtain a confession from the suspect (Kassin, 1997).

Being interrogated by the police for the purpose of extracting a confession is often considered to be inherently coercive. Imagine yourself being interrogated for the very first time. You would probably be in an environment that is foreign to you, faced with one, possibly two, police officers whom you have never met. You would know little of what the police officers are going to do to you (or what they can do to you) and would have no one to turn to for support. Even if you were innocent of the crime in question, the situation would no doubt be an extremely intimidating one. In large part, this is due to the fact that the police interrogators are part of a system that gives them certain powers over you, the suspect (Gudjonsson, 2003).

There is no question that police interrogations were coercive in the past. Consider police tactics in the mid-twentieth century, for example, when whipping was occasionally used to obtain confessions (e.g., *Brown v. Mississippi*, 1936). Or consider a more recent episode occurring in the 1980s, where New York City police officers jolted a suspect with a stun gun to extract a confession (Huff, Rattner, & Sagarin, 1996). Although these overt acts of physical coercion have become much less frequent with time, they have been replaced with more subtle, psychologically based interrogation techniques,

Police interrogation

A process whereby the police question a suspect for the purpose of obtaining a confession

such as lying about evidence, promising lenient treatment, and implying threats to loved ones (Leo, 1992). Although not all interrogators use these strategies, police officers sometimes view these techniques as a necessary evil to obtain confessions from uncooperative guilty persons. Indeed, leading authorities in the field of interrogation training openly state that, because offenders are typically reluctant to confess, they must often be tricked into doing so (Inbau, Reid, Buckley, & Jayne, 2004).

The Reid Model of Interrogation

Police officers around the world often receive specialized training in exactly how to extract confessions from suspects. Depending on where this training is provided, different approaches are taught. For example, as discussed later in this chapter, police officers in England and Wales are trained to use interrogation techniques that are far less coercive than those used in North America (Kassin & Gudjonsson, 2004; Sear & Williamson, 1999; Snook, Eastwood, Stinson, Tedeschini, & House, 2010). These different techniques are used primarily because courts in England have begun to recognize some of the potential problems associated with coercive interrogation practices, such as false confessions (Meissner & Russano, 2003). Before moving on to discuss these potential problems, let us look closely at the type of interrogation training provided to many police officers in the United States.

Perhaps the most common interrogation training program offered to police officers in the United States is based on a book written by Inbau et al. (2004) called *Criminal Interrogation and Confessions*. Within this manual, the authors describe the now-famous **Reid model** of interrogation, a technique originally developed by John E. Reid, a polygrapher from Chicago (Meissner & Russano, 2003). At a general level, the Reid model consists of a three-part process. The first stage is to gather evidence related to

Reid model

A nine-step model of interrogation sometimes used in North America to extract confessions from suspects

A police officer interrogates a suspect.

the crime and to interview witnesses and victims. The second stage is to conduct a nonaccusatorial interview of the suspect. The third stage is to conduct an accusatorial interrogation of the suspect (if he or she is perceived to be guilty) in which a nine-step procedure is implemented. The primary objective at this stage is to secure a confession (Inbau et al., 2004).

As described by Inbau et al. (2004), this nine-step sequential procedure in stage 3 consists of the following steps:

1. The suspect is confronted with his or her guilt. If the police do not have any evidence against the suspect at this time, then the interrogator can hide this fact and, if necessary, pretend that such evidence exists.
2. Psychological themes are developed that allow the suspect to justify, rationalize, or excuse the crime. For example, a suspected rapist may be told that the victim must have been asking for it given what she was wearing.
3. The interrogator interrupts any statements of denial by the suspect to ensure the suspect does not get the upper hand in the interrogation.
4. The interrogator overcomes the suspect's objections to the charges to a point at which the suspect becomes quiet and withdrawn.
5. Once the suspect has become withdrawn, the interrogator ensures that the suspect does not tune out of the interrogation by reducing the psychological distance between the interrogator and the suspect (e.g., by moving physically closer to the suspect).
6. The interrogator exhibits sympathy and understanding, and the suspect is urged to come clean. For example, the interrogator might try to appeal to the suspect's sense of decency.
7. The suspect is offered face-saving explanations for the crime, which makes self-incrimination easier to achieve.
8. Once the suspect accepts responsibility for the crime, typically by agreeing with one of the face-saving explanations, the interrogator develops this admission into a full confession.
9. Finally, the interrogator gets the suspect to write and sign a full confession.

In addition to the techniques included in these nine steps, Inbau et al. (2004) provide many other suggestions for how to effectively interrogate suspects. These suggestions include things such as using a plainly decorated interrogation room to avoid distractions, having the evidence folder in your hand when beginning the interrogation, and making sure that the suspect is alone in the interrogation suite prior to the interrogator entering the room.

The Reid model of interrogation is based on the idea that suspects do not confess to crimes they have committed because they fear the potential consequences that await them if they do (Inbau et al., 2004). In addition, their fear of the potential consequences of confessing is not sufficiently outweighed by the suspect's internal feelings of anxiety associated with remaining deceptive (i.e., by maintaining they did not commit the crime in question). The goal of the Reid model is to reverse this state of affairs, by making the consequences of confessing more desirable than the anxiety related to the deception (Gudjonsson, 2003). It is assumed that this can be done by using psychologically based strategies, such as the minimization and maximization techniques described below (Jayne, 1986). For example, many believe that providing the suspect with a way to rationalize his or her behavior can reduce the perceived consequences of confessing. Conversely, appealing to one's sense of morality can sometimes increase the anxiety associated with maintaining one's innocence when the suspect is in fact guilty.

Techniques used in the Reid model of interrogation can be broken down into two general categories. These categories are often referred to by different names, including *friendly and unfriendly techniques*, *Mutt and Jeff techniques*, and *minimization and maximization techniques*. Throughout this chapter, the labels *minimization* and *maximization* will be adopted since these terms appear to be the most commonly used.

Minimization techniques refer to "soft-sell" tactics used by police interrogators that are designed to "lull the suspect into a false sense of security" (Kassin, 1997, p. 223). These tactics include the use of sympathy, excuses, and justifications. For example, when the interrogator in the opening scenario suggested to Mark Jackson that the victim "had it coming" because he was a drug dealer, and that Mark "did everyone a favor" by shooting the victim, that interrogator was using minimization techniques. In contrast to minimization techniques, **maximization techniques** refer to "scare tactics" that interrogators often use "to intimidate a suspect believed to be guilty" (Kassin, 1997, p. 223). This intimidation is typically achieved by exaggerating the seriousness of the offense and by making false claims about evidence the police supposedly have. Reference to the nonexistent eyewitnesses in the opening scenario is an example of such a scare tactic.

Minimization techniques

Soft-sell tactics used by police interrogators that are designed to lull the suspect into a false sense of security

Maximization techniques

Scare tactics used by police interrogators that are designed to intimidate a suspect believed to be guilty

The Use of the Reid Model in Actual Interrogations

Simply because the Reid model of interrogation is a widely taught interrogation procedure in the United States does not necessarily mean that police officers rely on the model in practice. Currently, it is not possible to say with any degree of confidence how often police officers use Reid interrogation techniques, but studies are beginning to shed some light on this issue. One of these studies was conducted by Dr. Saul Kassin, who is profiled in Box 3.1. Other research carried out by Dr. Kassin will be discussed throughout this chapter.

Kassin et al. (2007) conducted a survey of 631 police investigators about their interrogation practices. As part of their survey, they had the officers rate, on a five-point scale ranging from never (1) to always (5), how often they used 16 different types of interrogation techniques, some of which are included in the Reid model of interrogation. The frequency of use varied drastically across interrogation techniques. For instance, interrogators commonly used techniques such as isolating suspects from friends and family (4.49/5) and trying to establish rapport with suspects to gain their trust (4.08/5). Other common but less frequently used techniques included confronting suspects with evidence of their guilt (3.90/5) and appealing to their self-interest (3.46/5). Less common still, but sometimes used, were techniques such as implying or pretending to have evidence (3.11/5) and appealing to the suspect's religion or conscience (2.70/5). Very rare were instances of threatening the suspect with consequences for not cooperating (1.86) and physically intimidating the suspect (1.43/5).

Potential Problems with the Reid Model of Interrogation

Because many police officers are trained to use the Reid model of interrogation, especially in North America, it has been the subject of extensive research. Collectively, this research indicates that the technique has a number of potential problems. Three problems in particular deserve our attention. The first two relate to the ability of investigators to

BOX 3.1   Researcher Profile: Dr. Saul Kassin

To those of us in the field of forensic psychology, the name Saul Kassin is synonymous with the study of police interrogations and confessions. It is fair to say that Dr. Kassin has probably contributed more to our understanding of these important issues than any other psychologist working in the United States today, if not the entire world.

Dr. Saul Kassin

Dr. Kassin's approach to studying these issues is heavily influenced by his education in social psychology, which he received while an undergraduate student at Brooklyn College and as a graduate student at the University of Connecticut. Indeed, much of his research today focuses on processes of social influence that take place in the context of a police interrogation.

Currently a Distinguished Professor of Psychology at John Jay College of Criminal Justice, Dr. Kassin is well known for his widely accepted taxonomy of false confessions (described in more detail below). However, he is perhaps best known for developing innovative experimental paradigms, which he uses in order to study confessions, including false confessions, in the lab.

For example, Dr. Kassin's classic "ALT-key" experiment, which you will read more about soon, allows researchers to examine the influence of interrogation tactics on people's willingness to confess to acts they have actually not committed. This experimental paradigm and recent variations of it are used by many researchers to study false confessions.

When asked to summarize his current research interests, Dr. Kassin indicates that he's interested in three things: (1) understanding why innocent people are sometimes targeted for interrogation by the police, (2) understanding why these people sometimes confess to crimes they did not commit, and (3) understanding the impact that this evidence has on juries.

When he's not conducting research on interrogations and confessions, or teaching his classes, Dr. Kassin is busy writing books about psychology. Some of these are standard textbooks for introductory psychology and social psychology courses, others relate to forensic topics. He also lectures frequently to judges, lawyers, psychiatrists, and law enforcement groups.

A past president of the American Psychology-Law Society and a long-serving faculty member at Williams College in Massachusetts, Dr. Kassin is the recipient of numerous awards. Most recently, he was awarded an American Psychological Association Presidential Citation for his pioneering work on false confessions and his efforts to reform interrogation practices in the United States.

---

detect deception (Memon, Vrij, & Bull, 2003) and to the biases that may result when an interrogator believes, perhaps incorrectly, that a suspect is guilty (Kassin, Goldstein, & Savitsky, 2003). The third problem has to do with the coercive nature of certain interrogation practices, and the possibility that these practices will result in false confessions (Ofshe & Leo, 1997). We will briefly discuss the first two problems here and reserve our discussion of false confessions for the next section of this chapter.

DETECTING DECEPTION   A more thorough discussion of **deception detection** will be provided in Chapter 4, so our discussion here will be limited to how deception detection relates to police interrogations. The issue of whether investigators are effective deception detectors is an important one, especially when using the Reid model of interrogation, because the actual interrogation of a suspect begins only after an initial interview has

Deception detection

Detecting when someone is being deceptive

allowed the interrogator to determine whether the suspect is guilty (Inbau et al., 2004). The decision to commence a full-blown police interrogation, therefore, relies on an accurate assessment of whether the suspect is being deceptive when he or she claims to be innocent during their nonaccusatorial interview (i.e., stage 2 of the Reid model).

As you will see in Chapter 4, very little research is currently available to suggest that police officers, or anyone else for that matter, can detect deception with any degree of accuracy (e.g., Memon et al., 2003). This finding often appears to be true even after people receive specialized training (Köhnken, 1987), although there are some recent exceptions to this, where certain training programs have been shown to increase lie detection accuracy (e.g., Porter, Juodis, ten Brinke, Klein, & Wilson, 2010; Porter, Woodworth, & Birt, 2000). As a result, it seems likely that the decision to interrogate a suspect when using the Reid model of interrogation will often be based on an incorrect determination that the suspect is guilty (Kassin et al., 2003).

Of course, procedural safeguards are in place to protect an individual during the transition to the interrogation phase of the Reid model (Kassin & Gudjonsson, 2004). Most notably in the United States are an individual's *Miranda* rights, which include a right to remain silent and the right to consult with an attorney (*Miranda v. Arizona*, 1966). It is only when suspects knowingly and voluntarily waive these rights that their statements can be used as evidence against them (Kassin & Gudjonsson, 2004). Research, however, has demonstrated that *Miranda*-type rights may not provide the protection that they are assumed to provide.

One significant problem is that many individuals do not understand their rights when they are presented to them. Particularly vulnerable populations in this regard appear to include young people and those with impaired intellectual capacity (Fulero & Everington, 2004; Oberlander & Goldstein, 2001), but healthy adults and even police recruits also exhibit problems with comprehension (Eastwood & Snook, 2010; Grisso, 1981; Gudjonsson, Clare, & Cross, 1992; Moore & Gagnier, 2008). Another major problem is that police in the United States sometimes employ methods that persuade suspects to waive their rights. According to Kassin and Gudjonsson (2004), these methods can include offering sympathy to the suspect, by presenting themselves as an ally, and by minimizing the importance of the process by describing it as a simple formality.

INVESTIGATOR BIAS   The second problem with the Reid model of interrogation occurs during the actual interrogation and results from the fact that when the police begin their interrogation they already believe the suspect to be guilty. The problem here is that when people form a belief about something before they enter a situation, they often unknowingly seek out and interpret information in that situation in a way that verifies their initial belief (Kassin et al., 2003). A study by Kassin et al. (2003) demonstrates some of the potential dangers that can result from this particular form of **investigator bias**.

Investigator bias

Bias that can result when police officers enter an interrogation setting already believing that the suspect is guilty

In a mock interrogation study, Kassin and his colleagues (2003) had students act as interrogators or suspects. Some of the interrogators were led to believe that the suspect was guilty of a mock crime (finding a hidden key and stealing $100 from a locked cabinet) while others were led to believe that the suspect was innocent. In reality, some of the suspects were guilty of the mock crime, whereas others were innocent. Interrogators were instructed to devise an interrogation strategy to use on the suspects, and the suspects were told to deny any involvement in the crime and to convince the interrogator of their innocence. The interrogation was taped, and a group of neutral observers then listened to the recording and were asked questions about the interrogator and the suspect.

A number of important results emerged from this study:

1. Interrogators with guilty expectations asked more questions that indicated their belief in the suspect's guilt. For example, they would ask, "How did you find the key that was hidden behind the DVD player?" instead of "Do you know anything about the key that was hidden behind the DVD player?"
2. Interrogators with guilty expectations used a higher frequency of interrogation techniques compared to interrogators with innocent expectations, especially at the outset of the interrogation.
3. Interrogators with guilty expectations judged more suspects to be guilty, regardless of whether the suspect was actually guilty.
4. Interrogators indicated that they exerted more pressure on suspects to confess when, unbeknownst to them, the suspect was innocent.
5. Suspects had fairly accurate perceptions of interrogator behavior (i.e., innocent suspects believed their interrogators were exerting more pressure).
6. Neutral observers viewed interrogators with guilty expectations as more coercive, especially against innocent suspects, and they viewed suspects in the guilty expectation condition as more defensive.

In sum, these findings suggest that biases can lead to coercive interrogations that cause suspects to appear more guilty to both the interrogator and neutral observers, even when the suspect has committed no crime.

Interrogation Practices and the Courts

The decision to admit confession evidence into court rests on the shoulders of the trial judge. In the United States, the key issues a judge must consider when faced with a questionable confession are whether the confession was made voluntarily and whether the defendant was competent when he or she provided the confession (Wakefield & Underwager, 1998). The reason for using these criteria is that involuntary confessions and confessions provided when a person's mind is unstable are more likely to be unreliable.

Unfortunately, what is meant by "voluntary" and "competent" is not always clear, which is why debate continues over the issue. What does seem clear, however, is that confessions resulting from overt forms of coercion will not be admitted in court. As Kassin (1997) states, "A confession is typically excluded if it was elicited by brute force; prolonged isolation; deprivation of food or sleep; threats of harm or punishment; promises of immunity or leniency; or, barring exceptional circumstances, without notifying the suspect of his or her constitutional rights" (p. 221). Conversely, confessions that result from more subtle forms of psychological coercion are sometimes admitted into court in the United States despite the fact that psychological coercion can have a powerful influence on people being interrogated.

For example, as discussed by Kassin et al. (2010), U.S. courts typically permit the use of deception by interrogators, though limits may be placed on the type of deceit that is permitted (e.g., making false assertions is permissible, whereas fabricating evidence is not). As an illustration of this, Kassin et al. discuss the U.S. Supreme Court ruling handed down in *Frazier v. Cupp* (1969), a ruling that stands to this day:

> In *Frazier*, police used a standard false evidence ploy—telling Frazier that another man whom he and the victim had been seen with on the night of the crime had confessed to

their involvement. The investigating detective also used minimization, suggesting to Frazier that he had started a fight with the victim because the victim made homosexual advances toward him. Despite the use of these deceptive tactics, the Court held that Frazier's confession was voluntary. This ruling established that police deception by itself is not sufficient to render a confession involuntary. Rather, according to *Frazier*, deception is but one factor among many that a court should consider. (p. 13)

An Alternative to the Reid Model

Because of the potential problems that can result from using coercive interrogation tactics, police agencies in several countries have recently introduced changes to their procedures, changes that may one day take place in the United States as well. Perhaps more than anywhere else, these changes have been most obvious in England and Wales, where courts have restricted the use of many techniques found in the Reid model of interrogation (Gudjonsson, 2003).

During the past 20 years, police agencies in England and Wales have gone through several phases of change in an attempt to reduce oppressive interrogation practices. Currently, these agencies use the so-called PEACE model to guide their interrogations. PEACE is an acronym for *planning* and *preparation*, *engage* and *explain*, *account*, *closure*, and *evaluation*. According to Meissner and Russano (2003), this model provides an inquisitorial framework within which to conduct police interrogations (compared with the accusatorial framework used in the Reid model) and is based on an interview method known as conversation management, which encourages accurate information gathering more than securing a confession.

In fact, police agencies in England and Wales have all but abandoned the term *interrogation* in favor of *investigative interviewing* to get away from the negative connotations associated with North American–style interrogation practices. Although little research has been conducted to examine the impact of the PEACE model, some research indicates that a decrease in the use of coercive interrogation tactics does not necessarily result in a substantial reduction in the number of confessions that can be obtained (Meissner & Russano, 2003). For example, one analysis shows that approximately 50% of all suspects confessed to crimes before and after the PEACE model was introduced (Milne & Bull, 1999).

Despite calls for change (e.g., Kassin et al., 2010), police agencies in the United States appear more hesitant to move toward a PEACE model of suspect interviewing. In part, this is because of a lack of research showing that this model can be used to effectively extract confessions from suspects in the American context. That being said, research on the topic is slowly beginning to accumulate and most of this research appears supportive of the PEACE model. If this trend continues, perhaps at some point in the future the British-based investigative interviewing approach will replace the Reid model as the interrogation method of choice.

False confession

A confession that is either intentionally fabricated or is not based on actual knowledge of the facts that form its content

FALSE CONFESSIONS

Perhaps the biggest problem that people have with the use of coercive interrogation tactics is that these techniques can contribute to the likelihood of suspects making **false confessions** (Kassin, 2008; Kassin & Gudjonsson, 2004). False confessions can be defined in a number of ways. However, Ofshe (1989) provides a definition that appears to be well accepted. He suggests that a confession should be considered false "if it is elicited in response to a demand for a confession and is either intentionally fabricated or is not based on actual knowledge of the facts that form its content" (p. 13). When false confessions do occur, they should be taken seriously, especially considering the weight that juries put on confessions when determining the guilt or innocence of a defendant (Kassin & Sukel, 1997). Research indicates that when people have been wrongfully convicted of a crime, a false confession is often to blame. For example, Scheck, Neufeld, and Dwyer (2000) discovered that, in the 70 cases of wrongful convictions they examined, 21% included confession evidence that was later found to be false.

Before examining the extent of this problem, it is important to define two additional terms that are often confused with false confessions: **retracted confessions** and **disputed confessions**. A retracted confession consists of an individual declaring that the confession he or she made is false, regardless of whether it actually is (Gudjonsson, 2003). Disputed confessions, on the other hand, are confessions that are disputed at trial, which does not necessarily mean the confession is false or that it was retracted. Instead, disputed confessions may arise because of legal technicalities, or because the suspect disputes the confession was ever made (Gudjonsson, 2003).

Retracted confession

A confession that the confessor later declares to be false

Disputed confession

A confession that is later disputed at trial

The Frequency of False Confessions

Most researchers readily admit that no one knows how frequently false confessions are made. The major problem with determining frequency is that in most cases it is almost impossible to determine whether a confession is actually false (Kassin, 1997). For example, as Kassin (1997) argues, the fact that a confession is coerced does not mean the confession is false, just as a conviction based on confession evidence does not mean the confession is true. As a result of this problem, researchers arrive at drastically different estimates of how frequently false confessions occur. For example, the incidence of self-reported false confessions among prison inmates has been found to vary from 0.6% (Cassell, 1998) to 12% (Gudjonsson & Sigurdsson, 1994). Regardless of the exact number, most researchers believe there are enough cases to treat the issue very seriously.

Different Types of False Confessions

One thing researchers do agree on is that there are different types of false confessions. While several different typologies exist for classifying false confessions (e.g., Gudjonsson, 2003; McCann, 1998), the most common typology still appears to be the one proposed by Kassin and Wrightsman (1985), which states that false confessions consist of voluntary false confessions, coerced-compliant false confessions, and coerced-internalized false confessions.

VOLUNTARY FALSE CONFESSIONS **Voluntary false confessions** occur when someone voluntarily confesses to a crime he or she did not commit without any elicitation from the police. Research has indicated that people voluntarily false confess for a variety of reasons. For example, Gudjonsson (1992) suggests that such confessions may arise out of (1) a morbid desire for notoriety, (2) the person being unable to distinguish fact from fantasy, (3) the need to make up for pathological feelings of guilt by receiving punishment, or (4) a desire to protect somebody else from harm.

Voluntary false confession

A false confession that is provided without any elicitation from the police

Although it may seem surprising, highly publicized cases do occasionally result in voluntary false confessions. Perhaps the most famous case was the kidnapping and murder of Charles Lindbergh's baby son. Charles Lindbergh was famous for being the first pilot to fly solo across the Atlantic Ocean in 1927. On March 1, 1932, Charles Lindbergh, Jr., was kidnapped at the age of 20 months. Two-and-a-half months later, the decomposed body of the baby was found with a fractured skull. It is estimated that some 200 people falsely confessed to the kidnapping and the murder (Note, 1953). In the end, only one man was convicted for the crime, a German immigrant named Bruno Richard Hauptman, who was executed for the crime in 1936, despite his repeated claims of being innocent. To this day, questions are still raised about Hauptman's guilt (e.g., Jones, 1997).

Another, more recent case involved the high-profile voluntary false confession made by John Mark Karr to the unsolved 1996 murder of JonBenet Ramsey, the 6-year-old American beauty pageant queen. Karr was living in Thailand when he confessed to being with JonBenet when she died, but claimed that her death was an accident (Aglionby, 2006). He was released to the U.S. authorities and returned to Boulder, Colorado, where the murder had taken place. Shortly after his arrival, prosecutors announced that they would not pursue charges against Karr because his version of events did not match details of the case and because his DNA did not match samples found at the scene (CNN, 2006). However, Karr was quickly extradited to California on several other child pornography charges.

Coerced-compliant false confession

A confession that results from a desire to escape a coercive interrogation environment or gain a benefit promised by the police

COERCED-COMPLIANT FALSE CONFESSIONS Coerced-compliant false confessions are those in which the suspect confesses to a crime, even though the suspect is fully aware that he or she did not commit it. This type of false confession is perhaps the most common (Gudjonsson & MacKeith, 1988). Unlike voluntary false confessions, these confessions are caused by the use of coercive interrogation tactics on the part of the police, such as the maximization techniques described earlier. Specifically, coerced-compliant confessions may be given so the suspect can (1) escape further interrogation, (2) gain a promised benefit, or (3) avoid a threatened punishment (Gudjonsson, 1992).

As with voluntary false confessions, a number of cases of coerced-compliant false confessions have been reported. For example, the 1993 movie *In the Name of the Father* starring Daniel Day-Lewis is based on such a case. Gerry Conlon, along with three other Irishmen, falsely confessed to bombing two pubs in Surrey, England, as a result of coercive police interrogations. The coercive tactics included making up false evidence and threatening to harm members of Conlon's family unless he confessed. Conlon and his acquaintances were subsequently convicted and sent to prison, but were later released (Gudjonsson, 2003).

Coerced-internalized false confession

A confession that results from suggestive interrogation techniques, whereby the confessor actually comes to believe he or she committed the crime

COERCED-INTERNALIZED FALSE CONFESSIONS The third, and perhaps the most bizarre type of false confession proposed by Kassin and Wrightsman (1985) is the **coerced-internalized false confession**. Here, individuals recall and confess to a crime they did not commit, usually after they are exposed to highly suggestive questions (Gudjonsson, 2003). In contrast to the coerced-compliant false confessor, however, these individuals actually end up believing they are responsible for the crime. According to Gudjonsson (1992), several vulnerability factors are associated with this type of false confession, including (1) a history of substance abuse or some other interference with brain function, (2) the inability of people to detect discrepancies between what they observed and what has been erroneously suggested to them, and (3) factors associated with mental state, such as severe anxiety, confusion, or feelings of guilt. Perhaps the most frequently cited case of a coerced-internalized false confession is that of Paul Ingram, which is discussed in more detail in Box 3.2.

Studying False Confessions in the Lab

It is obviously difficult to study if, and how, false confessions occur. Even in the research laboratory it is not an easy task because of obvious ethical constraints (Kassin & Kiechel, 1996). Nowadays, no university ethics committee would allow research participants to be led to believe they had committed crimes of the sort that Paul Ingram was accused of. As a result, researchers have attempted to develop innovative laboratory paradigms that allow them to study the processes that may cause false confessions to occur without putting their participants at risk. One such paradigm was proposed by Dr. Saul Kassin, who was profiled in Box 3.1.

BOX 3.2   The Curious Case of Paul Ingram

In 1988, Paul Ingram was accused by his two adult daughters of committing crimes against them, crimes that included sexual assault, rape, and satanic ritual abuse (Kassin, 1997). As if some of these allegations were not strange enough, Ingram confessed to the crimes after initially being adamant he had never committed them.

Ingram was eventually able to recall the crimes in vivid detail despite originally claiming he could not remember ever abusing his daughters. As a result, he ended up pleading guilty to six counts of rape and was sentenced to 20 years in prison (Kassin, 1997). In prison, Ingram came to believe he was not guilty of the crimes he confessed to. After having initial appeals rejected, Ingram was released from prison on April 8, 2003.

Many people feel that Ingram falsely confessed to the crimes he was sentenced for. Supporters of this position typically draw on two related pieces of evidence (see Olio & Cornell, 1998, for evidence to the contrary).

First, it is known that Ingram was exposed to highly suggestive interrogation techniques that have been shown to adversely influence people's memory of events. For example, over the course of five months, Ingram took part in 23 interrogations in which he was instructed (on some of these occasions) to visualize scenes of satanic cult activity that he could not remember (Wrightsman, 2001).

Second, a psychologist hired to evaluate the case, Dr. Richard Ofshe from the University of California, concluded that Ingram had been brainwashed into believing he was responsible for the crimes (Ofshe & Watters, 1994). To demonstrate this belief, Ofshe conducted an experiment in which he presented Ingram with a fabricated scenario: that Ingram had forced his son and daughter to have sex together while he watched (Olio & Cornell, 1998).

According to Olio and Cornell (1998), phase 1 of the experiment consisted of Ofshe asking Ingram if he could remember the incident (Ingram indicated that he could not). Ofshe then instructed Ingram to use the same visualization techniques he had used during his previous interview sessions. The next day, Ingram informed Ofshe he could now remember the incident and he produced a written confession providing details of his involvement. In phase 2 of the experiment, Ofshe pressured Ingram to retract his confession. Ingram was not willing to do so.

In their classic study, Kassin and Kiechel (1996) tested whether individuals would confess to a crime they did not commit. They had participants take part in what they thought was a reaction time study. A coconspirator read a list of letters out loud to a participant who had to type these letters into a computer. However, before each session began, the participant was warned that if he or she hit the ALT-key on the keyboard while typing in the letters, all the data would be lost. Sixty seconds after beginning the task, the computer automatically crashed, which brought the head researcher into the lab with accusations that the participant had hit the key.

Kassin and Kiechel were specifically interested in how two factors would affect participant reactions to the allegations. Participant vulnerability (defined as the participant's certainty concerning his or her own innocence) was manipulated by varying the speed that participants had to type. In the "not vulnerable" condition, letters were read at a rate of 43 letters per minute; in the "vulnerable" condition, letters were read at a rate of 67 letters per minute. The researchers also varied whether false evidence was presented. In the "no false evidence" condition, the coconspirator stated she did not see what happened; in the "false evidence" condition, she stated she saw the participant hit the ALT-key. The results from the study are presented in Figure 3.1.

Compliance

A tendency to go along with demands made by people perceived to be in authority, even though the person may not agree with them

To measure the degree to which participants exhibited **compliance** with the allegations, the researchers presented each participant with a written confession and recorded how many participants signed it. As indicated in Figure 3.1, many participants accepted responsibility for the crime despite the fact that they were innocent, particularly the vulnerable participants presented with false evidence. To measure the degree to which participants internalized their confession, the researchers recorded comments made by participants to another coconspirator outside the lab who asked them what had happened. If the participant accepted blame for the crime, he or she was recorded as exhibiting **internalization**. Based on the results from this study, many participants also internalized their confession. Again, this was especially true for vulnerable participants presented with false evidence. Finally, to measure the degree to which participants made up details to fit with their confession, known as **confabulation**, the researchers brought the participant back into the lab, read the list of letters again, and asked the participant to try to reconstruct where things had gone wrong. Vulnerable participants presented with false evidence were once again found to be particularly susceptible to confabulation.

Internalization

The acceptance of guilt for an act, even if the person did not actually commit the act

Confabulation

The reporting of events that never actually occurred.

Thus, Kassin and Kiechel's (1996) findings suggest that it is possible to demonstrate, under laboratory conditions, that people can admit to acts they are not responsible

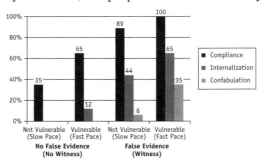

FIGURE 3.1   Compliance, Internalization, and Confabulation in Kassin and Kiechel's Study
Source: Based on data from "The social psychology of false confessions: Compliance, internalization, and confabulation" by Saul M. Kassin and Katherine L. Kiechel from *Psychological Science*, vol. 7, Sage Publications (1996).

for and come to believe in their guilt to such a point that they can reconstruct details of an act that never occurred (Kassin & Kiechel, 1996). However, whether these findings can be generalized to actual police interrogations is unclear because the Kassin and Kiechel paradigm fails to capture a number of important elements found in real-world interrogations: (1) while the participants in Kassin and Kiechel's study had nothing to lose if they couldn't convince others of their innocence, real suspects have much to lose if they are found guilty; (2) while all participants in the Kassin and Kiechel's study were actually innocent of the crime, all suspects in real interrogations aren't; and (3) while the participants in Kassin and Kiechel's study could have easily been confused about their guilt—they may have accidentally hit the key—real suspects typically aren't confused about their involvement in a crime (Russano, Meissner, Narchet, & Kassin, 2005).

Fortunately, more recent research is helping to clarify these issues (e.g., Horselenberg, Merckelbach, & Josephs, 2003; Russano et al., 2005). For example, Russano et al. (2005) dealt with these problems by devising a novel paradigm where only some of the participants were guilty of a crime (a crime that involved specific intent) and where a confession resulted in known consequences. Specifically, they paired participants with a confederate and were asked to solve a logic problem. The guilty condition included participants who provided help to the confederate when he asked them for an answer, despite the fact that this was not allowed. The innocent condition included participants who were never asked for assistance by the confederate. To examine the impact of various interrogation strategies on confessions, participants in both the innocent and guilty conditions were either presented with minimization tactics (e.g., face-saving excuses for committing the crime) or no minimizing tactics. The offer of a deal was also manipulated across conditions. In the deal condition, participants were told that if they confessed, the consequences would be less severe than if they didn't confess. In the no-deal condition, the consequences were consistent regardless of whether the participant confessed. The results were as expected. Guilty participants were much more likely to confess (71.6%) than innocent participants (20.3%). Participants were also more likely to confess when minimization tactics were used (57.4%) than when they were not used (34.5%). Finally, participants who were offered a deal were more likely to confess (54.1%) than participants who were not offered a deal (37.8%).

The Consequences of Falsely Confessing

False confessions cause problems for both the person making the false confession and the police agencies tasked with investigating the crime. The obvious problem that the person making the false confession faces is that if the confession is admitted into court, the jury could convict the suspect for a crime he or she did not commit (Leo & Ofshe, 1998). Recent studies have shown that jurors might be likely to convict a suspect based on confession evidence even when the jurors are aware that the suspect's confession resulted from a coercive interrogation.

For example, in one study, Kassin and Sukel (1997) presented participants with transcripts of a mock murder trial. One group of participants received a transcript in which the defendant immediately confessed to the police during questioning (the low-pressure condition). A second group of participants received a transcript in which the defendant was coerced into confessing by having his hands handcuffed behind his back and by being threatened by the interrogator (the high-pressure condition). A third group of participants received a transcript in which the defendant never confessed to the murder (the control condition). The results of the study indicate that those participants presented with a confession obtained in the high-pressure condition recognized the confession was involuntary and said it would not affect their decisions. However, when actual verdicts were examined across the three groups, the presence of a confession was found to significantly increase the conviction rate, even for those participants in the high-pressure condition. Thus, not only can people in mock jury studies be convicted of crimes they did not commit based on their false confession, this can happen even when the confession appears to have been obtained through coercive interrogation tactics.

A second and less commonly recognized consequence of false confessions involves the consequences for the police and, therefore, the public. When somebody makes a false confession, the police are diverted down a false trail that may waste valuable time—time that they could have used to identify and apprehend the real offender. Such was the case in both the Lindbergh kidnapping case and the Ramsey murder case, which were described above. Howitt (2002) also provides an example of this happening in the Yorkshire Ripper serial murder investigation that took place in England during the 1970s. At one point in the investigation, the police were sent several tape recordings supposedly from the Ripper himself. Howitt states that senior police officers on the case, believing the tapes to be genuine, used up valuable resources investigating the tapes. However, the tapes were not genuine, and these actions probably delayed the eventual arrest of Peter Sutcliffe, the real Yorkshire Ripper, and allowed further murders to take place.

Obviously the police have to be very concerned about false confessions and need to minimize the chance of them occurring. Read the scenario in the Case Study box and determine what you could do to reduce the likelihood of the suspect falsely confessing to the crime he is being questioned for.

CASE STUDY

YOU BE THE POLICE OFFICER

Edward Chen is a 42-year-old Chinese immigrant who has just been picked up by the police on suspicion of murdering Emily Jones, a 30-year-old nurse who was killed when coming home from a late shift at the hospital where she worked. Edward fits the suspect descriptions that were given by several eyewitnesses and he has no alibi for the night when the murder took place. He also has a criminal record, which consists of several drug charges. He denies knowing the victim and says he had nothing to do with the murder. When he is brought into the police station for questioning, he appears very anxious, shows potential signs of being slightly learning disabled, and does not speak fluent English.

Your Turn . . .

As a police officer working on this case, what approach would you suggest be taken when interrogating Edward? What should be the primary goals of the interrogation? What would you be concerned with when developing the interrogation strategy? Would you be worried about Edward possibly confessing to the crime even if he didn't commit it? Why or why not? If you think a false confession is a possibility, what could you do to prevent this from happening?

CRIMINAL PROFILING

To conduct interrogations, police need to have a viable suspect in custody. In some instances, the identification of probable suspects is relatively straightforward, because in many crimes the victim and the offender know each other and there is often a clear motivation for the crime, such as passion, greed, or revenge. But what about those crimes in which it is more difficult to identify a suspect, crimes in which the victim and offender are strangers and there is no clear motive? In these cases, the police often rely on unconventional investigative techniques, such as criminal profiling.

What Is a Criminal Profile?

Perhaps more than any other investigative technique, criminal profiling has caught the attention of the public, and Hollywood depictions of criminal profiling are common (as illustrated in the In the Media box below). But what is criminal profiling in reality? There is no single definition of criminal profiling (Alison, Bennell, Mokros, & Ormerod, 2002). Indeed, there is even little agreement as to what the technique should be called (Wilson, Lincoln, & Kocsis, 1997). However, the definition proposed by John Douglas and his former colleagues from the Federal Bureau of Investigation (FBI) fairly accurately describes the procedure: **criminal profiling** is "a technique for identifying the major personality and behavioral characteristics of an individual based upon an analysis of the crimes he or she has committed" (Douglas, Ressler, Burgess, & Hartman, 1986, p. 405).

Criminal profiling
A technique for identifying the background characteristics of an offender based on an analysis of the crimes he or she has committed

Although criminal profiling is now used in a range of contexts, it is most commonly used in cases of serial homicide and rape (Holmes & Holmes, 2002). In particular, profiling is thought to be most applicable in cases in which extreme forms of psychopathology are exhibited by the offender, including sadistic torture and ritualistic behavior (Geberth, 1990). Criminal profiling was originally intended to help the police identify the criminal in these sorts of cases, either by narrowing down a list of suspects or by providing new lines of inquiry. However, criminal profiling is now used for a number of purposes, including the following (Homant & Kennedy, 1998):

- To help set traps to flush out an offender
- To determine whether a threatening note should be taken seriously
- To give advice on how best to interrogate a suspect
- To tell prosecutors how to break down defendants in cross-examination

Although every criminal profile will undoubtedly be different in terms of the information it contains, some of the most common personality, behavioral, and demographic characteristics that profilers try to predict include the offender's age, sex, race, level of intelligence, educational history, hobbies, family background, residential location, criminal history, employment status, psychosexual development, and post-offense behavior (Holmes & Holmes, 2002). Often these predictions are made by forensic psychologists and psychiatrists who have either clinical or research experience with offenders (Wilson et al., 1997). In North America, however, the majority of profilers are experienced and specially trained law enforcement officers (Rossmo, 2000).

The Origins of Criminal Profiling

Criminal profiling is usually thought to have been developed by agents from the FBI in the 1970s. However, there are numerous examples of profiling techniques being used long

IN THE MEDIA   **Hollywood Depictions of Criminal Profiling**

Countless television shows and films have profiling built into their plots, and there seems to be no end in sight to Hollywood portrayals of this topic. We are often asked by students about these media depictions: "Do profilers like this actually exist?" "Can they actually do in real life what they are seen to do on the screen?" And most often, "What do I need to do to get that kind of job?"

We are sometimes tempted to tell these students that these shows are all fake—after all, the chance of gaining full-time employment as a profiler is very small. However, the truth is that these shows are not entirely fake, even though many aspects of them are. Indeed, audiences have become too smart, and too demanding, for Hollywood to pull the wool over their eyes entirely. Audiences require a degree of realism in these shows to stay interested; although we also need to have directors spice things up a bit.

In fact, audiences have gotten so demanding that it is now common practice to have researchers attached to these shows and to even hire technical consultants (real-life profilers) who help make the shows appear more realistic. These individuals provide information about what terms to use, what places to go to, and what names to drop so that there is a ring of truth to what the actors are saying and doing. It is then up to Hollywood to make this all sound (and look) sexy so that the audience keeps coming back for more.

Consider the following examples.

The Silence of the Lambs

Adapted from Thomas Harris's book, *The Silence of the Lambs*, much of this movie is set in Quantico, Virginia, where the FBI's Behavioral Sciences Unit (BSU) actually resides. In addition, parts of this film were largely based on the work of John Douglas, the previous chief of the BSU. Indeed, Scott Glenn's character (Jack Crawford) was largely modeled after Douglas and Douglas served as a technical consultant on the film (Douglas, 2010). The serial killer depicted in the movie, Buffalo Bill, was also based loosely on a real-life killer. In particular, many of the things that Buffalo Bill did, such as the skinning of bodies, resemble the crimes of Ed Gein, a Wisconsin man who was a frequent grave robber. Interestingly, on some DVD versions of this film, Douglas provides a commentary informing the audience as to what parts of the movie are real and what parts are fake.

Numb3rs

The first episode of the television series *Numb3rs* was broadcast on January 23, 2005. In that show, an FBI agent recruits his brother Charlie, who happens to be a mathematical genius, to help solve challenging crimes. One of the problems encountered in the first episode is to identify the residential location of an offender based on where he committed his crimes. Stumped, Charlie goes back to his university office and derives a formula for determining a "hot zone" where the offender is likely to live. The formula he comes up with was first proposed by Dr. Kim Rossmo, a former detective, who helped develop the field of geographic profiling while a Ph.D. student at Simon Fraser University in British Columbia, Canada (Devlin & Lorden, 2007).

before that time (Canter, 2000; Holmes & Holmes, 2002; Turvey, 2002; Woodworth & Porter, 1999). The investigation that you may be most familiar with is the famous case of Jack the Ripper (Harrison, 1993).

EARLY ATTEMPTS AT CRIMINAL PROFILING   In 1888, a series of murders was committed in the east end of London around an area known as Whitechapel. The victims were all women, and all were mutilated by the offender. At one point, the unknown offender sent a letter to the newspapers, and at the end of it he signed his name, Jack the Ripper (Holmes & Holmes, 2002). A police surgeon involved with the investigation of the murders engaged in a form of criminal profiling. As Woodworth and Porter (1999, p. 244) reveal:

> Dr. George Phillips attempted to create a reconstruction of various crime scenes and describe the wounds of the victims for the purpose of gaining a greater insight into the offender's psychological make-up. In particular, Phillips believed that a circumspect examination of the wound patterns of murder victims could provide clues about both the behavior and personality of the offender who committed the crimes.

This instance is probably one of the first times that criminal profiling was used in a criminal investigation. Unfortunately, it assisted little, evidenced by the fact that we still have no idea who Jack the Ripper actually was.

Another well-known case, often cited as an example of how accurate some profilers can be, is the case of New York City's Mad Bomber. Starting in 1940, an unknown offender began detonating bombs in public places around New York (Wrightsman, 2001). Stumped, the New York City Police Department turned to a local forensic psychiatrist, Dr. James Brussel, for help with the case. By examining the actions of the bomber, Brussel began to develop a profile of the unknown offender. Dr. Brussel's profile included characteristics such as the following: the offender would be a middle-aged male, he would suffer from paranoia, he would be pathologically self-centered, he would be reasonably educated, he would be unmarried and possibly a virgin, he would be Roman Catholic, and he would wear buttoned-up double-breasted suits (Turvey, 2002). In 1957, almost 17 years after the bombings started, the police finally arrested George Metesky. Reportedly, Metesky fit most of the characteristics that Dr. Brussel had profiled, even down to the double-breasted suit he wore to the police station (Holmes & Holmes, 2002). Metesky was subsequently sent to a mental institution for the criminally insane. He was released in 1973 and died in 1994.

THE FBI AND BEYOND   The next big milestone in the history of criminal profiling was the development of a criminal profiling program at the FBI in the 1970s (Turvey, 2002). Not only was this the first time that profiles were produced in a systematic way by a law enforcement agency, it was also the first time that training was provided in how to construct criminal profiles. Subsequent to the development of the FBI's Behavioral Sciences Unit in 1972, the National Center for the Analysis of Violent Crime was opened for the purpose of conducting research in the area of criminal profiling and providing formal guidance to police agencies around the United States that were investigating serial crimes. Similar units have now sprung up in police agencies around the world, including Canada, Germany, and England. These outfits typically provide operational support to police agencies in cases in which profiling may be useful, and many conduct their own research into criminal profiling.

INVESTIGATIVE PSYCHOLOGY   Since the early 1990s, some of the most important advances in the area of criminal profiling have been made by David Canter, the founder of a relatively new field of psychology that he has named *investigative psychology*.

The origins of this field can be traced back to Canter's involvement in the John Duffy (a.k.a. the Railway Rapist) rape/murder case. Canter was called in by Scotland Yard to provide a profile of the unknown offender, and in doing so, he drew on his knowledge of human behavior that he had gained as an academic psychologist (especially in the area of environmental psychology; Canter, 1994). Since that early successful contribution, Canter and his colleagues have spent the past 20 years developing the field of profiling into a scientific practice. These individuals have also made countless contributions to other areas of investigative psychology (Canter & Youngs, 2009).

How Is a Criminal Profile Constructed?

Profiles are constructed differently by different profilers. In fact, different "schools" of profiling now exist that guide the profile construction process (Hicks & Sales, 2006). However, regardless of what approach is taken to generate a profile, relatively little is known about the profiling process. While some individuals have attempted to change this (e.g., Canter, 2011), such attempts are not common. Indeed, the descriptions of the profiling process provided by many researchers and profilers are incredibly vague.

For example, in a now-classic study of criminal profiling, Pinizzotto and Finkel (1990) describe the process of profiling as an equation in the following form: WHAT + WHY = WHO. The WHAT of the crime refers to the material that profilers collect at the start of an investigation, such as crime scene photos, autopsy reports, and descriptions of victims. The WHY of the crime refers to the motivation for the crime and each crime scene behavior. The WHO of the crime refers to the actual profile that is eventually constructed once the WHAT and the WHY components have been determined. Although this conceptual model may make sense at a general level, it is clearly too vague to be useful. As Pinizzotto and Finkel (1990) themselves point out, the model "does not tell us precisely how . . . the profiler gets from the WHAT to the WHY, or from the WHY to the WHO" (p. 217).

Other conceptual models have also been produced, particularly by profilers at the FBI (e.g., Douglas & Burgess, 1986), but these models also lack the specificity required to truly understand the profiling process. Part of the problem with providing such detail is that profiling is still viewed primarily as an art, not a science. Although some are making an effort to change this (see Hicks & Sales, 2006, for a review), profiling is currently based to a large extent on the profiler's experience and intuition (Douglas & Olshaker, 1995). As a result, asking profilers to provide specific details of how they construct profiles may be similar to asking Picasso to explain how he painted.

Different Types of Profiling Methods

Deductive criminal profiling

Profiling the background characteristics of an unknown offender based on evidence left at the crime scenes by that particular offender

Although it is not clear how criminal profilers construct their profiles, it is evident that they can draw on different types of profiling methods (Hicks & Sales, 2006). Specifically, profilers can use two approaches: the deductive profiling method and the inductive profiling method. **Deductive criminal profiling** involves the prediction of an offender's background characteristics generated from a thorough analysis of the evidence left at the crime scenes by that particular offender (Holmes & Holmes, 2002). This method largely relies on logical reasoning, as indicated in an example provided by Canter (2000) in which the victim of an unidentified assailant noticed that the offender had short fingernails on his right hand and long fingernails on his left hand. According to Canter,

"Somebody with specialist knowledge suggested that this was a characteristic of people who are serious guitar players. It was therefore a reasonable deduction that the assailant was somebody who played the guitar" (p. 24). The primary disadvantage of this profiling method is that the underlying logic of the argument can sometimes be faulty. Take the prediction we just described. Although the argument appears to be logical, it is in fact wrong. The offender in this case did not play the guitar at all. Instead, the reason he had short fingernails on his right hand was that he had a job repairing old tires (Canter, 2000).

In contrast to deductive profiling, **inductive criminal profiling** involves the prediction of an offender's background characteristics generated from a comparison of that particular offender's crimes with similar crimes committed by other, known offenders. This method is based on the premise that "if certain crimes committed by different people are similar, then the offenders must also share some common personality traits" (Holmes & Holmes, 2002, p. 5). The inductive method of profiling relies largely on a determination of how likely it is an offender will possess certain background characteristics given the prevalence of these characteristics among known offenders who have committed similar crimes. An example of the inductive profiling method is provided by Aitken et al. (1996), who developed a statistical profile of a murderer of children. Based on their analysis of similar crimes committed by known offenders, they predicted that there was a probability of 0.96 that the offender would know the victim, a probability of 0.92 that the offender would have a previous criminal conviction, a probability of 0.91 that the offender would be single, a probability of 0.79 that the offender would live within 8 kilometers of the crime scene, and a probability of 0.65 that the offender would be under the age of 20. In the case of this child murderer, the profile turned out to be very accurate.

In contrast to deductive profiling, the major problem with the inductive method of profiling is with sampling issues (Turvey, 2002). The key problem is that it will never be possible to have a representative sample of serial offenders from which to draw profiling conclusions. That is, if we encounter a serial crime with behaviors A, B, and C, but no crimes in our database have behaviors A, B, and C, how do we construct an accurate profile?

Inductive criminal profiling

Profiling the background characteristics of an unknown offender based on what we know about other solved cases

THE ORGANIZED–DISORGANIZED MODEL   Many profilers today use an inductive profiling approach developed by the FBI in the 1980s. This model was developed largely through interviews with incarcerated offenders (some of whom were serial murderers) and has come to be called the **organized–disorganized model** (Hazelwood & Douglas, 1980). The model suggests that an offender's crime scene can be classified as either organized or disorganized (see Table 3.1). Organized crime scene behaviors reflect a well-planned and controlled crime, whereas disorganized behaviors reflect an impulsive crime, which is chaotic in nature. Similarly, an offender's background can be classified as either organized or disorganized (see Table 3.2). Organized background characteristics reflect a methodical individual, whereas disorganized characteristics reflect a disturbed individual, who is usually suffering from some form of psychopathology. The basic idea is that, when encountering a disorganized crime scene, the investigator should profile the background characteristics of a disorganized offender and likewise for organized crime scenes and organized background characteristics. Although little research has examined whether the organized–disorganized model actually works, the research that does exist raises serious doubts (e.g., Canter, Alison, Wentink, & Alison, 2004). Indeed, even the FBI has refined this model to account for the many offenders who display mixtures of organized and disorganized features (Douglas, Burgess, Burgess, & Ressler, 1992).

Organized– disorganized model

A profiling model used by the FBI that assumes the crime scenes and backgrounds of serial offenders can be categorized as *organized* or *disorganized*

TABLE 3.1	Organized and Disorganized Crime Scene Behaviors
Organized Behaviors	**Disorganized Behaviors**
Planned offense	Spontaneous offense
Use of restraints on the victim	No restraints used on the victim
Antemortem sexual acts committed	Postmortem sexual acts committed
Use of a vehicle in the crime	No use of a vehicle in the crime
No postmortem mutilation	Postmortem mutilation
Corpse not taken	Corpse (or body parts) taken
Little evidence left at the scene	Evidence left at the scene

Source: Based on data from "Sexual killers and their victims: Identifying patterns through crime scene analysis" by Robert K. Pessler et al. from *Journal of Interpersonal Violence*, vol. 1, Sage Publications (1986).

TABLE 3.2	Organized and Disorganized Background Characteristics
Organized Behaviors	**Disorganized Behaviors**
High intelligence	Low intelligence
Skilled occupation	Unskilled occupation
Sexually adequate	Sexually inadequate
Lives with a partner	Lives alone
Geographically mobile	Geographically stable
Lives and works far away from crimes	Lives and works close to crimes
Follows crimes in media	Little interest in media
Maintains residence and vehicle	Does not maintain residence and vehicle

Source: Based on data from "Sexual killers and their victims: Identifying patterns through crime scene analysis" by Robert K. Pessler et al. from *Journal of Interpersonal Violence*, vol. 1, Sage Publications (1986).

The Validity of Criminal Profiling

Because profiling is used by the police, it is important to consider whether the technique is actually reliable and valid. Profilers certainly claim that they have experienced much success with their profiles (Woodworth & Porter, 1999), and it appears that police officers hold generally positive (although somewhat cautious) views of profiling (e.g., Copson, 1995; Jackson, van Koppen, & Herbrink, 1993; Pinizzotto, 1984; Snook, Haines, Taylor, & Bennell, 2007; Trager & Brewster, 2001).

For example, according to Pinizzotto (1984), the results of a study conducted by FBI profiler John Douglas indicate that profiling advice was credited with solving the case in 46% of 192 instances where a FBI profile was requested. When respondents were asked to indicate the specific type of assistance provided by a criminal profile, 77.2% gave the response that it focused the investigation properly, 20.4% stated that it helped locate possible suspects, 17% stated that profiling identified suspects, and 5.6% stated that it assisted in the prosecution of suspects. Seventeen percent of responding agencies stated that criminal profiling was of no assistance.

There is also some, albeit very limited, empirical evidence for the basic assumptions underlying criminal profiling. For example, in a recent review of the profiling field, Alison, Goodwill, Almond, van den Heuvel, and Winter (2010) showed that under limited conditions it is possible to use certain crime scene behaviors to predict certain background characteristics of serial offenders.

Despite these findings indicating that criminal profiling may be useful, there is a large body of research that fails to support the assumptions underlying criminal profiling (e.g., Bateman & Salfati, 2007; Mokros & Alison, 2002), and the practice is still often criticized. Three criticisms in particular have received attention from researchers:

1. Many forms of profiling are based on a theoretical model of personality that lacks strong empirical support.
2. Many profiles contain information that is so vague and ambiguous they can potentially fit many suspects.
3. Professional profilers may be no better than untrained individuals at constructing accurate criminal profiles.

Let's now look at each of these criticisms in turn.

DOES PROFILING HAVE A STRONG THEORETICAL BASE?   There seems to be general agreement that most forms of profiling, including the FBI's organized–disorganized approach, rely on a **classic trait model** of personality that was popular in psychology before the 1970s (Alison et al., 2002). In this model, the primary determinants of behavior are stable, internal traits (Mischel, 1968). These traits are assumed to result in the expression of consistent patterns of behavior over time and across situations. In the criminal context, this consistency is thought to persist across an offender's crimes and into the offender's noncriminal lifestyle, thus allowing him or her to be accurately profiled (Homant & Kennedy, 1998). Thus, an offender characterized by a trait of "organization" is expected to exhibit organized behaviors across his or her crimes (e.g., the offender will consistently plan the crimes, use restraints, and use weapons), as well as in his or her noncriminal life (e.g., the offender will be highly intelligent, sexually adequate, and geographically mobile; Alison et al., 2002).

Although some researchers believe this classic trait model provides a solid basis for criminal profiling (e.g., Homant & Kennedy, 1998), other researchers disagree (e.g., Alison et al., 2002). Those who disagree draw on research from the field of personality psychology, which demonstrates that traits are not the only (or even primary) determinant of behavior (Cervone & Shoda, 1999). Rather, situational influences are also known to be very important in shaping our behavior, and some researchers argue that there is no reason to suspect that serial offenders will be any different (Bennell & Canter, 2002; Bennell & Jones, 2005). From a profiling perspective, the impact of various situational factors (e.g., an extremely resistant victim, an interruption during a crime, or a bad day at work) may create behavioral inconsistencies across an offender's crimes, and among different aspects of his or her life, making it very difficult to create an accurate profile of the offender.

Those who believe the classic trait model forms a strong basis for criminal profiling also acknowledge the "checkered past" that this model has experienced (e.g., Homant & Kennedy, 1998). However, these individuals refer to instances in which behavioral consistency has been found in the noncriminal context and highlight the fact that higher

Classic trait model

A model of personality that assumes the primary determinants of behavior are stable, internal traits

levels of behavioral consistency typically emerge when we examine pathological popula-tions (Pinizzotto & Finkel, 1990). Assuming that most serial offenders do in fact fall into this pathological population, these supporters argue that the level of behavioral consis-tency that they express may be adequate to develop accurate criminal profiles. Clearly, more empirical research dealing with this issue is required before any firm conclusions can be made. Until then, the debate over the validity of criminal profiling will continue.

WHAT IS THE IMPACT OF AMBIGUOUS PROFILES?   Another common criticism of criminal profiling is that many profiles are so ambiguous that they can fit many sus-pects. If one of the goals of profiling is to help to prioritize potential suspects, this con-cern clearly needs to be addressed. To examine this issue, Alison, Smith, Eastman, and Rainbow (2003) examined the content of 21 profiling reports and found that almost a quarter (24%) of all the profiling opinions provided in these reports could be consid-ered ambiguous (i.e., the opinion could be interpreted differently by different people). Of more direct relevance to the ambiguity criticism, however, is an interesting follow-up study conducted by Alison, Smith, and Morgan (2003), in which they examined whether ambiguous profiles could in fact be interpreted to fit more than one suspect.

Alison et al. (2003) provided details of a genuine crime to two groups of foren-sic professionals, including senior detectives. The crime involved the murder of a young woman. Each group of participants was then provided with a criminal profile constructed for this case by the FBI. They were asked to read the profile and compare it with the description of a suspect. Unbeknownst to the participants, each group was provided with a different suspect description. One group was provided with the description of the genuine offender, while the other group was provided with a suspect constructed by the researchers, who was different from the genuine offender on a number of key points. After comparing the profile with their suspect, each participant was asked to rate the accuracy of the pro-file and to state if (and why) he or she thought the profile would be operationally useful. Despite the fact that each group received different suspect descriptions, both groups of participants rated the profile as fairly accurate, with no significant difference between the groups. In addition, both groups viewed the profile as generally useful and indicated they thought it would allow the police to narrow down the list of potential suspects and develop new lines of inquiry. This study, therefore, provides preliminary support for the criticism that ambiguous profiles can in fact be interpreted to fit more than one suspect, even when those suspects are quite different from each other.

Although such a finding could have serious implications, we must be careful when interpreting these results. For example, it would be important to know how closely the profile used in this study matches the typical criminal profile provided in the field. In addition, we should emphasize that this study is far from realistic in that the crime scene details and suspect descriptions provided to the participants in this study contained much less information than would be the case in an actual police investigation. Also of note is a more recent study, which showed that a more up-to-date sample of profiles did not contain the same degree of ambiguity (13% instead of 24%; Almond, Alison, & Porter, 2007). This result suggests that in certain jurisdictions at least this potential prob-lem may be waning.

HOW ACCURATE ARE PROFESSIONAL PROFILERS?   The last criticism that we will deal with here is the possibility that professional profilers may be no more accurate in their profiling predictions than individuals who have received no specialized training. In early writings on criminal profiling, claims were even made that profilers may be no better than bartenders at predicting the characteristics of unknown offenders (Campbell, 1976). If this is in fact the case, the police must consider how much weight they will put on statements made by professional profilers. Unlike the previous two criticisms, this issue has been examined on numerous occasions and the results have been mixed (Kocsis, 2003; Pinizzotto & Finkel, 1990). In other words, profilers are sometimes found to be more accurate than other groups when asked to construct profiles under laboratory conditions, but at other times they are found to be no more accurate.

In a fairly representative study, Kocsis, Irwin, Hayes, and Nunn (2000) compared profile accuracy across five groups of individuals: profilers, psychologists, police officers, students, and psychics. All participants were provided with the details of a genuine crime, which they were asked to review. The participants were then given a questionnaire that dealt with various aspects of the offender's background, including his or her physical characteristics, cognitions related to the offense, pre- and post-offense behaviors, social history, and personality characteristics. The participants' task with this questionnaire was to select the alternatives that best described the unknown offender. For example, the various groups of participants were asked whether the offender was a male or a female and each participant had to try and select the correct option (i.e., male). Average levels of accuracy were determined for each group by comparing the responses from the participants to the correct answers (for each section of the questionnaire). The results from this study are presented in Table 3.3, which indicates the mean number of questions that each group got correct for each subset of characteristics (the higher the number in each column, the more accurate the predictions were for that group).

As you can see from this table, when compared to the other groups, professional profilers were the most accurate when it came to profiling cognitive processes (e.g., degree of planning) and social history (e.g., marital status). They also received the highest total accuracy score, which is an aggregate score for all subsets of characteristics,

TABLE 3.3	Comparing Profilers, Psychologists, Police Officers, Students, and Psychics*				
Measure	**Profilers**	**Psychologists**	**Police**	**Students**	**Psychics**
Cognitions	3.20	2.27	2.49	2.03	2.60
Physical	3.60	3.63	3.43	3.42	2.80
Offense	4.00	4.03	3.09	3.64	3.65
Social	3.00	2.63	2.60	2.94	2.25
Total	13.80	12.57	11.60	12.03	11.30
Personality	24.60	34.03	22.03	26.84	27.70

*Numbers refer to the mean number of correct questions. The total number of correct questions that participants could have predicted was 7 for cognitions, 6 for physical characteristics, 7 for offense behaviors, and 10 for social history (total accuracy is, therefore, out of 30). Kocsis and colleagues did not provide information relating to the total number of correct predictions for personality characteristics.
Source: Based on data from "Expertise in psychological profiling: A comparative assessment" by Richard N. Kocsis from *Journal of Interpersonal Violence*, vol. 15, Sage Publications (2000).

excluding personality predictions. On the other hand, psychologists were the most accurate when it came to profiling physical characteristics (e.g., offender age), offense behaviors (e.g., degree of control), and personality features (e.g., temperament).

When the results of the four nonprofiler groups were combined, Kocsis et al. (2000) found that the combined score of the nonprofiler group was lower than that of the profilers, leading them to conclude that "the collective skills of profilers are superior to the individual skills represented by each of the comparison groups" (p. 325). This result has recently been endorsed by other researchers who have reanalyzed the data by using sophisticated statistical techniques (Snook, Eastwood, Gendreau, Goggin, & Cullen, 2007). However, given the preliminary nature of these sorts of studies, the marginal accuracy differences between the groups, and the artificial conditions under which these studies are conducted, it seems likely that the debate over whether professional profilers can provide more accurate profiles than untrained individuals will continue (Bennell, Jones, Taylor, & Snook, 2006).

GEOGRAPHIC PROFILING

Geographic profiling

A technique that uses crime scene locations to predict the most likely area where an offender resides

In addition to criminal profiling, another form of profiling is commonly used by the police: **geographic profiling**. In simple terms, geographic profiling uses crime scene locations to predict the most likely area where the offender resides (Rossmo, 2000). As is the case with criminal profiling, geographic profiling is used most often in cases of serial homicide and rape, though it has also been used in cases of serial robbery, arson, and burglary. Geographic profiling is used primarily for prioritizing potential suspects. This prioritization is accomplished by rank ordering the suspects based on how close they live to the predicted home location, so the suspect who lives closest to the predicted home location would be focused on first (Rossmo, 2000). This task is important, especially considering the number of suspects who can enter a serial crime investigation. For example, in the Green River serial murder case in Washington State, which was solved in 2001, the police collected more than 18,000 suspect names (Rossmo, 1995).

The basic assumption behind geographic profiling is that most serial offenders do not travel far from home to commit their crimes and, therefore, it should be possible to make a reasonably accurate prediction about where an offender lives. Fortunately for the geographic profiler, research supports this assumption. Perhaps surprisingly, it turns out that serial offenders tend to be consistent in their crime site selection choices, often committing their crimes very close to where they reside (Rossmo, 2000). Indeed, even many of the most bizarre serial killers commit their crimes close to home (Canter, Coffey, Huntley, & Missen, 2000). For traveling offenders, particularly those who travel in a particular direction to commit their crimes, geographic profiling is typically not a useful investigative strategy. However, for the majority of serial offenders who do commit their crimes locally, a number of profiling strategies can be used (Snook, Zito, Bennell, & Taylor, 2005).

One of the first cases in which geographic profiling techniques were used was the case of the Yorkshire Ripper in England (Canter, 2003). After five years of unsolved murders, an advisory team was set up to review the investigation. Although some on the investigators felt the offender lived in a different part of the country from where the crimes were happening, the advisory team believed the offender was a local man. To provide support for this claim, the team constructed a type of geographic profile

(Kind, 1987). They plotted the 17 Ripper murders onto a map and calculated the center of gravity for the points (Canter, 2003). That is, by adding up the *x-y* coordinates for each crime and dividing by the 17 crimes, they could calculate the *x-y* coordinate for the center of gravity. In this case, the center of gravity was near Bradford, a city close to where the majority of the murders had taken place. When Peter Sutcliffe was eventually arrested for the crimes, he was found to reside in a district of Bradford (Canter, 2003).

Since the time of the Ripper murders, a number of individuals have built computerized **geographic profiling systems** that can assist with the profiling task (Canter et al., 2000; Levine, 2007; Rossmo, 2000). The locations of linked crime sites are input into these systems and are represented as points on a map. As described by Snook et al. (2005), the systems then perform calculations by using mathematical models of offender spatial behavior, which reflect the probability that the offender lives at particular points in the area where the offenses have taken place. Every single location on the map is assigned an overall probability and these probabilities are designated a color. For example, the top 10% of probabilities might be assigned the color red, and so on. The eventual output is a colored map, in which each color band corresponds to the probability that the offender lives in the area (see Figure 3.2). The police use this map to prioritize their investigative activities (Rossmo, 2000). Geographic profilers also consider other factors that may affect an offender's spatial behavior, such as the density of suitable victims in an area, but this probability map forms the basis of their prediction.

Whether these computerized geographic profiling systems are necessary for constructing accurate profiles, or whether less sophisticated and potentially more cost-effective

Geographic profiling systems

Computer systems that use mathematical models of offender spatial behavior to make predictions about where unknown serial offenders are likely to reside

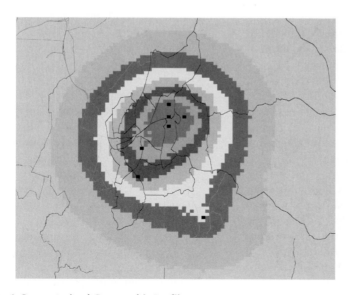

FIGURE 3.2   A Computerized Geographic Profile

The black squares represent the crime locations and the different colored bands (represented here by different shades of gray) correspond to the probability that the offender resides in that particular geographic area. The high-priority search area in this case centers on the four crimes in the upper half of the map. This profile was constructed by using Dragnet, a computerized geographic profiling system developed by David Canter.

Heuristics

Simple general rules that can be used to make decisions and solve problems

alternatives are possible, is a question that has recently begun to be explored (see Bennell, Taylor, & Snook, 2007). For example, Snook, Taylor, and Bennell (2004) examined whether individuals trained to use simple **heuristics** (e.g., predicting that serial offenders will live close to the locations of the majority of their crimes) would make profiling predictions that are as accurate as computerized systems. In that study, they found that, even before any training, approximately 50% of participants made predictions that were as accurate as a computerized system. After training, there was no difference between the average accuracy of the participants and the system, when accuracy was measured by calculating the distance between the actual and predicted home location. Such findings have resulted in a debate over the relative merits of various profiling approaches (e.g., Canter, 2005; Rossmo, 2005; Snook, Taylor, & Bennell, 2005), and research is currently being conducted in an attempt to resolve this debate.

Summary

1. One of the primary goals of a police interrogation is to obtain a confession from the suspect. Police officers in North America sometimes use the Reid model of interrogation to interrogate suspects. This model advocates the use of psychologically based interrogation tactics to break down a suspect's resistance to telling the truth. The tactics used in the Reid model of interrogation can be broken down into minimization and maximization techniques.

2. Three potential problems with the Reid model of interrogation are (1) the inability of police officers to accurately detect deception, (2) biases that result from presuming a suspect is guilty, and (3) an increased likelihood that suspects will make false confessions.

3. There are three types of false confessions, each having its own set of vulnerability factors. Voluntary false confessions occur when someone voluntarily confesses to a crime he or she did not commit without any elicitation from the police. Coerced-compliant false confessions are those in which the suspect confesses to a crime, even though the suspect is fully aware that he or she did not commit it. Coerced-internalized false confessions consist of individuals confessing to a crime they did not commit—and subsequently coming to the belief they committed the crime—usually after they are exposed to highly suggestible questions.

4. Various vulnerability factors are associated with false confessions. Voluntary false confessions may arise out of (1) a morbid desire for notoriety, (2) the person being unable to distinguish fact from fantasy, (3) the need to make up for pathological feelings of guilt, or (4) a desire to protect somebody else from harm. Coerced-compliant false confessions may be given so the suspect can (1) escape further interrogation, (2) gain a promised benefit, or (3) avoid a threatened punishment. Finally, several factors are associated with coerced-internalized false confessions: (1) a history of substance abuse or some other interference with brain function, (2) the inability of people to detect discrepancies between what they observed and what has been erroneously suggested to them, and (3) factors associated with mental state, such as severe anxiety.

5. Criminal profiling is sometimes used by the police in serial crime investigations. They use it for prioritizing suspects, developing new lines of inquiry, setting traps to flush out offenders, determining whether an offender's actions should be taken seriously, giving advice on how to interrogate suspects, and developing courtroom strategies. Despite its use, criminal profiling is often criticized. One major criticism centers on

the lack of a strong theoretical base underlying the approach. A second criticism relates to the fact that profiles sometimes contain ambiguous information and this may cause problems when police officers are asked to interpret the profile. A third criticism is that professionally trained profilers may be no better than other individuals at constructing accurate profiles.

6. Another common form of profiling is geographic profiling, which is defined as any technique that uses crime scene locations to predict the most likely area where the offender resides. Geographic profiling is often used to prioritize suspects, by rank ordering them based on the proximity of their residence to the predicted home location.

Key Concepts

classic trait model *73*
coerced-compliant false confessions *62*
coerced-internalized false confessions *62*
compliance *64*
confabulation *64*
criminal profiling *67*
deception detection *57*

deductive criminal profiling *70*
disputed confessions *61*
false confessions *60*
geographic profiling *76*
geographic profiling systems *77*

heuristics *78*
inductive criminal profiling *71*
internalization *64*
investigator bias *58*
maximization techniques *56*
minimization techniques *56*

organized–disorganized model *71*
police interrogation *53*
Reid model *54*
retracted confessions *61*
voluntary false confessions *61*

Discussion Questions

1. Many police agencies now video-record their interrogations, thus presenting potential advantages for the police, suspects, and the courts. Do you see any potential problems with using this procedure? What are some other possible ways to minimize the problems that result from modern-day interrogation practices?

2. Because the Reid model of interrogation can potentially increase the degree to which people falsely confess to crimes, people seem to agree that it should not be used with particular individuals (e.g., those with learning disabilities). However, few police agencies have policies in place to indicate when it is not appropriate to use the Reid model. Put yourself in the role of a police psychologist and develop a set of recommendations for when the technique should and shouldn't be used.

3. You are a criminal profiler who uses the inductive approach to profiling. You encounter a series of crimes in which the offender consistently attacks elderly women in their apartments at night. How would you go about constructing a profile in this case? What sorts of problems would a deductive profiler have with your profile? How could you attempt to counter some of their arguments?

4. Geographic profiling works in large part because offenders commit most of their crimes close to home. Why do you think offenders do this?

Deception

LEARNING OBJECTIVES

- Describe the two types of polygraph tests.

- Describe the most common types of errors made by the Comparison Question Test (CQT) and the Concealed Information Test (CIT).

- Describe physiologically based alternatives to the polygraph, including

event-related brain potentials and functional brain-imaging techniques.

- Outline the verbal and nonverbal characteristics of deception.

- Define malingering and list the three explanatory models of malingering.

- Differentiate among the types of studies used to examine malingering.

Dimitri Adonis is in trouble. He is a suspect in a vicious attack that occurred outside a popular nightclub. He was seen driving away from the scene of the attack. He has been asked by the police to take a polygraph exam. On the date of the first scheduled test, he tells the polygraph examiner that he has a bad cold. The police examiner asks him to come back the following week to take the exam. At the next exam, the police examiner informs him of his deceptive scoring and attempts to obtain a confession from him about his role in the attack. Dimitri maintains that he is innocent and the polygraph must be wrong.

How do we know whether someone is telling the truth or lying? A person may lie to the police about his or her involvement in a crime, lie to a psychologist about psychological symptoms, lie to a probation officer by claiming to be following conditional release requirements, or lie in a job interview. Several techniques have been developed to try to answer this question. As seen in Chapter 3, police attempt to detect whether someone is telling them the truth during an interrogation. Psychologists have participated in the development and testing of a variety of techniques to detect deception. In this chapter, we focus on several issues associated with deception, including the use of the polygraph and alternatives to the polygraph, the relationship between verbal and non-verbal cues to deception, and methods for detecting the malingering of mental disorders.

THE POLYGRAPH TECHNIQUE

Physiological measures have long been used in an attempt to detect deception. For example, at one time the Chinese forced suspects to chew on dry rice powder and then to spit it out. If the powder was dry, the suspect was judged to be lying (Kleinmuntz & Szucko, 1984). The rationale for this technique was that anxiety causes a person's mouth to be dry. A person telling the truth would not be anxious and, therefore, would not have a dry mouth. In contrast, a person lying would be anxious and would have a dry mouth. Polygraphy relies on the same underlying principle: deception is associated with physiological change. The origins of modern polygraphy date from 1917 when William Marston, a Harvard psychologist also trained as a lawyer, developed a systolic blood pressure test (Iacono & Patrick, 1999) and attempted to use this physiological response as evidence for a person's innocence (see Lykken, 1998). Marston's testimony was rejected by the courts in *Frye v. United States* (1923) because they felt the test had not gained acceptance by the scientific community, foreshadowing the debate associated with physiological measures that continues to the present day.

A **polygraph** (the word is a combination of two Greek words, *poly* = "many," and *grapho* = "write") is a device for recording an individual's autonomic nervous system responses. Measurement devices are attached to the upper chest and abdomen to measure breathing. The amount of sweat on the skin is measured by attaching electrodes to the fingertips. Sweat changes the conductance of the skin, which is known as the galvanic skin response. Finally, heart rate is measured by a partially inflated blood pressure cuff attached to an arm. Each of these measures is amplified and can be printed out on paper or stored in a computer to be analyzed. In a forensic context, a polygraph is used to measure a person's physiological responses to questions asked by an examiner.

Polygraph

A device for recording an individual's autonomic nervous system responses

Police polygraph testing room.

In the United States, the American Polygraph Association accredits independent polygraph schools. The polygraph courses vary in length but cover issues such as various techniques, interviewing practices, and scoring.

Applications of the Polygraph Test

Polygraph tests are used for a range of purposes. The police often use them to help in their criminal investigations. The police may ask a suspect to take a polygraph test as a means to resolve the case. If the suspect fails the polygraph test, that person may be pressured to confess, thereby giving the police incriminating evidence. Although not common, police may ask alleged victims of crimes to take a polygraph test to help verify whether a crime has occurred. Insurance companies may request a polygraph test to verify the claims of the insured. In addition, polygraph tests are used in the United States to assess and monitor sexual offenders on probation. **Polygraph disclosure tests** are used to uncover information about an offender's past behavior. Polygraph tests have been used to determine whether the offender is violating the conditions of probation or to test for evidence of risky behavior, such as sexual fantasies about children. At one time, the most widespread applications of polygraph testing in the United States were for the periodic testing of employees to identify those engaged in theft or using drugs at work and for the screening of prospective employees to weed out those with criminal tendencies or substance-abuse problems. However, the Employee Polygraph Protection Act of 1988 restricted private companies from using the polygraph for these purposes and limited the use of the polygraph to specific investigations of job-related wrongdoing. Nonetheless, some governmental agencies in the United States still use the polygraph as a general screening tool. For example, some police departments require applicants to take a polygraph test, and the Federal Bureau of Investigation and Central Intelligence Agency also require that their potential employees pass a polygraph test to verify information about drug and alcohol abuse and national security matters.

Types of Polygraph Tests

The polygraph does not detect lies per se, since the physiological states associated with lying share much in common with many other states, including anxiety, anger, embarrassment, and fear. Instead, polygraph tests rely on measuring physiological responses to different types of questions. Some questions are designed to elicit a larger physiological response in guilty individuals than in those who are innocent. The two main types of polygraph tests are reviewed below.

THE COMPARISON QUESTION TEST   The **Comparison Question Test** (CQT; also known as the Control Question Test) is the most commonly used test to investigate criminal acts. The typical CQT includes a pretest interview, followed by a series of questions administered while the suspect's physiological responses are measured (usually three separate question sequences are asked). The polygraph examiner then scores the charts and ends the CQT with a post-test interview in which the test results are discussed.

A critical component of this technique is the pretest interview. During the pretest interview, the polygraph examiner develops the comparison questions, learns about the background of the suspect, and attempts to convince the suspect of the accuracy of the polygraph test. The examiner will do this by quoting very high accuracy rates and conducting a stimulation test. For example, the suspect will pick a card with a number on it from a deck of cards, and the examiner will determine the number by examining the polygraph chart. The deck of cards is rigged so the examiner knows which card the suspect picked.

The examiner then asks ten questions to be answered with either "yes" or "no." Table 4.1 provides an example of a typical question series used in a CQT. Three types of questions are asked. Irrelevant questions, referring to the respondent's identity or personal background (e.g., "Is your first name Beatrice?"), are included as a baseline but are not scored. Relevant and comparison questions establish guilt or innocence. Relevant questions deal with the crime being investigated (e.g., "On June 12, did you stab your ex-wife?"). Probable-lie comparison questions (also known as control questions) are designed to be emotionally arousing for all respondents and typically focus on the

TABLE 4.1	Typical Question Series Used in a Comparison Question Test	
Type of Question	**Questions**	
Irrelevant	Do you understand that I will only be asking questions we have discussed before?	
Irrelevant	Do you live in the United States?	
Comparison	Between the ages of 18 and 26, did you ever deliberately plan to physically hurt someone?	
Relevant	Did you stab Petunia Bottoms on the night of March 10?	
Irrelevant	Is your first name Craig?	
Comparison	Prior to 2008, did you ever verbally threaten to hurt someone?	
Relevant	Did you use a knife to stab Petunia Bottoms?	
Irrelevant	Were you born in November?	
Comparison	During the first 26 years of your life did you do anything illegal?	
Relevant	On March 10, did you participate in any way in the stabbing of Petunia Bottoms?	

person's honesty and past history prior to the event being investigated (e.g., "Before the age of 25, did you ever try to seriously hurt someone?"). Polygraph examiners assume they can detect deception by comparing reactions to the relevant and comparison questions. Guilty suspects are assumed to react more to relevant questions than comparison questions. In contrast, innocent suspects are assumed to react more to comparison questions than relevant questions. The reasoning behind these assumptions is that innocent people know they are telling the truth about the relevant question so they will react more strongly to general questions about their honesty and past history.

Examiners in the past used global scoring, incorporating all available information—including physiological responses, the suspect's demeanor during the examination, and information in the case file—to make a decision about the guilt or the innocence of the suspect. Most examiners now numerically score the charts to ensure that decisions are based solely on the physiological responses. A polygraph test has three possible outcomes: truthful, deceptive, and inconclusive (examiner is not sure if the suspect is telling the truth or lying). During the post-test interview, the examiner tells the suspect the outcome, and if the outcome is deceptive the examiner attempts to obtain a confession.

Several psychologists have questioned the underlying rationale of the CQT (Cross & Saxe, 2001; Furedy, 1996; Iacono & Patrick, 2006). Imagine yourself being falsely accused of a serious crime and taking a polygraph exam. Being innocent, you might react more strongly to questions about a crime that you could get punished for (i.e., relevant questions) than about vague questions concerning your past behavior (i.e., comparison questions). In contrast, guilty suspects might actually respond more to comparison questions because they are novel or because they believe they have other crimes to hide. In addition, the guilty suspect may no longer react to the crime-relevant questions because he or she may have been asked repeatedly about the crime. The validity of the CQT is discussed later in the chapter.

Concealed Information Test

Type of polygraph test designed to determine if the person knows details about a crime

THE CONCEALED INFORMATION TEST This test was developed by Lykken (1960) and was originally called the Guilty Knowledge Test but is currently known as the **Concealed Information Test** (CIT). The CIT does not assess deception but instead seeks to determine whether the suspect knows details about a crime that only the person who committed the crime would know. The general form of the CIT is a series of questions in multiple-choice format. Each question has one correct option (often called the *critical option*) and four options that are foils—alternatives that could fit the crime but that are incorrect. A CIT question in the context of a homicide might take the following form: "Did you kill the person with (a) a knife, (b) an axe, (c) a handgun, (d) a crowbar, or (e) a rifle?" The guilty suspect is assumed to display a larger physiological response to the correct option than to the incorrect options. An innocent person, conversely, who does not know the details of the crime, will show the same physiological response to all options.

Underlying the CIT is the principle that people will react more strongly to information they recognize as distinctive or important than to unimportant information. Suspects who consistently respond to critical items are assumed to have knowledge of the crime. The likelihood that an innocent person with no knowledge of the crime would react most strongly to the critical alternative is one in five for each question. If 10 questions are asked, the odds that an innocent person will consistently react to the critical alternative are exceedingly small (less than 1 in 10,000,000). Critics of the CIT have warned that this test will work only if the suspect remembers the details of the crime (Honts & Schweinle, 2009). The most common physiological response measured when administering the CIT is palmar sweating (i.e., skin conductance response measured in the palm of the hand).

Although law enforcement in the United States does not routinely use the CIT, it is used regularly in a limited number of other jurisdictions, such as Israel and Japan (Ben-Shakhar & Furedy, 1990). Iacono and Patrick (1999) suggest two reasons for the lack of widespread acceptance of the CIT. First, since polygraph examiners believe in the accuracy of the CQT, they are not motivated to use the more difficult-to-construct CIT. Second, for law enforcement to use the CIT, salient features of the crime must be known only to the perpetrator. If details of a crime appear in the media, the crime-related details given cannot be used to construct a CIT.

Validity of Polygraph Techniques

TYPES OF STUDIES How is the accuracy of polygraph tests assessed? Accuracy is determined under ideal circumstances by presenting information known to be true and false to individuals and measuring their corresponding physiological responses. In practice, studies assessing the validity of polygraph techniques vary in how closely they are able to achieve this ideal. Studies of the validity of polygraph techniques can be classified into two types: laboratory and field studies.

Ground truth

As applied to polygraph research, the knowledge of whether the person is actually guilty or innocent

In laboratory studies, volunteers (often university students) simulate criminal behavior by committing a mock crime. Volunteers come to a laboratory and are randomly assigned to one of two conditions: committing a mock crime or not committing a mock crime. The main advantage of these studies is that the experimenter knows **ground truth** (i.e., who is truly guilty or innocent). In addition, laboratory studies can also compare the relative merits of different types of polygraph tests and control for variables such as the time between the crime and the polygraph exam. However, because of the large motivational and emotional differences between volunteers in laboratory studies and actual suspects in real-life situations, the results of laboratory studies may have limited application to real life. In laboratory studies, guilty participants cannot ethically be given strong incentives to "beat" the polygraph, and both guilty and innocent participants have little to fear if they "fail" the polygraph exam.

Field studies involve real-life situations and actual criminal suspects, together with actual polygraph examinations. Field studies often compare the accuracy of "original" examiners to "blind" evaluators. Original examiners conduct the actual evaluation of the suspect. Blind evaluators are provided with only the original examiner's charts and are given no information about the suspect or the case. Original examiners are exposed to extra polygraph cues—information about the case in addition to that obtained via the polygraph such as the case facts and the behavior of the suspect during the examination. Although polygraph examiners are taught to ignore these cues, Patrick and Iacono (1991) found that examiners are nonetheless significantly influenced by them.

The largest problem with field studies is establishing ground truth. Indicators of guilt, such as physical evidence, eyewitness testimony, or DNA evidence, are often not available. In such situations, truth is more difficult to establish. To deal with this problem, two additional ways of establishing ground truth have been developed: judicial outcomes and confessions. Judicial outcomes are problematic because some people are falsely convicted and some guilty people are not convicted. Confessions are also problematic. Although rare, some people may falsely confess. More significant, however, is the problem that confessions are often not independent from the polygraph examiner's decisions. Confessions are often elicited because a person fails a polygraph exam. Moreover, cases in which a guilty suspect beats the polygraph are not included in research studies. Thus, reliance on confessions to establish ground truth likely inflates polygraph accuracy rates (Iacono & Patrick, 2006). Most field studies have used confessions to establish ground truth.

POLYGRAPH TESTS: ACCURATE OR NOT?   The accuracy of the polygraph for detecting lies is controversial. Numerous laboratory studies have assessed the accuracy of the CQT and CIT (see Iacono & Patrick, 1999, for a review). However, as pointed out above, there are problems when relying on typical mock crime scenarios to estimate real-life accuracy. As a consequence, only field studies of the CQT will be described here. The situation concerning the CIT is different. Since the CIT is almost never used in the United States, no relevant North American data are available. Thus, we will describe assessments of the CIT based on laboratory and field studies done in Israel.

Although the CQT has been investigated for more than 30 years, its ability to accurately measure deception remains controversial (Furedy, 1996; National Research Council [NRC], 2003). Most of the studies have used confessions to classify suspects as guilty or innocent, and as noted above, there are problems with using this as the criterion. Most guilty suspects (84% to 92%) are correctly classified as guilty (Patrick & Iacono, 1991; Raskin, Honts, & Kircher, 1997). However, the picture for innocent suspects is less optimistic, with accuracy rates ranging from 55% to 78% (Honts & Raskin, 1988; Patrick & Iacono, 1991). Many of the innocent suspects were classified as inconclusive. Between 9% and 24% of innocent suspects were falsely identified as guilty. Such a high false-positive rate indicates that innocent people respond more to relevant than comparison questions, suggesting that the premise underlying the CQT does not apply to all suspects.

Table 4.2 presents data from several field studies comparing the accuracy of the original examiner with the blind evaluators. The accuracy rates of the original examiner are higher than those of the blind evaluator, especially for innocent suspects.

TABLE 4.2	Field Studies of the Comparison Question Test*					
Study	**Guilty Condition**			**Innocent Condition**		
	Guilty	Innocent	Inconclusive	Guilty	Innocent	Inconclusive
Honts & Raskin (1988)	92% (92%)	8% (8%)	0% (0%)	0% (15%)	91% (62%)	9% (23%)
Patrick & Iacono (1991)	98% (92%)	0% (2%)	2% (6%)	8% (24%)	73% (30%)	19% (46%)

*Blind examiners' results appear in parentheses.

Source: Based on data from "Physiological parameters and credibility; The polygraph" by A. Vrij from *Psychology and law: Truthfulness, accuracy, and credibility,* ed. A. Memon, A. Vrij, and R. Bull, McGraw Hill (1998).

For example, Patrick and Iacono (1991) examined the accuracy of original examiner opinions to blind scoring for 37 innocent verified cases. The hit rate (in this context, cases classified as innocent when actually innocent, excluding inconclusives) for original examiners was 90%, compared with 55% for blind scorers. The main reason original examiners are more accurate than blind examiners is that the original examiners appear to be using extra polygraph cues (such as the attitude of the suspect, other evidence about the case, and verbal cues), whereas blind chart evaluators have access only to polygraph information. Additional research is needed to confirm the source of these extra polygraphic cues used by examiners.

Mock-crime laboratory studies evaluating the CIT indicate that it is very effective at identifying innocent participants (hit rates of up to 95%) and slightly less effective at identifying guilty participants (hit rates between 76% and 85%) (Gamer, Rill, Vossel, & Gödert, 2005; Iacono & Patrick, 1988; Jokinen, Santilla, Ravaja, & Puttonen, 2006; Lykken, 1998). A meta-analysis of 80 CIT studies examined what factors are associated with higher accuracies (Ben-Shakhar & Elaad, 2003). Correct outcomes were better in studies that included motives to succeed, verbal response to alternatives, or five or more questions, and in laboratory mock-crime studies. Two published field studies, both done in Israel, have assessed the accuracy of the CIT. Elaad (1990) found that 98% of innocent suspects were correctly classified, but only 42% of guilty suspects were correctly classified. Elaad, Ginton, and Jungman (1992) measured both respiration and skin conductance and found that 94% of innocent and 76% of guilty suspects were correctly classified.

Based on the research described above, the CIT appears to be vulnerable to false-negative errors (falsely classifying guilty suspects as innocent), whereas the CQT is vulnerable to false-positive errors (falsely classifying innocent suspects as guilty). See Box 4.1 for a new way of measuring deception.

Can the Guilty Learn to Beat the Polygraph?

Countermeasures

As applied to polygraph research, techniques used to try to conceal guilt

Is it possible to use **countermeasures** to beat the polygraph? There are websites that describe the best ways to beat the polygraph. Honts, Raskin, and Kircher (1994) showed that 30 minutes of instruction on the rationale underlying the CQT was sufficient for community volunteers to learn how to escape detection in a mock-crime study. Participants were told to use either physical countermeasures (e.g., biting their tongue or pressing

BOX 4.1   Seeing Through the Face of Deception

If you travel by air, you will be subjected to intense scrutiny. Airport security officers have become increasingly vigilant in their attempts to detect passengers intent on harm. Technologies that can provide a rapid, accurate assessment of deceit are becoming more and more important.

Pavlidis, Eberhardt, and Levine (2002) examined whether high-definition thermal imaging of the face could be used to detect deceit. Thermal imaging measures the amount of facial warming, which is linked to regional blood flow. Imaging can be done quickly without the individual even knowing his or her facial temperature is being measured. Pavlidis and colleagues wanted to know whether facial warming was associated with deception. Individuals were randomly assigned to commit a mock crime (stab a mannequin and rob it of $20) or to a control condition in which they had no knowledge of the crime. Use of thermal imaging (in particular around the eyes) correctly classified 6 of the 8 guilty participants and 11 of the 12 innocent participants. This accuracy rate was similar to a polygraph exam administered to participants that correctly classified 6 of 8 guilty and 8 of 12 innocent participants. In the future, when security or customs officers ask you questions, they may be paying more attention to your facial temperature than to your answers.

their toes on the floor) or mental countermeasures (e.g., counting backward by 7 from a number greater than 200) when asked a comparison question during the polygraph exam. Both countermeasures worked, with 50% of the guilty suspects beating the polygraph test. In addition, the polygraph examiners were not able to accurately detect which participants had used the countermeasures.

Iacono, Cerri, Patrick, and Fleming (1992) investigated whether antianxiety drugs would allow guilty subjects to appear innocent on the CIT. Undergraduate students were divided into one innocent group (who watched a noncrime videotape) and four guilty groups. Participants in the guilty groups watched a videotaped crime and then were given one of three drugs (diazepam, meprobamate, or propranolol) or a placebo prior to being administered a CIT. None of the drugs had an effect on the accuracy of the CIT. In addition, the polygraph examiner was able to identify 90% of the participants receiving drugs.

Scientific Opinion: What Do the Experts Say?

Most knowledgeable scientists are skeptical about the rationale underlying the CQT and its accuracy. The National Research Council established a panel of 14 scientists and four staff to review the validity of the polygraph (NRC, 2003). In a comprehensive report, the committee concluded the following:

- "The theoretical rationale for the polygraph is quite weak, especially in terms of differential fear, arousal, or other emotional states that are triggered in response to relevant and comparison questions" (NRC, 2003, p. 213).
- "The existing validation studies have serious limitations. Laboratory test findings on polygraph validity are not a good guide to accuracy in field settings. They are likely to overestimate accuracy in field practice, but by an unknown amount" (p. 210).
- "In summary, we were unable to find any field experiments, field quasi-experiments, or prospective research-oriented data collection specifically designed

to assess polygraph validity and satisfying minimal standards of research quality" (p. 115).

- "What is remarkable, given the large body of relevant research, is that claims about the accuracy of the polygraph made today parallel those made throughout the history of the polygraph: practitioners have always claimed extremely high levels of accuracy, and these claims have rarely been reflected in empirical research" (p. 107).

Despite scientists' negative view of it, the CQT is still used by law enforcement as an investigative tool. To understand why, we have only to know that whatever its actual validity, the polygraph will cause many suspects to confess, thereby providing resolution of the criminal investigation.

Admissibility of Polygraph Evidence

Polygraph results were first submitted as evidence in court in the United States in *Frye v. United States* (1923). James Frye was denied the opportunity to have the results of a polygraph test conducted by William Marston admitted as evidence. This ruling led to the requirement that a technique must obtain "general acceptance" by the relevant scientific community before it can be admitted as evidence. This precedent was replaced by a new admissibility standard that required courts to render scientific decisions (*Daubert v. Merrell Dow Pharmaceuticals*, 1993) and was later extended to nonscientific experts who could provide unique specialized information to the court (*Kumho Tire Co. Ltd. v. Carmichael,* 1999). Some states permit the admission of polygraph evidence if there is a prior agreement between prosecuting and defense lawyers. The United States Supreme Court (*U.S. v. Scheffer*, 1998) rejected the admissibility of the polygraph because of the belief that polygraph evidence will usurp the role of the jury as determinant of the credibility of a witness. Justice Thomas ruled "Jurisdictions, in promulgating rules of evidence, may legitimately be concerned about the risk that juries will give excessive weight to the opinions of the polygrapher, clothed as they are in scientific expertise and at times offering, as in respondent's case, a conclusion about the ultimate issue in the trial" (p. 422).

BRAIN-BASED DECEPTION RESEARCH

Event-related brain potentials

Brain activity measured by placing electrodes on the scalp and by recording electrical patterns related to presentation of a stimulus

In the past decade, researchers have attempted to use brain-based responses to detect deception. **Event-related brain potentials** (ERPs) are a type of brain-based response that has been investigated for detecting deception. ERPs are measured by placing electrodes on the scalp and by noting changes in electrical patterns related to presentation of a stimulus. ERPs reflect underlying electrical activity in the cerebral cortex. One type of ERP that has shown promise is known as the P300. This ERP occurs in response to significant stimuli that occur infrequently. When using CIT procedures, guilty suspects should respond to such crime-relevant events with a large P300 response, compared with noncrime-relevant events. No difference in P300 responses to crime-relevant and irrelevant events should be observed in innocent suspects. One of the advantages of ERPs is that they have been proposed as a measure resistant to manipulation. (However, Rosenfeld, Soskins, Bosh, and Ryan [2004], have obtained results suggesting that participants who are knowledgeable about ERPs can evade detection.)

Several studies have been conducted to assess the validity of the P300 as a guilt detector (e.g., Abootalebi, Moradi, & Khalilzadeh, 2006; Allen & Iacono, 1997; Farwell & Donchin, 1991; Rosenfeld, Angell, Johnson, & Qian, 1991; Rosenfeld, Nasman, Whalen, Cantwell, & Mazzeri, 1987). Farwell and Donchin (1991) conducted one of the first studies on the use of the P300 to detect the presence of guilty knowledge. The study consisted of two experiments. In the first experiment, participants role-played one of two espionage scenarios, which involved the exchange of information with a foreign agent, during which they were exposed to six critical details (e.g., the color of the agent's hat). In the second experiment, participants were asked about details of minor offenses they had committed in their day-to-day lives. In the first experiment, using P300 as the measure, 18 of 20 participants were correctly classified in the guilty condition, and 17 of 20 were correctly classified in the innocent condition. In the second experiment, all four of the guilty participants were correctly classified, and three of the four innocent participants were correctly classified.

Although the results look impressive, there are several limitations to this study. First, guilty participants reviewed the crime-relevant details just prior to taking the CIT. In addition, there were no aversive consequences linked to performance in this study. Finally, the sample size, especially in the second experiment, was very small. Abootalebi and colleagues (2006) recently reported lower detection rates than previously reported (e.g., Rosenfeld et al., 1991) when employing the P300-CIT paradigm, with correct identification ranging from 74% to 80%, depending on the approach. In summary, although the P300 has shown potential for detecting deception, its application remains limited to laboratory settings.

More recently, investigators have also begun to use functional magnetic resonance imaging (fMRI) to determine which areas of the brain are associated with deception (Ganis, Kosslyn, Stose, Thompson, & Yurgelun-Todd, 2003; Langleben et al., 2002). For example, Ganis and colleagues (2003) examined which brain areas were activated when someone told a spontaneous or rehearsed lie. Lies that were part of a story and that had been rehearsed repeatedly produced a higher level of activation in the right anterior frontal cortex than did spontaneous isolated lies. In contrast, spontaneous isolated lies produced a higher level of activation in the anterior cingulate and posterior visual cortices. These findings and others indicate that brain-imaging techniques can differentiate which parts of the brain are involved in lying and can even indicate which areas are associated with different types of lying. A limitation of this research, however, is that it is typically based on averaging fMRI data across multiple participants, which constrains its use for detecting deception in individuals. More recent research has employed fMRI to detect deception at the individual level (Kozel et al., 2005; Langleben et al., 2005) and found increased prefrontal and parietal activity when someone is lying. Kozel and colleagues (2005) note that, to better treat and diagnose patients, this methodology is important for examining the neurological factors of disorders for which deception plays a prominent role (e.g., malingering or psychopathy).

Box 4.2 describes the case of Terry Harrington, a man convicted of murder who attempted to use the results of brain-based deception testing to prove his innocence.

Verbal and Nonverbal Behavior Cues to Lying

On average, North Americans tell one to two lies per day (Serota, Levine, & Boster, 2010). However, a small number of people are prolific liars. The most common method of deception detection is through the analysis of verbal characteristics and nonverbal

BOX 4.2	Brain Fingerprinting: Evidence for a New Deception-Detection Technology?

The case that put brain fingerprinting in the news was *Harrington v. State* (2003). On July 22, 1977, retired police officer John Schweer was shot and killed while working as a security guard for a car dealership in Iowa. Seventeen-year-old Terry Harrington and Curtis McGhee were arrested for the murder. At his trial, Terry Harrington claimed he was not at the crime scene and several witnesses testified that Harrington had been at a concert on the night of the murder. The prosecution's key witness was another teenager, Kevin Hughes, who testified that he was with Harrington and McGhee on the night of the murder. According to Hughes, the three teenagers decided to steal a car. They went to the car dealership. Hughes testified that he waited in the car while Harrington, who first removed a shotgun from the trunk, and McGhee went around a building at the car dealership. Hughes claims he heard a gunshot and Harrington and McGhee came running back to the car. Hughes testified that Harrington had stated he had just shot a cop. Both Terry Harrington and Curtis McGhee were convicted of first-degree murder and sentenced to life in prison without the possibility of parole.

Throughout his 25 years of imprisonment, Terry Harrington maintained his innocence, but all his attempts to appeal his conviction were unsuccessful. From his prison cell, Harrington heard about a new technology that might help his case. He contacted Lawrence Farwell, a cognitive psychophysiologist and head of Brain Fingerprinting Laboratories. On April 18 and 25, 2000, Farwell came to the Iowa State Penitentiary to test Harrington to determine if he had knowledge of the crime scene and of details about his alibi (the concert he claims he attended). Farwell measured the amplitude of Harrington's P300 brain potential to irrelevant and relevant crime scene and concert details. According to Farwell, Harrington's lack of P300 response to crime-relevant details indicated that Harrington had not participated in the murder. In contrast, Harrington showed a prominent P300 to alibi-relevant information.

Harrington's case received national attention in December 2001 when the CBS show *60 Minutes* featured Farwell's research and his testing of Harrington. In March 2002, Harrington's lawyer submitted a report describing the results of Farwell's testing to the Supreme Court of Iowa.

Although the results of the brain fingerprinting were entered as evidence, the judges relied on other evidence to overturn the murder conviction. During the hearing, three of the prosecution witnesses recanted their testimony. Kevin Hughes stated that he had made up the story about what happened the night of the murder. Hughes claimed that he lied to obtain the $5,000 reward being offered about the murder and to avoid being charged with the crime. In addition, the police failed to turn over all the police reports to Harrington's defense lawyer. These reports documented the police investigation of an alternative suspect. On February 26, 2003, the Supreme Court of Iowa overturned the murder conviction of Terry Harrington and the case was remanded for a new trial. On October 24, 2003, the Pottawattamie County Attorney announced that he was dropping the murder charges against Terry Harrington.

behaviors. The underlying assumption is the same as that for polygraphy: the act of deception produces a physiological change compared with telling the truth. The argument here is that it is more difficult for people to control aspects of their nonverbal behavior than their verbal behavior (DePaulo & Kirkendol, 1989). The typical experiment involves one group of participants (called the *message source*) who are told to provide either true or deceptive messages. For example, DePaulo, Lassiter, and Stone (1982) asked participants to honestly describe people they liked and disliked. They also asked participants to describe the same people dishonestly (i.e., to pretend to like the person they disliked and vice versa). Another group of participants was asked to detect when the message source participants were being truthful or deceptive. Participants who were instructed to focus their attention on the message source participants' tone of voice were more successful at detecting deception than those participants given no special instructions.

Researchers have also assessed facial cues and other nonverbal cues to deception. For example, Ekman and Friesen (1974) showed student nurses a film of an ocean scene and videotaped them describing what they were seeing and how they felt while watching the film. They also watched a gruesome medical training film (e.g., the amputation of a hand or a severe industrial burn) and were videotaped while pretending that the film they were watching was pleasant. To motivate the nurses watching the gruesome film, the researchers told them that to be successful in nursing, they would have to be able to mask feelings when dealing with unpleasant events. Ekman and Friesen found that the nurses focused on controlling their facial expressions when attempting to deceive. Observers who watched videotapes of the nurses attempting to deceive were more likely to detect deception when they were shown a videotape of the nurses' bodies (with the faces blacked out) than when shown a videotape of their faces. Subsequent research on whether nonverbal cues can be used as an indicator of deception is mixed (Vrij, 2008). Nonverbal behaviors such as gaze aversion, smiling, and self-manipulation (e.g., rubbing one's hands) are not reliable indicators of deception.

If a liar is not feeling excited, scared, or guilty, or when the lie is easy to fabricate, behavioral cues to deception will likely not be present. In a study of everyday lying, DePaulo, Kashy, Kirkendol, Wyer, and Epstein (1996) found that both college students and community members practiced deception daily. Most of the deception was not considered serious, and the participants reported they were not concerned or worried about being caught. Participants lied about their opinions, feelings, achievements, reasons for doing things, and possessions. Most of the lies were told for psychological reasons, such as protecting the liar from embarrassment. For example, "I told her Ted and I still liked each other when really I don't know if he likes me at all." The reason this person lied was "because I'm ashamed of the fact that he doesn't like me anymore."

Ekman (1992) has hypothesized that when people are attempting to conceal an emotion, the true emotion may be manifest as a micro facial expression. These microexpressions are brief facial expressions reflecting the true emotions the person is experiencing. In response to terrorists concerns, the United States has been training security officers at airports to use this technique (reading concealed emotions in people) to identify potential threats. Matsumoto, Hwang, Skinner, and Frank (2011) recommend that during interrogations investigators pay attention not only to what a suspect says but also to the suspect's facial expressions.

Strömwall, Hartwig, and Granhag (2006) explored the role of stress by creating a realistic deception scenario that used experienced police officers, employed long interrogations, and generated suspects who were motive driven and had adequate time to prepare their deception. Participants were offered $30 to tell a biographical story to a police officer and were randomly instructed to be honest or deceitful. To create motivation and higher risk, participants were offered an additional $20 if they were able to convince the officer that they were being truthful. Liars felt more anxious and stressed during the task when compared to truth-tellers. No differences in nonverbal behaviors were observed. For verbal strategies, the majority of truth-tellers claimed to "keep it real" (50%), whereas liars would "keep it simple" (46.7%). (For more on verbal cues to lying, see the next section).

Do students and offenders display similar cues to deception? Much of the deception research uses students as the participants but in the real-world students tend not to be crime suspects. Porter and his colleagues (2008) examined verbal and nonverbal behaviors while students and offenders told true and false stories about emotional events in their past history. Both groups provided fewer details when they were lying than when honest. Offenders also engaged in more self-manipulations and smiled less when lying about emotional events.

There are several types of verbal (e.g., saying "ah" and "umm", pitch of voice, rate of speech) and nonverbal (e.g., gaze aversion, smiling, blinking, body movements) indicators that have been studied to detect deception. The verbal indicator that has been most strongly associated with deception is voice pitch. Liars tend to speak in a higher-pitched voice than those telling the truth. Most studies have found increased use of speech fillers ("ah," "umm") and a slower rate of speech during deception (DePaulo et al., 1982; Fiedler & Walka, 1993; Sporer & Schwandt, 2006). However, if you ask participants only to conceal information or instruct them on what they should lie about, deception is associated with fewer speech fillers and a faster speech rate (Vrij, 1995). In summary, it appears that cognitively more difficult lies (lies in which you have to fabricate an answer) may be associated with one pattern of speech fillers, whereas cognitively simpler lies (lies in which you must conceal something) may be associated with a different pattern of speech disturbances.

Verbal Cues to Lying

In a comprehensive meta-analysis, DePaulo and colleagues (2003) coded 158 cues to deception from 120 samples of adults. Most of the verbal and nonverbal behaviors coded did not discriminate between liars and truth-tellers. One of the most reliable indicators was that liars provide fewer details than do truth-tellers. Liars also told less compelling accounts as compared with truth-tellers. For example, liars' stories were less likely to make sense (less plausible, lack logical structure, have discrepancies), were less engaging, and were less fluent than were truth-tellers' stories. Liars were also rated as less cooperative and more nervous and tense than truth-tellers. Finally, truth-tellers were more likely to spontaneously correct their stories and more likely to admit to a lack of memory than liars were. Deception cues were easier to detect when liars were motivated to lie or when they were attempting to cover up a personal failing or a transgression.

Can you detect a killer from a 911 call? Adams and Harpster (2008) analyzed a hundred 911 calls coding what the call was about, who the call was about, and how the call was made. Fifty of the calls were from innocent people calling for help, whereas the other 50 were from the perpetrator or the person who had arranged the murder. Innocent callers were more likely to make requests for help for the victim, were more likely to correct any misperceptions during the call, were more rude and demanding of immediate assistance, were cooperative, and the voice contained lots of emotion and was fast paced. Callers who had committed or organized the killing were more likely to provide irrelevant details, blame or insult the victim, state that the victim was dead, and be polite and patient, with little emotion displayed in the voice. If future research replicates these findings, these cues may help police investigators plan how they will interview 911 callers.

What about online deception? Computer-mediated communication is extremely common and researchers have begun to study when, where, and how people lie online. See Box 4.3 for an example of such research.

Are Some People Better at Detecting Deception?

If you believe what you see on the television there are lie detection wizards out there. See the In the Media box for a description of popular recent television series. Across studies, the ability to distinguish lies from truth tends to be only slightly better than

BOX 4.3   Quest for Love: Truth and Deception in Online Dating

Approximately 20 million Americans have used online dating services. There are a range of different types of electronic dating sites. On some sites the participants provide a profile for others to read (e.g., *match.com*), whereas at other sites participants pay a fee and complete a questionnaire about their personality traits, interests, attitudes, and beliefs (e.g., *eharmony*). Using the Internet to find potential mates has become increasingly popular.

How Accurate Are Internet Dating Profiles?

Most users of online dating sites believe that others misrepresent themselves (Gibbs, Ellison, & Heino, 2006) and some potential users avoid using these sites because of fear of deception. People who post profiles may embellish their profiles to attract potential mates. In contrast, users may want to ensure they present themselves accurately—quirks and all—since they are seeking a potential mate who will be compatible with their personality and interests. Do men and women engage in different types of impression management online? For example, are men be more likely to enhance their occupations and earnings, and women their youthfulness and physical attractiveness?

Toma, Hancock, and Ellison (2008) invited online daters to participate in a study on self-presentation in online dating profiles. Participants needed to be a subscriber to popular dating sites in which the users create their own profile (this requirement excluded sites such as *eharmony*, where subscribers are matched based on their responses to questionnaires). Forty men and 40 women were invited to the lab and the accuracy of their dating profiles was examined.

Self-Reported Accuracy

Participants self-reported they were most accurate about their relationship information (e.g., married, divorced, single) and whether they had children. However, when photos were included in profiles the participants rated them as less accurate than other information such as occupation, education, habits (e.g., smoking and drinking), and political and religious beliefs.

Observed Accuracy

In the study the participant's height and weight were measured and their age obtained from their driver's licenses. The majority (81%) of the participants provided inaccurate information about height, weight, or age. Participants were more likely to lie about their weight than their age or height. Men were more likely to overestimate their height, and women were more likely to underestimate their weight. Most of these deceptions were small in magnitude. However, in some cases they were larger in magnitude, such as a 3-inch difference in height, a 35-pound difference in weight, and an 11-year difference in age.

The authors conclude that "online daters in the present study used deception strategically as a resource in the construction of their online self-presentation and in the engineering of their romantic lives" (p. 1035).

chance. For example, a meta-analysis by Aamondt and Custer (2008) found that on average the accuracy rate for detecting deception for "professional lie catchers," such as police officers, judges, and psychologists, was 55.5%—a rate that is not much more accurate than that of students and other citizens (who had 54.2% accuracy). This poor performance in deception detection has been explained in two ways. First, people tend to rely on behaviors that lack predictive validity (Fiedler & Walka, 1993). Laypeople have a number of beliefs about lying. In a study that measured stereotypic beliefs about lying in 75 different countries, the Global Deception Research

IN THE MEDIA   TV and Lie Detection

Television shows about detecting deception are popular. In this box we describe three shows whose underlying premise is using physiological, linguistic, or behavioral cues to detect deception.

Lie to Me

Lie to Me's main character is Dr. Cal Lightman, a lie detection expert who has an uncanny ability to detect lies. He watches your face for microexpressions, reads your body language, listens to your voice, and monitors what you say. His only challenge is the stress caused by being able to detect all the lies told by those around him, even those told by his family and his friends. This TV drama launched in 2009 and was an instant success. Although the accuracy of Dr. Lightman's abilities is unrealistic, a true expert on lie detection comments on each episode.

Lie Detector

You may also have heard of the *Lie Detector*.

The most recent version of this show aired in 2005. Its premise was to provide people who have been accused of lying with the opportunity to vindicate themselves. This show featured Dr. Ed Gelb, a forensic psychophysiologist and a trained polygrapher examiner, who would conduct a polygraph examination on the show. Guests on the show ranged from a woman claiming to have contact with extraterrestrials, to Paula Jones, who claimed Bill Clinton sexually harassed her. Although some reality shows maintain their popularity, *Lie Detector* was cancelled after only one season.

The Moment of Truth

In this game show, contestants were asked increasingly embarrassing personal questions that they had to answer honestly to win money. To determine whether the person was telling the truth, a polygraph test was administered prior to the show. The polygraph results were used to determine whether the person was telling the truth or a lie. The show premiered in January 2008 and ended in August 2009.

Team (2006) found that the most common stereotype about liars is that they avoid eye contact. Police officers share belief in these stereotypes: they believe that two cues indicative of deceit are eye gaze and fidgeting. Liars are thought to avoid eye contact and to fidget. Unfortunately, these two cues have not been found to be related to deception (Vrij, 2008). Second, most people have a **truth-bias**. Truth-bias refers to the tendency of people to judge more messages as truthful than deceptive (Bond & DePaulo, 2006).

Several studies by Ekman and colleagues have investigated the abilities of diverse professional groups to detect deception. In the 1991 study by Ekman and O'Sullivan, forensic psychiatrists, customs agents, FBI agents, and judges all performed around chance levels in detecting deception. The only group that performed better than chance (64% correct) were U.S. Secret Service agents. About a third of Secret Service agents were 80% accurate or better. The most accurate participants were those who relied on multiple cues to assess credibility rather than on any one cue.

Truth-bias

The tendency of people to judge more messages as truthful than deceptive

More recently, Ekman, O'Sullivan, and Frank (1999) showed professional groups videotaped speakers describing a true or false opinion. Both federal law enforcement officers and clinical psychologists were able to detect deceit at above chance levels (around 70% correct). In a Canadian study, Porter, Woodworth, and Birt (2000) found that parole officers performed below chance levels (40% correct) at distinguishing videotaped speakers describing a truthful or fictitious stressful personal experience, such as an animal attack or a serious car accident. However, after attending a deception-detection workshop, they were significantly more accurate (77% correct). Thus, although detecting deception is difficult, it is possible to improve judgment accuracy through training.

In a review of 40 studies, Vrij (2000) found a 67% accuracy rate for detecting truths and a 44% accuracy rate for detecting lies. Table 4.3 presents the accuracy rates of professional lie-catchers. In most of the studies, the professional lie-catchers were not very accurate at detecting deception. The results also showed that in most studies, truthful messages were identified with more accuracy than deceptive ones. Thus, even professional lie-catchers have a truthfulness bias. One reason even professionals are not good at detecting lies is that they rely on the wrong cues. For example, Vrij and Semin (1996) found that 75% of police and customs officers believe that gaze aversion is a reliable indicator of deception, but empirical research has not found that belief to be true (Vrij, 1998). Mann, Vrij, and Bull (2004) examined police officers' ability to detect lies and truths told by suspects during police interrogations. These police officers were able to reach accuracy rates similar to those of more specialized law-enforcement groups, such as U.S. Secret Service agents (Ekman et al., 1999). There are two potential explanations for the higher-than-usual accuracy. First, the suspects were highly motivated to lie and research has shown that high-stakes lies are easier to detect than low-stakes ones.

TABLE 4.3	Accuracy Rates of Professional Lie Catchers		
Study	*Accuracy Rates*		
	Truth	Lie	Total
DePaulo & Pfeifer, 1996 (Experienced police)*	64%	42%	52%
DePaulo & Pfeifer, 1996 (New police recruits)*	64%	42%	53%
Ekman & O'Sullivan, 1991 (Federal polygraphers)			56%
Ekman & O'Sullivan, 1991 (Police officers)			56%
Ekman & O'Sullivan, 1991 (Secret Service)			64%
Köehnken, 1987 (Police officers)	58%	31%	45%
Vrij, 1994 (Police detectives)	51%	46%	49%
Ekman et al., 1999 (Federal law-enforcement officers)	66%	89%	73%
Ekman et al., 1999 (Sheriffs)	56%	78%	67%
Porter et al., 2000 (Parole officers)	41%	47%	52%
Mann et al., 2004 (Police officers)	64%	66%	65%

*Accuracy rates for experienced police and new recruits were collapsed together.

Source: Based on data from "Nonverbal communication and credibility" by A. Vrij from *Psychology and law: Truthfulness, accuracy, and credibility*, ed. A. Memon, A. Vrij, and R. Bull, McGraw Hill (1998).

Second, the police are more familiar with the setting and type of individual they were judging, namely, suspects. Box 4.4 looks at police detection of high-stakes lies.

Two factors one might think would be related to deception-detection ability are level of job experience and confidence in judgment. DePaulo and Pfeifer (1996) compared the proficiency of deception detection of university students, new police recruits, and experienced police officers. None of the groups were better than others at detecting deception; however, the experienced police officers reported being more confident in their decisions. This finding is consistent with more recent research (Ekman & O'Sullivan, 1991; Leach, Talwar, Lee, Bala, & Lindsay, 2004; Porter, Woodworth, et al., 2000) indicating that neither level of experience nor confidence in deception-detection ability is associated with accuracy rates. For example, in a meta-analysis examining the relationship between judges' accuracy at detecting deception and confidence in their judgments, DePaulo, Charlton, Cooper, Lindsay, and Muhlenbruck (1997) found that the average correlation was 0.04. The reason that confidence is unrelated to accuracy may be that people rely on cues they believe are related to deception and when they see these cues, their confidence increases. However, since the cues people believe are related to deception are often not valid, their accuracy tends to be poor.

Research by Bond and DePaulo (2008) has found that there are no specific traits related to detecting deception in others. They conclude that "deception judgments depend more on the liar than the judge (p. 489).

BOX 4.4   Detecting High-Stakes Lies

You are watching the news, and a mother is being interviewed outside her home, begging for the return of her two sons. She says that while stopped at a stop sign, a black man approached her car with a gun and demanded she get out of the car. Her two young sons were in the backseat. Frightened for her life, she got out of the car and the carjacker jumped into the car and drove off with the children in the back. Over the next nine days, she is often on the news pleading with the carjacker to return her sons. Your initial reaction is concern for the mother and hope that the children will be found unharmed. On the ninth day, the mother confesses to police that there was no carjacker and that she had driven her car to a local lake, left the car on the boat ramp in neutral, got out, and watched as the car slowly rolled into the lake and sank. The two children's bodies were found in the car, still in their car seats.

This story is the true case of 23-year-old Susan Smith. Smith was convicted of first-degree murder of 3-year-old Michael and 14-month-old Alex. During the penalty phase of the trial, the assistant prosecutor, Keith Giese, stated, "We're going to go back over the nine days of lies, the nine days of deceit, the nine days of trickery, the nine days of begging this country to help her find her children, while the whole time they lay dead at the bottom of that lake" (Reuter, 1995).

Would you have been able to detect if Susan Smith was lying by what she said or by her behavior during her numerous press conferences? Vrij and Mann (2001) asked a similar question. They asked 52 police officers to view videotaped press conferences of people who were asking for the public's help in locating their missing relatives or the murderers of their relatives. Vrij and Mann asked the officers to determine who was lying and who was telling the truth. What they didn't tell the officers was that every video showed people who had actually been found guilty of killing their own relatives. The officers were not very accurate at detecting the deception. Moreover, accuracy was not related to age, years of police work, level of experience interviewing suspects, or confidence.

Chapter 4 • Deception **97**

ASSESSMENT OF MALINGERING AND DECEPTION

Disorders of Deception

Deception is a central component of some psychological disorders. The disorders described below vary on two dimensions: (1) whether the person intentionally or consciously produces the symptoms, and (2) whether the motivation is internal or external.

The *Diagnostic and Statistical Manual of Mental Disorders*, Fourth Edition (*DSM-IV*) (American Psychiatric Association [APA], 1994), diagnostic criteria for a **factitious disorder** include (1) physical or psychological symptoms that are intentionally produced, (2) internal motivation to assume the sick role, and (3) an absence of external incentives. Eisendrath (1996) has suggested that patients with factitious disorders might be aware they are intentionally producing the symptoms, but they may lack insight into the underlying psychological motivation.

There are many different subtypes of factitious disorders, with most being rare. An example of a physical factitious disorder is **Munchausen syndrome**. In this syndrome, the patient intentionally produces a physical complaint, such as abdominal pain, and constantly seeks physician consultations, hospitalizations, and even surgery to treat the nonexistent illness. In some cases, patients will ingest poison or purposely infect wounds in order to maintain a patient role. This disorder often emerges by age 20, is difficult to treat, and is chronic in nature (APA, 1994). Meadow (1977) coined the term *Munchausen syndrome by proxy* (MBP) to describe cases in which parents or caregivers falsified symptoms in their children. A study by Rosenberg (1987) evaluated 117 reported cases of MBP and found 98% of the individuals were the biological mother of the child; in almost 9% of the cases, the child died. In a more recent review of this syndrome, Sheridan (2003) analyzed the characteristics of 451 MBP cases. Although the most common perpetrator was the child's biological mother (77%), other perpetrators were also identified (the father in 7% of cases). Most the victims were young (age 4 or younger), with 6% of the victims dying and 7% suffering long-term physical injuries. Nearly a third (29%) of the perpetrators had some symptoms of Munchausen syndrome.

The two key components of **somatoform disorders** include (1) physical symptoms that cannot be explained by an underlying organic impairment, and (2) the symptoms are not intentionally produced. In this disorder, patients truly believe they have a physical problem and often consult with their physicians for treatment of their physical problems. Somatoform disorders are rare and often co-occur with other disorders, such as depression or anxiety (Gureje, Simon, Ustun, & Goldberg, 1997).

The two key components to **malingering** are that (1) the psychological or physical symptoms are clearly under voluntary control and (2) there are external motivations for the production of symptoms. People typically malinger mental illness for one of the following external motivations:

- A criminal may attempt to avoid punishment by pretending to be unfit to stand trial, to have a mental illness at the time of a criminal act, or to have an acute mental illness in to avoid being executed.
- Prisoners or patients may seek drugs, or prisoners may want to be transferred to a psychiatric facility to do easier time or escape.

Factitious disorder

A disorder in which the person's physical and psychological symptoms are intentionally produced and are adopted to assume the role of a sick person

Munchausen syndrome

A rare factitious disorder in which a person intentionally produces a physical complaint and constantly seeks physician consultations, hospitalizations, and even surgery to treat the nonexistent illness

Somatoform disorders

A disorder in which physical symptoms suggest a physical illness but have no known underlying physiological cause and the symptoms are not intentionally produced

Malingering

Intentionally faking psychological or physical symptoms for some type of external gain

- Malingerers may seek to avoid conscription to the military or to avoid certain military duties.
- Malingerers may seek financial gain from disability claims, workers' compensation, or damages from alleged injury.
- Malingerers may seek admission to a hospital to obtain free room and board.

Any psychiatric or physical disorder may be malingered. As new syndromes are developed, such as post-traumatic stress disorder, they provide new opportunities for people to attempt to malinger them. Malingering varies in terms of severity from benign (e.g., "Not tonight, honey; I have a headache.") to serious (e.g., "I heard a voice telling me to kill my neighbor, so I obeyed it.").

Individuals with factitious and somatoform disorders often encourage and even insist on having physical tests and invasive procedures, whereas malingerers will often refuse to cooperate with invasive procedures to determine the veracity of their symptoms. The incidence of malingering in the general population is unknown. Patients who malinger rarely admit it. Thus, individuals who successfully malinger are never included in the statistics. Moreover, mental health professionals are often reluctant to label a patient as a malingerer.

The prevalence rate of malingering is relatively high in forensic contexts. For example, Frederick, Crosby, and Wynkoop (2000) reported that 45% of patients evaluated for competency or mental state at the time of offense produced invalid psychological test profiles. Rogers, Ustad, and Salekin (1998) reported that 20% of emergency jail referrals feigned psychological symptoms. Rogers (1986) reported that 4.5% of defendants evaluated for mental state at the time of offense were definite malingerers and another 20% were suspected. Given these large numbers, it is clear that malingering should be considered in all forensic evaluations. Estimates of malingering psychological symptoms following personal injury range widely. For example, Lees-Haley (1997) reported that about 25% of personal injury claimants were feigning post-traumatic symptoms in an attempt to receive financial compensation.

Defensiveness

Conscious denial or extreme minimization of physical or psychological symptoms

The opposite of malingering is called **defensiveness**. Defensiveness refers to the conscious denial or extreme minimization of physical or psychological symptoms. Patients or offenders of this sort seek to present themselves in a favorable light. Minimization of physical and psychological symptoms varies both in degree and motivation. Some people might want to appear to be functioning well to meet an external need, such as being a fit parent, or an internal need, such as unwillingness to acknowledge they are a "patient." Degree of defensiveness can range from mild, such as downplaying a minor symptom, to outright denial of a more serious psychological impairment, such as denying hearing command hallucinations.

Explanatory Models of Malingering

Based on motivations, Rogers (1990) described three explanatory models of malingering: pathogenic, criminological, and adaptational. The pathogenic model assumes that people are motivated to malinger because of an underlying mental disorder. According to this model, the patient attempts to gain control over his or her pathology by creating bogus symptoms. Over time, these patients experience more severe mental disorders and the true symptoms emerge. Little empirical support exists for this model.

The criminological model focuses on "badness": "a bad person (Antisocial Personality Disorder), in bad circumstances (legal difficulties), who is performing badly (uncooperative)" (Rogers, 1997, p. 7). This definition is similar to the malingering definition described in the *DSM-IV* (APA, 1994). According to this definition, malingering should be strongly suspected if two or more of the following factors are evident: (1) presence of antisocial personality disorder, (2) forensic assessment, (3) lack of cooperation, and (4) marked discrepancy between subjective complaints and objective findings. Like the pathogenic model, little empirical support exists for this model. No research indicates that persons with antisocial personality disorder are any more likely to malinger than are other offenders (Rogers, 1990). In addition, many different types of patients are uncooperative with evaluations, including those with eating disorders or substance-use problems. In contrast, some malingerers appear to be highly cooperative. Rogers (1990) found that *DSM-IV* indicators of malingering tended to overdiagnose malingering in a forensic sample.

According to the adaptational model, malingering is likely to occur when (1) there is a perceived adversarial context, (2) personal stakes are very high, and (3) no other viable alternatives are perceived. Research findings support this model in that there are higher rates of malingering in adversarial settings or when the personal stakes are high. This model provides the broadest and least pejorative explanation of malingering. Rogers, Sewell, and Goldstein (1994) asked 320 forensic psychologists to rate 32 items subdivided into pathogenic, criminological, and adaptational models on how important the item was to malingering. The adaptational model was rated the most important and the pathogenic model the least important. Dr. Richard Rogers, who proposed this model of malingering, is profiled in Box 4.5.

How to Study Malingering

Research comprises three basic designs: case study, simulation, and known groups. Each of these designs has its associated strengths and weaknesses. Although case studies are not used as often as they once were, they are useful for generating a wide variety of hypotheses that can be tested by using designs with more experimental rigor. In addition, a case study is the only way to examine rare syndromes such as MBP.

Most research on malingering has used a **simulation design** (similar to polygraph laboratory studies). Participants are told to malinger a specific disorder and are typically compared with two groups: (1) a control group randomly selected from the same population as the malingerers and (2) a clinical comparison group representing the disorders or symptoms that are being feigned. These studies address whether measures can detect malingering in nonclinical samples. However, individuals with mental disorders may also malinger. Studies have begun to ask patients with mental disorders to feign a different mental disorder or to exaggerate the severity of their symptoms. These studies address how effectively participants with mental disorders can malinger. In an early study using a clinical sample, Rogers (1988) reported that nearly half of the psychiatric inpatients either did not remember or did not follow the instructions to malinger. To examine the relative efficacy of detection methods for disordered and nondisordered samples, the optimal simulation design would use four groups: nonclinical experimental, nonclinical-control, clinical-experimental, and clinical-control.

The primary strength of the simulation design is its experimental rigor. The main disadvantage is its limited generalizability to the real world. Simulation studies are often limited in their clinical usefulness because of the minimal levels of preparation and level of motivation by participants. Early studies used brief and nonspecific instructions, such

Simulation design

As applied to malingering research, people are told to pretend they have specific symptoms of a disorder

BOX 4.5 **Researcher Profile: Dr. Richard Rogers**

Dr. Richard Rogers is an internationally known researcher on malingering and other assessment topics related to forensic evaluations. Dr. Rogers is currently a Regents Professor of Psychology at the University of North Texas. He began his studies with a love of literature and graduated summa cum laude from Worcester State College in 1972. Realizing that his true career aspirations laid in psychology, he scrambled to refocus on psychology and completed his M.S. from Assumption College in 1973. Subsequently, he was awarded his Ph.D. in clinical-counseling psychology from Utah State University in 1976.

More by happenstance than thoughtful deliberation, Dr. Rogers became involved in a juvenile forensic setting during his doctoral training and subsequently secured his first professional position at Chester Mental Health Center, the maximum security forensic hospital for Illinois. After two years and a

Dr. Richard Rogers

stint as a Unit Program Director, he was ready for a change. Fortuitously, a singular opportunity emerged in Chicago at Rush Medical School. Here, he joined a talented team of four—headed by Jim Cavanaugh, Jr., M.D.—to build an academically based Psychiatry and Law program. As an assistant professor of psychology and psychiatry, he thrived in the academic environment with its friendly competitiveness and multidisciplinary focus. His first major accomplishments involved an empirical basis to insanity evaluations with the development of the first standardized measure, the *Rogers Criminal Responsibility Assessment Scales (R-CRAS)*, and a companion book, *Conducting Insanity Evaluations*. It was also during the early 1980s that Dr. Rogers developed his deep and continuing interest in malingering and other response styles.

In 1984, Dr. Rogers "crossed the border" to join the Clarke Institute of Psychiatry and the faculty at the University of Toronto. His early empirical work on malingering bore fruition with the development of a psychological measure for feigned mental disorders, the *Structured Interview of Reported Symptoms (SIRS)* that is considered the gold standard for assessing malingering. As editor, he also synthesized research and clinical practice with the first edition of his award-winning book, *Clinical Assessment of Malingering and Deception*. In 1991, he returned to the United States to help rebuild the clinical Ph.D. program at the University of North Texas. Among other projects, Dr. Rogers developed programmatic research on competency to stand trial. With his colleagues, an important accomplishment was the *Evaluation of Competency to Stand Trial—Revised (ECST-R)*, a second-generation competency measure.

The current research by Dr. Rogers is bridging forensic practice and public policy in his investigations of *Miranda* warnings and waivers. With National Science Foundation support, he and his colleagues have explored the incredible diversity of *Miranda* warnings ranging from 55 to 374 words and requiring grade 3 to post-college reading levels. He continues to examine misconceptions about *Miranda* and how faulty reasoning has the potential for catastrophic results. His next project involves juvenile *Miranda* warnings, which paradoxically tend to be longer and more complex than those used with adult suspects.

Dr. Rogers' contributions to forensic psychology and psychiatry are nationally recognized by the American Academy of Forensic Psychology, the American Academy of Psychiatry and

(continued)

Law, the Society of Clinical Psychology, and the American Psychiatric Association. Most recently, he was honored by the American Psychological Association with the Distinguished Professional Contributions to Applied Research Award. He is justly proud of his research team, which has produced three students in the last 15 years whose achievements were recognized nationally by early-career research awards.

Beyond his career, Dr. Rogers is very involved in his family, his two-year-old granddaughter, and mentoring as a big brother. Summer "sabbaticals" on the sandy beaches of Cape Cod are greatly enjoyed, especially when he is able to write in the quiet of the early morning.

as "Appear mentally ill." Instructions are now more specific, with some studies giving participants a scenario to follow: For example, "Imagine you have been in a car accident and you hit your head. You have decided to exaggerate the amount of memory problems you are having to obtain a larger monetary settlement from the car insurance company." In addition, participants may be given time to prepare.

Some studies have coached participants by providing information about genuine mental disorders or by telling them about detection strategies. Research suggests that telling participants about disorders does not help them, whereas information about detection strategies does help them avoid detection (Baer, Wetter, & Berry, 1995; Storm & Graham, 2000). In contrast, Bagby et al. (2002) found that providing students with information about validity scales designed to detect deception did not enhance their ability to feign successfully.

Ethical concerns have been raised about whether participants should be taught how to become skilled malingerers. Ben-Porath (1994) has argued that such research does not "appear to have sufficient scientific justification to make up for the potential harm that might be caused by publishing such a study" (p. 150). A survey of lawyers and law students indicates that about 50% would provide information about psychological testing, including whether the test had any validity scales to detect deception (Wetter & Corrigan, 1995). See Box 4.6 for a discussion of the conflict between ethics and research design when doing this type of research.

When individuals engage in malingering in applied settings, the stakes are often high. For example, they may obtain funding for a disability or avoid a harsher sentence. Both the type and magnitude of incentives are typically limited in simulation studies. Studies that use incentives often offer monetary rewards to malingerers for being successful. The magnitude of the incentive ranges from very modest (e.g., $5) to more substantial (e.g., having their names placed in a lottery for the chance to win $100). Simulation studies have rarely used negative incentives. For example, the researcher could offer money for participating in a malingering study but take some of the money away if the participant is detected as unsuccessfully using deception.

Studies investigating malingering in applied settings would ideally use the known-groups design. The **known-groups design** involves two stages: (1) the establishment of the criterion groups (e.g., genuine patients and malingerers), and (2) an analysis of the similarities and differences between these criterion groups. The main strength of the known-groups design is its generalizability to real-world settings. Its chief limitation is the establishment of the criterion groups. Samples of the genuine patients likely include errors, and some of the classified malingerers may be genuine patients. Because of the difficulty with the reliable and accurate classification of criterion groups, this design is rarely used in malingering research.

Known-groups design

As applied to malingering research, it involves comparing genuine patients and malingerers attempting to fake the disorder the patients have

BOX 4.6   Ethics of Deception Research

Simulation laboratory studies are often used to study the accuracy of detection measures. To make these experiments more similar to real-world situations, rewards are given for successful deception, but punishment can be meted out for unsuccessful deception. In the studies described below, both positive and negative incentives were used to approximate real-life criminal investigation settings.

Psychopathy, Threat, and Polygraph Test Accuracy

The participants in a laboratory polygraph study by Patrick and Iacono (1989) were incarcerated Canadian male offenders. The experimenters wanted to "create a realistic threat context for the polygraph tests. . . . A failure to live up to group expectations can provoke responses much stronger than mere disapproval: Peer labeling in the prison environment frequently leads to ostracism, persecution, and physical brutality" (p. 348). Offenders were offered $10 for participating in the experiment and the potential of a $20 bonus. Offenders were told that if more than 10 offenders were judged by the polygraph examiner as deceptive, no one would receive the $20 bonus. To increase the offenders' motivation, they were told that a list of the names of participants who failed would be made public.

Offenders were randomly assigned to commit or not commit a mock crime. The mock crime consisted of sneaking into the doctor's office and removing $20 from the pocket of the doctor's jacket. Each participant was given a polygraph test. It was clear that some of the participants were concerned about their test outcomes. For example, one offender stated, "I hope they [the other inmates] don't beat my head if I fail" (Patrick & Iacono, 1989, p. 353).

At the end of the study, all participants were given the $20 bonus and participants' polygraph test outcomes were not made public.

Detecting Deceit and Different Types of High-Stakes Lies

In a study of observers' ability to detect deception, Frank and Ekman (1997) used both positive and negative incentives to motivate their participants. Participants engaged in a mock crime, which involved stealing $50 from a briefcase. They were told they could keep this money if they were able to convince an interviewer they had not taken the money (positive incentive). However, they were also warned that if the interviewer judged them as lying, they would have to give back the $50 and would not get the $10 for participating in the study (negative incentive). Some participants were also told that if they were unsuccessful liars, they would have to sit on a metal chair in a cold, small, darkened room and listen to repeated blasts of 110-decibel white noise for an hour (even more negative incentive). At the end of the experiment, all participants received their $10 and were told they did not need to face the additional punishment.

Researchers often have to balance ethical concerns with attempts to increase the validity of their research. In the two studies described here, deception was used to motivate the participants. Some researchers might consider that the level of deception borders on unethical, whereas others would argue that this level of deception is necessary to make the research meaningful. Researchers submit their research protocols to ethical committees for review to ensure the rights of participants are protected. Thus, although you may have some concerns about the level of deception, both of these studies were approved by ethical review.

Malingered Psychosis

How often people attempt to feign psychosis is unknown. Pope, Jonas, and Jones (1982) found nine patients with factitious psychosis in a sample of 219 consecutive admissions to a forensic psychiatric hospital. They followed these patients for seven years, and none went on to develop a psychotic disorder, although all were diagnosed with either borderline personality disorder (a personality disorder defined by instability in mood, self-image, and interpersonal relationships) or histrionic personality disorder (a personality disorder defined by excessive emotionality and attention-seeking behaviors). The presence of malingering does not negate the possibility that other psychiatric illnesses or psychological disorders are present. In fact, the term *instrumental psychosis* was developed to identify patients (many with psychiatric histories) attempting to feign symptoms to secure special accommodations (Waite & Geddes, 2006). Cornell and Hawk (1989) reported that 8% of 314 consecutive psychiatric admissions were diagnosed as malingering psychotic symptoms by experienced forensic psychologists. Box 4.7 describes one of the first studies of malingered psychosis.

BOX 4.7   Being Sane in Insane Places

In 1973, David Rosenhan published a paper in the journal *Science* titled "Being Sane in Insane Places." Rosenhan's goal was to investigate the accuracy of psychiatric diagnoses and the consequences of diagnostic labels. In the first part of his study, eight individuals with no history of a mental disorder tried to gain admission to several mental hospitals. Imagine you are one of the pseudo-patients taking part in Rosenhan's study. You go to your local hospital complaining that you have been hearing voices. When asked what the voices are saying, you reply that it is sometimes unclear but you think they are saying "empty," "hollow," and "thud." You state that you do not recognize the voice. Other than falsifying your name and occupation, everything else about your personal history is true. Like the actual eight pseudo-patients in the study, you also have no history of any serious pathology. To your surprise, you are immediately admitted to the psychiatric inpatient ward with a diagnosis of schizophrenia. Once you are admitted, you tell the staff that your auditory hallucinations have disappeared. Like the real pseudo-patients, you are feeling somewhat apprehensive about what might happen to you. You are cooperative and friendly toward staff and patients. When the staff member asks you how you are feeling, you answer, "I am fine." You follow the rules in the hospital and pretend to take the medication given to you. You have been told that you have to get out of the hospital on your own. So you try to convince the staff you are "sane." To deal with the boredom, you pace up and down the hall, engage staff and patients in conversation, and write extensive notes about your daily activities. The staff members do not question you about this behavior, although the other patients on the ward comment on your note-taking and accuse you of being "a journalist or a professor."

In the actual experiment, pseudo-patients were hospitalized from 7 to 52 days. Staff failed to recognize the lack of symptoms in the pseudo-patients. Not one of the pseudo-patients was identified as "normal" by staff. As noted by Rosenhan (1973), "once a person is designated abnormal, all of his other behaviors are colored by that label" (p. 253). For example, the nurses interpret your pacing behavior as a manifestation of anxiety and your note-taking as a behavioral manifestation of your pathology. Pseudo-patients' attempts to initiate conversations with staff were not very successful, since the staff would "give a brief response while they were on the move and with head averted, or no response at all" (Rosenhan, 1973, p. 255). An example of one conversation was,

> [PSEUDO-PATIENT]: "Pardon me, Dr. X. Could you tell me when I am eligible for grounds privileges?"

> [PHYSICIAN]: "Good morning, Dave. How are you today?" (Moves off without waiting for a reply.) (p. 255)

(continued)

BOX 4.7   *Continued*

This study raises concerns about the use of labels and how such labels can influence the meaning of behaviors. What are the consequences of psychiatric diagnoses? As stated by Rosenhan (1973), "A diagnosis of cancer that has been found to be in error is cause for celebration. But psychiatric diagnoses are rarely found to be in error. The label sticks, a mark of inadequacy forever" (p. 257).

WHAT ARE THE INDICATORS OF MALINGERED PSYCHOSIS?   Table 4.4 provides a list of the potential indicators of malingered psychosis. Resnick (1997) provides a comprehensive description of these indicators. Malingerers often tend to overact, believing the more bizarre they are, the more psychotic they will appear. Early observers have also reported this. For example, Jones and Llewellyn (1917) stated the malingerer "sees less than the blind, he hears less than the deaf, and is more lame than the paralysed. . . . He . . . piles symptom upon symptom and so outstrips madness itself" (p. 17). Malingerers are often willing to discuss their symptoms when asked, whereas actual patients with schizophrenia are often reluctant to discuss their symptoms. Some malingerers may attempt to control the assessment by behaving in an intimidating manner or by accusing the clinician of not believing them. In an interview, a malingerer may be evasive when asked to provide details, take a long time to answer, or answer "I don't know." Malingerers

TABLE 4.4   **Cues to Malingered Psychosis in Criminal Defendants**

- Understandable motive for committing crime
- Presence of a partner in the crime
- Current crime fits pattern of previous criminal history
- Suspicious hallucinations
  - Continuous rather than intermittent
  - Vague or inaudible hallucinations
  - Hallucinations with no delusions
  - Inability to describe strategies to diminish voices
  - Claiming all command hallucinations are obeyed
  - Visual hallucinations in black and white
- Suspicious delusions
  - Abrupt onset or termination
  - Eagerness to discuss delusions
  - Conduct markedly inconsistent with delusions
  - Elaborate delusions that lack paranoid, grandiose, or religious themes
- Marked discrepancies in interview versus noninterview behaviour
- Sudden emergence of psychotic symptoms to explain criminal act
- Absence of any subtle signs of psychosis

Source: Table from "Malingered psychosis" by P. J. Resnick from *Clinical assessment of malingering and deception* by Richard Rogers. Copyright © 1997 by Guilford Publications, Inc. Reprinted with permission.

often report rare or atypical symptoms, blatant symptoms, or absurd symptoms that are usually not endorsed by genuine patients. For example, a person attempting to malinger psychosis may claim to have seen "a large 60-foot Christ who told me to kill my mother."

Malingerers are more likely to report positive symptoms of schizophrenia such as delusions (a false belief that is persistently held) or hallucinations (a perceptual experience in absence of external stimulation), as compared with negative or subtle symptoms of schizophrenia, such as blunted affect, concreteness, or peculiar thinking. Both auditory and visual hallucinations are common in psychotic patients. When a person is suspected of malingering auditory hallucinations, he or she should be asked the vocal characteristics (e.g., clarity, loudness, duration), source (inside or outside of the head), characteristics (e.g., gender, familiar or unfamiliar voice, command), and response (insight into unreality, coping strategies, obeying them). Comparing genuine and feigned auditory hallucinations is one way to detect a malingerer. For example, actual patients often report coping strategies to make the "voices go away," such as watching television, seeking out interpersonal contact, or taking medications (Kanas & Barr, 1984). The malingerer may report there is nothing that will make the voices go away. In other cases, malingerers may report atypical auditory command hallucinations (hallucinations telling people to act in a certain way), such as "Go commit a sex offence" or "Rob, rob, rob."

Genuine visual hallucinations are usually of normal-sized people seen in color, and remain the same if eyes are open or closed. Atypical visual hallucinations, such as seeing "a green devil in the corner laughing" or "a dog that would change in size when giving messages" or seeing hallucinations only in black and white, are indicative of malingering. In the Case Study box you are asked to be a forensic psychologist doing a competency to stand trial assessment.

CASE STUDY

YOU BE THE FORENSIC PSYCHOLOGIST

Jason King is a 30-year-old, single, white man charged with aggravated sexual assault. He is being assessed for competency to stand trial at a pretrial jail. The police report indicated he acted alone and had stalked the victim prior to the sexual assault. The arresting police officers and correctional officers at the jail observed no signs of abnormal behavior in Jason. During the psychological evaluation, Jason rocked back and forth and sang songs. He constantly interrupted the psychologist and claimed he had ESP powers and was being held as a political prisoner.

He answered all the questions, although he refused to elaborate on some of his symptoms, and would often say "I don't know." He claimed his lawyer was a communist and was out to convert him. He also stated the courtroom was actually a circus with the judge being the ringmaster and the jury the audience.

Your Turn . . .

What are the clues that Jason might be malingering a mental disorder? If you were the forensic psychologist doing the assessment, which malingering tests would you use? Who else might you want interview to help with your assessment?

Assessment Methods to Detect Malingered Psychosis

INTERVIEW-BASED METHODS The Structured Interview of Reported Symptoms (SIRS) (Rogers, Bagby, & Dickens, 1992) was initially developed in 1985, and in its most recent version, it consists of 172 items that are scored from a structured interview. The items are organized into the following eight scales that represent different strategies that a person may employ when malingering:

1. Rare symptoms: symptoms that true patients endorse very infrequently
2. Symptom combinations: uncommon pairings of symptoms
3. Improbable or absurd symptoms: symptoms unlikely to be true, since true patients rarely endorsed them
4. Blatant symptoms: items that are obvious signs of mental disorder
5. Subtle symptoms: items that contain what most people consider everyday problems
6. Selectivity of symptoms: ratio of symptoms endorsed versus those not endorsed
7. Severity of symptoms: number of severe symptoms reported
8. Reported versus observed symptoms: discrepancy between self-report and observable symptoms

The SIRS has been extensively validated by using both simulation and known-groups designs, and research has consistently demonstrated differences in SIRS scores between honest and simulating samples, and between clinical samples and suspected malingerers (Rogers, 2008). The SIRS also correlates strongly with validity indices from the MMPI-2 (Boccaccini, Murrie, & Duncan, 2006; Edens, Poythress, & Watkins-Clay, 2007) and is used widely by clinical forensic psychologists (Archer, Buffington-Vollum, Stredny, & Handel, 2006).

Another interview-based method is the Miller-Forensic Assessment of Symptoms Test (M-FAST) (Miller, 2001), which was developed on 330 forensic patients and 216 undergraduate students and was intended as a brief, structured interview (25 items, 10-minute administration) to provide clinicians with a valid and reliable measure for detecting feigned mental illness. The M-FAST contains nine content items that resemble SIRS scales, including unusual hallucinations, reported versus observed symptoms, contradictory symptoms, extreme symptoms, trigger questions, rare combinations, negative image, unusual symptom onset, and suggestibility. A number of recent studies suggest that the M-FAST is a useful, reliable tool for detecting malingering (Guy, Kwartner, & Miller, 2006; Guy & Miller, 2004; Jackson, Rogers, & Sewell, 2005; Miller, 2001, 2005). The M-FAST is intended as a screening tool and is not recommended for use in isolation.

SELF-REPORT QUESTIONNAIRE The most widely used personality inventory to assess nonoffenders and offenders is the MMPI-2 (Butcher, Dahlstrom, Graham, Tellegen, & Kaemmer, 1989). The MMPI-2 includes several clinical scales to assess psychopathology but also includes several scales specifically designed to test "faking-bad" or malingering. For example, the items on the Infrequency (F) scale and the Back F (F_B) scale were developed to detect unusual or atypical symptoms and consist of items endorsed by less than 10% of a normative sample.

A comprehensive meta-analysis of the MMPI-2 and malingering found that the F and F_B scales were the most useful at detecting malingerers (Rogers, Sewell, Martin, & Vitacco, 2003). However, the optimal cut-off score to use varies across the samples studied. A study by Storm and Graham (2000) examined whether the MMPI-2 validity scales would be able to correctly classify college students who have been coached on malingering strategies, students told to malinger but given no coaching, and psychiatric inpatients. Some validity indicators were more susceptible to coaching whereas others, such as the Infrequency scale, could still discriminate coached malingerers from psychiatric inpatients. Recent research with criminal defendants, classified as malingerers or not based on the SIRS, has also supported the use of the Infrequency (F) scale to identify malingerers in forensic populations (Toomey, Kucharski, & Duncan, 2009).

Summary

1. The Comparison Question Test (CQT) is the most commonly used polygraph exam in North America. It consists of three types of questions: neutral, comparison (questions relating to past behaviors that are supposed to generate emotion), and relevant (questions relating to the crime being investigated). The Concealed Information Test (CIT) probes for whether the suspect has knowledge about the details of a crime that only the guilty person would have.

2. The CQT is quite accurate at detecting guilt but is not very good at determining a suspect's innocence (i.e., it has a high false-positive rate). The CIT is quite accurate in detecting innocence but is not very good at determining a suspect's guilt (i.e., it has a high false-negative rate).

3. Event-related brain potentials (ERPs) and brain-imaging techniques can be used to detect deception in laboratory settings. However, these techniques have not yet been used extensively in forensic settings.

4. Another method of attempting to detect whether someone is lying is through the analysis of verbal characteristics and nonverbal behaviors. The nonverbal indicator most strongly associated with deception is voice pitch. A verbal characteristic associated with deception is that liars provide fewer details when lying compared with those telling the truth.

5. The two key components to malingering are that the psychological or physical symptoms are clearly under voluntary control and that there are external motivations for the production of symptoms. Malingering should be considered in any forensic evaluation. Three explanatory models of malingering have been proposed: pathogenic, criminological, and adaptational. Only the adaptational model has received empirical support.

6. Malingering research utilizes three basic designs: case study, simulation, and known groups. The most common is the simulation design.

Key Concepts

Discussion Questions

1. You are a forensic psychologist hired to determine if a defendant is truly psychotic. What sorts of information would you base your assessment on? What clinical indicators would you look for?

2. Many of the studies designed to detect deception involve deceiving research participants. What ethical concerns have been raised? What types of studies should be allowed?

3. The Comparison Question Test is the polygraph test commonly used by police in North America. Do you think this test has sufficient validity for use by the police? Should it be admissible in court?

4. You recently got hired as a customs agent. Knowing what you do about nonverbal and verbal cues to deception, what cues would you watch out for to catch someone smuggling drugs?

Eyewitness Testimony

LEARNING OBJECTIVES

- Describe two categories of independent variables and three general dependent variables found in eyewitness research.

- Describe and explain the misinformation effect.

- Outline the components of the cognitive interview.

- Describe lineup procedures and how they may be biased.

- Summarize the debate surrounding expert testimony on eyewitness issues.

- Outline the recommendations for collecting eyewitness identification evidence.

Lucy Peluso went to the bank on her lunch hour. As she approached the teller, a man pushed her out of the way so that he could quickly exit the bank. Seconds later, Lucy found out that the man had robbed the teller. Lucy was an eyewitness. The police interviewed her along with the others in the bank. The witnesses were able to hear each other describe what they saw. Six months after the robbery, Lucy was asked to go to the police station to view a series of photographs. When she was asked whether the man who robbed the bank was pictured, Lucy very quickly pointed and said, "That's him, I'm certain."

Eyewitness evidence is one of the earliest and most widely studied topics in forensic psychology. As you read in Chapter 1, the German psychologist Albert von Schrenck-Notzing testified during a serial killer trial about the influence of pretrial media exposure on witnesses' memory. Today, both the police and the courts rely on eyewitness evidence. Eyewitness testimony is one of the most compelling types of evidence presented in criminal trials. Thus, information about the likelihood and types of mistakes made by eyewitnesses is vitally important in terms of justice.

In this chapter, we will focus on how memory works when it comes to remembering in an eyewitness context. We will consider various interview protocols police may use when interviewing eyewitnesses. Also, we will review the various identification procedures police may implement. As well, we will examine the various factors and police procedures that can influence how accurate eyewitnesses can be.

EYEWITNESS TESTIMONY: THE ROLE OF MEMORY

A large part of eyewitness testimony rests on memory. The concept of memory can be viewed as a process involving several stages. The encoding stage occurs first, when you perceive and pay attention to details in your environment. For example, you are perceiving and paying attention when you look at a stranger's face and notice his big, bushy eyebrows. To some extent, the stranger's face and eyebrows have been encoded. The encoded information then passes into your short-term holding facility, known as your short-term memory. Your short-term memory has a limited capacity. Consequently, in order to make room for other, new information, information in your short-term memory passes into your longer-term holding facility, known as your long-term memory. Information from long-term memory can be accessed or retrieved as needed. For example, if you are asked to describe the stranger you saw, you will retrieve the information you stored in your long-term memory and report that the stranger had bushy eyebrows. It is important to remember that not every piece of information will go through all the memory stages and also there are factors that can affect each stage. For example, not all details from an event will be encoded, nor will all information in short-term memory move to long-term memory. Using our example of Lucy Peluso witnessing a bank robbery, consider the factors that are occurring to affect memory and retrieval.

Look at this scene for five seconds.

Lucy is filling out a deposit slip so she will be ready for the bank teller. She is not paying attention to her environment (factor: inattention). Unexpectedly, there is a brief interaction between her and an unfamiliar male (factors: unexpectedness; amount of time to view environmental details). Lucy is now a witness and she is interviewed with several other people in the bank by police (factor: hearing others describe the same environmental details she saw). The police officer asks Lucy a few, brief questions (factor: the wording of the questions). Lucy is called six months after the crime to examine a lineup (factors: the amount of time elapsed between having witnessed the event and having to retrieve the information; type of lineup procedure used). Lucy is confident when she identifies the culprit (factor: relation between confidence and accuracy). Figure 5.1 delineates the stages of memory.

As you may have figured out by now, memory is not like a video recording in which an identical representation of the event is stored and then can be played on request (Loftus, 1979b). Our memory can change each time we retrieve the event; some parts of the event may be embellished or guessed at because we cannot remember all the details. Often in our everyday life, our memory fallibilities are insignificant. For example, remembering that you bought a coffee at a Starbucks when actually it came from a Dunkin Donuts is harmless, most likely. In contrast, remembering whether the culprit was right- or left-handed may be critical if police are going to arrest the guilty suspect.

FIGURE 5.1 Stages of Memory

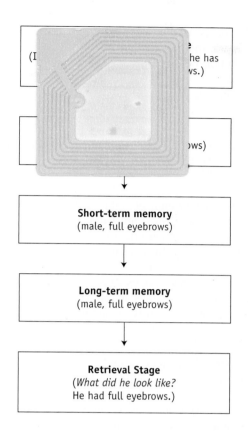

(I   he has
                                      vs.)

                                      ws)

Short-term memory
(male, full eyebrows)

↓

Long-term memory
(male, full eyebrows)

↓

Retrieval Stage
(*What did he look like?*
He had full eyebrows.)

Eyewitness memory retrieval can be broadly partitioned into either recall or recognition memory. **Recall memory** refers to reporting details of a previously witnessed event or person. For example, describing what the culprit did and what the culprit looked like are both recall tasks. In contrast, **recognition memory** refers to determining whether a previously seen item or person is the same as what is currently being viewed. For example, hearing a set of voices and identifying the culprit's voice or identifying clothing worn by the culprit during the crime are both recognition tasks.

Recall memory

Reporting details of a previously witnessed event or person

Recognition memory

Determining whether a previously seen item or person is the same as what is currently being viewed

HOW DO WE STUDY EYEWITNESS ISSUES?

Researchers interested in studying eyewitness issues can examine data from actual crimes. For example, they can use archival data such as police reports, or they can examine witnesses in naturalistic environments by accompanying police to crime scenes and interviewing witnesses after the police have done their job. Alternatively, they can conduct laboratory simulations. The laboratory simulation study is the most common paradigm used to study eyewitness issues and will be discussed below.

The Laboratory Simulation

To study eyewitness memory using a laboratory simulation, an unknowing participant views a critical event, such as a crime, either through a slide sequence, video recording, or live. The participant is unaware that he or she will be questioned about the event until after the event is witnessed. Now a witness, the participant is asked to describe what happened and the target/culprit involved. Following the descriptions of what was witnessed, the witness may be asked to examine a lineup. Many independent variables can be manipulated or examined; however, there are only three general dependent variables in eyewitness studies.

INDEPENDENT VARIABLES   Numerous independent variables can be manipulated or examined within the laboratory simulation. Wells (1978) has coined the terms *estimator variable* and *system variable* to help classify them. **Estimator variables** are those variables or factors that are present at the time of the crime and that cannot be changed. These can include the age of the witness, the amount of lighting, the presence of a weapon, and whether the witness was intoxicated. These are variables over which the criminal justice system cannot exert control. Thus, their effect on eyewitness accuracy can be estimated only after the crime. **System variables** are those variables or factors that can be manipulated to increase (or decrease) eyewitness accuracy, such as the type of procedure used by police to interview the witness or the type of lineup procedure used to present the suspect to the witness. These variables are under the control of the justice system. Both estimator and system variables can be manipulated in eyewitness laboratory studies.

DEPENDENT VARIABLES   The three general dependent variables in eyewitness studies are (1) recall of the event/crime, (2) recall of the culprit, and (3) recognition of the culprit.

Recall of the crime or culprit can take two formats. With **open-ended recall**, also known as a **free narrative**, witnesses are asked to either write or orally state all they remember about the event without the officer (or experimenter) asking questions. With this type of recall, the witness also may be asked to describe the culprit. With **direct question recall**, witnesses are asked a series of specific questions about the crime or the culprit. For example, the witness may be asked the color of the getaway car or the length of the culprit's hair.

A witness's recall of the crime or culprit can be examined for the following:

- *The amount of information reported.* How many descriptors of the crime do witnesses report? How many descriptors of the culprit do witnesses report?
- *The type of information reported.* What is the proportion of peripheral details versus central details? What is the proportion of culprit details versus environment details?
- *The accuracy of information reported.* What is the proportion of correct descriptors reported? What is the proportion of omission errors (information the witness failed to report)? What is the proportion of commission errors (details falsely reported to be present)?

As for the recognition of the culprit, the typical recognition task is a lineup. A culprit **lineup** is a set of people presented to the witness, who in turn must identify the culprit if he or she is present. Another type of lineup takes the form of a set of voices, and the witness is asked to identify the culprit's voice. Clothing lineups, in which the witness examines clothing that may have been worn by the culprit, sometimes also are used.

Estimator variables

Variables that are present at the time of the crime and that cannot be changed

System variables

Variables that can be manipulated to increase (or decrease) eyewitness accuracy

Open-ended recall/ free narrative

Witnesses are asked to either write or orally state all they remember about the event without the officer (or experimenter) asking questions

Direct question recall

Witnesses are asked a series of specific questions about the crime or the culprit

Lineup

A set of people presented to the witness, who in turn must state whether the culprit is present and, if so, which one

A witness's recognition response can be examined for the following:

- *Accuracy of decision.* What is the rate of correctly identifying the culprit in the lineup? What is the rate of correctly stating that the culprit is not present in the lineup?
- *Types of errors made.* What is the rate of identifying an innocent person? What is the rate of stating that the culprit is not present when he or she is actually in the lineup?

RECALL MEMORY

The primary goal for an officer interviewing an eyewitness is to extract from the witness a complete and accurate report of what happened (Fisher, Geiselman, & Raymond, 1987; Jackson, Sijlbing, & Thiecke, 1996). Insufficient information may provide the officer with few leads to pursue, resulting in a case that will not be solved. In this situation, the culprit will remain free to commit further crimes. If inaccurate information is supplied, an officer may pursue innocent suspects, thus reducing the likelihood that the guilty person will be caught.

Now test your own recall. Without looking back at the crime scene photo on page 110, how many details can you remember?

Interviewing Eyewitnesses

Fisher et al. (1987) were curious about the techniques police were using to interview eyewitnesses. They analyzed 11 tape-recorded interviews from a police department in Florida. Eight different detectives, who averaged 10.5 years of experience each, conducted these interviews. The researchers found that there was a lot of variation in how the interviews were conducted. In general, however, the researchers found that the officers would introduce themselves, ask the eyewitnesses to report what they remembered using an open-ended format, and then ask the witnesses a series of direct questions to determine specific information, such as the age or height of the culprit. The officers usually ended the interview by asking the eyewitnesses if there was any additional information that they could remember.

Fisher et al. (1987) found that the police officers' approach limited their ability to collect complete and accurate information in a number of ways. First, the researchers found that police often interrupted eyewitnesses when they were providing an open-ended recall report. The police may limit the amount of information eyewitnesses have in their conscious memory by preventing them from speaking or distracting them with questions.

Second, police questioned eyewitnesses with very short, specific questions. This type of question format uses a more superficial level of concentration than open-ended questions and tends to result in very short answers. The other problem with short, specific questions is that a police officer may not ask a relevant question that would provide critical information. For example, the culprit may have a tattoo, but if the officer does not ask about tattoos, the eyewitness may not report this feature. Thus, the police officer may miss a descriptor that could help in narrowing the suspect pool and arresting the culprit.

Third, police officers tended to ask questions in a predetermined or random order that was inconsistent with the information that witnesses were providing at the time. For example, a police officer may have asked a question about the culprit's voice while the witness was describing the culprit's clothing. Mixing visual and auditory questions has been found to decrease recall by approximately 19% (Fisher & Price-Roush, as cited in Fisher et al., 1987). Lastly, officers tended to ask questions that were "leading" or suggestive, which can be very dangerous when trying to collect accurate information.

The Leading Question—The Misinformation Effect

Elizabeth Loftus, one of the most prominent researchers in the area of leading questions, has conducted many experiments demonstrating that a witness's recall report can be altered by the phrasing of a question. See Box 5.1 to learn more about Dr. Loftus. In one study, Loftus and Palmer (1974) had university students watch a videotape of a car accident. After viewing the accident, the participants were asked the identical question with a variation in one critical word, hit: "About how fast were the cars going when they *hit* each other?" Hit was replaced with either *smashed, collided, bumped,* or *contacted.* Even though all participants saw the same videotape, the speed reported by the participants varied depending on which critical word was used. Participants reported the highest rate of speed when the word *smashed* was used and the lowest rates of speed when the words *bumped* and *contacted* were used.

The experiment did not end there. The researchers called participants back a week later and asked whether they had seen any broken glass. Participants who were questioned with the word *smashed* were more likely to recall seeing broken glass than were the other participants. However, there was no broken glass in the videotape. This study illustrates how the wording of a question can influence memory for the incident.

Loftus went on to demonstrate that simply introducing an inaccurate detail to witnesses could lead them to report that inaccurate detail when questioned later (Loftus, Altman, & Geballe, 1975). The **misinformation effect**, also called the **post-event information effect**, is a phenomenon in which a witness who is presented with inaccurate information after an event will incorporate that misinformation in a subsequent recall task (Loftus, 1975).

In one classic study, Loftus (1975) conducted four experiments demonstrating that how a question is worded can influence an eyewitness's recall at a later date. We'll discuss one of these experiments below.

Past misinformation studies have used a common method or paradigm. Participants were exposed to an event via slides, video, or live action. They were then given a series of questions about the event, some of which contained misinformation. Later, the participants were asked a series of questions about the event, probing their response to the misinformation introduced. They were asked to respond from a forced-choice/multiple-choice set. That is, they were given a set of responses to choose from, with one response being correct, one response containing the misinformation, and one or two incorrect responses.

EXPERIMENT   Forty university students watched a three-minute film clip of a class being interrupted by eight demonstrators. Following the clip, participants were given 20 questions. Half of the participants were asked "Was the leader of the 4 demonstrators who entered the classroom a male? The remaining participants were asked "Was the leader of the 12 demonstrators who entered the classroom a male?" All other questions were the same for the two groups. After a one-week delay, the participants

---

Misinformation effect/post-event information effect

Phenomenon in which a witness who is presented with inaccurate information after an event will incorporate that misinformation in a subsequent recall task

BOX 5.1   Researcher Profile: Dr. Elizabeth Loftus

One of the most influential psychologists of our time (making the top 100 list of the most eminent psychologists of the 20th century), Dr. Elizabeth Loftus studied mathematics and psychology at the University of California, Los Angeles (UCLA). She went on to complete her M.A. and Ph.D. at Stanford University on how people solve mathematical problems in a computer-assisted instructional setting.

Dr. Elizabeth Loftus

With an expertise in human memory and an interest in legal matters, Dr. Loftus began to study the memory of witnesses to crimes and accidents. One of Dr. Loftus's favorite studies and a classic found in many introductory psychology textbooks (and cognitive psychology textbooks) involves participants viewing a slide sequence of a simulated accident where a car goes through an intersection with a stop sign. Later, participants, now "witnesses," are probed with a leading question that insinuates that it was a yield sign (not a stop sign). Many participants report seeing a yield sign even though they actually saw a stop sign. The study shows the power of how post-event information can contaminate memory. Published in the late 1970s, this study and variations of it continue to be conducted today demonstrating the "misinformation effect."

After 30+ years of research in the area of psychology and law, Dr. Loftus would like to see more policies and procedures that reflect the science of memory. She provides the example of "blind" testing. "When it comes to witnesses identifying perpetrators, it would help if the investigator gathering the information did not know who the suspect is. That way, the investigators can't contaminate the process, even inadvertently."

Dr. Loftus has been called as an eyewitness expert in over 200 trials, including that of the serial murderer Ted Bundy, has appeared on numerous news and talk shows, including *60 Minutes* and *Oprah*, and has published many books and too many papers to count. Not surprisingly, she has received numerous awards including the Distinguished Scientific Award for the Applications of Psychology by the American Psychological Association in 2003. In 2004, Dr. Loftus was elected to the U.S. National Academy of Sciences.

Currently Dr. Loftus is a Distinguished Professor at the University of California at Irvine and holds positions in several departments plus the School of Law. She continues to research false memories and the types of people who are more susceptible to memory contamination.

To cap off her 12-hour+ workdays, Dr. Loftus loves socializing with friends.

---

were asked 20 new questions about the film. The critical question in this new set was "How many demonstrators did you see entering the classroom?" The participants that were asked a question about 12 demonstrators reported seeing an average of almost 9 demonstrators (8.85). Those who were asked about four demonstrators reported seeing an average of 6.40 demonstrators. Thus, incorporating the number of demonstrators into the question posed to witnesses affected the number of demonstrators witnesses recalled seeing later.

The misinformation effect occurs using a number of different types of questions and methodology. But why does it occur?

EXPLAINING THE MISINFORMATION EFFECT   Many studies have demonstrated that a witness's report can include misinformation that was previously supplied (Cole & Loftus, 1979; Loftus, 1979a), and these have fueled debates on how and why this phenomenon occurs (Loftus, Miller, & Burns, 1978; McCloskey & Zaragoza, 1985). Were witnesses' memories changed? Were the participants just going along with the experimenter (or guessing) and providing the answer they thought was wanted? Or maybe the witness had two memories, a correct one and an incorrect one, and could not remember where each memory came from. These are the three general positions that researchers have tried to advance or argue against, with each position having different implications for memory:

1. With changes in the methodology, some studies have found support for guessing or experimenter pleasing. Some witnesses will guess at the answer they think the ex-perimenter wants, resulting in the misinformation effect. This explanation is known as the **misinformation acceptance hypothesis** (McCloskey & Zaragoza, 1985).

2. Some studies have found that witnesses can recall both memories—the original, accurate one and the inaccurate one. However, witnesses cannot remember where each memory came from. When asked to recall what was seen, the witness chooses the incorrect memory. This explanation is called the **source misattribution hypothesis** (Lindsay, 1994).

3. Loftus is perhaps the biggest proponent of the **memory impairment hypothesis**. This hypothesis refers to the original memory being replaced/altered with the new, incorrect memory (Loftus, 1979b). The original memory is no longer accessible.

The debate on which explanation is responsible for the misinformation effect is far from over. Researchers continue to come up with different methodologies that point to alternative explanations. One issue that has been put to rest, though, is that the misinfor-mation effect happens. The misinformation effect is a real phenomenon.

How can the misinformation effect happen in real life? A witness can be exposed to inaccurate information in a number of ways:

1. An officer may make assumptions about what occurred or what was witnessed and then inadvertently phrase a question consistent with his or her assumption. For example, the officer may ask the witness, "Did you see *the* gun?" rather than ask-ing the more neutral question, "Did you see *a* gun?"

2. There may be more than one witness, and the witnesses overhear each other's statements. If there are discrepancies between the witnesses, a witness may change his or her report to make it consistent.

3. A police officer may incorporate an erroneous detail from a previous witness's interview. For example, the officer may ask the witness, "What was the culprit with the scar wearing?" The witness may subsequently report that the culprit had a scar when in fact there was none.

Misinformation acceptance hypothesis

Explanation for the misinformation effect where the incorrect information is provided because the witness guesses what the officer or experimenter wants the response to be

Source misattribution hypothesis

Explanation for the misinformation effect—where the witness has two memories, the original and the misinformation; however, the witness cannot remember where each memory originated or the source of each

Memory impairment hypothesis

Explanation for the misinformation effect where the original memory is replaced with the new, incorrect information

PROCEDURES THAT HELP POLICE INTERVIEW EYEWITNESSES

Psychologists have been instrumental in developing procedures that can be beneficial at eliciting accurate information from witnesses.

Hypnosis

In some cases, eyewitnesses may be unable to recall very much that was witnessed, pos-sibly because they were traumatized. With the help of hypnosis, they may be able to recall a greater amount of information. In a survey of 10 forensic hypnosis experts, all felt that hypnosis could help witnesses to remember crime details (Vingoe, 1995). It is assumed that a person under hypnosis is able to retrieve memories that are otherwise inaccessible. A hypnotized witness may be able to produce a greater number of details than a nonhypnotized witness; this phenomenon is termed *hypnotically refreshed memory* (Steblay & Bothwell, 1994).

According to Kebbell and Wagstaff (1998), two techniques that are often used in hypnosis are age regression and the television technique. With age regression, the witness goes back in time and reexperiences the original event. With the television technique, the witness imagines that he or she is watching an imaginary television screen with the events being played as they were witnessed. Further instructions stating that the eyewitness's memory will improve over time and in future sessions are provided once the witness has recalled the event. The witness is then awakened from the hypnosis.

Several reviews have examined the effectiveness of hypnosis in enhancing memory recall (e.g., Brown, Scheflin, & Hammond, 1998; Reiser, 1989; Steblay & Bothwell, 1994). These reviews find that individuals under hypnosis will provide more details, but those details are just as likely to be inaccurate as accurate (see also Fisher, 1995). Some researchers have suggested that one aspect of hypnosis that might help increase recall of details is when individuals close their eyes. Both visual and auditory information is recalled to a greater degree when individuals close their eyes compared to keeping their eyes open when trying to remember (Perfect et al., 2008). The hypnotized individual seems to be more suggestible to subtle cues by the interviewer than under normal conditions. The difficulty with using hypnosis is not being able to differentiate between the accurate and inaccurate details. Witnesses recall both accurate and inaccurate details with the same degree of confidence (Sheehan & Tilden, 1984), and as we will see later in this chapter, this confidence may be misleading.

Police are not interested in using hypnosis simply to collect more information—they are interested in collecting *accurate* information. For hypnosis to be useful in a forensic context, police need to know about the accuracy of the information recalled while under hypnosis. U.S. courts are somewhat divided on the admissibility of hypnotically elicited testimony. Many states exclude all testimony that was elicited through hypnosis. A few states allow all testimony through the use of expert witnesses and the jury's assessment of the reliability of the witness. A very few federal circuit courts decide on the admissibility of hypnotically recalled memory on a case by case basis.

The Cognitive Interview

Given the limitations of hypnosis, researchers have developed an interview procedure based on principles of memory storage and retrieval called the **cognitive interview** (Geiselman et al., 1984). The cognitive interview can be used with eyewitnesses, but it is not a procedure recommended for use with unwilling participants such as suspects (see Chapter 3).

Cognitive interview
Interview procedure for use with eyewitnesses based on principles of memory storage and retrieval

The cognitive interview is based on four memory-retrieval techniques (see Box 5.2) to increase recall: (1) reinstating the context, (2) reporting everything, (3) reversing order, and (4) changing perspective.

In an initial study, Geiselman, Fisher, MacKinnon, and Holland (1985) compared the "standard" police interview, hypnosis, and the cognitive interview to determine differences in the amount and accuracy of information recalled by witnesses. Participants watched a police training film of a crime. Forty-six hours after viewing the film, each

BOX 5.2	How the Cognitive Interview Components Are Implemented with Witnesses

Below are sample statements (from Geiselman, Fisher, MacKinnon, & Holland, 1986) that correspond to the cognitive interview memory-retrieval techniques:

1. *Reinstate the context:* "Try to reinstate in your mind the context surrounding the incident. Think about what the surrounding environment looked like at the scene, such as the room, the weather, and any nearby people or objects. Also think about how you were feeling at the time and think about your reactions to the incident" (p. 390).
2. *Report everything:* "Some people hold back information because they are not quite sure that the information is important. Please do not edit anything out of your report, report even things you think may not be important" (pp. 391–392).
3. *Recall the event in different orders:* "It is natural to go through the incident from beginning to end. However, you also should try to go through the events in reverse order. Or, try starting with the thing that impressed you the most in the incident and then go from there, going both forward in time and backward" (p. 391).
4. *Change perspectives:* "Try to recall the incident from different perspectives that you may have had or adopt the perspectives of others [who] were present during the incident. For example, try to place yourself in the role of a prominent character in the incident and think about what he or she must have seen" (p. 391).

Note that changing perspectives has been criticized for eliciting erroneous information. If a witness is asked to imagine what he or she saw from a different perspective, the witness might report details that are made up or inaccurate.

Source: "Eyewitness responses to leading and misleading questions under the cognitive interview" by Edweard R. Geiselman et al. from *Journal of Police Science and Administration*, vol. 14. Copyright © 1986 by The American Psychological Association.

participant was interviewed with one of the procedures by experienced law enforcement professionals. Compared with the "standard" police interview and hypnosis, the cognitive interview produced the greatest amount of accurate information without an increase in inaccurate details.

Bekerian and Dennett (1993) reviewed 27 studies that tested the cognitive interview. Across the studies, the cognitive interview produced more accurate information than the alternatives, such as the "standard" police interview. An approximately 30% increase in accurate information was obtained with the cognitive interview over other procedures, and there was an insignificant decrease in errors for the cognitive interview compared with other methods.

Over the years, Fisher and Geiselman (1992) expanded the cognitive interview into the **enhanced cognitive interview**, including various principles of social dynamics in addition to the memory-retrieval principles used in the original cognitive interview. The additional components include the following:

1. *Rapport building.* An officer should spend time building rapport with the witness and make him or her feel comfortable and supported.
2. *Supportive interviewer behavior.* A witness's free recall should not be interrupted; pauses should be waited out by the officer, who should express attention to what the witness is saying.

Enhanced cognitive interview

Interview procedure that includes various principles of social dynamics in addition to the memory retrieval principles used in the original cognitive interview

3. *Transfer of control.* The witness, not the officer, should control the flow of the interview; the witness is the expert—that is, the witness, not the officer, was the person who saw the crime.

4. *Focused retrieval.* Questions should be open ended and not leading or suggestive; after free recall, the officer should use focused memory techniques to facilitate retrieval.

5. *Witness-compatible questioning.* An officer's questions should match the witness's thinking; if the witness is talking about clothing, the officer should be asking about clothing.

The enhanced cognitive interview, the original cognitive interview, and the standard police interview have been compared (Memon & Bull, 1991). Both types of cognitive interviews produced more accurate information, without an increase in inaccurate information, than standard interviews. Significant differences between the two types of cognitive interviews have not been found (Köehnken, 1995). The question remains as to which components are responsible for the increase in accurate information (Kebbell & Wagstaff, 1998).

The cognitive interview has been tested in several countries including the United States and the United Kingdom. In the United Kingdom for example, with different-aged participants, including younger adults (age 17 to 31), older adults (age 60 to 74), and older-older adults (age 75 to 95), the cognitive interview increased the amount of accurate "person," "action," "object," and "surrounding" details for each age group without increasing the amount of inaccurate information recalled compared to a "standard" police interview (Wright & Holliday, 2007). The cognitive interview has also been shown effective with children and adults in the United States (e.g., Holliday, 2003).

Although some officers have been trained to conduct cognitive interviews, some are reluctant to use it, stating that it requires too much time to conduct and that the appropriate environment is not always available. However, trained officers report that they use some of the cognitive interview components on a regular basis when interviewing witnesses (see also Dando, Wilcock, & Milne, 2009).

RECALL OF THE CULPRIT

Along with a description of what happened, the witness will be asked to describe the culprit's appearance. Perusal of newspapers and news broadcasts find that descriptions are vague and apply to many. For example, a culprit may be described as white, male, between five-foot-nine and six feet tall, with short, brown hair. Think of how many people you know who fit this description.

Quantity and Accuracy of Descriptions

Research examining culprit descriptions provided by witnesses finds that descriptions are limited in detail and accuracy (Sporer, 1996). Lindsay, Martin, and Webber (1994) examined descriptions provided by adults in real and staged crimes. Witnesses to staged crimes reported an average of 7.35 descriptors. In contrast, witnesses to real crimes reported significantly fewer descriptors—3.94 on average. Hair and clothing items were commonly reported descriptors.

In a study examining real-life descriptions, Van Koppen and Lochun (1997) conducted an archival review of official court records examining descriptions of culprits from 400 robberies. Data were coded from 1,300 witnesses, and 1,650 descriptions of culprits were analyzed. Consistent with anecdotal evidence, witnesses provided few descriptors. On average, witnesses reported eight descriptors. The researchers found that sex and height were the items most often reported. Witnesses were correct 100% of the time when identifying the sex of the culprit. Unfortunately, sex is not a great discriminator. Only 52% of witnesses were accurate when identifying the height of the culprit.

Wagstaff and colleagues (2003) found that hair color and hairstyle were reported most accurately. Yarmey, Jacob, and Porter (2002) found that witnesses had difficulty correctly reporting weight (27% accuracy), eye color, (24% accuracy), and type of footwear (13% accuracy).

As you can see, culprit descriptions are limited in quantity and accuracy, which, in turn, limits their usefulness to the police in their investigation. Given the strides psychologists have made in other areas of police procedure, such as interviewing techniques, it would be worthwhile for psychologists to develop a technique or procedure that could be used to increase the amount and accuracy of witnesses' descriptions of culprits.

In one such attempt to increase the amount of descriptive information about an unfamiliar other, Kask, Bull, and Davies (2006) examined the effectiveness of having a "standard" for witnesses to use when answering questions about the target person. Participants saw an unfamiliar person interact with one of three experimenters. For half of the participants, the experimenter posed questions about the target stranger in reference to himself or herself (i.e., the experimenter functioned as a "standard" by which to be used as a reference). For example, when the experimenter was used as a "standard," he or she would ask the participant, "My hair is this long; how long was his hair?" For the participants in the no-standard condition, the experimenter would ask the participant, "How long was his hair?" Unfortunately, the researchers found that the use of a "standard" did not help witnesses to recall accurate person information. However, a "standard" did aid somewhat when it came to recalling descriptors that are not typically remembered well (e.g., appearance of eyes, nose, or mouth).

RECOGNITION MEMORY

As defined at the beginning of the chapter, recognition memory involves determining whether a previously seen item or person is the one that is currently being viewed. A witness's recognition memory can be tested in a number of ways including:

- Live lineups or photo arrays
- Voice identification

Lineup Identification

Suspect

A person the police "suspect" committed the crime, who may be guilty or not guilty of committing the crime in question

"It's number 5, I'll never forget that face!" The typical method used to gain proof about the identity of the culprit is to conduct a lineup identification, in which a witness views a group of possible suspects and determines whether one is the culprit.

WHY CONDUCT A LINEUP?   A critical distinction needs to be made between the terms *suspect* and *culprit*. A **suspect** is a person the police "suspect" committed the crime. However, a suspect may be guilty or not guilty of the crime in question. In contrast, a **culprit** is the guilty person who committed the crime.

Culprit

The guilty person who committed the crime

A lineup identification reduces the uncertainty of whether a suspect is the culprit beyond the verbal description provided (Wells, 1993). A witness identifying the suspect increases the likelihood that the suspect is the culprit. In contrast, not identifying the suspect decreases the likelihood that the suspect is the culprit.

An alternative view of a lineup identification is that it provides police with information about the physical similarity between the lineup member chosen and the culprit (Navon, 1990). Police will have some notion of what the culprit looks like based on the person selected from the lineup.

LINEUP DISTRACTERS   In addition to placing a suspect in a lineup, other lineup members may be included. These members are called **foils** or **distracters**, and they are known to be innocent of the crime in question. Police can use two types of strategies to decide on the physical appearance of the lineup distracters. A similarity-to-suspect strategy matches lineup members to the suspect's appearance. For example, if the suspect had brown hair, blue eyes, and a moustache, then each lineup member would have these characteristics. A difficulty with this strategy, however, is that there are many physical features that could be matched, such as width of eyebrows, length of nose, thickness of lips, and so on. If taken to the extreme, this strategy would produce a lineup of clones—everyone would look exactly like the suspect, making it virtually impossible to identify the culprit. In contrast, a match-to-description strategy sets limits on the number of features that need to be matched. With this strategy, distracters are matched only on the items that the witness provided in his or her description. For example, if a witness stated that the criminal had brown hair, blue eyes, a round face, and no facial hair, then those would be the features on which each lineup member is matched.

Lindsay et al. (1994) noted that some general characteristics that might not be mentioned would need to be included to produce a "fair" lineup. A **fair lineup** is one in which the suspect does not stand out from the other lineup members. For example, if skin color was not mentioned, then a lineup could be constructed with one white face (the suspect) and five black faces. Such a lineup would be unfair or biased. Some characteristics, such as sex and race, are known as default values and should be matched even if not mentioned in the witness's description.

To avoid a biased lineup, Luus and Wells (1991; Wells, Rydell, & Seelau, 1993) suggest that if a feature is provided in the witness's description but does not match the suspect's appearance, then the distracters should match the suspect's appearance on that feature. For example, if the culprit is described as having brown hair but the suspect has blond hair, then the distracters should have blond hair.

ESTIMATING IDENTIFICATION ACCURACY   When we are interested in finding out how often witnesses will make an accurate (or inaccurate) identification decision, we need to create the condition when police have arrested the right person, the guilty suspect. We also need to create the condition when police have arrested the wrong person, an innocent suspect. Thus, we create two lineups in our research. One lineup—the **target-present lineup**—contains a picture of the culprit. In the other lineup—the **target-absent lineup**—we substitute the culprit's picture with another photo. Identification decisions are different with each type of lineup. See Table 5.1 for the types of identification decisions possible as a function of type of lineup.

Three types of identification decisions can occur with a target-present lineup. The witness can identify the guilty suspect, which is a correct identification. If the witness

Foils/Distracters

Lineup members who are known to be innocent of the crime in question

Fair lineup

A lineup where the suspect does not stand out from the other lineup members

Target-present lineup

A lineup that contains the culprit

Target-absent lineup

A lineup that does not contain the culprit but contains an innocent suspect

TABLE 5.1	Possible Identification Decisions as a Function of Lineup Type				
Type of Lineup	*Identification Decision*				
	Correct Indentification	False Rejection	Foil Indentification	Correct Rejection	False Indentification
Target-present	X	X	X	Not possible	Not possible
Target-absent	Not possible	Not possible	X	X	X

Source: Table from "What do we know about eyewitness identification?" by Gary L. Wells from *American Psychologist.* Copyright © 1993 by The American Psychological Association.

identifies a foil, that is a foil identification. In addition, the witness may state that the culprit is not present, which is a false rejection.

Three types of identification decisions can occur with a target-absent lineup. The witness can state that the culprit is not present, which is a correct rejection. The witness can identify a foil, which is a foil identification. The witness can also identify an innocent suspect, in which case the witness makes a false identification. Sometimes, researchers will not make a distinction between false identifications and foil identifications from a target-absent lineup and will refer to these two errors simply as false positives.

IDENTIFICATION DECISION IMPLICATIONS The only correct decision with a target-present lineup is to make a correct identification. The only correct decision with a target-absent lineup is to make a correct rejection. The other decisions with each type of lineup are errors and have different implications for the witness and the justice system (Wells & Turtle, 1986):

- A foil identification (with either a target-present lineup or a target-absent lineup) is a known error to the police, so the person identified will not be prosecuted. The witness, however, may be perceived as having a faulty memory. Moreover, the other details provided by this witness may be viewed with some skepticism because a known recognition error was made.
- A false rejection is an unknown error and may result in the guilty suspect going free and possibly committing further crimes.
- A false identification also is an unknown error in real life and may result in the innocent suspect being prosecuted and convicted for a crime he or she did not commit. Moreover, with a false identification, the real criminal remains free to commit further crimes. False identifications may be the most serious type of identification error a witness can make.

LIVE LINEUPS OR PHOTO ARRAYS? Most often, police will use a set of photographs rather than live persons to assemble a lineup (Turtle, Lindsay, & Wells, 2003). *Photo array* is the term used for photographic lineups. Photo arrays are more common than lineups for a number of reasons:

- They are less time consuming to construct. The police can choose foils from their mug shot (pictures of people who have been charged with crimes in the past) files rather than find live persons.
- They are portable. The police are able to bring the photo array to the witness rather than have the witness go to the police department.

- The suspect does not have the right to counsel being present when a witness looks at a photo array. This right is present with live lineups.
- Because photos are static, the police need not worry that the suspect's behavior may draw attention to himself or herself, thus invalidating the photo array.
- A witness may be less anxious examining a photo array than a live lineup.

An alternative to photographs or live lineups is to use video-recorded lineups. Advantages to video lineups include the ability to enlarge faces or focus on particular features. Lineup members can be shown walking, turning, and talking. In a study by Cutler, Fisher, and Chicvara (1989), they found that correct identification and correct rejection rates did not differ across live and video-recorded lineups. Many jurisdictions in the United States use photographs. There has been some movement in the United Kingdom to use video-recorded lineups. Further research is needed to examine identification differences, if any, between video-recorded lineups and photo lineups.

LINEUP PRESENTATION PROCEDURES   Lineups can be presented in different formats or with different procedures to the witness. Perhaps most common is the procedure known as the **simultaneous lineup** (Wells, 1993). The simultaneous procedure presents all lineup members at one time to the witness. Wells suggested that this procedure encourages the witness to make a **relative judgment**, whereby lineup members are compared with each other and the person who looks most like the culprit is identified.

An alternative lineup procedure is the **sequential lineup**. This lineup procedure involves presenting the lineup members serially to the witness. The witness must make a decision as to whether the lineup member is the culprit before seeing the next lineup member (Lindsay & Wells, 1985). Also, with the sequential procedure, a witness cannot ask to see previously seen photos and the witness is unaware of the number of photos to be shown. Wells (1993) suggested that the sequential procedure reduces the likelihood that the witness can make a relative judgment. Instead, witnesses may be more likely to make an **absolute judgment**, whereby each lineup member is compared with the witness's memory of the culprit and the witness decides whether it is the culprit.

Lindsay and Wells (1985) compared the identification accuracy rate achieved with the simultaneous and sequential lineup procedures. University students witnessed a videotaped theft and were asked to identify the culprit from six photographs. Half the students saw a target-present lineup and the other half of students saw a target-absent lineup. Across target-present and target-absent conditions, the lineups were either presented using a simultaneous procedure or a sequential procedure.

Correct identification (target-present lineups) rates did not differ across lineup procedures. However, correct rejection rates were significantly different across lineup procedures. Only 42% of the participants made a correct rejection with a simultaneous lineup, whereas 65% of the participants made a correct rejection with a sequential lineup. In other words, if the culprit was not included in the lineup, witnesses were more likely to correctly indicate that he or she was not present if they were shown a sequential lineup than a simultaneous lineup. The higher correct rejection rate with the sequential procedure compared with the simultaneous procedure has been replicated numerous times (Steblay, Dysart, Fulero, & Lindsay, 2001). Across several studies however, correct identifications have been shown to decrease with the sequential lineup compared to the simultaneous lineup (Lindsay, Mansour, Beaudry, Leach, & Bertrand, 2009). The sequential lineup is the procedure used in some U.S. states, such as New Jersey. Recent research, however, has

Simultaneous lineup

A common lineup procedure that presents all lineup members at one time to the witness

Relative judgment

Witness compares lineup members to each other, and the person who looks most like the culprit is identified

Sequential lineup

Alternative lineup procedure where the lineup members are presented serially to the witness and the witness must make a decision as to whether the lineup member is the culprit before seeing another member. Also a witness cannot ask to see previously seen photos and is unaware of the number of photos to be shown.

Absolute judgment

Witness compares each lineup member to his or her memory of the culprit to decide whether the lineup member is the culprit

called into question the "sequential superiority effect" (McQuiston-Surrett, Malpass, & Tredoux, 2006). The researchers suggest that when certain methodological factors are considered, the simultaneous procedure produces similar correct rejection rates as the sequential procedure without a drop in correct identifications. Thus, the debate continues (see also Malpass, Tredoux, & McQuiston-Surrett, 2009).

Showup

Identification procedure that shows one person to the witness: the suspect

An alternative identification procedure to the lineup is a **showup**. This procedure shows one person to the witness: the suspect. The witness is asked whether the person is the culprit. Although an absolute judgment is likely with a showup, it has a number of other difficulties, making it a less-than-ideal procedure. Both courts and researchers have argued (*Stovall v. Denno*, 1967; Wells, Leippe, & Ostrom, 1979) that because there are no other lineup members shown, the witness is aware of whom the police suspect, and this knowledge may increase a witness's likelihood of making an identification that may be false.

Not everyone agrees with this view, however. In the early 1990s, a series of studies was conducted by Gonzalez, Ellsworth, and Pembroke (1993). They did not find false identifications to be higher with a showup than with a lineup. In fact, they found that witnesses were more likely to reject a showup than a lineup. Gonzalez et al. concluded that witnesses are more cautious with their decision making when presented with a showup rather than a lineup, and as a result will err on making a rejection rather than an identification. Yarmey, Yarmey, and Yarmey (1996), however, reached a different conclusion. They found that lineups produced lower false-identification rates than showups. In a recent meta-analysis comparing showups and lineups, Steblay, Dysart, Fulero, and Lindsay (2003) found that false identifications were higher with showups than with lineups. Also, in an analysis of 271 actual police cases, the suspect was more likely to be identified in a field showup (76%) than in a photographic lineup (48%) (Behrman & Davey, 2001). These results are consistent with the notion that showups are suggestive. Further research is needed to understand the discrepancy in identification rates for showups across studies.

For now, there are only two acceptable uses of a showup. It may be used for deathbed identifications, when there is a fear that the witness will not be alive by the time a lineup is assembled (Wells, Malpass, Lindsay, Turtle, & Fulero, 2000). Also, police may use a showup if a suspect is apprehended immediately at or near the crime scene.

Walk-by

Identification procedure that occurs in a naturalistic environment. The police take the witness to a public location where the suspect is likely to be. Once the suspect is in view, the witness is asked whether he or she sees the culprit

One other identification procedure that may precede a lineup identification is known as a **walk-by**. This identification occurs in a naturalistic environment. The police take the witness to a public location where the suspect is likely to be. Once the suspect is in view, the witness is asked whether he or she sees the culprit.

Biased lineup

A lineup that "suggests" who the police suspect and thereby who the witness should identify

LINEUP BIASES   Constructing a fair lineup is a challenging task. **Biased lineups** suggest who the police suspect and thereby who the witness should identify. In some way, the suspect stands out from the other lineup members in a biased lineup. The following biases have been investigated and found to increase false positives:

1. *Foil bias.* The suspect is the only lineup member who matches the description of the culprit. For example, the suspect has a beard and moustache while the other lineup members are clean-shaven (Lindsay, Lea, & Fulford, 1991).
2. *Clothing bias.* The suspect is the only lineup member wearing clothing similar to that worn by the culprit. For example, the culprit was described as wearing a blue baseball cap. The suspect is wearing a blue baseball cap while the foils are not (Dysart, Lindsay, & Dupuis, 2006; Lindsay et al., 1991; Lindsay, Wallbridge, & Drennan, 1987).

3. *Instruction bias.* The police fail to mention to the witness that the culprit may not be present; rather, the police imply that the culprit is present and that the witness should pick him or her out (Clark, 2005; Malpass & Devine, 1981; Steblay, 1997).

Voice Identification

Perhaps one of the first and most prominent cases involving voice identification (or "ear-witness" identification) occurred in the United States in 1937. The infant son of Charles Lindbergh, a well-known doctor and aviator, was kidnapped and murdered (see Chapter 2). Lindberg identified Bruno Hauptmann's voice as the one he heard three years earlier when he paid the ransom. The kidnapper had said, "Hey, doctor, over here, over here." Hauptmann was convicted of kidnapping and murder. At the time, no studies on voice identification existed. Unfortunately, little has changed during the past 65 years, as very few studies have been conducted in this area.

In one study examining many key voice variables, Orchard and Yarmey (1995) had 156 university students listen to a taped voice of a mock kidnapper that varied in length—either 30 seconds or 8 minutes. The voice was varied such that the kidnapper either had a distinctive or nondistinctive voice. The researchers also varied whether the speaker spoke in a whisper or a normal tone. Voice identification accuracy was tested using six-person voice lineups two days after the participants heard the taped voice. Here are some of the results:

- Identification accuracy was higher with longer voice samples.
- Whispering significantly decreased identification accuracy.
- Distinctiveness interacted with whispering, influencing identification accuracy.

FACTORS THAT DECREASE LIKELIHOOD OF CORRECT VOICE IDENTIFICATION   Other studies have found that the likelihood of a correct identification is decreased if a voice is changed by whispering or muffling, or through emotion (Bull & Clifford, 1984; Saslove & Yarmey, 1980). Orchard and Yarmey (1995) have stated that "when voices are disguised as whispers, or changed in tone between first hearing the perpetrator and the conduction of the voice lineup, identification evidence should be accepted with critical caution" (p. 259).

Kersholt, Jansen, Van Amelsvoort, and Broeders (2006) examined the question of whether the perpetrator and witness having different accents would affect voice identification. There was a trend for participants to be more accurate when the speaker had a familiar versus a different accent: 41% correct identifications versus 34% correct identifications, respectively, and 56% correct rejections versus 35% correct rejections, respectively.

In terms of target-voice position in a lineup, if the target voice occurs later in the lineup, correct identification decreases compared with an earlier presentation (Doehring & Ross, 1972). Cook and Wilding (1997) reported that when the target's face was visible when participants originally heard the voice at encoding, correct identification decreased greatly. Also, as the number of foils increased from four to eight voices, correct identification decreased (Clifford, 1980).

Are Several Identifications Better Than One?

If identification decisions for different pieces of evidence were combined, would the decision regarding the suspect's guilt be more accurate? Pryke, Lindsay, Dysart, and

Dupuis (2004) conducted two experiments examining the usefulness of multiple independent lineups to identify a culprit: for example, having the participants identify the clothing worn by the culprit in one lineup and identify the culprit's face in another lineup. If both of these identification decisions are of the suspect, then the likelihood that the suspect is the culprit should be greater than if just one identification decision implicates the suspect. In the first experiment, following exposure to a live target, participants were shown a face lineup, then a voice lineup, and lastly a body lineup (Pryke et al., 2004). In the second experiment, a clothing lineup was added to the other three lineups. The researchers found that exposing witnesses to more than one lineup, each consisting of a different aspect of the suspect, increased the ability to determine the reliability of an eyewitness's identification of the suspect. Thus, the likelihood of the suspect's guilt increased as the number of independent identifications of the suspect increased by any one witness. This research presents an interesting avenue for future research, with many questions still unanswered. For example, are certain types of lineups more diagnostic of a suspect's guilt than others?

Are Confident Witnesses Accurate?

In a landmark U.S. Supreme Court Case in 1972 (*Neil v. Biggers*), the Court stated that the confidence of a witness should be taken as an indicator of accuracy. This assertion implies that witnesses who are certain in their identification of the culprit are likely to be accurate. Many studies, however, have investigated this relationship and found a different result (Cutler & Penrod, 1989a, 1989b; Penrod & Cutler, 1995; Sporer, Penrod, Read, & Cutler, 1995). Overall, there appears to be a small positive correlation between accuracy and confidence. In addition, a number of moderator variables are available that can increase or decrease this relation.

Wells and his colleagues have investigated post-lineup identification feedback and its effect on the confidence–accuracy relationship (Bradfield, Wells, & Olson, 2002; Luus & Wells, 1994; Wells & Bradfield, 1998). In one study (Wells & Bradfield, 1998), after the witness made a lineup identification decision, the experimenter provided one of the following:

1. Confirming feedback: "Good, you identified the actual suspect."
2. Disconfirming feedback: "Actually, the suspect is number _____."
3. No feedback.

Participants were asked to make a number of judgments following the feedback or lack thereof. Of key interest were the ratings the participants made regarding how confident they were that they identified the correct person on a 1-to-7-point scale in which 1 means not at all certain and 7 means totally certain. See Figure 5.2 for the confidence ratings as a function of feedback condition.

Participants who were informed that they had identified the culprit reported significantly higher confidence ratings than did participants who received disconfirming feedback or no feedback. Thus, confidence can be manipulated and inflated, thereby affecting the confidence–accuracy relation. A recent meta-analysis of post-identification feedback has shown it to be a reliable and robust effect that has an impact on a number of factors, including how certain witnesses feel and how much attention they think they paid to the culprit (Douglass & Steblay, 2006).

Research also indicates that the more often you express a decision, the greater your confidence in subsequent reports (Shaw, 1996; Shaw & McClure, 1996). You can

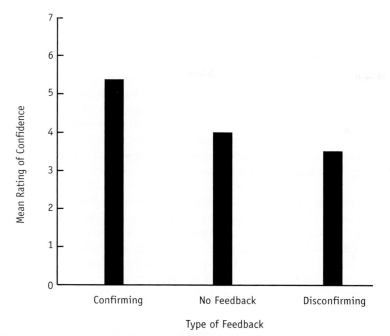

FIGURE 5.2   Mean Confidence Ratings as a Function of Feedback

Source: Figure from "'Good, you identified the suspect:' Feedback to eyewitnesses distorts their reports of the witnessing experience" by Gary L. Wells and Amy L. Bradfield from *Journal of Applied Psychology.* Copyright © 1998 by The American Psychiatric Association.

imagine that by the time a witness testifies in court, he or she has been interviewed many times. Consequently, the confidence the witness expresses in the courtroom may be inflated. Inflated confidence may be problematic given that it is an indicator used by fact finders (i.e., judges and juries) to assess accuracy. Moreover, mock jurors do not appear sensitive to "inflated confidence" (Bradfield & McQuiston, 2004). Wells et al. (1998) have recommended that police ask witnesses for their confidence rating immediately following their identification decision prior to any feedback and that this rating be used in court. This rating may be more informative with regard to accuracy. Also, it is recommended that the person administering the lineup not know who is the suspect to limit post-identification feedback.

Estimator Variable Research in Recognition Memory

Three estimator variables have received much attention in eyewitness research: age, race, and weapon focus.

AGE   Differences in the ability to make correct identifications have not been found between younger and older adults. Although older adults (over age 60) are just as likely as younger adults to correctly identify the culprit from a target-present lineup, older adults are more likely to make an incorrect decision from a target-absent lineup than are younger adults (Wells & Olson, 2003). In other words, older adults make a similar number of correct identifications but fewer correct rejections than do younger adults. This pattern of responding can also be found between children and young adults (Pozzulo & Lindsay, 1998; see Chapter 6 for more on this topic).

Memon and Gabbert (2003) tested younger (ages 18 to 30 years) and older (ages 60 to 80 years) witnesses' identification abilities. A crime video was shown, and target-present and target-absent lineups were presented using either a simultaneous or sequential lineup. Younger and older witnesses did not differ in their correct identification rate with the simultaneous lineup or the sequential lineup. Greater correct identifications were obtained with the simultaneous lineup than with the sequential lineup for both groups. Older witnesses made fewer correct rejections with the simultaneous and the sequential lineup than did younger witnesses. However, older witnesses made more correct rejections with a sequential lineup than with the simultaneous lineup (as did younger adults). Overall, though, older adult witnesses may have more difficulty than younger adult witnesses in making correct rejection decisions.

Cross-race effect/ other-race effect/ own-race bias

The phenomenon of witnesses remembering own-race faces with greater accuracy than faces from other races.

RACE   The **cross-race effect**, also known as the **other-race effect** and **own-race bias**, is the phenomenon of witnesses remembering faces of people of their own race with greater accuracy than they remember faces of people of other races. In a meta-analysis, Meissner and Brigham (2001) examined 30 years of research, including almost 5,000 participants, on the topic of cross-race identification. They found that own-race faces produced higher correct identifications and lower false positives than other-race faces.

A number of explanations for this phenomenon have been suggested. Below are three of the more common explanations.

Attitudes   One hypothesis to explain the other-race effect is based on attitudes. More specifically, people with fewer prejudicial attitudes may be more inclined to distinguish among members of other races. However, research to date does not support this explanation (Platz & Hosch, 1988; Slone, Brigham, & Meissner, 2000). Having said that, Meissner and Brigham (2001) do note that prejudicial attitudes may be related to the amount of contact a person has with other-race members, which, in turn, may help explain the other-race effect (see below).

Physiognomic Homogeneity   An alternative hypothesis to explain the other-race effect suggests that some races have less variability in their faces—"they all look alike." This hypothesis has not received much empirical support either. Goldstein (1979), for example, examined Japanese, black, and white faces and did not find that one group was more similar across members than the others were. Although physical similarity may not explain the other-race effect, some features may be more appropriate for discriminating among faces of certain races, such as hair color (Deregowski, Ellis, & Shepherd, 1975; Shepherd, 1981; Shepherd & Deregowski, 1981). Thus, persons from other races may not pay attention or encode relevant features that distinguish between members of a particular race. For example, paying attention to hair color for Asian faces may be less discriminating than hair color for Caucasian faces. This explanation, however, does not seem adequate at explaining the cross-race phenomenon.

Interracial Contact   Perhaps the hypothesis receiving the most attention examines the amount or type of contact people have had with other races. This hypothesis states that the more contact you have with other races, the better you will be able to identify them. In the 1970s, some researchers examined children and adolescents living in integrated neighborhoods versus those living in segregated neighborhoods. It was predicted that participants from integrated neighborhoods would be better at recognizing other-race faces than would those living in segregated neighborhoods. Some support for this prediction was found (Cross, Cross, & Daly, 1971; Feinman & Entwisle, 1976).

In another test of this hypothesis, Li, Dunning, and Malpass (as cited in Meissner & Brigham, 2001) examined the ability of white basketball "experts" (dedicated fans) and white basketball novices to recognize black faces. Given that the majority of U.S. professional basketball players are black, it was thought that the experts would have more experience distinguishing black faces because of their experience watching basketball. Indeed, the experts were better at identifying black faces than were the novices.

It is important to note that not all studies that have investigated interracial contact have found the predicted effect. For example, Ng and Lindsay (1994) examined university students from Canada and Singapore and the other-race effect was not completely supported.

A definitive conclusion on the contact hypothesis and how it factors into the other-race effect remains unclear. Further work in this area is needed.

WEAPON FOCUS   The term used to describe the phenomenon of a witness's attention being focused on the culprit's weapon rather than on the culprit is known as **weapon focus** (Steblay, 1992). The witness will remember less about the crime and culprit when a weapon is present than when no weapon is present. It is clear that this phenomenon occurs, but why it occurs is less clear. Two primary explanations have been offered for the weapon focus effect, namely, arousal and unusualness.

Weapon focus

Term used to describe the phenomenon of a witness's attention being focused on the culprit's weapon rather than on the culprit

Arousal   The **cue-utilization hypothesis** was proposed by Easterbrook (1959) to explain why a witness may focus on the weapon rather than other details. The hypothesis suggests that when emotional arousal increases, attentional capacity decreases. With limited attentional capacity, central details, such as the weapon, are more likely to be encoded than are peripheral details, such as the color of the culprit's hair. There is limited support for this hypothesis.

Cue-utilization hypothesis

Proposed by Easterbrook (1959) to explain why a witness may focus on the weapon rather than other details. The hypothesis suggests that when emotional arousal increases, attentional capacity decreases

Unusualness   An alternative explanation for the weapon focus phenomenon has to do with unusualness, in that weapons are unusual and thus attract a witness's attention. Because a witness is not paying attention to and encoding other details, these other details are not remembered (Mitchell, Livosky, & Mather, 1998; Pickel, 1998). To follow this line of thinking, you would predict that not only weapons but also other objects might produce a "weapon focus" effect, if they were unusual for the situation.

Pickel (1998) conducted two experiments to investigate the unusualness explanation. In one of the experiments, university students watched one of four videotapes in which a woman was approached by a man with a handgun. The scenarios differed in their location and the degree of threat posed to the witness. In one video, the interaction occurred at a baseball game in the stadium parking lot. In the other video, the interaction occurred at a shooting range. In the low-threat condition, the man kept the gun pointed to the ground. In the high-threat condition, the man pointed the gun at the woman. Participants provided less accurate descriptions of the man if he was carrying a gun in the parking lot rather than at the shooting range. The degree of threat did not influence the descriptions of the man. These data suggest that unusualness can produce the weapon focus phenomenon. However, it should be noted that identification of the target was not affected.

Thus, there is support for the unusualness explanation for the weapon focus effect. More research, however, is needed to definitively conclude why the weapon focus effect occurs. It may be encouraging to know that Pickel, Ross, and Truelove (2006) found that participants could be instructed/trained "not" to focus on a weapon, and thus reduce the weapon focus effect.

EXPERT TESTIMONY ON EYEWITNESS ISSUES

Eyewitness testimony is an area for which experts may be able to provide the courts with data that can help the fact finders with their decision making. However, not all eyewitness experts agree as to whether there is sufficient reliability across eyewitness studies and whether it is appropriate to apply the results of laboratory simulations to the real world. An additional criticism lodged against the testimony of eyewitness experts is that the information provided is common sense and, therefore, not necessary for the fact finder.

Kassin, Tubb, Hosch, and Memon (2001; Kassin, Ellsworth, & Smith, 1989) surveyed researchers to determine which eyewitness issues they felt were reliable enough to provide expert testimony in court. Issues that were deemed sufficiently reliable included lineup procedures, interview procedures, and the confidence–accuracy relationship.

There are, however, some dissenters (e.g., Egeth, 1993; McCloskey & Egeth, 1983). In one critique, Ebbesen and Konecni (1997) argue that eyewitness experts are overconfident in their conclusions and have thus misled the courts about the validity, consistency, and generalizability of the data. The researchers take issue with the lack of theory in the eyewitness area, and argue that the studies are too far removed from real-world eyewitness situations to be useful in predicting how "actual" witnesses would behave. They outline a number of weaknesses in eyewitness research that should limit its usefulness to real-world application and experts testifying:

1. Studies examining the same issue produce different results.
2. Most of the studies use university students; real-life witnesses vary in age and other demographic variables.
3. Most studies allow a witness to view the culprit for approximately six seconds; in reality, witnesses may view the culprit for five or more minutes.

In defense of eyewitness research, Leippe (1995) noted that eyewitness research uses a number of methodologies and types of participants (see also Loftus, 1983). In addition, a number of studies are highly reliable. In support of the laboratory simulation using staged crimes, Wells (1993) asks, "If subjects believe that they are witnessing real crime, for instance, in what important way are they different from people who witness a real crime?" (p. 555). Perhaps the eyewitness field will always have critics on each side.

Overall, several studies have suggested that the lay public may not be sufficiently knowledgeable about eyewitness issues to evaluate this evidence in court (e.g., Benton, Ross, Bradshaw, Thomas, & Bradshaw, 2006; Brewer, Potter, Fisher, Bond, & Luszcz, 1999). Furthermore, Yarmey (2001) has concluded that many results found with eyewitness studies are counterintuitive and contradict the commonsense beliefs of those in the community.

Currently, the American justice system tends to limit, and often does not allow, the testimony of eyewitness experts on these issues in court. How would you evaluate eyewitness testimony? See the Case Study box and you be the judge.

PUBLIC POLICY ISSUES AND GUIDELINES

In the mid-1990s, then-U.S. Attorney General Janet Reno commissioned a set of guidelines for the collection and preservation of eyewitness evidence. She was prompted by the large body of empirical literature on eyewitness issues. In addition, the more sensational factor that caught her attention involved a review of DNA exoneration cases (Wells et al., 2000). Specifically, in 1992, two law professors, Barry Scheck and Peter

CASE STUDY

YOU BE THE JUDGE

One Saturday evening in Vermont during the holiday season, Kenji Hattori (a Japanese tourist) stopped at a bank machine on his way back to his hotel after having several drinks at a nearby bar. He withdrew $200 and left the bank. As he walked back to his car in a nearby parking lot, he was approached by a Caucasian man with a knife who robbed him of his wallet, watch, and cell phone. Unfortunately, the incident occurred outside the view of the bank's security cameras and those passing by didn't seem to notice.

At the police station the police asked Mr. Hattori about the incident. Mr. Hattori stated that he was quite shaken up by the incident but he tried to provide as much information as he could about the appearance of the robber.

Three weeks later, the police had found a suspect who matched the description given by Mr. Hattori.

The police were certain they had the right man and asked Mr. Hattori to identify the robber from a simultaneous lineup. To ensure Mr. Hattori didn't make a mistake, they took a photo of the robber standing outside the bank where Mr. Hattori was held up. Mr. Hattori identified the suspect as the man who had robbed him. Mr. Hattori was certain he had selected the correct person. The police congratulated Mr. Hattori for picking out the robber.

Based on Mr. Hattori's identification, the police arrested and charged the suspect.

Your turn . . .

What factors do you think influenced Mr. Hattori's identification? Should Mr. Hattori's identification be admissible in court? Why or why not?

What recommendations would you make to police for future identifications?

Neufeld, at the Benjamin N. Cardozo School of Law at Yeshiva University formed the Innocence Project to assist prisoners who could be exonerated through DNA testing. Scheck and Neufeld used the following criteria in determining whether to take on a case at the time of conviction: DNA technology was not available; DNA must have been preserved to allow for testing with current technology; and the convicted individual must be claiming innocence. The Innocence Project is now an independent nonprofit organization affiliated with the Cardozo School of Law. Its mission is to exonerate people who are in prison serving time for crimes they did not commit and to bring reform to the justice system.

To date, the Innocence Project has obtained 266 exonerations through DNA testing in the United States with mistaken eyewitness identification the leading cause of conviction in 75% of these cases. Approximately 40% of these cases involved a cross-race identification. See Table 5.2 for some of the cases that involved wrongful conviction. See Box 5.3 for a case description of mistaken identification.

Eyewitness researchers, along with police officers and lawyers, constituted the Technical Working Group for Eyewitness Evidence (1999) that was commissioned in the United States to respond to Janet Reno's request. They developed a national set of guidelines known as *Eyewitness Evidence: A Guide for Law Enforcement.* In terms of

TABLE 5.2		DNA Exoneration Cases (United States)		
Name/State		**Crime**	**Years in Prison**	**Contributing Cause(s)***
Steven Barnes	NY	Rape	19.5 years	Witness ID, IFS
Ronnie Bullock	IL	Sexual Assault	10.5 years	Witness ID
Willie Davidson	VA	Rape	12 years	Witness ID, IFS
Frederick Daye	CA	Rape	10 years	Witness ID, IFS
Anthony Gray	MD	Murder	7 years	False Confession
Clarence Harrison	GA	Rape	17.5 years	Witness ID, IFS
Ray Krone	AZ	Murder	10 years	IFS
Clark McMillan	TN	Rape	22 years	Witness ID
Vincent Moto	PA	Rape	8.5 years	Witness ID
Miguel Roman	CT	Murder	18.5 years	Snitches

*ID = identification; IFS = improper forensic science.
Source: From Innocence Project webpage: "Profiles," "Facts Sheet," and "Charles Chapman case."
Copyright © 2011 by *The Innocence Project.* Reprinted with permission.

BOX 5.3 A Case of Wrongful Conviction

It was 1981, in a Dallas apartment when a 52-year-old woman was awakened by an African American intruder wearing a dark cap pulled over his head. After sexually assaulting the woman and tying her up, the intruder stole $15 from the woman and various household items. The victim heard a car door slam and a car drive away. The victim was able to free herself and call police.

The victim described the attacker as 5 feet, 7 inches, with black hair and facial hair. Although the victim typically wore glasses she did not have them on during the attack. She testified that she "got enough of a glance of his full face." On the day after the attack, the victim was shown a six-person photo lineup. She did not identify anyone. She then was shown another lineup that included Charles Chatman. She identified Chatman as the attacker. She also noted that she believed she had seen Chatman several times in her neighborhood during the past few years. Two weeks later, the victim was shown a live lineup that included Chatman. Once again, the victim identified Chatman.

Chatman was charged with aggravated rape and tried by jury in Dallas on August 12 and 13, 1981. In addition to the victim testifying, an expert testified that Chatman was a "type O secretor," which matched the sample of seminal fluid taken from the bed sheets. Forty percent of black men are "type O secretors."

Chatman was convicted and sentenced to 99 years in prison. In 2001, while Chatman continued to serve his sentence, Texas passed a law allowing inmates to seek DNA testing if it had the potential for exoneration. In 2002, Chatman's petition was granted to allow for DNA testing. It took two years to locate the evidence. Unfortunately there wasn't sufficient evidence for testing. After three more years, techniques had progressed and the sample could be tested. In 2007, the results indicated that Chatman was innocent and he was released on January 3, 2008, after having served more than 26 years in prison for a crime he did not commit.

Source: From Innocence Project webpage: "Profiles," "Facts Sheet," and "Charles Chapman case." Copyright © 2011 by *The Innocence Project.* Reprinted with permission.

lineup identification, Wells et al. (1998) proposed that the guidelines be limited to four recommendations:

1. The person who conducts the lineup or photo array should not know which person is the suspect.
2. Eyewitnesses should be told explicitly that the criminal may not be present in the lineup and, therefore, witnesses should not feel that they must make an identification.
3. The suspect should not stand out in the lineup as being different from the foils based on the eyewitness' previous description of the criminal or based on other factors that would draw extra attention to the suspect.
4. A clear statement should be taken from the eyewitness at the time of the identification and prior to any feedback as to his or her confidence that the identified person is the actual criminal.

Kassin (1998) added one more rule for lineup identification. He stated that the entire lineup procedure should be recorded on video to ensure accuracy in the process. In particular, the lineup and the interaction between the officer and the witness should be on video so that lawyers, the judge, and the jurors can later assess for themselves whether the reports of the procedure made by police are accurate. Will the recommendations ever make it into the real-life justice system? See the In the Media box to learn more about the eyewitness identification bill—Senate Bill 117 sponsored by Senator Rodney Ellis of Houston, Texas.

IN THE MEDIA   Eyewitness Identification Bill 117

Texas has the greatest number of known wrongful convictions in the United States. As you have read in this chapter, the leading cause of wrongful conviction is mistaken identification. Senator Rodney Ellis of Houston filed Bill 117, known as the Eyewitness Identification Bill, to mandate police agencies to adopt best practices around lineup identification processes. The bill included the following best practices based on 30 years of eyewitness research:

- Neutral lineup instructions stating that the perpetrator may or may not be present
- Lineup members chosen based on their match to features of the perpetrator
- Blind administration where the officer administering the lineup does not know who the suspect is.

Not everyone agrees with this bill however. Passing the bill would give defense attorneys the power to have lineup identifications not allowed into evidence if the process and procedures are inconsistent with the best practices outlined in the bill.

It was reported that Texas Governor Rick Perry would veto any bill that requires police to follow specific practices and that allows evidence to be excluded when those practices are not followed (http://www.austinchronicle.com/gyrobase/Issue/story?oid:764660).

Supporters of the bill thought it represented a major step toward reducing wrongful convictions. Currently, only a few Texas police agencies have written procedures for the administration of lineup identification.

Opponents of the bill felt that identification procedures should not be mandated by legislature. Moreover, they felt that using old examples of wrongful conviction was unfair and that, in fact, a number of changes have been made across police agencies in terms of how lineups are conducted.

The Bill "died in the House."

SB 117, Ellis.

Smith, J. (April 10, 2009). Eyewitness ID: Not seeing eye to eye. *The Austin Chronicle.* Retrieved from http://www.austinchronicle.com/gyrobase/Issue/story?oid:764660.

BOX 5.4   DNA Exoneration Fact Sheet

There have been 266 post-conviction DNA exonerations in the United States (and counting)

- First DNA exoneration took place in 1989.
- Exonerations have been won in 34 states.
- Seventeen of the 266 people exonerated through DNA served time on death row.
- The average length of time served by exonerees is 13 years.
- The average age of exonerees at the time of their wrongful conviction is 27.

Races of the 266 exonerees:

158 African Americans

80 Caucasians

21 Latinos

2 Asian American

5 whose race is unknown

- In 117 of the DNA exoneration cases the guilty suspect/perpetrator has been identified.
- Since 1989, there have been tens of thousands of cases where prime suspects were identified and pursued—until DNA testing (prior to conviction) proved they were wrongly identified.
- About 50% of the people exonerated through DNA testing have been financially compensated. In 27 states, the federal government and the District of Columbia have passed laws to compensate people who were wrongly incarcerated. Awards under these statutes vary from state to state.
- In 22% of cases closed by the Innocence Project since 2004, they were closed because of lost or missing evidence.
- Other causes of wrongful convictions include improper forensic science, false confessions and incriminating statements, and snitches.

Source: From Innocence Project webpage: "Profiles," "Facts Sheet," and "Charles Chapman case." Copyright © 2011 by *The Innocence Project*. Reprinted with permission.

With the implementation of these recommendations, it is hoped that fewer wrongful convictions will occur. See Box 5.4 for a list of facts regarding DNA exoneration. As science advances and our knowledge of eyewitness memory increases, we will continue to update recommendations and technology that will result in a fairer justice system.

Summary

1. Independent variables in the eyewitness area can be categorized as estimator or system variables. The effect of estimator variables on eyewitness accuracy can only be estimated after the crime. In contrast, system variables can be manipulated by the criminal justice system to increase (or decrease) eyewitness accuracy.

The three dependent variables in the eyewitness area are recall of the event, recall of the culprit, and recognition of the culprit.

2. The misinformation effect is a phenomenon in which a witness who is presented with inaccurate information after an event will incorporate that misinformation into a subsequent

recall task. This effect can occur as a result of a witness guessing what the officer wants the response to be. Alternatively, this effect can occur because a witness has two memories—one for the correct information and one for the incorrect information—but cannot accurately remember how he or she acquired each piece of information. The misinformation effect can also occur because the inaccurate information replaces the accurate information in memory.

3. The cognitive interview is based on four memory-retrieval techniques to increase recall: reinstating the context, reporting everything that comes to mind, recalling the event in different orders, and changing the perspective from which the information is recalled. In addition to these techniques, the enhanced cognitive interview includes five more techniques: building rapport, exhibiting supportive interviewer behavior, transferring control of the interview to the witness, asking for focused recall with open-ended questions, and asking the witness questions that match what the witness is recalling.

4. The simultaneous lineup, sequential lineup, showup, and walk-by are identification procedures used by police to determine whether the suspect is the culprit. Biased lineups suggest who the police suspect and thereby who the witness should identify. In some way,

the suspect stands out from the other lineup members in a biased lineup. Foil bias, instruction bias, and clothing bias have been investigated and shown to increase false-positive responding.

5. Not all eyewitness experts agree on the reliability of research findings and whether we can apply the results of laboratory simulations to the real world. An additional criticism lodged against the eyewitness expert testifying is whether the information provided is common sense and therefore not necessary for the fact finder.

6. Four rules were outlined to reduce the likelihood of false identification. First, the person who conducts the lineup should not know which member of the lineup is the suspect. Second, eyewitnesses should be told explicitly that the criminal may not be present in the lineup and, therefore, witnesses should not feel that they must make an identification. Third, the suspect should not stand out in the lineup as being different from the foils based on the eyewitness's previous description of the criminal or based on other factors that would draw extra attention to the suspect. Fourth, a clear statement should be taken from the eyewitness at the time of the identification (and prior to any feedback) as to his or her confidence that the identified person is the actual criminal.

Key Concepts

absolute judgment *123*
biased lineup *124*
cognitive interview *117*
cross-race effect *128*
cue-utilization
   hypothesis *129*
culprit *120*
direct question
   recall *112*
distracters *121*
enhanced cognitive
   interview *118*

estimator variables *112*
fair lineup *121*
foils *121*
free narrative *112*
lineup *112*
memory impairment
   hypothesis *116*
misinformation
   acceptance
   hypothesis *116*
misinformation
   effect *114*

open-ended recall *112*
other-race effect *128*
own-race bias *128*
post-event information
   effect *114*
recall memory *111*
recognition
   memory *111*
relative judgment *123*
sequential lineup *123*
showup *124*

simultaneous
   lineup *123*
source misattribution
   hypothesis *116*
suspect *120*
system variables *112*
target-absent lineup *121*
target-present
   lineup *121*
walk-by *124*
weapon focus *129*

Discussion Questions

1. Imagine you are a judge and are allowing an eyewitness psychological expert to testify. What factors would you consider appropriate for the expert to testify about? What factors would you disallow testimony on?

2. One of your friends is training to be a police officer. His training is almost complete, but he is worried that he has not received sufficient training on how to interview eyewitnesses. He asks whether you can describe some of the techniques you learned in your "forensic" class. Explain interview strategies to elicit complete and accurate recall, as well as a technique that may hinder the process.

3. A considerable amount of research has been conducted on the misinformation effect. Design an experiment to test whether the misinformation effect also occurs if participants witness a violent crime.

4. Police use different types of lineup procedures. Describe these different types of procedures, and distinguish among the types of identification decisions that can occur in both target-present and target-absent lineups.

6

Child Victims and Witnesses

LEARNING OBJECTIVES

- Differentiate between techniques that decrease versus increase the likelihood of accurate recall in child witnesses.

- Summarize children's ability to recall/describe appearances of people.

- Describe a lineup technique designed for children's identification.

- Outline the courtroom accommodations available for child witnesses.

- Explain child maltreatment categories and related consequences.

Suzie Sarandon lay asleep in the bed across from her older sister's when she heard something; someone was at the bedroom window. Suzie was 8 and Samantha (Sam) was 13. They shared a bedroom with a large pull-out window. In the summer it could get very warm in the city so they kept their window open most nights. As Suzie opened her eyes, she saw a tall, thin, white man cover her sister's mouth and say, "Don't scream and I won't hurt you." Suzie pretended she was still asleep but tried to peek at the man so she could describe him later. In a few seconds, Sam was gone with this man who had come through the window. Suzie started yelling for help immediately. Her parents rushed in and asked what had happened and where was Sam. They called 911 and within minutes police arrived to interview Suzie.

Suzie sat on her mother's lap as she recounted what had happened moments earlier. Unfortunately, Suzie did not provide a lot of detail. Many questions remained regarding the identity of the man. The police officer started to ask Suzie direct questions, such as "Did you ever see this man before? Did he have a weapon? How old was he? How tall was he? Did he have any facial hair?" When the abduction occurred, the only light in the room came from a dim nightlight between the beds. Suzie could not see much but she provided answers to all of the questions the officer asked.

A former gardener was arrested about three months after the crime and placed in a lineup for Suzie to identify her sister's abductor. Suzie stared at his picture but could not make an identification. It would be almost a year after the abduction that Sam was spotted at a Quickie Mart with a man fitting the description her sister had provided. The store clerk quickly called police and tried to detain the two. Police arrived to arrest the abductor and bring Sam back home to her family. The abductor was charged with numerous offences.

I n some cases, children may be the only eyewitnesses to criminal activity. Police will rely on children's ability to recall and recognize strangers that they have seen for only a short period of time. The conviction of guilty suspects may rest on a child's testimony.

How do we interview children? Should the justice system rely on children's memory? These are some of the questions that we will explore in this chapter. We will focus on the historical legal context around children testifying in court, children's memory abilities, how best to tap into children's memory, and, last, we will examine the various forms of child abuse and their consequences.

HISTORY

The way in which child victims and witnesses have been viewed by the justice system has changed dramatically over the years. Some early views can be traced back to the Salem witch trials in 1692, when children claimed to have witnessed the defendants perform supernatural feats and other falsehoods (Ceci & Bruck, 1993). Several years following the execution of the defendants for witchcraft, some of the children recanted their testimonies. For the most part, the prevailing legal attitude toward child witnesses for the following 300 years was that of skepticism.

Research testing the validity of these negative attitudes toward child witnesses started in Europe in the early 20th century. Reviews from this time seemed to conclude that young children were highly suggestible and had difficulty separating fact from fantasy, and thus were capable of providing inaccurate testimony, even if the testimony was of personal significance (Whipple, 1909, 1910, 1911, 1912). Unfortunately, little is known about the details of the research on which these conclusions were based. Also, the criminal justice system was not very interested in these reviews. As a result, few studies were conducted on children's competencies during the early and mid-20th century.

A flurry of research on children's witness abilities started in the 1970s and continues to this day. Ceci and Bruck (1993) outlined four factors that led to the renewed interest in child witnesses:

1. Expert psychological testimony was becoming more acceptable in the courtroom.
2. Social scientists were interested in research that could be applied to real-world problems.
3. Studies on adult eyewitness testimony were increasing.
4. The legal community became interested in behavioral science research regarding child witnesses.

This last point was in response to the increasing number of reported sexual and physical abuse cases where a child was a victim or witness. These cases often involved numerous children and numerous defendants. Box 6.1 describes the longest and most expensive criminal trial in American history when it ended in 1990 involving many child

BOX 6.1   Preschools on Trial

In 1983, Ray Buckey was working at his grandmother's preschool in Manhattan Beach, California (Ceci & Bruck, 1995; Garven, Wood, Malpass, & Shaw, 1998). Virginia McMartin had founded the preschool and Ray's mother, Peggy McMartin Buckey, was the school's administrator. The mother of a boy attending the preschool believed her son had been sexually assaulted by Ray Buckey. Several accusations of the sexual abuse of children by the preschool workers prevailed. The police were called and then sent a letter to the parents of the children of the preschool alerting them that Ray Buckey had been arrested for child molestation. Parents were urged to interview their children regarding things they may have experienced or witnessed pertaining to sexual abuse.

Hundreds of children who had attended the school or were then currently at the school were interviewed by Child Protective Services. The interviewing techniques would undergo empirical scrutiny may years later. Interviewing techniques included repeated questioning until the child gave the response the interviewer was looking for, rewards for providing the information the interviewers wanted, and false claims that other children had already reported abuse.

On March 22, 1984, Virginia McMartin, Peggy McMartin Buckey, Ray Buckey, Ray's sister Peggy Ann Buckey, and several teachers were charged with 115 counts of child abuse, which later extended into 321 counts of child abuse involving 48 children. Although several charges were dropped against several of the defendants citing weak evidence, Peggy McMartin's charges along with Ray Buckey's remained. After three years of testimony and nine weeks of deliberation, Peggy McMartin was acquitted on all counts. Although Ray Buckey eventually had his charges dropped, he had spent over five years in prison during this period without ever having been convicted.

At the Wee Care Nursery School located in Maplewood, New Jersey, a 23-year-old female teacher, Margaret Kelly Michaels, was accused of performing various sexual acts including rape on the young children under her care. The initial accusation happened in 1985 when a nurse took the temperature of a four-year-old boy with a rectal thermometer and the boy was reported as stating, "That's what my teacher does to me at nap time at school."

The school sent a letter to all parents informing them of an investigation of a former employee regarding serious allegations made by a child. A social worker made a presentation to the parents explaining that sexual abuse of children is very common, with one out of three children being victims of an "inappropriate sexual experience" by the time he or she is 18 years old. She encouraged parents to examine their children for genital soreness, nightmares, bed wetting, masturbation, or any noticeable changes in behavior and to have their doctor examine the children for injury.

For the next two months, several professionals interviewed the children and their families. Initially, children said that Michaels did nothing wrong. The investigators called this the "denial phase." Investigators would tell the children that others had already disclosed what Michaels did, even though this was untrue. Interviewers used suggestive questioning and kept pressing children for the answers they thought were correct. Children began to disclose abuse only after several interviews. Allegedly Michaels raped and assaulted three- to five-year-olds with spoons and Lego blocks. It also was alleged that she played the piano in the nude. According to the prosecutors, all of these events went unnoticed by other teachers, school administrators, and parents over the seven months Michaels worked at the school.

Two and half years after the first allegation was made, the trial began (*State v. Michaels, 1988*). Nineteen children provided testimony. Michaels was convicted of 115 counts of sexual abuse against 20 three- to five-year-old children. Michaels was sentenced to 47 years in prison. The Appeals Court of New Jersey reversed Michaels' conviction and she was released on bail after serving 5 years of her sentence (*State v. Michaels*, 1993). The prosecution appealed part

(continued)

BOX 6.1 *Continued*

of this decision to the Supreme Court of New Jersey but their appeal was denied (*State v. Michaels*, 1994). The court ruled that if the prosecution decided to retry the case, "they must first hold a pretrial taint hearing and show that despite improper interviewing techniques, the statements and testimony of the child witnesses are sufficiently reliable to admit them as witnesses at trial." The prosecution dropped all charges against Michaels in December 1994.

Source: Ceci & Bruck, 1993.

witnesses and the McMartin family, which operated a preschool. A second, similar example is that of a case occurring in Maplewood, New Jersey, in which children were the primary victims and witnesses.

RECALL FOR EVENTS

Are children able to recall events accurately? How does their performance compare with the recall of adults? The Wee Care Nursery School case and others similar to it may suggest that children do not make very reliable witnesses, even about events they supposedly experienced. However, studies have found that children are capable of accurately recalling forensically relevant details of events (e.g., Ceci & Bruck, 1993). Moreover, children are capable of recalling much that is accurate. The challenge, of course, is determining when children are recalling accurately and when they are **fabricating**—making false claims. Research suggests that the accuracy of children's reporting is highly dependent on how they are asked to report. Examine the Case Study box and decide how you would interview children about an event that occurred.

Fabricating

Making false claims

Free Recall versus Directed Questioning

When children are asked to report all they can remember, using a free narrative approach, their accuracy in reporting is comparable with adults' (Ceci & Bruck, 1993). Unfortunately, children tend to report very little information using a free narrative. Direct questions or probes, such as "What else do you remember?" or "Tell me more about what you remember," are often necessary to elicit the required information. The dilemma arises when we consider the accuracy of direct questioning.

As we have seen with adult eyewitnesses in Chapter 5, when children are asked leading, direct questions, they are more likely to produce an erroneous response than when they are asked nonleading, direct questions (Roebers, Bjorklund, Schneider, & Cassel, 2002). Generally, older children are more resistant to leading questions than are younger children, and adults are even more resistant to leading questions (Ceci & Bruck, 1993). Dr. Stephen Ceci has been a key researcher in the area of children's eyewitness memory and suggestibility. See Box 6.2 to learn more about Dr. Ceci and his research.

Direct questions that require a yes/no response or use a forced-choice format are particularly problematic for preschoolers (Peterson & Biggs, 1997). For example, Waterman, Blades, and Spencer (2004) interviewed children between the ages of five and nine years. An adult confederate went into children's classrooms and engaged

CASE STUDY

YOU BE THE FORENSIC PSYCHOLOGIST

Five-year-old Caitlin attends Sunshine Daycare in the city of Mar Vista in Los Angeles with a population of 55,000. One day when Caitlin's mother picked her up from day-care, Caitlin seemed upset. This was unusual for Caitlin. Typically Caitlin would run into her mother's arms, overjoyed to see her. When Caitlin's mom asked what was wrong, she didn't reply.

That night when Caitlin was getting into the tub for a bath, her mother noticed Caitlin had some red welts on her bottom. When Caitlin's mom asked, "Why is your bottom red?" Caitlin started crying. After calming Caitlin down, her mother asked again if something had happened at daycare today. Caitlin nodded yes. Mom then asked, what happened. Caitlin said that Miss Mimi got angry with the kids and hit them with a wooden spoon. Mom then asked if all the children got hit and Caitlin nodded yes.

After Caitlin went to bed, Caitlin's mom called some of the other mothers to find out if their kids had red marks as well and if there was anything unusual with their children's demeanor. The other mothers inspected their children and started asking them very specific questions. Some children had bruises and some children had other marks. The next morning, the mothers kept their children home and called the police and the Child Protective Services agency to report the physical abuse.

Children were interviewed by police officers and then again by social workers. Miss Mimi was ordered to close her daycare and was charged with the physical abuse of children.

Your Turn . . .

What would you do if you were Caitlin's mother or father? How should children be interviewed to increase the likelihood of reporting reliable information?

them on a discussion about familiar topics such as favorite pets and favorite foods for approximately 10 minutes. Children were shown four photographs: two of pets and two of food items. The children then were interviewed using yes/no (e.g., Did the lady show you a picture of a banana?) and "wh-" questions (e.g., What was the lady's name, Where does the lady live?). Half of both types of questions were unknown to the children (e.g., How did the lady get to school this morning") where the correct response should be "don't know." Children performed similarly across both types of questions when they were answerable. However, when questions were unanswerable, children were more likely to say "don't know" to wh- questions than yes/no questions. We see that yes/no questions are particularly problematic for children. Melnyk, Crossman, and Scullin (2006) suggest this may be the case because these questions rely on recognition rather than recall, thus increasing the likelihood of error. Using recall (e.g., tell me everything you remember) may elicit brief responses but those responses are more likely to be accurate. We will discuss recall and recognition in greater detail later in the chapter.

BOX 6.2   Researcher Profile: Dr. Stephen Ceci

Dr. Stephen Ceci started his academic career by earning a B.A. at the University of Delaware. He then completed a master's at the University of Pennsylvania and went on to complete a Ph.D. at the University of Exeter in England where his doctoral research focused on the development of young children's memory. Currently, Dr. Ceci is the H. L. Carr Chaired Professor of Developmental Psychology at Cornell University. Dr. Ceci's main research interests center on memory development, suggestibility of children's memory, and developmental forensic psychology. Dr. Ceci states that his interest in young children's memory has been so long-standing that he cannot remember how it started.

Dr. Stephen Ceci

Recently, Dr. Ceci has been working on some of his favorite studies with his colleagues Stanka Fitneva at Queens University (Ontario, Canada) and Wendy Williams at Cornell, examining the role of mental representation in children's memory and suggestibility (i.e., Ceci, Fitneva, & Williams, 2010). Dr. Ceci says, "I really loved doing these experiments because they all started with a weird observation in a pilot study; namely, 3-year-olds would claim they did not remember seeing a picture that had been previously presented. However, when we asked them to guess where it had been located, or guess what its background color was, these 3-year-olds could do so at accuracy rates higher than chance. The next experiments were designed to unravel this surprising claim of not recognizing items whose contexts they could identify."

Dr. Ceci says he sometimes feels that he lives a secret life. Indeed, Dr. Ceci has conducted much research on children's suggestibility, however his research interests don't end there. He also works in the area of intelligence, studying the reasoning ability of racetrack handicappers (e.g., Ceci & Liker, 1986) and he examines sex differences in cognition, with an emphasis on women in science—why they are underrepresented in math-intensive fields such as physics, computer science, engineering, economics, and mathematics (Ceci, Williams, & Barnett, 2009). "So, because students and colleagues know about part of my research life, but are wholly unaware of the other parts, I feel I lead a secret life." Overall, Dr. Ceci feels confident he will always be involved in young children's memory and its forensic implications, and even as he was being interviewed for this profile he was preparing to go on television to explain a child's testimony in a murder trial.

Perhaps the common theme across Dr. Ceci's research areas is the controversial nature of the topics. Dr. Ceci states, "At some level I must enjoy debating with colleagues. It certainly keeps me intrigued about these topics because it is often the case that no sooner have I published something on them that colleagues line up to criticize, revise, and extend my writings. I really enjoy this process and I think this give-and-take among researchers with different perspectives ultimately benefits science."

When not researching, Dr. Ceci teaches a course on Children and the Law both at the undergraduate and graduate levels. He has been doing this for the past 15 years and still really enjoys teaching it. Dr. Ceci says, "I bring in attorneys and judges of all stripes and we review actual cases and the students seem to enjoy it as much as I do."

Dr. Ceci balances his many research interests and teaching with running. Dr. Ceci runs seven or eight miles every other day.

Why Are Children More Suggestible Than Adults?

Generally, two directions have been taken to understand children's greater propensity toward suggestibility (Bruck & Ceci, 1999). One focus has investigated the "social characteristics" of the interview. It has been argued that children respond to interviewers in the manner they feel the interviewer desires, known as social compliance. The alternative area researchers have concentrated in to understand children's responding has been to investigate developmental changes in their cognitive or memory system.

SOCIAL COMPLIANCE OR SOCIAL PRESSURE   It has been suggested that children may respond to suggestive influences because they trust and want to cooperate with adult interviewers, even if the children do not understand or have the knowledge to answer the question. Children may infer the desired response in keeping with the "gist" or general idea of the question (Brainerd & Reyna, 1996). In a study by Hughes and Greive (1980), young children between the ages of five and seven were asked nonsensical questions such as "Is milk bigger than water?" and "Is red heavier than yellow?" Even though these questions are illogical and do not have correct responses, many children provided a yes/no answer rather than saying, "I don't know." Note, however, that although children may respond according to a suggestion provided, their memory for the actual event may remain intact, and, if later questioned, they may report the accurate response (if asked in a nonsuggestive manner).

CHANGES TO THE COGNITIVE SYSTEM   Some research has found developmental differences in the ways children and adults encode, store, and retrieve memories (Brainerd & Reyna, 2004). Moreover, differences between children and adults also have been found in terms of forgetting and retention. Also related to memory is the notion that children "misattribute" where information came from (Parker, 1995). For example, children may report on an event that they heard about (e.g., through suggestive questioning from an interviewer) as it being something they experienced. Children may not remember that Ms. Z suggested that the event occurred, and, when later asked about it, children report the "suggestion," believing that the event actually occurred.

Currently, researchers believe that an interaction of social and cognitive factors is likely responsible to explain children's suggestibility and their reporting of false information. The content and format of questions posed to child witnesses should be considered carefully. Interviewers need to balance asking direct questions with the risk of obtaining false information. Many would recommend relying on free recall as much as possible to obtain accurate information.

A number of techniques and protocols/procedures to aid child witnesses with recalling information have been investigated. Below, we describe some of these options for use with child witnesses and their efficacy for recalling accurate information.

Other Techniques for Interviewing Children

ANATOMICALLY DETAILED DOLLS   If children have difficulty providing a verbal account of what they witnessed or experienced, props may be useful. When interviewing children suspected of being sexually abused, some mental health professionals may introduce **anatomically detailed dolls**. Just as the name implies, anatomically detailed dolls, sometimes like a "rag doll," are consistent with the male or female anatomy. Dolls

Anatomically detailed dolls

A doll, sometimes like a rag doll, that is consistent with the male or female anatomy

Child testifying via closed-circuit television.

may be of an adult male or female or a young male or female. The assumption underlying the use of these dolls is that children may have difficulty verbalizing what occurred, and in their play with the dolls they will demonstrate the events they experienced (Vizard & Trantor, 1988). Is this assumption correct, though? The research provides some contradictory results (Aldridge, 1998).

In a field study, Thierry, Lamb, Orbach, and Pipe (2005) examined the impact of anatomically detailed dolls on reports provided by 3- to 12-year-old alleged sexual abuse victims. The children were separated into two groups: younger (ages 3 to 6) and older (ages 7 to 12). The number of details provided were comparable in response to open-ended questions, whether or not dolls were used. When direct questions were posed, children 3 to 6 years old were more likely to use the dolls to reenact what occurred than to report verbally. In contrast, 7- to 12-year-olds provided more verbal details rather than use the dolls to report. Younger children were more likely to play with the dolls in a suggestive manner and to contradict details that were reported verbally. Overall, both younger and older children reported proportionally more "fantastic" details with the dolls than without. Similar results were found by DeLoache and Marzolf (1995).

Contrary to the above results, Goodman, Quas, Batterman-Faunce, Riddlesberger, and Kuhn (1997) found that 3- to 10-year-olds who had been touched during an examination were more likely to report such touching with dolls than when questioned orally. In another study, Saywitz, Goodman, Nicholas, and Moan (1991) interviewed 5- and 7-year-old girls who had received a physical examination. For half the girls, a genital examination was included. In this study, many of the children failed to report genital touching when they were asked for a verbal report of their examination, or they failed to show on the dolls what had actually happened. However, when asked a direct question—such as "Did the doctor touch you here?"—many of the children correctly agreed. Children who had not received the genital examination never made false reports of genital touching in either the oral free recall or the doll-enactment conditions. For this group, very few errors were made when the experimenter pointed to the genital area of the doll and asked, "Did the doctor touch you here?"

SHOULD ANATOMICALLY DETAILED DOLLS BE USED? A number of difficulties have been identified for using these dolls to determine if sexual abuse occurred (Koocher et al., 1995). For example, no specifications or guidelines are available for manufacturers of these dolls. Consequently, wide variation exists and some mental health professionals even make their own dolls. Not only is there no standardization for what the dolls should look like, there also are no standard procedures for scoring the behaviors children exhibit when interacting with the dolls. Research is not available to answer how nonabused versus abused children play with the dolls. Moreover, it is not clear whether abused versus nonabused children play with the dolls differently. Thus, the use of anatomically detailed dolls for diagnosing sexual abuse can be inaccurate and dangerous (Dickinson, Poole, & Bruck, 2005).

CRITERION-BASED CONTENT ANALYSIS Developed in Germany in the 1950s by Udo Undeutsch (1989), **criterion-based content analysis** (CBCA) is used to facilitate distinguishing truthful from false statements made by children. It has gone through some revision over the years by Stellar and Kohnken (1989) and Raskin and Esplin (1991) (Stellar, 1989). CBCA is part of a more comprehensive protocol called **statement validity analysis** (SVA) for credibility assessment for sexual abuse allegations. SVA consists of three parts: (1) a structured interview with the victim, (2) a systematic analysis of the verbal content of the victim's statements using CBCA, and (3) the application of a statement validity checklist. Although some suggest the need to use the entire SVA system when assessing allegations, the CBCA is considered the most important part and is often used as a stand-alone protocol.

The underlying assumption of the CBCA is that descriptions of real events differ in quality and content from memories that are fabricated. Eighteen criteria were developed to discriminate between true and fabricated events of sexual abuse. See Table 6.1 for a list of CBCA criteria. It is assumed that true events are more likely to contain the CBCA criteria than fabricated events.

CBCA is not without its critics, however. For example, Ruby and Brigham (1997) noted a number of difficulties with CBCA, such as inconsistencies with the number of criteria that need to be present to conclude truthfulness and the different decision rules for reaching a conclusion. Research has shown that age of the interviewee is positively correlated with scores on the CBCA (e.g., Buck, Warren, Betman, & Brigham, 2002; Vrij, Akenhurst, Soukara, & Bull, 2002). Younger children do not possess the cognitive abilities and command of the language to provide statements as detailed as those of older children. As a result, truthful statements by younger interviewees may be judged as doubtful because the statements are missing certain CBCA criteria (Vrij, 2005). Also, Pezdek et al. (2004) raised concerns about the forensic suitability of the CBCA for discriminating between children's accounts of real and fabricated events. They note that CBCA scores are influenced by both how familiar the event is to the child and how old the child is.

Overall, CBCA scores are calculated using a truth–lie classification, which requires the assessor to classify the statement as truthful or not based on his or her own interpretation of the statement. As a result, this method is highly subjective and does not ensure inter-rater reliability. Despite the criticisms, CBCA and SVA are being used in parts of Europe to distinguish between children's truthful and false reports. Recently, SVA has also been applied to adult statements to distinguish between truthful and false reports, and studies report success (Parker & Brown, 2000) and may eventually be used in the United States.

STEP-WISE INTERVIEW An alternative procedure for interviewing children that aims to keep false claims at a minimum is the **step-wise interview** developed by Yuille and his colleagues (e.g., Yuille, Hunter, Joffe, & Zaparniuk, 1993). This interview protocol consists of a series of "steps" designed to start the interview with the least leading and directive type of questioning, and then proceeding to more specific forms of questioning

Criterion-based content analysis

Analysis that uses criteria to distinguish truthful from false statements made by children

Statement validity analysis

A comprehensive protocol to distinguish truthful or false statements made by children containing three parts: a structured interview of the child witness, a systematic analysis of the verbal content of the child's statements (criterion-based content analysis), and the application of the statement validity checklist

Step-wise interview

Interview protocol with a series of "steps" designed to start the interview with the least leading and directive type of questioning then proceeding to more specific forms of questioning, as necessary

TABLE 6.1	Criterion-Based Content Analysis Criteria

General Characteristics

1. Logical structure – Is the statement coherent? Do the statements fit together?
2. Unstructured production – Is the account consistently organized?
3. Quality of details – Are there specific descriptions of place, time, person, etc.?

Specific Contents

4. Contextual embedding – Is the action connected to other daily routine events?
5. Interactions – Are there reports of conversation between victim and perpetrator?
6. Reproduction of speech – Is conversation in its original form?
7. Unexpected complications – Was there an unplanned interruption in the sexual activity?
8. Unusual details – Are there details that are unusual but meaningful?
9. Superfluous details – Are peripheral details described in connection to the sexual event?
10. Accurately reported details misunderstood – Did the child describe a detail accurately but interpret it incorrectly?
11. Related external associations – Is there reference to a sexually toned event that is not related to the alleged offense?
12. Subjective experience – Did the child describe feelings or thoughts experienced at the time of the incident?
13. Attribution of the accused's mental state – Is there reference to the perpetrator's feelings or thoughts during the incident?

Motivation-Related Contents

14. Spontaneous corrections or additions – Were corrections offered or information added?
15. Admitting lack of memory or knowledge – Did the child indicate lack of memory or knowledge of an aspect of the incident?
16. Raising doubts about one's own testimony - Did the child express concern that some part of the statement seems incorrect?
17. Self-depreciation – Did the child describe some aspect of their behavior related to the alleged offense as inappropriate?
18. Pardoning the accused – Did the child make excuses for or fail to blame the alleged perpetrator?

Source: "Statement validity assessment: Interview procedures and content analysis of children's statements of sexual abuse" by David C. Raskin and Phillip W. Esplin from *Behavioral Assessment.* Copyright © 2012 by The American Psychological Association.

as necessary (see Table 6.2). The objective with this protocol is to provide the child with lots of opportunities to report using a free narrative before other types of questioning are used.

Lindberg, Chapman, Samsock, Thomas, and Lindberg (2003) have tested the stepwise procedure, along with a procedure they developed, the modified structured interview, and a procedure developed by Action for Child Protection in West Virginia that

TABLE 6.2	The Step-Wise Interview	
Step	**Goal**	**How**
1	Rapport building	Talk to the child about neutral topics, trying to make him or her feel comfortable.
2	Recall of two nonabuse events	Have the child describe two experienced events such as a birthday party and going to the zoo.
3	Explanation of truth	Explain truth in general and have the child agree to tell the truth.
4	Introduction of critical topic	Start with open-ended questions, such as "Do you know why you are talking with me today?" Proceed to more specific questions if disclosure does not occur, such as "Who are the people you like/don't like to be with?"
5	Free-narrative	Ask the child to describe what happened using a free-narrative approach.
6	General questions	Ask questions based on what the child said, in a manner the child understands.
7	Specific questions (if necessary)	Follow up and clarify inconsistencies with more specific questions.
8	Interview aids (if necessary)	Have the child draw if he or she is not responding. Dolls may be introduced only after disclosure has occurred.
9	Conclude	Thank the child for helping and explain what will happen next.

Source: Table from "Interviewing children in sexual abuse cases" by J. C. Yuille, R. Hunter, R. Joffe, and J. Zaparniuk from *Child victims, child witnesses: Understanding and improving testimony,* Ed. Gail S. Goodman and Bette L. Bottoms. Copyright © 1993 by Guilford Publications, Inc. Reprinted with permission.

uses doll play. The three procedures are similar in terms of rapport building and the general question phases. The major difference is in terms of specific questioning. With the step-wise procedure, specific questioning occurs through progressively more focused questions and probes information obtained from the more general questions. With the modified structured interview, specific questioning occurs through the use of who, what, where, and when questions. With the Action for Child Protection procedure, specific questioning occurs through doll play.

To test these three procedures, children in grades 1 and 2 watched a video of a mother hitting her son. The children were then randomly assigned to be interviewed using one of the three procedures. The interviewers were blind to what the children witnessed on the video. Interviews were transcribed and then coded for correct and incorrect statements. The results indicated that the procedure developed by the Action for Child Protection group was less effective than the other two, and the step-wise and modified interviews produced a comparable amount of information during the free-narrative portions. The modified procedure was superior to the step-wise or the Action for Child Protection procedure for *where* questions. Overall, the step-wise procedure is consistent with what we know about children's recall abilities and how to elicit accurate information.

Narrative elaboration

An interview procedure whereby children learn to organize their story into relevant categories: participants, settings, actions, conversation/ affective states, and consequences

NARRATIVE ELABORATION Saywitz and Snyder (1996) developed an interview procedure called **narrative elaboration**. With this procedure, children learn to organize stories into relevant categories:

- Participants
- Settings
- Actions
- Conversation/affective states
- Consequences

A card containing a line drawing is available for each category (see Figure 6.1 for four of them). These visual cues help children remember to state all that they can. Children practice telling stories with each card before being questioned about the critical event. Then, they are asked for a free narrative about the critical event—for example, "What happened?" Lastly, children are presented with each card and asked, "Does this card remind you to tell something else?"

To test the narrative elaboration procedure, children in grades 1 and 2 and children in grades 4, 5, and 6 witnessed a staged event (Saywitz & Snyder, 1996). The children were then interviewed with either the narrative-elaboration procedure (involving training in the use of reminder cue cards), exposure to the cue cards without training, or a "standard" interview without training or cue cards. Children interviewed with the narrative-elaboration procedure reported more accurate information but not more inaccurate information for the staged event compared with when just the cue cards were presented without training or the standard interview. Also, children did not fabricate more information with the narrative-elaboration procedure.

Participants

Setting

Actions

Conversation/Affective State

FIGURE 6.1
Line Drawings Appearing on Card Categories

Source: Figure from "Narrative elaboration: Test of a new procedure for interviewing children" by Karen J. Saywitz and Lynn Snyder from *Journal of Consulting and Clinical Psychology.* Copyright © 1996 by The American Psychological Association.

Given the positive effects of the narrative-elaboration procedure, Brown and Pipe (2003) considered whether they could further improve the procedure if it was coupled with mental reinstatement. The recall of six- to nine-year-olds was compared when they received narrative-elaboration training, the narrative-elaboration training with mental re-instatement, or the control condition without training for narrative elaboration. Children trained with the narrative elaboration reported almost twice as much information and the information was more accurate compared to the control group. Mental reinstatement did not increase accuracy. Moreover, research has found that simply asking children to report what they saw and heard or to talk about information across categories was sufficient to produce increases in the amount of information recalled (Quas, Schaaf, Alexander, & Goodman, 2000).

NATIONAL INSTITUTE OF CHILD HEALTH AND HUMAN DEVELOPMENT (NICHD) INTERVIEW PROTOCOL After having examined a number of interviewing protocols for use with children, Dr. Michael Lamb and his colleagues at the NICHD developed an interviewing procedure that relies on open-ended questioning with two types of prompts available to interviewers (Sternberg, Lamb, Esplin, Orbach, & Hershkowitz, 2002). Interviewers can use *time* prompts to have the child fill in details and a timeline. For example, the interviewer may ask, "What happened next?" Also, interviewers can use *cue question* prompts where details that the child has reported are used in the question and children are asked to elaborate. For example, the interviewer may ask, "You said, the teacher took off his belt. Tell me more about that." This protocol also provides direction on how to start the interview and how to introduce the topic of abuse. For example, children are initially engaged to describe neutral events (e.g., the child's guitar lessons) in a nonleading manner. The topic of abuse may be introduced by asking the child why he or she has come to talk to you. A number of studies have been conducted investigating the NICHD protocol with positive results (Lamb, Hershkowitz, Orbach, & Esplin, 2008).

COGNITIVE INTERVIEW As you may recall from Chapter 5, the cognitive interview that draws on cognitive principles can be adapted and used with children (Geiselman & Padilla, 1988). A meta-analysis found that children interviewed with the cognitive interview reported more accurate information than children interviewed in control conditions (Kohnken, Milne, Memon, & Bull, 1999; also Holliday & Albon, 2004).

As you can see, a number of protocols are available to those who interview children. These protocols limit the use of direct questions and attempt to have the child provide as much information as possible using a free-recall format (Larsson & Lamb, 2009). The interview protocols being used by police vary by jurisdiction.

RECALL MEMORY FOLLOWING A LONG DELAY

Is it possible to forget a traumatic event such as abuse, only to recall it many years later? This question is at the center of a heated debate about memory repression. Some argue that childhood sexual abuse memories are so traumatic for some individuals that they re-press them in their unconscious. It is only as adults, and through the help of therapy, that they come to recall the abuse, through what are known as recovered memories. Others argue that it is only through therapy and the use of suggestive techniques that clients come to believe that they were sexually abused as children when in fact they were not;

False memory syndrome

Term to describe clients' false beliefs that they were sexually abused as children, having no memories of this abuse until they enter therapy to deal with some other psychological problem such as depression or substance abuse

such recollections are known as false memories. Loftus (her research is described in Chapter 5) is among the proponents of this second group. **False memory syndrome** was a term coined to describe a client's false belief that he or she was sexually abused as a child. Clients may have no memories of this abuse until they enter therapy to deal with some other psychological problem such as depression or substance abuse (Read, 1999). See Box 6.3 for a case involving "delayed" memory.

Can Traumatic Memories Be Forgotten?

Perhaps the greatest point of contention regarding false memory syndrome is whether traumatic memories can be completely forgotten only to be remembered many years later.

In a study by Porter and Birt (2001), university students were asked to describe their most traumatic experience and their most positive experience. A number of different experiences were reported in each condition. Approximately 5% of their sample of 306 participants reported sexual assault or abuse as their most traumatic experience. The majority of these participants stated that they had consciously forced the memory out of their minds rather than never having a memory of it. Proponents of the false memory argument contend that not having any memory of abuse is different from preferring not to think about it. When there is absolutely no memory of abuse, and it is only through the use of suggestive techniques that the abuse is remembered, many argue that these memories should be interpreted cautiously.

BOX 6.3   Delayed Memory Goes to Court

In Redwood City, California, it was 1969 and eight-year-old Susan Nason was missing. She had left her house to return some shoes to a friend. She never returned. Susan was later found murdered. Eileen Franklin was a friend of Susan's. Twenty years had passed before Eileen started having memories of Susan's murder. Eileen recalled Susan sitting on a rock in a wooded area when she saw a man crush Susan's head with a rock. She claimed that it was her father, George Franklin, who had murdered her friend. Eileen met with detectives to describe Susan's rape and murder in vivid detail. Prosecutors felt that such vivid detail was indicative of an accurate memory. But was this assumption correct? Following Eileen's revelations, George Franklin was charged with first-degree murder.

Why did it take Eileen 20 years to remember this horrific event? Eileen told her brother she was in therapy and hypnotized and while under hypnosis she saw her father killing Susan. Eileen also told her mother that these memories came back during hypnosis. Perhaps feeling that being hypnotized would discredit her story, Eileen changed her story about being hypnotized and asked her brother to corroborate this new version.

What was the evidence against George Franklin? The only evidence was the memories of Eileen. Experts for both the prosecution and defense were called. For the defense, Dr. Elizabeth Loftus testified about her research into memory. She stated that although memories may feel real and may contain rich detail, they may not be accurate. Jury deliberations began on November, 29, 1990. The next day, the jury found George Franklin guilty of first-degree murder and sentenced to life in prison. In 1995, a federal judge in San Francisco overturned George Franklin's conviction. Prosecutors decided that they did not have enough evidence to retry George Franklin for the 1969 murder and he was set free. Do you agree with this decision?

Source: http://www.time.com/printout/0,8816970268,00.html.

Lindsay and Read (1995) suggest five criteria to consider when trying to determine the veracity of a recovered memory:

1. *Age of complainant at the time of the alleged abuse.* It is unlikely that anyone would have a memory (of abuse or otherwise) prior to age two.
2. *Techniques used to recover memory.* Techniques such as hypnosis and guided imagery heighten suggestibility and encourage fantasy.
3. *Similarity of reports across interview sessions.* Do the reports become increasingly more fantastic, or are they similar?
4. *Motivation for recall.* Is the client experiencing other psychological distress and wanting an answer to explain such feelings?
5. *Time elapsed since the alleged abuse.* It may be more difficult to recall abuse that occurred 25 years ago than 2 years ago.

Although some may "recover" memories of abuse and others never truly forget this traumatic experience, the courts are seeing a number of cases where there has been a delay in reporting the abuse. See Box 6.4 for a discussion regarding the phenomenon of **historic child sexual abuse** (HCSA).

Historic child sexual abuse

Allegations of child abuse having occurred several years, often decades, prior to when they are being prosecuted

---

BOX 6.4   **Delayed Prosecutions of Historic Child Sexual Abuse**

Courts are having to deal with a relatively new phenomenon known as historic child sexual abuse (HCSA)—that is, allegations of child abuse having occurred several years, often decades, prior to the time at which they are being prosecuted (Connolly & Read, 2006). Note that the vast majority of these cases involve memories of abuse that have been continuous. The alleged victim does not claim to have ever "forgotten" the abuse. From the results of a national survey in the United States, Smith and colleagues (2000) found that 47% of adults who reported having been abused as children delayed reporting the abuse for more than five years. Even more intriguing is that approximately 27% of this sample noted that they reported the abuse for the first time on the survey. Being male seems to be a reliable predictor of delayed reporting (Finkelhor, Hotaling, Lewis, & Smith, 1990).

In a number of countries, including the United States, there is no time limit during which a victim must report the sexual abuse. Connolly and Read (2006) examined 2,064 criminal complaints of HCSA in Canada with the objective of describing these criminal prosecutions. "Historic" abuse was defined as abuse in which the last offence occurred two or more years prior to the time of trial. Connolly and Read stated that the "typical" HCSA case had the following characteristics:

The complainant is probably female. On average, she was 9 years old when the abuse began, 12 years old when it ended, and 26 years old at trial. She is unlikely to be reported to have been in therapy, and she is very likely to report continuous memory for the offence. Her abuser is more likely than not to be a male relative and he is on average 23 years older than her. On average, he was 33 years old when the abuse began, 36 years old when it ended and 51 years old at trial. In the majority of cases, the complainant reports repeated abuse that was sustained over an average period of almost 4 years. A threat is probably not reported to have accompanied the abuse, but if one is reported, it is likely to be against the complainant's or her family's physical safety. (p. 424)

Read, Connolly, and Welsh (2006) examined the factors that predicted the verdicts in actual HCSA cases between 1980 and 2002 in Canada. Four hundred and sixty-six cases were heard

(continued)

BOX 6.4   *Continued*

before a jury, of which 434 cases resulted in a guilty verdict. Six hundred and forty-four cases were heard by judge alone; of those, 442 cases resulted in a guilty verdict. In each case, the complainant was 19 years old or younger when the alleged offense began, and two or more years had elapsed from the end of the alleged offense to the trial date. Eleven independent variables were examined: (1) length of delay, (2) age of complainant at the time the alleged abuse began, (3) repressed memory testimony, (4) involvement in therapy, (5) expert testimony, (6) frequency of alleged abuse, (7) intrusiveness of alleged abuse, (8) duration of alleged abuse, (9) presence of threat, (10) complainant's gender, and (11) relationship of accused to complainant. The researchers obtained the results discussed next for jury trials and judge-alone trials.

Results for Jury Trials

In 93% of the HCSAs prosecuted before a jury, a guilty verdict was reached. Guilty verdicts were lower with older-aged complainants (mean age = 12.67) than with younger-aged complainants (mean age = 9.52 years). Fewer guilty verdicts were obtained when experts provided an opinion for one side or the other, but not when there was an expert on each side. Surprisingly, when an expert testified on behalf of the Crown (i.e., prosecution), fewer guilty verdicts were obtained than when there was no expert testifying. An expert testifying for the defense also resulted in somewhat fewer convictions than when there was no expert. When the abuse was accompanied by threats (i.e., physical and/or emotional), guilty verdicts were more likely than when there were no threats. Also, guilty verdicts were higher for defendants who had a familial relationship with the complainant rather than a community connection to the complainant. Other independent variables did not differ significantly in their influence on the verdict.

Results for Judge-Alone Trials

In approximately 69% of the HCSAs prosecuted before a judge alone, a guilty verdict was reached. The increase in likelihood of acquittal corresponded with the increase in length of delay. The average delay period was 14.98 years for acquittals compared to an average delay of 12.36 years for guilty verdicts. Guilty verdicts were more likely when a claim of repression was made than when no repression claim was made by the complainant. Guilty verdicts were more likely with more intrusive sexual abuse than with less intrusive sexual abuse, such as sexual exposure or sexual touching. Judges were more likely to reach a guilty verdict when the defendant was a family member rather than someone in the community. When the defense had an unchallenged expert testify, guilty verdicts were less likely than if no expert testified.

RECALL FOR PEOPLE

Not only must children report the events that happened, it is likely they will have to describe the culprit, especially if he or she is a stranger. Culprit descriptions—also known as recall for people—by child witnesses have been examined in only a few studies relative to the number of studies that have examined recall for an event.

Describing the Culprit

In one study, Davies, Tarrant, and Flin (1989) asked for descriptions of a stranger from younger (ages 6 to 7) and older (age 10 to 11) children. The younger children recalled fewer items (M = 1 descriptor) than the older children (M = 2.21 descriptors). The researchers also found that older children recalled more interior facial features, such as freckles and nose shape, than younger children. Hair was the most frequently mentioned feature by both younger and older children.

The exterior feature of hair seems to be a dominant descriptor focused on by both children and adults (Ellis, Shepherd, & Davies, 1980; Sporer, 1996). Pozzulo and Warren (2003) found that exterior facial descriptors such as hair color and style were predominant and accurately reported by 10- to 14-year-olds and adults. Moreover, interior facial features were problematic for both youths and adults.

Height, weight, and age are descriptors commonly reported, and if they are not reported, police may ask about them directly. Unfortunately, children and youth may have considerable difficulty with their estimates of such characteristics. Davies, Stevenson-Robb, and Flin (1988) found that children/youths (ages 7 to 12 years) were inaccurate when asked to report the height, weight, and age of an unfamiliar visitor. Pozzulo and Warren (2003) found that accuracy for body descriptors such as height and weight were consistently problematic for youth. One possible explanation for this result is that children and youths may not understand the relation between height and weight—that is, taller people are heavier than shorter people of similar girth. Alternatively, children and youths simply may lack experience with height and weight. It is only in later adolescence that people become body conscious and more familiar with weight (and height proportions).

Leichtman and Ceci (1995) examined the effect of stereotypes and suggestions on preschoolers' reports. Children between the ages of three and six years were assigned to one of four groups:

- Control—no interviews contained suggestive questions.
- Stereotype—children were given expectations about a stranger who visited the class.
- Suggestion—children were given misinformation about acts committed by the stranger.
- Stereotype and suggestion—children were given expectations plus misinformation about the stranger.

Children witnessed a stranger by the name of Sam Stone visit their classroom. Sam was present for a story that was read by the teacher. All children were interviewed repeatedly after the event in one of the four conditions described above. For example, in the stereotype condition children were told that Sam was kind and well meaning but very clumsy and bumbling. In the suggestion condition, children were misled that Sam ripped a book and soiled a teddy bear during his classroom visit. So, which group was most accurate?

Using open-ended interviews, children were most accurate in the control condition and least accurate in the stereotype plus suggestion condition. Children in the stereotype condition produced a fair number of false reports. Children in the suggestion condition produced a great number of false reports. Overall, the older children were more accurate than the younger children.

In a follow-up study, Memon, Holliday, and Hill (2006) provided youngsters ages five to six years with picture books of a man called Jim Step who either paints his house, bakes a cake, or goes to the zoo. There were three versions of each story;

Jim was portrayed as a clumsy person (negative stereotype).

Jim was portrayed as a careful person (positive stereotype).

Jim was portrayed neutrally (no stereotype provided).

All children received post-storybook information that was consistent with the stereotype and inconsistent with the stereotype of Jim's character in the storybook.

The data revealed that children were more likely to accept positive, inaccurate information than negative, inaccurate information. Thus, negative information was more likely to be rejected and positive information was more likely to be accepted.

These studies illustrate that it is important for interviewers not to introduce their own biases or inaccurate information when interviewing children. Once again, the argument can be made that children should be asked to describe the culprit in terms of what he or she did and looked like using a free narrative. Given the few descriptors children provide, it may be important to probe this information for detail. Some of the techniques described above for event recall may be helpful with person recall. More research is needed on how to elicit person descriptions from children (as well as adults).

RECOGNITION

One other task a child victim or witness may be called on to perform is an identification of the culprit from a lineup. In a meta-analysis comparing children's identification abilities to adults', Pozzulo and Lindsay (1998) found that children over age five produced correct identification rates comparable to those of adults, provided the culprit was present in the lineup (target-present lineup). However, when the culprit was not in the lineup (target-absent lineup), children as old as age 14 produced greater false positives than adults. That is, children were more likely to select an innocent person from a lineup than were adults (see Chapter 5 for a review of general lineup identification issues).

Lineup Procedure and Identification Rates

Pozzulo and Lindsay (1998) examined whether identification rates differed between children and adults as a function of the lineup procedure used. As you may recall from Chapter 5, the sequential lineup has been demonstrated to decrease false-positive responding compared with simultaneous presentation for adults (Lindsay & Wells, 1985), although recently there has been some debate on the sequential superiority effect (McQuiston-Surrett, Malpass, & Tredoux, 2006). Nonetheless, we can examine whether the use of the sequential lineup with children decreases their false-positive responding. Pozzulo and Lindsay found that with sequential lineup presentation, the gap for false-positive responding between children and adults *increased*. Thus, the sequential lineup increased false-positive responding with child witnesses, whereas for adults the sequential lineup decreased false-positive responding.

AN IDENTIFICATION PROCEDURE FOR CHILDREN   In an attempt to develop an identification procedure that decreases children's false-positive responding, Pozzulo and Lindsay (1999) proposed a two-judgment theory of identification accuracy. The researchers postulated that to reach an accurate identification decision, witnesses conduct two judgments: relative and absolute. First, witnesses compare across lineup members and choose the most similar-looking lineup member to the culprit, a relative judgment. Second, witnesses compare the most-similar lineup member to their memory of the culprit and decide if it is in fact the culprit, an absolute judgment. Pozzulo and Lindsay speculated that children often fail to make an absolute judgment and thereby produce a greater number of false positives than adults.

The researchers explain how the failure to make an absolute judgment would result in more false positives. They argue that with target-present lineups, a relative judgment is sufficient to lead to a correct identification because it is likely that the culprit looks most like himself or herself compared with the other lineup members. Thus, the culprit is selected. In contrast, with target-absent lineups, solely relying on a relative judgment may lead to an identification of an innocent person because the most similar-looking lineup member is not the culprit—recall that with a target-absent lineup the culprit is not there. An absolute judgment is necessary with target-absent lineups. If children fail to conduct an absolute judgment, a greater false-positive rate may result.

Based on these notions, Pozzulo and Lindsay (1999) developed an identification procedure known as the **elimination lineup** for children that is consistent with the two-judgment theory of identification accuracy. The elimination lineup procedure requests two judgments from the child:

1. All lineup photos are presented to the child, and the child is asked to select the lineup member who looks most like the culprit (relative judgment). Once this decision is made, the remaining photos are removed.
2. The child is asked to compare his or her memory of the culprit with the most similar photo selected in the first stage and decide if the photo is of the culprit (absolute judgment).

Pozzulo and Lindsay (1999) tested variations of this procedure and the "standard" simultaneous procedure with children and adults. The elimination procedure was found to significantly decrease children's false-positive responding with target-absent lineups compared with the simultaneous procedure. In other words, children's correct rejection rate increased using the elimination procedure compared with the simultaneous procedure. Moreover, children's false-positive rate with the elimination procedure was similar to that of adults when the simultaneous procedure was used.

The elimination procedure continues to be tested with different-aged children and adults while varying the conditions under which an identification needs to be made in order to determine its robustness and viability for use in "real life" (e.g., Dempsey & Pozzulo, 2008; Pozzulo & Balfour, 2006; Pozzulo et al., 2008; Pozzulo, Dempsey, & Crescini, 2009). For example, in a study by Pozzulo and Balfour (2006), children ages 8 to 13 were tested along with adults when a culprit underwent a change in appearance following the commission of a theft. Simultaneous and elimination lineup procedures were examined under conditions when the culprit was or was not present in the lineup. The researchers found that correct identification rates decreased following a change in appearance regardless of age of witness and lineup procedure used. In terms of correct-rejection rates, children had an overall lower correct-rejection rate compared to adults. The elimination procedure compared with the simultaneous procedure was more effective at increasing correct rejections when there was no change in appearance from the time the crime was committed and a lineup was viewed. When a change occurred, however, correct-rejection rates were similar across the two identification procedures for both children and adults.

TESTIFYING IN COURT

Numerous countries including the United States have evidentiary rules where children must undergo a **competency hearing** before testifying. The notion behind the competency hearing is that children would demonstrate that they can communicate what they

Elimination lineup

Lineup procedure for children that first asks them to pick out the person who looks most like the culprit from the photos displayed. Next, children are asked if the most similar person selected is in fact the culprit

Competency hearing

Questions posed to child witnesses under age 14 to determine whether they are able to communicate the evidence and understand the difference between the truth and a lie, and in the circumstances of testifying, feel compelled to tell the truth witnessed or experienced. Also, it was felt that it is critical for children to understand the difference between saying the truth and lying and to feel compelled to tell the truth. It could be argued that the competency hearing was historically entrenched in the negative views of child witnesses discussed earlier in this chapter.

As stated in Shanks (2010), "Statues and case law from various states mandate that the following elements must be taken into consideration when deciding whether the child is competent to testify:

1. present understanding or intelligence to understand and an obligation to speak the truth
2. mental capacity at the time of the occurrence in question to observe and register the occurrence
3. memory sufficient to retain an independent recollection of the observations made
4. ability to translate into words the memory of those observations
5. ability to understand and respond to simple questions of the occurrence (Nestle, 2008)" (p. 11).

Each trial court develops its own manner of determination of competency. Not all of the elements above may be investigated. Some general questions may include the following:

- What grade are you in?
- What is your teacher's name?
- How many siblings do you have?

Children also may be questioned regarding their ability to distinguish between the truth and a lie, and must demonstrate an understanding of the meaning of oath. Common themes for questioning in this section include:

- Defining terms
- Religion and church
- Consequences of lying

In addition, some judges may hold up a black pen and ask the child what color it is. Then, they will ask the child if the pen is red. If the child correctly responds, judges then ask if they would call it a red pen whether that is the truth or a lie.

Legal scholars as well as social science researchers have identified several problems with these inquiries at actually establishing what they are intended to do (e.g., Shanks, 2010), however these inquiries continue.

Courtroom Accommodations

Child witnesses may experience extreme stress and trauma by having to testify in court while facing the defendant (Goodman et al., 1992). Alternatives are available for child witnesses and victims who need to testify. Alternatives vary by jurisdiction (National District Attorneys Office, 2009). Below are a list of possible alternatives:

1. A shield/screen to separate the child and defendant so that the child does not see the defendant's face. However, the child is visible to the defendant and the rest of the courtroom and may be able to see the defendant's feet.
2. The child is allowed to provide testimony via a closed-circuit television monitor. The child and lawyers are in a separate room from the courtroom and the child's

testimony is televised to the courtroom where the defendant, judge, and jury are present. The defendant can be in touch with his or her lawyer by telephone.

3. The child may have a support person with him or her while providing testimony. The child can decide whom he or she wants, although a person who is a witness in the same case cannot be a support person unless he or she has already provided testimony.

4. A child may be video-recorded while being interviewed about the details of the crime. The video may be admitted into evidence, so that the child does not have to repeat the details in court.

5. Generally, previous statements made by a witness are considered hearsay and not admissible. However, statements made by the child during the initial disclosure of the abuse may be allowed as evidence. For example, a mother may testify about what her child said when disclosing the abuse.

6. The judge may close the courtroom to the public and/or media to protect the privacy of the child. A publication ban prohibiting any information that would identify the complainant or any witness also may be granted to protect the child's identity.

CHILD MALTREATMENT

So far, we have highlighted sexual abuse against children; however, there are other forms of maltreatment that a child may experience. Other forms of maltreatment require the same considerations as sexual abuse. Generally, there are four categories of child maltreatment:

1. **Physical abuse** is the deliberate application of force to any part of a child's body that results or may result in a nonaccidental injury. Examples include shaking, choking, biting, kicking, burning, and poisoning.

2. **Sexual abuse** occurs when an adult or youth uses a child for sexual purposes. Examples include fondling, intercourse, incest, sodomy, exhibitionism, and exploitation through prostitution or the production of pornographic materials.

3. **Neglect/failure to provide** occurs when a child's caregivers do not provide the requisite attention to the child's emotional, psychological, or physical development. Examples include failure to supervise or protect leading to physical harm (such as drunk driving with a child), failure to provide adequate nutrition or clothing, failure to provide medical treatment, and exposing the child to unhygienic or dangerous living conditions. See Box 6.5 for a case of a mother forgetting her child in a hot car and how the court ruled on the case.

4. **Emotional maltreatment** includes acts or omissions by caregivers that cause or could cause serious behavioral, cognitive, emotional, or mental disorders. Examples are verbal threats, socially isolating a child, intimidation, exploitation, terrorizing, or routinely making unreasonable demands on a child.

It is likely that children experience multiple forms of maltreatment simultaneously. For example, it is hard to imagine that a child who is neglected is not also emotionally abused.

Government agencies have the authority and responsibility to remove children from their caregivers when the child is maltreated or at risk for maltreatment. Also, a child may be removed if caregivers are unwilling or unable to prevent abuse by a third

Physical abuse

The deliberate application of force to any part of a child's body that results in or may result in a nonaccidental injury

Sexual abuse

When an adult or youth uses a child for sexual purposes

Neglect/failure to provide

When a child's caregivers do not provide the requisite attention to the child's emotional, psychological, or physical development

Emotional maltreatment

Acts or omissions by caregivers that cause or could cause serious behavioral, cognitive, emotional, or mental disorders

BOX 6.5   A Case of Neglect or Forgetfulness?

On May 18, 2007, Haley Wesley's morning routine took a bit of a turn when she had to drop off a poster (Haley is a graphic artist) to a client before dropping her daughter, Maddison, off at day care and headed to work. Because the client's office was a bit away, Haley decided to drive her husband's car, which was more gas efficient than her truck. At about 9:00 a.m., she parked the car at Pacific Union College and headed to her desk. Around 3:30 she headed back to the car. Her plan was to drive home, tidy up a bit, and then go pick up Maddison. When she got home she went to pick something up from the passenger's side of the car, only to see her 10-month-old daughter in her car seat. It took about a second for Haley to realize that the only reason her daughter was in her car seat was because she forgot to drop her off in the morning—911 was quickly called, but Maddison was dead as a result of heatstroke and dehydration.

Three months later, Napa Country District Attorney Gary Lieberstein charged Haley with felony involuntary manslaughter. In a deal with prosecutors, Haley pleaded guilty to child endangerment and was sentenced to three years of probation and 120 hours of community service. As part of her community service, Haley spoke to parent groups about her experience. Currently, Haley is advocating that baby car seats be equipped with sensors to detect weight so that an alarm goes off if the driver gets out and forgets something (someone) in the baby seat.

According to the National Highway Traffic Safety Administration, during warm weather, a 78-degree temperature in a locked car can reach 100 degrees in approximately three minutes and can reach 125 degrees in about six to eight minutes. General Motors commissioned a study in 2001 to determine the number of children who had died of hyperthermia—that is, severe heatstroke or heat exhaustion (as cited in Picard, 2003). One hundred and twenty children were reported to have died from being left in hot, parked cars since 1996. Of course, not all cases are a result of forgetfulness.

Source: Picard, 2003; retrieved from: http://napavalleyregister.com/news/local/article_e21b1f5b-5a85-53d9-b150-82a8958e83fd.html. http://articles.sfgate.com/2008-03-28/bay-area/17167967_1_involuntary-manslaughter-sentenced-tragedy

party. For example, children may be removed from their caregivers' custody because of neglect, physical and sexual abuse, alcohol or other drug use, and mental illness. It is important to recognize that for children to be apprehended from Child Protective Services, these factors must have negative effects on parenting to the extent that the caregiver cannot adequately parent. The term **in need of protection** is used to describe a child's need to be separated from his or his caregiver due to maltreatment.

All 50 states, the District of Columbia, and the U.S. territories have mandatory child abuse and neglect reporting laws that require certain professionals and institutions to report cases of suspected child maltreatment to a child protective services (CPS) agency. Professionals who have a duty to report include health care providers and institutions, mental health care providers, teachers, school staff, social workers, police officers, foster care providers, and day care providers. Approximately a third of all cases reported to CPS are screened "out" and do not undergo further investigation. The remaining cases are screened "in" and undergo investigation by the CPS agency to assess whether maltreatment has been experienced or whether the child is at risk of maltreatment. Family members, the child, and other members who know the child and family may be interviewed and/or assessed. The CPS agency then makes a determination, called a disposition. Each state has its own definitions of child abuse and neglect based on minimum

In need of protection

A term used to describe a child's need to be separated from his or her caregiver due to maltreatment

standards set by federal law. The Child Abuse Prevention and Treatment Act (CAPTA; 42 U.S.C.A., 5106), as amended by the Keeping Children and Families Safe Act of 2003, defines child abuse and neglect as:

> Any recent act or failure to act on the part of a parent or caretaker which results in death, serious physical or emotional harm, sexual abuse or exploitation; or
>
> An act or failure to act which presents an imminent risk of serious harm.

The National Child Abuse and Neglect Data System (NCANDS) compiles and publishes statistics from state child protection agencies.

During 2008, approximately 3.3 million referrals were made that involved approximately 6 million children. Almost 63% were screened in, involving nearly 3.7 million children. Of these cases:

- 23.7% found at least one child to be a victim of abuse or neglect with the following dispositions: 22.3% substantiated, 0.9% indicated, and 0.5% alternative response victim
- 76.3% of the investigations found that the child was not a victim of maltreatment with the following dispositions: 64.7% unsubstantiated, 7.7% alternative response nonvictim, 1.7% "other," 1.9% closed with no finding, 0% intentionally false, and 0.1% unknown

The professionals most often reporting on suspected cases of child maltreatment were teachers (16.9%), law enforcement personnel (16.3%), and social services staff (10.6%).

The most common age group for victimization was children from birth to one year old with a rate of victimization of 21.7 per 1,000 children of the same age group in the national population. Slightly more than half the victims were female at 51.3%. Approximately 45% of victims were white, 20.8% were Hispanic, and 16.6% were African American.

Approximately 1,730 children died due to child abuse or neglect in 2008.

RISK FACTORS ASSOCIATED WITH CHILD MALTREATMENT

A number of risk factors—factors that are associated with an increased likelihood of abuse—have been identified for physical and sexual abuse. These can be categorized as child factors, parental factors, and social factors (see Table 6.3).

The risk factors for physical and sexual abuse differ. Physical abuse risk factors are varied and include a parent's past childhood physical abuse as well as the parent's attitude toward pregnancy. In contrast, sexual abuse risk factors tend to revolve around family composition.

Short-Term and Long-Term Effects of Physical Abuse

A number of short-term effects of physical abuse have been determined. These include greater perceptual-motor deficits, lower measured intellectual functioning, lower academic achievement, externalizing behavior such as aggression, and internalizing mental health difficulties such as hopelessness and depression (Ammerman, Cassisi, Hersen, & Van Hasselt, 1986; Conaway & Hansen, 1989; Lamphear, 1985).

TABLE 6.3	Risk Factors for Abuse	
	Type of Abuse	
	Physical Abuse	*Sexual Abuse*
Child Factors		
	Male sex	Female sex
Parental Factors		
	Young maternal age	Living in a family without a biological parent
	Single-parent status	Poor relationship between parents
	History of childhood physical abuse	Presence of a stepfather
	Spousal assault	Poor child–parent relations
	Unplanned pregnancy or negative attitude toward pregnancy	
	History of substance abuse	
	Social isolation or lack of social support	
Social Factors		
	Low socioeconomic status	
	Large family size	

Source: Table from "Child maltreatment: What we know in the year 2000" by Harriet L. MacMillan from *Canadian Journal of Psychiatry.* Copyright ©2000 by the Canadian Psychiatric Association. Reprinted with permission.

In a review of studies examining the long-term effects of physical abuse, Malinosky-Rummell and Hansen (1993) report strong relations between physical abuse and nonfamilial and familial violence. Physically abused persons, especially males, engage in more nonfamilial violence than nonabused persons. In terms of familial violence, about 30% of physically abused or neglected persons abuse their own children (Kaufman & Zigler, 1987; Widom, 1989a). Moreover, being abused as a child predicted inflicting and receiving dating violence in a sample of university students. Also, spouses who were abusive reported higher rates of physical abuse than nonabusive spouses. Thus, experiencing physical abuse appears to increase the likelihood of perpetrating physical abuse.

Short-Term and Long-Term Effects of Sexual Abuse

Kendall-Tackett, Williams, and Finkelhor (1993) examined 45 studies that considered the short-term effects of childhood sexual abuse. Common effects across the studies were behavior problems, lowered self-esteem, inappropriate sexuality, and symptoms consistent with post-traumatic stress disorder. Research has found that within two years of being abused, children report a number of physical difficulties such as sleep disturbance, eating disorders, stomach problems, and headaches (Adams-Tucker, 1982).

Putnam (2003) identified three categories of outcomes in adults with a history of childhood sexual abuse: (1) psychiatric disorders, (2) dysfunctional behaviors, and (3) neurobiological deregulation.

Under psychiatric disorders, major depression in adulthood has been found to be strongly related to sexual abuse in childhood (Paolucci, Genuis, & Violato, 2001). Sexualized behavior is one of the most closely related dysfunctional behaviors with those who have a history of childhood sexual abuse (Widom & Ames, 1994). In terms of neurobiological deregulation, magnetic resonance imaging (MRI) studies have found reduced hippocampal volume in adults who experienced sexual abuse as children, similar to that found in war veterans experiencing post-traumatic stress disorder (Stein, Koverola, Hanna, Torchia, & McClarry, 1997). Messman-Moore and Long (2003) reported that adults who were sexually abused as children have an increased risk of being sexually abused as adults. Other long-term risks for sexually abused children include depression, self-injurious behaviors, anxiety, and interpersonal distrust (Browne & Finkelhor, 1986).

In a retrospective study conducted from 1995 to 1997, more than 17,000 community members in California were surveyed (Dube et al., 2005). Participants were asked about abuse and dysfunction during childhood and other health-related issues. Childhood sexual abuse was reported by 16% of the male and 25% of the female respondents. If a person suffered childhood sexual abuse, it was found that there would be an increase in the risk of various outcomes. For example, suicide attempts were twice as likely among both men and women who had reported experiencing childhood sexual abuse compared to those who had not reported experiencing it. Also, there was an increased risk of alcohol problems, illicit drug use, and family problems when respondents had experienced childhood sexual abuse.

A recent survey in the United States found that roughly one in five young people is solicited for sex over the Internet or via social media each year (Mitchell, Finkelhor, & Wolak, 2001; see also Box 6.6). It is illegal to sexually exploit children via the Internet and there cannot be more than 4 years difference between children/youths engaging in intimate acts when a child is under age 15. Currently, the notion of "sexting," that is, sending sexually explicit text messages and photos, is undergoing legislative review. Recent cases have found young teens engaging in sexting and being prosecuted. In Greensboro, Pennsylvania, six teens were charged with child pornography when three girls sent sexually explicit photos to male classmates. Also, in Cincinnati, Ohio, an 18-year-old committed suicide after sending a naked picture of herself to someone who then forwarded it to her classmates. See the In the Media box to learn more about the media's involvement in battling online luring.

A CAVEAT TO THE OUTCOMES OF CHILD MALTREATMENT Although child maltreatment is always horrific, it is important to note that not all children who experience maltreatment will have negative outcomes. Just as some children who have experienced maltreatment will experience negative short-term and/or long-term effects, some children who have experienced maltreatment will not experience negative outcomes. Moreover, some children who have *not* experienced maltreatment will experience negative effects (and of course, some children who have not experienced maltreatment will not experience negative effects). A number of factors may increase or protect against negative outcomes (see Chapter 12 for a greater discussion on risk and protective factors for children and youth). Thus, it is important to keep in mind that no one factor in childhood can predict outcomes in adulthood with absolute accuracy.

BOX 6.6　Luring Children over the Internet

Advances in computer technology have provided a host of benefits to computer users. Unfortunately, however, this technology can be abused. With the internet, sexual predators have access to countless children while remaining anonymous, until they decide to meet the child. The child may assume he or she is meeting another child, but the Internet stranger may be a sexual predator. Some predators do not conceal their true age, however, as was the case with Timothy Robert Shea.

Mr. Shea was a 32-year-old cell phone salesman from Arvada, Colorado. A woman and her 13-year-old daughter went to buy a cell phone. Mr. Shea was their salesman. After the woman bought a cell phone, the 13-year-old mentioned a problem with her cell phone. Shea offered to send her a "test" text message to help fix the problem. Shortly thereafter, Mr. Shea sent the 13-year-old sexually suggestive messages. The teen told her mother who quickly contacted the police.

While under investigation, Mr. Shea had an online discussion with an undercover officer who pretended to be a teen. Allegedly Mr. Shea suggested meeting this underage teen for sexual purposes. Mr. Shea was arrested when he went to meet the underage teen. He was charged with Internet luring.

Source: Based on "Arvada cell phone salesman arrested over text messages teen reports messages to mother who contacts DA investigators" from TheDenverChannel.com, 2009.

IN THE MEDIA　To Catch a Predator

You may have heard of the show *To Catch a Predator*. *Dateline NBC*, a television show based in the United States, got into the business of crime busting with its series *To Catch a Predator*. It is estimated that one in four children are invited to meet for a sexual encounter. On this reality show, tables get turned on men who attempt to lure a child for a sexual encounter. Adult men chat online with youngsters, so they believe, and eventually, these men arrange to meet the child for a sexual encounter. The child, however, is an "operative"; an adult trained to pretend to be a child while "chatting" online. A predator has to use sexually explicit chat and be clear about his intent to meet for a sexual encounter with the underage child. When the male arrives at a prearranged location, he is met with a camera crew and is confronted by the host of the show. These men are shown on-air and the police may be contacted. The men's names and faces are shown to the viewing audience.

What happens when the predator is part of the criminal justice system? Louis Conradt, a 56-year-old Texas prosecutor, reportedly shot himself when police officers tried to arrest him for allegedly attempting to solicit a minor online. The cast and crew of *To Catch a Predator* were waiting outside to film the arrest in 2006. Allegedly Mr. Conradt attempted to set up a sexual encounter with a 13-year-old boy but failed to show up at the decoy house. A lawsuit against NBC was brought by Mr. Conradt's sister alleging that Mr. Conradt's civil rights were violated and the show intentionally inflicted emotional distress. Was NBC irresponsible? Should they be allowed to film these interactions? Should these men's faces be shown? Ms. Conradt sued for $100 million compensatory and punitive damages. The case was settled out of court. *Dateline NBC* has since decided to stop producing the *To Catch a Predator* shows.

Source: http://latimesblogs.latimes.com/showtracker/2008/06/nbc-resolves-la.html.

Summary

1. The accuracy of children's reporting is highly dependent on how they are asked to report. Requesting children to provide a free narrative provides recall from children as accurate as that of adults. A number of procedures and protocols to increase children's accurate reporting have been investigated (e.g., narrative elaboration). Leading questions and the use of anatomically correct dolls are problematic for accurate reporting.

2. Children report few person descriptors when asked to describe a stranger or culprit. Interior facial items such as freckles and nose shape are more likely to be reported by older children than younger children. However, accurately reporting these features is difficult. The exterior feature of hair is frequently mentioned by both children and adults. Height, weight, and age are unlikely to be reported accurately by children and youth.

3. Children produce correct identification rates that are comparable to those of adults when presented with a target-present lineup. However, children are more likely than adults to select an innocent person with a target-absent lineup. The elimination lineup procedure decreases children's false-positive responding compared with a simultaneous lineup procedure.

4. Prior to providing testimony, children undergo a competency hearing to assess their ability to recall details of the event under question and their ability to distinguish between the truth and a lie. A number of alternatives (e.g., screens, prerecorded interviews, and access to a support person) to in-court testimony are available for child witnesses.

5. Maltreatment can be categorized as sexual abuse, physical abuse, neglect/failure to provide, and emotional maltreatment. A number of short-term and long-term effects of physical abuse can result, for example, perceptual-motor deficits, lower measured intellectual functioning, lower academic achievement, externalizing behavior, internalizing mental health difficulties, and nonfamilial and familial violence. A number of short-term and long-term effects of sexual abuse can result, for example, behavior problems, lowered self-esteem, inappropriate sexuality, physical symptoms consistent with post-traumatic stress disorder, and being abused as an adult.

Key Concepts

anatomically detailed dolls *143*

competency hearing *155*

criterion-based content analysis *145*

elimination lineup *155*

emotional maltreatment *157*

fabricating *140*

false memory syndrome *150*

historic child sexual abuse *151*

in need of protection *158*

narrative elaboration *148*

neglect/failure to provide *157*

physical abuse *157*

sexual abuse *157*

statement validity analysis *145*

step-wise interview *145*

Discussion Questions

1. In your local community newspaper, you read of a seven-year-old boy who has been physically abused and then left abandoned. You wonder what difficulties this boy may experience in the next couple of years and when he becomes an adult. Describe the possible short-term and long-term effects of physical abuse.

2. Why is the use of anatomically correct dolls a controversial tool when assessing child sexual abuse?

3. After completing an undergraduate course in forensic psychology, you are interested in teaching your colleagues in the police department the best interview techniques to use with child witnesses. You decide to develop a mini-workshop on good and bad interview techniques. Put together a curriculum for your workshop.

4. An eight-year-old girl has witnessed the abduction of her best friend by an adult male. What factors will likely influence this child's ability to describe the kidnapper and what procedures should the police use when conducting a lineup with this child witness?

7

Juries: Fact Finders

LEARNING OBJECTIVES

- Differentiate between grand and petit juries.

- Describe jury selection.

- Distinguish between representativeness and impartiality.

- Describe the effects of pretrial publicity and the available options for dealing with it.

- Outline the stages to reaching a jury verdict.

- Describe the categories of variables that have been examined to predict the verdict.

Kathy Kramer was juror No. 10. She along with 11 others were seated in the jury box to listen to the evidence of how the defendant, Melissa Vincent, brutally murdered her roommate in a fit of rage when she found out her boyfriend and her roommate had had sex. Melissa wasn't your "typical" defendant; she was 21 years old and on an exchange program in Australia completing her undergraduate degree in psychology when the crime occurred. She came from a wealthy family with her parents both being surgeons. The prosecution argued that Melissa left the school library early one night and as she was walking to her apartment complex she saw her boyfriend, Mark Carson, leaving the building. Melissa is alleged to have confronted her roommate, Marcy Metcalfe, and when she learned that they were having a relationship behind her back, she became enraged, grabbed a kitchen knife and stabbed her roommate, leaving her dead. There is a phone record that shows Melissa calling Mark around the time the victim died. Melissa claimed she was just leaving the library then and asked Mark to meet her at the apartment. Melissa arrived after Mark was at the apartment and it was Mark who called the police to report the murder. Mark admits to the relationship with Marcy. He also claims Melissa was extremely jealous of the friendship he had with Marcy. Melissa argued that the apartment complex was located in a "rough" part of town with drug dealers and prostitutes all around. It was not uncommon to hear that apartments had been broken into for money or drugs. The murder weapon was never recovered. No one could verify what time Melissa left the library. Mark also did not have an alibi. What would your verdict be in this case? What factors are influencing your verdict?

I n the United States, the courts deal with both civil and criminal cases. State law pertaining to criminal issues can vary considerably (across states). Although we are not able to discuss each state separately, much of the material presented is common across states.

In this chapter, we will focus on the jury-selection process, how jury research is conducted, and how well we can predict verdicts. The information we provide in this chapter will focus on criminal trials exclusively unless otherwise stated.

GETTING TO TRIAL

Any citizen can file a criminal complaint. This complaint is then sent to the prosecutor's office in the county where the alleged crime occurred to assess whether the complaint should be presented to a "grand jury." A defendant may choose to waive this hearing and go directly to trial with a jury.

Grand Jury

The notion behind a grand jury is to determine whether there is sufficient evidence that a crime occurred and that the accused committed that crime. Note that the grand jury is *not* responsible for reaching a verdict for the defendant (this is the responsibility of the petit jury or trial jury discussed below); instead, the goal of the grand jury is to screen out bogus charges. The prosecution presents its evidence against the defendant and if the grand jury determines there is sufficient evidence to move forward then the case goes before a petit jury.

Following the presentation of the charge, the grand jury hears testimony and reviews the evidence against the defendant. Typically, the defendant and witnesses for the defense do not testify given that the purpose of the grand jury is to determine whether the prosecution has sufficient evidence against the accused. Grand jury hearings are not public so that witnesses may speak freely and in the event the case does not move forward the defendant will not be stigmatized. The grand jury can reach a "no bill," which means there is no indictment (i.e., formal charge) and the case does not move forward to a petit jury. Alternatively, the grand jury can reach a "true bill," which is an indictment. Each charge in an indictment is called a count. The defendant will have an arraignment (i.e., a hearing) where the judge will ask the defendant to enter a plea of "guilty" or "not guilty." A "not guilty" plea will result in a trial. Before the trial, an arraignment will be held in which the prosecution provides the defense with a list of all the witnesses it expects to call and the evidence it has against the defendant. Grand juries have 23 members (sometimes fewer and sometimes a few more depending on jurisdiction, charges, etc.) who deliberate. Grand juries do not need to reach a unanimous verdict.

Petit Jury

The petit jury is also known as the trial jury and it may have 12 members who deliberate; however, the number of jurors can vary between 6 and 12 depending on jurisdiction and charges and/or penalties. The petit jury will listen to the evidence and decide whether the defendant is guilty or not guilty. Petit juries hear civil cases, in addition to criminal cases. Petit juries typically are required to reach unanimous verdicts; however, this too may vary such that a majority verdict may be allowed.

JURY SELECTION

Jury Act

Outlines criteria for being a juror and the rules for jury selection

WHO CAN SERVE ON A JURY?   The Jury Selection and Service Act of 1968, also known as the **Jury Act**, outlines the criteria for being a juror and the rules for jury selection. An individual must be a U.S. citizen, at least 18 years old, and live in the county where the trial is being held. Jurors also must be able to read and understand English and be mentally and physically able to be a juror. You cannot be a juror if you have been convicted of an indictable offense.

Jury summons

A court order that states a time and place for jury duty

HOW IS A JURY SELECTED?   Random community members receive a questionnaire to assess their suitability for sitting on a jury. The court reviews the questionnaires and individuals are selected at random to receive a **jury summons**—that is, a court order that states a time and place for jury duty. Receiving a jury summons does not guarantee that you will be a juror, though. It simply means that you are expected to show up, typically at the courthouse, prepared to be a juror. If you ignore a summons and do not show up, you may incur a severe legal penalty such as a fine or jail time.

Voir dire

The question period when selecting people to serve on the jury

Typically, criminal trials will sit a 12-person jury with 2 alternate jurors. In the event someone from the jury cannot continue until a verdict is reached, this juror will be replaced with an alternate. Note, that once a jury starts the deliberation process no alternates will be used. If you are selected from the juror pool, you will be a juror unless one of the lawyers presents a challenge. Potential jurors from the jury pool are called up to the trial bench and may be asked questions by the prosecution, defense lawyer, or judge. This question period is known as the *voir dire* (the question period when selecting people to serve on the jury). During the *voir dire*, either the prosecution or defense (or the judge) may dismiss or reject a juror by using a "challenge." The *voir dire* starts with a brief statement about the case. The objective is to let the jurors know what the case is about and to identify the people involved, including the lawyers. The potential jurors are asked questions to determine any personal biases or if there is any relationship with those involved in the case.

Generally, lawyers can use two types of challenges to reject a potential juror: (1) peremptory challenges and (2) challenges for cause.

Both the prosecution and defense are allowed a limited number of peremptory challenges. The number of peremptory challenges allowed varies across state. In California, for example, where certain crimes can carry the death penalty, each side has 20 peremptory challenges. For other criminal cases, each side will have 10 peremptory challenges unless the punishment is less than 90 days in prison, in which case each side will have 6 peremptory challenges. Peremptory challenges can be used to reject jurors who are perceived to be unfavorable to the desired verdict. When using a peremptory challenge, the lawyer does not need to provide a reason for rejecting the prospective juror.

In contrast, when using a challenge for cause, the lawyer must give a reason for rejecting the prospective juror. We will discuss challenge for cause later in this chapter. Although a prospective juror may be challenged and not able to sit for one trial, he or she may be selected for another trial.

Predicting Who Will Be a Favorable Juror—Pro-Prosecution versus Pro-Defense

In a study examining lawyers' ability to select jurors favorable to their position, Olczak, Kaplan, and Penrod (1991) provided lawyers with the facts of a case and the demographic information for 36 potential jurors. The lawyers were asked to assume the role of the defense attorney in the case and to select 12 jurors who they would want on the jury and 12 jurors that they would want to reject. The results indicated that the lawyers were *not* very good at selecting favorable jurors. The lawyers were more likely to make erroneous decisions than accurate decisions; that is, they discarded jurors who found the defendant not guilty and selected jurors who found the defendant guilty. Thus, lawyer judgment may be insufficient for identifying favorable jurors. Perhaps a "jury consultant" can help?

Scientific Jury Selection

The idea behind **scientific jury selection** is that prospective jurors are evaluated based on predetermined characteristics to identify those who would be sympathetic or unsympathetic to the case. Many consulting firms in the United States are in the business of identifying these characteristics, which include demographic variables, personality traits, and attitudes, in order to determine whether potential jurors are likely to side with the prosecution or the defense. Some psychologists consult in this manner to determine which potential jurors may be more likely to favor one side over the other. Psychologists or other consultants may employ one of two approaches to scientific jury selection: broad based or case specific.

Scientific jury selection
Prospective jurors are evaluated on predetermined characteristics to identify those who would be sympathetic or unsympathetic to the case

BROAD-BASED APPROACH The broad-based approach to scientific jury selection starts with the presumption that there are certain traits or attitudes that make people more likely to be pro-prosecution versus pro-defense. Two traits that are commonly measured using a broad-based approach are authoritarianism (i.e., have right-wing political views and are conservative, rigid thinkers who acquiesce to authority) and dogmatism (i.e., rigid and close minded, but without the political overtones found with the authoritarianism construct). Individuals high on authoritarianism or dogmatism may be more likely to side with the prosecution. Thus, without knowing any of the evidence of a particular case, some individuals with these traits will be more inclined to favor the prosecution. Prospective jurors may be given questionnaires assessing these traits/attitudes so that lawyers will know whom they should and should not challenge. Alternatively, lawyers can ask prospective jurors questions to assess these traits directly during the *voir dire*. (We will discuss authoritarianism and dogmatism further under the Personality Traits section later in the chapter.)

CASE-SPECIFIC APPROACH In contrast to a broad-based approach, the case-specific approach to scientific jury selection starts with the issues and facts of the case. A specific questionnaire is developed to assess a number of characteristics that may influence the verdict. Individuals in the community from which the jury pool will be drawn are asked to complete the questionnaire. By analyzing the responses to the questionnaire items, profiles of the ideal juror for the prosecution and the ideal juror for the defense are developed. The trial lawyers can then ask each prospective juror relevant questions to decide whether he or she should be challenged. Some jurisdictions in the United States allow lawyers to distribute questionnaires to the actual jury pool prior to jury selection. The answers to the questionnaires are made available to the lawyers on both sides, who then can "prescreen" the prospective jurors prior to the *voir dire*.

The broad-based and case-specific approaches provide lawyers with information that they may use in an attempt to "stack the jury" in their favor. Trial consultants in the United States may be retained by lawyers throughout the duration of the trial to monitor and provide feedback on the jury's demeanor. As the trial is being conducted, notes are made about any verbal and nonverbal behavior exhibited by the jurors. This information can give lawyers an ongoing sense of whether they are "winning" the favor of the jurors. Lawyers can alter their strategy should they feel they are losing the jury. Moreover, trial consultants often can provide help with opening and closing statements, witness preparation, and demonstrative evidence (Strier, 1999). Jury consultants may be trained in psychology and can be psychologists.

Some recent cases (both criminal and civil cases) in the United States that have used scientific jury selection include those of O.J. Simpson, the Menendez brothers, Martha Stewart, and a case involving the fast-food chain McDonald's (Seltzer, 2006). Currently, many jury consultants *do not* claim they can predict a verdict. Rather, jury consultants try to predict attitudes that potential jurors may hold toward a particular case.

Methodology Used for Scientific Jury Selection

Two common methodologies are used for scientific jury selection: (1) telephone surveys and (2) focus groups/mock trials.

TELEPHONE SURVEYS   Jury-eligible respondents may be selected at random from the jurisdiction where the actual trial is being heard. Using this type of methodology, often questions are asked about demographics (e.g., age, race, sex) and religious affiliation. Also, a set of questions probing background attitudes believed to be relevant for the case at hand are asked (e.g., do they believe people accused of crimes are usually guilty). Lastly, respondents might be asked questions pertaining to the case (e.g., how much they know about the case and where they got their information).

FOCUS GROUPS/MOCK JURY TRIALS   Jury-eligible respondents may be called at random and asked if they are willing to participate in a focus group or mock trial that may take a half or full day. Jurors may view a videotape of the trial that may be staged for them so that opening and closing statements can be "tested." These mock jurors also may be asked to complete a questionnaire and their deliberations may be videotaped for analysis.

Representativeness

A jury composition that represents the community where the crime occurred

Impartiality

A characteristic of jurors who are unbiased

CHARACTERISTICS AND RESPONSIBILITIES OF JURIES

There are two fundamental characteristics of juries:

1. A composition that represents the community in which the crime occurred. This is known as **representativeness**.
2. A lack of bias on the part of jurors, known as **impartiality**.

Representativeness

In order for a jury to be considered "representative," it must allow any possible eligible person from the community the opportunity to be part of the jury. Representativeness is achieved through randomness. For example, a community's telephone directory or voter registration records are used as a pool from which to randomly draw 100 or so names for potential jury duty. Of course, one could argue that neither of these "pools" is truly representative of the community because there may be people who can serve on a jury but whose names do not appear on these lists. For example, a homeless person may not have a phone, but may be eligible to serve on a jury. Also, the Jury Act lists "exemptions" for those who cannot serve on a jury, thus limiting the true representativeness of the jury pool.

In some cases, the prosecution or the defense may be concerned about the composition of the jury, arguing that it does not represent the community on some characteristic. For example, in a case where the defendant is a minority, there may be a consideration to move the trial where the jury would be composed of members of a similar race to the defendant. One such case was the O.J. Simpson trial in the late 1990s. To learn more about this case see Box 7.1.

BOX 7.1　Balancing a Jury by Race

Former football great O.J. Simpson was charged with the murders of his ex-wife Nicole Brown Simpson and her friend Ron Goldman in 1994. The crime occurred in Santa Monica, California. The case was moved to downtown Los Angeles. A major difference in these two areas is the majority race of the community members. Santa Monica was a predominantly "white" community, whereas downtown Los Angeles was primarily African American. O.J. Simpson was African American and the two victims were Caucasian. Polls indicated that Caucasians were more likely to think Simpson was guilty, whereas African Americans were more likely to think Simpson was not guilty.

Jury selection started with 250 potential members. Both the prosecution and defense hired jury consultants. Potential jurors were requested to complete a 294-item questionnaire. Questions from the prosecution and defense were included. Questions involved beliefs about domestic violence, interracial marriages, their hobbies, and if they had read anything about DNA analysis.

Jury selection went on for two months. Johnnie Cochran, one of Simpson's lawyers, suggested that the prosecution was "challenging" potential jurors based on race, that is, African Americans. By early November, the jury had been selected. The jury consisted of eight African Americans, two Hispanics, one half Caucasian–half Native American, and one Caucasian. For this case, 15 alternates also were selected. The final jury was comprised of nine African Americans, one Hispanic, and two Caucasians. Other interesting details about the jurors included that none of them regularly read a newspaper but the majority watched tabloid TV shows. Five reported that they or a family member had a negative interaction with the police. Nine thought that Simpson was unlikely to be a murderer because he was a professional athlete.

Following almost a year of testimony, the jury deliberated for slightly under four hours and returned a "not guilty" verdict on all charges.

Source: Based on "The O. J. Simpson Trial: The jury" from http://law2.umkc.edu/.

Impartiality

The juror characteristic of impartiality centers on three issues:

1. For a juror to be impartial, he or she must set aside any preexisting biases, prejudices, or attitudes and judge the case based solely on the admissible evidence. For example, a juror must ignore that the defendant belongs to an ethnic group against which he or she holds a bias. An impartial juror will not let his or her prejudice cloud the evaluation of the evidence.
2. To be impartial also means that the juror must ignore any information that is not part of the admissible evidence. For example, prior to the start of a trial, a case may have received media attention highlighting facts about the defendant that are biased, irrelevant, or inadmissible.
3. It also is important that the juror have no connection to the defendant so that the juror does not view the evidence subjectively and does not unduly influence the other jurors.

THREATS TO IMPARTIALITY A number of threats to impartiality exist. For example, is it possible to forget the emotionally charged headlines that we read before going to jury duty? Typically, the media attention is negative for the defendant, and that could mean that the defendant will not receive a fair trial. Thus, the concern is that verdicts will be based on emotion and biased media coverage rather than on admissible evidence. Steblay, Besirevic, Fulero, and Jimenez-Lorente (1999) conducted a meta-analysis of 44 studies examining the effects of pretrial publicity. They found a modest, positive relationship between exposure to negative pretrial publicity and judgments of guilt. This relation means that as exposure to negative pretrial publicity increases, so do the number of guilty verdicts.

Pretrial publicity need not be negative however. Positive pretrial publicity also seems to impact verdict. In one study examining negative and positive pretrial publicity, Ruva and McEvoy (2008) had mock jurors read news clips with negative, positive, or unrelated pretrial publicity. Mock jurors watched a murder trial and rendered a verdict along with a number of other ratings. Pretrial publicity, whether positive or negative, influenced the verdict, perceptions of the defendant, and attorneys. Positive information biased jurors positively toward the defendant (e.g., fewer guilty verdicts) and negative information biased jurors negatively against the defendant (e.g., more guilty verdicts).

KEEPING POTENTIAL JURORS IMPARTIAL Some methods for increasing the likelihood of an impartial jury are as follows:

Change of venue

Moving a trial to a community other than the one in which the crime occurred

1. The prosecution or defense may argue that the trial should be moved to another community because it would be very difficult to obtain an impartial jury from the local community. This option is called a **change of venue**. The party raising the issue must demonstrate that there is a reasonable likelihood that the local community is biased or prejudiced against the defendant. Factors that may lead to a biased community include extensive pretrial publicity, a heinous crime, and a small community in which many people know the victim and/or the defendant (Granger, 1996). See Box 7.2 for a case where a change of venue was granted.

BOX 7.2   Change of Venue Granted

A young man in his early 20s from Guinea named Amadou Diallo immigrated to New York City where he sold gloves and socks on the sidewalk. Diallo was standing near his building in the Bronx in the early morning of February 4, 1999. Four New York City police officers, Kenneth Boss, Sean Carroll, Edward McMellon, and Richard Murphy, who were in plain clothes, thought he fit the description of a rapist that was on the loose and approached Diallo. The officers claim they identified themselves as police officers and Diallo ran up the steps to his apartment door. Police yelled for him to stop and to show his hands. Diallo seemed to reach in his pocket and pull something out. McMellon tripped over the curb and his gun fired. With dim lighting, seeing the suspect holding something, seeing an officer go down, and hearing gunfire, one of the officers yelled, "Gun."

The four officers, opened fire on Diallo firing 41 bullets. Diallo was shot dead. He did not have a criminal record, he did not have a gun (he had pulled out his wallet), and he was not the rapist. The officers were charged with second-degree murder and reckless endangerment. Although the murder took place in the Bronx, the defendants requested a change of venue to Westchester or a county outside New York City. The court granted the motion. The trial was moved to Albany. Some have suggested that counties such as Westchester and Albany are "police friendly" with a number of police officers living there.

The four police officers were found "not guilty" on all counts.

Source: Based on "Officers in bronx fire 41 shots, and an unarmed man is killed" by Michael Cooper, from *The New York Times*, February 5, 1999.

2. An alternative to moving a trial to a new community is to allow sufficient time to pass so that the biasing effect of any pretrial prejudicial information has dissipated by the time the trial takes place. Thus, the judge may call for an **adjournment**, delaying the trial until some time in the future. A major limitation to adjourning cases is that not only can prospective jurors' memories fade, so might those of the witnesses. Witnesses may forget critical details that they are to testify about. Also, witnesses may move or die. Consequently, courts infrequently call for an adjournment.

> **Adjournment**
>
> Delaying the trial until some time in the future

3. Another option that may be granted in cases for which bias is suspected among the prospective jury pool is known as a **challenge for cause**. The prosecution or defense may argue that, although the prospective jury pool may be partial, if questioned, these prospective jurors could be identified and rejected from serving on the jury. As with the change of venue, the side desiring the judge to allow a challenge for cause must demonstrate that there is reasonable partiality in the community from which the jury pool will be drawn. If the judge grants a challenge for cause, prospective jurors can be probed. See Box 7.3 for a case where potential jurors were questioned somewhat regarding their religious beliefs; however, a challenge for cause was not granted.

> **Challenge for cause**
>
> An option to reject biased jurors

When trying to evaluate whether a challenge for cause is useful for identifying biased individuals, a number of issues need to be considered:

1. The process may be conducted in open court, where the jury pool can hear the questions the lawyers ask and the responses provided. Moreover, they can hear the answers that lead to a positive or negative decision from the lawyers and judge. Thus,

BOX 7.3   Probing Jurors' Religious Biases

Homaidan Al-Turki was a Saudi Arabian citizen in graduate school at the University of Colorado. In November 2004, he and his wife, Sarah Khonaizan, were charged with unlawful sexual contact, extortion, false imprisonment, and a number of other charges based on accusations made by his housekeeper, known as "Z.A." Z.A. claimed she was kept as a sex slave. The parties involved in the case were Muslims.

It was agreed that potential jurors could be questioned about their beliefs toward Muslims and their ability to be fair and impartial. The prosecution and defense were given 45 minutes to question the potential jurors. Twelve jurors were selected from 106 potential jurors.

In 2006, Al-Turki was found guilty and sentenced to 28 years in prison. Sarah Khonaizan made a deal with the prosecution where she pleaded guilty to lesser charges. Her sentence included home detention, probation, and two months in jail. After completing her sentence, she was deported. Note that she did not fight deportation. Al-Turki has maintained his innocence and has appealed his verdict claiming jurors should have been further probed for potential bias. In 2010, the U.S. Supreme Court denied Al-Turki's appeal. However, the case did not end there. Al-Turki was resentenced following the outcome in another case under the Colorado Supreme Court. District Judge J. Mark Hannen reduced Al-Turki's sentence to 8 years to life, which means Al-Turki may be eligible for parole in a couple of years. Al-Turki's good behavior in prison was noted. Also, he will need to attend a sex offender treatment program before being released.

What does the research say about asking jurors about their religious biases? In one study by Park, Felix, and Lee (2007), they found that connecting Muslims to negative characteristics (during the questioning period, for example) can produce unconscious biases that can be hard to detect through direct questioning. Effects of religion can be complicated and may effect trials in different ways (Miller et al., 2011). More research is needed in this area.

What do you think, should jurors have been questioned about their beliefs and attitudes toward Muslims?

Source: Based on "Homaidan al-turki, colorado man who kept house keeper as slave, has appeal denied by supreme court," April 5, 2010.

it is possible for prospective jurors to alter their answers according to whether they want to serve on the jury.

2. Prospective jurors may find it difficult to be honest when answering questions about bias that may put them in an unflattering light, especially if the questioning is conducted in open court.

3. Prospective jurors must be aware of their biases and how their biases may influence their behavior. This may not be obvious. Some classic work by Nisbett and Wilson (1977) suggests that individuals are unaware of their biases and how their biases affect their behavior.

JURY FUNCTIONS

The main legal function of a jury is to apply the law, as provided by the judge, to the admissible evidence in the case and render a verdict of guilt or not guilty. As we will discuss, there are cases in which the jury will ignore the law and apply some other criteria to reach a verdict. In addition to the main legal function of juries, four other jury functions have been identified:

1. To use the wisdom of 12 (rather than the wisdom of 1) to reach a verdict
2. To act as the conscience of the community
3. To protect against out-of-date laws
4. To increase knowledge about the justice system

IGNORING THE LAW   The jury has a responsibility to apply the law as defined by the judge to the admissible evidence and to render a verdict. Ignoring that law and the evidence, and rendering a verdict based on some other criteria, is known as **jury nullification**. Juries may choose to ignore the law for a number of reasons. For example, they may believe the law is unfair given the circumstances of the case or the punishment accompanying a conviction is too harsh for the crime. In both of these instances, jury nullification may result. Jury nullification typically can occur when the case involves controversial issues such as abortion and euthanasia.

Jury nullification

Occurs when a jury ignores the law and the evidence, rendering a verdict based on some other criteria

    If juries are allowed to ignore the law and vote with their conscience, won't we end up with a biased or random system? Meissner, Brigham, and Pfeifer (2003) examined the influence of a jury nullification instruction in a euthanasia case. Mock jurors were more likely to find the defendant not guilty with a nullification instruction when the jurors had a positive attitude toward euthanasia. Intriguingly, when jurors were given a standard jury instruction, they reported relying on the legal aspects of the case to make their decisions. However, when they were given a nullification instruction they reported relying on their attitudes of euthanasia and their perceptions of the defendant's behavior. Overall, nullification instructions may influence jury decision making "producing both socially favorable (e.g., sympathetic) and socially unfavorable (e.g., prejudicial) verdicts" (Meissner et al., 2003, p. 253).

HOW DO WE STUDY JURY BEHAVIOR?

Now that we know how juries are selected, and what their characteristics, responsibilities, and functions are, we can start understanding and predicting their behavior. Many researchers in the forensic area have focused their careers on trying to predict verdicts and the variables that affect verdicts. We will now discuss four methodologies that have been used to gain understanding of juror and jury behavior.

Post-Trial Interviews

In trying to understand why juries reached particular verdicts, perhaps it seems most logical and simple to ask the jurors themselves why they reached the verdicts they did. You may have seen jurors go on television after a case is over to discuss their thoughts.

    The main strength of post-trial interviews is high external validity; that is, results come from using real cases and the actual jurors who deliberated. Consequently, results may be more likely to generalize to the real world. This methodology, however, also has a number of weaknesses. For one, jurors' accounts may not be reliable. For example, jurors may recall details inaccurately, they may forget critical aspects of the deliberation, they may embellish or downplay elements to present themselves more favorably, or they may be unaware of the reasons for their decisions and behavior. Thus, conclusions may be based on data that are unreliable. Moreover, a cause-and-effect relationship cannot be established with this type of methodology. At best, researchers can talk about variables that occur together. Alternative hypotheses cannot be ruled out with this methodology.

Mock-jurors deliberate.

Archives

Records of trials, such as transcripts and police interviews of witnesses, can be reviewed to uncover relationships among variables. The strength of this methodology is similar to that used for post-trial interviews in that external validity is high. A similar weakness, however, is the inability to establish cause-and-effect relationships. Also, the researcher is restricted to the data available in that the types of questions that can be posed are limited by the information that can be accessed. The researcher is unable to go back and collect more information. Furthermore, the researcher is unaware of how the information was collected and the reliability of that information. For example, police interviews may have been conducted using biased procedures.

Simulation

One of the most common methodologies used to investigate jury issues is a simulation. Researchers simulate a trial, or aspects of it, using a written, audio, or video format. Participants are presented with the trial information. The information that the participants receive about the trial can be varied and manipulated by the researcher. Examples of possible independent variables of interest include the age of the witness or the race of the defendant. Following the presentation of the trial, participants are asked to respond individually (juror research) or in groups (jury research). Typically, jurors and juries will be asked to render a verdict or make other judgments. Verdicts and other participants' responses can be compared to determine whether the independent variable(s) had an effect.

One of the major strengths of this methodology is its high internal validity; that is, the researcher can reveal cause-and-effect relationships because he or she systematically manipulated the independent variables. However, the control the researcher has over the independent variables limits the external validity of this methodology. For example, in simulations, cases are not real and there are no consequences to the verdicts or decisions the jurors render. Furthermore, the participants typically are university students, who may not be representative of real jury pools. These factors limit the generalizability of the results obtained with simulations.

Field Studies

This methodology involves using actual jurors while they are serving on jury duty, so cooperation from the courts and the jurors is required. Researchers are able to observe variables of interest as they are occurring. For example, they may be interested in how prospective jurors respond to questions posed during the *voir dire*. Alternatively, researchers may be able to introduce variables that they want to examine. The court may agree to let jurors take notes while the evidence is being presented, for example. Trials in which jurors were allowed to take notes can be compared with trials in which jurors were not allowed to take notes. A comparison of the verdicts can be undertaken across these cases.

The strength of field studies is high external validity. A number of limitations, however, also are present. For example, receiving approval from the courts for conducting the research may be difficult. Even when approval is granted, it is likely that only a small sample of participants will be available, and appropriate comparison groups may be too difficult to identify. Additionally, there are a host of confounding variables that the researcher may not be able to control, such as the gender of lawyers and witnesses.

As you can see, the researcher interested in juror/jury issues has a variety of methodologies to choose from. Each methodology has some strengths and weaknesses. By using all of these methodologies, we may be able to gain a more accurate understanding of juror and jury behavior.

REACHING A VERDICT

Once a jury has been selected, their work begins. Jurors must listen to the admissible evidence and disregard any evidence that the judge does not allow. Once the lawyers deliver their closing arguments, the judge provides the jury with the law that they must apply to the evidence in order to reach a verdict. The jury then makes its **deliberation**—that is, they discuss the evidence privately among themselves to reach a verdict, which is then provided to the court. We will discuss each stage involved in reaching a jury verdict and the factors that may affect each stage.

Deliberation

When jury members discuss the evidence privately among themselves to reach a verdict that is then provided to the court

Listening to the Evidence

Two innovations have been proposed as aids for jurors while they listen to the evidence: note-taking and asking questions. Advantages and disadvantages have been identified for each aid. We will discuss each aid in turn.

NOTE-TAKING   Trials can be lengthy and complex, resulting in missed or forgotten evidence by the time the jury is asked to deliberate. Some have suggested that allowing jurors to take notes may facilitate memory and understanding of the evidence (e.g., Heuer & Penrod, 1994). Moreover, note takers may be more attentive during the trial than those who do not take notes. Not everyone is in agreement, however, that allowing jurors to take notes is advantageous or even preferable. Two examples include:

- Jurors who take notes may exert influence while in deliberation over those who do not.
- If disagreements occur about the evidence, jurors will rely on those who took notes to clarify the issue.

A review of the research examining juror note-taking was conducted by Penrod and Heuer (1997). They reached the following conclusions regarding juror note-taking:

- Jurors' notes serve as a memory aid.
- Jurors do not overemphasize the evidence that they have noted at the expense of evidence they have not recorded.
- Notes do not produce a distorted view of the case.
- Note takers can keep up with the evidence as it is being presented.
- Note takers do not distract jurors who do not take notes.
- Note takers do not have an undue influence over those who do not take notes.
- Jurors' notes are an accurate record of the trial.
- Juror note-taking does not favor either the prosecution or the defense.

As you can see, allowing jurors to take notes does not appear to pose major difficulties. Hartley (2002) also concluded that note-taking does not significantly impact a juror's memory of the evidence. At present in many jurisdictions, jurors are permitted to take notes.

ASKING QUESTIONS   When watching trials on television, or if you have ever had the opportunity to listen to a trial in court, you may have found yourself wondering about a detail that was mentioned. Would it not help if you could stop the trial and ask a question? The courts have considered the issue of jurors being allowed to ask questions. Heuer and Penrod (1994) reported that typically juries have few questions (usually not more than three) and they tend to be concerned with the meaning of key legal terms such as reasonable doubt. In a review of the research examining juror questions, Penrod and Heuer (1997) reached the following conclusions:

- Jury questioning promotes juror understanding of the facts and issues.
- Juror questions do not clearly help get to the truth.
- Juror questions do not increase the jurors', judges', or lawyers' satisfaction with the trial and verdict.
- Jurors ask legally appropriate questions.
- If counsel objects, and the objection is sustained, the jury does not draw inappropriate inferences from unanswered questions.
- Jurors do not become advocates.

Thus, the research on allowing jurors to ask questions does not appear to be particularly harmful or helpful. Few courts, however, allow jurors to ask questions. When it is permitted, jurors submit their questions in writing to the judge who then reviews the questions with the lawyers and determines which questions are allowable. Questions that are permissible are posed by the judge. In one such case occurring in a D.C. Superior Court, the jurors had over 30 questions for the defendant, DeMarcus Yarborough, who was charged with killing a 16-year-old boy. Yarborough claimed it was self-defense. The jurors wanted to know who fired the gun first, what type of gun it was, and had Yarborough ever fired a gun in the past. Although not all questions were allowed, over 20 questions were allowed and read by the judge. The jury found Yarborough not guilty of killing Donald Brinkley who Yarborough thought was stealing his truck.

Does the relatively recent influx of forensic science television programming increase jurors' quest for scientific evidence? Shows such as *CSI: Crime Scene Investigation* and its two spin-offs, *CSI: Miami* and *CSI: New York*, "educate" potential jurors on the latest scientific evidence. Do the shows raise the bar too high? Do they influence the jury pool? See the In the Media box for a discussion of the "*CSI* effect."

Disregarding Inadmissible Evidence

Are jurors able to "forget" what they heard? This question is not only relevant when we consider pretrial publicity but also when judges request that jurors disregard inadmissible evidence. Often, juries will hear inadmissible evidence when lawyers or witnesses make statements that are not allowable according to legal procedure. Following an inadmissible statement or inadmissible evidence, the judge will instruct the jury to disregard it. The critical component to a fair trial and a just verdict is that only admissible statements and evidence are used by the jury. The question is, are jurors able to disregard evidence they have heard?

IN THE MEDIA   The *CSI* Effect

Do you watch any of the *CSI* shows? If you do, you are not alone. Approximately 60 million people tune into these programs each week. The *CSI* shows typically start with a crime, some evidence is collected, high-tech analysis is undertaken, and the crime is solved all in about 60 minutes. If only real life happened like this. Unfortunately, the more we watch these shows the more we begin to believe this is how our justice system should work and if it doesn't, we think the justice system has failed.

The "*CSI* effect" can be described as the education of jurors where they are more likely to convict if the procedures and techniques from television are used in real life. Why wasn't DNA collected? Is it a match? You can't beat DNA. The *CSI* effect has been around for about 10 years, shortly after the first *CSI* installment aired on television.

Are you a product of the *CSI* effect? You need not be a juror to be influenced by these television shows. Universities in the United States report a dramatic increase in "forensic science" type undergraduate and graduate programs (e.g., Triplett & Turner, 2009). A few programs include those offered at John Jay College, the University of Nebraska at Lincoln, and the University of South Florida.

Having watched these programs, jurors may rely on what they have seen on television to evaluate the evidence presented in real-life court. Jeffrey Heinrick (2006) reports on a number of cases where real-life investigation did not live up to the *CSI* shows. For example, a man from Illinois who was accused of trying to kill his ex-girlfriend was found not guilty by the jury reportedly because the police did not test the blood-stained sheets for DNA. Sadly, once he was released from jail he stabbed his ex-girlfriend to death. A jury also found a man from Phoenix not guilty because his blood-stained coat was not tested for DNA. Jurors now require expensive and sometimes unnecessary DNA tests, gun residue tests, and handwriting analyses, for example. Jurors also may not understand that some lab tests may take months and even years to complete.

Some argue that the *CSI* effect has a negative impact on the justice system, whereas others argue that it makes jurors more informed about what it takes to find someone guilty. Prosecutors argue that it raises the bar unfairly, making the case easier for the defense. What do you think?

A group of researchers from St. Mary's University in Canada, Drs. Smith, Patry, and Stinson (2008) found evidence that crime dramas do indeed influence the perceptions of forensic science and, in turn, what lawyers do in the courtroom. In terms of verdict, however, Kim, Barak, and Shelton (2009) found that watching *CSI* shows did *not* influence jurors' verdicts independently. The *CSI* effect was found to have an indirect influence on conviction in circumstantial cases where it raised expectations about scientific evidence. Perhaps the best conclusion at this point is that the jury is still out on whether and how crime shows influence the justice system. With no shortage of crime dramas on television, further research is needed in this area.

Sources: Heinrick, J. (2006, Fall). Everyone's an expert: The CSI effect's negative impact on juries. *The Triple Helix*. Arizona State University. Smith, S. M., Patry, M., & Stinson, V. (2008). Is the CSI effect real? If it is, what is it? In G. Bourgon, R.K. Hanson, J.D. Pozzulo, K.E. Morton Bourgon, & C.L. Tanasichuk (Eds.), *Proceedings of the 2007 North American Correctional & Criminal Justice Psychology Conference (User Report)*. Ottawa: Public Safety Canada.

Kassin and Sommers (1997) argued that whether jurors will follow a judge's instruction to disregard inadmissible evidence is related to the reason for the instruction rather than to the instruction itself. In their study, mock jurors were presented with a murder trial, and a piece of evidence was manipulated. Jurors in the control condition received only circumstantial and ambiguous evidence. In the experimental conditions, an audiotaped telephone conversation in which the defendant confessed to the murder was included. When this audiotape was admitted into evidence, the defense lawyer objected. The judge either overruled the objection, allowing it into evidence, or sustained the objection and asked jurors to disregard it because it was either illegally obtained or difficult to comprehend. When jurors were asked to disregard the evidence because it was illegally collected, their verdicts were similar to the jurors who received the ruling that the tape was admissible. In contrast, when jurors were instructed to disregard the tape because of comprehension difficulty, they rendered verdicts similar to the control jurors who had not heard about the inadmissible evidence. Thus, Kassin and Sommers concluded that jurors will disregard evidence when they are provided with a logical and legitimate reason for the judge's decision to disregard it.

One other interesting result has been found with the instruction to disregard. Some researchers have found that a judge's instruction to disregard evidence simply makes the evidence more memorable than if no instruction were given. This is known as the **backfire effect** (Paglia & Schuller, 1998). Thus, jurors are more likely to pay attention to inadmissible evidence following a disregard instruction than if no instruction was provided. Similarly, Pickel, Karam, and Warner (2009) found that if the inadmissible evidence was memorable, it was harder to ignore.

Overall, the influence of the disregard instruction is not straightforward. There are other factors that may come into play and interact with the effect of the instruction.

Backfire effect

When jurors are more likely to pay attention to inadmissible evidence following a disregard instruction than if no instruction was provided

Judge's Instructions

A number of studies have examined jurors' abilities to understand the legally dense instructions that the judge charges the jury with prior to deliberation. The results of these studies generally are not positive. Lieberman and Sales (1997) have concluded that jurors do not remember, understand, or accurately apply judges' instructions. Reifman, Gusick, and Ellsworth (1992) surveyed 224 citizens from Michigan who were called for jury duty. The goal was to assess jurors' comprehension of judges' instructions. These prospective jurors understood less than 50% of the instructions they received.

Four reforms for judges' instructions have been proposed: (1) rewriting instructions, (2) providing a written copy of the instructions to jurors, (3) pre- and post-evidence instructions, and (4) having lawyers clarify legal instruction during their presentation to the jury. However, these reforms do not necessarily significantly increase comprehension. These four proposed reforms have not been implemented with any consistency across jurisdictions.

JURY DECISION-MAKING MODELS

How do jurors combine the trial evidence to reach a verdict? Moreover, what is the process by which verdicts are reached? Although a number of models of juror/jury decision making have been proposed, they may be categorized as using either a mathematical or explanation-based approach.

A jury listens to evidence.

MATHEMATICAL MODELS   The common theme with mathematical models is that they view jurors as conducting a set of mental calculations regarding the importance and strength of each piece of evidence (Hastie, 1993). A guilty or not guilty verdict is determined by the outcome of the calculations for all the relevant evidence. For example, the evidence of an eyewitness who identified the defendant may be perceived as strong evidence and be weighed heavily toward a guilty verdict; however, learning that the DNA found at the crime scene does not match the defendant's decreases the likelihood of a guilty verdict. The verdict is a function of the calculation of all the relevant evidence.

Ellsworth and Mauro (1998) examined the congruency of mental calculations and how jurors perceive their process of reaching a verdict. They found that a mathematical approach was inconsistent with how jurors report that they reach verdicts. Jurors do not appear to provide a value for each piece of evidence presented. Moreover, it may be difficult to partition evidence into discrete pieces of evidence that can then be assigned a value. Perhaps an explanation-based approach is more consistent with how jurors process the trial evidence.

EXPLANATION MODELS   In contrast to mathematical models, explanation models suggest that evidence is organized into a coherent whole. Pennington and Hastie's (1986) explanation approach is called the *story model*. They proposed that jurors are active at understanding and processing the evidence. Jurors interpret and elaborate on the evidence and make causal connections, and in doing so, they create a story structure. These "stories" are then compared with each verdict option presented by the judge. The verdict option most consistent with the story is the verdict reached.

Of course, jurors listening to the same evidence may construct different stories that are consistent with alternative verdicts. That is to say, individual differences can influence the story-construction process. Jurors bring in their personal experiences, knowledge, beliefs, and attitudes when constructing their story. Thus, jurors may reach different decisions after hearing the same evidence.

To test the story model, Pennington and Hastie (1986) had 26 participants watch a simulated murder trial and then make individual verdicts at the end of the trial. Following their verdicts, participants were interviewed to determine how they thought about the evidence. The researchers found that participants put the evidence into a story format and different stories were related to different verdicts.

In a follow-up study, Pennington and Hastie (1988) varied how easily a particular story could be constructed by altering the order in which the evidence was presented. They found that when the evidence was presented in a chronological order, it was more likely that the verdict reached was consistent with that story order. This information could be useful to lawyers who may choose to present evidence in a story format that is consistent with the verdict they want. The story model seems to be consistent with how jurors process trial evidence and reach a verdict. The story model continues to be used to understand jury decision making.

Deliberations

As you may recall, criminal trials typically have a 12-person jury (although smaller juries are possible). As we previously mentioned, usually two alternate jurors (or more depending on the possible length of the case) are selected to hear the trial along with the jury in the event someone on the jury needs to be excused for illness or other reasons, during the trial.

Once all the evidence has been heard and the judge has delivered instructions to the jurors, the jury retires to a secluded room to deliberate. Juries can be sequestered (i.e., they are not allowed contact with anyone outside the jury and typically stay in a hotel for accommodations) until the final verdict is reached, after which the jury is dismissed by the judge. In high-profile cases that may garner a lot of attention during the trial, the judge may order that the jury be sequestered throughout the trial. Sequestering a jury means that the jury is not allowed to talk to anyone outside their 12-person panel, with the exception of the court-appointed officer in the event that they have a request or question.

Polarization

When individuals tend to become more extreme in their initial position following a group discussion

Leniency bias

When jurors move toward greater leniency during deliberations

The expectation from the justice system is that the jury reviews the evidence and determines the most consistent match between the verdict options that were provided by the judge and the admissible evidence. A number of factors can influence a juror's position on the case. A phenomenon known as **polarization** occurs when individuals tend to become more extreme in their initial position following a group discussion (Baron & Bryne, 1991). In contrast, a **leniency bias** also has been found whereby jurors move toward greater leniency following deliberations (MacCoun & Kerr, 1988).

The Final Verdict

Hung jury

A jury that cannot reach a unanimous verdict

Typically, a jury must reach a unanimous verdict. If not, the jury is said to be a **hung jury** or deadlocked and a mistrial is declared. Following a hung jury outcome, the prosecution must decide whether it will retry the case. The United States has permitted majority votes of 11 to 1, 10 to 2, and 9 to 3. Similarly, the United Kingdom has allowed juries to render 11-to-1 or 10-to-2 majority votes provided that the jury has deliberated for a minimum of two hours. In a meta-analysis examining the effects of jury size, Saks and Marti (1997) found that 6-person juries are less representative of the community, they remember less of the evidence, they return quicker verdicts, and they are more likely to reach a unanimous verdict than 12-person juries. Hastie, Penrod, and Pennington (1983) found that when a jury could retire with a majority vote, they tended to reach a decision faster and did not fully discuss both the evidence and law, compared with when the jury was required to reach a unanimous verdict.

In general, when a first verdict poll is taken, the final verdict tends to be consistent with the first poll in about 90% of cases (Kalvern & Zeisel, 1966; Sandys & Dillehay, 1995). MacCoun and Kerr (1988) conducted a meta-analysis of 12 studies examining juror preferences at the beginning of deliberation as well as final verdicts. They found that a pro-defense faction was more persuasive than a pro-prosecution faction. More specifically, if 7 or fewer jurors vote guilty at the beginning of deliberation, the jury will tend to render a not guilty verdict. If 10 or more jurors initially vote guilty, the final verdict will likely be guilty. If 8 or 9 jurors initially vote guilty, the final verdict is unpredictable.

Hastie, Penrod, and Pennington (1983) identified two broad styles that juries tend to adopt when trying to reach a verdict: verdict driven and evidence driven. Verdict-driven juries tend to start the deliberation process by taking an initial verdict poll. In contrast, evidence-driven juries tend to start the deliberation process by discussing the evidence. A verdict poll is not taken until much later during the deliberation. These two styles can influence the outcome of the initial verdict poll (Sandys & Dillehay, 1995).

PREDICTING VERDICTS

A great deal of research on juror characteristics has been conducted to determine whether verdicts can be predicted based on these characteristics. We will examine the following six types of variables that have been studied and their relation to the verdict: (1) demographic variables, (2) personality traits, (3) attitudes, (4) defendant characteristics, (5) victim characteristics, and (6) expert testimony.

Demographic Variables

Variables such as the gender, race, socioeconomic status, and education of jurors are types of demographic variables that have been examined, in part because they are readily available to lawyers but also because they can be used to challenge witnesses. For example, are female jurors more lenient? Are Caucasians more likely to render guilty verdicts?

Racial bias as it relates to jury decision making can be defined as disparate treatment of racial out-groups. In a recent meta-analysis examining racial bias on verdict and sentencing decisions, Mitchell, Haw, Pfeifer, and Meissner (2005) found a small significant effect of racial bias on jury decisions. Participants were more likely to render guilty verdicts for "other-race" defendants than for defendants of their own race. Also, participants rendered longer sentences for other-race defendants. Is it possible to reduce this effect? Cohn, Bucolo, Pride, and Sommers (2009) found that when a defendant's race was made salient, white juror racial bias toward a black defendant was reduced. Moreover, jurors' prejudicial beliefs were only related to verdict when the defendant's race was not made salient.

Other factors also may interact with defendant race. For example, Perez, Hosch, Ponder, and Trejo (1993) found that strength of the evidence may come into play along with race. When the evidence was weak or ambiguous (not clearly favoring one side), race similarity between defendant and jury led to leniency. When evidence was strong, race similarity between defendant and jury led to being punitive. This is known as the **black sheep effect** (Chadee, 1996).

Racial bias

The disparate treatment of racial out-groups

Black sheep effect

When evidence is strong, similarity between defendant and jury leads to being punitive

Eberhardt, Davies, Purdie-Vaughns, and Johnson (2006) examined racial stereotypes in a death sentence case. The researchers used photos of black defendants and had university students rate how stereotypically black they looked. They found that in cases where there was a white victim, black defendants who looked more stereotypical were more likely to be sentenced to death than those who looked less stereotypical.

Unfortunately, when using juror demographic variables to predict verdicts, results are less than reliable. Overall, only a small and inconsistent relation exists between juror demographic variables and jury verdicts (e.g., Bonazzoli, 1998).

Personality Traits

The two personality traits that have been commonly measured in connection to jurors are authoritarianism and dogmatism. As noted earlier in the chapter, individuals high in authoritarianism tend to have right-wing political views and are conservative and rigid thinkers who acquiesce to authority. Similarly, individuals high in dogmatism also tend to be rigid and close minded but without the political overtones found with the authoritarianism construct. Are personality traits better for predicting verdicts than demographic variables?

Given the underlying traits associated with dogmatism and authoritarianism, anyone would predict that jurors who score high on these constructs would be more likely to align themselves with the prosecution and, thus, render more guilty verdicts than jurors who score low on these constructs. In a meta-analysis that examined authoritarianism and juror verdicts across 20 studies, Narby, Cutler, and Moran (1993) found a moderate, positive relationship between authoritarianism and verdict such that those who score high on these traits tend to be more inclined to render guilty verdicts. That is, they have a pro-prosecution bias.

One also needs to consider that jurors are required to reach a unanimous decision, possibly by persuading other jurors. What type of person or what personality traits tend to be the most persuasive? In a study by Rotenberg, Hewlett, and Siegwart (1998), mock jurors who were extroverted and had higher moral reasoning were found to be more persuasive than other mock jurors. In another study, by Marcus, Lyons, and Guyton (2000), the "big five" personality dimensions were examined for persuasiveness:

- *Extroversion:* outgoing, sociable, and animated
- *Agreeableness:* altruistic, interpersonally pleasant, and positive
- *Conscientiousness:* self-disciplined, determined, and dutiful
- *Emotional stability:* calm, even-tempered, and able to handle stressful situations
- *Openness to experience:* imaginative, sensitive, intellectually curious, and unconventional

The researchers found that participants who showed a high level on conscientiousness were most likely to report being persuaded by other participants. In contrast, participants who scored high on openness were least likely to be persuaded by other participants. Those exhibiting high levels of extroversion were most persuasive, and being male wielded more influence than being female. Intriguingly, extroverted, tall males were even more persuasive than extroverted, shorter males. Jurors' personality traits seem to be more reliable for predicting verdicts than demographic variables.

Attitudes

Researchers have examined a variety of attitudes linked to specific topics or issues that may be present in cases, such as drunk driving, rape, child sexual abuse, and capital punishment. For example, Spanos, DuBreuil, and Gwynn (1991–1992) examined rape myths (e.g., a woman who wears provocative clothing is interested in having sex) in connection to a date-rape case. University students heard a version of a date-rape case involving expert testimony about rape myths and cross-examination of such, and then deliberated in small groups to reach a verdict. A gender split was observed in which females did not believe the defendant and voted him guilty more often than male mock jurors. However, regardless of the gender of the mock jurors, those with feminist attitudes were more likely *not* to believe the defendant's testimony.

Devine et al. (2001) reported that no group of attitudes or values has received sufficient investigation to reach a definitive conclusion at this point. The one notable exception is attitudes toward capital punishment. For example, Horowitz and Seguin (1986) reported that juries comprising death-qualified jurors (i.e., jurors who are willing to impose the death sentence) had a 19% higher conviction rate than non–death-qualified jurors. In general, death-qualified jurors are more likely than non–death-qualified jurors to vote for conviction at the end of a trial (Ellsworth & Mauro, 1998).

Overall, attitudes that are case specific seem to have more predictive power over verdict than more general attitudes do.

Defendant Characteristics

A number of studies have examined defendant characteristics and their influence on verdicts. For example, if jurors hear about a defendant's prior criminal record that contains one or more convictions, they are more likely to find the defendant guilty than if the jurors did not have this knowledge (Hans & Doob, 1976).

There also seems to be a small relationship between the attractiveness of the defendant and jury verdict. Izzett and Leginski (1974) provided mock jurors with either a picture of an unattractive defendant or an attractive defendant and found verdict preferences to be more lenient for the attractive defendant and more severe for the unattractive defendant. Patry (2008) examined whether defendant attractiveness and the act of deliberation would have an effect on guilt decision. Indeed, "plain-looking" defendants were more often found to be guilty when mock jurors did not deliberate. However, when mock jurors did deliberate, the attractive defendant was more likely to be found guilty.

Defendant characteristics often are examined in relation to other characteristics, such as victim characteristics. Pozzulo, Dempsey, Maeder, and Allen (2010) examined defendant gender, defendant age (15 years old vs. 40 years old), and victim gender in a sexual assault case of a 12-year-old student by her teacher. Male defendants received higher guilt ratings compared to female defendants. Female jurors found the victim more accurate, truthful, and believable than male jurors. In contrast, male jurors found the defendant more reliable, credible, truthful, and believable than female jurors. Female jurors held the defendant more responsible for the crime than male jurors. Overall, mock jurors perceived the younger defendant compared to the older defendant to have desired the event but only when the victim was a female compared to male.

Although a considerable amount of attention has been given examining differences in juror and jury perceptions of white versus black defendants, research has also considered the Hispanic defendant and juror. For example, Perez and colleagues (1993) examined the impact of ethnicity on jury decision making. White versus Hispanic jurors watched a videotaped trial of a white versus Hispanic defendant. Six-person juries that were primarily white were more likely to convict the defendant than were juries with primarily Hispanic jurors. A significant interaction found that primarily white juries were more lenient with the white defendant but the primarily Hispanic jurors did not differ in their conviction rates.

Dr. Bette Bottoms has conducted substantial juror decision-making research. She along with some of her colleagues have examined defendant characteristics in combination with other factors. For example, Wiley and Bottoms (2009) examined the sexual orientation of the defendant and the gender of the victim (10-year-old child) in a mock juror study. The researchers were interested in the stereotype of gay men being child molesters. Pro-prosecution judgments were made when the defendant was described as gay compared to straight especially when the victim was described as a boy. In general, female jurors were more pro-prosecution than male jurors; this is common in child sexual assault cases.

In another study, Stevenson and Bottoms (2009) investigated the race of the defendant and victim and the gender of the jurors on non–African American mock jurors' perceptions of crimes committed by young offenders. An interaction of defendant and victim race by juror gender was found. Male jurors (compared to female jurors) were more likely to judge the defendant more harshly when the victim was Caucasian and the defendant was African American. To learn more about Dr. Bottoms, see Box 7.4.

As you can see, a number of variables can interact and influence verdict as well as perceptions of the defendant and victim.

Victim Characteristics

Characteristics of the victim may become particularly relevant in cases of sexual assault in which a guilty verdict may hinge on the testimony of the alleged victim.

Bottoms, Davis, and Epstein (2004) examined a number of factors in a child sexual abuse case: defendant race, victim age, juror gender, and juror prejudice on jurors' decisions in child sexual abuse cases. Some of the findings included in Experiments 1 and 2 were that black and Hispanic child victims were perceived more responsible for their sexual abuse than white victims by mock jurors. In Experiment 3, more jurors found defendants more guilty in cases where the victim and defendant were of the same race compared to cross-race pairings. Interestingly also in Experiment 3, laypeople believed that same-race cases were more likely to have occurred.

Most jurisdictions have "rape shield" provisions that prevents lawyers from introducing a woman's prior sexual history into evidence in sexual assault cases. These rape shield provisions have not gone unchallenged by some however. For example, in the high-profile case involving basketball player Kobe Bryant in 2004, his lawyers argued that the alleged victim's sexual conduct was relevant because her injuries could have been a result of an encounter with someone other than Bryant after she and Bryant were together. The judge ruled against Bryant's lawyers and deemed Colorado's rape shield law as constitutional and valid.

Note, however, that there is some leeway with these provisions that would allow inquiry into a woman's sexual history at the judge's discretion only if a woman's sexual history was deemed relevant. How would you interpret a woman's sexual history in a "date rape" case? You be the juror—see Box 7.5.

Schuller and Hastings (2002) conducted a study in which the victim's sexual history was varied to include either sexual intercourse, kissing and touching, or no history

BOX 7.4 Researcher Profile: Dr. Bette Bottoms

As an undergraduate at Randolph-Macon Woman's College in Virginia (home of the first psychology laboratory in the South), Bette L. Bottoms became interested in psychology and the law. Dr. Bottoms would continue her fascination in the area through graduate work at the University of Denver and then on to a Ph.D. from State University of New York at Buffalo. Dr. Bottoms' dissertation examined jurors' perceptions of child witnesses in sexual abuse cases. Her graduate training and research interests are very broad, including a mix of cognitive, developmental, social, and even a little community and clinical psychology. Her work is unified by the theme of children, psychology, and law.

Dr. Bette Bottoms

Dr. Bottoms' current research is focused on children's eyewitness testimony and jurors' perceptions of that testimony, child abuse issues such as claims of repressed memory, and public perceptions of juvenile offenders, including perceptions of registry laws applied to juvenile sex offenders. What keeps Dr. Bottoms interested in this research is that these topics can both contribute to the science of psychology as well as reveal information that has real-world significance. Dr. Bottoms notes, "The legal system was designed for adults. Research can and has improved the legal system for children in important ways."

Along with her commitment to research, Dr. Bottoms is dedicated to training future psychologists. Dr. Bottoms believes that programs should be varied to develop the range of professionals needed in the field, from academic researchers interested in psychology and law research within traditional psychology departments to other researchers who conduct applied research within agencies, the legal system, and so forth. Dr. Bottoms enjoys teaching undergraduate courses in "Psychology and Law" as well as a graduate course that helps doctoral students learn how to teach and mentor. Dr. Bottoms has won a number of teaching awards, including the American Psychology-Law Society (APLS) Teaching and Mentoring award for her work advancing the psychology and law field through student training. Dr. Bottoms states, "Some of the best moments of my professional life have been sharing in the accomplishments of my students."

When Dr. Bottoms is outside of the classroom and her laboratory, she is active in the administration of the university. Dr. Bottoms enjoys being in a position to affect change that makes the university work better for faculty and students. Her administrative work also goes beyond the University of Illinois. Dr. Bottoms has served on numerous committees within APLS. She also served as president of the American Psychological Association (APA) Division 37: Society for Child and Family Policy and Practice, and as president of the APA Division 37 Section on Child Maltreatment. Dr. Bottoms notes that the presidential experiences were particularly rewarding because of the opportunities to accomplish much of practical value by translating research into public policy aimed at improving the lives of children and their families.

Dr. Bottoms has continued her illustrious career at the University of Illinois at Chicago where she has been for the past 18 years and is now Professor, Vice-Provost for Undergraduate Affairs, and DEAN of the Honors College.

Dr. Bottoms loves living in downtown Chicago, taking advantage of life in a big city during the week and retreating to a weekend house on a small lake in Michigan where she and her husband (Gary Raney, a cognitive psychologist) sail and swim.

information in a sexual assault trial. In addition, a judge's instructions limiting the use of the sexual history information were examined. Compared with the participants who heard no sexual history information, those who heard that the victim and defendant had sexual intercourse in the past were less likely to find the alleged victim credible, more likely to find her blameworthy, and more likely to believe she consented to sexual intercourse. Thus, they were more likely to find the defendant not guilty. It would appear that a judge's instruction to limit the use of the sexual history information is not effective. If a woman's sexual history is admitted into evidence, it is used to assess her credibility.

Expert Testimony

How well do jurors understand the evidence presented? Sometimes, jurors don't have the background knowledge to understand certain types of evidence, such as DNA. Lawyers may ask that an expert be allowed to testify to explain the evidence. What influence does expert evidence have on jurors' decisions?

A number of findings about expert testimony are available, but no simple conclusion has emerged. For example, Schuller, Terry, and McKimmie (2005) examined whether the expert's gender is used as a cue to evaluate the testimony provided. Along with the gender of the expert, the complexity of the testimony was varied such that the testimony was either more or less complex (e.g., using technical jargon). In a civil case that involved an alleged price-fixing arrangement between a crushed-rock supplier and a road construction company, the plaintiff was suing the two companies for damages of $490,000 due to the price-fixing agreement. When the testimony was more complex, higher damages were awarded to the plaintiff when the expert was male compared to female. When testimony was less complex, although not significantly so, higher damages were awarded when the expert was female compared to male. Participants may be using gender differently depending on their ability to process the testimony.

Expert testimony need not produce a positive effect, however, and jurors may disregard it completely. For example, Sundby (1997) examined the transcripts of 152 jurors who participated in 36 first-degree murder cases in California. Jurors were asked about their perceptions and reactions to three types of witnesses: professional experts, lay experts, and families/friends of the defendant. Professional experts were most likely to be viewed negatively and with little credibility along with hurting the side they were testifying for. Overall, expert testimony may be carefully considered by jurors.

A SPECIAL CASE OF EXPERT TESTIMONY ON BATTERED WOMEN'S SYNDROME

Dr. Regina Schuller and her colleagues have conducted a number of studies examining battered women who kill their abusers and the influence of expert testimony (Schuller, 1992, 1995; Schuller & Hastings, 1996; Schuller & Rzepa, 2002; Schuller, Smith, & Olson, 1994).

In one study, Schuller, Smith, and Olson (1994) examined the impact of four variables, including jurors' preexisting beliefs about wife abuse, jurors' beliefs in a "just world" (i.e., believing that you receive what you deserve), the presence or absence of expert testimony on battered women's syndrome, and sex of the juror (male versus female). Mock jurors listened to a homicide trial involving a woman who killed her abusive husband. They then made various judgments about the case. The mock jurors who heard the expert testimony were more likely to believe the woman's account of what happened

CASE STUDY

YOU BE THE JUROR

Jenny Jones was in her second year at university. She had met Matt Grayson in her introductory psychology class. They didn't know each other very well but had a few classes together and knew some of the same people. Jenny thought Matt was cute and told her friends that she'd go out with him if he asked.

Matt had been dating a female from his high school for almost three years. Matt had gone off to university and his girlfriend stayed in town and went to a local community college. Matt's girlfriend decided she no longer wanted a long-distance relationship. She broke up with Matt just before spring break. Matt was upset but decided there were lots of other women at university that he could go out with so it was her loss for leaving him. That weekend, a friend of Jenny's and Matt's had a house party to mark the end of spring break. Both Jenny and Matt went to the party.

At the party, Jenny and Matt started chatting and were having a good time together. Both Jenny and Matt had a couple of drinks but neither considered themselves drunk. As the party was breaking up around 2:00 a.m., Matt asked if Jenny wanted to go back to his dorm room to "hang out." Jenny said yes. While in Matt's room, Matt and Jenny started to get intimate. After a few minutes though, Jenny said she should go home. Matt asked her to stay and continued to kiss Jenny. Jenny repeated she should go. Jenny and Matt had intercourse and the next morning, Jenny claimed that Matt had sexually assaulted her. Matt agrees that they had sex but that it was consensual. Matt claimed that Jenny could have left at any time.

The case went to trial and the Judge allowed the defense to question Jenny on her sexual history. Jenny stated she had other boyfriends in the past who she had intercourse with but that she did not want to have intercourse with Matt that night. She also stated that she had intercourse the previous night.

Your Turn . . .

Do you think Matt sexually assaulted Jenny? Would you change your verdict if you did not know about Jenny's sexual history? Do you think an alleged victim's sexual history is relevant? Should it be allowed?

than were those who did not hear expert testimony. Those who had a weak belief in a just world were more lenient in their judgments and felt that the expert testimony was more relevant to the battered woman than did those who had a strong belief in a just world. Female mock jurors who had a weak belief in a just world were more likely to find the defendant not guilty.

Dr. Lenore Walker is a psychologist who has been a primary figure and expert on battered women's syndrome. She provides assessment, consultation, and testimony on the topic. Dr. Walker also has served on several task forces regarding practice and policy on battered women's syndrome. As you can see, psychologists can play a number of roles when it comes to jury decision making.

The effects of expert testimony can differ depending on the nature of the case, the expert, and the jurors' own beliefs.

Summary

1. Grand juries assess the evidence against the defendant to determine whether the case should go to trial. Petit juries are trial juries who listen to the evidence and determine whether the defendant is guilty or not guilty.
2. Prospective jurors are selected from a set of random names from the community. These prospective jurors receive a jury summons stating the time and place to go for jury duty. If you are randomly selected from this juror pool, you will be a juror unless one of the lawyers presents a challenge.
3. In order for a jury to be considered representative, it must allow any possible eligible juror from the community the opportunity to be part of the jury. Juror impartiality centers on three issues: (1) being able to set aside any pre-existing biases, prejudices, or attitudes to solely judge the case based on admissible evidence; (2) ignoring any information that is not part of the admissible evidence; and (3) not being connected to those involved in the case in any way.
4. Pretrial publicity threatens juror impartiality. The concern is that verdicts will be based on emotion and biased media coverage rather than on admissible evidence. To reduce or limit the negative effects of pretrial publicity, the judge can order a publication ban until the end of the trial. Other options for dealing with pretrial publicity include a change of venue, an adjournment, or a challenge for cause.
5. Once a jury has been selected, their work begins by listening to the admissible evidence and disregarding any evidence that the judge does not allow. Once the lawyers deliver their closing arguments, the judge provides the jury with the law that they must apply to the evidence to reach a verdict. The jury then deliberates to reach a verdict.
6. Categories that have been examined in terms of predicting verdicts include demographic variables, personality variables, attitudes, defendant characteristics, victim characteristics, and expert testimony.

Key Concepts

adjournment *171*

backfire effect *178*

black sheep effect *181*

challenge for cause *171*

change of venue *170*

deliberation *175*

hung jury *180*

impartiality *168*

Jury Act *166*

jury nullification *173*

jury summons *166*

leniency bias *180*

polarization *180*

racial bias *181*

representativeness *168*

scientific jury selection *167*

voir dire 166

Discussion Questions

1. Design a study to evaluate the advantages and disadvantages of jury aids (e.g., note-taking, asking questions).
2. A battered woman who shot and killed her sleeping abusive husband is standing trial for murder. The defense has retained a prominent forensic psychologist to give expert testimony. What impact do you think this expert will have on the jury? Discuss factors that can interact with expert testimony.
3. Should juries be permitted to ignore the law? Discuss the issues surrounding jury nullification.
4. To study juror decision making, researchers have used four different methodologies. Describe the advantages and disadvantages of each method.

8

The Role of Mental Illness in Court

LEARNING OBJECTIVES

- Outline the competency standard.
- Contrast competent and incompetent offenders.
- Explain the insanity standards used in the United States.

- State the explanations for high rates of mental illness in offender populations.
- Explain the various treatment goals and options for offenders with mental disorders.

Johnny Duchane became a ward of the state when he was two years old because his birth mother was a cocaine addict and his father was a drug dealer serving a life sentence for killing one of his drug runners. Johnny Duchane was adopted shortly thereafter by Mr. and Mrs. DeLaroche. Mr. and Mrs. DeLaroche were from a small town outside of Memphis. Once Johnny entered his teens, he started showing some odd behavior. Often Johnny was found talking to himself and seemed to think everyone was against him. Johnny thought that the only way to protect himself was to become a police officer. Johnny managed to be hired on as an officer but it quickly became clear that he was not well.

Johnny was diagnosed with paranoid schizophrenia. When he was on his medication, he could function in most daily activities. The only problem was that Johnny did not like how the medication made him feel. Johnny would go off his medication without warning. One time Mr. and Mrs. DeLaroche had not heard from their son in a month and could not find him. He wasn't in his apartment and he had been dismissed from the police force. While watching the news, Mr. and Mrs. DeLaroche heard that a local police officer was murdered outside the police station. This station was the one where Johnny had been employed. Mr. and Mrs. DeLaroche feared that Johnny's voices may have told him to kill. During a news report the next day, it was announced that former police officer Johnny Duchane had murdered the officer and was in custody awaiting a psychological assessment.

Although many people with mental illness do not commit crime, some do. People may become mentally ill while awaiting trial or during the proceedings. Alternatively, some may suffer mental illness during the commission of a crime. Competency and insanity are both psychological and legal concepts.

This chapter will consider mental illness as it relates to the ability to stand trial and to the commission of a crime. In this chapter, we will explore what is meant by the term *competency to stand trial* within the criminal justice system. We also will examine the defendant's mental state at the time an offense is committed. We will examine the notion of insanity as it pertains to criminal law and forensic psychology.

DIAGNOSING MENTAL DISORDERS

The notion of a mental disorder is that behavior can be defined as "normal" or "abnormal." The *Diagnostic and Statistical Manual of Mental Disorders*, known as the DSM, is the leading guide used to diagnose mental disorders in North America. The DSM was first published by the American Psychiatric Association (APA) in 1952 in order to facilitate the diagnosis of mental disorders and collect statistical information about the occurrence of different types of disorders. The original edition of the DSM was 130 pages long and listed 106 mental disorders. The manual was revised in 1968 (DSM-II), 1980 (DSM-III), and in 1994 (DSM-IV) the manual swelled to 494 pages with 265 disorders. The current version is known as the DSM-IV-TR (fourth edition, text revision, 2000). The DSM-V is scheduled for publication in 2013. Currently, the DSM is set up on a "multiaxial" system that divides the various disorders into categories to help with diagnosis:

Axis I: Clinical disorders, including mood disorders, anxiety disorders, phobias, schizophrenia, bipolar disorder, dissociative disorders, gender identity disorders, eating disorders, substance-related disorders, and developmental and learning disorders

Axis II: Mental retardation and personality disorders, including avoidant, dependent, obsessive-compulsive, histrionic, antisocial, borderline, narcissistic, paranoid, schizoid, and schizotypal disorders

Axis III: General medical conditions that may be related to the mental disorder or that might influence the choice of medications for treating the disorder

Axis IV: Psychosocial or environmental factors that contribute to disorders, including family problems, educational problems, economic problems, or problems with the legal system

Axis V: Assessment of the patient's general level of functioning

The DSM is not a perfect system and has had its critics (Baca-Garcia et al., 2007; Kendell & Jablensky, 2003). For example, it is not clear why certain disorders are included and how the symptoms for each disorder were selected. Some have argued that the DSM lacks a strong empirical or scientific basis. One other interesting note is that as revisions of the DSM have grown so has the number of disorders. Even David Kupler, the most recent chairperson for the new version of DSM, stated: "One of the raps against psychiatry is that you and I are the only two people in the U.S. without a psychiatric diagnosis" (Grossman, 2008). Despite criticism however, the DSM continues to be the default tool for diagnosing mental disorders in North America.

Many of the millions of people who are imprisoned worldwide experience serious mental disorders. There is an overrepresentation of serious mental disorders in prisons, with many prisoners suffering from anxiety and depressive disorders. In a meta-analysis of 62 studies from 12 Western countries, Fazel and Danesh (2002) reported the prevalence rates of psychotic illness, major depression, personality disorder, and antisocial personality disorder (ASPD) in offender samples. Prevalence rates for male (18,530 males) and female (4,260 females) offenders were, respectively, 3.7% and 4.0% for psychotic illness, 10% and 12% for major depression, and 47% and 21% for ASPD.

PRESUMPTIONS IN THE CRIMINAL JUSTICE SYSTEM

The cornerstone of English law identifies two elements that must be present for criminal guilt to be established: (1) a wrongful deed, also known as **actus reus**, and (2) criminal intent, also known as **mens rea**. Both of these elements (and the elements of the specific case) must be found beyond a reasonable doubt for a guilty verdict to be reached. Issues of competency, insanity, and mental disorders all call into question these two basic elements of criminal law.

Actus reus
A wrongful deed

Mens rea
Criminal intent

COMPETENCY TO STAND TRIAL

It is reasonable to expect that in order for individuals who are charged with the commission of a crime to be tried fairly, they should have some understanding of the charges and proceedings and be able to help in preparing their defense. A defendant who is deficient in these domains, possibly because of a mental disorder, may be considered **incompetent to stand trial**. Thus, incompetency to stand trial refers to the inability of a defendant to conduct a defense at any stage of the proceedings on account of a mental disorder. For example, a defendant may be found incompetent to stand trial if he or she is experiencing an episode of schizophrenia and lacks the ability to understand the situation and tell the lawyer the facts of the case. Competency issues also may occur at various stages throughout the trial process and can even occur at sentencing. The degree of impairment necessary for incompetency has been difficult to pinpoint, however.

Incompetent to stand trial

Refers to an inability to conduct a defense at any stage of the proceedings because of a person's mental disorder

The competency standard used in the United States was determined by the U.S. Supreme Court in *Dusky v. United States* (1960). In *Dusky*, the Court ruled that:

> It is not enough for a district judge to find that the defendant is oriented to time and place and has some recollection of events, but that the test must be whether he has sufficient present ability to consult with his lawyer with a reasonable degree of rational understanding—and whether he has a rational as well as factual understanding of the proceedings against him (p. 402).

In essence, a defendant should be able to conduct/instruct his or her defense at any stage of the proceedings, understand the nature of the proceedings against him or her, understand the consequences of the proceedings, and communicate with his or her counsel.

Raising the Issue of Competency

The issue of a defendant's competency may be raised at various points from the time of arrest to the defendant's sentence determination. Examples of instances in which the issue of competency may be raised include when a plea is entered, when a defendant chooses not to be represented by counsel, and during sentencing (Ogloff, Wallace, & Otto, 1991). A defendant is assumed to be competent to stand trial unless the court is satisfied on the balance of probabilities that he or she is incompetent. The defense or prosecution may raise the issue of a defendant's competency and even the court may raise it.

How Many Defendants Are Referred for Competency Evaluations?

Approximately 60,000 defendants a year are referred for competency evaluations (Bonnie & Grisso, 2000). Estimates are somewhere between 2% and 8% of all felony defendants are referred for competency evaluations in the United States (Hoge, Bonnie, Poythress, & Monahan, 1990). Note that great variability is seen in terms of the number of defendants who are referred and found competent (or incompetent) across jurisdictions (Skeem et al., 1998).

Who Can Assess Competency?

Traditionally, only medical practitioners have been allowed to conduct court-ordered assessments of such aspects as competency to stand trial and criminal responsibility—to be discussed later in the chapter (Viljoen, Roesch, Ogloff, & Zapf, 2003). The types of professionals allowed to conduct such assessments vary across countries. For example, both the United States and Australia allow psychologists to conduct court-ordered assessments. Farkas, DeLeon, and Newman (1997) reported that 47 U.S. states allow psychologists to conduct competency and criminal responsibility evaluations. In Canada, however, psychologists may only *assist* psychiatrists or other medical practitioners with the assessment of defendants who are referred for evaluation.

Competency Instruments

A number of screening instruments have been developed to help evaluators quickly screen out defendants who are competent to stand trial. Comprehensive competency assessments can then be reserved for those defendants who are "screened in." One popular competency tool is the MacArthur Competence Assessment Tool—Criminal Adjudication (MacCAT-CA). The MacCAT-CA (Hoge et al., 1992) is a semistructured interview containing 22 items that assess competencies in three areas:

- Factual understanding of the legal system and the adjudication process
- Reasoning ability
- Understanding of own legal situation and circumstances

These areas are assessed via hypothetical scenarios. Following the presentation of the scenario, the defendant is asked a series of specific questions. The evaluator assigns a score of 0, 1, or 2 based on the scoring criteria. For each area, score ranges are provided for three levels of impairment: none to minimal, mild, or clinically significant. For example, one scenario involves a bar fight between Fred and Reggie that then leads to an aggravated assault against Fred (Melton, Petrila, Poythress, & Slobogin, 1997). The defendant then gets asked a number of questions about Fred and the charge against him. One question asks the defendant to state what the judge's job is during the trial. A full response would include stating the following four items; "1) instructs the jury about the law, 2) rules on the admissibility of evidence, 3) ensures that rules are followed in order to ensure fairness, and 4) may be responsible for imposing a sentence" (p. 149). If a defendant does not provide at least two of these items, the evaluator provides the defendant with the functions and then the defendant is asked to paraphrase what was provided and then this paraphrase is scored for accuracy. The responses provided by the defendant give insight into his or her "capacities to comprehend the adjudicatory process; to evaluate the legal relevance of the given facts concerning the case; and to assess the advantages and disadvantages and the risks and benefits of Fred's going to trial versus accepting a plea offer" (p. 149).

See Box 8.1 for a look at some other competency instruments.

Distinguishing between Competent and Incompetent Defendants

In an early meta-analysis of 30 studies conducted in both the United States and Canada, Nicholson and Kugler (1991) found that competent and incompetent defendants differed on age, gender, race, and marital resources. Competent defendants were more likely to be older

---

BOX 8.1   Competency Instruments

Competency Screening Test (CST)

The CST (Lipsitt, Lelos, & McGarry, 1971) has 22 uncompleted sentences that the respondent must finish. For example,

- The lawyer told Bill that . . .
- When I go to court the lawyer will . . .
- Jack felt that the judge . . .

The items measure three constructs: the potential for a constructive relationship between the defendant and his lawyer, the defendant's understanding of the court process, and the ability of the defendant to emotionally cope with the criminal process. Responses are scored using a three-point scale (0, 1, 2) depending on the relation between the defendant's response and example responses provided in the scoring manual. A score of 0 would be assigned if the response demonstrated a low level of legal understanding. For example, "The lawyer told Bill that he is guilty" would receive 0 points (Ackerman, 1999). A score of 2 would be assigned if the response demonstrated a high level of legal understanding. For example, "The lawyer told Bill that he should plead guilty" would receive 2 points (Ackerman, 1999). Scores for each of the items are summed to produce a total CST score. The CST score, in addition to a brief psychiatric interview, is aimed at distinguishing between competent defendants who could proceed to trial and those defendants who should undergo a more complete competency assessment. A score of 20 or below suggests that the defendant should undergo a more comprehensive evaluation.

Competency to Stand Trial Assessment Instrument (CAI)

The CAI (Laboratory of Community Psychiatry, Harvard Medical School, 1973) was designed to accompany the CST in that the CAI is a semistructured interview. The CAI assesses 13 functions corresponding to a defendant's ability to participate in the criminal process on behalf of his or her best interests. Each function is represented in a statement with two or three sample questions that the evaluator may pose to the defendant. For example (Ackerman, 1999).

Function: Appraisal of available legal defenses

Statement: The defendant's awareness of possible legal defenses and how consistent they are with the reality of his or her particular circumstances

Question: How do you think you can be defended against these charges?

(continued)

BOX 8.1   Continued

Following a response to the question, the evaluator can ask follow-up questions to further probe the defendant's response if it is unclear or ambiguous. For each function, responses are rated on a scale from 1 (reflecting a total lack of capacity or function) to 5 (reflecting no impairment, defendant can function adequately). A score of 6 can be given when there is insufficient information to rate the function. The evaluator examines the scores for each function and then makes an overall determination.

Interdisciplinary Fitness Interview (IFI)

The IFI (Golding, Roesch, & Schreiber, 1984) was developed following an analysis of the CAI. As with the CAI, the IFI is a semistructured interview measuring three areas of competency: functional memory, appropriate relationship with lawyer, and understanding of the justice system. There are four main sections to the IFI:

Section A: Legal items

Section B: Psychopathological items

Section C: Overall evaluation

Section D: Consensual judgment

Each section has a number of subsections and areas within each subsection that can be assessed. The revision of the IFI (IFI-R) (Golding, 1993) retains the semistructured interview protocol; however, the revised version has only two sections: Current Clinical Condition and Psycho-Legal Abilities. Each section has a number of subsections. For example, the heading "Current Clinical Condition" has the following categories:

- Attention/consciousness
- Delusions
- Hallucinations
- Impaired reasoning and judgment
- Impaired memory
- Mood and affect

The evaluator assesses these major areas of clinical dysfunction. Responses are rated with a scale ranging from 0 (absent or does not bear on defendant's fitness) to 2 (symptom is likely to significantly impair the defendant's fitness).

The "Psycho-Legal Abilities" section has four subsections:

- Capacity to appreciate charges and to disclose pertinent facts, events, and motives
- Courtroom demeanor and capacity to understand the adversarial nature of proceedings
- Quality of relationship with attorney
- Appreciation of and reasoned choice with respect to legal option and consequences

Responses are rated on a scale ranging from 0 (no or minimal capacity) to 2 (substantial capacity). It also has been recommended that when conducting a competency assessment, the defendant's lawyer, previous mental health contacts, and jail personnel be interviewed. In addition, mental health reports, police reports, and prior arrest history should be reviewed (Golding, as cited in Ackerman, 1999).

females belonging to a minority group and to have fewer marital resources. Substantial research on competency to stand trial has been conducted since the 1990s. To examine this work, Pirelli, Gottdiener, and Zapf (2011) undertook another meta-analysis, examining 68 studies published between 1967 and 2008 that explored differences between competent and incompetent defendants. The researchers found that defendants given a psychotic disorder diagnosis were eight times more likely to be deemed incompetent than defendants without such a diagnosis. Also, incompetent defendants were twice as likely to have been previously hospitalized for a psychiatric disorder. One other robust difference that emerged was that incompetent defendants were twice as likely to be unemployed than employed.

A study that mirrors these results was conducted by Hubbard, Zapf, and Ronan (2003) who examined the competency reports of 468 defendants. Differences between competent and incompetent defendants were found on employment status, psychiatric diagnosis, ethnicity, and criminal charges. Incompetent defendants were less likely to maintain employment and had more serious mental illness than competent defendants. Also, more African American defendants were found incompetent compared to Caucasian defendants. Hubbard et al. (2003) also found that incompetent defendants were more likely to be charged with property and miscellaneous crimes rather than violent crimes compared to competent defendants.

In the following Case Study box, how would you rule on the defendant's competency? You be the judge.

CASE STUDY

YOU BE THE JUDGE

Jack Chow was a graduate student in psychology working on his Ph.D. He would often spend his days in the lab conducting file reviews of offenders for his dissertation research. Jack shared the lab with two other students who also were completing their graduate studies. One day, Jack accused his lab mates of tapping into his data set and changing the data. His lab mates didn't know what he was talking about. These accusations escalated when Jack accused them of going into his e-mail account and sending computer viruses to his friends who were contacts in his e-mail list. Jack's lab mates were getting tired of these accusations.

One Friday afternoon, Jack opened his data file and was convinced it had been tampered with. In a rage, Jack threw his chair at one of his lab mates and started punching him. A student walking by quickly called campus security and police. Jack was charged with assault. On the way to the police station, Jack started yelling that his lab mates had orchestrated his arrest so that they could steal his data and publish his groundbreaking research. Jack was given a court-appointed lawyer. In a preliminary hearing, Jack's lawyer stated Jack had no understanding of what he was being charged with and could not answer any of his questions. Jack kept repeating that he had to get back to his data and didn't have time for these games. He had a Nobel Prize to win. Jack's lawyer claimed Jack was incompetent to stand trial and requested an assessment.

Your Turn . . .

Would you grant Jack this assessment? Do you think Jack is showing signs of incompetency? What are some of your concerns regarding Jack's behavior?

How Is Competency Restored?

When a defendant is found incompetent to stand trial, the goal of the criminal justice system is to get the defendant competent. The most common form of treatment for competency is medication. A question facing the justice system concerning this form of treatment is whether a defendant has the right to refuse medication. This issue was raised in the U.S. Supreme Court case *Sell v. United States* (2003). Dr. Charles Sell was a dentist charged with several counts of insurance fraud who was found incompetent before being tried. He was sent to a mental health facility to receive treatment. However, Dr. Sell refused medication and treatment. The staff at the facility requested that Dr. Sell be mandated to take medication. The facility's medical review panel decided that Sell was mentally ill and dangerous and that medication would aid in his symptoms and could restore his competency to stand trial. Sell appealed the decision. The Court upheld the facility's decision. The Supreme Court ruled that antipsychotic medication could be given against the defendant's will provided it would restore competency but only in limited situations and that other factors, such as dangerousness, would be taken into account (see *Riggins v. Nevada*, 1992; *Washington v. Harper*, 1990).

In sum, although defendants sometimes may argue for *not* taking medication because of the serious side effects, a treatment order may be imposed by the court. The courts will take into account the individual's capacity to comprehend and appreciate the consequences of his or her actions and public safety. However, the courts also must grapple with having a heavily medicated defendant and whether this serves justice. It is important to note that the majority of incompetent defendants (approximately 70%) are fairly quickly restored to competency (Melton et. al., 1997). Often the medication used to restore competency can take effect within a few days of administration (Melton et al., 1997).

See Box 8.2 for a look at a case involving a defendant with a mental illness who stopped taking his medication while awaiting trial.

BOX 8.2	**Mentally Ill But Competent to Make Treatment Decisions?**

On April 25, 1998, police officers Dave Chetcuti and Seann Graham were conducting a routine traffic stop on Highway 101 in San Mateo County, California, when they stopped Marvin Patrick Sullivan. Chetcuti was killed by Sullivan who also tried to kill Graham.

In July 1999, Sullivan was declared incompetent to stand trial and sent to Napa State Hospital. Sullivan was diagnosed as a paranoid schizophrenic. Sullivan suffered from delusions that included his belief that he was an astronaut and at times a CIA agent.

Once Sullivan was declared competent and sent to jail to await his trial, he stopped taking his antipsychotic medication only to make him incompetent again to stand trial. This pattern of being declared competent and then stopping his medication while awaiting trial was repeated. Prosecutors requested that the Court force Sullivan to be medicated so that he could be deemed competent and be tried. The Court rejected the proposal citing insufficient legal precedent for such a recommendation.

However, should Sullivan become competent again, things may change if he once again decides to stop taking his medication while awaiting trial given the 2003 U.S. Supreme Court ruling described in the text above (*Sell v. United States*, 2003).

Source: Based on "Ruling offers hope for jailing accused cop killer" by M. Durand, *The Daily Journal*, January 7, 2004, San Mateo County.

What Happens after a Finding of Incompetency?

The proceedings against a defendant who is found incompetent to stand trial are halted until competency is restored. In the United States, almost all jurisdictions limit the time a defendant may be "held" as incompetent. In the landmark case of *Jackson v. Indiana* (1972), the U.S. Supreme Court stated that a defendant should not be held for more than a reasonable period of time to determine whether there is a likelihood of the person gaining competency. Of course, what constitutes a reasonable period of time is open to interpretation.

Following the *Jackson* decision, a number of states included alternatives to commitment in addition to limiting the length of time a defendant could be held (Roesch & Golding, 1980). The amount of time a defendant can be confined varies by state, with some states having specific time limits (e.g., 18 months), while other states base length of confinement on a proportion of the length of the sentence that would have been given had the defendant been convicted.

Even though a defendant may be restored to competency, it is possible that he or she will become incompetent once again during the trial proceedings. If incompetency occurs again, the proceedings stop until the defendant becomes competent. If a defendant becomes competent while in custody (e.g., detained in a mental facility) and there is reason to believe that he or she may become incompetent if released, the defendant will be required to remain in the mental facility until the trial is complete. Also, it is possible for a defendant to become incompetent while waiting to be sentenced (Manson, 2006); once again the goal is to restore competency if possible.

MENTAL STATE AT TIME OF OFFENSE

Insanity has been defined as not being of sound mind, and being mentally deranged and irrational (Sykes, 1982). Legal insanity definitions vary across jurisdictions; however, generally, insanity removes the responsibility for performing a particular act because of uncontrollable impulses or delusions, such as hearing voices. Two primary British cases shaped the current standards of insanity in the United States, that of James Hadfield and Daniel McNaughton (as cited in Moran, 1985). In addition, the landmark case of John Hinckley has greatly influenced the insanity standards in the United States. Each of these cases is described below.

Insanity

Impairment of mental or emotional functioning that affects perceptions, beliefs, and motivations at the time of the offense

The first British case regarding the issue of "insanity" was that of James Hadfield who in 1800 attempted to assassinate King George III. Hadfield had suffered a brain injury while fighting against the French. His lawyer successfully argued that he was out of touch with reality and therefore met the insanity standard of the time. Following this case, the Criminal Lunatics Act (1800) was established, and it stated the insanity standard of the day.

The second British case influencing insanity standards was that of Daniel McNaughton in 1843 (*R. v. McNaughton*, 1843). Daniel McNaughton was born and raised in Glasgow, Scotland. Eventually he found his way to London in July 1842. While in London, he purchased two pistols that he carried in his waistcoat. On Friday, January 20, 1843, he walked behind Edward Drummond, one of Prime Minister Robert Peel's secretaries, who was coming back from Drummond's bank. McNaughton approached Drummond from behind, took a pistol out of his pocket, and shot Drummond in the back. Drummond then turned to see who shot him and saw McNaughton and pointed to him. McNaughton reached for his other pistol and at that point was tackled by James Silver, a constable. McNaughton was handcuffed and his weapons were removed. Drummond died five days later.

There is some debate as to McNaughton's reason for shooting and whether Drummond or Prime Minister Robert Peel was the intended target.

McNaughton was charged with murder, and the judge interpreted his plea as "not guilty." McNaughton was found not guilty because of his mental status—insanity. He would serve out his life in a mental institute (see Dalby, 2006, for the full details of the story).

Five critical elements emerged from the McNaughton verdict, with three specific to the insanity defenses of today:

1. A defendant must be found to be suffering from a defect of reason/disease of the mind.
2. A defendant must not know the nature and quality of the act he or she is performing.
3. A defendant must not know that what he or she is doing is wrong.

The elements in the *McNaughton* standard emerged in legislation in parts of the United States, England, and Canada. Approximately half of the states in the United States use the *McNaughton* rule in defining insanity.

The *McNaughton* standard is considered a "cognitive test" of insanity because it focuses on the defendant's thought processes and perceptions at the time of the crime (Low, Jeffries, & Bonnie, 1986).

A variety of alternative insanity standards to *McNaughton* have emerged across the United States:

Irresistible Impulse Test If a defendant is cognitively aware of what is right or wrong, but cannot stop himself or herself from behaving in a particular way, the defendant could still be found not guilty by reason of insanity (Ogloff, Roberts, & Roesch, 1993). Twenty-eight states use a variation of the *McNaughton*/cognitive impairment test and another three use *McNaughton* plus the irresistible impulse test.

***Durham* Rule** In *Durham v. United States* (1954), the Court established a new insanity rule where the accused is not criminally responsible for unlawful behavior if it was a result of mental disease or defect. One concern that was raised with the *Durham* rule was that any clinical diagnosis could be used to establish "insanity" (Ogloff et al., 1993). Only the state of New Hampshire uses the *Durham* rule.

American Law Institute Rule This insanity standard occurred as a result of the case *United States v. Brawner* (1972). For this standard, a defendant is not criminally responsible if at the time of committing the crime, the defendant cannot appreciate his or her actions, as a result of mental disease or defect, or could not control his or her behavior consistent with the law as a result of mental disease or defect. As of 2006, 14 states used this standard (Melton et al., 2007).

The case of John Hinckley, Jr., also has had a large influence on a verdict of insanity. It was 1981 and Hinckley shot a number of people including President Ronald Reagan, a secret service agent, a police officer, and James Brady, who was Reagan's press secretary. Hinckley stated he was trying to impress movie star Jodie Foster who he had feelings for. Hinckley was tried and the jury returned a "not guilty by reason of insanity" verdict. The public was outraged that someone who committed such guilty acts would not be punished. Several pieces of legislation were introduced to eliminate or alter the insanity defense. What resulted was the Insanity Defense Reform Act of 1984.

Insanity Defense Reform Act Standard This standard is similar to *McNaughton* except it requires the defendant to experience severe mental disease or defect and places the burden on the defendant to prove this is the case. The burden of proof is higher with this standard than the *McNaughton* standard.

Mental Illness and Verdict

Two verdicts, guilty but mentally ill and not guilty by reason of insanity, acknowledging insanity are possible in some states. Thirteen states allow for a guilty but mentally ill (GBMI) verdict (Borum & Fulero, 1999). The defendant is found guilty but then is provided treatment at a state mental facility. Once the defendant is declared "sane," he or she is returned to prison to complete the sentence that would have been granted if the defendant did not suffer from mental illness. Note that criteria for a GBMI verdict and treatment conditions differ across states. The GBMI verdict has received a number of criticisms. For example, some argue that the treatment options available to defendants GBMI are no different than treatment available to offenders not given this verdict (Slobogin, 1985). See Box 8.3 for a description of a case in which the defendant was found GBMI.

A not guilty by reason of insanity (NGRI) verdict is available in some states where the defendant is sent to a psychiatric hospital and stays there as long as he or she continues to meet the criteria for his or her disorder. Many of these defendants end up being hospitalized longer than they would have been incarcerated for the same crime without the mental disorder (Borum & Fulero, 1999). One example of a failed NGRI is the

Psychiatric facility for defendants with active mental illness.

| BOX 8.3 | Multimillionaire John du Pont: A Mentally Ill Killer |

Perhaps you have heard the du Pont name before? John du Pont was heir to the du Pont fortune with an estimated value of approximately $200 million. Du Pont had an avid interest in athletics and seemed keen to support wrestling. In 1988, he turned his estate into an 800-acre wrestling camp in Delaware County, Pennsylvania. People who spent time around du Pont noticed his behavior becoming increasingly bizarre. For example, during his brief marriage, he accused his wife of being a spy and pointed a gun to her head.

David Schultz was an Olympic champion wrestler who was living on the du Pont property. It is not clear what transpired on January 6, 1996, other than that John du Pont shot David Schultz several times, killing him.

After the shooting, du Pont would not come out of his home. There was a standoff between du Pont and the police for two days. It was cold out so police decided to turn off du Pont's heat to try and get him to come out. When du Pont came out of his home to figure out what was wrong with the heating, police took him into custody and charged him with murder. There was no question that du Pont killed Schultz; at issue was du Pont's mental state. At trial, du Pont was described as a paranoid schizophrenic who believed Schultz was part of a conspiracy to kill him.

On February 25, 1997, the jury returned a guilty but mentally ill verdict for third-degree murder. Du Pont was sentenced to an incarceration term of 13 to 30 years. He is serving his time at the State Correctional Institute–Mercer, a minimum-security institution in Pennsylvania. Although du Pont was eligible for parole on January 29, 2009, he was denied. His maximum sentence would end on January 29, 2026, when he will be 87 years old.

Source: Based on "John du Pont found guilty, mentally ill" by D. Goldberg, Washington Post, February 26, 1997.

case of Jeffrey Dahmer who was charged with 15 murders in Milwaukee, Wisconsin, in 1991. Dahmer pleaded not guilty by reason of insanity. His defense lawyers argued that Dahmer knew what he was doing when he lured young men to his apartment, drugged them, and killed them. However, defense experts also argued that Dahmer could not stop killing because of his mental disorder and therefore should be found NGRI. The jury disagreed and convicted Dahmer for the murders and sentenced him to 15 life sentences. Dahmer was murdered while in a maximum security prison by another inmate in 1994.

Five states, Idaho, Kansas, Montana, Nevada, and Utah, do not allow for an insanity defense (Melton et al., 2007). However, in these states, the defense can introduce evidence of the defendant's mental status to try to disprove the mens rea element of the charge (Borum & Fulero, 1999).

Using the Insanity Defense

Numerous public perceptions regarding the insanity defense exist. Melton et al. (2007) detail four common perceptions of the insanity defense (p. 202):

1. A large number of defendants use the defense.
2. Most are successful (in part because defendants and their expert witnesses are able to deceive gullible juries).
3. Those acquitted by reason of insanity are released upon acquittal or shortly thereafter.
4. They are extremely dangerous.

Do you share these perceptions? These perceptions however should actually be labeled "*mis*perceptions." As Melton et al. (2007) note, the available data do not support these commonly held views.

Studies find that few defendants use the insanity defense. For example, in the United States, one study found that less than 1% of all felony cases will argue an insanity defense (Steadman et al., 1993). Moreover, the success rate of such a defense is variable. It has been reported that approximately 25% of defendants who argue an insanity defense succeed (Steadman et al., 1993). Dr. Henry Steadman has been conducting research with offenders who have mental illnesses for more than 40 years. To learn more about Dr. Steadman, see Box 8.4.

BOX 8.4   Researcher Profile: Dr. Henry (Hank) Steadman

Dr. Hank Steadman started out his career of understanding the mental health issues of inmates by getting postgraduate degrees in sociology. He received both his BA and his MA at Boston College and then moved to the University of North Carolina–Chapel Hill for his Ph.D.

Dr. Henry Steadman

One of Dr. Steadman's first job assignments was at the New York State Office of Mental Health where he undertook a longitudinal study of a cohort of 967 maximum security inmates in state prison mental hospitals who were mass transferred to state mental hospitals between March and August 1966 as a result of a landmark U.S. Supreme Court decision (*Baxstrom v. Herold*). Dr. Steadman's favorite study was the one following up on the *Baxstrom v. Herold* case. It was the first study showing empirically that psychiatrists were unable to accurately predict future violent behavior any better than chance and it directly shaped the "rest of my professional career," he states.

Dr. Steadman's research interests include the effectiveness of jail diversion programs for justice involving persons with mental illness, risk assessment of violence, and the operation and effectiveness of mental health courts.

When asked what keeps him interested in the field, Dr. Steadman notes, "There are about 2.3 million persons admitted to U.S. jails annually who are seriously mentally ill with acute symptoms who are among the most disadvantaged people in the U.S. I believe the research we do informs the development of much more effective programs and helps support advocacy to get scarce resources and develop political will."

Dr. Steadman's future research interests include trying to understand why the rates of serious mental illness are twice as high among women booked into U.S. jails compared to men.

There are a few things Dr. Steadman would like to see changed in the criminal justice system. For example, he would like to see the Rockefeller Drug Laws in New York dropped to reduce the unnecessary long-term incarceration of relatively low-level drug offenses.

In terms of how he would like to see future forensic psychologists trained, he notes the importance of students having a combination of rigorous methodological and statistical research training with solid clinical understanding that is linked to a clear picture of how the criminal justice system actually works. He also believes that internships in real-world settings are essential.

Currently, Dr. Steadman is the president of Policy Research Associates, Inc., where his group conducts research and evaluations and offers technical assistance.

When Dr. Steadman isn't working, he enjoys watching his four thoroughbred horses race. And when they aren't racing, Dr. Steadman is. Dr. Steadman has completed 14 marathons and numerous other road races. Although now he states, "my arthritic hips have put me on the Injured Reserve List."

In an attempt to examine the annual number of insanity cases for each state, Cirincione and Jacobs (1999) were able to collect data from 36 states. They found that for the 36 states surveyed, the average number of insanity acquittals was 33.4% per state per year. They found that California (134) and Florida (110.5) had the highest average number of insanity acquittals per year and that New Mexico (0) and South Dakota (0.1) had the lowest, with six states reporting no more than 1 insanity acquittal a year.

Assessing Insanity

Just as with competency to stand trial, an insanity defense requires a psychiatric assessment. Richard Rogers developed the first standardized assessment scales for criminal responsibility: the Rogers Criminal Responsibility Assessment Scales (R-CRAS) (Rogers, 1984).

The R-CRAS is the only instrument of its kind. It has 25 individual scales examining a number of factors such as:

- Patient reliability of what occurred
- Possible organic conditions
- Presence of mental health issues
- Thought and language disturbances

The ratings on each of these 25 scales are then summarized into categories (Melton et al., 1997, p. 255):

- Presence of organicity
- Presence of major psychiatric disorder
- Loss of cognitive control (i.e., whether the person lacked the ability to comprehend the criminality of his or her behavior)
- Loss of behavioral control (i.e., whether the person was unable to change, monitor, or control his or her criminal behavior)
- A judgment of whether the assessed loss of control was a direct result of the organic or psychiatric disturbance

The decisions are then plotted in a decision tree to produce an outcome: sane, insane, or no opinion.

It is important to note that the R-CRAS was developed to standardize evaluations and ensure that particular areas are evaluated, rather than produce a cutoff score to indicate criminal responsibility (Rogers & Ewing, 1992). The clinician is to take all the information into account and use it as the basis for a decision regarding the defendant's mental status and criminal responsibility. One issue with using these types of tests is that they typically assess current functioning; however, the issue with insanity is prior mental state (i.e., mental state at the time of the crime). As such, a broad-based assessment protocol is usually implemented including defendant interviews, third-party information about the crime scenario, social history examination, prior medical/psychiatric records, intellectual/personality testing, and medical scans (Melton et al., 1997, p. 267).

What Happens to a Defendant Found "Insane"?

Although the public may think a NGRI verdict means the defendant "gets off easily" and is released back into the community after a short stint in a hospital, in reality, NGRI defendants often spend more time committed in psychiatric facilities than they would

sentenced to prison if they were simply found "guilty" (Silver, 1995). The notion behind commitment to a psychiatric facility is that defendants are treated until they are no
longer dangerous, at which point they are released. In some states, defendants may be
committed for an indeterminate amount of time (i.e., until they are no longer considered
dangerous).

DEFENDANTS WITH MENTAL DISORDERS

If a defendant does not receive an incompetent finding or a verdict of insanity, this does
not necessarily mean that he or she does not have mental health difficulties. A substantial number of offenders in the United States also have mental health needs. For example, 25% of offenders incarcerated in Colorado suffer from mental illness (O'Keefe &
Schnell, 2007). Also, it is important to note that offenders who have mental illnesses are
likely to have more than one mental health issue. It is estimated that approximately 75%
of offenders with a mental illness (in the United States) have dual diagnoses (Chandler,
Peters, Field, & Juliano-Bult, 2004).

Why Are There Such High Rates
of Mental Illness in Offender Populations?

A variety of explanations have been postulated to understand the high rates of mental illness in offender populations (Bland et al., 1990):

1. Individuals with a mental illness are likely to be arrested at a disproportionately
   high rate compared with those who do not have a mental illness.
2. Individuals with a mental illness are less adept at committing crime and therefore
   more likely to get caught.
3. Individuals with a mental illness are more likely to plead guilty, possibly because
   of an inability to access good representation or to understand the consequences of
   their plea.

It is possible that all of these explanations are appropriate. Moreover, there may be
alternative explanations to the high rates of mental illness in offender populations that
have yet to be articulated. Further research is needed to explain this phenomenon.

Dealing with Offenders Who Are Mentally Ill

Police have great latitude in how they deal with offenders who are mentally ill in the
community. Mental health legislation grants police two options for handling these offenders. If an individual has a mental disorder and poses a threat to him- or herself or to
others, the police may take the individual to a hospital or mental health facility for assessment and possible treatment. As an alternative, the police may charge and arrest the
individual. In this scenario, mental health services may be obtained through the criminal
justice system. Thus, the mental health system and the criminal justice system are both
available to police, providing two alternative routes for dealing with people with a mental
illness. Some have argued that people with a mental illness are more likely to be processed through the justice system because of the difficulty of obtaining services for them
through the mental health system (Teplin, 1984).

Bias against Offenders Who Are Mentally Ill

The association between mental illness and criminality/violence has been studied for over 20 years with mixed results. Some researchers have found a link between mental disorder and criminality/violence, and others report that use of alcohol and drugs is responsible for the elevated base rates of criminality and violence in individuals with mental disorders.

In one study, individuals with mental illness, according to police records, were twice as likely to be at risk for coming back into contact with the criminal justice system compared to other offenders (Hartford, Heslp, & Stitt, 2005). In a six-year follow-up study, Teplin, Abram, and McClelland (1994) examined the relationship between postrelease arrest rate for violent crime and mental disorders. Offenders with either schizophrenia or a major affective disorder had a 43% likelihood of rearrest. Those with substance abuse had a similar rearrest rate of 46%. Moreover, offenders with a prior history of violent crime were twice as likely to be rearrested as those with no prior history. Offenders with a history of hallucinations and delusions (i.e., schizophrenia symptoms) were not more likely to be subsequently arrested.

Offenders with mental disorders may be treated cautiously by the criminal justice system because of a presumption that they are a greater risk for committing more crime. A number of factors, however, can be related to rates of rearrest, not just mental illness.

Are People with Mental Illnesses Violent?

A commonly held belief is that those who have a mental illness are violent predators. Does the research support this view? Recently, Elbogen and Johnson (2009) examined the relationship between mental disorder and violence in a longitudinal study. In phase 1 of the study, 34,653 Americans were interviewed and assessed for serious mental disorders. Participants were interviewed again about three years later and asked if they had engaged in any of the following behaviors in that time: used a stick, knife, or gun in a fight; started a fire on purpose to destroy someone's property; hit someone so hard that they were injured or had to see a doctor; or forced someone to have sex with them against their will. The rates of violence for people with serious mental illness were relatively low. However, individuals with substance dependence and those with co-occurring severe mental illness had the highest rates of violence. It is important to note that the vast majority of people with serious and co-occurring mental illnesses did not commit any violence.

Cirincione, Steadman, Clark-Robbins, and Monahan (1992) examined the degree to which a diagnosis of schizophrenia was predictive of violence, after controlling for arrest history. Two cohorts, one from 1968 and one from 1978, in a New York State psychiatric facility were reviewed. Results differed across cohorts. Prior arrest was a significant predictor of violence in both cohorts. A schizophrenia diagnosis was predictive of violence in the 1968 cohort but not in the 1978 cohort. For those without a history of prior arrest, a diagnosis of schizophrenia did not predict engaging in later violence. This research indicates that prior violence and substance abuse seem to have much greater effects on the likelihood of future violence than psychiatric diagnoses such as schizophrenia.

A meta-analysis examining the recidivism of over 15,000 offenders with mental disorders was conducted by Bonta, Law, and Hanson (1998). The disordered offenders were followed for an average of 4.8 years in the community after having been released from prisons and hospitals. Offenders with mental disorders were found less likely to recidivate violently than offenders who did not have major psychological or psychiatric disorders. The researchers suggest that some data find a greater likelihood of violence when an individual is experiencing a psychotic phase with symptoms of a paranoid nature. Overall, the notion that people with mental illness are more violent may not be a completely accurate view. Numerous factors (e.g., how psychosis is defined and measured) have been found to moderate the association between psychosis and violence (Douglas, Guy, & Hart, 2009). See the In the Media box for a further discussion on the community's perception of people with mental illness.

Treatment of Offenders with Mental Disorders

The goals for treatment for offenders with mental disorders vary greatly and are somewhat dependent on whether the offender is dealt with through the mental health system or the criminal justice system. Some of the treatment goals identified for those with mental

---

IN THE MEDIA **Are Offenders with Mental Illness Really Violent?**

You're standing at the bus station when a man walks up to you and starts attacking you with a brick. You did not know the man and the attack was unprovoked. A few weeks later, a man walks into a fast-food restaurant with a gun and kills three random patrons. A few weeks after that attack, you learn of a man who sat beside a sleeping teenager on a train ride home; the man pulled out a knife and killed the teen. The man did not know the teen. These are all attacks that have actually occurred. The one common denominator is that the attackers all suffered some form of mental illness and these cases made headlines.

Given the media attention to these cases, it is not difficult for the public's perception to be that people with mental illness are violent. But what does the research show? In fact, not all people with mental illness are violent.

Certain factors may be more predictive of violence than mental illness. For example, having committed violence in the past increases the likelihood that you will commit violence in the future. Substance abuse also may increase your likelihood of being violent. Moreover, in terms of mental illness, it is more likely that should violence occur, it will happen when the individual is experiencing "active" symptoms—for example, having delusions or experiencing the lows of depressions—compared to when symptoms are controlled.

Some may argue that if people who are mentally ill refuse to take their medication, they should be hospitalized and forced to take medication. This extreme view, however, impinges on the civil rights of people with mental illness and in reality there simply aren't enough facilities to house everyone. An alternative view has been proposed by the National Alliance of the Mentally Ill who proposes a "Program of Assertive Community Treatment" that attempts to provide 24-hour care outside of a hospital setting for individuals with severe mental illness. Involvement in these programs is often mandatory. For example, "Kendra's Law" in New York is a law named for a young woman pushed in front of a Manhattan subway train by a man with a long history of untreated mental illness. The law allows the authorities to order outpatient treatment for those people who are mentally ill and who refuse get help. Although people with mental illnesses who are violent make headlines, many people with mental illness are not violent. Of course, there are many individuals who are violent, but do not have a mental illness.

Source: Mulvey, E., & Fardella, J. (2000, November 1). Are the mentally ill really violent? *Psychology.* Retrieved from Today http//www.psychologytoday.com/node/22419.

disorders include symptom reduction, decreased length of stay in the facility, and no need to be readmitted to hospital (Test, 1992). Of course, reducing the risk of recidivism has garnered much attention as a treatment goal among those in the criminal justice system (Lipsey, 1992).

A number of types of facilities exist at which offenders with mental disorders can receive treatment: psychiatric institutions, general hospitals, and assisted housing units. There appears to be little agreement on which type of treatment is appropriate for offenders with mental disorders (Quinsey & Maguire, 1983). However, for those who experience active psychotic symptoms such as delusions, hallucinations, suspicion, and noncompliance with medication, two key treatment options are used: antipsychotic drugs and behavior therapy (Breslin, 1992). Medication can help control psychotic symptoms, while behavior therapy can help to ensure that patients take the medication consistently. The critical aspects of behavior therapy appear to be in providing positive social and material reward for appropriate behavior, while decreasing or eliminating attention for symptomatic behavior (Beck, Menditto, Baldwin, Angelone, & Maddox, 1991; Paul & Lentz, 1977).

The availability of facilities and the treatment programs offered vary across the country. Moreover, the willingness of an offender to engage in a particular program will vary. Even if an offender is motivated to receive treatment, an appropriate program may not be available at a particular facility. Thus, there are difficulties in matching programs to offenders' needs and willingness to participate.

One overarching treatment goal of many offender programs is to reintegrate the offender into society. The mental health and criminal justice systems have developed options with this goal in mind. For example, a **community treatment order** allows the offender who has a mental illness to live in the community, with the stipulation that he or she will agree to treatment or detention in the event that his or her condition deteriorates. Another option for the courts dealing with offenders with mental illness who are facing minor charges is **diversion**—that is, diverting them directly into a treatment program rather than having them go through the court process. Generally, only defendants who are willing to participate in treatment will be diverted.

Hodgins et al. (2007) identified five components of community treatment programs that are related to success with offenders with a mental illness. They are (1) multifaceted, intense, and highly structured, and the treating clinician (2) accepts the dual role of treating the mental disorder and preventing violence, (3) takes responsibility for ensuring that the patient follows the treatment program, (4) rehospitalizes the patient if it is needed to stabilize acute symptoms or if there is an increase in risk for violence, and (5) obtains court orders, if necessary, to ensure patients comply with their treatment program.

Treatment can be critical for offenders who have certain mental disorders such as schizophrenia.

A NEW COURT FOR PEOPLE WITH MENTAL ILLNESS: THE MENTAL HEALTH COURTS

A new court is in town, designed for people in need of competency and criminal responsibility assessments and those wanting to plead guilty and for sentencing hearings. The first mental health courts in the United States were established in the late

Community treatment order

Sentence that allows an offender who has a mental disorder to live in the community, with the stipulation that the person will agree to treatment or detention in the event his or her condition deteriorates

Diversion

A decision not to prosecute a young offender, but rather have him or her undergo an educational or community-service program. Also an option for the courts dealing with offenders with mental illnesses who are facing minor charges. The court can divert the offender directly into a treatment program rather than have him or her go through the court process.

1990s with the first court opening in Broward County, Florida, in 1997. In 2000, the Clinton administration and Congress signed the America's Law Enforcement and Mental Health Project Act into law. This act provided funding for 100 mental health courts nationwide, with plans for more if those succeeded. Currently, the United States has more than 150 mental health courts. These courts attempt to redirect those with mental health needs back into the mental health care system (rather than the criminal justice system). Mental health courts have four main objectives (Schneider, Bloom, & Heerema, 2007):

1. To divert accused people who have been charged with minor to moderately serious criminal offenses and offer them an alternative
2. To facilitate a defendant's competency to stand trial evaluation
3. To ensure treatment for a defendant's mental disorders
4. To decrease the cycle that offenders with mental illness experience by becoming repeat offenders

In general, mental health courts offer a rehabilitative reaction to behavior that would otherwise have been dealt with through the criminal justice system. Alternatives to serving a sentence in prison for less serious offenses such as theft, shoplifting, property damage, and minor assaults are available. One goal for these courts is to ensure that defendants and offenders receive the proper assessments and treatments. The courts make referrals to medical experts, as well as case workers who help develop a "release plan" (e.g., provide clothes, find housing, and treatment options) once the accused is in the community.

Are Mental Health Courts Effective?

At the outset, it must be noted that little research has been conducted to evaluate mental health courts. What we do know is that there is a lot of variability across different courts. For example, courts may differ on how defendants are referred, the criteria for a defendant's eligibility, and the quality and quantity of services available. Data are now available for the first multisite follow-up study on mental health courts with treatment and control groups (Steadman, Redlich, Callahan, Robbins, & Vesselinov, 2011). Participants were 447 individuals in four mental health courts in San Francisco County (California), Santa Clara County (California), Hennepin County (Minneapolis), and Marion County (Indianapolis). Six hundred participants were in the control condition of "treatment as usual." In the 18 months following treatment, defined as entry into the mental health court, the mental health court participants had a lower rearrest rate and fewer days of incarceration compared to the control group. These data show mental health courts meeting their objectives.

It also appears to be the case that defendants going through mental health courts are more likely to be connected to services than those not going through such a court (Schneider et al., 2007). Those having gone through the mental health system also report being more satisfied with the process and perceiving higher levels of fairness, lower levels of coercion, and increased confidence with the administration of justice.

Summary

1. A defendant is found to be incompetent if he or she is unable, due to a mental disorder, to understand the nature of the proceedings, understand the consequences of the proceedings, or communicate with counsel.

2. Differences between competent and incompetent defendants were found on psychiatric diagnosis, prior hospitalization, and employment. Incompetent defendants were more likely to have psychiatric diagnoses, prior hospitalization for mental illness, and less likely to be employed than competent defendants.

3. A variety of insanity standards are used in the United States. Five states do not acknowledge an insanity defense. Generally, the defendant is not criminally responsible for an act that was committed (or omitted) while he or she was suffering from a mental disorder to the extent that he or she could not appreciate the nature or quality of the act or of knowing that it was wrong.

4. A number of explanations have been suggested for the high rates of mental illness in offender populations. For example, individuals with a mental illness may be less adept at committing crime and, therefore, more likely to get caught.

5. Treatment goals for offenders with mental disorders vary greatly. Some goals are symptom reduction, decreased length of stay in the facility, no need to be readmitted to hospital, and reduced recidivism.

Key Concepts

actus reus *191*

community treatment order *206*

diversion *206*

incompetent to stand trial *191*

insanity *197*

mens rea *191*

Discussion Questions

1. While having dinner with your parents, your father mentions an article that he read in the newspaper highlighting the dangerousness of offenders with mental disorders. He makes the inference that mental illness leads to violent offending. Describe the data that call your father's conclusion into question.

2. When you show up for your part-time job at the grocery store, you are informed that the store manager has been arrested for voyeurism. When he was arrested, he was confused and incoherent. He is scheduled to undergo a competency evaluation. Your coworkers mention that they heard a rumor about the manager having some sort of mental illness. Describe the characteristics associated with incompetent defendants and the process the store manager will undergo following an incompetence determination.

3. Design a study to evaluate the various dispositions/options the criminal justice system has for offenders with mental illness and their influence on recidivism—the likelihood of reoffending.

4. You have been hired by the police department to help police quickly identify those who may need psychiatric services rather than be processed through the criminal justice system. Develop a brief checklist for police to use when they come in contact with disorderly individuals so that they can take the most appropriate action.

CHAPTER 9

Sentencing in the United States: Practices and Public Opinions

LEARNING OBJECTIVES

- Describe the structure of the court system in the United States.

- List the primary purposes and principles of sentencing.

- Describe some of the sentencing options available in the United States.

- Define the term *sentencing disparity* and explain how it might be reduced.

- List the principles that form the basis for effective correctional interventions.

- Outline some of the opinions Americans have toward the criminal justice system.

In a Baltimore courtroom, Jamie Harrison was just found guilty of burglary, and Judge Singh, who presided over the case, has made the difficult decision to incarcerate him for his crime. In part, the decision was based on the seriousness of the crime—more than $10,000 worth of valuables was stolen from the property Jamie burglarized—but it didn't help that this was not Jamie's first crime.

In fact, starting from a very young age, Jamie has had a lot of encounters with the police and he has a long criminal record to show for it. Most of his crimes have involved property offenses, but he has also been charged with a serious assault and drug possession. Jamie has also been incarcerated on several other occasions, and he has always managed to find trouble very quickly upon his release.

Given all of these facts, Judge Singh feels he has few options for Jamie. He is not confident that prison will turn Jamie's life around, but given the seriousness of the crime and Jamie's constant reoffending, he thinks that prison is probably the best place for him. Judge Singh also hopes that a prison sentence will send a message to other criminals in the community that the sort of behavior exhibited by Jamie will not be tolerated by the criminal justice system.

A lthough not studied as much as some other topics in the field of forensic psychology, sentencing is a crucial aspect of the criminal justice system, and one that deserves our attention. Obviously, sentencing has a direct and significant impact on offenders. However, sentencing also impacts the public in a variety of ways. For example, not only will our safety potentially be affected by the sorts of sentences judges hand down to offenders, but so will our finances, given that we will ultimately have to help pay for many of the sanctions offenders receive. Thus, it is important for us to understand the sentencing process, and reviewing research conducted by criminologists, psychologists, and other criminal justice professionals can assist with this task.

Throughout this chapter, we will discuss the sentencing of offenders in the United States by focusing on some of the issues raised in the opening vignette. We will first describe the structure of the court system and briefly discuss the sentencing process, focusing specifically on the purposes and principles that often guide sentencing decisions. We will also briefly discuss some of the sentencing options available to judges like Judge Singh. Our attention will then turn to one of the major problems that can result from this process and a potential solution that has been proposed to solve this problem. Specifically, we will focus on sentencing disparity, which often results from the high degree of discretion judges have when deciding on appropriate sentences, and sentencing guidelines as a way of decreasing this disparity. We will finish our discussion of sentencing by reviewing research that examines whether the goals of sentencing are actually achieved. To conclude the chapter, we will present research findings that deal with public opinions toward sentencing, and the criminal justice system more generally, and discuss where these opinions might come from.

THE STRUCTURE OF THE U.S. COURT SYSTEM

The court system is one component of a larger criminal justice system that includes policing agencies and correctional institutions. Some of the major roles of courts in the United States include hearing evidence presented at trial, determining guilt and innocence, and rendering sentencing decisions. As already indicated, in this chapter we will focus on the sentencing aspect of the U.S. court system. However, before we do that, we will first briefly discuss the structure of the court system.

The court system in the United States is relatively unique in that it is made up of two separate systems, the federal court system and the state court system, which are both separated into levels of legal superiority (i.e., courts are essentially bound by the rulings of courts positioned above them in the hierarchy). Historically, the separation of federal and state courts is due to the Constitution, which established a sharing of powers between the individual governments of the various states and that of the national governing body (United States Courts, 2011a).

The structure of the federal court system is relatively straightforward; however, there is no consistent court structure at the state level, with variations existing across jurisdictions (although, as described below, many commonalities also exist). Given the complexities associated with the state court system, we will only briefly mention it here. We will spend most of our time in this section, and subsequent sections, talking about the federal court system.

Although the federal court system is often viewed as a three-tier hierarchy with U.S. district (or trial) courts at the bottom, U.S. appeal courts in the middle, and the Supreme

Court of the United States (SCOTUS) at the top, the court system can be deconstructed even further. For example, there are a wide variety of federal courts and administrative agencies that actually operate outside of the judicial system. These include the U.S. Tax Court, U.S. military courts, and various U.S. administrative offices and boards, such as the IRS Appeals Office. Despite this, U.S. district courts are often considered to form the bottom layer of the federal court system. District courts are essentially the federal trial courts, where civil and criminal cases are heard, facts are decided, and sentences are handed out. Above the district courts are the U.S. appellate courts. The primary function of the U.S. appellate courts is to review appeals from the district courts. Finally, at the top of the federal court system is the SCOTUS.

The SCOTUS is the final court of appeal in the United States. However, before the SCOTUS will hear an appeal, the case must typically have been appealed in the relevant courts lower in the hierarchy, namely, the U.S. appellate courts, and even then people still have limited rights to appeal to the SCOTUS. Indeed, of the 7,000+ cases that the SCOTUS is asked to hear each year, between 100 and 150 are actually accepted (United States Courts, 2011a). The SCOTUS also provides guidance to the federal government on law-related matters (e.g., interpretation of the Constitution). An example of such a case was the groundbreaking 1954 trial, *Brown vs. Board of Education*, which was discussed in Chapter 1. Recall that in this case, the Supreme Court ruled that racial segregation in American schools was unconstitutional. The SCOTUS currently consists of eight judges plus the chief justice (as of 2012, John G. Roberts). These judges are all appointed by the president of the United States and affirmed by the federal government through the Senate (United States Courts, 2011a).

The Supreme Court of the United States.

Each of the U.S. states also has its own court system. As previously stated, many differences can be seen across the systems. However, commonalities also exist. In fact, the basic structure of most state systems resembles the three-tier hierarchy of the federal court system, with trial courts on the bottom, appellate courts in the middle, and state supreme courts at the top (the names of these courts are often jurisdiction dependent). Generally speaking, these different courts will deal with the same types of issues that are heard in federal courts positioned at similar levels in the hierarchy.

As indicated in Table 9.1, state and federal courts have different mandates in terms of the matters with which they tend to deal. However, the two systems can and do interact, and there are circumstances under which federal courts can become involved in state cases (United States Courts, 2011b). For example, as highlighted in the last column of Table 9.1, the Fourteenth Amendment to the U.S. Constitution allows this to happen when one makes the argument in state cases that certain constitutional rights are being violated (e.g., right to counsel, right against self-incrimination, right to a speedy trial, etc.; see United States Court System, 2011b).

TABLE 9.1	Matters Dealt with by Courts in the State and Federal System.	
State Courts	**Federal Courts**	**State or Federal Courts**
Crimes under state legislation	Crimes under statuses enacted by Congress	Crimes punishable under both federal and state law
State constitutional issues and cases involving state laws or regulations	Most cases involving federal laws or regulations (for example, tax, Social Security, broadcasting, civil rights)	Federal constitutional issues
Family law issues	Matters involving interstate and international commerce, including airline and railroad regulation	Certain civil rights claims
Real property issues		"Class action" cases
Most private contract disputes (except those resolved under bankruptcy law)	Cases involving securities and commodities regulation, including takeover of publicly held corporations	Environmental regulations
Most issues involving the regulation of trades and professions	Admiralty cases	Certain disputes involving federal law
Most professional malpractice issues	International trade law matters	
Most issues involving the internal governance of business associations such as partnerships and corporations	Patent, copyright, and other intellectual property issues	
	Cases involving rights under treaties, foreign states, and foreign nationals	
Most personal injury lawsuits	State law disputes when "diversity of citizenship" exists	
Most workers' injury claims	Bankruptcy matters	
Probate and inheritance matters	Disputes between states	
Most traffic violations and registration of motor vehicles	*Habeas corpus* actions	
	Traffic violations and other misdemeanors occurring on certain federal property	

Source: Jurisdiction of state and federal courts, U.S. courts from administrative office of the U.S. courts on behalf of the federal judiciary.

SENTENCING IN THE UNITED STATES

Probably the most visible and controversial component of the court system in the United States is the sentencing process, whereby judges determine the appropriate legal sanction to hand down to a person convicted of an offense. According to Roberts (1991), sentencing is a highly visible process because, unlike the majority of decisions made in the criminal justice system (e.g., police arrests, prison placements, release decisions), sentencing decisions are made in the open and presented before the court. The sentencing process is highly controversial because of the many problems that can potentially result from the sentencing process, such as issues with sentencing effectiveness and sentencing disparity, which will be discussed in more detail below.

The Purposes of Sentencing

To understand the sentencing process in the United States, we must begin by discussing the reasons why we sentence offenders. Although the United States has two separate court systems, judges trying cases in these two systems are generally attempting to accomplish the same thing. For example, one obvious goal of sentencing in either system is to contribute to respect for the law and to maintain a just, peaceful, and safe society (U.S. Sentencing Commission, 2011a). In addition to this purpose, judges also sentence offenders in order to change their behavior or to change the behavior of potential offenders (i.e., us) who reside in the community. More specifically, offenders are often sentenced to reduce the probability that they, and the rest of the community, will violate the law in the future. These sentencing goals are referred to as **specific deterrence** and **general deterrence**, respectively. Other potential objectives involved in sentencing include the following:

- To denounce unlawful conduct
- To separate offenders from society (e.g., in order to enhance public safety)
- To assist in rehabilitating offenders
- To provide **reparations** for harm done to victims or the community

At present, it is not clear if one of these sentencing goals is any more dominant or important than another. The following facts, however, do seem clear:

1. Judges in the United States often consider more than one goal when handing down a sentence. For example, an offender may be sentenced to prison by a judge in an attempt to reduce the probability that he or she will commit another crime and also to separate that offender from society (e.g., for the public's safety).
2. Many of the goals that have been listed above can, at times, be incompatible with one another. For example, handing down a long prison sentence to an offender will separate that individual from society, at least for a time. However, as will be discussed later in this chapter, long sentences may not be an effective way of rehabilitating an offender (i.e., reducing the probability that the person will reoffend in the future or become prosocial members of society when they are released).
3. Different judges across the United States likely hand down sentences for different reasons, even when dealing with offenders and offenses that are similar. For example, under similar circumstances, one judge may hand down a sentence that he or she feels is likely to assist in the rehabilitation of the offender, while another judge may hand down a sentence primarily intended to deter the general public from violating the law.

Specific deterrence

Sentencing to reduce the probability that an offender will reoffend in the future

General deterrence

Sentencing to reduce the probability that members of the general public will offend in the future

Reparations

A sentence where the offender has to make a monetary payment to the victim or the community. See *restitution* on page 214.

The Principles of Sentencing

Just as there are numerous reasons for imposing sanctions on offenders, there are also numerous principles in the United States that help guide the sentencing decisions of judges. Often these principles are not explicitly stated, but are embedded within the sentencing guidelines that judges draw on to make sentencing decisions. For example, as will be discussed more thoroughly below, sentencing guidelines exist at the federal level (U.S. Sentencing Commission, 2011a). Within these guidelines, one of the fundamental principles of sentencing appears to be that sentences should be proportionate to the gravity of the offense. In other words, when handing down a sentence, judges are meant to consider the seriousness of the offense: the more serious the crime, the more serious the sentence should be. In addition, according to federal guidelines, judges need to consider the criminal history of the offender when deciding on sentences (U.S. Sentencing Commission, 2011a). Like crime seriousness, sentences should be proportionate to the seriousness of the offender's criminal history.

In addition to these primary principles, judges are also meant to take into account a range of other factors when deciding on sentences (U.S. Sentencing Commission, 2011a). For example:

- A sentence should be adjusted to account for any relevant aggravating or mitigating circumstances relating to the offense or the offender. For example, if the offender abused a position of authority when committing his or her offense, this should be considered in the sentencing decision.
- Sentences should be similar for similar offenders committing similar offenses under similar circumstances. Indeed, this principle is a driving force behind the development of sentencing guidelines, which are ultimately meant to result in fair and uniform sentencing decisions.
- Although disagreement surrounds this issue, there also seems to be a degree of consensus, especially for juvenile offenders, that individuals should not be deprived of liberty (e.g., imprisoned) if less restrictive sanctions are appropriate under the circumstances (i.e., can accomplish the goals of sentencing). The increased use of restorative justice in the United States perhaps reflects this sentencing principle (see below).

Sentencing Options in the United States

In addition to the purposes and principles of sentencing, it is important to understand the various options available to judges when it comes to the types of sentences they can hand out. As just discussed, certain guidelines in the United States describe the various sentencing options available for particular offenses and the minimum and maximum penalties that can be handed down. These are federal guidelines, but they can be drawn on by state judges as well (Kauder & Ostrom, 2008). However, in the vast majority of cases, especially in state courts when relatively minor offenses are being heard, judges have a great deal of discretion when deciding on appropriate sentences.

For example, while it may be possible to sentence a petty criminal to prison, it is highly likely that some other sentencing option will be used instead, such as a fine. Sometimes this high degree of discretion can result in very unusual sentences, such as those described in Box 9.1. Instead of describing all the various sentencing options available to judges in the United States, which is a task that would take up a large portion of this book, we describe instead some of the most commonly used sanctions, or at least the most commonly talked about.

Depending on the offense being considered, and the jurisdiction where the offense is being tried, judges in the United States have many sentencing options available to them, some of which are used in combination, including the following (see Caputo, 2004, for more details about many of these options):

Fine

A sentence where the offender has to make a monetary payment to the courts

Restitution

A sentence where the offender has to make a monetary payment to the victim or the community

- A common sentencing option is the **fine**. Fines can be given alone or in combination with other sentencing options, such as probation (see below). According to the U.S. Sentencing Commission (2011a), a court that fines an offender will set the amount of the fine, the way the fine is to be paid, and the time by which the fine must be paid. If an offender, without a reasonable excuse, does not pay the fine, then the person can serve a term of imprisonment (see below).
- **Restitution** is a payment made by an offender to the victim to cover expenses resulting from a crime, such as monetary loss resulting from property damage.

There appears to be a movement in many jurisdictions to rely on alternatives to imprisonment when sentencing offenders, especially for crimes that are relatively minor. As we discuss in the section on sentencing effectiveness, this seems to be a wise move, and one that is likely to save taxpayer dollars, improve the probability of rehabilitation, and reduce the overcrowding problem in many prisons. Some judges seem to be extremely creative in their sentencing decisions, however, as indicated in these recent examples that have been reported in the media.

- Three men who were involved in a prostitution ring were sentenced to spend time in chicken suits in Painesville, Ohio. The men were ordered to put on the chicken suits and to stand outside the courthouse with signs reading "No Chicken Ranch in Painesville," which referred to the brothel in the movie *The Best Little Whorehouse in Texas*.
- Also in Ohio, this time in Coshocton, two men were given the choice of a jail sentence or being forced to dress as women and walk around the town square after being convicted of throwing bottles at a woman's car. They were also fined $250 each.
- An Illinois judge in Champaign County sentenced a man to listen to 20 hours of classical music as a punishment for playing his hip-hop music excessively loud from his car. If he did, his fine would be reduced from $135 to $35. After about 15 minutes of the classical music, the man decided to pay the high fine instead.
- Offenders convicted of domestic violence or fighting in the courtroom of Judge Frances Gallegos in Santa Fe, New Mexico, have been sentenced to new age anger management classes, held in the lobby of the courtroom, which is transformed with candles, mirrors, and aromatherapy.

Sources: Based on Azpiri, 2008; Leinwand, 2004; Martin, 2007; Reuters, 2001.

When someone is injured, restitution can also be used to cover medical bills, lost income, etc.

- **Probation** refers to a court-mandated period of supervision in the community (Caputo, 2004). An offender on probation is released into the community and must follow a set of conditions for a specific period of time and report regularly to a probation officer. Often a set of mandatory conditions accompanies all probation orders (e.g., the offender must not commit another crime), as well as conditions that the judge deems appropriate given the circumstances surrounding the particular offender and crime (e.g., the offender must not possess any weapons) (U.S. Sentencing Commission, 2011a). If an offender breaks these rules, the person may be required to serve the remainder of his or her sentence in prison (Caputo, 2004).

  Probation

  A court-mandated period of supervision in the community, often accompanied by a set of conditions that the offender has to abide by

- A variety of other sentencing options exist between the two extremes of probation and imprisonment, which are referred to generally as **intermediate sanctions** (Caputo, 2004). These include house arrest, community confinement (e.g., in a halfway house), community service, and mandatory treatment. According to Caputo, intermediate sanctions are generally used as a way to punish offenders who have committed crimes that are more severe than those crimes where probation is an appropriate sentence, but less severe than crimes that allow for imprisonment.

  Intermediate sanctions

  A set of sentencing options that range between the extremes of probation and imprisonment (e.g., community confinement)

- Imprisonment continues to be one of the most commonly used methods of punishment in the United States for those offenders committing serious crimes. Although differences exist across states, the term of incarceration for misdemeanors (i.e., less serious crimes) is usually no more than one year, whereas those convicted of felonies (i.e., more serious crimes) often receive a sentence of more than one year (Caputo, 2004). In 2006, for instance, the average sentence length for offenders convicted of a felony in state courts was 4 years and 11 months (U.S. Bureau of Justice Statistics, 2009). Typically, offenders convicted of misdemeanors serve their time in local jails, whereas those convicted of felonies are confined to state or federal prisons (Caputo, 2004).

- The death penalty, which is the most serious of all sentences, remains a sentencing option for offenders in many states, the federal government, and the military. States without the death penalty will often sentence offenders to life imprisonment without parole as an alternative (Death Penalty Information Center, 2011). In practice, the death penalty is rarely used and is usually reserved for murder involving aggravating factors. In the majority of the states with the death penalty, the jury holds the primary responsibility of sentencing someone to death.

Despite the fact that the sentencing options presented above vary with respect to their level of severity, they are all punishment-based strategies. Given this, it is important to mention that a different approach for achieving justice is growing in popularity in the United States (especially for juvenile offenders). Indeed, during the past few years, the United States has joined many other countries, such as Canada, in considering the use of **restorative justice** options in place of (or in addition to) punishment-based strategies (Bradshaw & Roseborough, 2005). Although no single definition or practice of restorative justice exists, generally speaking, restorative justice "reconceptualizes the purpose of justice by focusing on the three major stakeholders in the process of restoration and healing: the victim, offender, and community" (Bradshaw & Roseborough, 2005, p. 15).

The goal when using restorative justice options is typically for the victim of a crime, the offender, and members of the community to voluntarily meet in an attempt to restore the imbalance that was caused by the crime. According to the Department of Juvenile Justice (2010) in Alaska, the primary objectives of restorative justice are to prevent further damage from occurring (community safety), to ensure that the offender is made responsible for the crime and "repays" the victim and/or the community (accountability), and to provide the offender with whatever he or she needs (e.g., with respect to skill development) to become a law-abiding citizen in the future (competency development).

Restorative justice
An approach for dealing with the crime problem that emphasizes repairing the harm caused by crime. It is based on the philosophy that when victims, offenders, and community members meet voluntarily to decide how to achieve this, transformation can result.

Factors That Affect Sentencing Decisions

As indicated above, various factors should be taken into account when judges decide on sentences in the United States. These include the seriousness of the offense, the offender's criminal record, various aggravating and mitigating factors, the harshness of the sentence, and so forth. Some researchers suggest that these legally relevant factors can explain most of the variation that occurs in sentencing decisions across judges (e.g., Andrews, Robblee, & Saunders, 1984). This clearly is as it should be. However, other researchers argue that many judges appear to rely on extra-legal factors (i.e., legally irrelevant factors) when making their sentencing decisions, which is obviously cause for concern.

For example, an important study by Hogarth (1971) found that "only about 9% of the variation in sentencing could be explained by objectively defined facts, while more than 50% of such variation could be accounted for simply by knowing certain pieces of information about the judge himself" (p. 382). Likewise, in a slightly more recent study, Ulmer (1997) found that a variety of extra-legal factors influence sentencing even when relevant factors, such as crime seriousness and prior criminal history, are held constant (e.g., in Pennsylvania, black offenders were approximately 50% more likely than white offenders to be incarcerated for their crimes). Very recent research continues to confirm the fact that legally irrelevant factors are still influencing the sentences handed down by judges in the United States (Spohn, 2009). Primary among these factors is the gender of the offender, as discussed in Box 9.2.

Obviously the task that judges face when handing down sentences is an extremely difficult one and this is largely because they need to remain objective while also considering the range of factors that need to be considered when making sentencing decisions. Review the case of Steve Patterson in the Case Study box and determine what factors you would consider when handing down a sentence.

BOX 9.2	Do Male Offenders Get the Short End of the Stick When It Comes to Sentencing?

One of the most consistent findings in criminological research is that men commit more crime than women. It is difficult to think of any type of crime where a man is not more likely than a woman to be the person responsible for the crime. It should not be a surprise then to see a higher number of men represented in criminal justice statistics, especially for violent crimes, and published arrest rates, conviction rates, and incarceration rates bear this out (e.g., U.S. Department of Justice, 2010).

But, what should happen if two offenders (one man and one woman) are being tried for a very similar type of crime in the same jurisdiction and they possess a very similar criminal history? If there are no aggravating or mitigating factors that are unique to one of the cases, a neutral and fair criminal justice system would presumably result in both offenders receiving the same sentence. Interestingly, this is not what the research reveals.

In fact, researchers who examine these types of issues consistently report that women are treated more leniently than men, at least in state courts, and this holds true even when variables such as crime seriousness, prior criminal record, dangerousness, and child care responsibilities are statistically controlled for (e.g., Spohn, 2009). The lack of research examining federal offenders makes it more difficult to draw strong conclusions, but here too the data suggest a gender bias (e.g., Albonetti, 1997).

The degree of gender disparity reported in these studies is not trivial. For example, Spohn (2009) presents data on offenders convicted of felony crimes in Cook County, Illinois, in 1993 that show clear evidence of a gender bias in sentencing decisions. Even when controlling for variables that might lead to justifiable differences in the sentences handed down, such as prior record and the use of a weapon in the crime, male offenders were significantly more likely than female offenders to be sentenced to prison (49.4% vs. 28.4% for those offenders who were convicted of drug possession with intent to deliver).

What is less clear currently is why female offenders are treated more leniently than male offenders. Some researchers have proposed that even when committing similar crimes, women are viewed by judges as being less culpable, less dangerous, and more remorseful than men (Steffensmeier et al., 1998). Others have suggested that family circumstances, while factored in for both male and female offenders, may have a more pronounced mitigating impact on female offenders (Daly, 1989). Clearly more research on this important topic is urgently needed.

CASE STUDY

YOU BE THE JUDGE

Steve Patterson, a young man of 26, has pleaded guilty to robbery. Late one night, Steve entered a local grocery store. Pointing a plastic replica gun at the cashier, Steve demanded that he hand him all the money from the cash register. Steve ran out of the store with over $500 in cash, but the police picked him up later that night.

This is the first time Steve has ever been charged with a crime. For the last four years, he had been working as a forklift driver, but he was recently laid off from the company because it went bankrupt. Steve tells the court he robbed the store to buy food for his wife and newborn child. He pleads with the judge to spare him from prison and states that his wife and child depend on him.

Your Turn . . .

If you were the judge presiding over this case what sort of sentence do you feel Steve should receive? What factors would you consider when determining an appropriate sentence and why? What goals would you try to achieve by handing down your sentence and how confident would you be that those goals would actually be achieved?

Sentencing disparity

Variations in sentencing severity for similar crimes committed under similar circumstances

Warranted sentencing disparity

Variations in sentencing severity for similar crimes committed under similar circumstances that result from a reliance on legally relevant factors (e.g., laws that differ across jurisdictions)

Unwarranted sentencing disparity

Variations in sentencing severity for similar crimes committed under similar circumstances that result from reliance by the judge on legally irrelevant factors

Sentencing Disparity

One of the reasons that it is important to appreciate the various factors that affect sentencing decisions is so that we can understand **sentencing disparity**. Sentencing disparity is defined as "any difference in severity between the sentence that an offender receives from one judge on a particular occasion and what an identical offender with the identical crime would receive from either the same judge on a different occasion or a different judge on the same or a different occasion" (McFatter, 1986, pp. 151–152). Because sentencing disparity can lead to serious injustices, it is commonly viewed as a major problem within the criminal justice system (Spohn, 2009).

SOURCES OF UNWARRANTED SENTENCING DISPARITY Given the complexity of the U.S. judicial system, and the differences that exist across jurisdictions with respect to both laws and resources, a degree of sentencing disparity should be expected. When sentencing disparity exists because of these differences, this is referred to as **warranted sentencing disparity** (Spohn, 2009). For example, as Spohn discusses, if the range of possible penalties for a burglary is 5 to 10 years in one jurisdiction and 7 to 10 years in another, the fact that similar offenders who are convicted of burglaries in these two jurisdictions receive different sentences (one receiving 5 years and the other receiving 7 years) reflects warranted disparity because both judges are relying on the guidelines that are in place within their jurisdictions regarding the minimum sentence that is permissible for this offense.

The real problem is not warranted sentencing disparity, but rather disparities in sentencing that occur because of a reliance on extra-legal factors. In this case, we can refer to the disparity as **unwarranted sentencing disparity** (Spohn, 2009). Unwarranted sentencing disparity can result from many factors, and researchers have attempted to classify these factors into groups. For example, McFatter (1986) discusses two major sources of unwarranted sentencing disparity: **systematic disparity** and **unsystematic disparity**. Systematic disparity represents *consistent* disagreement across judges about sentencing, such as how lenient they feel sentences should be. Sources of systematic disparity can include differences among judges in terms of their personality, philosophy, experience, and so on. Unsystematic disparity, conversely, results from a given judge's *inconsistency* over occasions in judging the same type of offender or crime. This type of disparity can also arise from a number of sources, including fluctuations in mood, focusing on irrelevant stimuli, or the way in which the facts of the case are interpreted by the judge on any particular day (McFatter, 1986).

Another factor that may result in unwarranted sentencing disparity is the reliance on public opinion surrounding a particular case. As indicated in the In the Media box below, the likelihood of this happening has increased with the emergence of social media technology, such as Twitter and Facebook. Why is it important to understand these different sources of sentencing disparity? As McFatter (1986) suggests, only by understanding the various sources of sentencing disparity can we come up with effective strategies to combat its existence.

STUDYING SENTENCING DISPARITY   Researchers in this area typically use one of two procedures to study sentencing disparity: the examination of official sentencing statistics in an attempt to uncover variations in judicial sentencing decisions (e.g., Mustard, 2001) or the use of laboratory-based simulation studies (e.g., McFatter, 1986). The value of relying on official statistics to examine issues of sentencing disparity is that the research is based on the decisions of real judges who are trying genuine cases committed by actual offenders. Thus, the results from these studies likely generalize to naturalistic settings. However, because it is very difficult to control for all of the potential factors that might influence sentencing decisions, including factors that are legally relevant, it is sometimes difficult in these studies to establish why sentencing disparity occurred.

Simulation studies tend to be the method of choice in this area, largely because the researcher is in a better position to design studies that can pinpoint the causes of sentencing disparity. In a simulation study, mock judges or real judges are presented with the details of trials, and the researcher manipulates particular variables of interest, such as the defendant's age, ethnicity, or gender. The goal in these studies is to manipulate these variables while attempting to control for as many other variables as possible, so that if evidence for sentencing disparity is found, the researcher can be fairly confident as to what caused it.

The experiment conducted by McFatter (1986) provides an example of a simulation study. He provided six judges with 13 crime and offender descriptions, which included brief details of the crime and the offender's age, prior record, drug use, and employment status. The descriptions were chosen to represent a wide range of typical crimes (that differed in severity) and offender descriptions. For example, the crimes ranged from a fight that broke out after a minor traffic accident to a rape and murder of an 11-year-old girl. In the first phase of the study, judges were asked to rate various aspects of the crime, such as its seriousness, and to recommend a sentence. Approximately two months later, the judges were given the same crime and offender descriptions and were asked to make ratings and recommend sentences once again. In both phases, the severity of sentences

Systematic disparity

Consistent disagreement among judges about sentencing decisions because of factors such as how lenient judges think sentences should be

Unsystematic disparity

Inconsistencies in a judge's sentencing decisions over time when judging the same type of offender or crime because of factors such as the judge's mood

IN THE MEDIA — Twitter Goes to Court: The Role of Social Media in the Casey Anthony Case

In an era of ever-increasing connectivity and media exposure, the coverage of legal trials has become more complicated. Updates are immediately disseminated to members of the public on social networking sites and conclusions are often drawn before the full story can be analyzed. Increasing media coverage of sensationalized legal trials may actually have a negative impact on the public's opinion of a case.

An example demonstrating this is the recent, highly publicized Casey Anthony murder trial in Florida. Casey Anthony was accused of the first-degree murder of her two-year-old daughter, Caylee, as well as the associated charges of aggravated child abuse, manslaughter of a child, and other misdemeanors. The prosecution alleged that Casey had used chloroform to render Caylee unconscious, suffocated her, and then disposed of the girl's body. The trial was a media sensation and was often covered nightly by news outlets, where every detail of the case was scrutinized. Many media pundits would also provide commentary from a legal perspective on various aspects of the case.

Social networking media were also heavily utilized in the case. Numerous people who were following the case provided commentary through websites such as Twitter and Facebook, voicing their opinions of the defense and prosecution, as well as Casey Anthony herself. Ultimately, Casey Anthony was found not guilty of murder and released after her judgment.

The not guilty verdict triggered a significant amount of public outcry, with many members of the public believing the verdict unjust. Many people, including politicians, celebrities, and other members of the public expressed their disappointment with the verdict. However, it was remarked in the media that many commentators had already decided the fate of Casey Anthony and proclaimed her guilty before a verdict was reached, a feeling that seemed to be echoed by the general public.

This well-publicized case is likely one of the first examples of social networking allowing individuals to immediately express their opinions on a legal outcome. In addition, it has been suggested that the influence of social media had a direct impact on the handling of the case. Indeed, it appears that members of Casey Anthony's legal team would analyze various online opinions to assist in their defense strategy by attacking or supporting various witnesses based on the public's opinion of them. This may have allowed them to strategize their tactics to influence the jurors (and perhaps the judge's) opinion.

For example, one news report suggested that the defense team hired social media consultants who analyzed more than 40,000 online opinions in order to use this information to help them develop their strategies. When the public learned of an alleged affair that Casey's father had they started attacking him online. Based on this reaction, the defense team increased their attack on him too. When Casey's mother testified that it was her, not Casey, who had searched for the word "chloroform" on the home computer, many people indicated online that they believed she lied out of motherly instinct and felt sorry for her. Based on this reaction, the defense team decided to go relatively easy on her in their closing arguments.

It has been found that television coverage can influence opinions in court, but no research has examined how social media might impact the opinions of those playing a role in a trial. Certainly no research has examined how social media might impact legal strategies used in the courtroom or the sentencing decisions that are made. This is an area that needs to be explored and researched. As members of the public become more connected and able to express their opinions more rapidly, their influence on the legal system may be profound.

Sources: Banfield, Kunin, Dolak, & Ng, 2011; Bowden, 2011; Conley, 2011; Greene, 1990; Mann, 2011; Reuters, 2011.

TABLE 9.2	Sentencing Severity Scores	
Sentence		**Severity Score**
Fine or suspended sentence		1
Probation (months)		
1–12		1
13–36		2
Over 36		3
Split sentence (jail and probation)		4
Prison		
1–6 months		3
7–12 months		5
13–24 months		7
25–36 months		9
(Add 2 points for every year up to 50 years)		
50 years		103
Life imprisonment or death		103

Source: Tables from "Sentencing disparity" by Robert M. McFatter from *Journal of Applied Social Psychology.* Copyright © 1986 by John Wiley and Sons. Reprinted with permission.

handed down by judges was transformed into numbers by using the scale developed by Diamond and Zeisel (1975), which is provided in Table 9.2.

The raw severity scores for the sentences handed down by the judges in each phase of McFatter's (1986) experiment are presented in Table 9.3. Three interesting things emerge from these data. First, the results indicate that there is a good deal of agreement among judges about the severity of sentences appropriate for each crime. Second, despite these similarities, there are also many instances of unwarranted sentencing disparity (e.g., crime 9). Third, much of this disparity comes from unsystematic sources where the same judge handed down different sentences when presented with the same information on different occasions (e.g., judge 4 for crimes 12 and 13).

REDUCING SENTENCING DISPARITY Regardless of how sentencing disparity is studied, the conclusion is often that a reasonably high degree of disparity exists across sentences handed down by different judges considering similar crimes and across sentences handed down by the same judge when considering similar crimes on different occasions. As discussed above, a number of sources can account for this disparity, but ultimately, sentencing disparity exists because judges in the United States are allowed a great deal of discretion when making sentencing decisions.

Although certain forms of sentencing disparity are inevitable, there has been a move within the United States to try to reduce unwarranted disparity. One common approach for doing this is to implement **sentencing guidelines**. These guidelines attempt to provide a more consistent, structured way of arriving at sentencing decisions in order to reduce disparity, while also accomplishing other goals (e.g., increasing the likelihood that sentences

Sentencing guidelines

Guidelines that are intended to reduce the degree of discretion that judges have when handing down sentences

TABLE 9.3	Sentencing Severity Scores for the Judges										
					Judge	(Phase)					
Crime	1(1)	1(2)	2(1)	2(2)	3(1)	3(2)	4(1)	4(2)	5(1)	5(2)	6(1)	6(2)
1	1	1	2	4	2	2	2	3	1	4	1	4
2	3	2	4	4	1	2	2	2	1	4	3	2
3	2	1	5	4	4	2	3	4	2	2	2	3
4	5	5	9	9	3	3	3	3	3	3	2	3
5	3	3	4	9	4	4	3	4	7	4	7	3
6	5	2	7	7	4	4	3	3	3	3	3	13
7	2	4	5	4	3	3	4	5	13	3	4	13
8	4	3	5	9	23	5	13	4	1	4	4	3
9	53	39	53	43	2	5	13	5	3	4	13	23
10	103	103	103	103	5	103	23	23	12	23	103	53
11	63	103	103	103	103	43	13	13	103	103	13	23
12	103	103	103	103	103	103	53	103	103	103	103	103
13	103	103	103	103	103	103	53	103	103	103	103	103

Source: Tables from "Sentencing disparity" by Robert M. McFatter from *Journal of Applied Social Psychology.* Copyright © 1986 by John Wiley and Sons. Reprinted with permission.

reflect the severity of the offenses). In some cases these guidelines are referred to as presumptive guidelines. Such guidelines force a judge to make specific sentencing decisions unless they have important reasons for departing from the recommendation (Roberts, 1991). However, voluntary guidelines also exist in some jurisdictions (Roberts, 1991).

In the United States, presumptive guidelines have been proposed by the U.S. Sentencing Commission with the goal being to increase the appropriateness of sentences handed down to offenders who are convicted of federal crimes (U.S. Sentencing Commission, 1989). The guidelines essentially limit disparity by imposing restrictions on the sentences that judges can hand down when dealing with individuals who are at the same level of offense severity and criminal history (Mustard, 2001). As illustrated in Table 9.4, the guidelines take the form of a table, with rows representing different levels of offense severity, columns indicating different categories of criminal history, and cells showing the range of appropriate sentences (in months) (U.S. Sentencing Commission, 2011b). After assigning an offender to a cell, the judge is to follow the guidelines, deviating only if circumstances warrant such a decision. Research suggests that deviations occur in the minority of cases. For example, of the 77,236 offenses examined by Mustard (2001), 27.1% of sentences deviated from the guidelines (with most sentences being adjusted downward).

Although relatively little research has examined the impact of sentencing guidelines, the research that does exist provides mixed results. Some studies in the United States have indicated that sentencing guidelines have little impact on sentencing disparity (e.g., Cohen & Tonry, 1983), whereas other research has shown a positive effect (e.g., Kramer & Lubitz, 1985; Moore & Miethe, 1986). Why might sentencing guidelines work in some jurisdictions, but not others? Moore and Miethe suggest that some of

TABLE 9.4	The U.S. Sentencing Commission Guidelines.

Criminal History Category

Offense Level	I (0 or 1)	II (2 or 3)	III (4, 5, 6)	IV (7, 8, 9)	V (10, 11, 12)	VI (13 or more)
1	0–6	0–6	0–6	0–6	0–6	0–6
2	0–6	0–6	0–6	0–6	0–6	1–7
3	0–6	0–6	0–6	0–6	2–8	3–9
4	0–6	0–6	0–6	2–8	4–10	6–12
5	0–6	0–6	1–7	4–10	6–12	9–15
6	0–6	1–7	2–8	6–12	9–15	12–18
7	0–6	2–8	4–10	8–14	12–18	15–21
8	0–6	4–10	6–12	10–16	15–21	18–24
9	4–10	6–12	8–14	12–18	18–24	21–27
10	6–12	8–14	10–16	15–21	21–27	24–30
11	8–14	10–16	12–18	18–24	24–30	27–33
12	10–16	12–18	15–21	21–27	27–33	30–37
13	12–18	15–21	18–24	24–30	30–37	33–41
⋮	⋮	⋮	⋮	⋮	⋮	⋮
43	Life	Life	Life	Life	Life	Life

Source: Table from The United States sentencing commission guidelines, from http://www.ussc.gov/.

Note: With respect to offense level, every type of offense is assigned a base level and then points are added or subtracted based on various aggravating and mitigating factors (e.g., whether the crime caused death or serious injury). Likewise, the criminal history category is determined by examining the number and severity of previous crimes committed, while also taking into account other factors (e.g., whether the offender was on probation when he committed these crimes).

the differences might be explained by the fact that different types of guidelines are used in different states (e.g., advisory guidelines, which are only followed on a voluntary basis, might not be effective).

Are the Goals of Sentencing Achieved?

Recall from the beginning of this chapter that sentencing has many different goals. As a result, the question of whether the goals of sentencing are achieved is a difficult one to answer because, to a large extent, the answer depends on what goal we are most concerned with. For some goals, the answer to this question is often "yes." For example, if a judge sentences an offender to a term in prison, we can be confident that the offender will be separated from society for a period of time. However, with respect to some other goals the answer is less clear-cut. In particular, there is an ongoing debate as to whether current sentencing practices in the United States achieve the goals of deterring people from committing crimes and whether they assist in the rehabilitation of offenders. Various researchers have played a crucial role in this debate. One of these researchers is Dr. Frank Cullen, who is profiled in Box 9.3.

BOX 9.3   Researcher Profile: Dr. Francis Cullen

After receiving his B.A. in psychology from Bridgewater State College in Bridgewater, Massachusetts, Dr. Cullen went on to complete postgraduate training in sociology and education at Columbia University. During his graduate training, Dr. Cullen was taught how social welfare was being used to justify repressive controls over poor and deviant populations. According to Dr. Cullen, it was this view that inspired many scholars in the 1970s to reject rehabilitation as an ideology within the criminal justice context.

Dr. Francis Cullen

This general view—that rehabilitation has untoward consequences—led Dr. Cullen to begin thinking about offender rehabilitation while taking part in a seminar at the University of Virginia in 1979. As part of that seminar, he wrote a 10-page paper in which he considered whether the criminal justice system would in fact be better off if rehabilitation was stripped away. He concluded that it would not be, and during the next few years that 10-page paper turned into one of Dr. Cullen's most important books, *Reaffirming Rehabilitation*.

Interestingly, *Reaffirming Rehabilitation* was published in 1982 by Cincinnati-based Anderson Publishing Company on the very same day that Dr. Cullen was interviewing for an academic position at the University of Cincinnati. It turned out to be a good day, with the book receiving high praise and Dr. Cullen landing the Cincinnati job. He moved from Western Illinois University in 1982, where he had been teaching, and has been at the University of Cincinnati ever since.

During his time in Cincinnati, Dr. Cullen has published widely in many areas, including offender rehabilitation. Much of Dr. Cullen's early work on this topic was on a policy level, essentially challenging the view that moving away from social welfare was a good thing. He also conducted several important public opinion surveys, which indicated that the American public strongly supports the idea of offender rehabilitation and thinks that offender treatment should play an important part in the correctional system.

More recently, Dr. Cullen has tried to determine what makes offender rehabilitation effective. This has included some important meta-analytic studies that have helped identify several core principles of effective correctional practice (see the text). In many of his publications, Dr. Cullen has argued that correctional policy and practice should be evidence based by drawing on the available "research knowledge about what is the 'best bet' to reduce recidivism."

For his many contributions to the field of criminology and criminal justice, Dr. Cullen has won numerous awards, including the prestigious Edwin H. Sutherland Award from the American Society of Criminology in 2010. He is past president of this society, he currently serves on the Office of Justice Programs Advisory Board for the U.S. Department of Justice, and he is a Distinguished Research Professor in the School of Criminal Justice at the University of Cincinnati.

When Dr. Cullen is not conducting research on crime-related issues he spends much of his time following one of his other passions: cheering on the Bearcats, the University of Cincinnati's basketball team. In fact, Dr. Cullen is such a big fan of the team that in the mid-1990s, when building an attachment to his house, he installed red and black bathroom fixtures, the official colors of Cincinnati's school teams. Dr. Cullen's wife was relieved that he relented on his plans to do the same thing to their master bedroom.

Sources: Cullen, 2002; Cullen & Gendreau, 2000.

A great deal of recent research has focused specifically on the effectiveness of "get tough" strategies (Cullen & Gendreau, 2000), which include a range of punishment-based sentencing options, some consisting of incarceration. Other strategies fall under the heading of intermediate strategies, as discussed above, which are less severe than incarceration but more severe than probation (Gendreau, Goggin, Cullen, & Andrews, 2001). Examples of intermediate strategies include house arrest, curfews, and electronic monitoring. It has long been assumed that experiencing one of these sanctions would change the antisocial behavior of offenders and reduce the likelihood that they will reoffend. However, recent research does not support this hypothesis (Gendreau et al., 2001).

In a review, Gendreau et al. (2001) examined the rehabilitative and deterrent effect of various community-based sanctions and prison sentences. These researchers used the technique of meta-analysis to summarize findings from research studies that examined the impact of specific sanctions. For our purposes here, the most important measures to focus on from the study are the rate of recidivism for offenders who experienced the sanction, the rate of recidivism for offenders who experienced regular probation (used as a control group), and the average effect size that resulted from a comparison of these two rates. The consideration of effect size is particularly important since this measure summarizes the impact that a particular sanction was found to have across a range of studies. In this case, effect sizes can range from $+1.00$ to -1.00, with positive effect sizes indicating that the sanction increased recidivism (i.e., compared with probation, those offenders who received the sanction reoffended at a higher rate) and negative effect sizes indicating that the sanction decreased recidivism (i.e., compared with probation, those offenders who received the sanction reoffended at a lower rate).

Based on the results from this study, some of which are summarized in Table 9.5, it must be concluded that there is very little evidence that community sanctions lead to substantial decreases in recidivism rates (compared with regular probation). Indeed, most of the average effect sizes listed in Table 9.5 are positive, which indicates that, on average, the particular sanctions listed in this table resulted in small increases in recidivism. Only two sanctions (fines and restitution) resulted in average effect sizes that were negative, and in these cases the observed decreases in recidivism rates were very small (-0.04 and -0.02, respectively). In addition, this study found that sanctions consisting of incarceration also had little impact on recidivism. In fact, longer periods of incarceration led to slightly higher rates of recidivism across the studies that were examined ($+0.03$). In addition, those offenders who were sent to prison for brief periods of time also exhibited higher rates of recidivism compared with offenders who received a community-based sanction ($+0.07$).

Why don't get tough strategies work? Why do we not see lower rates of criminal recidivism when we punish offenders for their criminal behavior? Many theories have attempted to explain why punishment doesn't work in the criminal justice system. As we will discuss in more detail below, one of the major reasons is that get tough strategies typically fail to target factors that strongly predict involvement in crime (Cullen & Gendreau, 2000). Another reason is that the sort of punishment-based sanctions that are used in the criminal justice system do not replicate the conditions under which punishment is known to be effective for reducing unwanted behavior in other contexts. For example, punishment can effectively reduce unwanted behavior if it is presented immediately after the expression of the unwanted behavior, in a consistent fashion, and with a high level of intensity (Andrews & Bonta, 2006). Get tough strategies in the criminal

TABLE 9.5	Effects of Community-Based Sanctions and Incarceration on Recidivism	
Type of Sanction	Sample Size	Average Effect Size
Supervision program	19,403	0.00
Arrest	7,779	0.01
Fine	7,162	−0.04
Restitution	8,715	−0.02
Boot camp	6,831	0.00
Scared straight	1,891	0.07
Drug testing	419	0.05
Electronic monitoring	1,414	0.05
More versus less prison	68,248	0.03
Prison versus community	267,804	0.07

Source: Table from "The effects of community sanctions and incarceration of recidivism" by Paul Gendreau, Paula Smith, and Claire Goggin from *Compendium 2000 on effective correctional programing* (p. 18–21). Copyright © 2001 by The Minister of Public Works and Government Services Canada. Reprinted with permission.

justice system, however, rarely if ever meet these criteria (e.g., punishments often come long after the commission of a crime).

See Box 9.4 for a discussion of these issues as they relate to one popular get tough strategy, the Scared Straight program.

WHAT WORKS IN OFFENDER TREATMENT?

So, given the results of studies like those conducted by Gendreau et al. (2001), does this mean that nothing can be done to deter or rehabilitate offenders? Historically, some researchers have taken the view that nothing will work with offenders, most notably Martinson (1974), but new research suggests that this is not the case. In fact, several principles of effective correctional intervention have been proposed, and a growing body of research is beginning to show the value of these principles (Andrews & Bonta, 2006; Latessa, Cullen, & Gendreau, 2002). Although quite a large number of principles are emerging as potentially important (Latessa et al., 2002), we will focus on three that appear to be particularly valuable in determining which correctional interventions will be effective.

Need principle

Principle that correctional interventions should target known criminogenic needs (i.e., factors that relate to reoffending)

The first of these principles is known as the **need principle**. It states that effective intervention will target known criminogenic needs (i.e., factors that are known to contribute to reoffending), including (1) antisocial attitudes, beliefs, and values; (2) antisocial associates; (3) antisocial personality factors (such as impulsivity, risk-taking, and low self-control); and (4) antisocial behaviors (Cullen & Gendreau, 2000).

Risk principle

Principle that correctional interventions should target offenders who are at high risk to reoffend

The second principle is known as the **risk principle**. It states that effective interventions will focus on those offenders who are at high risk of reoffending (Cullen & Gendreau, 2000). Not only are low-risk offenders unlikely to reoffend, their chances of reoffending may actually increase if exposed to an intervention, because of the fact that they will be brought into contact with people who hold antisocial attitudes (Andrews, 2001).

BOX 9.4   The Ineffectiveness of Scaring Kids Straight

One approach commonly used to prevent juvenile offenders (or at-risk youth) from committing more crimes is to try to "scare them straight." The basic approach involves taking the youths to prison in order to show them firsthand what's in store for them if they continue committing crimes. Usually current prisoners are recruited to take part in the programs. Often these prisoners are violent offenders who speak about the harsh realities of prison life. Themes of prison violence are common in the sessions with youth and often include exaggerated stories of prison rape and murder. Some prisoners verbally threaten the young people, making it clear what they would do to them if they ever did end up in prison.

Historically, these Scared Straight programs were deemed highly successful. Reductions in reoffending on a scale of 80% to 90% were being reported, and programs being run across the country generated extensive media attention. In 1979, *Scared Straight*, a documentary narrated by Peter Falk, was released. It followed a group of juvenile delinquents taking part in a Scared Straight program at Rahway State Prison in New Jersey. The documentary won an Academy Award as well as an Emmy. The popularity of these programs has grown since that time and they continue to be used in the United States today.

Unfortunately, the empirical research that has evaluated Scared Straight programs is less promising. For example, the original program run out of Rahway Prison was evaluated in 1982 and not only was the program found to be ineffective, the youth who took part in it were actually more likely to be arrested compared to kids in a control group. (As an interesting anecdote, Angelo Speziale, one of the original Scared Straight members, was convicted in 2010 (at age 49) for the rape and murder of the teenage girl who lived next door to him).

Meta-analytic research has since confirmed these results. For example, a well designed meta-analysis was conducted in 2003 that analyzed nine methodologically sound studies conducted between 1967 and 1992 in eight different states. This meta-analysis found that Scared Straight programs actually caused more harm than good. Indeed, kids taking part in the programs were almost twice as likely to reoffend compared to kids who did not participate in the programs.

Such findings have caused some agencies to stop and think about whether these programs should be used. Recently, formal decisions have been made about the status of Scared Straight programs. For example, on January 11, 2011, the U.S. Department of Justice formally declared Scared Straight programs ineffective and indicated that all funding to such programs should be suspended. Following this, a number of states have closed down their programs, including Maryland and California.

Why are Scared Straight programs ineffective? There are many potential reasons and each probably has merit. For example, some researchers suggest that juvenile delinquents feel alienated and may see prison as one of the few places where they fit in. Prison visits or interactions with prisoners may simply reinforce that view. Others argue that Scared Straight programs end up romanticizing lifers and other prison inmates in the impressionable minds of delinquent youths. Many young offenders may even look up to the offenders they meet.

Another possible explanation is that Scared Straight programs don't work because they are based on a flawed theory, a deterrence theory of criminal behavior, which assumes that offenders think about the consequences of their offending behavior before they act. Unfortunately, this does not appear to be the case for most offenders, especially young offenders. As a result, fear of official punishment—scaring kids with stories of prison life—will not be a strong predictor of criminal behavior.

Source: ABC News, 2011; Schembri, n.d.

Responsivity principle

Principle that correctional interventions should match the general learning style of offenders

The third principle is known as the **responsivity principle**. It states that effective interventions will match the general learning styles, motivations, and abilities of the offender being targeted as well as more specific factors such as the offender's personality, gender, and ethnicity (Cullen & Gendreau, 2000).

The often-cited meta-analytic study conducted by Andrews and colleagues (1990) was one of the first attempts to determine whether interventions, which consist of these core principles, do in fact lead to reductions in recidivism. These researchers examined 80 program evaluation studies and coded the interventions in each study as appropriate, inappropriate, or unspecified. Interventions were defined as appropriate if they included the three principles of effective intervention described above (most of these programs involved the use of behavioral and social learning principles, which included techniques such as behavioral modeling, rehearsal, role-playing, and reinforcement). Interventions were coded as inappropriate if they were inconsistent with these principles (many of these programs were based on get tough or psychodynamic strategies). Interventions were coded as unspecified if they could not be categorized as appropriate or inappropriate because of a lack of information. The hypothesis in this study was that offenders exposed to appropriate interventions would exhibit lower rates of recidivism compared with offenders exposed to inappropriate interventions. This is exactly what was found. Offenders taking part in appropriate programs exhibited a decrease in recidivism, whereas offenders taking part in inappropriate programs exhibited an increase in recidivism. Offenders taking part in unspecified programs exhibited a decrease in recidivism, though less of a decrease compared with offenders in appropriate programs.

Since this study, this same general pattern of results has been found on numerous occasions, for various offending groups (e.g., Andrews, Dowden, & Gendreau, 1999; Antonowicz & Ross, 1994; Pearson, Lipton, & Cleland, 1996). This has led correctional researchers to conclude that something can be done to deter and rehabilitate offenders. By focusing on current research in the area of forensic psychology, and drawing on these principles of effective correctional treatment, interventions can be developed that significantly reduce the chance that offenders will go on to commit further crimes. Certainly, this does not suggest that all new sentencing options will be effective, since many of these new options will not be consistent with the principles of effective correctional programming. However, a number of options have been developed—many in the United States—that do correspond with these principles. Early indications suggest that they hold promise for achieving some of the goals of sentencing that we discussed at the beginning of this chapter.

PUBLIC ATTITUDES TOWARD SENTENCING

Having examined in some detail the sentencing process in the United States, let us now focus our attention on the attitudes that Americans have about this process, and other aspects of the criminal justice system. Studying these attitudes is important. For example, Roberts (2007) highlights the fact that public confidence in the criminal justice system is important to its functioning, in that the system relies on victims reporting crimes to the police and in assisting with the prosecution of accused persons. The general public will carry out these duties only if they have confidence in the criminal justice system.

A fair amount of research has examined public opinion of the criminal justice system in the United States. This research typically involves the use of one of the following research methods: public opinion surveys, simulation studies, or focus groups (in which a small number of people are brought together for an in-depth discussion of their views on a particular topic). Mostly, the results that emerge from these three different approaches are similar, so we will focus our discussion on the results from public opinion surveys because they are the most commonly used.

As summarized by several researchers, as well as several national polls, a number of general trends can be observed from the results of public opinion surveys. For example, details of opinion polls from the U.S. Bureau of Justice Statistics (2011a) reveal some consistent trends in opinions of the criminal justice system, some of which are listed below.

1. Overall, Americans often express a lack of confidence in the criminal justice system. For example, only 28% of Americans report a "great" deal of confidence in the criminal justice system (Sourcebook of Criminal Justice Statistics, 2011b). This is followed by a further 42% who indicate "some" confidence. Although these views vary somewhat across the United States, among different age groups and geographic areas, results remain fairly consistent. This is in contrast to other nations, which report higher levels of confidence. For example, the majority of Canadian citizens (57%) report a great deal or quite a lot of confidence in their justice system (Halman, 2001; cited by Roberts, 2007).

2. This result must be qualified by the fact that Americans possess different levels of confidence in different branches of the criminal justice system. For example, respondents to two surveys in 2011 indicated that Americans have a relatively high degree of confidence in the police (56%) (U.S. Bureau of Justice Statistics, 2011c), but a lower level of confidence in the Supreme Court (37%) (U.S. Bureau of Justice Statistics, 2011d). These findings tend to be consistent across gender and income levels, although there are substantial differences in police confidence when comparing different ethnicities. According to Roberts (2007), the finding that confidence tends to be higher for the police than the courts is stable across public opinion polls conducted in other countries.

3. In part, the findings listed above can be explained by the fact that many Americans think offenders are treated too leniently by the courts. For example, when respondents are asked about how their local criminal justice institutions deal with offenders, their view is that the courts consistently do not treat criminals harshly enough (U. S. Bureau of Justice Statistics, 2011e). However, it is important to note that Americans also consistently underestimate how harshly criminals are treated in reality. In comparison to other Western countries, the United States has a very high degree of punitiveness, which often leads to longer incarceration periods (Van Kesteren, 2009).

4. In general, Americans support alternatives to prison and believe that those alternatives may be more effective at reducing recidivism. For example, approximately 77% of Americans believe that supervised probation, community service, and/or rehabilitative services are the most appropriate sentence for nonviolent offenders who don't have a serious criminal record (Hartney & Marchionna, 2009). However, they feel that jail may be appropriate for these offenders if those alternatives fail. In addition, more than half of Americans (54%) do not believe that serving time will necessarily reduce the likelihood that a person will commit future crimes (Hartney & Marchionna, 2009).

The Media's Influence on Public Opinion

Many researchers have claimed that public opinion on issues like sentencing does not fairly reflect the state of affairs in the United States (e.g., Van Kesteren, 2009). It has been suggested that this discrepancy between public opinion and reality often occurs because of an inadequate understanding on the part of the public of crime and the criminal justice system (Roberts, 2007). Certainly, the results of public opinion surveys support the idea that the public lacks the knowledge required to develop accurate perceptions of the criminal justice system. For example, a very common finding in public opinion surveys is that the public believe that violent crime in general is increasing in the United States (Saad, 2007). This perception, however, does not correspond to actual crime trends in the United States, which indicate a general decreasing trend in the levels of violent crime (Federal Bureau of Investigation, 2009).

So, if public opinion is not based on fact, where does public opinion come from? As we have tried to demonstrate in some of the In the Media boxes you have encountered in this textbook, one obvious source of public opinion is the media. Research has found that the media can influence public attitudes toward crime and criminal justice issues (Dowler, 2003; Surette, 1990). If the media presented an accurate depiction of crime and the criminal justice system's response to it, this might not be a bad thing. Unfortunately, many studies have shown that the media tend to present a biased picture of crime-related issues. For example, studies have indicated that the media focus disproportionately on violent crime and portray the criminal justice system as being more ineffective than it actually is (e.g., Gerbner, Gross, Morgan, & Signorielli, 1980; Surette, 1990). According to some researchers, "members of the public do not adequately correct for the unrepresentative [stories] they hear about in the news media. . . . As a result, the negative feelings and perceptions of leniency that the news media create are perpetuated" (Sprott & Doob, 1997, p. 276).

A lot of research has now been conducted to specifically look at how the media influences fear of crime among the general public and whether fear of crime relates to attitudes toward criminal justice issues. Generally, the research indicates that television viewing is positively related to fear of crime (e.g., Dowler, 2003; Gerbner et al., 1980; Weaver & Wakshlag, 1986). However, the relationship appears complicated and depends on a number of factors, including both audience and message variables (e.g., Heath & Gilbert, 1996). For example, exposure to large amounts of local news coverage increases fear of crime among viewers, however exposure to large amounts of non-local crime does not, and can actually result in viewers feeling safer (Liska & Baccaglini, 1990).

Research generally indicates that media-induced fear of crime can also impact public attitudes toward the criminal justice system, although here too the relationship is complex. For example, television viewing appears to increase feelings that the criminal justice system should be more punitive (e.g., Barille, 1984), but some research has indicated that this is only the case when reality-based crime shows are viewed rather than fictional crime shows (Oliver & Armstrong, 1995).

Research is clearly needed to clarify the role of all these variables (and others) in explaining public opinion toward criminal justice issues and how the media impacts these opinions. Only once we understand where these opinions come from can attempts be made to correct opinions that are uninformed.

Summary

1. The U.S. court system is one component of the larger criminal justice system. The court system in the United States is divided into a federal system and a state system. The federal court system has three layers with U.S. district courts at the bottom, U.S. appellate courts in the middle, and the U.S. Supreme Court at the top. Although the state system can often be characterized in a similar fashion, there is no consistent court structure at the state level, with variations existing across jurisdictions.

2. Sentences are supposed to serve a number of different purposes in the United States. Deterring people from committing crimes and offender rehabilitation are two of the primary purposes. Sentencing is also guided by numerous principles, such as the fact that a sentence should be proportionate to the seriousness of the offense. Such principles are meant to provide judges with guidance when handing down sentences.

3. Judges have many sentencing options at their disposal. The most serious option (in some states) is the death penalty. Other sentencing options include fines, probation, and imprisonment. A range of intermediate sanctions (falling between probation and incarceration) are becoming more common (e.g., house arrest) as are restorative justice options.

4. One of the major problems with sentencing in the United States is unwarranted sentencing disparity, which refers to differences in the severity of sentences handed down by different judges (or the same judge on different occasions) because of a reliance on extra-legal factors. These factors can include the judge's personality, philosophy, experience, and so on. One of the primary strategies for reducing sentencing disparity is to implement sentencing guidelines.

5. Research examining the impact of punishment-based sentences suggests that such sentences are not effective for reducing recidivism. In contrast, correctional interventions based on core correctional principles show more promise. These principles include the need principle (effective interventions target criminogenic needs), the risk principle (effective interventions target high-risk offenders), and the responsivity principle (effective interventions match the general learning style and the particular characteristics of the offender).

6. Public opinion polls reveal that Americans do not have a great deal of confidence in the criminal justice system, although they do have more confidence in policing compared to the courts. To some extent this can be explained by the fact that the American public believes that offenders are treated too leniently by the courts, though the American public also consistently underestimates how punitive the courts actually are. Americans also support alternatives to imprisonment for certain types of offenders and do not believe that incarceration is necessarily the best sentencing option to achieve offender rehabilitation.

Key Concepts

fine *214*
general deterrence *213*
intermediate
   sanctions *215*
need principle *226*
probation *215*

reparations *213*
responsivity
   principle *228*
restitution *214*
restorative justice *216*
risk principle *226*

sentencing
   disparity *218*
sentencing
   guidelines *221*
specific deterrence *213*
systematic disparity *219*

unsystematic
   disparity *219*
unwarranted sentencing
   disparity *218*
warranted sentencing
   disparity *218*

Discussion Questions

1. You have just been hired as a research assistant by one of your professors. She is working on a government project looking at ways to deal with sentencing disparity. Together, you and your professor must propose strategies, beyond the sentencing guidelines that currently exist, that could be used to reduce unwarranted sentencing disparity. What types of strategies would you propose?

2. Your neighbor thinks that the government is getting soft on crime by providing community "rehabilitation" programs. He thinks the only way to really rehabilitate offenders is to lock them up in cells with nothing to do but ruminate on the crimes they've committed. Do you think your neighbor is right? Explain.

3. Recent results from public opinion polls suggest that, even when the public is told that the death penalty has little impact as a crime deterrent, many people still support it. Why do you think this happens?

4. Beyond the factors we have discussed in this chapter, what might account for the inaccurate perceptions of the public when it comes to sentencing practices in the United States? What can be done, if anything, to decrease these inaccurate perceptions?

CHAPTER

10

Risk Assessment

LEARNING OBJECTIVES

- Define the components of risk assessment.

- List what role risk assessments play in the United States.

- Describe the types of correct and incorrect risk predictions.

- Differentiate among static, stable, and acute dynamic risk factors.

- Describe unstructured clinical judgment, actuarial prediction, and structured professional judgment.

- List the four major types of risk factors.

Joanne Marshall has served two years of a three-year sentence for aggravated assault. The assault occurred late one evening after Joanne had returned home from drinking with her friends. She got into a heated argument with her boyfriend, grabbed a knife from the kitchen, and stabbed him in his shoulder. A prison psychologist completed a risk assessment and is supporting her application for parole. Joanne is going to appear before the three-member parole board to discuss the offense she committed, her plans if released, and what intervention programs she has participated in. The parole board members will need to consider what level of risk Joanne poses for reoffending, including whether or not she will engage in another violent act. They will also attempt to determine whether she has developed more appropriate ways of dealing with interpersonal conflict.

E very day, individuals make judgments about the likelihood of events. Predictions are made about being admitted into law school, recovering from an episode of depression, or committing a criminal act after release from prison. Our legal system frequently requires decisions about the likelihood of future criminal acts that can significantly influence the lives of individuals. With the possibility that offenders could spend years or even the remainder of their lives in confinement, decisions by psychologists can have a significant impact. Predicting future violence has been described as "one of the most complex and controversial issues in behavioral science and law" (Borum, 1996, p. 945).

Although it is clear that significant advances have taken place since the 1990s, risk assessment and prediction remain imperfect. Bonta (2002) concludes that "risk assessment is a double-edged sword. It can be used to justify the application of severe sanctions or to moderate extreme penalties. . . . However, the identification of the violent recidivist is not infallible. We are not at the point where we can achieve a level of prediction free of error" (p. 375). Nonetheless, the systematic assessment of risk provides judicial decision makers, such as judges and parole commission members, with much needed information to help them make challenging decisions.

The goal of this chapter is to explore the major issues associated with risk prediction in a forensic context. In particular, the focus will be on understanding the task of assessing risk and predicting violence.

WHAT IS RISK ASSESSMENT?

In the past two decades, we have seen a change in the way risk is viewed. Prior to the 1990s, risk was seen as a dichotomy—the individual was either dangerous or not dangerous. Nowadays, risk is regarded as a range—the individual can vary in the degree to which he or she is considered dangerous (Steadman, 2000). In other words, the shift has added a dimension of probability to the assessment of whether a person will commit violence. The focus on probability reflects two considerations. First, it highlights the idea that probabilities may change across time. Second, it recognizes that risk level reflects an interaction among a person's characteristics, background, and possible future situations that will affect whether the person engages in violent behavior.

The process of risk assessment includes both a "prediction" and a "management" component (Hart, 1998). The prediction component describes the probability that an individual will commit future criminal or violent acts. The focus of this component is on identifying the risk factors that are related to this likelihood of future violence. The management component describes the development of interventions to manage or reduce the likelihood of future violence. The focus of this component is on identifying what treatment(s) might reduce the individual's level of risk or what conditions need to be implemented to manage the individual's risk. As described by Hart (1998), "the critical function of risk assessments is violence *prevention*, not violence *prediction*" (emphasis in the original; p. 123).

RISK ASSESSMENTS: WHEN ARE THEY CONDUCTED?

Risk assessments are routinely conducted in civil and criminal contexts. The phrase *civil contexts* refers to the private rights of individuals and the legal proceedings connected with such rights. *Criminal contexts* refers to situations in which an individual has been charged with a crime. Common to both contexts is a need for information that would enable legal judgments to be made concerning the probability of individuals committing some kind of act that would disrupt the peace and order of the state or individuals within the state.

Civil Setting

A number of civil contexts require risk assessment:

- *Civil commitment* requires an individual to be hospitalized involuntarily if he or she has a mental illness and poses a danger to him- or herself or others. A mental health professional, usually a psychiatrist or psychologist, would need to know the probability of violence associated with various mental symptoms and disorders and be able to identify whether the circumstances associated with individual patients would affect the likelihood that they would harm others or themselves.
- Assessment of risk in *child protection* contexts involves the laws that are in place to protect children from abuse. The risk of physical or sexual abuse or neglect is considered when a state or local child protective services agency decides whether to temporarily remove a child from his or her home or to terminate parental rights. To provide assistance to protection agencies, professionals need to be familiar with the risk factors that predict childhood maltreatment.
- *Immigration* laws prohibit the admission of individuals into United States if there are reasonable grounds for believing they will engage in acts of violence or if they pose a risk to social, cultural, or economic functioning of United States society.
- *School* and *labor regulations* also provide provisions to prevent any kind of act that would endanger others.
- Mental health professionals who are assessing or treating a client, are required to inform a third party if they believe their client poses a risk of violence to an identifiable third party. This responsibility is called a *duty to warn*.

Mental health professionals are expected to consider the likelihood that their patients will act in a violent manner and to intervene to prevent such behavior. The most well-known case involving mental health professionals and duty to warn is the *Tarasoff* case. This case involved Prosenjit Poddar, an Indian graduate student studying at the University of California at Berkeley. He dated another student, Tatiana Tarasoff, a couple of times (including kissing her a few times) and believed he had a special relationship. Poddar became depressed when Tarasoff indicated she was not interested in him. He went to the University Health Clinic and was seen by a psychologist. Poddar disclosed to the psychologist that he wanted to get a gun and shoot Tarasoff. The psychologist sent a letter to the campus police requesting them to take Poddar to a psychiatric hospital. The police interviewed Poddar and were convinced he was not dangerous and told him to stay away from Tarasoff. When the psychiatrist in charge of the University Health Clinic returned from vacation he ordered the letter to the police be destroyed and no further action be taken.

Two months later Poddar stabbed Tarasoff to death. Tarasoff's parents sued the campus police, Heath Service employees, and the University of California for failing to warn them that their daughter was in danger. The parents settled out of court for an undisclosed amount. Poddar served four years of a five-year sentence for manslaughter. His conviction was overturned due to faulty jury instructions on diminished capacity. However, a new trial was not held when Poddar agreed to return to India. The Supreme Court of California (*Tarasoff v. Regents of the University of California,* 1974) ruled that mental health professionals have a duty to warn a potential victim of potential harm. In a 1976 rehearing of the case (*Tarasoff v. Regents of the University of California,* 1976), the court ruled that the mental health professional has a duty to protect the intended victim. Thus the mental health professional must take reasonable steps to protect the victim, such as notifying the police or warning the intended victim. This case assumes mental health professionals are able to determine if a person will act in a violent manner.

Criminal Settings

The assessment of risk occurs at nearly every major decision point in the criminal justice and forensic psychiatric systems, including pretrial, sentencing, and release. A person can be denied bail if there is a substantial likelihood that he or she will commit another criminal offense.

Although risk assessment is a routine component of many sentencing decisions, it is a critical component of certain kinds of decisions. For example, in 1990 Washington State was the first to enact the Sexually Violent Predator (SVP) Act. This act permits the civil confinement of sexual offenders for an indefinite period of time after the completion of their sentence. Many other states have also passed similar SVP acts. Generally SVP laws have three requirements: first, a conviction for a sexually violent crime; second, a mental abnormality (most often pedophilia) or a personality disorder (most often psychopathy); and third, a likelihood the offender will sexually reoffend if released. Thus, risk assessment is a core component of this legislation.

Risk assessment can also play a crucial role in the sentencing phase of a capital murder case. In cases where the jury has found a person guilty of capital murder, during the penalty phase, jurors are asked to determine the number of aggravating and mitigating factors present. Aggravating factors are those that make the harshest punishment appropriate (i.e., deciding for the death penalty), whereas mitigating factors are those that would cause the jurors to vote for a lesser sentence. Each state has its own list of aggravating and mitigating factors. For example, in several states (e.g., Washington) an aggravating factor is whether the defendant is a future danger. In these cases, a mental health professional will often testify concerning the probability the defendant will commit future violence (see Box 10.2 later in this chapter for a Texas example).

Risk assessment is also required for decisions concerning release from correctional and forensic psychiatric institutions, such as parole. For example, a federal offender serving a sentence of more than one year can be released on parole after completion of one-third of his or her sentence (although some offenses are not eligible for parole such as use of a firearm during commission of a federal crime). A federal offender can apply to the U.S. Parole Commission to get early release. Commission members use a variety of sources of information (including risk assessments provided by correctional psychologists) to decide the likelihood that the offender will commit another offense if released. Finally, a patient who has been found not guilty by reason of insanity (see Chapter 8) can be released from a secure forensic psychiatric facility only after a review panel has determined the presence and severity of mental illness and the risk of future violence.

Clearly, risk assessment plays an integral role in legal decision making, both in civil and criminal settings, allowing informed decisions that weigh the likelihood that an individual will engage in a dangerous or criminal act in the future. In the sections that follow, we will look at the predictive accuracy of these assessments, as well as the factors that actually predict violence.

TYPES OF PREDICTION OUTCOMES

Predicting future events will result in one of four possible outcomes. Two of these outcomes are correct, and two are incorrect. The definitions provided below are stated in terms of predicting violent acts but could be used for any specific outcome (see also Table 10.1):

- A **true positive** represents a correct prediction and occurs when a person who is predicted to be violent engages in violence.
- A **true negative** is also a correct prediction and occurs when a person who is predicted not to be violent does not act violently.
- A **false positive** represents an incorrect prediction and occurs when a person is predicted to be violent but is not.
- A **false negative** is also an incorrect prediction and occurs when a person is predicted to be nonviolent but acts violently.

The last two types of errors are dependent on each other. Minimizing the number of false-positive errors results in an increase in the number of false-negative errors. The implication of these errors varies depending on the decisions associated with them, and in many cases the stakes are high. A false-positive error has implications for the individual being assessed (such as denial of freedom), whereas a false-negative error has implications for society and the potential victim (such as another child victimized by a sexual offender). In some cases, it is perhaps tolerable to have a high rate of false positives if the consequences of such an error are not severe. For example, if the consequence of being falsely labeled as potentially violent is being supervised more closely while released on parole, the consequence may be acceptable. However, if the consequence of being falsely labeled as potentially violent contributes to a juror's decision to decide in favor of the death penalty, then this price is too high to pay. As in many legal settings, the consequences for the individual must be weighed in relation to the consequences for society at large.

The Base Rate Problem

A problem with attempting to predict violence is determining base rates. The **base rate** represents the percentage of people within a given population who commit a criminal or violent act. It is difficult to make accurate predictions when the base rates are too high or too low. A problem that emerges when attempting to predict events that have a

True positive
A correct prediction that occurs when a person who is predicted to engage in some type of behavior (e.g., a violent act) does so

True negative
A correct prediction that occurs when a person who is predicted not to engage in some type of behavior (e.g., a violent act) does not do so

False positive
An incorrect prediction that occurs when a person is predicted to engage in some type of behavior (e.g., a violent act) but does not

False negative
An incorrect prediction that occurs when a person is predicted not to engage in some type of behavior (e.g., a violent act) but does

Base rate
Represents the percentage of people within a given population who engage in a specific behavior or have a mental disorder

TABLE 10.1 **Predictions: Decisions versus Outcomes**

Decision	Outcome	
	Does not reoffend	**Reoffends**
Predicted not to reoffend	True negative (correct prediction)	False negative (incorrect prediction)
Predicted to reoffend	False positive (incorrect prediction)	True positive (correct prediction)

Deadly violence: students escape from a school shooter.

low base rate is that many false positives will occur. For example, the past decade has seen several high-profile school shootings. However, although these events generate much media coverage, they occur infrequently. For example, in 2008–2009 less than 2% of youth homicides occurred at school. During the 2008–2009 school year, a total of 15 youth homicides occurred at school in the United States (Roberts, Zhang, & Truman, 2010). Any attempt to predict which individual youths might engage in a school shooting would result in many youths being wrongly classified as potential shooters.

The base rate can vary dramatically depending on the group being studied, what is being predicted, and the length of the follow-up period over which the individual is monitored. For example, the base rate of sexual violence tends to be relatively low, even over extended follow-up periods, whereas the base rate for violating the conditions of a conditional release is very high. The base rate problem is not such a concern if predictions of violence are limited to groups with a high base rate of violence, such as incarcerated offenders. The general rule is that it is easier to predict frequent events than infrequent events.

A HISTORY OF RISK ASSESSMENT

Before 1966, relatively little attention was paid to how well professionals could assess risk of violence. In the 1960s, civil rights concerns provided the rare opportunity to study the accuracy of mental health professionals to predict violence. In the case of *Baxstrom v. Herald* (1966), the U.S. Supreme Court ruled that the plaintiff Johnnie Baxstrom had been detained beyond his sentence expiry and was ordered released into the community. As a result of this case, more than 300 offenders with mental illness from the Dannemora State Hospital for the Criminally Insane and another state hospital were released into the community or transferred to less secure institutions. Steadman and Cocozza (1974) followed 98 of these patients who were released into the community but had been considered by mental health professionals as too dangerous to be released. Only 20 of these patients were arrested over a four-year period, and of these, only 7 committed a violent offense.

In a larger study, Thornberry and Jacoby (1979) followed 400 forensic patients released into the community because of a similar civil rights case in Pennsylvania (*Dixon v. Attorney General of the Commonwealth of Pennsylvania,* 1971). During an average three-year follow-up period, 60 patients were either arrested or rehospitalized for a violent incident.

The two studies we have just described are known as the Baxstrom and Dixon studies. These cases and similar ones call into question the ability of mental health professionals to make accurate predictions of violence. Two key findings emerged from the research. First, the base rate for violence was relatively low. For example, in the Baxstrom study, 7 out of 98 (roughly 7%) violently reoffended, as did 60 out of 400 (15%) in the Dixon study. Second, the false-positive rate was very high. In the Baxstrom and Dixon studies, the false-positive rates for violent reoffending were 93% and 85%, respectively. These findings indicate that in the past many forensic patients with mental disorders were needlessly kept in restrictive institutions based on erroneous judgments of violence risk.

Ennis and Litwack (1974) characterized clinical expertise in violence risk assessment as similar to "flipping coins in the courtroom" and argued that clinical testimony be barred from the courtroom. Other researchers have gone even further, concluding that "no expertise to predict dangerous behavior exists and . . . the attempt to apply this supposed knowledge to predict who will be dangerous results in a complete failure" (Cocozza & Steadman, 1978, p. 274).

This pessimism continued into the 1980s. John Monahan, a leading U.S. researcher, summarized the literature in 1981 and concluded that "psychiatrists and psychologists are accurate in no more than one out of three predictions of violent behavior over a several-year period among institutionalized populations that had both committed violence in the past (and thus had a high base rate for it) and who were diagnosed as mentally ill" (Monahan, 1981, p. 47). See Box 10.1 for a profile of Dr. Monahan.

Notwithstanding the above conclusion, U.S. courts have ruled that predictions of violence risk do not violate the basic tenets of fundamental justice, nor are they unconstitutional. In *Barefoot v. Estelle* (1983), the U.S. Supreme Court determined the constitutionality of a Texas death-penalty appeal decision. Thomas Barefoot burned down a bar and shot and killed a police officer. Barefoot was convicted of capital murder and, at the sentencing phase of the trial, testimony was presented from two psychiatrists (one being Dr. James Grigson, whom we will discuss later in the chapter) about the threat of future dangerousness posed by Thomas Barefoot. Both psychiatrists testified, based on a hypothetical fact situation, that the individual described would be a threat to society. The judge sentenced Barefoot to death. The U.S. Supreme Court rejected the defendant's challenge that psychiatrists were unable to make sufficient accurate predictions of violence and ruled that the use of hypothetical questions to establish future dangerousness was admissible. The court concluded that mental health professionals' predictions were "not always wrong . . . only most of the time" (p. 901).

| BOX 10.1 | Researcher Profile: Dr. John Monahan |

Dr. Monahan became interested in psychology when he read Carl Rogers' *On Becoming a Person* in college. In graduate school at Indiana University, he took several law courses and was fascinated by the ways that social science could contribute to the law, but was not doing so. In the early 1980s, Monahan wrote a monograph on the clinical prediction of violent behavior for Saleem Shah at the National Institute of Mental Health. It was a turning point in Monahan's career, and the topic has stayed with him since.

Dr. John Monahan

Dr. Monahan's first job, at the University of California, Irvine, was in a new program called Social Ecology. There, he learned to thrive in an interdisciplinary academic setting. In 1980, he moved to the University of Virginia School of Law, where he is currently the John S. Shannon Distinguished Professor of Law and also a professor of psychology and of psychiatry and neurobehavioral sciences. At Virginia, Monahan began to collaborate with his Law School colleague Laurens Walker on a series of articles on the uses of psychology and other social sciences in the courtroom. Their casebook, *Social Science in Law*, is now in its seventh edition and has recently been published in Chinese. Shortly after moving to Virginia, Dr. Monahan became the founding president of the Division of Psychology and Law of the American Psychological Association.

In the mid-1980s, Dr. Monahan was asked by the John D. and Catherine T. MacArthur Foundation to direct a Research Network on Mental Health and the Law. The network chose to focus its studies on three topics: the competence of people with a mental illness to make legally relevant decisions, such as to consent to treatment or to plea bargain; the relationship between mental illness and violence; and whether coerced institutional treatment could increase decision-making competence or reduce violence risk. One product that came out of this effort was the development of the first violence risk assessment software, the *Classification of Violence Risk*, published with the sociologist Henry Steadman and other colleagues. When this project was finished, the MacArthur Foundation asked Monahan to direct a second network, this one on the effectiveness of mandated treatment in communities rather than in institutional settings—for example, civil commitment to outpatient treatment or outpatient treatment as a condition of probation. Often, community treatment is mandated in order to reduce violence risk. This network is just completing its work. Monahan is now planning on extending what he has learned about the risk assessment of violence in general to the risk assessment of violent terrorism in particular.

When recently asked what advice he would give people at the start of their careers in forensic psychology, Monahan offered three thoughts:

"First, don't get hung up on disciplinary labels. If you do good work no one will care where you came from. Second, choose your research topics well and your research collaborators better. Science is increasingly a group effort. Plus, work is much more fun when you're doing it with people that you actually like. Finally, travel to professional meetings as much as you can. Even in a digital world, there is no substitute for being there in the flesh, when new ideas are being fleshed out and exciting projects are on the drawing board."

METHODOLOGICAL ISSUES

Risk assessment assumes that risk can be measured. Measurement, in turn, assumes that an instrument exists for the measurement of risk. What would be the ideal way to evaluate an instrument designed to measure risk? The way to proceed would be to assess a large number of offenders and then, regardless of their risk level, release them into the community. The offenders would then be tracked to see if they commit another criminal act. This way, the risk instrument could be evaluated to determine if it could accurately predict future criminal acts. However, although this is an ideal scenario from a research perspective, it is not ethically feasible to release high-risk individuals into the community. In reality, the sample available for evaluating a risk assessment instrument is limited to those with a relatively low risk of reoffending. This constrains the kinds of conclusions that can be drawn when risk assessment is evaluated in the real world.

Monahan and Steadman (1994) have identified three main weaknesses of research on the prediction of violence. The first issue concerns the limited number of risk factors being studied. Violent behavior is due to a complex interaction between individual dispositions and situational factors. In other words, people engage in violence for many different reasons. Thus, many risk factors are likely involved, including the person's background, social situation, and biological and psychological features. Many studies have focused on only a limited number of risk factors. Assessment of risk may be improved by measuring more of the reasons why people engage in violence.

The second issue concerns how the criterion variable (the variable you are trying to measure) is measured. Researchers have often used official criminal records as their criterion measure. However, many crimes may never be reported to police. Thus, many false positives may be undiscovered true positives. Even violent crimes may go undiscovered and many violent sexual crimes are recorded as simply violent in nature. Some research shows that the number of recorded *violent* crimes of sexual offenders is a better estimate of the number of *sexual* crimes they may have committed (Rice, Harris, Lang, & Cormier, 2006). In short, use of official records underestimates violence. When official records are combined with interviews with patients or offenders and with collateral reports (information from people or agencies who know the patient or offender), the rate of violence increases. The MacArthur Violence Risk Assessment Study (Steadman et al., 1998) illustrates the effect of using different measures. Using official agency records, the base rate for violence was 4.5%, but, when patient and collateral reports were added, the base rate increased to 27.5%, a rate of violence six times higher than the original base rate.

Finally, how the criterion variable is defined is a concern. In some studies researchers will classify their participants as having either engaged in violence or not. Monahan and Steadman (1994) recommend that researchers expand this coding to include the severity of violence (threatened violence versus severe violence), types of violence (spousal violence versus sexual violence), targets of violence (family versus stranger), location (institutions versus community), and motivation (reactive [unplanned violence in response to a provocation] versus instrumental [violence used as an instrument in the pursuit of some goal]). It is likely that some risk factors will be associated with certain forms of violence; for example, a history of sexual offenses may predict future sexual offenses but not future bank robberies.

JUDGMENT ERROR AND BIASES

How do psychologists make decisions when conducting risk assessments? Researchers have identified the typical errors and biases in clinical decision making (Elbogen, 2002). The shortcuts people use to help to make decisions are called *heuristics* (Tversky & Kahneman, 1981). These heuristics may lead to inaccurate decisions. Clinicians may

Illusory correlation

Belief that a correlation exists between two events that in reality are either not correlated or correlated to a much lesser degree

make several types of decision errors. Clinicians include traits they intuitively believe to be important or assume to be associated with the risk but that actually are not (Odeh, Zeiss, & Huss, 2006). Chapman and Chapman (1967) define an **illusory correlation** as the belief that a correlation exists between two events that in reality are either not correlated or correlated to a much lesser degree. For example, a clinician might assume a strong correlation between a diagnosis of mental disorder and high risk for violent behavior. Although some forms of mental disorder are related to an increased risk, a relationship has not been consistently found (Monahan & Steadman, 1994). Clinicians also tend to ignore base rates of violence (Monahan, 1981). Clinicians working in prisons or forensic psychiatric facilities may not be aware of how often individuals with specific characteristics act violently. For example, the base rate for recidivism in homicide offenders is extremely low. Other investigators (Borum, Otto, & Golding, 1993) have noted the tendency to rely on highly salient or unique cues, such as bizarre delusions.

In general, people tend to be overconfident in their judgments (see Kahneman & Tversky, 1982). Clinicians who are very confident in their risk assessments will be more likely to recommend and implement intervention strategies. However, people can be very confident in their risk assessments but be completely wrong. Desmarais, Nicholls, Read, and Brink (2010) investigated the association between clinicians' confidence and accuracy of predicting short-term inpatient violence. Clinicians completed a structured professional judgment measure designed to assess the likelihood of violent behavior (i.e., verbal and physical aggression, self-harm) and indicated on a 5-point scale their level of confidence. Most clinicians were highly confident, however, the association between confidence and accuracy was minimal. The pattern of findings suggested clinicians tended to have an overconfidence bias.

APPROACHES TO THE ASSESSMENT OF RISK

Unstructured clinical judgment

Decisions characterized by a substantial amount of professional discretion and lack of guidelines

What are the existing methods of risk assessment? Three methods of risk assessment are most commonly described. **Unstructured clinical judgment** is characterized by a substantial amount of professional discretion and lack of guidelines. There are no predefined rules about what risk factors should be considered, what sources of information should be used, or how the risk factors should be combined to make a decision about risk. Thus, risk factors considered vary across clinicians and vary across cases (Grove & Meehl, 1996; Grove, Zald, Lebow, Snitz, & Nelson, 2000). Grove and Meehl (1996) have described this type of risk assessment as relying on an "informal, 'in the head,' impressionistic, subjective conclusion, reached (somehow) by a human clinical judge" (p. 294). See Box 10.2 for an example of a mental health professional using this type of risk assessment.

Actuarial prediction

Decisions are based on risk factors that are selected and combined based on their empirical or statistical association with a specific outcome

In contrast, mechanical prediction involves predefined rules about what risk factors to consider, how information should be collected, and how information should be combined to make a risk decision. Thus, risk factors do not vary as a function of the clinician and the same risk factors are considered for each case. A common type of mechanical prediction is called **actuarial prediction**. With actuarial prediction, the risk factors used have been selected and combined based on their empirical or statistical association with a specific outcome (Grove & Meehl, 1996; Grove et al., 2000). In other words, a study has been done in which a number of risk factors have been measured, a sample of offenders has been followed for a specific period, and only those risk factors that were actually related to reoffending in this sample are selected (for an example of an actuarial scale, see the Violence Risk Appraisal Guide described later in this chapter).

BOX 10.2	Dr. Death: A Legendary (Notorious) Forensic Psychiatrist

Dr. James Grigson was a Dallas psychiatrist who earned the nicknames *Dr. Death* and *the hanging shrink* because of his effectiveness at testifying for the prosecution in death-penalty cases. For nearly three decades, Dr. Grigson testified in death-penalty cases in Texas.

Death-penalty trials are divided into two phases. First, the defendant's guilt is decided. Next, if the defendant is found guilty, the same judge and jury decide whether to impose life in prison or to sentence the defendant to die. One of the issues the jurors must decide on is "whether there is a probability that the defendant would commit criminal acts of violence that would constitute a continuing threat to society." Psychiatrists and psychologists are often hired to testify about the likelihood of future violence.

Dr. Grigson's testimony was very effective. He often diagnosed defendants as being sociopaths and stated with 100% certainty that they would kill again. For example, in *Estelle v. Smith* (1981), Dr. Grigson testified on the basis of a brief examination that the defendant Smith was a "very severe sociopath," who, if given the opportunity, would commit another criminal act. The diagnosis of sociopath appears to have been based on the sole fact that Smith "lacked remorse."

Dr. Grigson has been proven wrong. In the case of Randall Dale Adams (documentarian Errol Morris made a movie about Adams' story in 1988, called *The Thin Blue Line*, which helped to get the case reopened), Dr. Grigson testified that Randall Adams was a "very extreme" sociopath and would continue to be a threat to society even if kept locked in prison. Dr. Grigson based his assessment on a 15-minute interview in which he asked about Adams' family background, had Adams complete a few items from a neuropsychological test designed to measure visual-motor functioning (Bender Gestalt Test), and asked Adams the meaning of two proverbs: *A rolling stone gathers no moss* and *a bird in the hand is worth two in a bush*. Randall Adams was sentenced to death. However, after spending 12 years on death row, his conviction was overturned and he was released (another inmate confessed to the murder Adams had been convicted of). It has been 13 years since Randall Adams has been released. He is now married, employed, and living a nonviolent life. Dr. Grigson was wrong in this case—and potentially in how many others?

In 1995, Dr. Grigson was expelled from the American Psychiatric Association (APA) for ethical violations. He was expelled for claiming he could predict with 100% certainty that a defendant will commit another violent act (and, on at least one occasion, testifying that the defendant had a "1,000%" chance of committing another violent act). The APA was also concerned that Dr. Grigson often testified in court based on hypothetical situations and diagnosed an individual without even examining the defendant. Dr. Grigson often diagnosed defendants as sociopaths on the basis of his own clinical opinion and not on any structured assessment procedures.

When Dr. Grigson died in 2004 at the age of 72, he had testified in 167 trials. How many of these defendants fell victim to Dr. Grigson and his misguided attempt to protect society is unknown.

A debate in the literature exists concerning the comparative accuracy of unstructured clinical versus actuarial prediction. The first study to compare actuarial and unstructured clinical judgment was conducted by sociologist Ann Burgess in 1928. Burgess compared the accuracy of 21 objective risk factors (e.g., age, number of past offenses, length of sentence) to clinical judgments of three psychiatrists in predicting parole failure in a sample of 3,000 criminal offenders. The actuarial scale was markedly superior to the psychiatrists in identifying which offenders would fail on parole. In a review of 20 studies, Paul Meehl (1954) concluded that actuarial prediction was equal to or better than unstructured clinical judgment in all cases. A similar conclusion was reached almost 50 years later, when Meehl and his colleagues (Grove et al., 2000) conducted a meta-analysis of prediction studies for human health and behavior (including criminal behavior). In sum, the weight of the evidence clearly favors actuarial assessments of risk (Ægisdóttir et al., 2006; Mossman, 1994), even with samples of offenders with mental disorders (Bonta, Law, & Hanson, 1998; Phillips et al., 2005) and sex offenders (Hanson & Morton-Bourgon, 2009). A criticism of many actuarial assessments has been their sole reliance on static risk factors, which do not permit measuring changes in risk over time or provide information relevant for intervention (Wong & Gordon, 2006).

Arising from the limitations associated with unstructured clinical judgment and concern that the actuarial method did not allow for individualized risk appraisal or for consideration of the impact of situational factors to modify risk level, a new approach to risk assessment has emerged—**structured professional judgment** (SPJ) (Borum, 1996; Webster, Douglas, Eaves, & Hart, 1997). According to this method, the professional (the term *professional* is used to acknowledge that it is not only clinicians who make evaluations of risk but a diverse group, including law enforcement officers, probation officers, and social workers) is guided by a predetermined list of risk factors that have been selected from the research and professional literature. The professional considers the presence and severity of each risk factor, but the final judgment of risk level is based on the evaluator's professional judgment. The reliability and predictive utility of these risk summary judgments are only beginning to be assessed.

Types of Risk Factors

Clinicians and researchers might use hundreds of potential risk factors to predict antisocial and violent behavior. A **risk factor** is a measurable feature of an individual that predicts the behavior of interest, such as violence. Traditionally, risk factors were divided into two main types: static and dynamic.

Static risk factors are factors that do not fluctuate over time and are not changed by treatment. Age at first arrest is an example of a static risk factor, since no amount of time or treatment will change this risk factor. **Dynamic risk factors** fluctuate over time and are amenable to changing. An antisocial attitude is an example of a dynamic risk factor, since it is possible that treatment could modify this variable. Dynamic risk factors have also been called *criminogenic needs* (see Chapter 9 for a discussion).

More recently, correctional researchers have begun to conceptualize risk factors as a continuous construct (Douglas & Skeem, 2005; Grann, Belfrage, & Tengström, 2000; Zamble & Quinsey, 1997). At one end of the continuum are the static risk factors described above. At the other end are acute dynamic risk factors. These risk factors change rapidly within days, hours, or minutes and often occur just prior to an offense. Factors at this end of the continuum include variables such as negative mood and level of intoxication. In the middle of the continuum are stable dynamic risk factors. These risk factors change but only over long periods of time, such as months or years, and are variables that should be targeted for treatment. These factors include criminal attitudes, coping ability, and impulse control.

Recent research has found that dynamic risk factors are related to the imminence of engaging in violent behavior. Quinsey, Jones, Book, and Barr (2006) had staff make monthly ratings of dynamic risk factors in a large sample of forensic

---

Structured professional judgment

Decisions are guided by a predetermined list of risk factors that have been selected from the research and professional literature. Judgment of risk level is based on the evaluator's professional judgment

Risk factor

A measurable feature of an individual that predicts the behavior of interest (e.g., violence or psychopathology)

Static risk factor

Risk factor that does not fluctuate over time and is not changed by treatment (e.g., age at first arrest). Also known as *historical risk factor*

Dynamic risk factor

Risk factors that fluctuate over time and are amenable to change

psychiatric patients. Changes in dynamic risk factors were related to the occurrence of violent behaviors.

IMPORTANT RISK FACTORS

Since the late 1980s, a great deal of research has investigated what factors are associated with future violence. These can be classified into historical, dispositional, clinical, and contextual risk factors. **Historical risk factors** (sometimes called *static risk factors*) are events experienced in the past and include general social history and specific criminal history variables, such as employment problems and a history of violence. **Dispositional risk factors** are those that reflect the person's traits, tendencies, or style and include demographic, attitudinal, and personality variables, such as gender, age, criminal attitudes, and psychopathy. **Clinical risk factors** are the symptoms of mental disorders that can contribute to violence, such as substance abuse or major psychoses. **Contextual risk factors** (sometimes referred to as *situational risk factors*) are aspects of the individual's current environment that can elevate the risk, such as access to victims or weapons, lack of social supports, and perceived stress.

Some of these factors are likely relevant to risk assessment only, while others are relevant to both risk assessment and risk management. These factors vary in terms of how much they are subject to change. For example, some are fixed (e.g., gender), some cannot be undone (e.g., age of onset of criminal behavior), and some may be resistant to change (e.g., psychopathy), whereas others (e.g., social support or negative attitudes) may be subject to intervention or may vary across time.

Several meta-analytic reviews have examined the predictors of general and violent recidivism in adult offenders, sexual offenders, and patients with mental disorders (Bonta et al., 1998; Gendreau, Little, & Goggin, 1996; Hanson & Morton-Bourgon, 2005). Two key findings have emerged. First, factors that predict general recidivism also predict violent or sexual recidivism. Second, predictors of recidivism in offenders with mental disorders overlap considerably with predictors found among offenders who do not have a mental disorder.

Dispositional Factors

DEMOGRAPHICS   Researchers in the 1970s identified young age as a risk factor for violence (Steadman & Cocozza, 1974). The younger the person is at the time of his or her first offense, the greater the likelihood that person will engage in further criminal behavior and violence. Dozens of studies have firmly established age of first offense as a risk factor for both general and violent recidivism in both offenders with mental disorders (Bonta et al., 1998) and offenders without mental disorders (Gendreau et al., 1996). Offenders who are arrested prior to age 14 tend to have more serious and more extensive criminal careers than those who are first arrested after age 14 (DeLisi, 2006; Piquero & Chung, 2001). Males are at higher risk than are females for general offending (Cottle et al., 2001; Gendreau et al., 1996). Notably, males engage in more serious violent acts, such as sexual assaults, homicides, and assaults causing bodily harm (Odgers & Moretti, 2002). Some studies using self-report measures have found that females engage in similar or even higher rates of less serious violence (Nichols, Graber, Brooks-Gunn, & Botvin, 2006; Steadman et al., 1994).

Historical risk factor

Risk factor that refers to events that have been experienced in the past (e.g., age at first arrest). Also known as *static risk factor*

Dispositional risk factor

Risk factor that reflects the individual's traits, tendencies, or styles (e.g., negative attitudes)

Clinical risk factors

Types and symptoms of mental disorders (e.g., substance abuse)

Contextual risk factor

Risk factor that refers to aspects of the current environment (e.g., access to victims or weapons). Sometimes called *situational risk factor*

PERSONALITY CHARACTERISTICS Two personality characteristics have been extensively examined: impulsiveness and psychopathy. Not being able to regulate behavior in response to impulses or thoughts increases the likelihood of engaging in crime and violence (Webster & Jackson, 1997). Lifestyle impulsivity (being impulsive in most areas of life) distinguishes recidivistic rapists from nonrecidivistic rapists (Prentky, Knight, Lee, & Cerce, 1995).

Psychopathy is a personality disorder defined as a callous and unemotional interpersonal style characterized by grandiosity, manipulation, lack of remorse, impulsivity, and irresponsibility (see Chapter 11 for more information on psychopaths and the Hare Psychopathy Checklist–Revised [PCL-R], the most widely used measure of psychopathy). Given these features, it is not surprising that psychopathic individuals engage in diverse and chronic criminal behaviors. A recent meta-analysis has found that psychopathy is moderately related to general and violent recidivism (Leisticio, Salekin, DeCoster, & Rogers, 2008) and moderately related to violence in a prison setting (Guy, Edens, Anthony, & Douglas, 2005). Psychopathy predicts reoffending across different countries (e.g., Canada, the United States, the United Kingdom, Belgium, Germany, the Netherlands, New Zealand, Sweden) (Hare, 2003), in both male and female offenders (Richards, Casey, & Lucente, 2003), offenders with mental disorders (Nicholls, Ogloff, & Douglas, 2004; Steadman et al., 2000; Strand, Belfrage, Fransson, & Levander, 1999), male adolescent offenders (Corrado, Vincent, Hart, & Cohen, 2004; Forth, Hart, & Hare, 1990; Gretton, Hare, & Catchpole, 2004; Murrie, Cornell, Kaplan, McConville, & Levy-Elkon, 2004), and sexual offenders (Barbaree, Seto, Langton, & Peacock, 2001; Rice & Harris, 1997a). However, psychopathy may be weakly related or unrelated to violent reoffending in adolescent females (Odgers, Repucci, & Moretti, 2005; Schmidt, McKinnon, Chattha, & Brownlee, 2006; Vincent, Odgers, McCormick, & Corrado, 2008).

Several studies have found that the combination of psychopathy and deviant sexual arousal predicts sexual recidivism (Hildebrand, de Rutter, & de Vogel, 2004; Olver & Wong, 2006; Rice & Harris, 1997a). Deviant sexual arousal is defined as evidence that the sexual offender shows a relative preference for inappropriate stimuli, such as children or violent nonconsensual sex. For example, Rice and Harris (1997a) found that about 70% of sexual offenders with psychopathic features and evidence of deviant sexual arousal committed a new sexual offense, compared with about 40% of the other offender groups.

Historical Factors

PAST BEHAVIOR The most accurate predictor of future behavior is past behavior. Past violent behavior was first identified as a predictor in the 1960s and 1970s (see Cocozza, Melick, & Steadman, 1978) and has consistently been associated with future violence in diverse samples, including adolescents and adults, correctional offenders, offenders with mental disorders, and civil psychiatric patients (Farrington, 1991; McNiel, Sandberg, & Binder, 1988; Phillips et al., 2005). Interestingly, it is not only past violent behavior that predicts violence, but also past nonviolent behavior (Harris, Rice, & Quinsey, 1993; Lipsey & Derzon, 1998). For example, offenders who have a history of burglary offenses are at an increased risk for future violence.

AGE OF ONSET As noted earlier, individuals who start their antisocial behavior at an earlier age are more chronic and serious offenders (Farrington, 1991; Tolan & Thomas, 1995). For example, Farrington (1991) found that 50% of the boys who committed a violent offense prior to age 16 were convicted of a violent offense in early adulthood. In another longitudinal study, Elliott (1994) reported that 50% of male youth who committed their first violent acts prior to age 11 continued their violent behavior into adulthood, compared with 30% whose first violence was between the ages of 11 and 13, and only 10% of those whose first violent act occurred during adolescence. Age of onset is not as strong a predictor for female offenders (Piquero & Chung, 2001).

CHILDHOOD HISTORY OF MALTREATMENT Having a history of childhood physical abuse or neglect is associated with increased risk for violence (Smith & Thornberry, 1995; Zingraff, Leiter, Johnsen, & Myers, 1994). In a large-scale study of childhood abuse, Widom (1989b) reported that victims of sexual abuse were no more likely than those who were not sexually abused to commit delinquent or violent offenses. Those who were victims of physical abuse or who were victims of neglect were much more likely to commit criminal acts compared with those who were not abused. Being abused in childhood predicts initiation into delinquency, but continued abuse predicts chronic offending (Lemmon, 2006). Physical abuse in adolescence is also directly related to adolescent offending and may be related to some types of offending in adulthood as well (Fagan, 2005; Smith, Ireland, & Thornberry, 2005).

Clinical Factors

SUBSTANCE USE Drug and alcohol use has been associated with criminal behavior and violence. However, the drug–violence link is complex because of both direct effects (e.g., the pharmacological effects of the drugs) and indirect effects (e.g., the use of violence to obtain drugs; Hoaken & Stewart, 2003). The obvious link between drugs and crime is that the use, possession, and sale of illegal drugs are crimes. In some cases, the individual commits offenses to support a drug habit (Klassen & O'Connor, 1994). For example, Chaiken and Chaiken (1983) found that severe drug users commit 15 times as many robberies and 20 times as many burglaries as compared with non–drug-using offenders. The drug that has been most associated with crime is heroin (Inciardi, 1986). A large study of 653 opiate users in Edmonton, Montreal, Quebec City, Toronto, and Vancouver concluded that individuals with greater heroin and crack use are at the greatest risk of committing property crimes (Manzoni, Brochu, Fischer, & Rehm, 2006). Not all classes of drugs are related to the same degree with criminal behavior and violence, and in some cases the strength of the association depends on the amount of the drug used (Hoaken & Stewart, 2003).

Dowden and Brown (2002) conducted a meta-analysis of 45 studies to examine the association between substance abuse and recidivism. Alcohol and drug use problems were moderately related to general recidivism. Zanis and colleagues (2003) followed a sample of 569 offenders with a prior history of substance abuse or dependence for two years after release from prison on parole. Factors relating to a new conviction included the number of prior convictions, younger age, parole without treatment, and cocaine dependence.

Drug abusers also come in contact with antisocial people, thus leading to violent confrontations. Laboratory research (Taylor & Sears, 1988) has found that aggression displayed by intoxicated individuals is a joint function of the pharmacological effects of alcohol intoxication (disinhibition effects), expectancies, and the situation (what is happening in the environment). Neuropsychological deficits (i.e., executive functioning) also play a role in the effects of alcohol on aggression (Giancola, Parrott, & Roth, 2006).

In one of the largest surveys done, Swanson (1994) interviewed 7,000 individuals in two U.S. cities (Durham, North Carolina, and Los Angeles), asking about the presence of substance abuse, psychiatric disorders, and violent behavior. Based on data from the previous year, less than 3% of men and women with no psychiatric diagnosis committed violence. However, for those with a diagnosis of substance abuse, the rates of violence for men and women were 22% and 17%, respectively.

MENTAL DISORDER   Much controversy exists over the connection between major mental disorder and violence. The general public believes that these two items are linked (Pescosolido, Monahan, Link, Stueve, & Kikuzawa, 1999). Although most people with mental disorders are not violent, a diagnosis of affective disorders and schizophrenia has been linked to higher rates of violence (Swanson, 1994). Hillbrand (1995) reported that in a sample of forensic psychiatric patients, those with a history of suicide attempts and engaging in self-harm behaviors were more likely to engage in verbal and physical aggression than were other patients.

In a recent meta-analysis of 204 studies, Douglas, Guy, and Hart (2009) concluded that psychosis was associated with between a 49% to 68% increase in the odds of violence. However, the strength of the psychosis violence link depended on several factors including study design (settings, comparison group), measurement (types of symptoms), and timing of the symptoms and the violence.

Contextual Factors

LACK OF SOCIAL SUPPORT   This risk factor refers to the absence of strong support systems to help individuals in their day-to-day life. Henggeler, Schoenwald, Borduin, Rowland, and Cunningham (1998) describe four kinds of support: (1) *instrumental*, to provide help for a problem; (2) *emotional*, to express compassion and love; (3) *appraisal*, to support the person with his or her decision making; and (4) *information*, to provide new information to help the person. Assessing the kinds and levels of support a person has and what types of support must be created will help to evaluate that person's level of risk. Those with serious mental illnesses often have a narrow range of social contacts with others. If these relationships provide inadequate support or if there is conflict within these relationships, this may predispose to violence (Estroff and Zimmer, 1994; Klassen and O'Connor, 1989).

ACCESS TO WEAPONS OR VICTIMS   If the offender is released into an environment that permits easy access to weapons or victims, then the potential for another violent act increases. An offender who moves into a skid-row rooming house that houses many other antisocial individuals and provides easy access to drugs may start associating with antisocial people or using drugs (Monahan & Steadman, 1994). If the offender has engaged in violence with other associates or under the influence of substances, then releasing the offender to live in the same circumstances that led to past violence may induce future

IN THE MEDIA   Megan's Law: Attempting to Prevent Crime

The purpose of Megan's Laws is to help police track high-risk sexual offenders. If a child is abducted, the police need to know if there are any high-risk child molesters living or visiting where the abduction has occurred. Laws vary across the states but most include a sex offender registry and community notification. Sex offenders are required to register with the local police when they move into a neighborhood and local authorities must inform the community of the sex offender's presence. The first law was launched in New Jersey in 1994 just a month after the rape and murder of seven-year-old Megan Kanka by a convicted sexual offender (Jesse Timmendequas) who had moved across the street from her home. Below provides a summary of key events relating to Megan Kanka's rape and murder and Jesse Timmendequas' past:

- April 15, 1961: Jesse Timmendequas born.
- 1979: Pleaded guilty to attempted aggravated sexual assault on a five-year-old. He was given a suspended sentence but failed to attend treatment and sentenced to nine months.
- 1981: Pleaded guilty to assault and attempted sexual assault of a seven-year-old girl and was sentenced to six years. According to therapists at the treatment institution Timmendequas failed to participate in treatment and one therapist predicted Timmendequas would commit another sex crime.
- July 29, 1994: Timmendequas lures Megan Kanka into his house (he was sharing with two other sexual offenders) by offering to show her a puppy. After raping her, he slams her head into a dresser, puts two plastic bags over her head, and strangles her with a belt. He placed her body in a toy chest and left her body in a nearby park. When investigated by the police, Timmendequas confessed and showed police to the body.
- May 30, 1997: Found guilty of capital murder.
- June 1997: Jesse's younger brother Paul testifies for the defense during the sentencing phase of the capital hearing. Paul claims that both he and Jesse were repeatedly raped by their father and that when they were children they saw their father brutally rape a seven-year-old girl.
- June 20, 1997: Jurors sentence Jesse Timmendequas to death.
- August 9, 1999: Jesse Timmendequas' brother Paul is given a seven-year sentence for sexually assaulting two teenage girls.
- December 17, 2007: Jesse Timmendequas' sentence is commuted to life in prison without parole after New Jersey Legislature abolishes the death penalty.
- 2010: Jesse Timmendequas is serving his sentence at New Jersey State Prison.

How effective are Megan's Laws at protecting children? The premise is that if parents and others know that there are sex offenders living in their communities they can take steps to protect their children. Despite Megan's Laws being in effect for over a decade, little research has been conducted to determine their effectiveness. Researchers have asked sex offenders about the impact notification laws have had on them. These sex offenders report experiencing social stigmatization, loss of relationships, exclusion from housing, emotional harm to their family, verbal threats, and physical assaults (Tewksbury & Lees, 2006). Some researchers have suggested that these laws may result in greater stress for sex offenders trying to transition to life in the community (Presser & Gunnison, 1999). The greater stress and lack of perceived support may result in an increased risk of recidivism. A recent study (Zgoba, Witt, Dalessandro, & Veysey, 2008) has compared sexual offense rates pre– and post–Megan's Law implementation and the costs associated with this law in New Jersey. The researchers concluded that Megan's Law did not reduce sexual recidivism, it had no effect on time to first rearrest, and it had no effect on reducing the number of victims. They reported that costs associated with the program

(*continued*)

increase each year and in 2007 totaled about $3.9 million. They concluded "Despite wide community support for these laws, there is little evidence to date, including this study, to support a claim that Megan's Law is effective in reducing either new first-time sex offenses or sexual re-offenses" (p. 41). In a recent media release, Maureen Kanka, Megan's mother, said in response to the above study "The purpose of the law was to provide an awareness to parents. It was put there for parents to know where the offenders are living. It's doing what it is supposed to do" (Livio & Spoto, 2009).

Since 2002 there have been more than 9 million visits to the New Jersey sex offender notification website. On this website you can search by geographic region or by name of sex offender. Currently, 3,221 registered sex offenders are listed on the New Jersey website. The website provides information about current address, date of birth, weight, height, race, and hair color of the sex offender.

violence. In addition, if offenders who have assaulted their spouses and refused treatment for domestic violence return to live with their spouses, they have a much higher likelihood of violence than those who do not have easy access to a past victim.

RISK ASSESSMENT INSTRUMENTS

Many of the factors affecting risk assessment that we've discussed above serve as the basis for various kinds of risk assessment instruments. Some instruments have been developed to predict specific kinds of risk, while others utilize particular strategies outlined above, such as actuarial or structured clinical assessments. Examples of an actuarial risk assessment and a structured professional judgment are described below. See Box 10.3 for a look at some other risk assessment instruments.

An actuarial risk for violence instrument developed in Canada is the Violence Risk Appraisal Guide (VRAG) (Harris et al., 1993). The VRAG is an empirically derived 12-item measure designed to assess the long-term risk for violent recidivism in offenders with mental disorders. Researchers coded about 50 risk factors from institutional files in a sample of 618 male adult patients with mental disorders who had been transferred to less secure institutions or released into the community. Statistical analyses were used to select the 12 best predictors of violence from childhood history, adult adjustment, offense history, and assessment results. The 12 predictors varied in terms of how strongly they were related to violent recidivism and included the following (ordered from most to least predictive):

- Hare Psychopathy Checklist–Revised score
- Elementary school maladjustment
- Diagnosis of any personality disorder
- Age at index offense (young age, higher risk)
- Separation from biological parents prior to age 16
- Failure on prior conditional release
- Prior nonviolent offenses
- Single marital status at time of offense
- Diagnosis of schizophrenia (lower risk)

BOX 10.3   Risk Assessment Instruments

Level of Service–Case Management Inventory (LS-CMI)

The LS-CMI (Andrews, Bonta, & Wormith, 2004) is the most recent version of structured professional judgment scale initially published in 1982 (this scale was called the Level of Supervision Inventory). The LS-CMI is a comprehensive risk/need assessment and treatment planning system. It consists of 11 sections that are evaluated based on a semistructured interview and review of the offender's file information (e.g., specific risk factors, institutional experience, special responsivity considerations, progress report, discharge summary). Section 1 consists of 43 items that are summed to yield a total risk score. These items are designed to measure the "Central Eight" risk factors that have been reliably associated with recidivism and include:

- Criminal history
- Education/employment
- Family/marital
- Leisure/recreation
- Companions
- Alcohol/drug problems
- Procriminal attitude/orientation
- Antisocial pattern

Iterative Classification Tree (ICT)

The ICT (Steadman et al., 2000) is an actuarial scale developed to predict violence in a community sample of patients. In the development sample, researchers coded 134 potential risk factors in 939 male and female civil psychiatric patients admitted to hospital in the United States. Patients were followed up for 20 weeks after discharge to determine if they engaged in violence toward others (violence was defined as physical violence resulting in injury, sexual assaults, assaults with a weapon, and threats with a weapon). The ICT contains 12 risk factors that form six risk groups. A classification tree approach places patients in different risk levels depending on the particular combination for risk factors. Depending on how the patient scores on the initial risk factor, the clinician considers other risk factors. Recently, a software program based on the ICT has been developed, called the Classification of Violence Risk (COVR; Monahan et al., 2005). Using this new software program, Monahan et al. (2005) followed a sample of 157 civil psychiatric patients for 20 weeks. The researchers found that 9% of the low-risk patients were violent compared to 49% of the high-risk patients. This study suggests that the COVR may be helpful to mental health professionals making decisions about when to discharge patients from hospitals.

Spousal Assault Risk Assessment (SARA)

The SARA (Kropp, Hart, Webster, & Eaves, 1999) is a 20-item structured professional judgment scale designed to assess the risk for spousal violence. It consists of 10 general violent risk factors (Part 1) and 10 spousal violent risk factors (Part 2). Part 1 items code for past history of violence and substance use problems, as well as relationship and employment problems. Part 2 items code for the nature and severity of violence in the most recent spousal assault incident, attitudes supportive of spousal assault, and violations of "no contact" orders. Researchers have often summed the individual risk factors to create a numerical total score. However, users are encouraged to make a summary risk judgment of low, moderate, or high.

(continued)

BOX 10.3   Continued

In a meta-analysis of 18 studies, Hanson, Helmus, and Bourgon (2007) found that the SARA total score and risk judgment were moderately related to spousal assault recidivism.

Static-99

The Static-99 (Hanson & Thornton, 1999) is a 10-item actuarial scale designed to predict sexual recidivism. All items on this scale are static in nature. Scores on the Static-99 can range from 0 to 12, with scores being associated with four risk categories: low, moderate-low, moderate-high, and high. Items on the Static-99 include:

- Young age at time of release
- Ever lived with intimate partner
- Any prior nonsexual violent convictions
- Any index nonsexual violent convictions
- Number of prior sex offenses
- Number of prior sentences
- Any male victims
- Any unrelated victims
- Any stranger victims
- Any noncontact sex offenses

The Static-99 was tested on three development samples in Canada and a fourth cross-validation sample in the United Kingdom. The Static-99 showed good predictive validity in the combined sample of 1,208, and the authors provided observed recidivism rates for both violent and sexual reoffense at 5-, 10-, and 15-year intervals (Hanson & Thornton, 2000). More recently, the developers have provided a set of recidivism norms for samples from Canada, the United States, Europe, and New Zealand for different aged sex offenders (Helmus, Thornton, Hanson, & Babchishin, in press). The developers have also developed the Static-2002 (Hanson & Thornton, 2003), which includes additional risk factors, such as persistence of sexual offending, deviant sexual interests, and general criminality.

A meta-analysis of the Static-99 (Hanson & Morton-Bourgon, 2009) reported moderate to strong predictive validity across more than 60 studies and 24,000 offenders.

- Victim injury (less injury, higher risk)
- History of alcohol problems
- Victim gender (female victim, lower risk)

Using scores on each of these risk factors, nine risk categories—or "bins"—were created. Each risk bin has a probability of violent recidivism within 10 years ranging from 9% (bin 1) to 35% (bin 5) to 100% (bin 9).

The Historical Clinical Risk Management-20 (HCR-20; Webster et al., 1997) was designed to predict violent behavior in correctional and forensic psychiatric samples. The HCR-20 uses the structured professional judgment approach to risk assessment developed by a group of researchers in British Columbia, Canada. In this approach, the evaluator conducts a systematic risk assessment and refers to a list of risk factors, each having specific coding criteria and a demonstrated relationship with violent recidivism based on the existing professional and empirical literature. The HCR-20 stands for the list of 20 items organized into three main scales that align risk factors into past (historical), present (clinical), and future (risk management):

Historical (primarily static in nature):

- Past violence
- Age at first violent offense
- Relationship instability
- Employment instability
- Relationship problems
- Substance use problems
- Major mental disorder
- Psychopathy
- Early maladjustment
- Personality disorder
- Prior supervision failure

Clinical (reflect current, dynamic risk factors):

- Lack of insight
- Negative attitudes
- Active mental disorder symptoms
- Impulsivity
- Treatability

Risk management (future community or institutional adjustment of the individual):

- Feasibility of plans
- Exposure to destabilizers
- Level of personal support
- Stress
- Likelihood of treatment compliance

Table 10.2 presents the results of a recent meta-analysis comparing the predictive effectiveness of several risk assessment measures for institutional violence and violence recidivism (Campbell, French, & Gendreau, 2009). The values in the table are effect sizes. All the effect sizes are positive, indicating all the measures were predictive of institutional violence and violent reoffending. All the scales were equally predictive of violent recidivism, whereas both the HCR-20 and LSI-R were the most predictive of institutional violence.

TABLE 10.2	The Predictive Accuracy of Different Risk Assessment Measures	
Measure	**Institutional Violence**	**Violent Recidivism**
HCR-20	0.31	0.25
LSI/LSI-R	0.24	0.25
PCL/PCL-R	0.15	0.24
VRAG	0.17	0.27

Source: Based on Campbell et al., 2009.

CURRENT ISSUES

Where is the Theory?

Much of the focus in risk assessment research has been on perfecting the prediction of violence. This focus is especially true for actuarial methods of risk assessment in which risk factors are selected based on their statistical relation to a specific outcome. There is less attention as to *why* these risk factors are linked to violence. Understanding the causes of violence will aid in the development of prevention and intervention programs. Box 10.4 presents one model that explains criminal recidivism. Recently, Silver (2006) has recommended that researchers use criminological theories to help to guide "the next generation of empirical research in the area of mental disorder and violence" (p. 686).

What about Female Offenders?

Most of the risk assessment measures have been developed and validated with male offenders. How well these measures generalize to women is an empirical question. If the causes and explanations for female and male criminality are similar, then risk assessment measures developed with male offenders likely can be used with female offenders. However, if there are important differences in male and female criminality, then it may be inappropriate to apply measures developed with male offenders to females. There are a number of gender differences in criminality. First, women engage is much less criminal behavior than men. In addition, women are arrested for different crimes than men. The only type of crime women commit more often than men is prostitution. When women engage in violence, they are more likely to target family members than are men. Second, women reoffend at a lower rate than do men. Third, childhood victimization is more prevalent in female offenders than male offenders. For example, 50% of incarcerated female offenders report childhood sexual abuse and 70% experienced childhood physical abuse (Shaw, 1994). Finally, female offenders are more likely to have a serious mental disorder, such as schizophrenia, bipolar disorder, depression, and anxiety disorders than are men (Warren et al., 2002).

Gender-specific risk factors may exist, however the research to date has found more similarities than differences in both adolescents and adults (Andrews & Bonta, 2006; Blanchette & Brown, 2006; Simourd & Andrews, 1994). Blanchette and Brown (2006) provide a review of static and dynamic risk factors in female offenders. They conclude that many of the static risk factors associated with recidivism in men, such as criminal history and age, are also predictors with women. Similar dynamic risk factors for women and men include substance abuse, antisocial attitudes, and antisocial associates. Evidence also suggests that women have further risk factors, such as a history of self-injury or attempted suicide and self-esteem problems. Overall, additional research is needed to understand the static and dynamic risk factors for recidivism in female offenders. Further research is also needed to fully understand protective factors that may improve women's success in the community upon release from prison. For example, Benda (2005) found that being married was a protective factor for men but a risk factor for women.

How well do the risk assessment instruments predict reoffending in female offenders? One risk assessment scale that has been well researched with female offenders is the LSI-R and its most recent version the LS-CMI (see Box 10.4 for a description). In a recent meta-analysis, Smith, Cullen, and Latessa (2009) reported that the LSI-R predicted general recidivism as well for women as for men (effect sizes of 0.27 and 0.26 for men

BOX 10.4   Coping-Relapse Model of Criminal Recidivism

Zamble and Quinsey (1997) have attempted to explain why an individual will commit another offense after release. Figure 10.1 illustrates the recidivism process and how each level interacts. According to the model, the first event is some type of environmental trigger. What will be considered a trigger varies across individuals and can range from stressful life events, such as losing a job or having relationship problems and financial difficulties, to more mundane daily events, such as being stuck in a traffic jam. Once the event has occurred, the individual will invoke both an emotional and cognitive appraisal of the event. If this appraisal process results in the experience of negative emotions (e.g., anger, hostility, fear) or elevated levels of stress, the individual will attempt to deal with these unpleasant feelings. If the individual does not possess adequate coping mechanisms, a worsening cycle of negative emotions and maladaptive cognitions occurs, eventually resulting in criminal behavior. The model also posits that how an individual perceives and responds to an environmental trigger is dependent on two factors: individual and response mechanisms.

Individual influences include factors such as criminal history and enduring personality traits (e.g., psychopathy, emotional reactivity). These factors influence how an individual will perceive an event and the likelihood he or she will engage in criminal conduct, both of which are relatively stable. For example, research has found that psychopathic individuals are impulsive and are more likely to interpret ambiguous events as hostile (Serin, 1991). These factors increase the likelihood of engaging in criminal behavior.

Available response mechanisms also influence how an individual will perceive a situation, which, in turn will mediate that person's response. These factors are considered to be more dynamic in nature and thus important targets for intervention. Examples of these factors include coping ability, substance use, criminal attitudes and associates, and social supports. Imagine an individual who loses his job. He becomes angry and upset, and reverts to drinking to deal with these negative feelings. His drinking angers his intimate partner who becomes less and less supportive of him. These factors increase the likelihood that he will resume his criminal behavior.

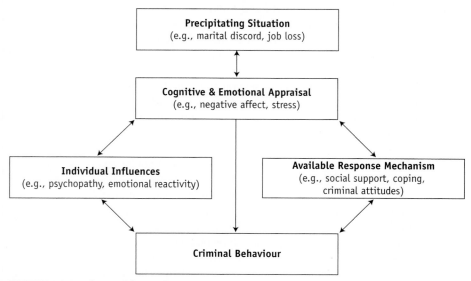

FIGURE 10.1   The Recidivism Process

Sources: Table from *The criminal recidivism* process by Vernon L. Quinsey and Edward Zamble. Copyright © 1997 by Cambridge University Press. Reprinted with the permission of Cambridge University Press.

and women, respectively). In addition, the LSI-R was also predictive of general recidivism in a sample of female offenders convicted of serious violent offenses (Manchak, Skeem, Douglas, & Siranosian, 2009).

     The above research indicates that some risk assessment instruments developed and validated with male offenders may also be used with women. However, it is not appropriate to assume that this will always be the case, and a considerable amount of research still needs to be conducted. Using the information about risk assessment you have learnt in the chapter, read the case presented in the Case Study and experience some of the difficulties a member of the parole board might have when making release decisions.

CASE STUDY

YOU BE THE PAROLE BOARD MEMBER

Jason Booth is a 26-year-old second-time state prisoner in California serving a 5-year sentence for robbery, carrying a concealed weapon, and probation violation. He pled guilty to all these charges. He has served two years of his sentence and has applied for parole to the Board of Parole Hearings.

     Official records indicate that Mr. Booth was in possession of a handgun at the time of his arrest. He robbed a drugstore threatening the cashier with the gun. At the time of his arrest, he was on probation from a previous conviction and, therefore, this constituted a breach of probation. He had been released from custody only 2 weeks prior to committing the current offenses. He is currently incarcerated at a medium-security state prison.

     Official records indicate that Mr. Booth has been previously sentenced by the courts six times (four times in youth court and two times in adult court) for a total of 12 convictions (8 in youth court and 4 in adult court) including assaults, assault with a weapon, carrying a concealed weapon, stalking, obstructing a peace officer, larceny, failure to attend court, unlawfully at large, and failure to comply with a probation order.

     Mr. Booth has violated probation several times and has engaged in violence in institutions (e.g., spitting in a correctional officer's face, stabbing another inmate with a pen). He has also engaged in violence in the community (e.g., assaulting his girlfriend, threatening to kill a bouncer at a bar).

     In his parole hearing, Mr. Booth explained that he committed the current offenses because he had just been released from prison and would not be receiving any social assistance for 2 weeks. He seemed to feel that the only way to obtain money was to rob the drugstore. He was unable to generate any prosocial alternatives by which he could have obtained assistance. In addition, Mr. Booth minimized his criminal history and the harm he has done to his victims. For example, he stated that one of his past victims, a woman who he had stalked and threatened to kill, was "a spoiled brat who deserved what she got." Most of Mr. Booth's friends are criminals.

     In the psychological report, Mr. Booth was described as hostile, arrogant, manipulative, impulsive, and lacking in remorse. Mr. Booth denies any current problems with drugs or alcohol. Neither drugs or alcohol have been involved in his current or past offenses.

Mr. Booth was reportedly diagnosed with attention-deficit/hyperactivity disorder at 9 years of age. He was never interested in school and was expelled numerous times. He completed grade 9 but was absent for most of grade 10. He dropped out of school when he was 16 years of age. Mr. Booth's employment history consists of several short-term jobs with the longest job lasting 1 year. He has few employment skills and tends to get into altercations with his boss and other employees. He was fired from his last job for stealing merchandise from the warehouse. During his current incarceration he has refused educational and vocational training.

Mr. Booth's biological father, who reportedly has been incarcerated himself, left his mother when he was 3 years of age. He was raised by his biological mother and an alcohol-abusing stepfather. His stepfather reportedly threw Mr. Booth out of the house when he was 13 years old due to his stealing and other disruptive behaviors. He was subsequently placed in a series of foster and group homes. He was often moved from home to home due to his aggressive and disruptive behavior.

In terms of his intimate partners, there is evidence of assaults on his partners. Past reports indicate Mr. Booth can be jealous, overly controlling, and hold unreasonable expectations in relationships with women. He reportedly has two children of his own, but does not maintain contact with either of them. He said that he has reentered a relationship with his ex-common-law spouse, the partner he assaulted in the past, and that they plan to be together when he is released.

When released he plans to go live with his mother. However, she does not want him to stay with her. Mr. Booth typically lives on social assistance or obtains money from criminal behaviors when in the community.

There is no evidence that Mr. Booth has ever successfully completed either institutional or community programming. Mr. Booth is typically uncooperative with attempts at assessment and treatment. However, he has recently expressed an interest in treatment programs.

Your Turn . . .

What risk factors for future reoffending are present? Are any protective factors present? How likely is Mr. Booth to commit another nonviolent or violent offense if you decide to release him? Which risk assessment instrument would you recommend Mr. Booth be assessed with?

What about Protective Factors?

Various historical, dispositional, clinical, and contextual risk factors have been shown to have predictive utility. **Protective factors** are factors that mitigate or reduce the likelihood of antisocial acts or violence in high-risk offenders (Borum, 1996). Understanding the positive attributes could help to explain why some individuals with many risk factors do not become violent. For example, a youth may have antisocial parents at home (a risk factor) but also be strongly attached to school (a protective factor). Like risk factors, protective factors vary across time, and the impact they have depends on the situation. Most of the research on protective factors has been conducted with children and youth. The following factors have been identified as protective factors: prosocial involvement, strong social supports, positive social orientation (e.g., school, work), strong attachments

Protective factors

Factors that mitigate or reduce the likelihood of a negative outcome (e.g., delinquency, aggression)

(as long as attachment is not to an antisocial other), and intelligence (Caldwell, Silverman, Lefforge, & Silver, 2004; Caprara, Barbaranelli, & Pastorelli, 2001; Hoge, Andrews, & Leschied, 1996; Lipsey & Derzon, 1998). More research on protective factors in adult offenders is beginning. A variable identified as a potential protective factor for high-risk offenders is employment stability, whereas strong family connections appears to be a protective factor for lower-risk male offenders (DeMatteo, Heilbrun, & Marczyk, 2005).

Risk Assessment: Risky Business?

Risk assessments have limitations that forensic evaluators and decision makers need to be aware of (Glazebrook, 2010). Most actuarial risk assessment measures provide probability statements about reoffending based on group data. However, currently there is no method of determining what the specific risk level is for an individual (see Hart, Michie, & Cooke, 2007, for a review). In contrast to actuarial measures, structured professional judgment measures typically ask evaluators to state the level of risk in terms of low, moderate, or high. However, researchers have found that forensic evaluators do not agree on what is meant by low, moderate or high risk (Hilton, Carter, Harris, & Sharpe, 2008; Mills & Kroner, 2006). Numerous risk assessment measures have been developed for several different types of outcomes (e.g., predicting sexual reoffending, spousal assault reoffending, and violent reoffending). Measures developed in one country or in one population may not generalize to another country or population (Austin, 2006). For example, Boccaccini, Murrie, Caperton, and Hawes (2009) reported that the Static-99 was not as predictive of sexual reoffending in a sample of sex offenders in United States as compared to the published norms for this measure. Risk assessment measures need to be validated in the community on which they will be used.

Recently some concerns have also been raised about the field reliability of risk assessment measures. For example, researchers using the PCL-R have reported excellent inter-rater reliabilities. However, in a study comparing prosecution and defense PCL-R scores in an adversarial context (sexual violent predator evaluations) very poor agreement was found (Murrie, Boccaccini, Johnson, & Janke, 2008). Finally, clinicians who are writing risk assessment reports or providing evidence to decision makers (e.g., an expert testifying in court) must ensure they use terminology that can be understood by the decision makers (e.g., juries, judges, lawyers, probation officers).

Are Decision Makers Using the Scientific Research?

Despite the considerable strides that have been made in refining methods of violence prediction, many practitioners are not using these instruments. This gap in integrating science and clinical practice represents a significant challenge to this area. A survey by Boothby and Clements (2000) asked 820 correctional psychologists what tests they used in their assessments. The most commonly used test was the Minnesota Multiphasic Personality Inventory (MMPI), which was used by 87% of the psychologists. The MMPI was not designed as a risk assessment measure, although it is being used by the majority of psychologists. Only 11% of the respondents mentioned using the Hare PCL-R, and less than 1% mentioned using the VRAG or the LSI-R. It is not clear why so few correctional psychologists are using these instruments. Research is needed to understand the obstacles to the adoption of new risk assessment measures. One potential reason is that these newer instruments have not been part of the training programs for psychologists.

What impact do psychologists' recommendations have on forensic decision making? Past research has found that judicial decision making relies heavily on recommendations made by mental health professionals (Konecni & Ebbesen, 1984). In Canada, decisions to release forensic patients are strongly related to recommendations by clinicians (Quinsey & Ambtman, 1979), and reports by clinicians about treatment gains made by sex offenders strongly influence decisions about granting parole (Quinsey, Khanna, & Malcolm, 1998). Another related question is whether decision makers are relying on results of the newly developed actuarial risk instruments. Hilton and Simmons (2001) studied the influence of VRAG scores and clinical judgments on decisions made to transfer offenders with mental disorders in a maximum-security facility to less secure institutions. Review board decisions were not related to scores on the VRAG but to senior clinicians' testimony at the review board hearing. Patients who caused few institutional problems, who were compliant with medication, who were more physically attractive, and who had less serious criminal histories were more likely to be recommended by the clinician for transfer. Clinicians make more accurate decisions when they are given a statement that summarizes an individual's risk along with case information (i.e., "64% of people in Mr. Smith's risk category reoffended violently within 10 years after release") (Hilton, Harris, Rawson, & Beach, 2005). Clinicians also are able to make accurate decisions when they are provided with the information that relates to risk.

Why Do Some Individuals Stop Committing Crimes?

Much of the research discussed in this chapter focuses on the risk factors related to engaging in crime and violence. However, if we want to prevent or reduce crime, knowledge about the factors relating to desistance from crime is probably equally important (Farrington, 2007). **Desistance** occurs when an individual who has engaged in criminal activities stops committing crimes. Research even shows that a majority of offenders show large declines in their criminal activity in early adulthood (Blumstein & Cohen, 1987; Piquero et al., 2001). As many as 70% of offenders show significant declines in crime (and only a small percentage of offenders maintain criminal activity well into adulthood; Piquero et al., 2001). Yet, the reasons why offenders give up crime is poorly understood. Some research shows that the factors that relate to the onset of a criminal career do not necessarily explain desistance from crime (Stouthamer-Loeber, Wei, Loeber, & Masten, 2004). The desistance process occurs over time and may be related to such factors as "good" work or "good" marriages (Sampson & Laub, 2005; Maume, Ousey, & Beaver, 2005; Uggen, 1999).

Desistance
The process of ceasing to engage in criminal behavior.

Age is strongly related to criminal behavior, and the age-related decline in criminal offending is connected to the maturation process (Menard & Huizinga, 1989). LeBlanc (1993) defines maturation as the "development of self- and social control" (p. 65). Shover and Thompson (1992) have suggested that as people age, they become less interested in a criminal lifestyle and are more able to understand and fear the consequences of engaging in crime. Recently, Serin and Lloyd (2009) have developed a model that proposes the transition between criminal offending and desistance is influenced by several intrapersonal moderators such as crime expectancies (what benefits do they see from not engaging in crime), beliefs about their ability to change (how hard will it be to change), and attributions for engaging in crime. See Box 10.5 for excerpts from a study that examines why high-risk offenders stop offending.

BOX 10.5	Why Do High-Risk Violent Offenders Stop Offending?

In a study entitled "Against All Odds: A Qualitative Follow-Up of High-Risk Violent Offenders Who Were Not Reconvicted," Haggard, Gumpert, and Grann (2001) explored what factors were related to why repeat violent offenders stopped reoffending. To be eligible to participate in the study, the offender had to score high on the historical subscale of the HCR-20, to have been convicted of at least two violent crimes, and not to have been convicted for any crime for at least 10 years. From a sample of 401 violent offenders, only 6 individuals were eligible to participate. Of these 6, only 4 consented to be interviewed. The participants reported that the following factors are related to desistance. For each factor, a quotation from one of the participants is provided.

- *Insight triggered by negative events connected to their criminal lifestyle.* "It grows within during a long time, the insight, but you have to reach a point where it feels wrong. . . . To me, it was mostly due to the last time, when I was admitted to the forensic psychiatric hospital. The whole thing was crazy, and then I realized how off track I was—when you strike down a person with an axe because of a trivial thing . . . then you start wondering. I did anyway" (p. 1055).
- *Social avoidance.* "I have a terrible temper and I can become violent, very violent. . . . You have to avoid different situations, you have to think about it all the time so that you don't put yourself in situations you can't handle" (p. 1057).
- *Orientation to the family.* "After I served my sentence, I became more committed to my children. To help them not to make the same mistake I did" (p. 1057).

Summary

1. An assessment of risk requires two components: (1) an analysis of the likelihood of future criminal or violent acts and (2) the development of strategies to manage or reduce the risk level.

2. Risk assessments are routinely conducted in the civil and criminal contexts. Risk assessments in civil contexts include civil commitments, child protection, immigration, and duty to warn. In criminal settings, the assessment of risk occurs at pretrial, sentencing, and release stages.

3. Different types of errors occur when attempting to make predictions. Each of these errors has different consequences. False-positive errors affect the offender, whereas false-negative errors affect society and the victim.

4. Risk factors vary in terms of how fixed or changeable they are. Static factors either do not change or are highly resistant to change. Dynamic factors are changeable and are often targeted for intervention.

5. Various approaches have been developed to assess violent prediction. These include unstructured clinical judgment, actuarial prediction, and structured professional judgment. There are advantages and disadvantages to each approach.

6. Major risk factors can be classified into historical, dispositional, clinical, and contextual factors. Historical risk factors include general social history and specific criminal history variables, such as employment problems and past history of violence. Dispositional factors include demographic, attitudinal, and personality variables, such as gender, age, negative attitudes, and psychopathy. Clinical factors refer to those things that contribute to violence, such as substance abuse or major psychoses. Contextual factors refer to aspects of the individual's situation that can elevate the risk, such as access to victims or weapons, lack of social supports, or perceived stress.

Key Concepts

actuarial prediction *242*
base rate *237*
clinical risk factors *245*
contextual risk
    factors *245*
desistance *259*
dispositional risk
    factors *245*

dynamic risk factors
    244
false negative *237*
false positive *237*
historical risk
    factors *245*
illusory correlation *242*

protective factors *257*
risk factor *244*
static risk
    factors *244*
structured professional
    judgment *244*
true negative *237*

true positive *237*
unstructured clinical
    judgment *242*

Discussion Questions

1. You have decided to take a summer job working at your state's Department of Corrections. You are asked to help devise a study to evaluate the accuracy of a new instrument designed to predict hostage taking by state offenders. How would you approach this task?
2. You think there should be more research on why offenders decide to stop offending. Describe a study you would conduct, focusing on the methodology and what factors you would measure that might relate to the desistance process.
3. Researchers have developed several risk assessment instruments, but not all psychologists conducting risk assessments are using these scales. Why is this? What could be done to encourage forensic psychologists to start using these instruments?
4. A school board wants to know how to identify the next potential school shooter and has contacted you for your expertise. Describe what you know about problems with trying to identify low-base-rate violent acts.

11

Psychopathy

LEARNING OBJECTIVES

- Define psychopathy.
- Outline the different assessment methods developed to measure psychopathy.
- Explain the two main theories of psychopathy.

- Describe the association between psychopathy and violence.
- Identify the concerns associated with labeling a youth as a psychopath.
- Describe the effectiveness of treatment programs for adolescents and adults with psychopathic traits.

Jason Roach is a 19-year-old working in a convenience store. He dropped out of college and spends most of his time partying, getting drunk and stoned. He decides that he does not want to spend the rest of his life working in a convenience store—a job he describes as "menial." One of his 16-year-old friends, Shawn, has been complaining about his parents and has started talking about wanting to "get rid of them." Jason offers to help, stating that if he helps he wants half of the insurance money. Jason convinces another 17-year-old friend with a car to help them with their murderous plan. Jason knows that they will need to have an alibi, so on the night of the murder they go to the nearby town to a strip club. Jason gets into an altercation with the bouncer to ensure the bouncer will remember them. Around midnight, armed with a baseball bat and a tire iron, they enter Shawn's house and beat his parents and his 14-year-old sister. While the beatings are taking place, Jason pours gasoline downstairs. As the offenders leave, Jason sets the house on fire. Two people die, and one is severely injured. Jason and his two friends are all charged and convicted of first-degree murder. At his trial, Jason describes himself as the "puppet master," appears proud of his ability to manipulate his younger friends, and shows no remorse for his actions.

P sychopaths have been called intraspecies predators (Hare, 1993). They seek vulnerable victims to use for their own benefit. Sometimes they get what they want
by charming their victims; at other times they use violence and intimidation to
achieve their goals. Lacking a conscience and feelings for others, they satisfy their own
selfish needs by preying on others. **Psychopathy** is a personality disorder defined by
a collection of interpersonal, affective, and behavioral characteristics. Psychopaths are
dominant, selfish, manipulative individuals who engage in impulsive and antisocial acts
and who feel no remorse or shame for behavior that often has a negative impact on others. Jason in the above vignette manifests many psychopathic traits.

    Descriptions of psychopathy exist in most cultures. Murphy (1976) found that the
Inuit in Alaska use the term *kunlangeta* to describe an individual who "repeatedly lies and
cheats and steals things and does not go hunting and, when the other men are out of the
village, takes sexual advantage of many women—someone who does not pay attention to
reprimands and who is always being brought to the elders for punishment" (p. 1026). When
Murphy asked an Inuit elder what the group would typically do with a kunlangeta, he replied,
"Somebody would have pushed him off the ice when nobody else was looking" (p. 1026).

    In this chapter, we focus on methods for the assessment of psychopathy, how prev-
alent psychopathy is, its overlap with other disorders, the relationship between psychopathy and violence, and the effectiveness of treating psychopathy.

Psychopathy

A personality disorder
defined by a collection
of interpersonal,
affective, and
behavioral
characteristics
including
manipulation, lack of
remorse or empathy,
impulsivity, and
antisocial behaviors

ASSESSMENT OF PSYCHOPATHY

Hervey Cleckley (1976), a psychiatrist in Georgia, provided one of the most comprehensive clinical descriptions of the psychopath in his book *The Mask of Sanity*. Cleckley
described 16 features ranging from positive features (e.g., good intelligence, social
charm, and absence of delusions and anxiety), emotional-interpersonal features (e.g., lack
of remorse, untruthfulness, unresponsiveness in interpersonal relations), and behavioral
problems (e.g., inadequately motivated antisocial behavior, unreliability, failure to follow any life plan).

    Currently, the most popular method of assessing psychopathy in adults is the **Hare
Psychopathy Checklist–Revised** (PCL-R) (Hare, 1991, 2003). This assessment instrument was developed by Robert Hare at the University of British Columbia in Canada
and is now being used around the world. The development of the PCL-R was strongly
influenced by the work of Hervey Cleckley. The PCL-R is a 20-item rating scale that
uses a semistructured interview and a review of file information to assess interpersonal
(e.g., grandiosity, manipulativeness), affective (e.g., lack of remorse, shallow emotions),
and behavioral (e.g., impulsivity, antisocial acts) features of psychopathy. Each item is
scored on a 3-point scale: 2 indicates that the item definitely applies to the individual;
1 that it applies to some extent; and 0 indicates that the symptom definitely does not
apply. The items are summed to obtain a total score ranging from 0 to 40. Researchers
have often subdivided those administered the PCL-R into three groups: a high-PCL-R
group (often called psychopaths) defined by a score of 30 or greater; a middle-scoring
group (mixed group), with scores between about 20 and 30; and a low-scoring group
(often called nonpsychopaths), with scores of below 20.

    Initial factor analyses (a statistical procedure to identify clusters of traits within a
measure) of the PCL-R indicated that it consisted of two correlated factors (Hare et al.,
1990). Factor 1 reflects the combination of interpersonal and affective traits, whereas
factor 2 is a combination of unstable and socially deviant traits. Researchers have

**Hare Psychopathy
Checklist–Revised**

The most popular
method of assessing
psychopathy in adults

examined the differential correlates of these two factors and found that factor 1 is more strongly related to predatory violence, emotional processing deficits, and poor treatment response (Hare, Clark, Grant, & Thornton, 2000; Patrick, Bradley, & Lang, 1993; Seto & Barbaree, 1999; Woodworth & Porter, 2002), whereas factor 2 is strongly related to reoffending, substance abuse, lack of education, and poor family background (Hare, 2003; Hemphill, Hare, & Wong, 1998; Porter, Birt, & Boer, 2001; Rutherford, Alterman, Cacciola, & McKay, 1997). Some researchers have argued for a three-factor model of psychopathy (Cooke & Michie, 2001). These three factors are (1) arrogant and deceitful interpersonal style, (2) deficient affective experience, and (3) impulsive and irresponsible behavioral style. This factor structure splits the original factor 1 into two factors and removes some of the antisocial items from factor 2. The most recent factor analysis of the PCL-R includes these three factors plus a fourth factor called *antisocial* that includes the antisocial items (Hare, 2003).

A considerable amount of research supports the use of the PCL-R in a range of samples, including male and female offenders, forensic psychiatric patients, sexual offenders, and substance abusers (Hare, 2003).

Another way of assessing for psychopathic traits is via self-report questionnaires. Using self-report measures has a number of advantages. First, they are able to measure those attitudes and emotions that are not easily observed by others (e.g., feelings of low self-esteem). Second, they are easy to administer (they can be administered on the web for research), quick to score, and relatively inexpensive. Third, it is not necessary to worry about inter-rater reliability because only the individual is completing the score. Finally, although there are concerns about psychopaths lying on self-report measures (see below), some questionnaires include measures of response styles to detect faking good or faking bad.

The use of self-report measures to assess for psychopathy also has a number of challenges (Lilienfeld & Fowler, 2006). First, as noted above, psychopaths often lie. Some psychopaths are "master manipulators" and will say whatever will be in their best interests. For example, they may malinger and claim they have a mental disorder to avoid facing more serious sanctions. Second, psychopaths may not have sufficient insight to accurately assess their traits. For example, psychopaths may not consider themselves as arrogant, dominant, or opinionated, whereas others might. Finally, it will likely be difficult for a psychopath to report on specific emotions if they have not experienced these emotions. For example, if asked if they feel remorse for the suffering they have caused others, they may mistake this feeling with the regret they feel for the consequences of getting caught.

Two of the most widely used self-report scales are the Psychopathic Personality Inventory–Revised (PPI-R; Lilienfeld & Widows, 2005) and the Self-Report Psychopathy Scale (SRP; Paulhus, Neumann & Hare, in press). The PPI-R is a 154-item inventory designed to measure psychopathic traits in offender and community samples. It consists of eight content scales, two validity scales (to check for carelessness and positive or negative response styles), and measures two factors (fearless dominance and self-centered impulsivity). The SRP is a 64-item self-report measure designed to assess psychopathic traits in community samples. It consists of four factors: erratic lifestyle (e.g., "I'm a rebellious person"), callous affect (e.g., "I am more tough-minded than other people"), interpersonal manipulation (e.g., "I think I could 'beat' a lie detector"), and criminal tendencies (e.g., "I have been arrested by the police"). See Box 11.1 for research using self-report psychopathy scales in university students.

BOX 11.1	Subclinical Psychopaths: University Samples

Psychopathic traits are dimensional, meaning that people vary on the number and severity of psychopathic features exhibited. Although most research has been conducted with offenders or forensic psychiatric patients, an increasing amount of research has examined people outside institutional settings. Much of this research has used self-report psychopathy measures. Several studies that investigated a range of different behaviors in university students are described below.

Detecting Vulnerable Victims (Wheeler, Book, & Costello, 2009)

Method: University students were unknowingly videotaped walking down a hallway and were classified as being vulnerable or not based on their self-report of experienced victimization. Male university students were asked to pretend to be a mugger and rated the videotapes on vulnerability.

Results: Students with higher SRP scores were more accurate at detecting victim vulnerability.

Defrauding a Lottery (Paulhus, Williams, & Nathanson, 2002)

Method: A student participates in a study and has a chance of winning $100. After the study has been completed, all study participants are sent an e-mail in which the experimenter states that he has lost the information about who was supposed to receive the five $100 prizes. Participants are asked to e-mail the experimenter to let him know it they had previously been a winner.

Results: Students scoring higher on the SRP were more likely to try to defraud the experimenter and claim they were the "true" winner.

Cheating on Exams (Nathanson, Paulhus, & Williams, 2006)

Method: The experimenters obtained computerized multiple-choice exam answers and seating plans from the instructors of several large introductory psychology classes. The experimenters wanted to determine which personality traits were related to cheating.

Results: Four percent of students were identified as cheating pairs, in which one student copied the answers from an adjacent student. Psychopathic traits, as measured by the SRP, were the strongest predictors of cheating.

Owning "Vicious" Dogs (Ragatz, Fremouw, Thomas, & McCoy, 2009)

Method: A large sample of 869 university students completed an anonymous online questionnaire assessing ownership of types of dog breeds, criminal behaviors, tolerance of animal abuse, and psychopathic traits. Owners of the following six breeds of dogs were classified as owning "vicious" dogs: Akita, Chow, Doberman, Pit bull, Rottweiler, and Wolf mix.

Results: Students classified as owning a "vicious" dog engaged in more criminal behaviors and scored higher on the primary psychopathy scale (measures selfishness, carelessness, and manipulation) of the Levenson Primary and Secondary Psychopathy Scale (Levenson, Kiehl, & Fitzpatrick, 1995), but were not more tolerant of animal abuse than other students.

PSYCHOPATHY AND ANTISOCIAL PERSONALITY DISORDER

According to the Diagnostic and Statistical Manual of Mental Disorders (DSM-IV; American Psychiatric Association, 1994), **Antisocial personality disorder** (APD) refers to a personality disorder in which there is evidence for conduct disorder before age 15

Antisocial personality disorder

A personality disorder characterized by a history of behavior in which the rights of others are violated and a chronic pattern of disregarding the rights of others since age 15. The DSM-IV is a manual used by mental health professionals to diagnose mental health disorders in children and adults. After age 15, a person diagnosed with APD would need to display three or more of the following symptoms:

- Repeatedly engaging in criminal acts
- Deceitfulness
- Impulsivity
- Irritability
- Reckless behaviors
- Irresponsibility
- Lack of remorse

Sociopathy

A label used to describe a person whose psychopathic traits are assumed to be due to environmental factors

Additional confusion surrounds the diagnosis of APD and its relationship to both psychopathy and **sociopathy**. The three terms are sometimes used interchangeably, whereas a general consensus among most researchers is that the constructs of APD, psychopathy, and "sociopathy" are related but distinct (Hare & Neumann, 2008). The term *sociopath* was coined in 1930 by Partridge to describe those people who had problems with or refused to adapt to society. Lykken (2006) proposed that sociopaths manifest similar traits as psychopaths but develop these traits as a result of poor parenting and other environmental factors, whereas psychopaths are genetically predisposed to a temperament that makes them difficult to socialize. The term *sociopath* is rarely used in the empirical literature and no assessment instruments have been developed to identify this construct.

Although psychopathy and APD share some features, APD places more emphasis on antisocial behaviors than does the PCL-R. The prevalence of APD is very high in prisons, with up to 80% of adult offenders being diagnosed with this disorder (Hare, Forth, & Strachan, 1992; Motiuk & Porporino, 1991). Using a cut-off of 30 on the PCL-R, 10% to 25% of adult offenders can be classified as psychopaths (Hare, 2003). An asymmetrical relation exists between these two disorders: nearly all psychopathic offenders meet the diagnostic criteria for APD, but most offenders diagnosed with APD are not psychopaths. APD symptoms are most strongly related to the behavioral features of psychopathy and not to the interpersonal or affective features. Another difference is that APD is recognized as one of the personality disorders in the DSM-IV (APA, 1994), whereas psychopathy is not. However, this situation might change with the upcoming changes to DSM being proposed. Figure 11.1 illustrates the overlap between psychopathy and APD in incarcerated offenders.

WHAT MAKES THEM TICK?: COGNITIVE AND AFFECTIVE MODELS OF PSYCHOPATHY

Response Modulation Deficit

Theory that psychopaths fail to use peripheral cues to change their behavior

A number of theories have been proposed to help forensic psychologists to understand the development of psychopathy. Two of the most prominent theories of psychopathy place emphasis on either cognitive or affective (emotional) processes. Newman, Brinkley, Lorenz, Hiatt, and MacCoon (2007) have proposed that psychopaths have a **response modulation deficit**. According to this theory, psychopaths fail to use contextual cues that are peripheral to a dominant response set to modulate their behavior. In other words, if psychopaths are engaging in a specific rewarded behavior, they will not pay attention to other information that might inhibit their behavior. This theory has been used to

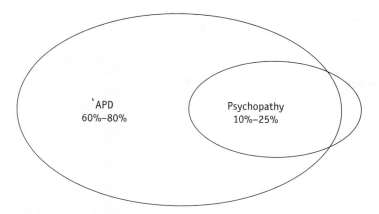

FIGURE 11.1

DSM-IV Antisocial Personality Disorder and PCL-R Psychopathy: Construct Overlap in Offenders

Sources: DSM-IV Antisocial personality disorder and PCL-R Psychopathy: Construct overlap in offenders, Copyright © 1994 by American Psychological Association.

explain why psychopaths fail to learn to avoid punishment (i.e., have poor passive avoid-ance). Dr. Newman has been studying psychopaths for over 30 years, see Box 11.2 for a profile and an overview of his research.

The other theory proposes that psychopaths have a deficit in the experience of certain critical emotions that guide prosocial behavior and inhibit deviance (Blair, 2006a; Hare, 2007; Patrick, 2007). Hervey Cleckley (1976) was the first person to theorize that psychopaths had a deep-rooted emotional deficit that involved the disconnection between cognitive-linguistic processing and emotional experience. In one of the first experimental studies to measure this deficit, Williamson, Harpur, and Hare (1991) showed that psychopaths fail to show the nor-mal, faster reaction times to emotional words on a lexical-decision task ("Is the word you see on the screen a real word or a nonword"?). In addition, the study found that psychopaths' brain wave activity does not differentiate between emotional and neutral words.

Researchers have used measured affective processing in a range of different para-digms. For example, Blair, Budhani, Colledge, and Scott (2005) asked children to iden-tify the emotions in neutral words spoken with intonations conveying happiness, disgust, anger, sadness, and fear. Boys with many psychopathic traits were impaired at recogniz-ing fearful vocal affect. In adults, Patrick and colleagues (1993) compared startle reflexes of psychopathic and nonpsychopathic sexual offenders to slides of positive (e.g., puppies, babies, eroticism), neutral (e.g., table, glass), and negative (e.g., baby with tumor, injured kitten, homicide scene) stimuli. The startle-elicited blinks of nonpsychopathic offenders were smaller when watching positive slides, moderate when watching neutral slides, and enhanced when watching negative slides. In contrast, the psychopathic offenders' startle-elicited blinks did not differ in magnitude across the different types of slides.

These findings of emotional deficits in psychopaths have led some researchers to propose an amygdala dysfunction theory (Blair, 2006b, 2008). The amygdala is a small almond-shaped structure located in the medial temporal lobes. The amygdala is part of the limbic system, which regulates the expression of emotion and emotional memory. It is linked to many other brain regions responsible for memory, control of the auto-nomic nervous system, aggression, decision making, approach and avoidance behavior,

BOX 11.2   Researcher Profile: Dr. Joseph Newman

Dr. Joseph Newman

Dr. Joseph Newman was fascinated by the compelling psychological explanations for abnormal behavior in his first-year psychology course. These explanations included psychodynamic, behavioral, cognitive, affective, and physiological mechanisms for psychopathology. While doing research on the learned helplessness model of depression as a graduate student, he became interested in the effects of lesions to the septo-hippocampal system because such lesions had been shown to prevent the development of learned helplessness. In 1980 he (and his collaborator, Ethan Gorenstein) proposed a physiological model of psychopathy (septo-hippocampus-orbitofrontal model). This model attempted to clarify the psychobiological mechanisms underlying psychopathy and other syndromes of disinhibition. Testing this model became the focus of much of Dr. Newman's research endeavors.

Dr. Newman completed his Ph.D. in clinical psychology at Indiana University–Bloomington. His dissertation was an investigation of the role of response perseveration in the learning deficits of psychopaths and was the first test of the Gorenstein and Newman septo-hippocampus-orbitofrontal model of psychopathy. Dr. Newman's first job was at the University of Wisconsin–Madison where he continues to work as a professor in the Department of Psychology.

When asked what keeps him interested in research, Dr. Newman says, "The excitement of testing new hypotheses and gaining new insights into the nature of psychopathy and other forms of disinhibitory psychopathology; working with extraordinary students who bring fresh ideas and insights to our research collaborations; and the desire to demonstrate the value of using basic research findings to treat psychopathology and enhance mental health more generally."

Dr. Newman typically uses the Hare Psychopathy Checklist–Revised to assess psychopathy. He and his students have developed computerized tasks to identify factors that moderate the cognitive and affective deficits associated with psychopathy. In addition, they are currently using emotion-modulated startle paradigms and event-related potentials (ERPs) to study cognitive-affective interactions in psychopathy. He is extremely enthusiastic about his recent collaborative work with John Curtin and Arielle Baskin-Sommers in which they found that psychopathic offenders display normal fear-potentiated startle when task instructions focus participants' attention on threat cues but abnormal fear-potentiated startle when threat cues are peripheral to their primary focus of goal-directed behavior (Newman, Curtin, Bertsch, & Baskin-Sommers, 2010; Baskin-Sommers, Curtin, & Newman, 2010). What Dr. Newman finds particularly encouraging about these studies, beyond demonstrating a potentially important emotion deficit, is the identification of a specific psychological process that may prove useful in treating psychopaths.

Dr. Newman enjoys teaching courses that help students to think scientifically and apply psychobiological mechanisms to understand human behavior. To balance his busy academic life, Dr. Newman has recently returned to a sport he enjoys immensely—running. Most recently, he finds great enjoyment interacting with his first grandchild.

and defense reactions. Other researchers have proposed that other brain areas are implicated and have suggested a paralimbic model to explain the emotional deficits seen in psychopaths. Recently, Newman and colleagues (2010) have argued that the emotional deficits seen in psychopaths can be explained by an attention deficit and are not due to an amygdala-mediated deficit.

PSYCHOPATHY AND VIOLENCE

The characteristics that define psychopathy are compatible with a criminal lifestyle and a lack of concern for societal norms. Characteristics that ordinarily help to inhibit aggression and violence, such as empathy, close emotional bonds, and internal inhibitions, are lacking or relatively ineffective in psychopaths. Psychopathy is significant because of its association with criminal behavior in general and violence in particular. Although psychopaths make up a relatively small proportion of the population, their involvement in serious repetitive crime and violence is out of proportion to their numbers. As stated by Hart (1998), "The two are so intimately connected that a full understanding of violence is impossible without consideration of the role played by psychopathy" (p. 367). See Box 11.3 for a description of a psychopath.

Psychopaths are high-density (prolific), versatile offenders. The crimes of psychopaths run the gamut from minor theft and fraud to cold-blooded murder. Compared to nonpsychopathic offenders, they start their criminal career at a younger age and persist longer, engage in more violent offenses, commit a greater variety of violent offenses, engage in more violence within institutions, and, as seen in Chapter 10, are more likely to be violent after release (Hare, 2003).

The nature of psychopaths' violence also differs from other types: "Psychopathic violence is more likely to be predatory in nature, motivated by readily identifiable goals, and carried out in a callous, calculated manner without the emotional context that usually characterizes the violence of other offenders" (Hare, 2003, p. 136). Several studies have found that offenders who engage in instrumental (planned and motivated by an external goal) violence score significantly higher on measures of psychopathy than do offenders engaging in reactive violence (Cornell et al., 1996; Walsh, Swogger, & Kosson, 2009). One study by Williamson, Hare, and Wong (1987) found that when nonpsychopaths commit violence, they are likely to target people they know and their violent behavior is likely to occur in the context of strong emotional arousal. In contrast, psychopaths are more likely to target strangers and be motivated by revenge or material gain. Several studies of adolescent offenders have found that youth who engaged in instrumental violence were more psychopathic than other youth (Flight & Forth, 2007; Vitacco, Neumann, Caldwell, Leisticio, & Van Rybroek, 2006).

Psychopaths' use of instrumental motives extends to homicide. Woodworth and Porter (2002) investigated the association between psychopathy and the nature of homicides committed by 135 Canadian offenders. Using PCL-R scores to divide the offenders into the three groups described above—nonpsychopaths (PCL-R scores of less than 20), medium scorers (PCL-R scores between 20 and 30), and psychopaths (PCL-R scores of 30 or greater)—the percentage of homicides that were primarily instrumental were 28%, 67%, and 93%, respectively. The researchers concluded that psychopaths engage in "cold-blooded" homicides much more often than nonpsychopaths.

BOX 11.3 A Psychopath among Us: Serial Killer Ted Bundy

Although Ted Bundy was executed in 1989, he remains one of the most high-profile psychopaths in U.S. history. Bundy exhibited the classic traits of psychopathy: arrogance, superficial charm, deceit, grandiosity, and a lack of remorse or compassion. Perhaps one of the most accurate descriptions of Bundy is from his own self-description provided to police after his 1978 arrest for the murder of a 12-year-old girl: "I'm the most cold son of a bitch you have ever met."

Theodore Bundy was born November 24, 1946. He grew up believing his mother was his older sister and his maternal grandparents were his parents. As a teenager he began shoplifting and would forge ski tickets in order to go skiing. He graduated from high school and was given a scholarship to the University of Puget Sound. After two seminars he transferred to the University of Washington and majored in psychology. (While at university he volunteered at Seattle's Suicide Hot Line where he met Anne Rule, another volunteer, who was a former police officer and a fledgling crime writer. Rule later wrote the book *The Stranger Beside Me*, a biography of Bundy.) In 1967 Bundy dated a fellow university student but she ended the relationship after a year, claiming he was too immature and lacked ambition. He dropped out of university and managed the local campaign office of Presidential candidate Nelson Rockefeller. Bundy returned to university and graduated in 1972 with a BA in psychology. In the fall of 1973 he started law school but dropped out in the spring of 1974 due to skipping classes and failing grades. It is not clear when Bundy committed his first murder. He gave differing accounts ranging from 1969 to 1974. It is known that around midnight on January 4, 1974, he broke into an 18-year-old university student's basement apartment and raped and beat her. She survived but was in a coma for 10 days. His first known murder occurred February 1, 1974, when he murdered Lynda Anne Healey. From that point on, young university students began disappearing about once a month. Witnesses reported that they saw a man in either a leg cast or arm sling approaching women asking them to help carry books to his car. On July 14, 1974, Bundy approached several women at a park. He had his arm in a sling, said his name was "Ted" and asked them to come help remove a sailboat from his VW Beetle. Five women refused but two agreed and both were murdered. Police put up fliers with a description of Bundy and his vehicle. In an ironic twist, Bundy's former co-volunteer, Ann Rule, called the police saying that Ted Bundy appeared to fit the description. Others also called to identify Bundy, including one of his former psychology professors. However, because the police were overwhelmed by the large number of other tips, Bundy was not immediately identified as a suspect. In the fall of 1974 he moved to Utah to attend Law School at the University of Utah. While in Utah Bundy continued abducting, raping, and murdering young women. He killed three women in October 1974 including the 17-year-old daughter of a police chief.

On November 8, 1974, he approached Carol DeRonch in a shopping mall. He pretended to be a police officer and told her someone had broken into her car and that she needed to come with him to the police station. After driving for a short time, Bundy pulled over and attempted to put handcuffs on her. She struggled and he attached both cuffs to the same wrist. He attempted to hit her with a crowbar but she managed to escape from his car.

In the winter of 1975, Bundy started to go to ski resorts in Colorado to hunt for victims. He would be on crutches and ask women to help carry his ski boots to his car. Bundy was arrested on August 15, 1975, for failing to stop for a police officer. The police found handcuffs, a ski mask, rope, crowbar, gloves, and an ice pick in his car. After investigating, police linked Bundy to the kidnapping of Carol DeRonch and she selected him from a police line-up. He was convicted of kidnapping in Utah and sentenced to 15 years.

Bundy was then extradited to Colorado to stand trial for murder. Bundy escaped on June 7, 1977, by jumping out of a second-story window at the courthouse. He was captured 1 week

(continued)

later. Amazingly, he escaped again on December 30, 1977, by using a hacksaw to saw through a metal plate in the ceiling of his cell. Bundy hitchhiked his way to Denver, caught a plane to Chicago, took a train to Ann Arbor, Michigan, where he stole a car, and drove to Atlanta, Georgia, and then took a bus to Tallahassee, Florida. Within 1 week, at 3 a.m. on January 15, 1978, he broke into the Florida State University Chi Omega sorority house, killing two students and severely injuring two others. After leaving the scene he broke into another home and severely injured another Florida State University student. He stole a van and drove to Lake City, Florida, where on February 9, 1978, he abducted, raped, and murdered a 12-year-old girl. Bundy was captured and went to trial for the two murders of the Florida State University students. He acted as his own attorney which gave him the opportunity to cross-examine witnesses. Based on both eyewitness testimony and bite mark evidence (Bundy had bitten one of the murdered students on her buttocks and a forensic odontologist matched Bundy's teeth to this bite mark), he was convicted of capital murder and given a death sentence. He was given a second death sentence for the murder of the 12-year-old Lake City girl. On February 9, 1980, while a former coworker, Carole Boone, was on the stand testifying on his behalf, Bundy asked her to marry him. She agreed and in 1982 she gave birth to a daughter (Bundy and Boone were given several conjugal visits). Boone and her daughter moved back to Washington State in 1986 where she divorced Bundy.

Bundy was interviewed by FBI agents in an attempt to convince him to confess to several unsolved murders. How many murders did Bundy commit? The total number is unknown. He confessed to 30 murders with 20 known victims (all females ages 12 to 26 years) across seven states.

On January 23, 1989, the day before Bundy was executed by electric chair, he spoke with psychologist Dr. James Dobson about what contributed to him to becoming a serial killer. According to Bundy, at the age of 12 or 13 he started looking at soft-core pornography that escalated to more violent pornography he found in the garbage around his neighborhood. As Bundy stated "The most damaging kind of pornography—and I'm talking from hard, real, personal experience—is that that involves violence and sexual violence. The wedding of those two forces—as I know only too well—brings about behavior that is too terrible to describe."

At 7:06 a.m. on January 24, 1989, Bundy was strapped into "Old Sparky," the electric chair at Florida State Prison. At 7:16 a.m., after 2 minutes of 2,000 volts of electricity, he was pronounced dead. Outside the prison gates several hundred people gathered; some carried signs that read "Thank God It's Fryday," "Bundy Bar-B-Q," and "Roast in Peace." When it was announced that Bundy was dead, they cheered and clapped. A smaller crowd of anti–death-penalty activists was also present.

In a study of post-homicide behaviors, Häkkänen-Nyholm and Hare (2009) measured psychopathic traits in 546 Finnish homicide offenders. Higher PCL-R scores were found for cases with multiple versus single offenders, stranger victims, male victims, for offenders who left the scene of the murder, and for offenders who denied responsibility for the murder. Rather than experiencing remorse for the murder they had committed, psychopathic offenders shifted the blame and focused on "saving their own skin."

Recent evidence for psychopaths' ability to manipulate the criminal justice system comes from a study by Porter, ten Brinke, and Wilson (2009). Psychopathic offenders (both sexual and nonsexual offenders) were given early release from prison more often than nonpsychopathic offenders. However, when followed up, the psychopathic offenders were less successful than the nonpsychopathic offenders. It is critical that people making decisions about release be familiar with psychopathy and the psychopath's abilities to engage in impression management (i.e., telling people what they want to hear).

PSYCHOPATHS IN THE COMMUNITY

Much of the research in community samples has used the Hare Psychopathy Checklist–Screening Version (PCL-SV; Hart, Cox, & Hare, 1995). This 12-item version takes less time to administer and places less emphasis on criminal behavior for scoring than the PCL-R. In the general population psychopathy is relatively rare. Coid, Yang, Ullrich, Roberts, and Hare (2009) assessed 301 male and 319 females in the community and found that 0.6% of the sample had scores of 13 or greater on the PCL:SV (only one person scored above the cut-off score of 18), with 71% of the sample having no psychopathic traits (i.e., scoring 0 on the PCL-SV). In another community sample in the United States (Neumann & Hare, 2008), about 75% of the sample had scores of 2 or less and only 1.2% had scores in the "potential psychopathic" range (i.e., scores of 13 or greater on the PCL-SV). Regardless of sample, females consistently score lower than males on the PCL-SV and other psychopathy measures (Dolan & Völlm, 2009).

Not all psychopaths are violent, nor do they all end up in prison. As Hare (1993) notes, "[We] are far more likely to lose our life savings to an oily tongued swindler than our lives to a steely-eyed killer" (p. 6). Paul Babiak (2000), an organizational psychologist, consulted with six companies undergoing dramatic organizational change, such as merging and downsizing. In each of these companies, Babiak found employees with many psychopathic features to be at the root of some of the company problems. These employees were skilled at getting information on other employees, spreading unwarranted vicious rumors about others, and causing dissension among employees. What they were not doing was pulling their own weight on the job. They were particularly good at manipulating the key players in the organization (employees who can provide them with information about upper management) and blaming others for their failures (see Babiak, 1995, for a case study of the corporate psychopath).

More recently, Babiak, Neumann, and Hare (2010) assessed psychopathic traits in 203 corporate professionals. The average PCL-R score was 3.6; however, eight professionals (or 4.9%) scored above the 30-point cutoff for a diagnosis of psychopathy. The professionals with psychopathic traits were less likely to be team players, had poorer management skills, and had poorer performance appraisals than professionals with few psychopathic traits. However, the more psychopathic professionals were more creative, engaged in more strategic thinking, and had stronger communication skills than the less psychopathic professionals.

One area of research that has been vastly neglected is research with victims of psychopaths. To date there is only one published study exploring the experiences of victims of psychopaths. Through semistructured phone interviews with 20 female victims, Kirkman (2005) aimed to identify the behavioral and personality characteristics of nonincarcerated psychopathic males who may or may not have abused their partners. Eight characteristics of male psychopaths in heterosexual relationships were extracted from the interviews: (1) talking victim into victimization, (2) lying, (3) economic abuse, (4) emotional abuse/psychological torture, (5) multiple infidelities, (6) isolation and coercion, (7) assault, and (8) mistreatment of children. Future research using a larger, more diverse sample of victims needs to be conducted. See the In the Media box for how psychopaths are portrayed in the media.

IN THE MEDIA	Mean on the Screen: Media's Portrayal of Psychopaths

When you think of the term *psychopath*, who comes to mind? If you think of psychopaths in movies, the first character that most people think of is Hannibal Lecter. This character was introduced in Thomas Harris's book *Red Dragon*, which was published in 1981. In 1988, the sequel was turned into the popular movie *Silence of the Lambs* with lead actor Anthony Hopkins playing Hannibal Lecter. Lecter is a psychiatrist who happens also to be a cannibalistic serial killer who is in a secure forensic psychiatric institution. A trainee FBI agent is sent to interview Lecter in hopes he will help her capture another serial killer. The film revolves around Lecter's manipulation of this agent and his escape. Although Lecter has many psychopathic traits, most psychopaths are not serial killers, nor as intelligent or as successfully manipulative as Lecter.

What about psychopaths on television shows? In recent years, the most popular psychopathic television character is Dexter Morgan. The *Dexter* series follows the day-to-day life of Dexter, a blood-splatter analyst who also happens to be a serial killer. However, Dexter is a serial killer with some morals, since he targets killers who have escaped justice. In reality, most serial killers target vulnerable victims, such as children, sex-trade workers, runaways, or the homeless, not other violent criminals.

Both Hannibal Lecter and Dexter Morgan experienced serious trauma in their early childhood. At age 8, Lecter's parents are killed in an explosion and his sister murdered and cannibalized in front of him. He is put in an orphanage and starts having deviant violent fantasies focused on avenging his sister's death.

Dexter witnessed the murder of his mother at age 3 and was adopted by Harry, a police officer. Harry recognizes Dexter's "psychopathic traits" and teaches him to channel his passion for killing to murder other killers. Harry also realizes that Dexter has no emotions and teaches Dexter to fake emotions.

Is experiencing a traumatic event in childhood related to the development of psychopathy? Although some psychopaths do experience trauma many do not, which suggests that trauma is not a necessary precursor for psychopathy. Also, although these fictional psychopaths may have some characteristics associated with psychopathy, they are definitely not "typical" psychopaths.

PSYCHOPATHY AND SEXUAL VIOLENCE

Psychopathy and sexual violence have been the focus of much research. As noted above, psychopathy is associated with violent offenses. However, it is only weakly associated with sexual offenses. For example, Brown and Forth (1997) reported that in a sample of 60 rapists, their PCL-R score was associated with their number of prior offenses but not the number of prior sexual offenses. In a larger sample of offenders, Porter, Fairweather, and colleagues (2000) found that psychopaths engaged in significantly more violent offenses than nonpsychopaths (7.3 versus 3.0, respectively), but engaged in fewer sexual offenses (2.9 versus 5.9, respectively). One potential explanation for this finding is the high rate of sexual offending found in child molesters, who tend not to be psychopaths.

In general, offenders who commit **sexual homicides** (homicides that have a sexual component or in which sexual arousal occurs) are the most psychopathic, followed by mixed sexual offenders (those who sexually assault both children and adults), followed by rapists, with the lowest psychopathy scores found among child molesters (Brown & Forth, 1997; Firestone, Bradford, Greenberg, & Larose, 1998; Porter, Fairweather, et al., 2000; Quinsey, Rice, & Harris, 1995).

Sexual Homicide

Homicides in which there is a sexual component

Other studies have evaluated the motivations of psychopaths when committing sexual crimes. Brown and Forth (1997) examined specific motivations for psychopathic and nonpsychopathic rapists. The Massachusetts Treatment Center Rapist Typology (MTC: R3; Knight & Prentky, 1990) identifies different types of rapists based on motivation and level of social competence. Brown and Forth reported that 81% of psychopathic rapists were opportunistic or vindictive, compared with 56% of the nonpsychopathic rapists. Nonpsychopaths were more likely to report feelings of anxiety or alienation in the 24-hour period leading up to the rape, whereas psychopaths reported positive emotions. Porter, Woodworth, Earle, Drugge, and Boer (2003) investigated the relation between psychopathy and severity of violence in a sample of 38 sexual homicide offenders. Level of sadistic violence (evidence for overkill and that the offender obtained enjoyment from hurting the victim) was related to the PCL-R total scores and with the interpersonal and affective features of psychopathy.

In a recent study of 100 male German forensic patients (all sexual offenders), Mokros, Osterheider, Hucker, and Nitschke (2010) studied the association between psychopathy and **sexual sadism**. Sexual sadists are those people who are sexually aroused by fantasies, urges, or acts of inflicting pain, suffering, or humiliation on another human (American Psychiatric Association, 2000). PCL-R total scores, affective deficits facet, and antisocial facets were all related to sexual sadism.

PSYCHOPATHY IN YOUTH

Research is increasingly focused on identifying the emergence of psychopathic traits in youth. The assumption is that psychopathy does not suddenly appear in adulthood but instead gradually develops from various environmental and biological antecedents. In line with this viewpoint, several measures have been recently developed to identify psychopathic traits early in development. Two assessment instruments have been adapted from the PCL-R: one for use with children and the other for adolescents. The **Antisocial Process Screening Device** (APSD) (Frick & Hare, 2001) is designed for assessing the precursors of psychopathic traits in children. The child is assigned a rating on various questions by parents or teachers. A self-report version of this scale also has been developed for use with adolescents. Frick, Bodin, and Barry (2000) found that the APSD has a three-dimensional structure consisting of a callous/unemotional factor, an impulsivity factor, and a narcissism factor. The **Hare Psychopathy Checklist–Youth Version** (PCL-YV) (Forth, Kosson, & Hare, 2003) is a rating scale designed to measure psychopathic traits and behaviors in male and female adolescents between the ages of 12 and 18 years.

Reservations have been raised concerning the appropriateness of applying the construct of psychopathy to children and adolescents (Edens, Skeem, Cruise, & Cauffman, 2001; Seagrave & Grisso, 2002; Zinger & Forth, 1998). One concern has been the use of the label *psychopath*, a label that has many negative connotations for the public and for mental health and criminal justice professionals. As stated by Murrie, Cornell, Kaplan, McConville, and Levy-Elkon (2004), "The use of the label 'psychopath' has ominous connotations that may adversely influence treatment decisions, social service plans, and juvenile justice determinations" (p. 64). Studies examining the effects of the *psychopathy* label in adults and juveniles are described in Box 11.4.

Sexual sadism

People who obtain sexual arousal through fantasies, urges, or acts of inflicting pain, suffering, or humiliation on another human

Antisocial Process Screening Device

Observer rating scale used to assess psychopathic traits in children

Hare Psychopathy Checklist–Youth Version

Scale designed to measure psychopathic traits in adolescents

BOX 11.4　Psychopathy Label: The Potential for Stigma

If an individual is called a psychopath in court, are judges and juries likely to be more puni-tive toward him or her? The results from mock juror decision-making trials have been mixed. Two studies examined the effect of the psychopath label in a death-penalty trial: one in which the defendant was an adult (Edens, Colwell, Deforges, & Fernandez, 2005) and one in which the defendant was a juvenile (Edens, Guy, & Fernandez, 2003). In both studies, undergrad-uates were presented with written descriptions of a defendant in a murder case. All aspects about the case presented to the students were the same except that the authors manipulated the diagnosis or personality traits of the defendant. In the Edens et al. (2005) study, the defendant was described as a psychopath, as psychotic, or as having no mental disorder. As can be seen in Figure 11.2, mock jurors were more likely to support the death penalty for the psychopathic defendant than for the psychotic or nondisordered defendant.

Edens et al. (2003), a study that examined the influence of psychopathic traits, presented undergraduates with one of two versions of a modified newspaper clipping about a 16-year-old facing the death penalty. In one version, the juvenile defendant was described as having psy-chopathic traits; he was "the kind of teenager who did not feel remorse for his behavior or guilt when he got into trouble . . . a pathological liar who manipulated people . . . arrogant" (p. 22). In contrast, the nonpsychopathic traits version described the youth as "the kind of teenager who felt remorseful and guilty when he got into trouble . . . a trustworthy adolescent who never conned people . . . modest and humble (p. 22). In this study, the mock jurors presented with the psychopathic traits version were more likely to support the death penalty and to be less support-ive of the defendant receiving intervention in prison. As can be seen in Figure 11.2, mock jurors also were less likely to support the death penalty for juveniles than for adults.

Murrie, Cornell, and McCoy (2005) investigated the potential influence of a diagnosis of psychopathy, conduct disorder, or no diagnosis with juvenile probation officers. In con-trast to the above studies, the diagnostic label was not strongly related to probation officers'

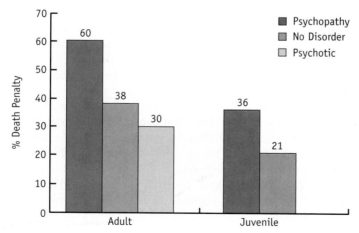

FIGURE 11.2
Death-Penalty Verdicts Based on Mental Disorder of Offender and Age of Offender

Sources: Table from "Psychopathic traits predict attitudes toward a juvenile capital murderer" by Krissie Fernandez, John F. Edens, and Laura S. Guy from *Behavioral Sciences & The Law.* Copyright © 2003 by John Wiley and Sons. Reprinted with permission.

(continued)

BOX 11.4 **Continued**

recommendations of type of sanction, risk level, or treatment amenability. Murrie et al. state, "There was little evidence that a specific diagnosis of psychopathy affected JPO [juvenile probation officer] judgments" (p. 338). Murrie and his colleagues have also studied the impact of the psychopathy label on juvenile court judges, community eligible jurors, and clinicians (Boccaccini, Murrie, Clark, & Cornell, 2008; Murrie, Boccaccini, McCoy, & Cornell, 2007; Rockett, Murrie, & Boccaccini, 2007). These researchers have found that the language used to describe the defendant makes a difference. Researchers stating the defendant "is a psychopath" have found stronger biasing effects as compared to researchers stating the defendant "meets criteria for psychopathy" or "has a psychopathic personality disorder."

Psychopathy in adults is associated with violence, is assumed to be a stable trait, and is resistant to intervention attempts. Whether psychopathic traits in youth are stable has recently been studied. For example, a study using the APSD has indicated fairly high stability across a 4-year period (Frick, Kimonis, Dandreaux, & Farell, 2003). The only longitudinal study to assess psychopathic traits in youth and to reassess for psychopathy in adulthood was recently completed by Lynam, Caspi, Moffitt, Loeber, and Southamer-Loeber (2007). The results indicated that there was a moderate degree of stability in psychopathic traits from age 13 to age 24. Another concern that has been raised is whether "scores on measures of psychopathy arguably may be inflated by general characteristics of adolescence" (Edens, Skeem, et al., 2001, p. 59). Arguing against this last point are the few studies measuring psychopathic traits in community youth that have found the scores on psychopathy measures to be very low (Forth et al., 2003; Sevecke, Pukrop, Kosson, & Krischer, 2009).

Research has provided some support for extending the construct of psychopathy to youth. For example, boys who score high on the callous/unemotional dimension of the APSD have more police contacts, more conduct problems, and are more likely to have a parent with APD than are children who score low on this dimension. Research using the PCL-YV has found that adolescents with many psychopathic traits become involved in criminal behaviors at an earlier age, engage in more violence in institutions and in the community, and are at a higher risk of reoffending once released as compared with other adolescents (Corrado, Vincent, Hart, & Cohen, 2004; Forth et al., 2003; Kosson, Cyterski, Steuerwald, Neumann, & Walker-Matthews, 2002; Murrie et al., 2004). In contrast, however, more recent research has questioned the utility of the PCL-YV to predict violence in adolescent female offenders (Odgers, Reppucci, & Moretti, 2005; Schmidt, McKinnon, Chattha, & Brownlee, 2006). Research has also looked at the association between psychopathic traits and other symptoms in youth. For example, Campbell, Porter, and Santor (2004) found that psychopathic traits were related to delinquency and aggression but not to anxiety or depression symptoms in a sample of male and female adolescent offenders.

One aspect of psychopathy in youth that may differ from its adult counterpart is that youth with psychopathic traits may be more responsive to interventions (Salekin, Rogers, & Machin, 2001). In contrast, however, O'Neill, Lidz, and Heilbrun (2003) examined treatment outcome in a sample of 64 adolescent substance abusers and found that youth scoring high on the PCL-YV showed poor program attendance, poor quality of participation, and less clinical improvement, and were more likely to reoffend after completing the program. Caldwell, Skeem, Salekin, and Van Rybroek (2006) compared the treatment outcome of two groups of incarcerated youth, both with very high PCL-YV scores. Youth who were given intensive treatment at a juvenile treatment center were compared with youth who were given treatment at a juvenile correctional center. Youth who were released from the correctional center violently reoffended at twice the rate in a 2-year follow-up as compared with the youth receiving the intensive treatment at the treatment center. These results suggest that with the appropriate intensive treatment, youth with many psychopathic traits are amenable to treatment (Caldwell, McCormick, Umstead, & Van Rybroek, 2007).

PSYCHOPATHY: NATURE VS NURTURE?

The nature versus nurture debate focuses on the relative importance of a person's innate characteristics (nature) as compared with his or her personal experiences (nurture). Growing evidence suggests a strong genetic contribution to psychopathy.

In all research designed to tease apart the role of genes (nature) and environment (nurture) in the development of psychological traits, investigators try to hold constant the effect of either genes or environment. Typically, this involves comparing individuals who have similar genes but who are raised in different environments. Variations on this basic idea can take several forms. Identical twins (who have identical genes) can be compared when raised apart from each other. This method holds genetic influences constant while allowing the environment to vary. In this kind of study, the twins are usually compared with randomly paired individuals. Also, fraternal twins (who share half their genes) raised together can be compared with identical twins (who share all their genes) raised together. Finally, biological siblings (who share half their genes) raised together can be compared with adoptive siblings (who share no genes but who are raised in the same environment).

To date, the only type of studies that have been done to measure the heritability of psychopathic traits are studies comparing identical and fraternal twins. Several twin studies have been done and all have yielded similar findings. In a study of adult male twins, Blonigen, Carlson, Krueger, and Patrick (2003) had each pair of identical and fraternal twins complete the Psychopathic Personality Inventory (PPI) (Lilienfeld & Andrews, 1996). Identical twins were much more similar in their PPI scores than were fraternal twins. Genetic influences accounted for between 29% and 59% of the variance for each of the different PPI subscales. In a recent adolescent twin study in Sweden, Larsson, Andershed, and Lichtenstein (2006) also found a strong genetic influence using the Youth Psychopathic Traits Inventory (Andershed, Gustafson, Kerr, & Håkan, 2002). Finally, in a sample of 7-year-old twin pairs in the United Kingdom, Viding, Blair, Moffitt, and Plomin (2005) found that callous/unemotional traits were moderately to highly heritable. These studies point to the importance of genetic factors, but environmental factors such as adverse family background may influence how these innate traits are expressed.

Does Family Matter?

The best research method to determine whether family experiences are related to the development of psychopathy is to do a prospective longitudinal study. Such research would study a group of young children and follow them through childhood, adolescence, and into adulthood, measuring family background variables and psychopathic traits. The strength of this type of study is that it allows researchers to avoid retrospective bias (the tendency to reconstruct past events so that they are consistent with an individual's current beliefs) and to establish causal order. Unfortunately, there are very few prospective longitudinal studies that specifically investigate the development of psychopathy.

The Cambridge Study in Delinquent Development is a 40-year prospective study of antisocial behavior of 411 London boys who have been followed from age 8 to age 48. At age 48, the men were assessed by using the PCL-SV (Hart et al., 1995). Farrington (2006) reported that of those men scoring 10 or more, 97% had been convicted of an offense and 48.5% of these men were chronic offenders (i.e., convicted more than 10 times). Measuring family background variables between ages 8 and 10, the best predictors of adult psychopathy were having a criminal father or mother, being a son whose father was uninvolved with him, having a low family income, coming from a disrupted family, and experiencing physical neglect.

In another longitudinal study, Weiler and Widom (1996) used court records to identify over 900 children who had been abused or neglected prior to age 11 and compared them with a control group matched on age, race, gender, elementary school class, and place of residence. Children were followed up after 20 years and assessed on a modified PCL-R. Children who had been abused had slightly higher modified PCL-R scores compared with the control sample.

Likely no single variable or combination of family background variables is responsible for the development of psychopathy. Current research is consistent with the view that there are multiple pathways to the development of psychopathy, some of which involve family background and others in which psychopathy emerges irrespective of family background.

PSYCHOPATHY AND TREATMENT

Are psychopathic adults responsive to treatment? Most clinicians and researchers are pessimistic, although some (e.g., Salekin, 2002) are more optimistic. As Hare (1998) states, "Unlike most other offenders, they suffer little personal distress, see little wrong with their attitudes and behavior, and seek treatment only when it is in their best interests to do so (such as when seeking probation or parole)" (p. 202).

The best-known study of treatment outcome in psychopaths was a retrospective study by Rice, Harris, and Cormier (1992). These researchers investigated the effects of an intensive therapeutic treatment program on violent psychopathic and nonpsychopathic forensic psychiatric patients. Using a matched group design, forensic patients who spent 2 years in the treatment program (treated group) were paired with forensic patients who were assessed but not admitted to the program (untreated group). Using file information, all patients were scored on the PCL-R using file information and were divided into psychopaths (scores of 25 or greater) and nonpsychopaths (scores of less than 25). Patients were followed for an average of 10 years after release. The violent recidivism rate was 39% for untreated nonpsychopaths, 22% for treated nonpsychopaths, 55% for untreated psychopaths, and 77% for treated psychopaths. Treatment was associated with a reduction in violent recidivism among nonpsychopaths, but an increase in violent recidivism among psychopaths. Some clinicians have concluded from the above study that we should not bother to treat psychopaths, since treatment will only make them worse. However, a more accurate conclusion from the above study would be: "This was the wrong program for serious psychopathic offenders" (Quinsey, Harris, Rice, & Cormier, 1998, p. 88).

Caution is required in interpreting the results of studies such as that carried out by Rice et al. (1992). Although at first glance such research implies that psychopaths are untreatable, an alternative but perhaps equally plausible account is that the treatments for psychopaths that have been tried so far have not worked (Hare et al., 2000; Richards, Casey, & Lucente, 2003; Seto & Barbaree, 1999). Reasons why a treatment may not work include the use of an inappropriate treatment and problems in implementing the treatment, such as inadequate training of those administering it or lack of support from management.

A more promising treatment outcome study has been reported by Olver and Wong (2009). These researchers found that although psychopathic sex offenders who dropped out of treatment were more likely to violently reoffend, those psychopathic sex offenders who stayed in treatment showed positive treatment gains and were less likely to violently reoffend. We hope that in the future, with better understanding of what causes psychopathy, treatment programs can be developed to target potentially changeable factors linked to why psychopaths engage in crime and violence.

FORENSIC USE OF PSYCHOPATHY

Several studies have surveyed the use of expert testimony regarding the assessment of psychopathy in criminal and civil court proceedings. Recent studies by DeMatteo and Edens (2006) and Walsh and Walsh (2006) reviewed cases in which an expert testified about psychopathy using the PCL-R. These researchers found that psychopathy has played a role in a diverse range of criminal cases, with the majority of testimony regarding psychopathy being associated with an increased severity of disposition. In the United States, the PCL-R was also used in sexual violent predator evaluations and death-penalty sentencing and in civil cases for child custody decisions. For example, in death-penalty hearings in the United States, prosecutors have sometimes implied that psychopathy is an aggravating factor because it is associated with an increased risk for violence. Several researchers have raised concerns about the use of the PCL-R in death-penalty hearings (Edens, Petrila, & Buffington-Vollum, 2001). These researchers argue that since the PCL-R does not reliability predict prison violence among incarcerated U.S. prisoners (prison violence is the only issue in these cases since the offender will never be released), it should not be used.

Psychopathy and Law Enforcement

According to O'Toole (2007), "psychopathy can be described as one of law enforcement's greatest challenges" (p. 305). Psychopaths engage in high rates of crime, including violent offenses. Thus, law enforcement personnel will often come into contact with psychopaths. In some cases, the contact can lead to lethal consequences. For example, Pinizzotto and Davis (1992) conducted a study of the characteristics of killers of police officers. Almost half of these killers had personality and behavior features consistent with psychopathy. O'Toole describes the potential crime scene characteristics manifested by a psychopathic violent offender. For example, impulsivity (a feature of psychopathy) can be manifested at a crime scene by injury pattern to the victim, choice of weapon, and time and location of crime. Some psychopaths are charming and manipulative and will be more likely to use a con to minimize the threat they pose when approaching a victim. For example, a prolific serial killer convinced sex-trade workers that he was not a threat by having children's toys visible in his car and a photograph of his young son on the dashboard.

Another challenge for law enforcement personnel is to develop effective methods for interrogating psychopathic suspects. For example, when interrogating a suspected psychopathic serial killer, trying to get the suspect to confess by saying such things as "Think about the family of the victims" or "You will feel better if you tell us about it" will likely be counterproductive. Instead, appealing to the psychopath's sense of grandiosity and need for status might be more productive. Quayle (2008), a police officer in the United Kingdom, suggests that psychopathic suspects are likely to engage in the following types of behaviors during an interrogation:

- Try to outwit the interrogator (they may consider the interrogation a "game" to win)
- Enjoy being the focus of attention (they may act like they are holding a press conference)
- Attempt to control the interrogation (they may attempt to "turn the tables" and become the interrogator)
- Will not be fooled by bluffs (they are adept at conning others and may "see through" interrogators' attempts to obtain a confession)
- Attempt to shock (they may speak in a matter-of-fact manner about how they have treated other people)

Quayle (2008) has offered several suggestions for interviewing a psychopathic suspect including the following:

- Be familiar with the case (interrogators should be extremely familiar with the evidence in order to counteract the psychopath's evasiveness and deceitfulness)
- Convey experience and confidence (interrogators need to be able to control the interview and create an atmosphere of 'authority')
- Show liking or admiration (psychopaths respond to thinking interrogators want to "learn" from them and will encourage them to keep talking)
- Avoid criticism (psychopaths may become hostile and stop the interview)
- Avoid conveying emotions (interrogators should avoid conveying their own emotions about the offense or lack of progress in the case)

Psychopathy is a complex disorder but one that causes a substantial amount of damage to society. Research during the past 30 years has led to many advances in how to measure psychopathy, associations with aggression, genetic and environmental origins, and treatment. Within the next few years, new research will provide further insights in how to prevent the development of this devastating disorder. There is still much research to be done to understand psychopathy. Read the scenario in the Case Study and develop your own study to determine if psychopaths have an affective deficit.

CASE STUDY

YOU BE THE RESEARCHER

You have just finished reading Hervey Cleckley's book *The Mask of Sanity*. According to Cleckley, psychopaths are fundamentally deficient in the capacity for emotional experience. This lack of emotional response enables psychopaths to manipulate and exploit others without feeling any remorse for their actions. In Cleckley's view, the psychopath's characteristic "mask of sanity," results in the psychopath attempting to simulate emotional reactions to obtain what he or she wants. You are intrigued by Cleckley's ideas about the psychopath's core deficit in emotional experience and reactions.

Develop a study to test whether psychopaths have a core emotional deficit. First, decide what sample you will study and how you will measure psychopathic traits. Second, what stimuli or task will you use; that is, how will you try to elicit emotions? Finally, how will you measure emotions? That is, will you ask them how they are feeling? Will you measure their physiological responses? Will you code their facial expressions?

Summary

1. Psychopathy is a personality disorder defined by a cluster of interpersonal, affective, and behavioral features. Psychopathy, sociopathy, and antisocial personality disorder are overlapping but distinct constructs.

2. The Hare Psychopathy Checklist–Revised is the most popular tool used to measure psychopathic traits in adults. Several self-report measures have been developed to assess psychopathic traits in community samples.

3. Two of the most prominent theories of psychopathy place emphasis on either cognitive or affective processes. Newman and his colleagues have proposed that psychopaths have a response modulation deficit. According to this theory, psychopaths fail to use contextual cues that are peripheral to a dominant response set to modulate their behavior. The other theory proposes that psychopaths have a deficit in the experience of certain critical emotions that guide prosocial behavior and inhibit deviance. This latter theory has been related to an amygdala dysfunction.

4. Psychopaths begin their criminal career earlier, persist longer, and are more violent and versatile than other offenders. Most of the murders committed by psychopaths are instrumental.

5. Research is increasingly focused on identifying the emergence of psychopathic traits in youth, and assessment instruments have been developed to measure psychopathic traits in children and adolescents with some success. Concerns have been raised about the potential problems with labeling youth as psychopaths. These concerns have focused on (1) the issue of labeling a youth as a psychopath, (2) the stability of psychopathic traits from late childhood to early adulthood, and (3) the possibility that characteristics of psychopathy are common features of normally developing youth.

6. Psychopaths are difficult to treat. They are not motivated to change their behavior and some research has shown that after treatment psychopaths were more likely to violently reoffend. However, some recent research has obtained more promising treatment outcome effects, especially with adolescent offenders with many psychopathic traits.

Key Concepts

antisocial personality disorder *265*

Antisocial Process Screening Device *274*

Hare Psychopathy Checklist– Revised *263*

Hare Psychopathy Checklist–Youth Version *274*

psychopathy *263*

response modulation deficit *266*

sexual homicides *273*

sexual sadism *274*

sociopathy *266*

Discussion Questions

1. Your friend has recently met a man via an online dating site. She has been dating him for a few months but is starting to feel uneasy about the stories he has been telling her. She knows you have been studying forensic psychology and asks you about psychopathy. Describe what you know about psychopathy and what red flags your friend might want to watch for.

2. Motives for violence have been classified into instrumental and reactive types. Psychopaths commit both types of violence. What are the treatment implications for a psychopath whose violence is reactively motivated?

3. You want to know how important childhood abuse and poor parenting is to the development of psychopathy. Describe the methodology you would use and the variables you would measure.

4. You have been hired by the police department to consult on a serial killing case. You suspect the serial killer might be a psychopath. Describe to the homicide investigators the key features of psychopathy, the potential crime scene characteristics of psychopathic serial killers, and any suggestions you have for the interrogation of this suspect.

12

Assessment and Treatment of Juvenile Delinquency

LEARNING OBJECTIVES

▪ Describe the history of juvenile courts.

▪ Identify the psychiatric diagnoses and their trajectories to young offenders.

▪ Differentiate between the theories of antisocial behavior.

▪ List the risk and protective factors associated with externalizing disorders in youth.

▪ Distinguish between primary, secondary, and tertiary interventions for children, youth, and young offenders.

As a child, Alex Kelly was no angel. He got into fights at school and in his neighborhood on a daily basis. He would pick fights not only with children his own age and older, but even with adults. His teacher also reported that on several occasions, Alex sneaked into the school during recess and rummaged through the other children's backpacks, taking toys or other belongings that he wanted. It was not uncommon for Alex to throw a temper tantrum when he did not get his way. He often refused to follow rules and would argue until the adults gave in to his demands.

When both the school and Alex's mother failed to get Alex to change his behavior, his mother took him to a psychologist for an assessment. Alex refused to cooperate with the psychologist, throwing a stuffed bear at her and telling her that she could assess it instead. Based on the psychologist's observations, parent interviews, and teacher ratings, Alex was diagnosed with oppositional defiant disorder (ODD), a diagnosis that puts Alex at an increased risk for interactions with the criminal justice system.

Are there programs that decrease Alex's risk for future involvement with the criminal justice system? Does Alex have other risk factors or protective factors? Numerous questions often are asked about youngsters who display difficult behavior and whether these youngsters become youth who get involved with the criminal justice system.

In this chapter, we will focus on young offenders and the behaviors they may have displayed when they were younger. We will consider the assessment and treatment of young offenders along with the types of crimes they commit. We also will provide a discussion regarding the legal options available when dealing with this group.

YOUNG OFFENDERS

Adolescents (i.e., those younger than 18 years) who come into contact with the criminal justice system pose several challenges to the adult-based system. Legislation has changed over the years in an attempt to address the special needs of adolescents. Moreover, it is critical to consider the developmental paths to young offending in order to prevent and rehabilitate. A number of treatment options have been developed for juveniles with varying success rates. Ultimately, the goal is to prevent juvenile delinquency from starting and should it occur, provide intervention to stop it from continuing into adulthood.

HISTORICAL OVERVIEW

Up until the late 1800s, youth who committed criminal acts were treated as adult offenders. The criminal justice system made no accommodations or considerations for how youngsters were charged, sentenced, or incarcerated. They were kept in the same facilities as adults while awaiting their trials, received the same penalties as adults, and served their sentences with adults. Even in cases involving the death penalty youth were dealt with in a similar manner as adults. See Box 12.1 for a discussion of the death penalty for youth.

In 1899, the first juvenile court was established in Chicago, Illinois (Steinberg, 2009). Over the years and across the states, the juvenile justice system has gone through numerous changes. The system has moved from a "parental" model to a much more punitive model with harsher sanctions and more youth transferred to adult court. In the early 1990s, the American public perceived a juvenile crime epidemic that facilitated several changes to the justice system.

Modern Day

Each state varies in how its juvenile offenders are processed. Below is a general description of the various decision points that are common across states. Note that states vary with regards to the minimum age a youngster can be charged with a criminal offense. The age range is from 6 (e.g., North Carolina) to 12 years. However, not all states have a minimum age. In these states, common law is used, which means that someone must be at least 7 years old and for federal crimes the age is set at 10 years. Those who commit criminal acts at ages younger than these minimum ages are usually processed through Social Services where the youngster and family may receive support services such as counseling and parental skills training.

For those youngsters who meet the minimum age for arrest, law enforcement must decide to either pursue the case further into the justice system or divert the case out of the system into an alternative program. This decision may be based on such considerations as the nature of the crime, the victim, the juvenile (e.g., age, prior history), and his or her parents. In 2007, approximately 70% of juveniles committing criminal acts were sent to "juvenile court."

Once a case has been referred to juvenile court, the juvenile probation department and/or the prosecutor's office must decide to either dismiss the case, handle the case

BOX 12.1   The Death Penalty for Juveniles?

Should juveniles who kill be sentenced to death? In 1989, the United States Supreme Court found that the death penalty for 16- and 17-year-olds who murdered was lawful. A key case in the juvenile death penalty debate was that of *Roper v. Simmons* (03-0633).

In 1993, Christopher Simmons was convicted of killing his neighbor, Shirley Crook, in St. Louis County, Missouri. Simmons confessed to the murder and was given the death penalty. This sentence was appealed.

It wasn't until 2005 that this ruling was reversed. States with the death penalty could no longer sentence juveniles to death. In a close decision, the Supreme Court ruled 5–4 that juveniles who kill could no longer face the death penalty. The death penalty for juveniles was found unconstitutional.

The dissenters, however, see this ruling as not necessarily the final word and there may be a time when the ruling is reversed and the death penalty could reemerge under special circumstances.

For those who argue against the death penalty, they point to the scientific evidence that finds youth are less able to control their impulsiveness and have difficulty exhibiting self-control and sound judgment, compared to adults.

In 2005, approximately 70 juveniles were on death row. With the Supreme Court ruling outlawing the death penalty for juveniles, these death sentences are now void.

A related issue to consider is whether a juvenile should be sentenced to life in prison without being eligible for parole in nonmurder cases. One such case is that of Terrance Jamar Graham who was convicted of armed home invasion while on probation for another crime. He was sentenced to life without parole in 2006. His lawyer argued that adolescents do not have all the same capacities as adults and that adolescents are still in their formative stage. The Appeal Court of Florida reversed the original sentence, arguing that a juvenile who did not commit murder must be given a reasonable opportunity to be released before the end of his or her sentence.

Sources: Based on "High court: Juvenile death penalty unconstitutional slim majority cites 'evolving standards' in american society" by Bill Mears, from CNN Washington Bureau, March 1, 2005 and *Graham v. Florida* from http://www.scotusblog.com/.

---

informally, or request formal intervention by the juvenile court. In making this decision, the evidence for the allegation is considered. The case is dismissed if there is insufficient evidence. If there is sufficient evidence, the probation officer and/or prosecutor will determine if formal court intervention is necessary. Cases can be handled informally and may be dismissed if the juvenile agrees to certain conditions for a specific period of time (e.g., being home by 10:00 p.m.)—these conditions are written in an agreement called a consent decree. In these cases, the juvenile often must admit to having committed the crime. If the juvenile fulfills the agreement, the case is dismissed. If the juvenile does not meet the conditions outlined, then formal proceedings against the juvenile will occur.

Across all states, juveniles will undergo a detention hearing typically within 24 hours of being charged. The goal of the detention hearing is to determine if the juvenile needs to be detained further or released until the case is adjudicated (decided).

Prosecutors can choose to file a case in juvenile court or criminal court. When a juvenile commits a serious, violent offense, it is not uncommon for it to be filed in criminal court. A case going to criminal court means that the juvenile will be treated like an adult defendant. See Box 12.2 for a case where a teen killer was declared an adult. Back in juvenile court, two types of petitions can be filed; either a delinquency

BOX 12.2 The Dartmouth Murders

On January, 27, 2001, two popular university professors, Half and Susanne Zantop, were murdered in their house in New Hampshire. The Zantops had been on the faculty at Dartmouth College since the 1970s. The murderers were two teens, James Parker, who was 16, and Robert Tulloch, who was 17.

On the morning of the murders, Parker and Tulloch went to the Zantops' home pretending to be students working on a school survey. Wanting to help, Half invited the teens in the house while Susanne was preparing lunch. While Half had his back turned, Tulloch stabbed him (and he ultimately died). Susanne tried to stop him but Parker killed her too. Tulloch and Parker took $340 from Half's wallet and left the house, leaving behind the knives they used for the murders.

The bodies were found by a family friend. The police found the knives and a bloody footprint. The knives were traced back to Parker who acknowledged buying the knives with Tulloch claiming the knives were to build a fort. They were later apprehended by police.

The community where Parker and Tulloch lived were stunned. Both youth seemed popular, good students who didn't act out. Tulloch was president of his senior class. There was no connection between the Zantops, who lived in Hanover, New Hampshire, and Tulloch and Parker, who lived in Vermont.

Parker was declared an adult and accepted a plea bargain to testify against Tulloch. Parker pleaded guilty to second-degree murder and received a 25-year–life sentence with the possibility of parole after 16 years. Tulloch who initially pleaded not guilty by reason of insanity eventually changed his plea and pleaded guilty and was given a life sentence without parole.

Sources: http://www.nytimes.com/2002/04/02/us/youth-may-change-to-guilty-plea-in-dartmouth-professors'-death
http://www.nytimes.com/2002/04/05/us/teenagers-are-sentenced-for-killing-two-professors
http://www.nytimes.com/2002/05/18/us/youth-dreamed-ofadventure-but-settled-for-killing-a-couple

petition or a waiver. "A delinquency petition states the allegations and requests the juvenile court to determine that the juvenile is a delinquent and should be made a ward of the court" (Office of Juvenile Justice and Delinquency Prevention, 2012. p. 2). In contrast, in criminal court, the defendant would be convicted and sentenced.

With a delinquency petition, an adjudicatory hearing (trial) is scheduled where typically only a judge hears the evidence and decides the case. A waiver petition is filed when the prosecutor believes the case would be more appropriately dealt with through a criminal court. With these cases, the facts are reviewed to determine the likelihood the juvenile committed the crime and, if so, the court decides whether the case should go to criminal court. A key issue regarding a juvenile transfer to criminal court is whether the juvenile is open to treatment.

Once a juvenile is determined to be delinquent, a disposition (outcome) will be imposed. A dispositional hearing occurs where dispositional recommendations are made. Sometimes the courts will request psychological testing or evaluation that may inform a disposition or supervision plan. Ultimately, the judge determines the disposition. Many juveniles receive probation in addition to other dispositions such as drug counseling and repaying the victim. The probation period may be specific or open. Review hearings are scheduled throughout the probation period to assess the juvenile's progress.

It is possible for the judge to send the juvenile to a residential facility that may be a secure facility (similar to prison) or open (similar to a home setting). Once a juvenile

CASE STUDY

YOU BE THE POLICE OFFICER

Jimmy Jones was the neighborhood "bad boy." He and his mother had lived in one of the government-subsidized housing units since Jimmy was about 4; now Jimmy was 14. Jimmy was well known at school and to his neighbors. As a young boy, Jimmy would take toys from the other children and often would become aggressive if he didn't get his way. At school, the teachers would have to call Ms. Jones on a weekly basis because they could not manage Jimmy's aggression and tantrums. Jimmy would bully other kids and was cruel to his pet dog.

Jimmy's problems just seemed to keep escalating. Jimmy started hanging around with some of the older teenaged boys known to belong to a local street gang. Jimmy liked how the gang boys always had money. He soon began selling drugs for the gang leader. At first, Jimmy was selling drugs at the high schools in the neighborhood. The high schools had police officers trying to work with the "drug dealers" to change their ways. The police knew Jimmy well.

One night, Jimmy's gang leader said he needed Jimmy to do him a favor. A rival gang had set up shop in an abandoned warehouse and were trying to get in on the drug dealing. Jimmy was asked to set a fire to burn down the warehouse. Jimmy knew that if he could do this successfully he would be rewarded financially and would move up in the gang hierarchy. Jimmy agreed to set the fire. Although Jimmy did not want to hurt anyone, some of the rival gang members were in the warehouse when the fire was started. Three rival gang members received serious burns resulting from the fire. Police were informed that Jimmy set the fire.

Your Turn . . .

How should police handle Jimmy's case? Should police keep Jimmy out of the criminal justice system? Should Jimmy be dealt with using alternative measures? If so, which ones?

---

is released, he or she is often on parole as would be an adult. The juvenile would have to follow the conditions set out by the court during parole and should those conditions not be fulfilled, the juvenile will be returned to the facility. Examine the Case Study box, where you are the police officer, to consider how would you deal with a youth engaged in unlawful behavior.

YOUTH CRIME RATES

Generally, the total number of crimes committed by youth has been decreasing for the past few years. This pattern also can be seen for violent offenses. Males compared to females are responsible for more juvenile arrests, accounting for approximately 70% of the arrests. See Table 12.1 for a distribution of some of the young offender cases by some of the major crime categories.

Taken from *Crime in the United States*, October 2011, http://www.fbi.gov/about-us/cjis/ucr/ucr#ucr_cisu.

TABLE 12.1	Number of Youth under 18 Years Arrested in the United States in 2010 (Partial List)
Offense	**2010 Number of Arrests**
Total	1,288,615
Partial List	
Murder/Negligent Manslaughter	784
Forcible Rape	2,198
Robbery	21,110
Aggravated Assault	35,001
Burglary	51,298
Larceny-Theft	223,207
Motor Vehicle Theft	12,268
Arson	3,578
Other Assaults	163,370
Stolen Property	11,608
Vandalism	60,591
Weapons	24,518
Prostitution	804
Sex Offense	10,147
Drug Abuse	132,921
Gambling	1,040
Driving under the Influence (DUI)	9,352
Liquor laws	75,889
Drunkenness	10,030
Disorderly Conduct	121,276
All other offenses (except traffic)	232,702

Source: Number of youth under 18 years arrested in the United States in 2010 (partial list) from FBI.gov.

ASSESSMENT OF YOUNG OFFENDERS

Assessing Those under Age 12

A clinician will often obtain two levels of consent before commencing the assessment of a child or adolescent. Because children and adolescents are not legally capable of providing consent, consent will be sought from parents or guardians and, assent or agreement to conduct the assessment will be sought from the child or adolescent. Although court-ordered assessments do not necessarily require consent or assent, clinicians often will seek consent/assent before beginning the assessment.

Broadly, children's and youth's emotional and behavioral difficulties can be categorized as internalizing or externalizing problems (Rutter, 1990). **Internalizing problems** are emotional difficulties such as anxiety, depression, and obsessions.

Internalizing problems

Emotional difficulties such as anxiety, depression, and obsessions experienced by a youth

Externalizing problems are behavioral difficulties such as delinquency, fighting, bullying, lying, and destructive behavior. Externalizing problems have been considered more difficult to treat and more likely to have long-term persistence (Ebata, Peterson, & Conger, 1990; Robins, 1986). Externalizing disorders have been known to be quite stable, though symptoms often peak in teenage years and decrease when people reach their late twenties (Rutter, 1995). Males are more likely to have externalizing difficulties than females, with a ratio of about 10:1 (Barkley, 1997; Rutter, 1990). Note that internalizing problems might co-occur with externalizing difficulties; these issues also should be assessed and treated.

To assess externalizing problems, multiple informants are necessary to obtain an accurate assessment because the child or youth may not be aware of his or her behavior or the influence it has on others (McMahon, 1994). Parents, teachers, and peers may be interviewed or asked to rate the child or adolescent. Also, it is important that behavior be viewed within a developmental context. For example, rebelling against rules set by parents may be normative for adolescents but worrisome if younger children are oppositional and continually refuse to comply with parents' requests. The duration, severity, and frequency of troublesome behaviors should be measured.

Three childhood psychiatric diagnoses occur with some frequency in young offenders: **attention-deficit/ hyperactivity disorder** (ADHD), **oppositional defiant disorder** (ODD), and **conduct disorder** (CD). ADHD is described in the *DSM-IV* as an inattention and restlessness (APA, 1994). Some examples of features associated with ADHD include the following: does not appear to listen when spoken to, has difficulty in organization, loses items, fidgets, and talks excessively. To qualify for an ADHD diagnosis, a number of symptoms must be present, occur in two or more settings, and persist for at least six months. When making an ADHD diagnosis, it is important to consider the age of the child. In young children, many of the symptoms of ADHD are part of normal development and behavior and may not lead to criminal activity later. However, there may be some hyperactive-impulsive or inattentive symptoms before the age of 7 years that can cause impairment. Many children with ADHD also receive diagnoses of ODD or CD (Barkley, 1991).

ODD is described as a "pattern of negativistic, hostile, and defiant behavior" (APA, 1994, p. 93). Some examples of features associated with ODD include the following: loses temper, deliberately annoys others, and is vindictive. Approximately 40% of children with ODD develop CD (Loeber, Keenan, Lahey, Green, & Thomas, 1993). If a child with ODD qualifies for a CD diagnosis, an ODD diagnosis is not used. Some examples of features associated with CD include the following: initiates physical fights, is physically cruel to animals, sets fires, lies for gain, and is truant before 13 years of age. Approximately 50% of children meeting the criteria for CD go on to

A juvenile vandalizes a wall in a community.

Externalizing problems

Behavioral difficulties such as delinquency, fighting, bullying, lying, or destructive behavior experienced by a youth

Attention-deficit/ hyperactivity disorder

A disorder in a youth characterized by a persistent pattern of inattention and hyperactivity or impulsivity

Oppositional defiant disorder

A disorder in a youth characterized by a persistent pattern of negativistic, hostile, and defiant behaviors

Conduct disorder

A disorder characterized by a persistent pattern of behavior in which a youth violates the rights of others or age-appropriate societal norms or rules

receive diagnoses of antisocial personality disorder in adulthood (APA, 1994; Loeber & Farrington, 2000). Thus, CD often is the precursor to antisocial personality disorder. ODD and CD are not diagnosed if the individual is 18 years or older (the individual may meet criteria for antisocial personality disorder). Dr. Rolf Loeber has conducted extensive research into antisocial behavior and delinquency. To learn more about Dr. Loeber see Box 12.3.

Assessing the Adolescent

Once an adolescent's antisocial behavior receives the attention of the courts, a court-ordered assessment may be issued. In such cases, the adolescent need not provide consent/assent. The issue for the courts is to determine what level of risk the young person poses for reoffending. In other words, does having a young offender in the community pose a risk for others? Does the young offender have the potential to change in a positive

---

BOX 12.3   **Researcher Profile: Dr. Rolf Loeber**

Dr. Rolf Loeber

Dr. Rolf Loeber is the quintessential international researcher. He received his BA and MA at the University of Amsterdam in the Netherlands. He then went to Canada and completed his Ph.D. at Queen's University in Kingston, Ontario. Currently, Dr. Loeber is a distinguished professor at the University of Pittsburgh and professor at the Free University, Amsterdam, Netherlands.

Dr. Loeber's dissertation focused on the condition of therapists in their interaction with patients. So how did this lead to his research into juvenile delinquency? Dr. Loeber notes that he became encouraged by the work of juvenile delinquency researchers Drs. Patterson and Farrington.

Dr. Loeber's research areas include antisocial and delinquent behavior, developmental psychopathology, longitudinal studies, and the developmental transition between the juvenile years and young adulthood.

When asked what keeps him interested in this work, Dr. Loeber states, "Working closely with my wife, and with our research team of about 60 people, the topics that I work on with my colleagues are intrinsically interesting and new topics emerge every month." Dr. Loeber often uses an extensive database that has followed children into their youth and young adulthood in Pittsburgh. This database allows for longitudinal data analyses where he can examine how children and youth develop over time.

Dr. Loeber states that he would like to see "juvenile sentences shortened on the basis of what is known about longitudinal careers and individuals' risk patterns" and more done for prevention. When asked about the secret of his success, Dr. Loeber states, "My career would not have taken me where I am now without the stimulation and camaraderie of my wife. Working with her continues to be the best thing in my life. I found that getting the best balance in life is to limit the number of hours per day that I work and to have other interests as well. Over the years, I have developed a profound interest in Irish history, literature, and architecture, and have become skilled in each of these fields."

manner? Young offenders are assessed so that resources can be used effectively and the risk to the community reduced.

The instruments used to assess a young offender's risk generally include a "checklist" where items are scored on a scale, the points are summed, and a cut-off value is set for either detaining or releasing the young offender. Risk assessment instruments collect information about a set of factors, both static (i.e., factors that cannot change, such as age of first arrest) and dynamic (i.e., factors that can change, such as antisocial attitudes). Interviews with the young offender as well as case files and histories may be used to complete a risk assessment. A total risk score is then obtained. Generally, the notion is that the more relevant risk factors that are present, the more likely the youth will reoffend. Any number of professionals (front-line staff in institutions, probation staff, credentialed professionals) may be responsible for conducting the risk assessment.

The task of identifying risk factors for young offenders who will reoffend is different than for adults (Mulvey, 2005). For example, history of behavior often is considered in the risk assessment of adult offenders. This may be limited for and ambiguous for young offenders—young offenders simply do not have the years behind them that can be examined. Child and adolescent behavior may be more influenced by context than enduring character. Children and adolescents may display behavior that is adaptive to the environment they are in rather than the behavior being a demonstration of their character across all situations (Masten & Coatsworth, 1998). A child who is disruptive in one school may not be disruptive in another, so interpreting a behavior problem may be inaccurate. Children and adolescents experience more change developmentally and in character than adults. It is a challenge to separate developmental issues from persistent personality for the prediction of future offending. See Box 12.4 for a review of the Columbine massacre where the teen killers may have had some risk factors for antisocial behavior. Some researchers argue further that risk assessment may differ between adolescent boys and girls (Odgers, Moretti, & Reppucci, 2005).

Rates of Behavior Disorders in Youth

It has been estimated that approximately 5% to 15% of children display severe behavioral problems (Rutter, 1990). This estimate may, however, be too low. Researchers have found that behavioral disorders commonly co-occur. For example, 20% to 50% of children with ADHD also have symptoms consistent with CD or ODD (Offord, Lipman, & Duku, 2001).

TRAJECTORIES OF YOUNG OFFENDERS

When examining the aggressive histories of young offenders, two categories emerge. Young offenders may be categorized as those who started with social transgressions and behavioral problems in very early childhood (child-onset, life-course persistent) or those whose problem behaviors emerged in the teen years (adolescent-onset, adolescent limited; Moffitt, 1993). Thus, two developmental pathways to youthful antisocial behavior have been suggested: childhood onset versus adolescent onset.

Age of onset is a critical factor in the trajectory to adult offending. A number of researchers have found that early onset of antisocial behavior is related to more serious and persistent antisocial behavior later in life (Fergusson & Woodward, 2000; Loeber &

BOX 12.4 Teen Killers

Dylan Klebold was 18 and Eric Harris was 17 when they walked into their high school, Columbine High, with loaded guns and bombs to take revenge on their classmates and their teachers. These two teens murdered 13 people and injured 21 others before they killed themselves.

After the massacre, everyone wanted to know how could this happen, whether it could have been predicted, and whether there were any warning signs. The murders occurred on April 20, 1999, and we are still asking these questions after more than 10 years have passed.

Harris and Klebold were described as unpopular students who were often bullied. In retrospect, some have suggested that these two teenagers were showing signs of trouble. However, it is important to keep in mind that many adolescents experience distress and difficulties but do not go on to murder and commit crime. Harris and Klebold played violent video games and they wrote in journals and blogs about killing and how to make bombs. It has been claimed that they were part of the Goth subculture, belonging to a group known as the Trench Coat Mafia. They also had a previous arrest and charge for the theft of some tools. There is some question to whether Harris and Klebold felt rejected, isolated, and helpless. Harris was depressed and taking antidepressants.

More recently, a report suggests that much of what we believed about Harris and Klebold was false (Toppo, 2009, http://www.usatoday.com/news/nation/2009-04-13-columbine-myths_N.htm). Perhaps we will never know the truth.

Although Harris and Klebold may have had some "risk factors," most teens with these risk factors do not go on to become murderers.

It is important to note that school shootings are exceedingly rare (despite being highly publicized) and not easily predicted through simple methods (Borum & Cornell, 2010).

Sources: Based on http://www.nytimes.com/1999/04/21/us/terror-littleton-overview-2-students-colorado-school-said-gun-down-many-23-kill.html?ref=columbinehighschool
http://topics.nytimes.com/top/reference/timestopics/organizations/c/columbine_high_school/index.html
http://www.nytimes.com/1999/04/22/us/terror-in-littleton-the-suspects-portrait-of-outcasts-seeking-to-stand-out.html?ref=columbinehighschool

---

Farrington, 2000). Those with a childhood onset also may have a number of other difficulties, such as ADHD, learning disabilities, and academic difficulties (Hinshaw, Lahey, & Hart, 1993). The childhood-onset trajectory is a less frequent occurrence than adolescent onset, with about 3% to 5% of the general population showing a childhood-onset trajectory (Moffitt, 1993). It is important to remember, however, that most young children with behavioral difficulties do not go on to become adult offenders (or even young offenders for that matter).

The adolescent-onset pattern occurs in about 70% of the general population (Moffitt, 1993). Many young people engage in social transgressions during their adolescence, but adolescents who only engage in a few antisocial acts do not qualify for a CD diagnosis. Although it is more common for adolescent-onset youth to desist their antisocial behavior in their early adulthood than for those with a childhood onset, some of these adolescent-onset youth continue to engage in antisocial acts in adulthood (Moffitt, Caspi, Harrington, & Milne, 2002).

In a study by Brame, Nagin, and Tremblay (2001), a group of boys from Montreal in Canada were followed from the time they entered kindergarten through to their late teen years. The researchers found that participants' overall level of aggression decreased at they got older regardless of how high it was when the participants were youngsters. It was notable, however, that for a small proportion of youngsters with high levels of aggression, these high levels continued into their teen years. A much larger proportion of youngsters with high levels of aggression reported little to no aggression in their teen years. Thus, for a small group of youngsters with high levels of aggression, these levels will continue into later years.

THEORIES TO EXPLAIN ANTISOCIAL BEHAVIOR

Biological Theories

To explain why some youth engage in antisocial acts, researchers have examined the relation between frontal lobe functioning and antisocial behavior. The frontal lobe is responsible for the planning and inhibiting of behavior. Moffitt and Henry (1989) have found that conduct-disordered youth have less frontal lobe inhibition of behavior. Thus, the likelihood that these youth will act impulsively is increased, making it more likely that they will make poor behavioral choices.

Physiologically, conduct-disordered youth have been found to have slower heart rates than youth who do not engage in antisocial behavior (Wadsworth, 1976). Genetic studies have found a relation between paternal antisocial behavior and child offspring antisocial behavior (Frick et al., 1992). Moreover, adoption and twin studies also find a biological link to young offending. That is, children who have an antisocial biological father are more likely to engage in antisocial behavior, even when raised apart from the biological father (Cadoret & Cain, 1980; Jarey & Stewart, 1985). Overall, the research explaining the relation among biology, physiology, genetics, and behavior is just beginning.

Cognitive Theories

To understand delinquency using cognitive theories, the focus is on an individual's thoughts that occur during social interactions. Kenneth Dodge and his colleagues proposed a model of conduct-disordered behavior that considers the thought processes that happen when engaged with others (Crick & Dodge, 1994; Dodge, 2000). Thought processes start when individuals pay attention to and interpret social and emotional cues in their environment. The following step in the model is to consider alternative responses to the cues. Finally, a response is chosen and performed. Delinquent youth demonstrate cognitive deficits and distortions (Fontaine, Burks, & Dodge, 2002). These youth often attend to fewer cues and misattribute hostile intent to ambiguous situations. Moreover, conduct-disordered youth demonstrate limited problem-solving skills, producing few solutions to problems, and these solutions are usually aggressive in nature. Cognitive deficits are likely to be present in early childhood and may contribute to child-onset conduct disorder (Coy, Speltz, DeKlyen, & Jones, 2001).

Dodge and his colleagues also have distinguished between two types of aggressive behavior—reactive aggression and proactive aggression (Dodge, 1991; Schwartz et al., 1998). Reactive aggression is described as an emotionally aggressive response to a perceived threat or frustration. In contrast, proactive aggression is aggression directed at achieving a goal or receiving positive reinforcers. Referring to Dodge's model, deficiencies in the process occur at different points for reactive and proactive aggression. Reactively aggressive youth are likely to demonstrate deficiencies early in the cognitive process, such as focusing on only a few social cues and misattributing hostile intent to ambiguous situations. In contrast, proactive aggressive youth are likely to have deficiencies in generating alternative responses and often choose an aggressive response. Furthermore, reactive and proactive aggressors tend to have different trajectories. Reactive aggressors tend to have an earlier onset of problems than proactive aggressors (Dodge, Lochman, Harnish, Bates, & Pettit, 1997).

Social Theories

Social learning theory

A theory of human behavior based on learning from watching others in the social environment and reinforcement contingencies

Bandura's (1965) **social learning theory** suggests that children learn their behavior from observing others. Children are more likely to imitate behavior that receives positive reinforcement than behavior that receives negative reinforcement or punishment. As children are developing, numerous models are available to imitate, including parents, siblings, peers, and media figures. Studies have found that children who are highly aggressive and engage in antisocial behavior often have witnessed parents, siblings, or grandparents engage in aggression and antisocial behavior (Farrington, 1995; Waschbusch, 2002). This is a pattern of intergenerational aggression, in which one aggressive generation produces the next generation, which also is aggressive (Glueck & Glueck, 1968; Huesmann, Eron, Lefkowitz, & Walder, 1984).

Watching extremely violent television and movies in which actors are rewarded for their aggression also increases children's likelihood of acting aggressively (Bushman & Anderson, 2001). In addition, playing aggressive video games presents a forum for youth to be reinforced for their aggression and, in turn, may increase the likelihood of children acting aggressively in real life (Anderson & Dill, 2000). Moreover, some data find a link between violent video exposure and aggressive behavior to brain processes believed to be associated with desensitization to real-world violence (Barthlow, Bushman, & Sestir, 2006). See the In the Media box for a case where the obsession to play a particularly violent video game may have led to murder.

RISK FACTORS

Risk factor

A factor that increases the likelihood for emotional and/or behavioral problems

A number of individual and social factors, known as **risk factors**, place children at increased risk for developmental psychopathology, such as emotional and behavioral problems (Coie, Lochman, Terry, & Hyman, 1992; Fitzpatrick, 1997; Hart, O'Toole, Price-Sharps, & Shaffer, 2007; Jessor, Turbin, & Costa, 1998; Rutter, 1988, 1990; Wasserman & Saracini, 2001; Werner & Smith, 1992). It is important to remember that it is not just one risk factor but rather multiple risk factors that can lead to negative child outcomes (Rutter, 1979).

Individual Risk Factors

A variety of genetic or biological factors have been linked to behavioral problems. Even before a child is born, there are factors that can operate to increase the likelihood for later behavioral difficulties. For example, a parent's own history of ADHD or behavioral difficulties are known risk factors for their offspring, especially sons (Cohen, Adler, Kaplan, Pelcovitz, & Mandel, 2002; National Crime Prevention Council, 1995, 1997).

IN THE MEDIA Do Video Games Desensitize Teens?

What could make a teen kill his parents? Video games have become increasingly popular over the years and have increased in violence.

Daniel Petric was from Wellington, Ohio, and liked playing video games. He was like many 16-year-olds. Daniel enjoyed playing a very violent game named Halo 3 on his Xbox 360. Daniel's parents thought the game was inappropriate given the degree of violence and adult rating of the game. That didn't stop Daniel, however—he purchased the game without informing his parents. While recovering from a snowboarding injury, Daniel would often play the game for 18 hours without taking a break. Daniel's parents took his game away once they found out about it. They locked it in a safety box that also contained a handgun.

On October 20, 2007, approximately one month after the game was taken away from him, Daniel took his dad's lockbox key to get his game back and the gun. Daniel asked his parents to close their eyes because he had a surprise for them. When they did, Daniel shot them both in the head. Daniel's mother was killed, but his father survived the shooting. After shooting his parents, Daniel gave his father the gun and then took his game and went out to the family van to play it.

Daniel's attorney argued that Daniel was playing the game for so long that he did not understand the consequences of shooting someone and that death was real. The prosecutor disagreed and said that Daniel showed no remorse and tried to make the killing look like a suicide by placing the gun in his father's hand. Daniel was found guilty by the judge who sentenced him to 23 years in prison.

Do you think that violent videogames desensitize teens to kill?

Sources: http://www.timesonline.co.uk/tol/news/world/us_and_americas/article5512446.ece
http://www.cbsnews.com/8300-504083_162-504083.html?keyword=Daniel+Petric

A pregnant woman's use of drugs and alcohol can place the fetus at risk for later behavioral problems (Cohen et al., 2002). Once the child is born, diet and exposure to high levels of lead are risk factors for externalizing disorders (Cohen et al., 2002; National Crime Prevention Council, 1995, 1997).

A child's temperament also can be a risk factor. For example, children who are difficult to soothe or have a negative disposition can be at risk for later behavioral difficulties (Farrington, 1995). It also has been found that children who are impulsive are at risk for behavioral problems (Farrington, 1995).

Familial Risk Factors

Parents play a critical role in the development of their children. Children of parents who are neglectful (Shaw, Keenan, & Vondra, 1994) or children who do not attach securely to their parents are at risk for later behavioral problems (Fagot & Kavanagh, 1990). Divorce and familial conflict are risk factors for children (Amato & Keith, 1991; Cummings, Davies, & Campbell, 2000). Parenting style also can be problematic. For example, parents who are inconsistent, overly strict, and apply harsh discipline pose a risk to the child (Dekovic, 1999). In addition, not properly supervising a child presents a risk factor to the child for later behavioral problems (Dekovic, 1999; Farrington, 1995; Hoge, Andrews, & Lescheid, 1996; National Crime Prevention Council, 1995, 1997; Patterson, Reid, & Dishion, 1998; Rutter, 1990).

It has been suggested that parents who drink heavily are less likely to respond appropriately to their children's behavior, thus increasing the likelihood of future negative behavior (Lahey, Waldman, & McBurnett, 1999). Also, heavy drinking has been implicated in inept monitoring of children and less parental involvement, both being familial risk factors (Lahey et al., 1999).

Consequences of child abuse may be psychological, physical, behavioral, academic, sexual, interpersonal, self-perceptual, or spiritual (Wasserman et al., 2003). Boys, in particular, may respond to abuse by acting aggressively and later engaging in spousal abuse (Fergusson & Lynskey, 1997; Loos & Alexander, 1997). Cohen et al. (2002) found that physical abuse experienced during adolescence increases the risk for developing lifetime mental health difficulties and behavior problems.

Numerous other family variables have been reported as risk factors, including low socioeconomic status, large family size, and parental mental health problems (Frick, 1994; Patterson et al., 1998; Waschbusch, 2002). Recently, easy access to firearms at home has been found to increase the likelihood of violent offending that persists into adulthood (Ruback, Shaffer, & Clark, 2011). Moreover, family problems and antisocial behavior while a juvenile is in treatment have been associated with recidivism for young offenders (Mulder, Brand, Bullens, & van Marle, 2010).

School and Social Risk Factors

Having trouble reading and having a lower intelligence are both risk factors for antisocial behavior (Elkins, Iacono, Doyle, & McGue, 1997; Rutter, 1990). The school environment also provides an opportunity for peer influences on behavior. Young children who play with aggressive peers at an early age are at risk for externalizing behavior (Fergusson & Horwood, 1998; Laird, Jordan, Dodge, Petit, & Bates, 2001). Children with early CD symptoms who do not end up with CD tend to associate with less delinquent peers compared with children who later qualify for a CD diagnosis (Fergusson & Horwood, 1996). As children get older they may get involved in gangs. See Box 12.5 for a discussion of youth gangs.

Social disapproval and being rejected are likely to occur with aggressive children and adolescents (Coie, Belding, & Underwood, 1988; Ebata et al., 1990; Rutter, 1990), and these rejected, aggressive children are at risk for behavioral problems (Parker & Asher, 1987; Rudolph & Asher, 2000).

Resilient

Characteristic of a child who has multiple risk factors but who does not develop problem behaviors or negative symptoms

Protective factors

Factors that mitigate or reduce the likelihood of a negative outcome (e.g., aggression, psychopathology)

PROTECTIVE FACTORS

Although children may experience a similar environment and adversity, children's responses and outcomes vary, with some children prevailing and prospering, and others having a number of difficulties and negative outcomes. The child who has multiple risk factors but who can overcome them and prevail has been termed **resilient**. Resilience has been described as the ability to overcome stress and adversity (Winfield, 1994).

It has been suggested that resilient children may have **protective factors** that allow them to persevere in the face of adversity. The notion of protection and protective factors was introduced in the early 1980s (Garmezy, 1985). Garmezy (1991) identified a number of areas in which protectiveness can be present: genetic variables, personality dispositions, supportive family environments, and community supports. There is some debate

| BOX 12.5 | Running Around with the Wrong Crowd: Gangs |

There are three key elements to a youth gang:

1. The individuals involved must identify themselves as a group (they may have a group name, group colors, etc.).
2. Other people see the members as a distinct group.
3. Group members commit "delinquent" acts, often imposing on the rights of others in the community.

The National Gang Center is part of the Office of Juvenile Justice and Delinquency Prevention and reports many statistics on youth gangs.

Although anyone can be a gang member, gangs are often comprised of individuals from lower socioeconomic backgrounds who belong to a minority ethnic group. In 2008, the National Gang Center estimated that 32.4% of all jurisdictions in the United States surveyed experienced gang problems. This rate has increased about 15% from 2002. In terms of actual persons involved, approximately 774,000 gang members and 27,900 gangs were found to be active in 2008 in the United States. Compared to 2002, there was a 28% increase in the number of gangs and a 6% increase in gang members in 2008.

In a study that compared youth who were delinquent and nondelinquent who belonged to gangs, those involved in gangs were more likely to engage in serious and violent offenses (Esbensen, 2000; Battin-Pearson et al., 1998).

The Office of Juvenile Justice and Delinquency Prevention supported a series of studies examining gang membership in Denver, Seattle, and Rochester. Using self-report measures, gang members were found to be responsible for a large proportion of both violent and nonviolent criminal acts compared to those not in a gang. More specifically, in Denver, gang members committed three times more crime than non–gang members. In Seattle, gang members committed five times more crime than non–gang members and it was seven times more in Rochester (Howell, 1998).

Erickson and Butters (2006) examined the relationship between gangs, guns, and drugs in Toronto and Montreal, Canada. A total of 904 male high school students, school dropouts, and young offenders were interviewed. The researchers found that as gang presence in schools increased, so did the number of guns and amount of drugs. Almost 19% of boys ages 14 to 17 in Toronto and 15% in Montreal brought a gun to school. Dropouts who sell drugs are more likely to be engaged in gun violence than dropouts who do not sell drugs.

over the definition of protective factors and how protective factors work. Many agree, however, that protective factors help improve or sustain some part of an individual's life (Leadbeater, Kuperminc, Blatt, & Hertzog, 1999). Rutter (1990) identifies four ways that protective factors are effective:

1. Protective factors reduce negative outcomes by changing the risk level of the child's exposure to a risk factor.
2. They change the negative chain reaction following exposure to risk.
3. They help develop and maintain self-esteem and self-efficacy.
4. They avail opportunities to children they would not otherwise have.

Protective factors can be grouped into three categories: individual, familial, and social/external factors (Grossman et al., 1992).

Individual Protective Factors

Protective factors that reside within the individual, known as resilient temperaments (Hoge, 1999), include exceptional social skills, child competencies, confident perceptions, values, attitudes, and beliefs within the child (Vance, 2001).

Work from twin studies has suggested that social support may have a heritable component, which is influenced by personality. For example, likable children may respond to good role models in a positive manner, thus promoting a positive and continuing relationship.

Familial Factors

Protective familial factors are those positive aspects of the child's parents/guardians and home environment. For example, a child who has a positive and supportive relationship with an adult may display less negative behavior. Thus, a good parent/adult–child relationship is a protective factor for the child who is growing up in an underprivileged community.

Social/External Protective Factors

Peer groups can have a strong effect on child outcomes (Vance, 2001). Associating with deviant peers is a risk factor for antisocial behavior. The converse is a protective factor. That is, associating with prosocial children is a protective factor against antisocial behavior (Fergusson & Horwood, 1996).

Just as there are risk factors leading to increased negative outcomes, so too are there protective factors that may reduce negative outcomes in the presence of risk factors (Grossman et al., 1992; Masten, Best, & Garmezy, 1990). Protective factors may counteract risk (Loeber & Farrington, 1998a; Rutter, 1988). Further research is necessary to understand the role protective factors play in positive outcomes.

Primary intervention strategies

Strategies that are implemented prior to any violence occurring, with the goal of decreasing the likelihood that violence will occur later on

Secondary intervention strategies

Strategies that attempt to reduce the frequency of violence

Tertiary intervention strategies

Strategies that attempt to prevent violence from reoccurring

PREVENTION, INTERVENTION, AND TREATMENT OF YOUNG OFFENDING

Prevention, intervention, and treatment of young offending can be conceptualized as occurring at three levels: primary, secondary, and tertiary (DeMatteo, Heilbrun, & Marczyk, 2005; Flannery & Williams, 1999; Mulvey, Arthur, & Reppucci, 1993). **Primary intervention strategies** are implemented prior to any violence occurring with the goal of decreasing the likelihood that violence will occur later. **Secondary intervention strategies** attempt to reduce the frequency of violence. **Tertiary intervention strategies** attempt to prevent violence from reoccurring.

Primary Intervention Strategies

At the primary level of intervention, the goal is to identify groups (of children) that have numerous risk factors for engaging in antisocial behavior at a later time. The belief is that if the needs of these children are addressed early, before violence has occurred, then the likelihood that they will go on to become young offenders is reduced. Because "groups" (rather than specific individuals) are targeted, often these intervention strategies occur at broad levels such as in the family, at school, and in the community (Mulvey et al., 1993). Examples of primary intervention approaches are discussed next.

FAMILY-ORIENTED STRATEGIES Targeting the family may be an effective means of preventing young offending, given that family poses a number of risk factors (Kumpfer & Alvarado, 2003). According to Mulvey et al. (1993), family-based intervention efforts generally can be classified as either parent focused or family supportive. **Parent-focused interventions** are directed at assisting parents to recognize warning signs for later young violence and/or training parents to effectively manage any behavioral problems that arise. **Family-supportive interventions** connect at-risk families to various support services (e.g., child care, counseling, medical assistance) that may be available in their community.

An example of a family-oriented strategy is a popular parent-education program known as "The Incredible Years Parenting Program," a 12-week training program that starts with building a strong emotional attachment between parent(s) and child, then teaches parents how to set behavioral expectations for their children, monitor children's behavior, reinforce positive behavior, provide consequences for inappropriate behavior, and develop and use effective communication skills (Webster-Stratton, 1992). Videos are used to demonstrate parenting techniques and enhance parent learning. Although parent-focused approaches have shown some success in the shorter term, the most common research finding is that parents of high-risk children tend to discontinue the training at rates of more than 50% (Mulvey et al., 1993). With such high attrition rates, particularly among families with the greatest need for these services, it is unlikely that parent-focused approaches are a reliable mechanism for preventing youth violence. Parenting programs usually are not "stand alone" and are part of more comprehensive programs that may involve a child component, school component, and/or community program.

SCHOOL-ORIENTED STRATEGIES Given the amount of time children spend in school and the number of difficulties that can arise there, school is a common environment for primary prevention strategies. School-based prevention programs include preschool programs (e.g., Project Head Start, which incorporates The Incredible Years Parenting Program); social skills training for children, which may include cognitive behavioral therapy; and broad-based social interventions designed to alter the school environment (Loeber & Farrington, 1998a; Mulvey et al., 1993).

Project Head Start is designed for children from low socioeconomic backgrounds. A number of social services are provided to these children and families (e.g., nutrition, structured activities, academic tutoring, and medical services) to reduce disadvantages that may interfere with learning. Preschool programs can produce some positive outcomes in the short term; however, the positive effects at reducing antisocial behavior over the long term are questionable (Loeber & Farrington, 1998a; Mulvey et al., 1993).

It is not uncommon to recommend a social skills program to children showing some early signs of interpersonal and behavioral difficulties. Social skills training may involve a structured program with a limited number of sessions (e.g., 12), teaching alternative methods for conflict resolution, adjusting social perceptions (recall that a cognitive theory approach suggests that aggressive children may interpret ambiguous situations aggressively; e.g., Lochman, Whidby, & Fitzgerald, 2000), managing anger, and developing empathy. Cognitive behavioral therapy usually is a component of social skills programs. The cognitive behavioral component focuses on children's thought processes and social interactions. Concrete strategies for handling interpersonal conflict are outlined, that children practice through role-playing and modeling with others in the class.

Parent-focused interventions

Interventions directed at assisting parents to recognize warning signs for later youth violence and/or training parents to effectively manage any behavioral problems that may arise

Family-supportive interventions

Interventions that connect at-risk families to various support services

Program evaluations have suggested that social skills training with cognitive behavior therapy can be beneficial in the short term, although long-term follow-up suggests that the effects on reducing antisocial behavior may be small (e.g., Denham & Almeida, 1987). Larger effects may be obtained if social skills programs are combined with others such as parent education (Webster-Stratton & Hammond, 1997).

"Social process intervention" is another school-based approach that alters the school environment (Gauce, Comer, & Schwartz, 1987; Mulvey et al., 1993). Changes include increasing the connection among students with learning problems, assisting the transition from elementary school to high school, improving the perception of safety in school, and providing students with experiences in the community (Mulvey et al., 1993). Although these efforts may improve academic success, their influence on reducing the likelihood of young offending is unclear.

COMMUNITY-WIDE STRATEGIES   Community approaches include providing structured community activities for children's participation and increasing a community's cohesion. Few community-based programs exist for children and youth. The SafeFutures initiative was a federal-based initiative to connect the research on risk and protective factors to prevent and control delinquency (Office of Juvenile Justice and Delinquency Prevention, 2000). A main focus of SafeFutures is to use community-wide approaches to fight the fragmentation of various services such as health, social, educational, and juvenile justice. Nine components make up the SafeFutures initiative:

1. After-school programs
2. Juvenile mentoring programs
3. Family strengthening and support services
4. Mental health services for at-risk and adjudicated youth
5. Delinquency prevention programs
6. Comprehensive community-wide approaches to gang-free schools and communities
7. Community-based day treatment programs
8. Continuum-of-care services for at risk and delinquent girls
9. Serious, violent, and chronic juvenile offender programs

As you can see, a number of programs culminate to form SafeFutures representing a broad-based approach that spans not only programs but the developmental range to young offending.

Secondary Intervention Strategies

Secondary intervention strategies are directed at young offenders who have either had contact with the police or criminal justice system or have demonstrated behavioral problems at school. The goal of these strategies is to provide social and clinical services so that young offenders do not go on to commit serious violence. Many of the same approaches used in primary intervention strategies are used here. One of the main differences is the "target" (i.e., which children are involved in the program) rather than the content of the intervention. Common secondary intervention strategies include diversion programs, alternative and vocational education, family therapy, and skills training (see Mulvey et al., 1993).

Diversion programs "divert" youth offenders from the young justice system into community- or school-based treatment programs. The belief is that the justice system may cause more harm than good in reducing offending. Intervention and treatment in the community may be more successful at reducing the likelihood that young offenders will escalate their offending. Alternative and vocational education programs offer the option of mainstream schooling. Family therapy and skills-training programs incorporate the youth and their family. Diversion and certain school-, family-, and community-based interventions have shown some success at reducing antisocial behavior in youth (e.g., Davidson & Redner, 1988; Kazdin, 1996).

One particular secondary intervention program that has undergone considerable evaluation is Multisystemic Therapy (MST). MST examines a child across the contexts or "systems" in which they live—family, peers, school, neighborhood, and community (Henggeler & Borduin, 1990; Henggeler, Melton, & Smith, 1992; Henggeler, Schoenwald, Borduin, Rowland, & Cunningham, 1998; Henggeler, Schoenwald, & Pickrel, 1995). This intensive program is used for difficult offenders between 12 and 18 years of age. Often the cases involve repeat offenders with a history of difficulties. MST workers can be contacted 24 hours a day, seven days a week, if needed. The workers are involved with the offender, parents/caregivers, the school, and the community. Often the focus is on providing parents/caregivers skills and parenting strategies to help with the offender. The offender is engaged to try to finish school and/or is given job training. Also, the offender and parents/caregivers may be informed and encouraged to access recreational activities and sports in the community to divert the offender from negative activity.

MST has been implemented in various parts of the United States and Canada. To evaluate its effectiveness, Timmons-Mitchell, Bender, Kishna, and Mitchell (2006) examined MST compared to "typical treatment" that is provided to juvenile offenders in the United States. Ninety-three juvenile offenders on probation from a Midwestern state were randomly assigned to receive either MST or typical treatment services (e.g., drug counseling, anger management, family therapy). These juveniles were followed for 18 months following treatment completion to assess rearrest rates and 6 months for youth functioning. Rearrests and new arrests for the MST group were significantly lower than for the juveniles who received typical treatment services. More positive functioning also was found with the MST group compared to the typical treatment group. Various studies evaluating MST in the United States have found it more effective than incarceration, individual counseling, and probation (Henggeler et al., 1986, 1992, 1995). Overall, MST provides a promising model for intervention.

Tertiary Intervention Strategies

Tertiary intervention strategies are aimed at youth who have engaged in criminal acts and who may have already been processed through formal court proceedings (Flannery & Williams, 1999). As such, these intervention efforts are actually more "treatment" rather than prevention, and the recipients are often chronic and serious young offenders. The goal of tertiary intervention strategies is to minimize the impact of existing risk factors and foster the development of protective factors, which may reduce the likelihood that the at-risk adolescent will engage in future offending.

Tertiary intervention strategies include inpatient treatment (i.e., institutional, residential) and community-based treatment (Mulvey et al., 1993). The approach can be one of retribution or rehabilitation. For those who favor retribution, they believe that young offenders should be held accountable for their actions, punished accordingly, and separated from society. Treatment for these young offenders should be provided in an institutional setting (e.g., youth detention center). By contrast, those who favor rehabilitation believe that treatment based in the community is a more effective way to reduce the likelihood of reoffending. One meta-analysis reported that shorter stays (rather than longer stays) in institutional settings and greater involvement with community services are more effective for violent young offenders (Wooldredge, 1988).

Summary

1. In 1899 the first juvenile court was established to respond to youth who engaged in criminal behavior. When a juvenile first comes into contact with law enforcement, a decision must be made about whether to divert the juvenile out of the justice system or engage the juvenile court, which then commences the process into the justice system.

2. Three common disorders are diagnosed in young offenders: attention-deficit/hyperactivity disorder (ADHD), oppositional defiant disorder (ODD), and conduct disorder (CD). Young children diagnosed with conduct disorder are at greatest risk for young and adult criminal offending.

3. Biological theories focus on genetic and physiological differences between young offenders and those who do not behave antisocially. Cognitive theories propose a model of antisocial behavior that focuses on thought processes that occur in social interactions. Social theories are based in social learning theory, which proposes that children learn behavior from observing others and through reinforcement contingencies.

4. Risk factors increase the likelihood of behavioral (and emotional) disorders in children and youth. Protective factors provide a buffer against the risk factors a child may experience. Risk factors include individual (e.g., temperament), familial (e.g., attachment to parent), and school and social (e.g., social disapproval) factors. Protective factors include individual (e.g., resilient temperament), familial (e.g., good parent–child relationship), and social/external (e.g., peer group) factors.

5. Primary intervention strategies are implemented prior to any violence occurring with the goal of decreasing the likelihood that violence will occur later. Secondary intervention strategies attempt to reduce the frequency of violence. Tertiary intervention strategies attempt to prevent violence from reoccurring.

Key Concepts

attention-deficit/hyperactivity disorder *289*
conduct disorder *289*
externalizing problems *289*
family-supportive interventions *299*
internalizing problems *288*

oppositional defiant disorder *289*
parent-focused interventions *299*
primary intervention strategies *298*
protective factors *296*

resilient *296*
risk factors *294*
secondary intervention strategies *298*
social learning theory *294*
tertiary intervention strategies *298*

Discussion Questions

1. Sixteen-year-old Andrew Smith is appearing before Judge Brown in youth court for the third time in two years. Andrew's most current offenses are robbery and possession of a handgun. How would you recommend this case be processed? Why?

2. In your opinion, what factors should the courts consider when determining whether a young offender should be tried as an adult?

3. Various unconventional treatment approaches have been proposed as a way of dealing with young offenders, for example, taking young offenders to prison to witness firsthand the prison environment or taking young offenders to the morgue. Do you think these sorts of approaches will successfully rehabilitate young offenders? Why or why not?

4. You decide to volunteer at the local Boys and Girls Club on Saturday mornings. You participate in a program for 4- to 6-year-olds. You notice that a few of the children in the group are showing early signs of aggressive behavior. Design a program to reduce young children's aggression. Each program runs for eight weeks. What elements would you include in your program? Why?

Intimate Partner Violence

LEARNING OBJECTIVES

- Differentiate among the different forms of abuse, and outline the prevalence of intimate partner violence.

- Explain why some women remain in, or return to, abusive relationships.

- Outline how social learning theory has been used to explain intimate partner violence.

- Describe the various types of male batterers.

- Outline the effectiveness of intimate partner violence offender treatment.

- Define stalking and identify the various types of stalkers.

Nelson Grann is serving a sentence for stalking, threatening, and aggravated assault. His abusive behavior started when his wife was pregnant with their first child. He engaged in verbally abusive behavior, calling her names and threatening to use violence against her. After the baby was born, the verbal abuse escalated and he started physically abusing his wife (i.e., slapping her, shoving her into walls, punching her). After the birth of their second child, he became very controlling and refused to allow his wife to have contact with her family or friends unless he was present.

After a particularly brutal beating, she left him and took the children to her sister's home and told Nelson she wanted a divorce. For eight weeks, Nelson phoned her and on several occasions he showed up at the home demanding to see his wife and children. The police were called and Nelson was charged with stalking. One evening Nelson broke into the house, threatened to kill his brother-in-law, and repeatedly punched his wife. He was arrested and charged with threatening and aggravated assault. He was sentenced to seven years in prison and has been attending the high-risk intimate partner violence treatment program for the past two months. The program consists of individual and group therapy. One therapist thinks Nelson is making considerable progress in treatment, whereas the other therapist is less optimistic. In group therapy, Nelson is evasive when challenged, has been vindictive toward other group members, and is continually testing boundaries. The therapist who has been concerned with Nelson's attitudes and behavior thinks that Nelson is not genuinely interested in changing.

Violence occurring within the family has a major impact on victims and society. Violence and its aftermath is also a major focus of forensic psychology, with psychologists involved in developing assessment and intervention programs for victims and offenders. Reading the opening vignette raises a number of questions. How common is this sort of behavior? Why would someone hurt a person he or she claims to love? After being caught, does the violence stop? What can be done to prevent the development of attitudes supportive of abuse? Are treatment programs effective at reducing risk for future violence? We will address these and other questions in this chapter.

The term **domestic violence** refers to any violence occurring among family members. Domestic violence typically occurs in private settings, and historically authorities were reluctant to violate the privacy of families. Although not necessarily condoned, it was tolerated and was not subject to effective legal sanctions. Reasons for this were varied, but religious and cultural attitudes generally positioned women and children in deferential roles within families. In the United States, little attention was paid to intimate partner violence prior to the 1980s. The women's liberation movement and the growth of feminism gave women the courage to speak out against such violence. Since that time, intimate partner violence has become a major focus of research and legal action.

Domestic violence

Any violence occurring among family members

In this chapter, we will focus on violence occurring between intimate partners who are living together or separated (called spousal violence or **intimate partner violence**). Abuse and aggression within intimate relationships has a long history and is, unfortunately, still common. We will review the different types of abuse experienced and the prevalence of intimate partner violence. We will present theories that attempt to explain why some people engage in violence against their partners. Research examining the different types of spousal violent men will be provided. In addition, some of the major approaches to treatment will be presented and research on their effectiveness will be reviewed. Finally, research examining the prevalence of stalking and types of stalkers will be summarized.

Intimate partner violence

Any violence occurring between intimate partners who are living together or separated. Also known as spousal violence

A victim of intimate partner violence.

TYPES OF VIOLENCE AND MEASUREMENT

Violence against partners is varied in terms of types and severity and includes physical (e.g., hitting, punching, stabbing, burning), sexual, financial (e.g., restricting access to personal funds, forcing complete financial responsibility, theft of paychecks), and emotional abuse (e.g., verbal attacks, degradation, threats about hurting family members or pets, isolation from family members, unwarranted accusations about infidelity).

The scale most commonly used to measure intimate partner violence has been the Conflict Tactics Scale (CTS) (Straus, 1979). This scale consists of 18 items intended to measure how the person and his or her partner resolve conflict. The items range from constructive problem solving (e.g., discussing the item calmly) to verbal or indirect aggression (e.g., swearing or threatening to hit) to physical aggression (e.g., slapping or using a gun). Respondents are asked how frequently they have engaged in the behavior and how often they have experienced these acts. One of the most influential researchers in the area of intimate partner violence is Dr. Murray Straus, who is profiled in Box 13.1.

| BOX 13.1 | Researcher Profile: Dr. Murray Straus |

Murray Straus's work blends basic and applied research together in a remarkable interdisciplinary mix: he has made a major contribution to understanding why people engage in partner violence (both men and women), developed the most widely used measure of partner violence (the Conflict Tactics Scale), and has challenged the effectiveness of using corporal punishment.

Dr. Murray Straus

Dr. Straus obtained his Ph.D. in sociology at the University of Wisconsin, Madison, in 1956. His dissertation was on child-rearing practices and their effects on children in an urban and village sample in Ceylon (now Sri Lanka). Currently, he is a professor of sociology at the University of New Hampshire, where he conducts research on family violence including child abuse, partner violence, and corporal punishment.

Dr. Straus became interested in studying violence within the family when he found out that a quarter of the students in one of his classes had been hit by their parents when they were seniors in high school. Initially, he thought the one-quarter value reported was due to sampling error, but when he asked other classes in the late 1960s, he found that this was a stable estimate.

When asked about what keeps him interested in research, Dr. Straus replied, "I believe that reducing violence against children, which goes under the euphemism of "spanking," can contribute greatly to human well-being."

Dr. Straus has two favorite research topics. These topics also happen to correspond to the titles of two of his books: *Behind Closed Doors: Violence in the American Family* and *Beating the Devil Out of Them: Corporal Punishment in American Families and Its Effects on Children.*

Behind Closed Doors: Violence in the American Family, first published in 1980, is a classic and a must-read for students interested in understanding family violence. In it, Straus demonstrated that valid data on partner violence and child abuse could be obtained from nationally representative samples. Almost all the results in the book have been confirmed by other researchers during the past 30 years.

Beating the Devil Out of Them: Corporal Punishment in American Families and Its Effects on Children was first published in 1994. In the book Straus described research on spanking

(continued)

BOX 13.1   Continued

and other legal forms of corporal punishment by parents and presented new research on nationally representative samples of American children. He found that almost all American children (97%) experienced violent socialization in the form of spanking when they were toddlers. Straus linked spanking to a series of harmful side effects in children such as increased aggression, including violence against partners when an adult, depression, lower economic achievement, and an increased probability of masochistic sexual interests. Dr. Straus hopes that those who read the book will be moved to end the violent childrearing practices that have been the norm in American society and most other nations.

Based on his research, Straus would like to see two changes to current legislation. First, he hopes the United States and Canada will follow the lead of many European countries and ban the use of corporal punishment. Second, he wants an end to regulations in many states that prohibit couples therapy and anger management therapy as court-ordered alternatives to punishment for spousal violence. These regulations restrict treatment of spousal violence to so-called Duluth programs, which numerous studies have found to be ineffective.

Dr. Straus enjoys teaching seminars on research methods and family violence. He encourages future researchers in forensic psychology to take an interdisciplinary approach and to learn about the social causes of crime. A perk Dr. Straus enjoys as an academic is the opportunity to travel. Dr. Straus has taught at the University of Minnesota, Cornell University, the University of Wisconsin, Washington State University, the University of Ceylon (Sri Lanka), the University of Kentucky, the University of Bombay (India), the University of York (England), Columbia University, and the University of Leuven (Belgium).

Archer (2002) conducted a meta-analysis of 48 studies using the CTS and found that females are more likely to engage in minor physical aggression, such as slapping, kicking, or hitting with an object, whereas men are more likely to beat up or to choke their partners. Sex differences varied across community, university student, and treatment samples (couples in treatment for the husband's violence). Within treatment samples, men engage in much higher rates of minor and severe physical violence compared with students and community samples. Within community and university student samples, males and females commit equal amounts of violence. Comparing self- and partner reports, respondents report fewer violent acts than their partners, and men are more likely to underreport than women.

Although commonly used, the CTS is often criticized for a number of reasons (Dobash & Dobash, 1979; Ratner, 1998):

1. The way it is introduced to respondents has been criticized. Respondents read the following: "No matter how well a couple get along, there are times when they disagree, get annoyed with the other person or just have spats or fights because they're in a bad mood or for some other reason. They also use many different ways of trying to settle their differences" (Straus, 1990, p. 33). The introduction to a questionnaire is crucial since it provides respondents with information on what to focus on. In the case of the CTS, the focus is on how couples settle disputes. However, some acts of violence are not precipitated by an argument and therefore the respondent may not report these.

2. The CTS does not include the full range of potential violent acts. For example, sexual aggression is not included.

3. The CTS does not take into account the different consequences of the same act for men and women. For example, treating a punch by a woman and a man as equivalent ignores the difference in the injury that might be inflicted (Nazroo, 1995). Surveys have consistently shown that women are more likely than men are to suffer both physical and psychological consequences from spousal violence (Saunders, 2002). Tjaden and Thoennes (2001) reported an injury rate of 42% for women versus 19% for men in the most recent violent episode. Canadian women reported that they had been physically injured in 44% of all cases of intimate violence, and in 13% of cases they sought and received medical care.

4. The CTS does not assess motive for violence and therefore offensive violence is treated as equal to a defensive response. For example, consider the case of a couple arguing. If he threatens to punch her, and she pushes him away from her, both acts would be included on the CTS.

In response to these and other criticisms, Straus, Hamby, Boney-McCoy, and Sugarman (1996) revised the CTS (CTS2), deleting some items and adding new items. For example, physically aggressive acts, such as slamming a person against a wall, burning them on purpose, and sexual aggression, have been included. The verbal aggression scale was renamed psychological aggression and additional items were added (e.g., did something to spite partner). Moreover, the consequence (physical injury) has also been added. Researchers are using the CTS2 in studies of spousal violence. Box 13.2 provides more details about the prevalence and severity of mutual violence, as well as sex-specific differences.

Intimate Partners: A Risky Relationship

The most recent U.S. survey on intimate partner violence was the National Crime Victimization Survey in 2008 (Catalano, Smith, Snyder, & Rand, 2009). This survey includes measures of physical and sexual violence in intimate relationships. In 2008, the annual rate of violence per 1,000 was 4.3 for females and 0.8 for males. Black females experienced higher rates of intimate violence than white females. The rate of intimate rape and sexual assault was 0.3 for females and 0.1 for males. Nearly all of the violence committed against females was perpetrated by males (99%), whereas 83% of the violence committed against males was perpetrated by females. Between 1993 and 2008 there was a decrease in the rate of intimate violence (54% decrease for females and 53% decrease for males). Respondents were asked about whether the violence was reported to police. In 2008, 72% of violence experienced by male victims was reported to the police as compared to 49% of violence experienced by female victims. In 2007, 1,640 women were killed by their intimate partners and 700 men. Females are much more likely to be killed by their intimate partners than males. For example, in 2007 intimate partners were responsible for 45% of females murdered, but only 5% of males murdered. There is less research on the rates of intimate violence within same-sex partners. However, recent research suggests that the rate of intimate violence between same-sex partners is comparable to that of heterosexual couples (see Walters, 2011, for review). Partners of same-sex abuse often feel isolated and are hesitant to seek help due to the lack of acknowledgment and support for victims of same-sex violence.

What is the prevalence of dating violence in university students? The International Dating Violence Study (Chan, Strauss, Brownridge, Tiwari, & Leung, 2008) examined

BOX 13.2   Husband Battering Does Exist

Intimate partner violence is certainly not exclusively initiated by men. However, some researchers have minimized the impact of such abuse. For example, Berk, Berk, Loseke, and Rauma (1983) note that "While there are certainly occasional instances of husbands being battered, it is downright pernicious to equate their experiences with those of the enormous number of women who are routinely and severely victimized" (p. 210). In a review of the literature on women as perpetrators of intimate violence, Carney, Buttell, and Dutton (2007) address the following questions.

- Is intimate partner violence invariably male initiated?
  The answer is "no." It appears that women engage in the same amount of violence as men, and some studies found that women engaged in more minor violence than men (Archer, 2002). Williams and Frieze (2005) analyzed the different violence patterns of 3,519 couples and found that the most common type of violence was mutual mild violence, followed by mutual severe violence. Thus, the long-assumed gender gap does not exist. As Carney et al. (2007) conclude, "Female violence is common, [and] occurs at the same rate as male violence" (p. 113).
- Do males suffer any serious consequences of female-initiated violence?
  The answer is "yes." Based on their review of the literature, Carney et al. (2007) concluded that "(1) women are injured more than men but (2) men are injured as well and are not immune to being seriously injured" (p. 110).
- Is there a gender bias in police responses to intimate partner violence?
  The limited research indicates the answer is "yes." Brown (2004) studied differences in arrest rates in cases of injury and no-injury assaults. When the female partner was injured, the male was charged in 91% of the cases; however, when the male was injured, the female was charged 60% of the time. When no injury occurred, the female was charged in 13% of cases as compared with 52% of the time for males.
- Do the courts treat men and women charged with intimate partner violence the same way?
  The answer is "no." Women are more likely to have the charges against them dropped by prosecutors and are less likely to be found guilty. For example, Brown (2004) reported that in severe injury cases, 71% of men and 22% of women defendants were found guilty. A major factor for why such a low percentage of women were found guilty was that the male victim was not willing to testify.

the prevalence of dating violence in 14,252 university students across 32 countries. The CTS2 scale was administered to students, asking whether they had engaged in any physical and sexual violence with their dating partner and whether they had experienced any physical and sexual violence by their dating partners. Students responded to items about any assaults, including minor violence (e.g., something that could hurt them thrown at them, being slapped, having their arm twisted) to serious violence (e.g., being choked by partner, being beaten up by partner, being threatened by a knife or gun by partner). Rates of perpetration and victimization of sexual coercion (pressuring someone to engage in unwanted sexual activity) ranged from minor acts (e.g., was made to have sex without a condom, partner insisted on sex when they did not want to) to more severe acts (e.g., was forced to have oral or anal sex, had sex because of partner threats). Table 13.1 presents the perpetration and victimization results across male and female students. Female students were less likely to be perpetrators of serious assaults and sexual coercion as compared with male students. The median rates across all the countries of having physically

TABLE 13.1	Rates of Violence as Reported by American University Students		
Measure	**Total (%)**	**Men (%)**	**Women (%)**
Perpetration of any assault	30.3	33.1	28.7
Victim of any assault	28.3	35.3	24.5
Perpetration of serious assault	8.8	16.1	4.9
Victim of serious assault	9.5	17.4	5.3
Perpetration of sexual coercion	28.6	36.1	24.6
Victim of sexual coercion	31.8	34.0	30.6

Source: Chan et al. 2008.

assaulted their partners was 29.8% for any assaults, 5.8% for serious assaults, and 21.5% for any sexual coercive acts. American dating physical violence rates were in the upper half of countries surveyed; about one in four American university students reported having experienced physical assault by their dating partner in the past 12 months. In addition, American students had higher rates of sexual coercion as compared with other countries. These findings suggest that dating violence is a substantial problem. Moreover, if university students are committing dating violence, this violence will likely continue in future intimate relationships.

THEORIES OF INTIMATE PARTNER VIOLENCE

Some researchers believe that a patriarchal society contributes to the spousal assault of women by men (e.g., Dobash & Dobash, 1979; Ellis, 1989; Straus, 1977). The theory of patriarchy was first described in the 1970s and is often associated with sociology and feminism. **Patriarchy** refers to a broad set of cultural beliefs and values that support the male dominance of women. As stated by Dobash and Dobash (1979), "the seeds of wife beating lie in the subordination of females and in their subjection to male authority and control" (p. 33). Smith (1990) has proposed a distinction between "social" patriarchy (male domination at the social level) and "familial" patriarchy (male domination within the family). To study the association between patriarchy and spousal abuse, Yllo and Straus (1990) compared the rates of spousal abuse across American states with the degree to which each state was characterized by patriarchal structure. States with male-dominant norms had much higher rates of spousal assault than those with more egalitarian norms.

Patriarchy likely influences the development of individual expectations about the appropriate level of authority within intimate relationships. One difficulty for patriarchal accounts of spousal violence is that it does not predict which individuals within a system will engage in intimate violence. Other factors operating within the community (e.g., work, peers), family (e.g., communication level between partners), and individual (e.g., coping skills, empathy) are needed to provide an explanation (Dutton, 1995). For example, consider two men who are raised to value the same cultural beliefs, who have similar social supports and identical levels of conflict in the home; one man may react with violence whereas the other does not.

Social learning theory was developed by Bandura (1973) to explain aggression and has been applied by Dutton (1995) to explain spousal assault. Social learning theory

Patriarchy

Broad set of cultural beliefs and values that support the male dominance of women

Social learning theory

A theory of human behavior based on learning from watching others in the social environment and reinforcement contingencies has three main components: origins of aggression, instigators of aggression, and regulators of aggression. One way people acquire new behaviors is via **observational learning**. Bandura (1973) describes three major sources for observational learning: family of origin, the subculture the person lives in, and televised violence. Studies of the family background of male batterers have found they are much more likely to have witnessed parental violence than are nonviolent men (Kalmuss, 1984; Straus et al., 1980). Not all behavior that is observed, however, will be practiced. Social learning theory posits that in order for a person to acquire a behavior, it must have functional value for him or her. Behavior that is rewarded increases in likelihood of occurrence and behavior that is punished decreases in likelihood of occurrence.

Observational learning

Learning behaviors by watching others perform these behaviors

The next requirement is that even acquired behaviors are only manifested if there is an appropriate event in the environment to act as a stimulus for the behavior. These events are called **instigators**. Dutton (1995) describes two types of instigators in intimate partner assault: aversive instigators and incentive instigators. Aversive instigators produce emotional arousal and how a person labels that emotional arousal will influence how he or she responds. Studies with male batterers have found that they tend to label many different emotional states as anger (Gondolf, 1985, labels this the *male-emotional funnel system*). Incentive instigators are perceived rewards for engaging in aggression. When people believe they can satisfy their needs by using aggression, they may decide to be violent.

Instigators

In social learning theory, these are events in the environment that act as a stimulus for acquired behaviors

Social learning theory assumes that behavior is regulated by its consequences. Two types of **regulators** include external punishment and self-punishment. An example of external punishment would be if the person were arrested for engaging in violence. An example of self-punishment would be if the person felt remorse for engaging in violence. If the consequences outweigh the rewards for engaging in the behavior and if alternatives are provided to cope with instigators, the likelihood of violence should diminish.

Regulators

In social learning theory, these are consequences of behaviors

Another helpful way to conceptualize the interaction among factors related to violence within intimate relationships is in terms of the nested ecological model first proposed by Dutton (1995). This model focuses on the relationship among the multiple levels that influence intimate violence, such as the following:

- Macrosystem: This level considers the broad sets of societal and cultural beliefs and attitudes, for example, patriarchy and social norms, that condone or promote gender inequality, male domination, and aggression.
- Exosystem: This level considers the social structures that connect the individual to the wider society (e.g., social supports, employment, friends) and can influence the likelihood of intimate violence. For example, job stress or unemployment can increase the likelihood of violence, whereas family or friends who provide emotional support or corrective feedback can decrease the likelihood of violence.
- Microsystem: This level focuses on the immediate environment in which abuse occurs such as the interaction pattern that exists among the family members. For example, the couple's pattern of communication or level of conflict, or each spouse's method of coping with conflict.
- Ontogenic level: This level focuses on the psychological and biological features of the individual, for example, the individual's abuse history, exposure to violent models, and abilities to manage emotions.

Dutton's model is useful because it recognizes the importance of various levels of explanation and acknowledges the importance of the interactions that can occur among levels.

WHY DO BATTERED WOMEN STAY?

One of the more perplexing questions is "If a woman is in an abusive relationship, why doesn't she just leave?" Although intimate violence is no longer sanctioned in the United States, negative myths and stereotypes concerning battered woman still prevail. These myths include that a battered woman has a masochistic desire to be beaten, that she is emotionally disturbed, that the violence cannot be as bad as she claims, and that the woman is partially to blame for her victimization (Ewing & Aubrey, 1987; Harrison & Esqueda, 1999; Walker, 1979). Box 13.3 describes some of the other myths associated with intimate partner violence.

BOX 13.3	Myths and Realities Concerning Intimate Partner Violence

Intimate partner violence is associated with many myths. A list of these myths appears below, accompanied by facts that challenge these false beliefs.

Myth 1: Intimate partner violence is not a common problem.

Because of the private nature of intimate partner violence and the shame and embarrassment that inhibits many victims from talking about the issue, it is impossible to determine exactly how many people are subject to violence. In United States, about one in four women have experienced sexual or physical abuse by their past or current intimate partner. You likely know someone who has been assaulted by his or her partner or who is currently in an abusive relationship. The highest rates of intimate partner violence are experienced by women between the ages of 15 and 25.

Myth 2: Only heterosexual women get battered. Men are not victims and women never batter.

Such myths ignore and deny the realities of violent relationships. Men can be and are victims of intimate partner violence. Women can be and are batterers. Even when two people are of the same sex, in a same-sex relationship, partner abuse can and does occur.

Myth 3: When a woman leaves a violent relationship, she is safe.

The most dangerous time for a battered spouse is after separation. Of all spousal homicides, 75% occur after separation. At this time, the abusive partner is losing control, which may cause an escalation of abuse in an attempt to regain control.

Myth 4: Alcohol and/or drugs cause people to act aggressively.

Although abuse of alcohol or drugs is often present in incidents of spousal abuse, it is not the alcohol or drug that causes the violence. However, people will often use this to excuse or to

(continued)

rationalize their behavior by saying, "I wasn't myself" or "I hit you because I was drunk." Blaming alcohol or drugs takes the responsibility away from the abusive person and can prevent that person from changing.

Myth 5: When a woman gets hit by her partner, she must have provoked him in some way.

No one deserves to be hit; whether or not there was provocation, violence is always wrong. It never solves problems, although it often silences the victim.

Myth 6: Maybe things will get better.

Once violence begins in a relationship, it usually gets worse without some kind of intervention. Waiting and hoping the abusive partner will change is not a good strategy. Partners in an abusive relationship need help to break the abusive pattern.

The extent to which people believe such myths varies (Ewing & Aubrey, 1987; Greene, Raitz, & Lindblad, 1989). To examine myths about battered women, Ewing and Aubrey gave community samples a hypothetical scenario about a couple having ongoing marital problems, including a description of an incident in which the husband assaulted his wife (the husband accused his wife of cheating on him and then grabbed her and threw her to the floor). The percentage of males and females agreeing with each statement are shown in parentheses:

- The female victim "bears at least some responsibility." (Males = 47%; females = 30%)
- The battered woman could simply leave her battering husband. (Males = 57%; females = 71%)
- The battered woman who stays is "somewhat masochistic." (Males = 24%; females = 50%)
- The woman can prevent battering by seeking counseling. (Males = 86%; females 81%)
- Battering is an isolated event. (Males = 40%; females = 27%)
- The woman can rely on the police to protect her. (Males = 18%; females = 15%)

Researchers have asked victims of intimate partner violence why they stay in abusive relationships, and for those who returned after separating, why they did so. The decision to stay with, to leave, or to return to an abusive partner is complex, especially because the violence experienced is often not constant. Walker (1979) proposed that a three-phase cycle of abuse occurs. First, there is a tension-building phase occurring prior to the assault with increasing conflict and stress between partners. Second, there is the acting-out phase when the batterer engages in intimate partner violence. Third, there is the honeymoon phase, when the batterer apologizes and often promises not to engage in future violence. According to Walker, the cycle repeats itself with the honeymoon phase sometimes disappearing. Figure 13.1 illustrates the cycle of violence phases.

Critiques of the cycle of abuse claim that not all abuse is as predictable as the cycle of abuse model suggests and that many abusers do not cycle through the different stages. Another reason why some women may remain in abusive relationships is learned helplessness (Walker, 1979). Learned helplessness was originally described by Seligman and colleagues (Abramson, Seligman, & Teasdale, 1978), who investigated the reaction of

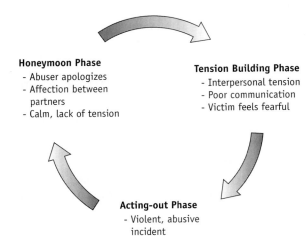

Honeymoon Phase
- Abuser apologizes
- Affection between
  partners
- Calm, lack of tension

Tension Building Phase
- Interpersonal tension
- Poor communication
- Victim feels fearful

Acting-out Phase
- Violent, abusive
  incident

FIGURE 13.1 Lenore Walker's Cycle of Violence (adapted from Walker, 1979)

Sources: Based on Lenore Walker's Cycle of violence by Walker, 1979.

punished dogs to their environment. They found that dogs who could not avoid an electric shock essentially "gave up," a finding that has parallels with how humans deal with unavoidable aversive stimuli. Walker (1979) applied this theory of learned helplessness to abused women to help explain their passivity in response to repeated abuse and their lack of effort to leave the abusive situation. This theory has been critiqued because some women may be passive on purpose in order to placate their abuser. In addition, many women do make active attempts to leave their abusive partner.

In a study by Anderson and colleagues (2003) of victims of intimate violence, 400 women who sought help from a domestic violence advocacy center were asked, "If you never left your mate or returned to your mate after separating, check those factors that affected your decision" (p. 152). Thirty-two potential factors were listed and most women endorsed several different reasons, including the following:

- Mate promised to change (71%)
- Lack of money (46%)
- Mate needed me (36%)
- Nowhere to go or stay (29%)
- Threats of mate to find me and kill me (22%)
- Children [with me] wanted to go back (19%)
- Shelter was full (5%)

This study and others point to the environmental, socialization, and psychological barriers that exist for victims. For a woman to leave, she needs resources such as money, a place to go, and support from the criminal justice system (examples of environmental barriers). Women are socialized to be the primary caretaker in relationships and appear to place a high value on the promises of the abuser to change. In addition, they return because they do not want their children to suffer (35%). Psychological barriers also exist. Some victims reported that they felt safer remaining in the relationship than leaving, because they knew what the abuser was doing (22%).

Recently, researchers have begun to study the link between family violence and animal maltreatment. Growing evidence suggests that batterers often threaten or harm their partners' pets and that one reason women delay leaving is out of concern for the welfare of their animals (Ascione, 1998; Faver & Strand, 2003; Flynn, 2000). Box 13.4 describes one such study. Although a link between maltreatment of animals and intimate partner violence may appear insignificant in relation to other factors, it underscores the complexity of the variables associated with remaining in a violent relationship.

A HETEROGENEOUS POPULATION: TYPOLOGIES OF MALE BATTERERS

An increasing body of empirical research demonstrates that not all batterers are alike. Categories of male batterers have been developed to help understand the causes of intimate violence. Holtzworth-Munroe and Stuart (1994) divided male batterers into three

---

BOX 13.4 **Woman's Best Friend: Pet Abuse and Intimate Violence**

Only recently have researchers started to investigate the link between animal maltreatment and violence against women (Ascione, 1998; Ascione et al., 2007; Faver & Strand, 2003). In a study of women in intimate partner violence shelters, Ascione reported that 72% said their partners had either threatened to harm or actually had harmed their pets. Moreover, 54% reported that their pets had actually been injured or killed by their abusive partners. Compared with women who said they had not experienced *intimate violence*, Ascione et al. found that women in intimate partner violence shelters were 11 times more likely to indicate that their partners had hurt or killed pets. Faver and Strand questioned 50 abused women who owned pets and found that 49% reported their partners had threatened their pets and 46% indicated that their partners had actually harmed their pets.

Flynn (2000) asked a series of questions about the women's experiences with their pets:

1. In dealing with the abuse, how important has your pet been as a source of emotional support?
2. Has your partner ever threatened to harm your pet, actually harmed your pet, or killed your pet?
3. Where is your pet now?
4. Did concern about your pet's safety keep you from seeking shelter sooner?

Flynn divided the sample of 42 battered women into a pet-abuse group ($n = 20$) and a no-pet-abuse group ($n = 22$). Ninety percent of the women in the pet-abuse group considered their pet a source of emotional support, compared with 47% of the no-pet-abuse group. About half of the pets in both groups were left with the abusive partner. In light of the partner's history of pet abuse, it is not surprising that 65% of the women in the pet-abuse group worried about the safety of their pets, whereas only 15% of the women in the no-pet-abuse group were concerned. Eight women actually delayed leaving their abusive partners out of concern for their pets' safety, with five of these women reporting that they delayed leaving for more than two months. Flynn concluded that "efforts to prevent and end such violence must not only recognize the interconnections, but grant legitimacy to all victims, human and animal" (p. 176).

A recent study of 860 university students found a robust overlap among experiencing childhood abuse, witnessing animal abuse, and witnessing intimate partner violence. The researchers concluded, "There is a significant overlap between these various forms of abuse within the home and that, in particular, the identification of animal cruelty in a home (perpetrated by parents or children) may serve as a reliable red flag for child maltreatment or severe intimate partner violence" (DeGue & DiLillo, 2009, p. 1053).

types based on severity of violence, generality of violence, and personality disorder characteristics: family-only, dysphoric/borderline, and generally violent/antisocial.

The **family-only batterer**

Family-only batterer

A male spousal batterer who is typically not violent outside the home, does not show much psychopathology, and does not possess negative attitudes supportive of violence

- Of all types of batterers, engages in the least amount of violence
- Typically neither is violent outside the home nor engages in other criminal behaviors
- Does not show much psychopathology, and if a personality disorder is present, it would most likely be passive-dependent personality
- Does not report negative attitudes supportive of violence and has moderate impulse-control problems
- Typically displays no disturbance in attachment to his partner

The **dysphoric/borderline batterer**

Dysphoric/borderline batterer

A male spousal batterer who exhibits some violence outside the family, is depressed and has borderline personality traits, and has problems with jealousy

- Engages in moderate to severe violence
- Exhibits some extrafamilial violence and criminal behavior
- Of all types of batterers, displays the most depression and borderline personality traits, and has problems with jealousy
- Has moderate problems with impulsivity and alcohol and drug use
- Has an attachment style that would be best described as preoccupied

The **generally violent/antisocial batterer**

Generally violent/ antisocial batterer

A male spousal batterer who is violent outside the home, engages in other criminal acts, has drug and alcohol problems, has impulse-control problems, and possesses violence-supportive beliefs

- Engages in moderate to severe violence
- Of all types of batterers, engages in the most violence outside of the home and in criminal behavior
- Has antisocial and narcissistic personality features
- Likely has drug and alcohol problems
- Has high levels of impulse-control problems and many violence-supportive beliefs
- Shows a dismissive attachment style

Several studies have provided support for this typology both in offender and in community samples of male batterers (Tweed & Dutton, 1998; Waltz, Babcock, Jacobson, & Gottman, 2000).

CRIMINAL JUSTICE RESPONSE

Mandatory charging policies

Policies that give police the authority to lay charges against a suspect where there is reasonable and probable grounds to believe an intimate partner assault has occurred

For centuries, wife battering was seen as a private family matter and police were reluctant to become involved (Dobash & Dobash, 1979). When called to an intimate partner violence scene, police would attempt to calm the people involved and, once order was restored, they would leave (Jaffe, Hastings, Reitzel, & Austin, 1993). Since the 1980s, however, mandatory charging policies have been in effect in most jurisdictions in the United States. **Mandatory charging policies** give police the authority to lay charges against a suspect when there are reasonable and probable grounds to believe that an assault has occurred. Prior to mandatory charging, women were required to bring charges against their husbands. Women were often too intimidated to do so as they feared further violence; as a result, charges were usually not laid. Box 13.5 describes the case of Tracey Thurman, a battered woman whose case changed legislation.

The first experimental study to examine the specific deterrence effect of arrest on spousal violence was conducted by Sherman and Berk (1984) in Minneapolis. This study

BOX 13.5	Tracey Thurman: Calls for Help Ignored

Tracey Thurman, 22 years of age, made numerous pleas to the City of Torrington Police Department for help. Her estranged husband, Charles Thurman, had made several threats to kill her and their two-year old son, Charles, Jr. The police often failed to respond to her and other's calls for assistance and failed to arrest Charles Thurman for violating his restraining order. On June 10, 1983, Charles Thurman attempted to murder Tracey. Tracey Thurman suffered horrific injuries and sued the City of Torrington and 24 police officers for failing to provide her with adequate protection. In 1984 she won the lawsuit and was awarded almost $2 million in damages. This case was the impetus for changing legislation. In 1986 the state of Connecticut passed the Tracey Thurman Law, which requires police to arrest the abuser if they believe an assault has occurred. In 1989, Tracey Thurman's story was made into a TV movie *A Cry for Help: The Tracey Thurman Story.*

Below is a chronology of some key events:

October 1982: Tracey Thurman is attacked by Charles Thurman at the home of her friends. Her friends go to the police station and ask that Charles Thurman be kept off their property.

November 5, 1982: Charles Thurman, using physical force, removes his son from the place where Tracey Thurman is staying. Tracey Thurman and her friend go to the police station, but a police officer refuses to accept a complaint against Charles Thurman.

November 9, 1982: A police officer witnesses Charles Thurman scream threats at Tracey Thurman while she is sitting in her car. The police officer only arrests Charles Thurman after he breaks the windshield of Tracey's car.

November 10, 1982: Charles Thurman is convicted of breach of peace, given a suspended sentence of six months and a two-year conditional sentence, and is told to stay completely away from Tracey Thurman and her friend's house where she is living.

December 31, 1982: Charles Thurman goes to residence where Tracey Thurman is living and threatens to kill her. She calls the police but the police make no attempt to locate Charles Thurman or arrest him.

January 1 and May 4, 1983: Tracey Thurman makes repeated calls to the police about continued threats being made by Charles Thurman. She asks that Charles Thurman be arrested for these threats and for violating his conditional discharge. He is not arrested.

May 4, 1983: Tracey Thurman goes to the police department stating that Charles Thurman has threatened to shoot her. Tracey Thurman is told to return three weeks later on June 1, 1983.

May 6, 1983: Tracey Thurman files an application for a restraining order against Charles Thurman. Court orders Charles Thurman to stop harassing, threatening, and assaulting Tracey Thurman.

May 27, 1983: Tracey Thurman returns to Torrington Police Department requesting Charles Thurman be arrested. She is told she would have to wait until after the Memorial Day weekend.

May 31, 1983: Tracey Thurman returns to Torrington Police Department. She is told that the only officer who can help her is on vacation. Her brother-in-law calls the Torrington Police Department to complain about the lack of action with Tracey's complaints. He is told Charles Thurman would be arrested on June 8, 1983. Charles Thurman is not arrested.

June 10, 1983: Charles Thurman arrives at the residence where Tracey Thurman is staying, demanding to talk to her. Tracey Thurman calls the police. After waiting for 15 minutes, Tracey goes outside to talk to Charles Thurman. He attacks her and stabs her 13 times in the

(continued)

> ### BOX 13.5   Continued
>
> face, neck, shoulders, and chest. Twenty-five minutes after the call to police a lone officer arrives. He witnesses Charles Thurman standing beside Tracey Thurman holding a bloody knife. Upon seeing the police officer, Charles Thurman drops the knife, kicks Tracey in the head, and flees into the residence. Charles Thurman returns holding Charles, Jr., and drops the child on his mother's wounded body. Charles Thurman again kicks Tracey in the head. When three other officers arrive Charles Thurman is arrested.
>
> **1984:** Charles Thurman convicted and given a 20-year sentence. The sentence is reduced upon appeal to 14 years.
>
> **April 12, 1991:** Charles Thurman is released after serving 7 years of his 14-year sentence.
>
> **January 27, 2000:** Charles Thurman is given a one-year probation term for violating a restraining order against another woman. He had stopped beside his ex-girlfriend's car and waved at his son. The restraining order was given because Charles Thurman's ex-girlfriend reported he had forced her to have sex and threatened to kill her.
>
> *Source: Thurman v. City of Torrington,* http://cyber.law.harvard.edu/vaw00/thurmanexcerpt.html

involved the random assignment of 314 intimate partner assault calls to three police responses: separation (order for suspect to leave premises for at least eight hours), mediation (provide advice to victim), or arrest. A six-month follow-up of the men was conducted by using both police reports and victim reports. Figure 13.2 presents the recidivism rates across the groups for both police and victim reports. The recidivism rates for the arrested

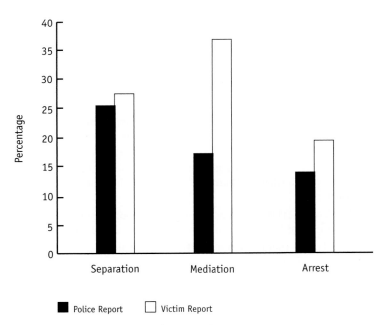

FIGURE 13.2   Rates of Recidivism for Different Police Responses

Source: Based on Sherman and Berk, 1984.

men were much lower than those of men in the separation or mediation groups. Attempts to replicate this finding have met with mixed results. Tolman and Weisz (1995) also found a deterrent effect for arrest, whereas Hirschell, Hutchison, and Dean (1992) did not. In an attempt to replicate their findings, Sherman, Schmidt, and Rogan (1992) randomly assigned police calls of intimate partner violence to nonarrest or arrest. Using police and victim reports, lower rates of recidivism were reported in the short term (30 days after police contact) for both arrest and nonarrest groups. However, in the long-term follow-up (seven to nine months after police contact) the arrest group had slightly higher rates of recidivism than did the nonarrest group. The authors found that arrest did not work for those offenders who were unemployed. In other words, arrest worked as a deterrent only for those men who had something to lose.

Do mandatory arrest policies increase the probability of intimate partner abusers being arrested? Arrest rates for intimate partner violence have increased dramatically since mandatory arrest policies were implemented. For example, in the 1970s and 1980s, arrest rates in Canada and the United States ranged from 7% to 15%, whereas more recent rates of 30% to 75% have been reported. However, one unanticipated outcome of these policies has been an increase in dual arrests (Hirschell & Buzawa, 2002). If the police are unable to determine the identity of the primary aggressor, and if there are minor injuries to both parties, then the police will charge both the man and woman.

Another consequence of the increase in the number of arrests for intimate partner assault has been the dramatic increase in the number of men who are court mandated to attend treatment. Because most batterers are not motivated to attend treatment programs, having judges impose a treatment order forces men to obtain treatment. If the man fails to attend treatment, then the judge can impose a prison term. The use of court-mandated treatment is based on the belief that it is possible to treat male batterers. However, the effectiveness of treatment for batterers is still very much in question.

EFFECTIVENESS OF TREATMENT OF MALE BATTERERS

A number of different procedures have been developed to treat male batterers. The two most common forms of intervention are feminist psychoeducational group therapy (also referred to as the Duluth model, since the treatment was designed at the Duluth Intimate Partner Abuse Intervention Project in Minnesota) and cognitive-behavioral group therapy. According to the Duluth model (Pence & Paymar, 1993), the primary cause of intimate partner violence is patriarchal ideology. Group therapy in this model focuses on challenging the man's perceived right to control his partner. The atmosphere in treatment often has a blaming, punitive orientation, which can result in very high drop-out rates (up to 75%).

The Duluth model has been criticized on several grounds. First, the entire focus is on violence done by men to women. This restricted gendered approach limits its usefulness for dealing with women's use of violence (which is common) against men, and women-to-women violence within same-sex relationships. Second, violence is viewed as one sided and not as an interaction between people. Much of violence in relationships is mutual. For the treatment to be effective, it cannot be only the man in these relationships who needs to change. Third, the focus of the Duluth model is on shaming the man, and therapists fail to establish a therapeutic bond with their clients. Finally, there is a limited focus on changing the man's attitudes about power and control in relationships. The cause of intimate partner violence is multi-determined and focusing solely on power and control is not sufficient to effect change. In a review of the effectiveness of the Duluth model, Dutton and Corvo (2006) concluded this model has "negligible success in reducing or eliminating violence among perpetrators" (p. 462).

The other, more common treatment program is cognitive-behavioral therapy, which subscribes to the beliefs that violence is a learned behavior and that use of violence is reinforcing for the offender because he or she obtains victim compliance and reduces feelings of tension (Sonkin, Martin, & Walker, 1985). Cognitive-behavioral therapy focuses on the costs of engaging in violence. Alternatives to violence are taught, such as anger management and communication skills training. Some cognitive-behavioral treatment programs also address perpetrators' attitudes about control and dominance. The rationale for using group therapy is to help to break through the barriers of denial and minimization.

Babcock, Green, and Robie (2004) conducted a meta-analysis of 22 studies to evaluate the efficacy of treatment for male batterers. Studies were included only if the outcome was measured by either police reports or partner reports of violence (i.e., studies using only batterer self-report were not included). Studies were also divided into three types of treatment: the Duluth model, cognitive-behavioral, and other (e.g., couples therapy). There were no differences in efficacy among the three treatment types in terms of recidivism rates. Based on partner reports, the effect size for quasi-experimental studies was $d = 0.34$ and for experimental studies it was $d = 0.09$. The authors conclude that "regardless of reporting method, study design, and type of treatment, the effect on recidivism rates remains in the small range" (p. 1044). Based on experimental studies and the use of partner reports, these results mean there is a 5% increase in success rate because of treatment. This small effect does not mean we should abandon attempts to treat batterers. As stated by the authors, "a 5% decrease in violence . . . in [the] United States . . . would equate to approximately 42,000 women per year no longer being battered" (p. 1044). Although the effects appear to be small, they are similar to treatment effects for alcohol abuse when abstinence from alcohol is the outcome (Agosti, 1995).

Recent research, however, is more optimistic about the promise of intimate partner violence treatment. Bennett, Stoops, Call, and Flett (2007) found that even when controlling for differences in the history of violence, personality, demographic variables, and motivation, men who completed treatment were less than half as likely to be rearrested for intimate partner violence than those who did not finish the intervention program. Bowen and Gilchrist (2006) identified participant characteristics that predict program attrition, including youthful age, having served a previous prison sentence, and self-reporting a low level of partner violence. The researchers recommended using these static factors to tailor intimate partner violence treatment and to prevent program attrition so that participants can benefit from treatment. In another study, Lee, Uken, and Sebold (2007) recommended the inclusion of more self-determined goals for offenders in treatment, based on their study of 88 male perpetrators of intimate partner violence participating in court-mandated treatment. They found that goal specificity and the facilitator's agreement with the participant's goals positively predicted offenders' confidence to achieve their goals, which in turn had a negative relationship with recidivism.

Future research should examine the treatment response of specific subsamples, such as types of batterers (e.g., family-only, borderline/dysphoric, and generally violent/antisocial), batterers with substance abuse problems, and batterers at different levels of motivation. As Saunders (2001) has asserted, "The best intervention outcomes for men who batter may be obtained when the type of offender is matched to the type of treatment"

(p. 237). Failure to match a batterer to treatment services may lead to a batterer completing a program that does not meet his or her specific treatment needs. Cavanaugh and Gelles (2005) point out that a victim could thus be led to having a "false sense of security, with the belief that she is now safer when, in fact, she is not" (p. 162). According to Gondolf and Fisher (1988), the variable most predictive of whether a woman will return to a violent partner after a shelter stay is if the batterer has sought treatment. In addition, future research needs to focus on women's use of violence and to develop interventions for intimate partner violent women. Review the case of Francine Hughes in the Case Study box and determine what factors were related to her staying in this abusive relationship.

CASE STUDY

YOU BE THE JUDGE

On March 9, 1977, 29-year-old Francine Hughes bundled her four children into the car and then walked back into the house. Moments later she rushed out to the car, crying hysterically as flames burst through the windows of the downstairs bedroom. Her ex-husband, Mickey Hughes, who was sleeping, died in the fire.

For 13 years, Francine had experienced regular beatings by Mickey. He had a violent temper and had repeatedly threatened Francine with death if she left him. Mickey drifted from job to job and often spent whatever money he had on alcohol. Mickey's first violent episode occurred within weeks of marrying Francine (she was 16 and he was 18 years old). He became upset over what she was wearing and ripped off her clothes. Mickey also engaged in animal abuse. He broke the neck of a kitten his daughter had brought into the house (he had earlier told her not to bring any animals into the house). He also refused to allow their pregnant dog in the house or to be taken to the vet. The dog died while having puppies.

On the day of the murder, Francine had come back from school and was confronted by an upset and intoxicated Mickey who demanded his dinner. Having no groceries in the house, she went shopping and returned with TV dinners. Mickey punched her repeatedly, claiming he did not like the smell of TV dinners. When Mickey started strangling her, she yelled out to her children who were locked out of the house to go next door and call the police. When the police arrived, Mickey had calmed down. The police asked Francine if they could take her somewhere but she declined. She felt she had nowhere to go and that Mickey would find her if she did leave.

The police left and Francine put the TV dinners in the oven. During dinner Mickey again became angry and told the children to go upstairs and not to come downstairs. He began to beat Francine again, with each blow telling her she would have to quit school. Finally Francine agreed and Mickey made her gather her school books and materials and burn them. He then demanded she bring him dinner in bed and have sex with him. He fell asleep in the downstairs bedroom. Francine released her children from their upstairs bedrooms and watched TV with them for a couple of hours. Later that evening she decided the time had come to finally do something about her situation—she decided to leave Mickey. She went to the basement and picked up a

(continued)

gasoline container. She reported she kept hearing a voice saying "Do it. Do it. Do it." She put her children into the car, went back into the house, and poured gasoline around the bed where Mickey lay sleeping. Francine then set the gasoline on fire. Her children told her to drive to the police station because that was where they could go to get help. She drove to the police station and told them that she had set fire to her house.

Francine was charged with first-degree murder and spent nine months in jail awaiting her murder trial. At her trial a jury of 10 women and two men heard how Mickey Hughes had battered his wife mercilessly for 13 years and had threatened her with death if she tried to leave him. Their verdict was a surprise to everyone—not guilty by reason of temporary insanity and Francine was released. This was the first time a battered woman who had killed her abuser successfully used this defense. Feminist groups were quick to use Francine Hughes as an example of how a battered woman has a right to self-defense against violence. Mickey Hughes' relatives, although acknowledging the violence, felt that Mickey needed help and that Francine had gotten away with murder.

Francine Hughes' life was made into a book and movie, *The Burning Bed*, and a song titled "The Ballad of Francine Hughes" by Lyn Hardy.

Why do you think Francine Hughes did not leave Mickey Hughes? What was the trigger for the homicide? What sort of sentence do you think she should have been given?

STALKING: DEFINITION, PREVALENCE, AND TYPOLOGIES

Awareness of stalking has increased dramatically during the past decade. Often, it has been the cases of celebrity stalking that have caught the attention of the media. However, celebrities aren't the only people who get stalked. Stalking can occur when an abusive relationship ends. All 50 states, the District of Columbia, and the U.S. territories have criminal laws to prohibit **stalking**, although the legal definition varies across jurisdictions. Some jurisdictions require the victim to feel fear and emotional distress, whereas others only require that a reasonable person would feel fear. In addition, jurisdictions vary on the threshold of fear required. In some jurisdictions, in order for the police to charge someone with stalking, the victim needed to fear serious bodily harm or death, whereas in other jurisdictions the victim needed to have suffered emotional distress.

Stalking

Crime that involves repeatedly following, communicating with, watching, or threatening a person directly or indirectly

The prevalence of stalking can be measured via official statistics or by victimization studies. Stalking arrests are very low and are nowhere near the number of actual stalking cases. In 2006, the National Crime Victimization Survey added a Supplemental Victimization Survey (SVS) to include stalking. A total of 65,270 respondents ages 18 years and older were surveyed. Stalking was defined as "a course of conduct directed at a specific person that would cause a reasonable person to feel fear" (Baum, Catalano, Rand, & Rose, 2009, p. 1). The prevalence of victims being harassed was also measured. *Harassment* included the same stalking behaviors experienced, but where the victim did not report being fearful. Table 13.2 summarizes the prevalence of different stalking behaviors for stalking and harassed victims.

Between 2005 and 2006, an estimated 3.4 million Americans ages 18 years and older were stalked. Women were more likely to be victims of stalking than men (women,

TABLE 13.2	Types of Stalking Behaviors Experienced by Victims	
Behaviors	Stalked Victims (%)	Harassed Victims (%)
Unwanted phone calls and messages	66	57
Spreading rumors	36	20
Following or spying	34	11
Showing up at places	31	10
Unwanted letters or emails	31	29
Waiting for victim	29	8
Leaving unwanted presents	12	5

Source: Based on Baum et al., 2009.

20 per 1,000, versus men, 7 per 1,000). Young women between the ages of 18 to 24 years old experience the highest stalking rates (Baum et al., 2009). The SVS also found that intimates were most likely to be stalked, with the highest rate (34 per 1,000) for divorced or separated victims. In about 1 in 10 cases the stalking went on for more than five years. In 21% of the stalking cases, the offender attacked the victim. Prevalence of stalking is more common in university students than the general public. Studies measuring stalking in students have found rates of between 9% and 30% for university females and between 11% and 17% for university males (Bjerregaard, 2002; Fremouw, Westrup, & Pennypacker, 1997). The prevalence rates vary depending on the definition of stalking used and the time period (e.g., last 12 months versus ever).

Most stalking victims know their stalkers. In a meta-analysis of 175 studies of stalking, Spitzberg and Cupach (2007) reported that 79% of stalking victims knew their stalker. The most common type of relationship was romantic (49%). According to the SVS, a female victim is most likely stalked by a male offender (67% of cases). Some researchers have suggested that more males are actually stalked by ex-intimates than the surveys indicated (Kropp, Hart, & Lyon, 2002). However, these men do not report they have been stalked since the behavior does not cause them to fear for their safety.

If you are a victim of stalking, you are often worried whether the stalker will assault you. A meta-analysis has attempted to discriminate between stalkers who represent a significant risk of violence and those who pose less of a risk (Rosenfeld, 2004). Rosenfeld analyzed 10 studies that included 1,055 stalking offenders. Violence occurred in 38.6% of the cases. The following variables were significantly related to violence:

- *Clinical variables.* Substance-abuse disorder, personality disorder, and the absence of a psychotic disorder predicted violence.
- *Case-related variables.* A former intimate relationship between offender and victim and threats toward the victim predicted violence.

Stalking offenders who are at the greatest risk for continuing stalking behavior after release from prison are those who have both a personality disorder and a history of substance abuse (Rosenfeld, 2004).

Imagine being in constant fear of what might happen to you. Stalking victims suffer intense stress, anxiety, sleep problems, and depression, as well as disruptions in social functioning and work. In the SVS, 29% of the victims reported they feared the stalking would never end. Overall, victims of stalking experience a decrease in the quality of their lives (Davis & Frieze, 2000; Fisher, Cullen, & Turner, 2002; Spitzberg & Cupach, 2007). McFarlane, Campbell, and Watson (2002) examined the prevalence and type of stalking behaviors 12 months prior to an attempted or actual murder or assault by an ex-partner. This study consisted of 821 women, of which 174 had survived an attempt on their lives by their intimate partners (attempted femicides), 263 had been killed by their intimate partners (actual femicides), and 384 had been physically abused or threatened with physical harm but no attempt on their lives had been made (controls). Stalking was more common in the attempted/actual femicide group (68%) than in the controls (51%). Women who were spied on or followed were twice as likely to become attempted or actual homicide victims. In addition, in cases in which threats of harm were made to children, if the woman did not return to the stalker, the likelihood of attempted or actual homicide increased by nine times. This study suggests that certain types of stalking behaviors are associated with increased risk of lethal violence and stalking victims and police need to be aware of these risk factors.

Stalking victims often change their behaviors to try to protect themselves. Victims in the SVS survey, for example, reported taking a number of countermeasures, including asking friends for assistance (43%), changing their day-to-day activities (22%), installing caller ID/call blocking (18%), getting pepper spray (6%), or getting a gun (3%). One in seven victims moved out of their home to try to avoid their stalker.

According to the SVS, 41% of the stalking victims contacted the police, with the most common police response being taking a report (55% of cases). In only 8% of cases were charges laid against the stalker. In a detailed study of 346 male stalkers arrested in Kentucky, only 20% were subsequently convicted (Jordan, Logan, Walker, & Nigoff, 2003). In contrast, much higher conviction rates are found in intimate partner violence arrests with 64% of those arrested being convicted (Garner & Maxwell, 2009).

Categories of stalkers have been developed to help to understand the causes of stalking. Several different typologies have been proposed with the types overlapping. Beatty, Hickey, and Sigmonet al. (2002) have proposed a four-type typology of stalkers. The four are (1) simple obsession stalkers, (2) love obsession stalkers, (3) erotomanic stalkers, and (4) vengeance stalkers. The case vignette described at the beginning of this chapter is an example of a love obsession stalker. See the In the Media box for an example of John Hinckley, who fits the profile of a love obsession stalker, and Margaret Ray, who fits the profile of an erotomanic stalker. An illustration of a vengeance stalker type is a student who receives a failing grade in a course and then begins to stalk and harass the professor.

Simple obsession stalker

A stalker who engages in stalking after the breakup of an intimate relationship

The **simple obsession stalker**

- Is the most common type and is usually a male
- Engages in stalking after the breakup of an intimate relationship where there is usually a prior history of intimate partner violence
- Targets his or her former intimate partner
- Is an individual who is disgruntled or estranged, and who is unable to let go of his or her partner
- Is an individual who desires reconciliation or revenge
- Is the type most likely to escalate to murder

The **love obsession stalker**

- Is a rare type
- Is an individual who has never had an intimate relationship with the victim
- Targets casual acquaintances, coworkers, or in some cases strangers including celebrities or politicians
- Has intense emotional feelings for the victim, and he or she hopes that the victim will develop feelings for him or her
- Has poor self-esteem and is often depressed

The **erotomanic stalker**

- Is a rare type
- Is an individual who has never had any relationship with the victim, but the stalker mistakenly believes that a relationship exists
- Often targets a celebrity, media figure, or politician
- Is often diagnosed with delusional disorders or schizophrenia

The **vengeance stalker**

- Is a rare type
- Is an individual who knows the victim, but has not had an intimate relationship with the victim
- Is not seeking an intimate relationship with the victim
- Is an angry individual seeking revenge for a perceived injustice
- Wants to frighten the victim

Love obsession stalker

A stalker who has intense emotional feelings for a victim but who has never had an intimate relationship with the victim

Erotomanic stalker

A stalker who suffers from delusions and who wrongly believes he/she has a relationship with a victim

Vengeance stalker

A stalker who knows the victim and is angry at the victim for some perceived injustice

---

IN THE MEDIA   **Dangerous Fixations: Celebrity Stalkers**

Although most stalking takes place in the context of ex-partners or prior acquaintances, it is the stalking of celebrities that catches the attention of the media. It was the stalking of celebrities that prompted several countries to introduce criminal code offenses. In 1990, California was the first state to introduce antistalking laws in the aftermath of the Rebecca Schaffer murder. Three high-profile cases of celebrity stalkers are described below.

Rebecca Schaffer

Born in 1967, Rebecca Schaffer was the only child of a clinical psychologist and a writer. She lived in Los Angeles and starred in the TV series *My Sister Sam*. In 1986, John Bardo (born in 1970) who was working as a fast-food cook living in Tucson, Arizona, developed an obsession with Schaffer and started sending her letters. She responded to these fan letters and sent him a response signed "with love Rebecca." In 1987, he travelled to Burbank Studios with a teddy bear and a bouquet of roses and demanded to see Schaffer. The security guards refused to allow him entrance. Bardo sent hundreds of letters to Schaffer and his bedroom was decorated with dozens of photos of her.

At the age of 21, Bardo saw Schaffer in the movie *Scenes from the Class Struggle in Beverly Hills* in which Schaffer was shown in a sex scene with a male actor. Bardo was extremely upset and asked his older brother to buy him a gun. Bardo sent his older sister a letter, which stated that if he could not have Rebecca no one could. In July 1989 he travelled to Hollywood and hired a private investigator to find out where Schaffer lived. On the morning of July 18,

(continued)

1989, he rang her doorbell. When she answered he told her he was her biggest fan. She asked him to leave. He returned an hour later and shot her twice, killing her. Bardo was convicted of capital murder and was sentenced to life without eligibility of parole. He is currently serving his sentence at a maximum-security prison in California. On July 27, 2007, Bardo was stabbed 11 times by another inmate but survived.

David Letterman

Margaret Ray (born 1958) developed an obsession with David Letterman in the mid-1980s after the breakup of her marriage. Ray was diagnosed with schizophrenia. She was first arrested in 1988 when she stole Letterman's Porsche and was caught driving it with her three-year-old son. She told the police that she was Letterman's wife and the child was Letterman's son. During the next few years she repeatedly showed up at Letterman's house, leaving letters, books, and cookies. She was charged with trespassing eight times. In the early 1990s, she served a 10-month prison sentence for harassing Letterman. After her release, she shifted her obsession to astronaut Story Musgrave. In 1998, Ray committed suicide by kneeling in front of a train. Both Letterman and Musgrave expressed sympathy upon her death.

Jodie Foster

In 1976, John Hinckley (born 1955) watched the movie *Taxi Drive* in which Jodie Foster played a child prostitute. Hinckley became obsessed with Foster. When Foster when to Yale University, Hinckley followed her there, called her, and left messages and poems in her mailbox. These attempts failed to get Foster to notice him. Hinckley then planned to get Foster's attention by assassinating the president of the United States. He spent a couple of months trailing President Carter but was stopped at Nashville Airport for carrying handguns in his luggage. He was fined and released. On March 30, 1981, he fired six shots at President Ronald Reagan, injuring him and three others. Just prior to the shooting, he sent a letter to Foster stating:

"As you well know by now I love you very much. Over the past seven months I've left you dozens of poems, letters and love messages in the faint hope that you could develop an interest in me. Although we talked on the phone a couple of times I never had the nerve to simply approach you and introduce myself . . . the reason I'm going ahead with this attempt now is because I cannot wait any longer to impress you."

Hinckley was found not guilty by reason of insanity and was sent to a secure forensic psychiatric hospital. In 1999, he was allowed supervised visits to his parents' house. However, in 2004, these visits were temporarily halted because he smuggled materials about Foster back into the hospital. In 2009, he was allowed to visit his mother for nine days at a time.

Summary

1. The prevalence rates of intimate partner violence are difficult to estimate accurately since the violence often occurs in private. Intimate partner violence can be classified into the following types: physical abuse, sexual abuse, financial abuse, and emotional abuse.

2. Abused women remain in, or return to, abusive relationships for a number of reasons. Environmental, socialization, and psychological barriers exist that make it difficult for abused women to leave these relationships.

3. Social learning theory has been used to explain intimate partner violence. The three main components of social learning theory are origins of aggression, instigators of aggression, and regulators of aggression. One way people acquire new behaviors is via observational learning. Instigators are events in the environment that act as stimuli for the behavior, and behavior is regulated by the prospect of its consequences. Behaviors that are rewarded increase in frequency, and behaviors that are punished decrease in frequency.

4. Holtzworth-Munroe and Stuart (1994) divided male batterers into three types based on severity of violence, generality of violence, and personality disorder characteristics: family-only, dysphoric/borderline, and generally violent/antisocial.

5. Treatment for intimate partner violent offenders involves modifying attitudes that condone violence; enhancing conflict resolution skills; learning to manage emotions; and developing relapse-prevention plans. The effectiveness of treatment programs for male batterers varies, with some cognitive-behavioral treatment programs showing promising results.

6. Research on stalking has found (a) most stalkers know their victims; (b) males are more likely to be stalkers and females are more likely to be victims; (c) spying, following, and making threats of violence are related to an increased risk for lethal violence; and (d) the most common type is the simple obsession stalker.

Key Concepts

domestic violence *305*
dysphoric/borderline batterer *316*
erotomanic stalker *325*
family-only batterer *316*
generally violent/antisocial
    batterer *316*

instigators *311*
intimate partner violence *305*
love obsession stalker *325*
mandatory charging policies *316*
observational learning *311*
patriarchy *310*

regulators *311*
simple obsession stalker *324*
social learning theory *310*
stalking *322*
vengeance stalker *325*

Discussion Questions

1. What are the barriers to some battered women leaving an abusive relationship? What could be done at both an individual and a societal level to help battered women?

2. You are having a discussion with your friends about dating-related violence and one of them states that women engage solely in self-defense violence. Describe the data that call your friend's statement into question.

3. You are interested in doing a study on the association between animal abuse and intimate partner violence. Describe the methodology you would use and what variables you would measure.

4. Your friend has recently broken up with her boyfriend. She tells you that her boyfriend falsely accused her of cheating on him and had become very controlling. She left her boyfriend after he had punched her for failing to call him when he told her to. She tells you that he has been sending her repeated e-mail messages and calling her cell phone daily. What advice can you give her?

Sexual and Homicidal Offenders

LEARNING OBJECTIVES

- List the different typologies of rapists and child molesters.
- Outline the treatment targets for sexual offenders.
- Describe the effectiveness of treatment for sexual offenders.
- Describe the characteristics of homicide in the United States.
- Differentiate between instrumental and reactive violence.
- Describe different types of murderers.

Trevor Cook was 26 years old when the police finally caught up with him. For years he had been terrorizing women in the city where he lived. Known as a womanizer throughout his teenage years and a conman who was always trying to make a quick buck, the first of Trevor's crimes could be traced back to when he was 16 years old. He had just started dating a 17-year-old girl and they were sexually active. One night, the girlfriend wasn't feeling well and denied his sexual advances. Upset at being rejected, Trevor pushed his girlfriend onto the bed and held her down as he forced her to have intercourse. Similar incidents occurred with several other girlfriends and Trevor's behavior toward women quickly became more parasitic and aggressive. He would regularly steal money from his girlfriends, he would frequently cheat on them, and he was emotionally and verbally abusive toward them. By the time he was in his early 20s, Trevor's behavior had escalated to the point where he was committing sexual assaults against women he met while at bars. He would spot a young woman at a bar that he thought was attractive and would follow her home. The first few times Trevor attacked women, he would put on a ski mask, fondle the woman, and run away. However, that didn't satisfy him for long and when he was 23 years old Trevor raped and beat one of the women he followed home in a back alley outside of her house. He would commit many more rapes that year, with each rape being more vicious than the previous one. Trevor's crimes ended when one of his victims finally got away before he could attack her. This woman had ripped Trevor's ski mask off him and had gotten a good look at his face. The description she gave to the police ultimately led to his arrest.

The police had been searching for Trevor for more than five years. By the time he was arrested at the age of 27, Trevor had raped 12 women. Given the escalation of his behavior, the police were confident that Trevor would have eventually gone on to kill.

V iolence of the sort displayed by Trevor in the opening vignette has a major impact on victims and society. The victims of such crimes can be scarred for life and the family members of these victims often fare no better. In addition, the media often focuses on violent crimes and as a consequence, violence is often on the minds of the American public. Indeed, when pollsters ask the public about the concerns they have, fear of violent crime is a common response (Warr, 2000). Given this response, it is perhaps unsurprising that violent crime is also talked about a lot by politicians. It is rare for politicians not to play the crime card in an attempt to get elected, and once elected, much energy is invested by politicians in showing the country how they are dealing with the violent crime problem.

Violence and its aftermath are major focuses of forensic psychology. For example, many forensic psychologists are involved in developing theories to explain why people become violent, they conduct research to understand the nature of this violence, they develop procedures to assess violent offenders, and they implement intervention programs to rehabilitate these offenders. This chapter discusses some of this work. In the first part of the chapter we cover some of these issues with respect to sexual violence; in the second part of the chapter we examine acts of homicide.

SEXUAL OFFENDERS

Nature and Extent of Sexual Violence

In 2009, just over 88,000 forcible rapes were reported to the police in the United States (U.S. Department of Justice, 2011a). The rate per 100,000 population was 28.7, which represents a slight drop compared to previous years (e.g., the rate 10 years earlier was 32.8 per 100,000). However, official statistics do not necessarily provide an accurate measure of the true incidence of rape, or for sexual assaults more generally, because the majority of people who are victimized by sex offenders do not report the crime to the police (Kilpatrick, 2000; Yurchesyn, Keith, & Renner, 1992). For example, in one report it was estimated that only 36% of completed rapes, 34% of attempted rapes, and 26% of sexual assault cases are reported to the police (Rennison, 2002). The major reasons for not reporting sexual offenses include the fact that victims often don't feel that the matter is important enough, they believe the matter has already been dealt with, they feel the matter is too personal, or they simply don't want to involve the police (Brennan & Taylor-Butts, 2008; Kilpatrick, Edmunds, & Seymour, 1992).

In contrast to what is revealed by official police statistics, when people are asked whether they have been a victim of sexual assault it becomes clear that sexual assault does in fact affect a large percentage of the U.S. population. For example, high victimization rates are reported among children and youth in the United States (roughly 1 in 12; Finkelhor, Ormrod, Turner, & Hamby, 2005) and among adult women (roughly 1 in 6 report being raped at some time in their lives; Tjaden & Thoennes, 2006). Community-based self-report surveys, which look at offending behavior, also indicate the seriousness of the problem. For example, in studies of community samples (e.g., university students) in which respondents are assured there will be no negative consequences of reporting, 10% to 20% of men admit to sexually assaulting women or children at some point in their past (Hanson & Scott, 1995; Lisak & Roth, 1988).

Given these statistics, it is not surprising that sexual offenders admit to having many victims. For example, Abel, Becker, Mittelman, and Cunningham-Rathner (1987) investigated the number of victims reported by 127 rapists, 224 female-victim child molesters, and 153 male-victim child molesters. High victim rates were reported, with rapists having on average 7 victims, female-victim child molesters having 20 victims, and male-victim child molesters averaging 150 victims!

Definition of Sexual Violence

In the United States, the definitions of rape and sexual assault have undergone substantial change during the past four decades. Historically, rape was defined as carnal knowledge of a woman (not one's wife) gained by force or against her will. This definition was refined in 1962 such that "A man who has sexual intercourse with a female not his wife is guilty of rape if . . . he compels her to submit by force or threat of force or threat of imminent death, serious bodily injury, extreme pain, or kidnapping" (Epstein & Langenbahn, 1994, p. 7). During the 1970s, many other reforms occurred, including the rape shield laws that protect victims of rape by not allowing the victim's past relationships or any history of promiscuity to be used in court (Orenstein, 2007). Criticisms of narrow definitions of rape, such as those that do not allow for a spouse to be charged with rape (Bergen, 2006), have led to further reforms.

At present, the definitions of sexual assault, rape, and child molestation can differ slightly from state to state because each state contains its own criminal code. For example, while some states hold the terms "sexual assault" and "rape" to be synonymous, others differentiate between them. Currently, the United States Federal Code splits sexual assault into two categories: sexual abuse and aggravated sexual abuse (see Legal Information Institute, 2012a). The definitions of these crimes include gender neutral language, do not use the term "rape," and differentiate abuse depending on the type of abuse and the degree of force or threat of force used (Title 18, Chapter 109A, Sections 2241-2248). Under the Federal Code, "aggravated sexual abuse" replaces what was once referred to as "forcible rape," though that term is still sometimes used. Chapter 109A also includes the sexual abuse of minors [Sections 2241(c); 2243]. If found guilty of sexual abuse in the United States, possible sentencing penalties differ from state to state and are determined by the jurisdiction where the crime(s) occurred.

Consequences for Victims of Sexual Violence

Sexual aggression has serious psychological and physical consequences for victims. For example, child victims of sexual abuse develop a wide range of short- and long-term problems. In the year following disclosure of the abuse, up to 70% of children experience significant psychological symptoms. Longer-term problems include substance abuse, depression, eating disorders, and prostitution (Hanson, 1990). Victims of rape also report high levels of stress and fear that often disrupt social, sexual, and occupational functioning, while also generating high levels of anxiety and depression (Hanson, 1990). Physically, Koss (1993) reports that up to 30% of rape victims contract sexually transmitted diseases, and pregnancy results in about 5% of cases. Psychologically, a wide range of negative consequences have been reported, as discussed below.

In 1974, Burgess and Holmstrom first proposed the term **rape trauma syndrome** to describe the psychological aftereffects of rape. Burgess and Holmstrom interviewed 92 women who had been raped. The first interview took place within 30 minutes of the women's arrival at the hospital and the second interview took place one month later. The effects of rape identified by the researchers were divided into two phases: an acute crisis phase and a long-term reactions phase.

According to Burgess and Holmstrom (1974), the acute crisis phase lasts for a few days to several weeks and the symptoms are often quite severe. These symptoms can include very high levels of fear, anxiety, and depression. Victims of rape also often ask questions about why the rape happened to them and commonly engage in self-blame (Janoff-Bulman, 1979), which is perhaps unsurprising given the common myth that rape victims sometimes "ask for it" by the way they dress or act (see Box 14.1 for a discussion of other rape myths). The long-term reactions phase is more protracted, lasting anywhere from a few months to several years. One-quarter of women who have been raped do not significantly recover, even after several years (Resick, 1993). Long-term reactions include the development of phobias, such as the fear of being left alone or the fear of leaving the house. Other long-term reactions include the development of sexual problems and depression (Burgess & Holmstrom, 1974).

The psychological consequences of rape victimization can also include **post-traumatic stress disorder** (PTSD). The *DSM-IV* defines PTSD as an anxiety disorder that can develop in response to exposure to an extremely traumatic event (American Psychiatric Association, 1994). PTSD symptoms include frequent, distressing, and intrusive memories of the event, avoiding stimuli associated with the traumatic event, and persistent anxiety or increased arousal symptoms. Rothbaum, Foa, Riggs, Murdock, and Walsh (1992) assessed the PTSD symptoms in 95 female rape victims over a nine-month follow-up period. One month after the rape, 65% of victims were diagnosed with PTSD and at nine months 47% were classified as having PTSD. Some victims continue to experience PTSD symptoms years after the rape. In one study, 16.5% of rape victims had PTSD 15 years after the rape (Kilpatrick, Saunders, Veronen, Best, & Von, 1987). Thankfully, effective treatment programs have been developed to help rape victims overcome the emotional suffering caused by this trauma (Foa & Rothbaum, 1998).

Classification of Sexual Offenders

Sexual offenders are usually divided into categories based on the type of sexually deviant behavior they exhibit, the relationship between victim and offender, and the age of the victim. **Voyeurs** obtain sexual gratification by observing unsuspecting people, usually strangers, who are either naked, in the process of undressing, or engaging in sexual activity. **Exhibitionists** obtain sexual gratification by exposing their genitals to strangers. These two types of sexual offenders are sometimes referred to as hands-off or no-contact sexual offenders. **Rapists** are offenders who sexually assault victims who are not considered children. The term *pedophilia* means "love of children." Thus, the term **pedophile** is often used to refer to an adult whose primary sexual orientation is toward children. Other researchers use the term **child molester** to refer to individuals who have actually

Rape trauma syndrome

A group of symptoms or behaviors that are frequent aftereffects of having been raped

Post-traumatic stress disorder

Anxiety disorder that can develop in response to exposure to an extremely traumatic event. Symptoms include frequent, distressing, and intrusive memories of the event, avoiding stimuli associated with the traumatic event, and persistent anxiety or increased arousal symptoms

Voyeur

People who obtain sexual gratification by observing unsuspecting people, usually strangers, who are either naked, in the process of undressing, or engaging in sexual activity

Exhibitionist

Someone who obtains sexual gratification by exposing his or her genitals to strangers

Rapist

Person who sexually assaults victims who are not considered children

Pedophile

Person whose primary sexual orientation is toward children

Child molester

Someone who has sexually molested a child

| BOX 14.1 | Sexual Assault: Discounting Rape Myths |

Rape myths are stereotypic ideas people have about rape (Burt, 1980). Rape myths appear to be accepted across many levels of society (Gylys & McNamara, 1996; Kershner, 1996; Szymanski, Devlin, Chrisler, & Vyse, 1993), though men appear to be more accepting of rape myths than are women (Bohner et al., 1998). Many myths are associated with sexual assault or rape. Here is a list of myths associated with sexual assault or rape, followed by facts that challenge these false beliefs:

Myth 1: Sexual assault is not a common problem.

Statistics suggest that one in every four women and one in every six men have experienced some type of sexual assault. You likely know someone who has been sexually assaulted.

Myth 2: Sexual assault is most often committed by strangers.

Women face the greatest risk of sexual assault from men they know, not from strangers. About half of all rapes occur in dating relationships. In about 80% of cases, victims of sexual assault know the attacker.

Myth 3: Women who are sexually assaulted "ask for it" by the way they dress or act.

Victims of sexual assault range across the age span (from infants to elderly) and sexual assaults can occur in almost any situation. No woman "deserves" to be sexually assaulted regardless of what she wears, where she goes, or how she acts. Blaming sexual assault on how a victim behaves would be like blaming a mugging on a person for carrying a wallet.

Myth 4: Avoid being alone in dark, deserted places, such as parks or parking lots, and this will protect you from being sexually assaulted.

Most sexual assaults occur in a private home and many in the victim's home.

Myth 5: Women derive pleasure from being a victim.

Sexual assault is associated with both short- and long-term serious problems. High rates of anxiety, fear, depression, and post-traumatic stress disorder are seen in survivors of sexual assault. Some women are physically injured during an assault.

Myth 6: Women lie about sexual assault.

False accusations happen, but are very rare. Sexual assault is a vastly underreported crime and most sexual assaults are not reported to the police.

Intra-familial child molesters

People who sexually abuse their own biological children or children for whom they assume a parental role, such as a stepfather or live-in boyfriend. Also known as incest offenders

Extra-familial child molester

Someone who sexually abuses children not related to them

sexually molested a child. Child molesters are often divided into two types: intra-familial and extra-familial. **Intra-familial child molesters** (also called incest offenders) are those who sexually abuse their own biological children or children for whom they assume a parental role, such as a stepfather. **Extra-familial child molesters** sexually abuse children outside the family.

BOX 14.2	Is Resisting a Sexual Attack a Good Idea?

One question often posed by women is "If attacked, should I fight back or not?" Responses to this answer are common and websites abound where advice is given to women so that they can prevent themselves from being victimized. Unfortunately, the answer to the question is complicated. For example, based on the sex offender typologies described in this chapter, the answer to the question will likely depend on the type of offender under consideration.

Research with incarcerated rapists indicates that they search for vulnerable victims in certain areas and attack women they believe cannot or will not resist the attack (Stevens, 1994). That being said, some studies of women who were raped or who avoided being raped have found that forceful verbal resistance, physical resistance, and fleeing are all associated with rape avoidance (Ullman & Knight, 1993; Zoucha-Jensen & Coyne, 1993), whereas nonresistance strategies (e.g., pleading with rapists, crying, reasoning) are not.

However, the association between victim injury and resistance is inconclusive. For example, Zoucha-Jensen and Coyne (1993) found no association between victim resistance and injury. In contrast, Ullman and Knight (1993) found that if the offender had a weapon, women who resisted the rape suffered more physical injury than those who did not resist.

In a review of universities' sexual assault prevention programs, Söchting, Fairbrother, and Koch (2004) conclude that the most promising prevention program is teaching self-defense skills. This strategy is also one that is recommended by many of the agencies in the United States who provide advice to women on how to better protect themselves against rapists.

RAPIST TYPOLOGIES   As discussed in Box 14.2, it is important to understand that rapists are not part of a homogeneous group and do not all engage in sexual assault for the same reasons. Several different rapist typologies have been proposed, primarily based on research with male offenders. One of the most commonly used typologies came out of an ambitious project during the 1990s that was undertaken at the Massachusetts Treatment Center by Raymond Knight and Robert Prentky (see Box 14.3 for a profile of Dr. Knight). Their goal was to develop and empirically validate a typology for rapists. The resulting classification system, what is now referred to as the *Massachusetts Treatment Center Rapist Typology, Version 3* (MTC: R3; Knight & Prentky, 1990), consists of five primary subtypes of rapists based on motivational differences:

1. The opportunistic type commits sexual assault that is generally impulsive, void of sexual fantasies, controlled primarily by situational or contextual factors, and void of gratuitous violence. These offenders often engage in other criminal behaviors. For example, a rapist who breaks into a home with the intention of stealing, but who rapes the female occupant could be classified as opportunistic.

2. The pervasively angry type has a high level of anger that is directed toward both men and women. These offenders tend to be impulsive, use unnecessary force, cause serious victim injury, and are void of sexual fantasies.

3. The sexual type is distinguished from the other types in that these offenders' crimes are primarily motivated by sexual preoccupation or sexual fantasies.

4. The sadistic type is differentiated from the sexual type in that there must be a sadistic element to the offense.

5. The fifth type is labeled vindictive. In contrast to the pervasively angry type, the vindictive rapist's anger is focused solely on women. These offenders are not impulsive, nor are they preoccupied by sexual fantasies. The goal of this type of rapist is to demean and degrade the victim.

BOX 14.3   Researcher Profile: Dr. Raymond Knight

As a Ph.D. student in the Department of Psychology at the University of Minnesota in the late 1960s and early 1970s, Dr. Raymond Knight was exposed to all sorts of interesting ideas. Few universities at the time could teach students the intricacies of experimental psychology, while also training them in a wide range of psychotherapeutic orientations, but Minnesota was such a place. Being a student at the University of Minnesota also meant that Dr. Knight was exposed to many influential psychologists, such as the late Dr. Paul Meehl, who Dr. Knight describes as his early hero.

Dr. Raymond Knight

Paul Meehl taught Dr. Knight one of the most important lessons that any psychology student can be taught: the importance of developing carefully thought-out theoretical models to explain the phenomenon of interest and the need to ruthlessly challenge these models in an attempt to disconfirm them. As Dr. Knight's stellar career has shown, this approach to conducting psychological research often leads to important, replicable discoveries.

Describing himself as an empiricist, Dr. Knight lives by the motto that, whether a researcher or a clinician, one must always follow the data. And this is what he has done throughout his long career at Brandeis University, first in his early research examining the cognitive deficiencies of those suffering from schizophrenia, and later in his investigations of sexual aggression and psychopathy. Together with his students and colleagues, Dr. Knight has made many important discoveries in each of these domains, including the development (with Robert Prentky) of the *Massachusetts Rapist Typology*, which is described in your textbook.

Currently, Dr. Knight is conducting research in a number of different areas, beyond the classification of sexually coercive males. These include the etiology and prognosis of psychopathology among sex offenders and patients with schizophrenia, and the continued development of the *Multidimensional Inventory of Development, Sex, and Aggression* (MIDSA). The MIDSA is a computerized inventory that allows researchers to assess multiple aspects of sexual aggression and identify multiple targets of intervention that are relevant to sexual offending. In contrast to the "one size fits all" approach that characterizes many treatment programs, the MIDSA will allow treatment to be individualized, which, according to Dr. Knight is crucial given the heterogeneous nature of sexual offenders.

Given the nature of what Dr. Knight studies, many of the cases that Dr. Knight has worked on over the years have been disturbing. So, what keeps him interested in studying sexual aggression? To him, the answer is easy: not only does he enjoy working with his colleagues and students, he also views the problems that he's tackling as complex and fascinating. Dr. Knight believes that researchers in this area are making serious headway in addressing many of the problems he studies and this is extremely gratifying to him, both intellectually and because of the positive consequences the research can have for society and public safety.

Currently Dr. Knight is the Mortimer Gryzmish Professor of Human Relations at Brandeis University and he is a past president of the Society for Research in Psychopathology and the Association for the Treatment of Sexual Abusers. A self-declared optimist when it comes to the effectiveness of treatment for sex offenders, and a brilliant and committed researcher, Dr. Knight will no doubt make many more important discoveries as he continues to "follow the data" in his attempt to better understand sexual aggression and how best to treat it.

Source: Carich, 2007.

The opportunistic, sexual, and vindictive subtypes are further subdivided based on their level of social competence. The sadistic type is also further subdivided into overt or muted sadists based on the presence or absence of gratuitous violence (Knight & Prentky, 1990). Research using the MTC: R3 has found that these types differ on prevalence of psychopathy (Barbaree, Seto, Serin, Amos, & Preston, 1994; Brown & Forth, 1997), rates of sexual recidivism (Knight, Prentky, & Cerce, 1994), and treatment needs (Knight, 1999). Knight and Guay (2006) describe a restructuring of the MTC: R3 in which the muted sadistic type of sexual offender has been dropped since the existence of this type of sexual offender has not been supported by research.

Another typology that uses motivations to classify rapists was proposed by Groth (1979). Groth suggested that rapists can be divided into three main types: anger rapists, power rapists, and sadistic rapists.

The features of the **anger rapist** include:

- The use of more force than necessary to obtain compliance and engagement in a variety of sexual acts to degrade the victim
- High levels of anger directed solely toward women
- Not being motivated primarily by sexual gratification

Most of these rapes are precipitated by conflict or perceived humiliation by some significant woman, such as the offender's wife, mother, or boss. Approximately 50% of rapists fit this type.

The features of the **power rapist** include:

- The intention to assert dominance and control over the victim
- Variation in the amount of force used depending on the degree of submission shown by the victim
- Not being motivated primarily by sexual gratification
- Frequent rape fantasies

About 40% of rapists fit into this category.

The features of the **sadistic rapist** include:

- Obtaining sexual gratification by hurting the victim
- High levels of victim injury, including torture and sometimes death
- Frequent violent sexual fantasies

Approximately 5% of rapists fit this type.

There is considerable overlap between the MTC: R3 and Groth's typology. For example, both typologies describe a sadistic rapist. The vindictive rapist is similar to the anger rapist and the pervasively angry rapist shares some of the features of the power rapist.

CHILD MOLESTER TYPOLOGIES With respect to child molesters, the most widely used typology is Groth et al.'s typology of the fixated and regressed child molester (Groth, Hobson, & Gary, 1982). Groth developed his typology based on research with incarcerated child molesters.

Fixated child molesters tend to have the following features:

- Their primary sexual orientation is toward children and they have little or no sexual contact with adults.
- Their sexual interest in children begins in adolescence and is persistent.

Anger rapist

A rapist, as defined by Groth, who uses more force than necessary to obtain compliance from the victim and who engages in a variety of sexual acts to degrade the victim

Power rapist

A rapist, as defined by Groth, who seeks to establish dominance and control over the victim

Sadistic rapist

A rapist, as defined by Groth, who obtains sexual gratification by hurting the victim

Fixated child molester

A child molester, as defined by Groth and his colleagues, who has a long-standing, exclusive sexual orientation preference for children

- Male children are their primary targets.
- Precipitating stress is not evident.
- Their offenses are planned.
- They are emotionally immature, have poor social skills, and are usually single.
- They usually have no history of alcohol or drug abuse.
- They often feel no remorse or distress over their behavior.

Regressed child molester

A child molester, as defined by Groth and his colleagues, whose primary sexual orientation is toward adults, but whose sexual interests revert to children after a stressful event or due to feelings of inadequacy

Regressed child molesters usually have the following characteristics:

- Their primary sexual orientation is toward adults.
- Their sexual interest in children begins in adulthood and is episodic.
- Female children are their primary targets.
- Precipitating stress and feelings of inadequacy are usually present.
- Their offenses are more impulsive.
- They are often married and are having marital problems.
- Many of their offenses are related to alcohol use.
- They are more likely to report feeling remorse for their behavior.

Groth also subdivided child molesters into two types based on the type of coercion they used. The *sex-pressure* child molester uses persuasion or entrapment to make the child feel obligated to participate in sexual acts. For example, this type of child molester may buy the child gifts or take the child on fun outings. The *sex-force* child molester threatens or uses physical force to overcome any resistance by the child. This latter group has been divided into the exploitative type who uses the threat of force to obtain compliance and the sadistic type who obtains gratification from hurting a child. The sadistic type of child molester is, fortunately, very rare.

Adolescent Sexual Offenders

Prior to the 1980s, sexually aggressive behavior by adolescents was not deemed serious and was discounted by some as normal experimentation. However, crime reports and victimization surveys indicate that a large number of sexual offenses are committed by adolescents. For example, about 20% of rapes and between 30% and 50% of child sexual abuse appear to be committed by adolescents (Davis & Leitenberg, 1987).

Like their adult counterparts, adolescent sexual offenders consistently report having been victims of sexual abuse themselves. The prevalence rate for sexual abuse committed against adolescent sexual offenders ranges from about 40% to 80% (Friedrich & Luecke, 1988; Ryan, Miyoshi, Metzner, Krugman, & Fryer, 1996). However, although early sexual victimization and later sexual offending are related, the majority of sexually abused children do not go on to become adolescent or adult sexual offenders and prior history of childhood sexual victimization is not related to sexual recidivism in samples of adult sexual offenders (Hanson & Bussière, 1998) or samples of adolescent sexual offenders (Worling & Curwen, 2000). Clearly, being the victim of sexual abuse is only one factor that affects later sexual offending. Rasmussen, Burton, and Christopherson (1992) suggest that in addition to sexual abuse, other factors such as social inadequacy, lack of intimacy, and impulsiveness also play a role.

In a national sample of 1,616 adolescent sex offenders undergoing treatment, Ryan et al. (1996) investigated offender, victim, and offense characteristics and found many interesting trends. For example, the age of sex offenders in their sample ranged from

5 to 21 years, with the majority being between 10 and 18. Male offenders were much more common than female offenders, comprising 97.4% of the overall sample. Traumatic experiences were common in the backgrounds of the youths, with an estimated 41.8% of the youths experiencing physical abuse and 39.1% experiencing sexual abuse. The majority of the youths (63%) had committed other nonsexual offenses. In terms of their sexual offenses, the offenders tended to sexually abuse young female victims. In fact, the researchers found that 63% of the adolescent sexual offenders' victims were younger than age nine. The victims were frequently known to their offenders and the offenses were characterized by a wide range of sexually abusive behavior.

Female Sexual Offenders

Research on female sexual offenders is severely limited. This lack of attention is probably because relatively few incarcerated sex offenders are female. However, some researchers have suggested that sexual abuse of children by women is more prevalent than previously believed.

The rates of sexual abuse by females vary dramatically depending on the definition used and there is certainly debate about what should, and should not, be considered abuse. For example, should a female be classified as a sexual abuser if she knew that her husband was sexually abusing their child and did nothing to stop the abuse? Does a mother sleeping with her child constitute sexual abuse in the absence of sexual touching? What if the child is a teenager who becomes sexually aroused by sleeping with his mother? Most people would agree that it is sexual abuse for a 20-year-old woman to have sexual contact with an 8-year-old boy, but not if the boy is 16. But what if the boy is 14? If the 14-year-old boy initiates the sexual act and views it positively, should this be classified as sexual abuse?

Retrospective surveys of university students have found that a large percentage of sex assault perpetrators are in fact female. For example, Fritz, Stoll, and Wagner (1981) reported that of the 5% of college men who report being molested as children, 60% say they were molested by females, most being older female adolescents. In a large survey of 2,972 university students that used broad criteria for sexual abuse, Risin and Koss (1987) reported that 7.3% were abused. They found that almost half of the perpetrators were female (43%), and of these, almost half were female adolescent babysitters. Similar to other studies, about half of the male respondents reported that they participated in the sexual acts voluntarily and did not feel victimized. In contrast to these studies, fewer female perpetrators have been reported by other researchers (Finkelhor, 1984; Reinhart, 1987). For example, Finkelhor found that only 6% of university women and 16% of university men who reported childhood sexual abuse indicated that the offender was a woman.

Some researchers have speculated that the rate of sexual abuse by females is underestimated. Some potential reasons for this underreporting include the following (Banning, 1989; Groth, 1979):

- Women are able to mask their sexually abusive behaviors through caregiving activities and thus are more difficult to recognize.
- Female sex offenders are more likely to target their own children, who are less likely to disclose the abuse.
- Boys are more frequent targets than girls, and boys are less likely to disclose abuse.

Research designed to determine the characteristics of female sexual offenders has generally been plagued with very small sample sizes. Whether the findings will generalize to larger samples of female sexual offenders remains to be investigated. Keeping this limitation in mind, Atkinson (1996) suggests there are four types of female sexual offenders:

1. *Teacher/lover.* These offenders initiate sexual abuse of a male adolescent that they relate to as a peer. The offender is often in a position of authority or power. It is unknown how common this type of female sex offender is because the victim rarely reports the abuse to authorities. This type of offender has not likely experienced childhood sexual abuse, although substance-use problems are common. These offenders often are not aware that their behavior is inappropriate. Teacher/lovers often describe themselves as being "in love" with the victim. Victims often report that they participated voluntarily and do not feel victimized.

2. *Male-coerced.* These offenders are coerced or forced into sexual abuse by an abusive male. Often the victim is the female offender's own daughter. These offenders are unassertive, dependent on men, and are relatively passive partners in the abuse.

3. *Male-accompanied.* These offenders also engage in sexual abuse with a male partner. However, they are more willing participants than are the male-coerced type. Victims are both inside and outside the family.

4. *Predisposed.* This offender initiates the sexual abuse alone. She has often experienced severe and persistent childhood sexual abuse and has been a victim of intimate violence. This type of offender often reports having deviant sexual fantasies, the offenses are more violent and bizarre, and they typically involve younger children. Victims are often their own children, and they also frequently physically abuse and neglect the victim.

In a study of 40 female sexual offenders, Faller (1987) reported that most had significant psychological and social functioning problems. Most of the offenders (29 out of the 40, or 73%) were classified as engaging in poly-incestuous abuse, which involved two perpetrators and generally two or more victims. The male offender usually instigated the sexual abuse, while the women played a secondary role. In another study, Vandiver and Teske (2006) compared 61 juvenile female sex offenders to 122 juvenile male sex offenders using sex offender registration data and criminal records. The female offenders were found to be younger than their male counterparts at the time of their arrest. The female offenders also had younger victims and chose both male and female victims equally while male offenders chose female victims more often.

Theories of Sexual Aggression

It is important that we understand why child molestation and rape occur, and a number of theories have been proposed to account for these forms of antisocial behavior. One of the most popular and widely cited theories for understanding child sexual abuse is Finkelhor's (1984) precondition model of child molestation. Finkelhor's theory of child molesting proposes that in order for sexual abuse to occur there are four preconditions:

1. The offender must be motivated to sexually abuse. Motivation is due to three factors: (1) emotional congruence, which is the offender's desire for the child to satisfy an emotional need; (2) sexual attraction to the child; and (3) blockage of emotional outlets for the offender to meet his sexual and emotional needs.

2. The next precondition relates to the offender's lack of internal inhibitions. For example, alcohol and impulse-control problems can weaken the offender's ability to restrain the behaviors that lead to abuse.

3. The offender must overcome external inhibitors for the abuse to occur. For example, the offender might need to create opportunities to be alone with the child.
4. The offender must overcome the child's resistance. Offenders will reward the child with attention or bribes in order to encourage the child to cooperate. Alternatively, some offenders will use the threat of harm to intimidate the child.

Marshall and Barbaree (1990) have proposed an integrated model of sexual aggression that includes biological factors, childhood experiences, sociocultural influences, and situational events. They argue that males normally learn to inhibit sexually aggressive behavior via a socialization process that promotes the development of strong, positive attachments. The authors suggest that sexual offenders fail to acquire effective inhibitory control because they experienced childhood abuse (emotional, physical, or sexual abuse) or because they were raised in extremely dysfunctional families (e.g., harsh and inconsistent punishment, lack of supervision, hostility). They also acknowledged the importance of the structure of society that reinforces the use of aggression and the acceptance of negative attitudes toward women.

More recently, Ward and Siegert (2002) have proposed a pathway model of child sexual abuse that integrates Finkelhor's precondition model, Marshall and Barbaree's integrated model, and Hall and Hirschman's quadripartite model (Hall & Hirschman's model is not discussed here; for more information on their model, see Hall & Hirschman, 1992). The pathway model proposes that there are different causal pathways that lead to sex offending, each having its own set of dysfunctional mechanisms, including inappropriate emotions, deviant sexual arousal, cognitive distortions, and intimacy deficits. For example, one pathway, labeled *emotional dysregulation*, focuses on individuals who have problems controlling their emotions and who use sex as an emotional coping strategy. For these offenders, the association between sex and negative emotions increases the probability they will sexually molest a child.

A number of theorists have also applied evolutionary theory to sexual offending (Quinsey & Lalumière, 1995; Thornhill & Palmer, 2000). Evolutionary theories focus on how behavior is the product of our ancestral history and how offense behaviors that are related to reproductive success become more frequent. Quinsey (2002) provides a clear example of a mating strategy that would not be very successful: "Consider a man in an ancestral environment who preferred trees as sexual partners. We can surmise that this man is very unlikely to be among our ancestors if his tree preference was caused by genes, because these genes would decrease in frequency over generations" (p. 2). Quinsey and others view rape as a consequence of a mating strategy that was selected for because it previously resulted in a reproductive advantage for males (Lalumière, Harris, Quinsey, & Rice, 2005). Evolutionary theories of sexual aggression have been criticized both for having a limited scope and lacking explanatory depth (see Ward & Siegert, 2002, for a detailed criticism).

Assessment and Treatment of Sexual Offenders

Much of the assessment of sexual offenders is to help determine future risk for reoffending, to identify treatment needs, and to evaluate whether or not the treatment has had the desired effect. Risk factors for sexual reoffending were discussed in Chapter 10, as was risk assessment more generally. The focus of this section will be on the assessment of treatment needs and the effectiveness of treatment programs.

Most treatment programs are designed to address the following: denial, minimizations, and cognitive distortions; victim empathy; enhanced social skills; substance-abuse problems; modification of deviant sexual interests; and the development of relapse prevention plans (Marshall, 1999).

DENIAL, MINIMIZATIONS, AND COGNITIVE DISTORTIONS   As clearly illustrated in the Case Study box, sex offenders often deny or fail to take full responsibility for their sexual offending (i.e., they claim they didn't do what they are accused of or that the victim consented; Barbaree, 1991). Often blame is shifted to someone else, including the victim or some external factor. For example, sex offenders will often say, "The victim wanted to have sex with me" or "I was drunk and didn't know what I was doing." Assessments of denial and acceptance of responsibility are most often conducted using self-report questionnaires such as the Clarke Sex History Questionnaire (Langevin, Handy, Paitich, & Russon, 1985) or by a comparison of police and victim reports with what the offenders admit in interviews. Most research has not found a link between denial and sexual recidivism. Recently, however, Nunes and colleagues (2007) have found that in low-risk sexual offenders and incest offenders, denial is related to increased sexual recidivism.

Cognitive distortions

Deviant cognitions, values, or beliefs that are used to justify or minimize deviant behaviors

Cognitive distortions are deviant cognitions, values, and beliefs that are used by the sexual offender to justify deviant behaviors. For example, a child molester might state, "Having sex with a child in a loving relationship is a good way to teach a child about sex"; or an incest offender might claim, "It was better for her to have her first sexual experience with me since I love her, rather than with some teenager who would just want to use her." Both of these child molesters are reporting cognitive distortions that are self-serving and inhibit them from taking full responsibility for their offenses.

Some treatment programs refuse to accept deniers. The reason for this is that if the person refuses to admit to having committed a sexual offense, it is difficult for that person to fully participate in the treatment, since the focus is on sexual offending. In treatment, offenders are asked to disclose in detail what happened before, during, and after the sexual abuse. The therapist has access to the police and victim reports in order to challenge an offender who is denying or minimizing aspects of the event. Other group members are encouraged to also challenge what the offender discloses.

EMPATHY   Although some sex offenders have a general deficit in empathy (e.g., psychopathic sex offenders), most have a specific deficit in empathy toward their victims (Marshall, Barbaree, & Fernandez, 1995). Empathy is the ability to perceive others' perspectives and to recognize and respond in a compassionate way to the feelings of others. Empathy problems in sexual offenders arise in part due to cognitive distortions. Because they minimize the amount of harm they have done, they do not think the victim has suffered, and therefore they do not empathize with the victim. Measures of empathy have focused on self-report scales such as the Rape Empathy Scale (Deitz, Blackwell, Daley, & Bentley, 1982) and interviews.

Empathy training typically focuses on getting the offender to understand the impact of the abuse on the victim and the pain caused, and to develop feelings such as remorse. Offenders read survivor accounts of rape and child abuse and compare these accounts with how their victim likely felt. Videos of victims describing the emotional damage they have suffered and the long-term problems they experience are often used. Some therapy programs use role-playing, with the offender taking the part of the victim. Finally, although controversial, some programs may have sexual offenders meet with adult survivors of rape or child sexual abuse. Only those sexual offenders who are demonstrating empathy are permitted to take part in these meetings.

CASE STUDY

YOU BE THE FORENSIC PSYCHOLOGIST

You have just been hired as a psychologist at a forensic psychiatric hospital. Larry Wilkins is a child molester who has been at the hospital for some time. He has just been assigned to your caseload and you are now responsible for developing a treatment plan for Larry and working with him to address his serious sexual offending problem.

Most of Larry's victims have been very young girls. When talking to him, Larry doesn't seem to see anything wrong with the fact that he regularly engages in sexual interactions with girls. Usually, it just involves touching the girls, he says, and not much else. In fact, he thinks he has been a good influence on many of the girls and says that they rarely resist his advances. He says that occasionally the girls make the first move and they are usually very affectionate toward him. He assures you that he never actually hurts the girls; just the opposite. He frequently buys them presents, takes them on nice outings, and always says nice things to them.

Larry also says he is aware of research that indicates sexual relations between men and children may be healthy for kids because it provides them with a sense of belonging and shows them that they are loved. Before being caught by the police, he actually belonged to an organization that promotes sexual relations between adults and kids and he assures you that many men think the same way he does. He has heard them say so at meetings.

Your Turn . . .

As the psychologist working with Larry, what are some of the issues you would need to deal with and how would you proceed with his treatment?

Sex offenders take part in a group therapy session.

SOCIAL SKILLS   Sexual offenders have been found lacking in a variety of social skills, including self-confidence in interpersonal relations, capacity for intimacy, assertiveness, and dealing with anger (Bumby & Hansen, 1997; Marshall, Anderson, & Champagne, 1997; Marshall et al., 1995). Self-report questionnaires, interviews, and responses to scenarios have all been developed to assess social skill deficits (see Marshall, 1999, for a review). Treatment programs for sexual offenders vary in terms of which social skill deficits are targeted. Some programs focus on anger and communication skills (Pithers, Martin, & Cumming, 1989), whereas others target relationship skills, anger control, and self-esteem (Marshall et al., 1997).

SUBSTANCE ABUSE   Substance-abuse problems are common in nonsexual offenders and sexual offenders (Lightfoot & Barbaree, 1993). It is likely that some sexual offenders use alcohol to facilitate offending by reducing their inhibitions. Self-report measures are often used to assess problems with alcohol and drugs.

Sexual offenders with substance-abuse problems are often referred to substance-abuse programs. These programs are usually based on the relapse prevention model developed by Marlatt and his colleagues, which is described in more detail below (Marlatt & Gordon, 1985).

DEVIANT SEXUAL INTERESTS   Deviant sexual interests motivate some sexual offenders. However, many other salient motives also play a role, including power and control over others, anger toward others, and a desire for emotional intimacy. One of the most popular methods to assess deviant sexual interests is the use of **penile phallometry** (Marshall, 1999). Penile phallometry involves placing a measurement device around the penis to measure changes in sexual arousal. For example, to measure deviant sexual interests in child molesters, photos of naked male and female children and adults are presented, as well as rapists' recorded descriptions of nondeviant and deviant sexual behavior. Phallometric assessments have been used to differentiate extra-familial child molesters from nonoffenders. However, most intra-familial child molesters do not differ in their phallometric responses from nonoffenders (see Marshall, 1999, for a review). Research with rapists is mixed. Some studies have found differences between rapists and nonrapists (Quinsey, Chaplin, & Upfold, 1984), whereas others have not (Marshall & Fernandez, 2003).

Many different techniques have been developed to train offenders to eliminate deviant thoughts and interests, and to increase the frequency of appropriate sexual thoughts and interests. For example, in **aversion therapy** the offender is sometimes given an aversive substance to smell (e.g., ammonia) whenever he has a deviant sexual fantasy. The underlying goal is to reduce the attractiveness of these deviant fantasies by pairing them with a negative event.

Another approach is called masturbatory satiation. In this treatment, the offender is told to masturbate to ejaculation to a nondeviant fantasy. After ejaculation, he is told to switch to a deviant fantasy, thus pairing the inability to become aroused with this deviant fantasy. The effectiveness of these techniques in changing deviant sexual interests has been questioned by several researchers (e.g., Quinsey & Earls, 1990).

Pharmacological interventions appear to be effective at suppressing deviant sexual desires (Bradford & Pawlak, 1993). However, drugs used in the past acted to suppress all sexual interests and compliance was a serious problem (Langevin, 1979). The use of selective serotonin-reuptake inhibitors (SSRIs) has shown to be effective at controlling deviant sexual fantasies and not eliminating all sexual functioning (Federoff & Federoff, 1992).

Penile phallometry

A measurement device placed around the penis to measure changes in sexual arousal

Aversion therapy

The pairing of an aversive stimulus with a deviant fantasy for the purpose of reducing the attractiveness of these deviant fantasies

RELAPSE PREVENTION   Sexual offenders need to identify their offense cycle (e.g., emotional states and stress factors that put them at risk) and develop ways to avoid these problems or to deal with them.

Programs with a **relapse prevention** (RP) component usually consist of two main parts. First, offenders are asked to list emotional and situational risk factors that lead to either fantasizing about sexual abuse or actually committing the abuse. For example, for a rapist, perhaps feelings of anger toward women would be a risk factor; whereas for a child molester, feeling lonely and sitting on a bench, watching children in a playground might be a risk factor. Second, offenders need to develop plans to deal more effectively with their problems (e.g., meeting their emotional needs in a prosocial way) and ways to avoid or cope with high-risk situations. Box 14.4 describes in more detail how the relapse prevention model has been applied with sexual offenders.

Relapse prevention

A method of treatment designed to prevent the occurrence of an undesired behavior (e.g., sexual assault)

Effectiveness of Treatment for Sexual Offenders

If we are going to treat sexual offenders, it is important to know whether the treatment actually works. There is a lack of consensus about whether sex offender treatment is

---

BOX 14.4   Relapse Prevention with Sexual Offenders

Relapse prevention (RP) is a self-control program designed to teach sexual offenders to recognize risky situations that could lead to reoffending and to learn coping and avoidance strategies to deal with those situations. The RP model was initially developed for the treatment of addictive behaviors such as smoking, alcohol abuse, and overeating (Marlatt & Gordon, 1985). Sexual offenders are asked to develop a personalized sexual offense cycle that identifies their pre-offense thoughts, feelings, and behaviors. At each step of the cycle, the offender generates options or alternative behaviors that interrupt the offense cycle. RP is not considered a cure, but it helps the sexual offender to manage the urge to offend sexually. RP is a way of teaching sexual offenders to think and look ahead in order to prevent committing another sexual offense. In order for RP to be successful, the sexual offender must be motivated to stop offending.

The following are some relevant terms (used in Figure 14.1) associated with relapse prevention:

- *Lapse:* Any occurrence of fantasizing about sexual offending or engaging in behaviors in the offense cycle
- *Relapse:* Occurrence of a sexual offense
- *High-risk situation:* Any situation that increases the likelihood of a lapse or relapse
- *Apparently irrelevant decisions:* Conscious or unconscious decisions made by offenders that put them in high-risk situations
- *Coping response:* Development of avoidance strategies to sidestep high-risk situations and escape plans if the high-risk situation cannot be avoided
- *Abstinence violation effect:* Refers to how the offender reacts to a lapse. Both cognitive reactions (e.g., lack of willpower) and emotional states (e.g., feeling guilty) are considered. If the offender views the lapse as an irreversible failure, this can promote a relapse. Alternatively, if the lapse is seen as a reasonable mistake in a learning process, the offender can become more confident in his ability to avoid or handle future lapses.

Figure 14.1 presents the sequences of events that may lead to a relapse in a child molester.

(continued)

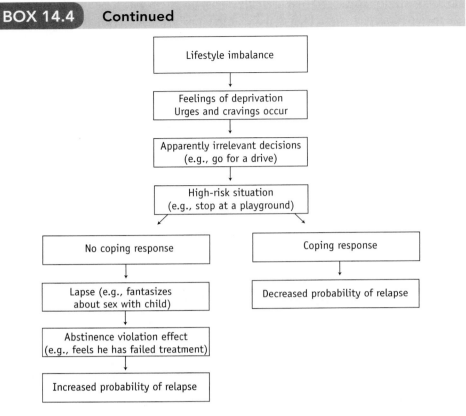

| BOX 14.4 | Continued |

FIGURE 14.1
Sequence of Events Leading to Relapse in a Child Molester

effective. Some researchers argue that treatment does not work (Quinsey, Harris, Rice, & Lalumière, 1993), whereas others are more optimistic (Marshall, Eccles, & Barbaree, 1991). What we do know is that incarceration does not appear to be an effective deterrent for many sexual (or other) offenders (e.g., Nunes, Firestone, Wexler, Jensen, & Bradford, 2007) and increasing prison time for offenders doesn't appear to result in less reoffending (e.g., Langan, Schmitt, & Durose, 2003). Certainly, incarceration may be the only effective method for handling high-risk sexual offenders. However, for some sex offenders, community alternatives may be a more effective and less expensive option.

Numerous problems face researchers wanting to evaluate the effectiveness of sexual offender treatment programs. The main problem is that it is unethical to carry out the ideal controlled study. The optimal design would randomly assign motivated sexual offenders (i.e., offenders all wanting treatment) to either treatment or no treatment. Then, both treated and untreated sexual offenders would be released at the same time, followed up for several years, and rates of reoffending would be measured. Most treatment outcome studies have not used this design (see Marques, 1999, for one of the few studies to use random assignment). Indeed, it is unlikely that many sexual offenders would agree to participate in this ideal study since untreated sexual offenders are held in custody longer than treated offenders. In addition, not treating motivated sex offenders would likely place the community at risk because the offenders are more likely to reoffend if left untreated.

Another challenge for researchers has been the relatively low base rates of sexual recidivism, even in untreated offenders (Barbaree, 1997). For example, on average, the 265 male sex offenders from the Massachusetts Treatment Center that were examined by Prentky, Lee, Knight, and Cerce (1997) exhibited a 9% recidivism rate for new sexual offenses in the first year of follow-up (post-release) and thereafter, an additional 2% to 3% of offenders recidivated per year through the fifth year of follow-up. Similar results have been found in other countries, such as Canada (e.g., Hanson & Bussière, 1998; Hanson & Thornton, 2000). Thus, in order for researchers to detect any differences between treatment and comparison groups, they need to wait many years. As a way of trying to deal with this problem, some researchers have begun to use unofficial data, such as child protection agency files or self-reports to detect reoffending (see Marshall & Barbaree, 1988).

Despite the challenges described above, a number of meta-analyses of sexual offender treatment programs have been published (e.g., Alexander, 1999; Gallagher, Wilson, Hirschfield, Coggeshall, & MacKenzie, 1999; Hall, 1995; Hanson et al., 2002; Lösel & Schmucker, 2005). For example, in one well-cited meta-analytic study, Hanson et al. examined 42 separate studies with a total of 5,078 treated sex offenders and 4,376 untreated sex offenders. Averaged across the different types of treatment, the sexual recidivism rate was 12.3% for the treated sex offenders and 16.8% for the untreated sexual offenders. The following results were also found:

- Sexual offenders who refused treatment or who dropped out of treatment had higher sexual recidivism rates compared to those who completed the treatment.
- Treatment effects were equally effective for adolescent and adult sex offenders.
- Both institutional treatment and community treatment were associated with reductions in sexual recidivism.

Based on their findings, Hanson et al. (2002) concluded that "The treatments that appeared effective were recent programs providing some form of cognitive-behavioral treatment, and, for adolescent sex offenders, systemic treatment aimed at a range of current life problems (e.g., family, school, peers)" (p. 189). In contrast, the treatment approach that Lösel and Schmucker (2005) reported to be the most effective was surgical castration. However, this form of treatment has been considered by some to be unethical. In addition, the sexual offenders willing to participate in this form of intervention are a very select group of highly motivated offenders.

However, as noted above, not all studies have reported positive effects of sexual offender treatment. For example, Hanson, Broom, and Stephenson (2004) compared the sexual recidivism rates of 403 treated sexual offenders with 321 untreated sexual offenders. In a 12-year follow-up, the rates of sexual reoffending were almost identical: 21.1% for the treated group and 21.8% for the untreated group.

HOMICIDAL OFFENDERS

The ultimate violent act is homicide and there is substantial fear and fascination about homicide among the general public. This fear and fascination is often fueled by newspaper stories and television shows that focus on homicide and homicidal offenders, particularly offences that are bizarre or offenders who have killed multiple victims. In this section, we describe what research has revealed about various types of homicidal offenders, including mass and serial murderers, we discuss some of the potential causes of homicidal violence, and we present results regarding the effectiveness of violent offender treatment programs, which often target offenders who commit homicide.

Nature and Extent of Homicidal Violence

In the United States, specific definitions of homicide, and the range of sanctions for committing different types of homicide, vary from state to state. For a particular case, the relevant definitions and sanctions are determined by the jurisdiction where the crime(s) occurred. Here, we will provide general definitions and do not address the many differences that exist from state to state.

Homicide is an umbrella term in the United States and includes murder and manslaughter (see Legal Information Institute, 2012b). Murder is considered more serious than manslaughter, and in the United States, definitions of murder are separated by degree (Title 18, Chapter 51, Section 1111). **First-degree murder** is a term generally used to describe any homicide that is willful, deliberate, malicious, and premeditated, or homicides that occurred during the commission of another violent offense (e.g., sexual assault) regardless of whether the murder was unplanned or deliberate. **Second-degree murder**, on the other hand, is a term reserved for cases of homicide where the killing was deliberate, but the murder was not planned in advance. Manslaughter also tends to be separated into two types (Section 1112). **Voluntary manslaughter** refers to intentional killings, but where no prior intent to kill is present and the offender acted under circumstances where his or her functioning was impaired. The most common cases of voluntary manslaughter include killings that occur in the "heat of passion." For example, if a man returned home unexpectedly from a business trip and found his wife in bed with her lover, and during the ensuing altercation he grabbed a rifle and shot and killed the lover, the man would be charged with voluntary manslaughter. **Involuntary manslaughter**, on the other hand, is a term reserved for homicides that were unintentional or due to negligence, such as when a drunk driver kills a fellow motorist. There is a type of homicide in the United States that is not a crime. It is known as "justifiable homicide." While the specific legal definition of justifiable homicide varies somewhat from state to state, all definitions cover cases where killings occurred to save lives (e.g., self-defense), to protect the state (e.g., war), or as part of one's job (e.g., a police officer).

Although the homicide rate in the United States is substantially higher than that found in other countries, the U.S. homicide rate has been steadily declining during the past two decades (U.S. Department of Justice, 2011b). In 1990, for example, 23,438 murders (and non-negligent manslaughters) were known to the police, representing a per capita homicide rate of 9.4 per 100,000 inhabitants. Nearly 20 years later, in 2009, the number of homicides has decreased to 15,421, representing a per capita rate of 5.0.

Additional details relating to homicide in the United States include the following (U.S. Department of Justice, 2011b):

- The vast majority of murder victims in 2009 were male (77%). The same is also true of offenders who committed murder (89.7% male).
- With respect to the race of murder victims in 2009, approximately half were black (48.6%) and half were white (48.7%). A similar breakdown applies to offenders, with approximately half being black (51.6%) and the other half white (46.3%).

First-degree murder

Homicides that are planned and deliberate, or committed during the commission of another violent offense

Second-degree murder

Homicides that are deliberate, but not planned in advance

Voluntary manslaughter

Homicides that are intentional, but where no prior intent to kill is present and the offender's emotional or mental functioning was impaired. Also known as "crimes of passion"

Involuntary manslaughter

Homicides that are unintentional or due to negligence

- Approximately 54% of homicide victims in 2009 knew their offender (e.g., acquaintance) with another 24% being killed by a family member. In cases where females were killed, a large percentage (approximately 35%) of the victims were killed by their husband or boyfriend.
- A large percentage of homicides in 2009 (41.2%) occurred during an argument. Another 23% occurred during the commission of another crime (e.g., rape, robbery, burglary, etc.).
- Police reported 667 justifiable homicides in 2009, with 406 being committed by law enforcement officers and 261 being committed by private citizens (e.g., an individual killing the perpetrator of a crime during the commission of the crime).

Bimodal Classification of Homicide

During the past few decades, a number of researchers have attempted to characterize aggression in animals and humans in a bimodal manner. For example, Kingsbury, Lambert, and Hendrickse (1997) proposed a bimodal classification scheme for the study of aggression and homicide in humans, in which homicides are classified as **reactive aggression** (or affective aggression) and **instrumental aggression** (or predatory aggression). Reactive homicide is defined as impulsive, unplanned, immediate, driven by negative emotions, and occurring in response to some perceived provocation. Instrumental homicide is defined as proactive rather than reactive, and is a premeditated, calculated behavior, motivated by some goal. This goal could be to obtain money, power, control, or even the gratification of sadistic fantasies (Meloy, 1997).

Reactive homicide occurs more often among relatives, and instrumental homicide among strangers (Daly & Wilson, 1982). The majority of homicides are reactive in nature. In a large-scale study, Miethe and Drass (1999) coded 34,329 single-victim, single-offender homicides in the United States between 1990 and 1994. Eighty percent were classified as reactive, and 20% as instrumental. In this study, the victim–offender relationship was divided into three categories: strangers, acquaintances, and family members/intimates. Most of the homicides involved acquaintances (55%), with most of these being classified as reactive (80%). Family members and intimate partners accounted for 28% of the cases, with nearly all of these homicides being classified as reactive (93%). Finally, in 17% of the cases, the victim was a stranger, with 52% being classified as reactive.

Reactive aggression
Violence that is impulsive, unplanned, immediate, driven by negative emotions, and occurring in response to some perceived provocation. Also known as *affective violence*

Instrumental aggression
Violence that is premeditated, calculated behavior, motivated by some goal. Also known as *predatory violence*

Filicide: When Parents Kill

The killing of a child by a parent is difficult to understand. The term **filicide** refers to the killing of children by their biological parents or step-parents and includes neonaticide (killing a baby within 24 hours of birth) and infanticide (killing a baby within the first year of life). Attitudes toward parents killing their children vary across cultures and time. For example, in ancient Rome, a father had a right to kill his children (Finkel, Burke, & Chavez, 2000). A few cultures have also sanctioned the gender-based killing of children. Notably, in China and India, female children are more likely to be killed due to the greater value these societies place on male children. In the past, certain Inuit societies killed infants that had birth defects or killed one infant when twins were born (Garber, 1947).

Child murder in the United States is a relatively uncommon, but still significant problem (U.S. Department of Justice, 2011c). In 2009, for example, 1,348 children and

Filicide
The killing of children by their biological parents or step-parents; includes neonaticide (killing a baby within 24 hours of birth) and infanticide (killing a baby within the first year of life)

youth under the age of 18 were killed, representing approximately 10% of all victims. According to the U.S. Department of Justice, the majority of these young victims were male (67.7%), with about half being white (48.5%) and half being black (47.4%). Firearms were responsible for the majority (50.7%) of these homicides, followed by personal weapons (e.g., hands, fists, feet), which accounted for 20% of homicides. When examining child homicides specifically, a significant portion of the homicides are perpetrated by family members, often a parent (Farooque & Ernst, 2003). Fathers appear to be more likely than mothers to kill their children, especially stepfathers (Daly & Wilson, 1996). However, differences between fathers and mothers tend to be less apparent when infants are killed, with some studies even suggesting that mothers are responsible for a higher proportion of infant deaths than fathers (U.S. Department of Justice, 1999).

Mothers Who Kill

Why would a mother kill her child? Several studies have classified maternal filicides (Cheung, 1986; Resnick, 1970). Stanton and Simpson (2002) reviewed these and other studies of child murder and concluded that there are three broad types of maternal filicides: (1) neonaticides, (2) those committed by battering mothers, and (3) those committed by mothers with mental illnesses.

The neonaticide group, those who kill their children within 24 hours of birth, are typically young, unmarried women with no prior history of mental illness, who are not suicidal, and who have concealed their pregnancy, fearing rejection or disapproval from their family. Battering mothers have killed their children impulsively in response to the behavior of the child. These mothers have the highest rates of social and family stress, including marital stress and financial problems. The group with mental disorders tends to be older and married. They are likely to have killed older children, to have multiple victims, and to be diagnosed with a psychosis or depression, and they are the group most likely to attempt suicide after the murder. Some researchers have used the term "altruistic filicide" (Resnick, 1969) to describe mothers who kill out of love. In these cases, the murder is in response to the mother's delusional beliefs that the child's death will somehow protect the child.

INFANTICIDE AND MENTAL ILLNESS Does childbirth trigger mental illness? The assumption underlying the offense of infanticide is that women who kill their infants are suffering from a mental illness related to childbirth. Three types of mental illness have been identified during the postpartum period (the period after childbirth): postpartum blues, postpartum depression, and postpartum psychosis.

The most common type of mental illness is postpartum blues (experienced by up to 85% of women), which includes crying, irritability, and anxiety beginning within a few days of childbirth and lasting from a few hours to days but rarely continuing past day 12 (Affonso & Domino, 1984; O'Hara, 1995). Given the onset and short time span of postpartum blues, it has not been considered a causal factor in filicide.

Postpartum depression (experienced by 7% to 19% of women) occurs within the first few weeks or months after birth and usually lasts for several months (O'Hara, 1995). The symptoms are identical to clinical depression and include depressed mood, loss of appetite and concentration, sleep problems, and suicidal thoughts. Recent studies have found that postpartum depression is not a mental illness that occurs as a consequence of childbirth (O'Hara, 1995).

The most severe and rare type of mental illness that has been associated with child-birth is postpartum psychosis (afflicting about 1 in 1,000 new mothers). Postpartum psychosis usually involves delusions, hallucinations, and suicidal or homicidal thoughts within the first three months after childbirth (Millis & Kornblith, 1992). Research does support a link between childbirth and postpartum psychosis (Kendell, Chalmers, & Platz, 1987). Box 14.5 describes the case of Andrea Yates, the Houston mother who killed her five children. This case illustrates the potential lethality of postpartum psychosis.

Fathers Who Kill

Fathers rarely commit neonaticide, but fathers are more likely than mothers to commit **familicide**, which occurs when a spouse and children are killed. In fact, familicide is

Familicide

The killing of a spouse and children

BOX 14.5	**From Devotion to Depression: A Mother Who Killed**

Postpartum depression affects about 10% of new mothers; this rate increases to about 20% to 30% for those who have had previous depressive episodes. If a mother has experienced postpartum depression with one child, she has about a 50% chance of developing postpartum depression if she has another baby.

Postpartum psychosis is the rarest but also the most severe postpartum mental illness. It afflicts about 1 in 1,000 mothers within six months of birth. Symptoms include hearing voices, seeing things, and feeling an irrational guilt that they have somehow done something wrong. Without treatment, women may try to harm themselves or their infants. The following case illustrates the potential lethality of postpartum depression and psychosis.

Andrea Yates had been diagnosed with postpartum depression after the birth of her fourth son, Paul. She had attempted suicide twice, was hospitalized, and was given antidepressant medication. After the birth of her daughter, Mary, Yates also experienced severe postpartum depression, was hospitalized twice, and was given antidepressants. According to her defense lawyers and mental health experts, Andrea Yates was not only experiencing postpartum depression but also postpartum psychosis.

On June 20, 2001, after her husband had left to go to work and prior to her mother arriving to help her, Andrea Yates drowned each of her five children—Noah (age seven), John (five), Luke (three), Paul (two), and Mary (six months)—in a bathtub at their family home. According to the defense lawyers, Yates was delusional when she murdered her children, believing that she had to murder them in order to save them from Satan. The prosecution agreed that Andrea Yates had a mental illness, but argued that she knew what she was doing and knew that killing the kids was wrong.

In March 2002, it took a jury four hours to reject Andrea Yates's insanity plea and find her guilty of capital murder. A week later, the same jury took 40 minutes to reject the death penalty but to sentence her to life in prison. The Texas Court of Appeals later reversed Yates's convictions because of false testimony given by a psychiatrist witness for the prosecution. A new trial ended on July 26, 2006, when Yates was found not guilty by reason of insanity and committed to a state mental hospital.

Treatment of postpartum depression and postpartum psychosis is possible. Continuing research holds the promise of improved treatment and, ultimately, the prevention of these devastating illnesses.

Sources: Based on Diamond, 2008; McLellan, 2006; Yardley, 2002.

almost always committed by a man, and is often accompanied by a history of spousal and child abuse prior to the offense. Wilson, Daly, and Daniele (1995) examined 109 Canadian and British cases and found that in about half of the cases the killer committed suicide. They also found that those who killed their spouse and their own children (i.e., genetic offspring) had a greater likelihood of committing suicide than those who killed their spouse and their stepchildren. Wilson et al. also described two types of familicide murderers: the despondent nonhostile killer and the hostile accusatory killer. The despondent nonhostile killer is depressed and worried about an impending disaster for himself or his family. He kills his family and then commits suicide. Past acts of violence toward children and spouse are not characteristic of this type of killer. The hostile accusatory killer, however, expresses hostility toward his wife, often related to alleged infidelities or her intentions to terminate the relationship. A past history of violent acts is common for this type of killer.

Youth Who Kill

In 2009, law enforcement agencies in the United States reported that 923 youths under the age of 18 had committed a murder (U.S. Department of Justice, 2011d). Although this number represents only a small proportion of murders committed in the United States, homicide by youth holds a particular fascination in the mind of the public. What motivates youth to kill? What factors underlie homicide by youth?

Corder, Ball, Haizlip, Rollins, and Beaumont (1976) compared 10 youths charged with killing parents, 10 youths charged with killing relatives or acquaintances, and 10 youths charged with killing strangers. Youth charged with parricide (killing parents) were more likely to have been physically abused, to have witnessed spousal abuse, and to report amnesia for the murders, compared with the other youth who committed murder. More recently, Darby, Allan, Kashani, Hartke, and Reid (1998) examined the association between family abuse and suicide attempts in a sample of 112 adolescents convicted of homicide. Abused youth were younger, more often Caucasian, and more likely to have attempted suicide prior to the homicide than nonabused youth.

Cornell, Benedek, and Benedek (1987) developed a typology of juvenile homicide offenders based on the circumstances of the offense. The types of homicide were labeled psychotic (youth who had symptoms of severe mental illness at the time of the murder), conflict (youth who were engaged in an argument or conflict with the victim when the killing occurred), and crime (youth who killed during the commission of another crime, such as robbery or sexual assault). When the classification system was applied to 72 juveniles charged with murder, 7% were assigned to the psychotic subgroup, 42% to the conflict subgroup, and 51% to the crime subgroup. Differences across these homicide subgroups with respect to family background, criminal history, and psychopathology have been reported (Greco & Cornell, 1992).

Spousal Killers

Femicide

The killing of women

In 2009 in the United States, 609 wives and 141 husbands were killed by their spouses (U.S. Department of Justice, 2011e). As this statistic makes clear, husbands are much more likely to kill their wives than wives are to kill their husbands. **Femicide** is the general term applied to the killing of women. Uxoricide is the more specific term denoting the killing of a wife by her husband and matricide is the term denoting the killing of a husband by his wife.

Why do men kill their spouses? Crawford and Gartner (1992) found that the most common motive for uxoricide (in 43% of cases) was the perpetrators' anger over either estrangement from their partner or sexual jealously about perceived infidelity. Comparing police records in Canada, Australia, and the United States, Wilson and Daly (1993) found that recent or imminent departure by the eventual victim was associated only with a husband killing his wife and not with a wife killing her husband. A study of risk factors for femicide in abusive relationships by Campbell, Webster, and Koziol-McLain (2003) found that the following factors increased the risk for homicide: the offender had access to a gun, previous threats with a weapon, estrangement, and the victim having left for another partner.

Serial Murderers: The Ultimate Predator

The term **serial murder** was first coined in the early 1980s, and there is a considerable amount of disagreement regarding the definition of this term. For example, how many victims are needed for a set of murders to be considered a serial murder case? Should the motive for killing matter? Should the relationship between murderer and victim be considered? Most definitions of serial murder include the criterion that a minimum of three people are killed over time, although some have recommended that this number be decreased to two victims (Federal Bureau of Investigation, 2008). The time interval between the murders varies and has been called a "cooling-off period." Subsequent murders occur at different times, often have no apparent connection to the initial murder, and are usually committed in different locations (Fox & Levin, 2012). While serial murder causes far less damage than more traditional murders, with respect to the overall number of individuals who are victimized in a given time period, serial murder is an important problem that we need to understand.

Serial murder
The killing of a minimum of three people over time, usually at different locations, with a cooling-off period between the murders

CHARACTERISTICS OF SERIAL MURDERERS Although serial killers are a heterogeneous group, many serial killers appear to have certain characteristics in common (Hickey, 2006). These include the following:

- Most serial murderers are male. For example, in a review of 399 serial murderers in the United States between 1825 and 1995, Hickey (2006) reported that 83% were male and 17% were female.
- Most serial murderers operate on their own. However, there are team murders that are committed by two or more offenders working together. Between 1875 and 1995, there were 47 serial killer teams in the United States (Hickey, 2006). For example, the Hillside Stranglers, who committed their crimes in Los Angeles, California, in 1977 and 1978, were Kenneth Bianchi and his cousin Angelo Buono.
- Most serial murderers in the United States are Caucasian. Hickey (2006), in his review, reported that 73% of serial murderers were Caucasian and 22% African American.
- Victims of serial murderers are usually young females who are not related to the murderer. However, the age and sex of the victim can vary. For example, Dr. Harold Shipman, England's most prolific serial murderer, is suspected of having killed 215 people, mostly elderly women who were his patients. Other serial killers, such as the Chicago-based John Wayne Gacy, killed young men.

FEMALE SERIAL MURDERERS Like female offenders in general, female serial murderers have not been the focus of much research. One reason is that serial killing by females is extremely rare. Most female serial killers are either "black widows," those who kill husbands or family members for financial gain, or "angels of death," nurses who kill their patients. For example, Dorothea Puente was charged with nine murders of her tenants and, in 1993, convicted of three of the murders. The murders were supposedly done in order for Puente to collect the tenants' Social Security checks. Puente claims that the seven people whose bodies were found in her yard had all died of natural causes and that she is innocent (Vronsky, 2007).

Aileen Wuornos is one of the few female serial murderers who did not kill family members or for financial gain (although she stole cash, belongings, and some of the victims' cars). In 1989 and 1990, she killed seven men she had agreed to have sex with. Initially, Wuornos claimed she had killed each of them in self-defense because they had become violent with her (Vronsky, 2007). Wuornos was executed in Florida in 2002. In 2003, the life and crimes of Wuornos were portrayed in the hit movie, *Monster*, starring Charlize Theron as the serial killer.

Table 14.1 summarizes the differences between male and female serial murders. Compared to male serial murderers, female serial murders are more likely to have no

---

TABLE 14.1 Differences between Male and Female Serial Murderers

Point of Comparison	Male Serial Murderers	Female Serial Murderers
Prior criminal history	Males tend to have a prior criminal history.	Females tend not to have a prior criminal history.
Accomplice	Only about 25% of males have an accomplice.	About 50% of females have an accomplice.
Murder method[a]	Males are more likely to use a firearm or to strangle or stab their victims.	Females are much more likely to use poison.
Murder motive[b]	Males are more likely to kill for sexual gratification or for control.	Females are more likely to kill for money.
Victim type[c]	Males are more likely to kill strangers.	Females are much more likely to kill family members.
Geographic type	Males tend to be more geographically mobile.	Females are more likely to be place specific (i.e., to carry out all killings in one location).

[a]*Hickey (2006) reported that 35% of female serial murderers killed using poison, compared to only 5% of male serial murderers.*

[b]*Hickey (2006) reported that in 74% of female serial murders, money played a role, compared to only 26% of male serial murders. In contrast, he reported that sexual gratification played a role in 55% of male serial murders, compared to only 10% of female serial murders.*

[c]*Hickey (2006) found that 50% of female serial murderers had killed at least one family member, compared to 1% of males.*

Source: Based on data from *Serial murderers and their victims* by Eric W. Hickey, Cengage Learning (2006).

prior criminal record, have an accomplice, use poison, kill for money, and kill a family member or someone they know (Hickey, 2006).

TYPOLOGIES OF SERIAL MURDERERS A number of classification systems have been developed to classify serial murderers, although most have yet to be subjected to empirical verification. One typology that focuses on crime scenes and offenders is the organized-disorganized model proposed by the FBI in the 1980s. This typology was described in Chapter 3.

In 1998, Holmes and Holmes proposed another typology. They used 110 case files of serial murderers to develop a classification system based on victim characteristics and on the method and location of the murder. They proposed four major types of serial murders: (1) **visionary**, (2) **mission-oriented**, (3) **hedonistic**, and (4) **power/control-oriented**.

The visionary serial murderer kills in response to voices or visions telling him or her to kill. This type of serial murderer would most likely be diagnosed as delusional or psychotic. The mission-oriented serial murderer believes there is a group of undesirable people who should be eliminated, such as homeless people, sex-trade workers, or a specific minority group. Hedonistic serial murderers are motivated by self-gratification. These killers have been divided into three subtypes, based on the motivation for killing: **lust serial murderer**, **thrill serial murderer**, or **comfort serial murderer**. The lust serial murderer is motivated by sexual gratification and becomes stimulated and excited by the process of killing. The thrill murderer derives excitement from seeing his or her victims experience terror or pain. The comfort serial murderer is motivated by material or financial gain. The power/control-oriented serial murderer is not motivated by sexual gratification but by wanting to have absolute dominance over the victim.

The above typology is compelling, but it has been criticized for the following reasons. First, there is considerable overlap among categories. For example, lust, thrill, and power/control murders are all characterized by a controlled crime scene, a focus on process (i.e., an enjoyment of the act of killing), and a selection of specific victims. Second, the typology's developers have failed to test it empirically. Recently, Canter and Wentink (2004) tested whether or not the characteristics within each type of murderer would tend to co-occur in 100 serial murderers who committed crimes in the United States. The researchers failed to find support for the proposed typologies. One reason for the lack of support for this typology is that murderers' motives may change over the course of their killings.

Keppel and Walter (1999) applied the motivational rapist typology proposed by Groth, Burgess, and Holmstrom (1977) to classify sexual murder. They proposed two types of sexual murders that reflect the theme of power (power-assertive and power-reassurance) and two types reflecting the theme of anger (anger-retaliation and anger-excitation). The authors describe how these types differ with regard to crime scene characteristics. For example, the power-reassurance type commits a planned rape that escalates to an unplanned overkill of the victim. In contrast, the anger-excitation type commits a planned rape and murder of the victim. Using prison files from the Michigan Department of Corrections, Keppel and Walter classified 2,475 sexual homicide offenders as follows: 38% power-assertive, 34% anger-retaliation, 21% power-reassurance, and 7% anger-excitation. How well this typology will apply to serial sexual murders and whether or not it will help with the identification of serial sexual homicides remains to be tested.

Visionary serial murderer

A murderer who kills in response to voices or visions telling him or her to kill

Mission-oriented serial murderer

A murderer who targets individuals from a group that he or she considers to be "undesirable"

Hedonistic serial murderer

A murderer who is motivated by self-gratification. This type of killer is divided into three subtypes: lust, thrill, and comfort

Power/control-oriented serial murderer

A murderer who is motivated not by sexual gratification but by wanting to have absolute dominance over the victim

Lust serial murderer

A murderer who is motivated by sexual gratification

Thrill serial murderer

A murderer who is motivated by the excitement associated with the act of killing

Comfort serial murderer

A murderer who is motivated by material or financial gain

HOW MANY SERIAL MURDERERS ARE THERE? Based on statistics from the United States, it appears that there has been an increase in the number of serial murderers over time. However, it is difficult to know the true prevalence rate of serial murderers. For example, the apparent increase in the number of serial murderers may be due to better police investigations and communication among law enforcement agencies, which has led to better detection. What is clear from official statistics is that the percentage of murder victims killed by strangers or unknown persons has increased dramatically in the United States. Egger (1999) has suggested that some of this increase is due to an increase in the number of drug-related murders, but that at least part of it is the result of an increase in serial murder.

There do appear to be regional differences in the rate of male serial killers. For example, DeFronzo, Ditta, Hannon, and Prochnow (2007) measured the rate of serial killers per 10 million in various locations in the United States, and found 18.6 in California, 10.3 in Florida, 7.0 in Texas, 6.3 in New York, and 3.0 in Pennsylvania. The researchers propose that sociocultural factors may help explain these differential rates. For example, cultures that are supportive of violence (as measured, for example, by the ratio of executions to homicides) appear to have higher rates of serial homicide.

Mass Murderers

Mass murder

The killing of four or more victims at a single location during one event with no cooling-off period

Mass murder is often defined as the killing of four or more victims at a single location during one event with no cooling-off period (Fox & Levin, 2012). School shootings such as those at Columbine and, more recently, Virginia Tech are examples of mass murder. In fact, to date, the Virginia Tech massacre is the most deadly mass murder in North America. It occurred on April 16, 2007, when Seung-Hui Cho killed 32 people (27 students and 5 faculty members) on the campus of Virginia Tech before committing suicide (Hickey 2010). The 23-year-old Cho was a student majoring in English at Virginia Tech and was described as being a loner. Professors had encouraged him to seek counseling due to the violent themes in his writing and he had been investigated for stalking two female students (Hickey, 2010). In the suicide note he left, Cho expressed his hatred of wealthy students, but little more is known of his underlying motivations. The Virginia Tech shooting has raised a fierce debate over the importance of civil liberty on the one hand and public safety on the other in domains including media coverage (e.g., whether or not to show videos made by Cho), mental health treatment, and firearms regulations.

Despite what the mass media might portray, "a majority of mass killers target victims who are specially chosen . . . the indiscriminate slaughter of strangers by a crazed killer is the exception to the rule" (Fox & Levine, 2012, p. 142). Indeed, most mass murderers plan their crimes and they often obtain semiautomatic guns in order to maximize the number of deaths. In other words, mass murderers do not "just snap," but in fact display warning signs that if recognized by others may help to prevent a tragedy. In addition, mass murderers often plan to commit suicide or get killed by law enforcement officers (Fox & Levin, 2012).

As discussed by Fox and Levin (2012), mass murderers are not all motivated by the same reasons. Mass murderers are often depressed, angry, frustrated individuals who believe they have not succeeded in life. They are often described as socially isolated and lacking in interpersonal skills. In some cases, the murder is triggered by what they perceive as a serious loss. In most cases, these offenders select targets that represent who they hate or blame for their problems. Mass murderers can also feel rejected by others and come to regard suicide and homicide as justified acts of revenge.

Theories of Homicidal Aggression

While numerous theories have been proposed to explain the emergence of specific forms of aggression (e.g., Hickey's, 2006, trauma-control model to explain why serial murderers kill), most of our thinking about homicidal aggression is guided by general theories of aggression. Although many theories of aggression exist (see Anderson & Bushman, 2002), we will focus on just three theories that have been particularly influential in the field of forensic psychology: social learning theory, evolutionary theory, and the general aggression model.

According to social learning theorists, aggressive behavior is learned the same way nonaggressive behavior is, through a process of reinforcement. Specifically, the likelihood of engaging in aggressive behavior is thought to increase as a function of how rewarding aggressive behavior has been in an individual's past (Akers, 1973). Rewards for aggressive behavior are often experienced directly, such as when an individual beats up a schoolmate and experiences an increase in status among his friends (as being "tough" or "cool"). However, social learning theorists also place a lot of emphasis on rewards that are not experienced directly, but vicariously, as a result of observing others. Social learning theory highlights several major sources that can influence behavior in this indirect fashion, including the family circle, the peer group, and the mass media (Akers, 1973). Aggressive behavior can be common in each of these settings and research has confirmed that observing aggressive behavior being reinforced in each context can increase the likelihood that the observer will model that aggressive behavior (e.g., Anderson et al., 2003; Loeber & Stouthamer-Loeber, 1986; Pratt & Cullen, 2000).

IN THE MEDIA   **The Mass Media and Antisocial Behavior**

In 1998, Oregon teenager Kip Kinkel, who was fascinated with the 1996 violent remake of *Romeo and Juliet* and the controversial music of Marilyn Manson, killed his mother and father. He then drove to Thurston High School, where he went on a shooting rampage that left two students dead and 25 wounded (Ramsland, 2009). In 1999, Eric Harris and Dylan Klebold shot 12 students and a teacher at Columbine High School before killing themselves. Both individuals were avid players of the online game *Doom*, and reportedly referred to the shooting in a prerecorded video, saying it was going to be "just like *Doom*" (Cullen, 1999).

If one were to trust the news stories surrounding these tragic events, we'd have to conclude that much of the violence in our society can be attributed, at least in part, to the television programs, movies, music, and video games that today's children and adolescents are exposed to. But, what does the research actually say about this issue? How does violence in the media influence aggressive behavior?

According to leading experts, it is certainly the case that the youth of today are exposed to an incredible amount of violence in the media (Anderson et al., 2003). It also appears to be true that exposure to media violence can have a small to moderate effect on the expression of antisocial behavior, especially in young viewers who are already characterized as being aggressive (Anderson et al., 2003). However, there also seem to be a range of factors that can counteract this positive relationship between exposure to violent media and antisocial behavior. For example, the relationship can be reduced by effective parental monitoring (e.g., discussing the inappropriateness of television violence with our children; Anderson et al., 2003).

See the In the Media box for a more detailed discussion of how the mass media may influence aggressive behavior.

As mentioned above, evolutionary theories of crimes, including violent crimes such as homicide, are also popular. The focus in evolutionary theories is on how crime can be thought of as adaptive behavior, developed as a means for people to survive (and pass on genes) in their ancestral environment (Daly & Wilson, 1988). In an ancestral environment characterized by recurring challenges or conflicts, such as finding mates or securing shelter, certain physiological, psychological, and behavioral characteristics became associated with reproductive success. From an evolutionary perspective, homicide emerged as one approach to best competitors who were competing for limited resources, and modern man has simply inherited this strategy from his successful ancestors (Buss & Shackelford, 1997). Notwithstanding criticisms made against this theory, a growing body of research is exploring these ideas and showing how they can be used to account for different forms (and rates) of homicide (e.g., Daly & Wilson, 1997).

Finally, the general aggression model (GAM) is one of the more recent theories of aggression (Anderson & Bushman, 2002). As its name implies, the GAM is a general theory of human aggression in that it integrates a number of domain-specific theories to explain the emergence of all types of aggression. The model is complex and a full discussion of it is beyond the scope of this book. However, we will discuss its main components, which are highlighted in Figure 14.2.

The first component is referred to as inputs, which refer to biological, environmental, psychological, and social factors that influence aggression in a specific social encounter. Inputs are categorized into person factors (e.g., traits, attitudes, genetic predispositions) and situation factors (e.g., incentives, provocation, frustration). According to the authors of the GAM, inputs influence behavior via the internal states that they create within an individual. Specifically, input variables are thought to influence cognitions (e.g., hostile thoughts), emotions (e.g., anger), and arousal, and these three routes are also thought to influence one another (e.g., hostile thoughts can lead to increases in anger). These internal states in turn influence behavioral outcomes through a variety of appraisal

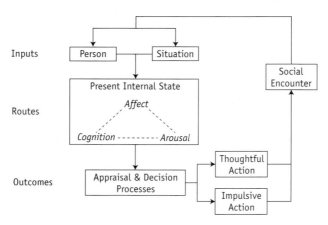

FIGURE 14.2
The General Aggression Model (Source: Anderson & Bushman, 2002)

Sources: Table from "Human aggression" by Craig A. Anderson and Brad J. Bushman from *Annual Review of Psychology* volume 53. Copyright © 2002 by Annual Reviews. www.annual reviews.org. Reproduced with permission.

and decision processes. Some of the outcomes reflect relatively automatic, impulsive actions, whereas other actions are thoughtful in nature. These outcomes influence the social encounter, which impacts the inputs in the next social encounter. Research supports many of the links proposed in the GAM (e.g., see Anderson & Bushman, 2002), and the model appears useful, not only for understanding human aggression, but also for developing interventions to reduce aggression, a topic we turn to next.

Treatment of Homicidal Offenders

The treatment of homicidal offenders has not received the same degree of attention in the research literature as the treatment of sexual offenders (Serin, Gobeil, & Preston, 2009). While this may be unsurprising in the case of serial or mass murderers, given the very long sentences these offenders will likely receive and their low potential for rehabilitation, it is more surprising for other types of homicide offenders. Indeed, given the serious consequences of their actions it is remarkable that so little attention has been given to the development and evaluation of treatment programs for offenders who have committed homicide.

Like sexual offending, nonsexual violent offending has a multitude of interacting causes and these causes inform treatment programs for violent offenders. While there is no such thing as a "typical" treatment program for violent offenders, many treatment programs are designed to target some or all of the following factors: anger (and emotions) management, self-regulation (i.e., self-control), problem solving, interpersonal skills, and social attitudes (e.g., beliefs supporting violence) (Polaschek & Collie, 2004).

Given these factors, it makes sense that some of the intervention programs used for sexual offenders (e.g., relapse prevention programs) are sometimes also used to treat nonsexual violent offenders. However, a wide variety of other programs are also used to intervene with violent offenders (see Jolliffe & Farrington, 2007; Polaschek & Collie, 2004). When it comes to the effectiveness of these treatment programs, there are few well-controlled evaluations (Polaschek & Collie, 2004). However, there have been some attempts recently to fill this gap using meta-analysis techniques.

For example, the recent meta-analysis by Jolliffe and Farrington (2007) was designed to evaluate treatment effectiveness for violent (male) offenders specifically (the study was not restricted to homicide offenders, but it excluded domestic and sexual offenders). These researchers included eight studies in their analysis, where treated and untreated violent offenders were compared to one another, and they calculated an average effect size to determine the impact of treatment. In each of these studies, violent reoffending (in addition to general reoffending) was used as the outcome measure of interest.

With positive effect sizes indicating lower rates of reoffending in the treated group and negative effect sizes indicating higher rates of reoffending in the treated group, Jolliffe and Farrington (2007) found the average effect to be about 0.13 when comparing the reoffending rates of violent offenders who did, or did not, participate in treatment. Thus, their results indicate that the treatment programs that they examined were effective to some extent, though the effect wasn't extremely large.

Like the meta-analysis conducted by Hanson et al. (2002), where various moderators of effectiveness for sexual offender treatment were identified, Jolliffe and Farrington (2007) also found that not all violent offender treatment programs were equally effective. Whether a treatment program resulted in reductions in violent reoffending depended partially on what the treatment program targeted. For example, treatment programs that targeted anger control were associated with an average effect size of 0.14. On the other hand, treatment programs that provided empathy training were associated with an average effect size of –0.05 (i.e., reoffending actually increased).

Beyond the content of the intervention, other factors that impacted the effectiveness of treatment included features of the study (e.g., providing longer treatment sessions increased effectiveness), the mode of treatment delivery (e.g., having the intervention delivered by correctional staff versus a rehabilitation professional increased effectiveness), and the methodology of the study (e.g., restricting the samples to offenders who completed the treatment increased effectiveness).

Summary

1. Rapists are offenders who sexually assault adults, and child molesters are offenders who sexually assault children. Typologies of both rapists and child molesters have been proposed that focus on the motives for sexual abuse. Rapists have been classified into the following five primary types based on research by Knight and Prentky (1990): opportunistic, pervasively angry, sexual, sadistic, and vindictive. Groth (1979) proposes a different rapist typology consisting of the following three types: angry, power, and sadistic. Groth proposes that child molesters be classified into two main types: regressed and fixated.

2. Treatment for sexual offenders involves recognizing denial, minimizations, and cognitive distortions; gaining victim empathy; enhancing social skills; dealing with substance-abuse problems; modifying deviant sexual interest; and developing relapse prevention plans.

3. Meta-analyses of sexual offender treatment programs have found the following: (a) sexual offenders who complete treatment have lower rates of sexual recidivism than do dropouts or treatment refusers, (b) treatment is effective for both adolescent and adult sexual offenders, (c) both institutional and community treatment programs are associated with reductions in sexual recidivism, and (d) cognitive-behavioral treatments are more effective than other forms of treatment.

4. Although homicide receives extensive media coverage, the homicide rate in the United States has been steadily declining during the past two decades. Certain trends are present in homicide statistics: the majority of victims and offenders are male; blacks and whites are equally likely to be victims and offenders; over half of all homicide victims know their offenders, and many are killed by family members; many homicides occur during arguments and a significant number occur during the commission of another crime; and a reasonably high number of justifiable homicides are committed each year, mostly by police officers, but also by private citizens.

5. Reactive homicide is defined as impulsive, unplanned, immediate, driven by negative emotions, and occurring in response to some perceived provocation. Instrumental homicide is defined as proactive rather than reactive and is a premeditated, calculated behavior, motivated by some goal.

6. Different types of homicides can be identified, based largely on who the victims and offenders are. Some murders include multiple victims. Serial murder is the killing of at least three people over time, usually at different locations, with an emotional cooling-off period between each murder. Mass murder is the killing of four or more victims at a single location during one event, with no cooling-off period.

Key Concepts

anger rapist *335*
aversion therapy *342*
child molester *331*
cognitive
   distortions *340*
comfort serial
   murderer *353*
exhibitionist *331*
extra-familial child
   molester *332*
familicide *349*
femicide *350*
filicide *347*
first-degree murder *346*

fixated child
   molester *335*
hedonistic serial
   murderer *353*
instrumental
   aggression *347*
intra-familial child
   molester *332*
involuntary
   manslaughter *346*
lust serial murderer *353*
mass murder *354*
mission-oriented serial
   murderer *353*

pedophile *331*
penile phallometry *342*
post-traumatic stress
   disorder *331*
power rapist *335*
power/control-oriented
   serial murderer *353*
rape trauma
   syndrome *331*
rapist *331*
reactive aggression *347*
regressed child
   molester *336*
relapse prevention *343*

sadistic rapist *335*
second-degree
   murder *346*
serial murder *351*
thrill serial
   murderer *353*
visionary serial
   murderer *353*
voluntary
   manslaughter *346*
voyeur *331*

Discussion Questions

1. You are interested in doing a study on the association between childhood sexual abuse and sexual offending later in life. Describe the methodology you would use and what variables you would measure.
2. Several typologies have been proposed for child molesters and rapists. What are the similarities and differences between these typologies?
3. A treatment center has proposed a new treatment program for sexual offenders. You have been hired by the center to develop an evaluation of the program to determine whether it would be effective. Describe how you plan to evaluate this program.
4. Homicide offenders have been classified into instrumental and reactive types. What are the treatment implications for these two types of murderers?

GLOSSARY

Absolute judgment Witness compares each lineup member to his or her memory of the culprit to decide whether the lineup member is the culprit

Actuarial prediction Decisions are based on risk factors that are selected and combined based on their empirical or statistical association with a specific outcome

Actus reus A wrongful deed

Adjournment Delaying the trial until some time in the future

Anatomically detailed dolls A doll, sometimes like a rag doll, that is consistent with the male or female anatomy

Anger rapist A rapist, as defined by Groth, who uses more force than necessary to obtain compliance from the victim and who engages in a variety of sexual acts to degrade the victim

Antisocial personality disorder A personality disorder characterized by a history of behavior in which the rights of others are violated

Antisocial Process Screening Device Observer rating scale used to assess psychopathic traits in children

Assessment center A facility in which the behavior of police applicants can be observed in a number of situations by multiple observers

Attention-deficit/hyperactivity disorder A disorder in a youth characterized by a persistent pattern of inattention and hyperactivity or impulsivity

Aversion therapy The pairing of an aversive stimulus with a deviant fantasy for the purpose of reducing the attractiveness of these deviant fantasies

Backfire effect When jurors are more likely to pay attention to inadmissible evidence following a disregard instruction than if no instruction was provided

Base rate Represents the percentage of people within a given population who engage in a specific behavior or have a mental disorder

Biased lineup A lineup that "suggests" who the police suspect and thereby who the witness should identify

Black sheep effect When evidence is strong, similarity between defendant and jury leads to being punitive

Challenge for cause An option to reject biased jurors

Change of venue Moving a trial to a community other than the one in which the crime occurred

Child molester Someone who has sexually molested a child

Classic trait model A model of personality that assumes the primary determinants of behavior are stable, internal traits

Clinical forensic psychologists Psychologists who are broadly concerned with the assessment and treatment of mental health issues as they pertain to the law or legal system

Clinical risk factors Types and symptoms of mental disorders (e.g., substance abuse)

Coerced-compliant false confession A confession that results from a desire to escape a coercive interrogation environment or gain a benefit promised by the police

Coerced-internalized false confession A confession that results from suggestive interrogation techniques, whereby the confessor actually comes to believe he or she committed the crime

Cognitive ability tests Procedure for measuring verbal, mathematical, memory, and reasoning abilities

Cognitive distortions Deviant cognitions, values, or beliefs that are used to justify or minimize deviant behaviors

Cognitive interview Interview procedure for use with eyewitnesses based on principles of memory storage and retrieval

Comfort serial murderer A murderer who is motivated by material or financial gain

Community treatment order Sentence that allows an offender who has a mental disorder to live in the community, with the stipulation that the person will agree to treatment or detention in the event his or her condition deteriorates

Comparison Question Test Type of polygraph test that includes irrelevant questions that are unrelated to the crime, relevant questions concerning the crime being investigated, and comparison questions concerning the person's honesty and past history prior to the event being investigated

Competency hearing Questions posed to child witnesses under age 14 to determine whether they are able to communicate the evidence and understand the difference between the truth and a lie, and in the circumstances of testifying, feel compelled to tell the truth

Compliance A tendency to go along with demands made by people perceived to be in authority, even though the person may not agree with them

Concealed Information Test Type of polygraph test designed to determine if the person knows details about a crime

Conduct disorder A disorder characterized by a persistent pattern of behavior in which a youth violates the rights of others or age-appropriate societal norms or rules

Confabulation The reporting of events that never actually occurred

Contextual risk factor Risk factor that refers to aspects of the current environment (e.g., access to victims or weapons). Sometimes called situational risk factor

Countermeasures As applied to polygraph research, techniques used to try to conceal guilt

Criminal profiling A technique for identifying the background characteristics of an offender based on an analysis of the crimes he or she has committed

Criterion-based content analysis Analysis that uses criteria to distinguish truthful from false statements made by children

Cross-race effect/other-race effect/own-race bias The phenomenon of witnesses remembering own-race faces with greater accuracy than faces from other races

Cue-utilization hypothesis Proposed by Easterbrook (1959) to explain why a witness may focus on the weapon rather than other details. The hypothesis suggests that when emotional arousal increases, attentional capacity decreases

Culprit The guilty person who committed the crime

***Daubert* criteria** A standard for accepting expert testimony, which states that scientific evidence is valid if the research upon which it is based has been peer reviewed, is testable, has a recognized rate of error, and adheres to professional standards

Deception detection Detecting when someone is being deceptive

Deductive criminal profiling Profiling the background characteristics of an unknown offender based on evidence left at the crime scenes by that particular offender

Defensiveness Conscious denial or extreme minimization of physical or psychological symptoms

Deliberation When jury members discuss the evidence privately among themselves to reach a verdict that is then provided to the court

Desistance The process of ceasing to engage in criminal behavior

Direct question recall Witnesses are asked a series of specific questions about the crime or the culprit

Dispositional risk factor Risk factor that reflects the individual's traits, tendencies, or styles (e.g., negative attitudes)

Disputed confession A confession that is later disputed at trial

Diversion A decision not to prosecute a young offender, but rather have him or her undergo an educational or community-service program. Also an option for the courts dealing with offenders with mental illnesses who are facing minor charges. The court can divert the offender directly into a treatment program rather than have him or her go through the court process

Domestic violence Any violence occurring among family members

Dynamic risk factor Risk factors that fluctuate over time and are amenable to change

Dysphoric/borderline batterer A male spousal batterer who exhibits some violence outside the family, is depressed and has borderline personality traits, and has problems with jealousy

Elimination lineup Lineup procedure for children that first asks them to pick out the person who looks most like the culprit from the photos displayed. Next, children are asked if the most similar person selected is in fact the culprit

Emotional maltreatment Acts or omissions by caregivers that cause or could cause serious behavioral, cognitive, emotional, or mental disorders

Enhanced cognitive interview Interview procedure that includes various principles of social dynamics in addition to the memory retrieval principles used in the original cognitive interview

Erotomanic stalker A stalker who suffers from delusions and who wrongly believes he/she has a relationship with a victim

Estimator variables Variables that are present at the time of the crime and that cannot be changed

Event-related brain potentials Brain activity measured by placing electrodes on the scalp and by recording electrical patterns related to presentation of a stimulus

Exhibitionist Someone who obtains sexual gratification by exposing his or her genitals to strangers

Experimental forensic psychologists Psychologists who are broadly concerned with the study of human behavior as it relates to the law or legal system

Expert witness A witness who provides the court with information (often an opinion on a particular matter) that assists the court in understanding an issue of relevance to a case

Externalizing problems Behavioral difficulties such as delinquency, fighting, bullying, lying, or destructive behavior experienced by a youth

Extra-familial child molester Someone who sexually abuses children not related to them

Fabricating Making false claims

Factitious disorder A disorder in which the person's physical and psychological symptoms are intentionally produced and are adopted to assume the role of a sick person

Fair lineup A lineup where the suspect does not stand out from the other lineup members

False confession A confession that is either intentionally fabricated or is not based on actual knowledge of the facts that form its content

False memory syndrome Term to describe clients' false beliefs that they were sexually abused as children, having no memories of this abuse until they enter therapy to deal with some other psychological problem such as depression or substance abuse

False negative An incorrect prediction that occurs when a person is predicted not to engage in some type of behavior (e.g., a violent act) but does

False positive An incorrect prediction that occurs when a person is predicted to engage in some type of behavior (e.g., a violent act) but does not

Familicide The killing of a spouse and children

Family-only batterer A male spousal batterer who is typically not violent outside the home, does not show much psychopathology, and does not possess negative attitudes supportive of violence

Family-supportive interventions Interventions that connect at-risk families to various support services

Femicide The killing of women

Filicide The killing of children by their biological parents or step-parents; includes neonaticide (killing a baby within 24 hours of birth) and infanticide (killing a baby within the first year of life)

Fine A sentence where the offender has to make a monetary payment to the courts

First-degree murder Homicides that are planned and deliberate, or committed during the commission of another violent offense

Fixated child molester A child molester, as defined by Groth and his colleagues, who has a long-standing, exclusive sexual orientation preference for children

Foils/Distracters Lineup members who are known to be innocent of the crime in question

Forensic psychiatry A field of medicine that deals with all aspects of human behavior as it relates to the law or legal system

Forensic psychology A field of psychology that deals with all aspects of human behavior as it relates to the law or legal system

General acceptance test A standard for accepting expert testimony, which states that expert testimony will be admissible in court if the basis of the testimony is generally accepted within the relevant scientific community

General deterrence Sentencing to reduce the probability that members of the general public will offend in the future

Generally violent/antisocial batterer A male spousal batterer who is violent outside the home, engages in other criminal acts, has drug and alcohol problems, has impulse-control problems, and possesses violence-supportive beliefs

Geographic profiling systems Computer systems that use mathematical models of offender spatial behavior to make predictions about where unknown serial offenders are likely to reside

Geographic profiling A technique that uses crime scene locations to predict the most likely area where an offender resides

Ground truth As applied to polygraph research, the knowledge of whether the person is actually guilty or innocent

Hare Psychopathy Checklist–Revised The most popular method of assessing psychopathy in adults

Hare Psychopathy Checklist–Youth Version Scale designed to measure psychopathic traits in adolescents

Hedonistic serial murderer A murderer who is motivated by self-gratification. This type of killer is divided into three subtypes: lust, thrill, and comfort

Heuristics Simple general rules that can be used to make decisions and solve problems

Historic child sexual abuse Allegations of child abuse having occurred several years, often decades, prior to when they are being prosecuted

Historical risk factor Risk factor that refers to events that have been experienced in the past (e.g., age at first arrest). Also known as static risk factor

Hung jury A jury that cannot reach a unanimous verdict

Illusory correlation Belief that a correlation exists between two events that in reality are either not correlated or correlated to a much lesser degree

Impartiality A characteristic of jurors who are unbiased

In need of protection A term used to describe a child's need to be separated from his or her caregiver due to maltreatment

Incompetent to stand trial Refers to an inability to conduct a defense at any stage of the proceedings because of a person's mental disorder

Inductive criminal profiling Profiling the background characteristics of an unknown offender based on what we know about other solved cases

Insanity Impairment of mental or emotional functioning that affects perceptions, beliefs, and motivations at the time of the offense

Instigators In social learning theory, these are events in the environment that act as a stimulus for acquired behaviors

Instrumental aggression Violence that is premeditated, calculated behavior, motivated by some goal. Also known as predatory violence

Intermediate sanctions A set of sentencing options that range between the extremes of probation and imprisonment (e.g., community confinement)

Internalization The acceptance of guilt for an act, even if the person did not actually commit the act

Internalizing problems Emotional difficulties such as anxiety, depression, and obsessions experienced by a youth

Intimate partner violence Any violence occurring between intimate partners who are living together or separated. Also known as spousal violence

Intra-familial child molesters People who sexually abuse their own biological children or children for whom they assume a parental role, such as a stepfather or live-in boyfriend. Also known as incest offenders

Investigator bias Bias that can result when police officers enter an interrogation setting already believing that the suspect is guilty

Involuntary manslaughter Homicides that are unintentional or due to negligence

Inwald Personality Inventory An assessment instrument used to identify police applicants who are suitable for police work by measuring their personality attributes and behavior patterns

Job analysis A procedure for identifying the knowledge, skills, and abilities that describe a good police officer

Jury Act Outlines criteria for being a juror and the rules for jury selection

Jury nullification Occurs when a jury ignores the law and the evidence, rendering a verdict based on some other criteria

Jury summons A court order that states a time and place for jury duty

Known-groups design As applied to malingering research, it involves comparing genuine patients and malingerers attempting to fake the disorder the patients have

Leniency bias When jurors move toward greater leniency during deliberations

Lineup A set of people presented to the witness, who in turn must state whether the culprit is present and, if so, which one

Love obsession stalker A stalker who has intense emotional feelings for a victim but who has never had an intimate relationship with the victim

Lust serial murderer A murderer who is motivated by sexual gratification

Malingering Intentionally faking psychological or physical symptoms for some type of external gain

Mandatory charging policies Policies that give police the authority to lay charges against a suspect where there is reasonable and probable grounds to believe an intimate partner assault has occurred

Mass murder The killing of four or more victims at a single location during one event with no cooling-off period

Maximization techniques Scare tactics used by police interrogators that are designed to intimidate a suspect believed to be guilty

Memory impairment hypothesis Explanation for the misinformation effect where the original memory is replaced with the new, incorrect information

Mens rea Criminal intent

Minimization techniques Soft-sell tactics used by police interrogators that are designed to lull the suspect into a false sense of security

Minnesota Multiphasic Personality Inventory An assessment instrument for identifying people with psychopathological problems

Misinformation acceptance hypothesis Explanation for the misinformation effect where the incorrect information is provided because the witness guesses what the officer or experimenter wants the response to be

Misinformation effect/post-event information effect Phenomenon in which a witness who is presented with inaccurate information after an event will incorporate that misinformation in a subsequent recall task

Mission-oriented serial murderer A murderer who targets individuals from a group that he or she considers to be "undesirable"

Munchausen syndrome A rare factitious disorder in which a person intentionally produces a physical complaint and constantly seeks physician consultations, hospitalizations, and even surgery to treat the nonexistent illness

Narrative elaboration An interview procedure whereby children learn to organize their story into relevant categories: participants, settings, actions, conversation/affective states, and consequences

Need principle Principle that correctional interventions should target known criminogenic needs (i.e., factors that relate to reoffending)

Neglect/failure to provide When a child's caregivers do not provide the requisite attention to the child's emotional, psychological, or physical development

Observational learning Learning behaviors by watching others perform these behaviors

Occupational stressors In policing, stressors relating to the job itself

Open-ended recall/free narrative Witnesses are asked to either write or orally state all they remember about the event without the officer (or experimenter) asking questions

Oppositional defiant disorder A disorder in a youth characterized by a persistent pattern of negativistic, hostile, and defiant behaviors

Organizational stressors In policing, stressors relating to organizational issues

Organized–disorganized model A profiling model used by the FBI that assumes the crime scenes and backgrounds of serial offenders can be categorized as organized or disorganized

Parent-focused interventions Interventions directed at assisting parents to recognize warning signs for later youth violence and/or training parents to effectively manage any behavioral problems that may arise

Patriarchy Broad set of cultural beliefs and values that support the male dominance of women

Pedophile Person whose primary sexual orientation is toward children

Penile phallometry A measurement device placed around the penis to measure changes in sexual arousal

Physical abuse The deliberate application of force to any part of a child's body that results in or may result in a nonaccidental injury

Polarization When individuals tend to become more extreme in their initial position following a group discussion

Police discretion A policing task that involves discriminating between circumstances that require absolute adherence to the law and circumstances where a degree of latitude is justified

Police interrogation A process whereby the police question a suspect for the purpose of obtaining a confession

Police selection procedures A set of procedures used by the police to either screen out undesirable candidates or select in desirable candidates

Polygraph disclosure tests Polygraph tests that are used to uncover information about an offender's past behavior

Polygraph A device for recording an individual's autonomic nervous system responses

Post-traumatic stress disorder Anxiety disorder that can develop in response to exposure to an extremely traumatic event. Symptoms include frequent, distressing, and intrusive memories of the event, avoiding stimuli associated with the traumatic event, and persistent anxiety or increased arousal symptoms

Power rapist A rapist, as defined by Groth, who seeks to establish dominance and control over the victim

Power/control-oriented serial murderer A murderer who is motivated not by sexual gratification but by wanting to have absolute dominance over the victim

Primary intervention strategies Strategies that are implemented prior to any violence occurring, with the goal of decreasing the likelihood that violence will occur later on

Probation A court-mandated period of supervision in the community, often accompanied by a set of conditions that the offender has to abide by

Protective factors Factors that mitigate or reduce the likelihood of a negative outcome (e.g., aggression, psychopathology)

Protective factors Factors that mitigate or reduce the likelihood of a negative outcome (e.g., delinquency, aggression)

Psychological debriefing A psychologically oriented intervention delivered to police officers following exposure to an event that resulted in psychological distress

Psychology and the law The use of psychology to examine the operation of the legal system

Psychology in the law The use of psychology in the legal system as that system operates

Psychology of the law The use of psychology to examine the law itself

Psychopathy A personality disorder defined by a collection of interpersonal, affective, and behavioral characteristics including manipulation, lack of remorse or empathy, impulsivity, and antisocial behaviors

Racial bias The disparate treatment of racial out-groups

Rape trauma syndrome A group of symptoms or behaviors that are frequent aftereffects of having been raped

Rapist Person who sexually assaults victims who are not considered children

Reactive aggression Violence that is impulsive, unplanned, immediate, driven by negative emotions, and occurring in response to some perceived provocation. Also known as affective violence

Recall memory Reporting details of a previously witnessed event or person

Recognition memory Determining whether a previously seen item or person is the same as what is currently being viewed

Regressed child molester A child molester, as defined by Groth and his colleagues, whose primary sexual orientation is toward adults, but whose sexual interests revert to children after a stressful event or due to feelings of inadequacy

Regulators In social learning theory, these are consequences of behaviors

Reid model A nine-step model of interrogation sometimes used in North America to extract confessions from suspects

Relapse prevention A method of treatment designed to prevent the occurrence of an undesired behavior (e.g., sexual assault)

Relative judgment Witness compares lineup members to each other, and the person who looks most like the culprit is identified

Reparations A sentence where the offender has to make a monetary payment to the victim or the community.

Representativeness A jury composition that represents the community where the crime occurred

Resilient Characteristic of a child who has multiple risk factors but who does not develop problem behaviors or negative symptoms

Response Modulation Deficit Theory that psychopaths fail to use peripheral cues to change their behavior

Responsivity principle Principle that correctional interventions should match the general learning style of offenders

Restitution A sentence where the offender has to make a monetary payment to the victim or the community

Restorative justice An approach for dealing with the crime problem that emphasizes repairing the harm caused by crime. It is based on the philosophy that when victims, offenders, and community members meet voluntarily to decide how to achieve this, transformation can result

Retracted confession A confession that the confessor later declares to be false

Risk factor A factor that increases the likelihood for emotional and/or behavioral problems

Risk factor A measurable feature of an individual that predicts the behavior of interest (e.g., violence or psychopathology)

Risk principle Principle that correctional interventions should target offenders who are at high risk to reoffend

Sadistic rapist A rapist, as defined by Groth, who obtains sexual gratification by hurting the victim

Scientific jury selection Prospective jurors are evaluated on predetermined characteristics to identify those who would be sympathetic or unsympathetic to the case

Second-degree murder Homicides that are deliberate, but not planned in advance

Secondary intervention strategies Strategies that attempt to reduce the frequency of violence

Selection interview In recruiting police officers, an interview used by the police to determine the extent to which an applicant possesses the knowledge, skills, and abilities deemed important for the job

Sentencing disparity Variations in sentencing severity for similar crimes committed under similar circumstances

Sentencing guidelines Guidelines that are intended to reduce the degree of discretion that judges have when handing down sentences

Sequential lineup Alternative lineup procedure where the lineup members are presented serially to the witness and the witness must make a decision as to whether the lineup member is the culprit before seeing another member. Also a witness cannot ask to see previously seen photos and is unaware of the number of photos to be shown

Serial murder The killing of a minimum of three people over time, usually at different locations, with a cooling-off period between the murders

Sexual abuse When an adult or youth uses a child for sexual purposes

Sexual Homicide Homicides in which there is a sexual component

Sexual sadism People who obtain sexual arousal through fantasies, urges, or acts of inflicting pain, suffering, or humiliation on another human

Showup Identification procedure that shows one person to the witness: the suspect

Simple obsession stalker A stalker who engages in stalking after the breakup of an intimate relationship

Simulation design As applied to malingering research, people are told to pretend they have specific symptoms of a disorder

Simultaneous lineup A common lineup procedure that presents all lineup members at one time to the witness

Situational test A simulation of a real-world policing task

Social learning theory A theory of human behavior based on learning from watching others in the social environment and reinforcement contingencies

Social learning theory A theory of human behavior based on learning from watching others in the social environment and reinforcement contingencies

Sociopathy A label used to describe a person whose psychopathic traits are assumed to be due to environmental factors

Somatoform disorders A disorder in which physical symptoms suggest a physical illness but have no known underlying physiological cause and the symptoms are not intentionally produced

Source misattribution hypothesis Explanation for the misinformation effect—where the witness has two memories, the original and the misinformation; however, the witness cannot remember where each memory originated or the source of each

Specific deterrence Sentencing to reduce the probability that an offender will reoffend in the future

Stalking Crime that involves repeatedly following, communicating with, watching, or threatening a person directly or indirectly

Statement validity analysis A comprehensive protocol to distinguish truthful or false statements made by children containing three parts: a structured interview of the child witness, a systematic analysis of the verbal content of the child's statements (criterion-based content analysis), and the application of the statement validity checklist

Static risk factor Risk factor that does not fluctuate over time and is not changed by treatment (e.g., age at first arrest). Also known as historical risk factor

Step-wise interview Interview protocol with a series of "steps" designed to start the interview with the least leading and directive type of questioning then proceeding to more specific forms of questioning, as necessary

Structured professional judgment Decisions are guided by a predetermined list of risk factors that have been selected from the research and professional literature. Judgment of risk level is based on the evaluator's professional judgment

Suspect A person the police "suspect" committed the crime, who may be guilty or not guilty of committing the crime in question

System variables Variables that can be manipulated to increase (or decrease) eyewitness accuracy

Systematic disparity Consistent disagreement among judges about sentencing decisions because of factors such as how lenient judges think sentences should be

Target-absent lineup A lineup that does not contain the culprit but contains an innocent suspect

Target-present lineup A lineup that contains the culprit

Tertiary intervention strategies Strategies that attempt to prevent violence from reoccurring

Thrill serial murderer A murderer who is motivated by the excitement associated with the act of killing

True negative A correct prediction that occurs when a person who is predicted not to engage in some type of behavior (e.g., a violent act) does not do so

True positive A correct prediction that occurs when a person who is predicted to engage in some type of behavior (e.g., a violent act) does so

Truth-bias The tendency of people to judge more messages as truthful than deceptive

Unstructured clinical judgment Decisions characterized by a substantial amount of professional discretion and lack of guidelines

Unsystematic disparity Inconsistencies in a judge's sentencing decisions over time when judging the same type of offender or crime because of factors such as the judge's mood

Unwarranted sentencing disparity Variations in sentencing severity for similar crimes committed under similar circumstances that result from reliance by the judge on legally irrelevant factors

Use-of-force continuum A model that is supposed to guide police officer decision making in use-of-force situations by providing the officer with some guidance as to what level of force is appropriate given the suspect's behavior and other environmental conditions

Vengeance stalker A stalker who knows the victim and is angry at the victim for some perceived injustice

Visionary serial murderer A murderer who kills in response to voices or visions telling him or her to kill

Voir dire The question period when selecting people to serve on the jury

Voluntary false confession A false confession that is provided without any elicitation from the police

Voluntary manslaughter Homicides that are intentional, but where no prior intent to kill is present and the offender's emotional or mental functioning was impaired. Also known as "crimes of passion"

Voyeur People who obtain sexual gratification by observing unsuspecting people, usually strangers, who are either naked, in the process of undressing, or engaging in sexual activity

Walk-by Identification procedure that occurs in a naturalistic environment. The police take the witness to a public location where the suspect is likely to be. Once the suspect is in view, the witness is asked whether he or she sees the culprit

Warranted sentencing disparity Variations in sentencing severity for similar crimes committed under similar circumstances that result from a reliance on legally relevant factors (e.g., laws that differ across jurisdictions)

Weapon focus Term used to describe the phenomenon of a witness's attention being focused on the culprit's weapon rather than on the culprit

REFERENCES

Aamodt, M.G. (2004). *Research in law enforcement selection.* Boca Raton, FL: Brown Walker Press.

Aamodt, M.G., & Stalnaker, N.A. (2006). *Police officer suicide: Frequency and officer profiles.* Retrieved from PoliceOne.com website: http://www.policeone.com/health-fitness/articles/137133-Police-Officer-Suicide-Frequency-and-officer-profiles

Aamondt, M.G., & Custer, H. (2008). Who can best catch a liar? A meta-analysis of individual differences in detecting deception. *The Forensic Examiner, 15.1,* 6–11.

ABC News (2011). *Md., Calif. suspend "Scared Straight" programs.* Retrieved from http://abcnews.go.com/Entertainment/comments?type=story&id=12845875#.T0UQT4dumSo

Abdollahi, M.K. (2002). Understanding police stress research. *Journal of Forensic Psychology Practice, 2,* 1–24.

Abel, G.G., Becker, J.V., Mittelman, M., & Cunningham-Rathner, J. (1987). Self-reported sex crimes of non-incarcerated paraphiliacs. *Journal of Interpersonal Violence, 2,* 3–25.

Abootalebi, V., Moradi, M.H., & Khalilzadeh, M.A. (2006). A comparison of methods for ERP assessment in a P300 based GKT. *International Journal of Psychophysiology, 62,* 309–320.

Ackerman, M.J. (1999). *Forensic psychological assessment.* New York, NY: John Wiley & Sons.

Adams, K. (1999). *What we know about police use of force.* Washington, DC: U.S. Department of Justice.

Adams, S.H., & Harpster, T. (2008, June). 911 homicide calls and statement analysis: Is the caller the killer? *FBI Law Enforcement Bulletin, 77*(6), 22–31.

Adams-Tucker, C. (1982). Proximate effects of sexual abuse in childhood: A report on 28 children. *American Journal of Psychiatry, 139,* 1252–1256.

Ægisdóttir, S., White, M.J., Spengler, P.M., Maugherman, A.S., Anderson, L.A., Cook, R.S., . . . Rush, J.D. (2006). The meta-analysis of clinical judgment project: Fifty-six years of accumulated research on clinical versus statistical prediction. *The Counseling Psychologist, 34,* 341–382.

Affonso, D.D., & Domino, G. (1984). Postpartum depression: A review. *Birth: Issues in Perinatal Care and Education, 11,* 231–235.

Aglionby, J. (2006). Thai police hold maid for JonBenet murder. *Guardian.co.uk.* Retrieved from http://www.guardian.co.uk/world/2006/aug/17/usa.johnaglionby

Agosti, V. (1995). The efficacy of treatments in reducing alcohol consumption: A meta-analysis. *International Journal of the Addictions, 30,* 1067–1077.

Ainsworth, P.B. (1993). *Psychological testing and police applicant selection: Difficulties and dilemmas.* Paper presented to the European Conference on Law and Psychology, Oxford, England.

Aitken, C.C.G., Connolly, T., Gammerman, A., Zhang, G., Bailey, D., Gordon, R., & Oldfield, R. (1996). Statistical modelling in specific case analysis. *Science & Justice, 36,* 245–256.

Akers, R. L. (1973). Deviant behavior: A social learning approach. Belmont, CA: Wadsworth.

Albonetti, C.A. (1997). Sentencing under the federal guidelines: Effects of defendant characteristics, guilty pleas, and departures on sentence outcomes for drug offences, 1991–1992. *Law & Society Review, 31,* 789–822.

Aldridge, N. (1998). Strengths and limitations of forensic child sexual abuse interviews with anatomical dolls: An empirical review. *Journal of Psychopathology and Behavioral Assessment, 20,* 1–41.

Alexander, D.A., Innes, G., Irving, B.L., Sinclair, S.D., & Walker, L.G. (1991). *Health, stress and policing: A study in Grampian policing.* London, England: The Police Foundation.

Alexander, M.A. (1999). Sexual offender treatment efficacy revisited. *Sexual Abuse: Journal of Research and Treatment, 11,* 101–116.

Alison, L.J., Bennell, C., Mokros, A., & Ormerod, D. (2002). The personality paradox in offender profiling: A theoretical review of the processes involved in deriving background characteristics from crime scene actions. *Psychology, Public Policy, and Law, 8,* 115–135.

Alison, L.J., Goodwill, A.M., Almond, L., van den Heuvel, C., & Winter, J. (2010). Pragmatic solutions to offender profiling and behavioural investigative advice. *Legal & Criminological Psychology, 15,* 115–132.

Alison, L.J., Smith, M., Eastman, O., & Rainbow, L. (2003). Toulmin's philosophy of argument and its relevance to offender profiling. *Psychology, Crime and Law, 9,* 173–183.

Alison, L.J., Smith, M., & Morgan, K. (2003). Interpreting the accuracy of offender profiles. *Psychology, Crime and Law, 9,* 185–195.

Allen, J.J., & Iacono, W.G. (1997). A comparison of methods for the analysis of event-related potentials in deception detection. *Psychophysiology, 34,* 234–240.

Almond, L., Alison, L., & Porter, L. (2007). An evaluation and comparison of claims made in behavioural investigative advice reports compiled by the National Policing Improvements Agency in the United Kingdom. *Journal of Investigative Psychology & Offender Profiling, 4,* 71–83.

Alpert, G.P., & Dunham, R. (1999). *The force factor: Measuring and assessing police use of force and suspect resistance.* Washington, DC: U.S. Department of Justice.

Amato, P.R., & Keith, B. (1991). Parental divorce and the well being of children: A meta-analysis. *Psychological Bulletin, 110,* 26–46.

American Psychiatric Association. (1994). *Diagnostic and statistical manual of mental disorders* (4th ed.). Washington, DC: Author.

American Psychological Association. (1993). Award for distinguished contribution to research in psychology: Linda A. Teplin. *American Psychologist, 48,* 370–372.

American Psychological Association. (2007). *Psychology and the law: Jenkins v. United States.* Retrieved from http://www.apa.org/psyclaw/jenkins.html

Ammerman, R.T., Cassisi, J.E., Hersen M., & Van Hasselt, V.B. (1986). Consequences of physical abuse and neglect in children. *Clinical Psychology Review, 6,* 291–310.

Andershed, H.A., Gustafson, S.B., Kerr, M., & Hakån, S. (2002). The usefulness of self-reported psychopathy-like traits in the study of antisocial behaviour among non-referred adolescents. *European Journal of Personality, 16,* 383–402.

Anderson, G. (2012). Forensic entomology: The use of insects in death investigations. Retrieved May 17, 2012 from http://www.sfu.ca/~ganderso/forensicentomology.htm

Anderson, C.A., & Bushman, B.J. (2002). Human aggression. *Annual Review of Psychology, 53,* 27–51.

Anderson, C.A., & Dill, F.E. (2000). Video games and aggressive thoughts, feelings, and behavior in the laboratory and in life. *Journal of Personality and Social Psychology, 78,* 772–790.

Anderson, M., Gillig, P.M., Sitaker, M., McCloskey, K., Malloy, K., & Grigsby, N. (2003). "Why doesn't she just leave?": A descriptive study of victim reported impediments to her safety. *Journal of Family Violence, 18,* 151–155.

Andrews, D. (2001). Principles of effective correctional programs. In L. Motiuk and R. Serin (Eds.), *Compendium 2000 on effective correctional programming* (pp. 9–17). Ottawa, ON: Correctional Service Canada.

Andrews, D., Dowden, C., & Gendreau, P. (1999). *Clinically relevant and psychologically informed approaches to reduced re-offending: A meta-analytic study of human service, risk, need, responsivity, and other concerns in justice contexts.* Unpublished manuscript, Carleton University, Ottawa, ON.

Andrews, D., Robblee, M., & Saunders, R. (1984). *The sentencing factors inventory.* Toronto, ON: Ontario Ministry of Correctional Services.

Andrews, D.A., & Bonta, J. (2006). *The psychology of criminal conduct* (4th ed.). Cincinnati, OH: Anderson Publishing.

Andrews, D.A., Zinger, I., Hoge, R.D., Bonta, J., Gendreau, P., & Cullen, F.T. (1990). Does correctional treatment work? A clinically relevant and psychologically informed meta-analysis. *Criminology, 28,* 369–404.

Anshel, M.H. (2000). A conceptual model and implications for coping with stressful events in police work. *Criminal Justice and Behavior, 27,* 375–400.

Anson, R.H., & Bloom, M.E. (1988). Police stress in an occupational context. *Journal of Police Science and Administration, 16,* 229–235.

Antonowicz, D., & Ross, R. (1994). Essential components of successful rehabilitation programs for offenders. International *Journal of Offender Therapy and Comparative Criminology, 38,* 97–104.

Archer, J. (2002). Sex differences in physically aggressive acts between heterosexual partners: A meta-analytic review. *Aggression and Violent Behavior, 7,* 313–351.

Archer, R.P., Buffington-Vollum, J.K., Stredny, R.V., & Handel, R.W. (2006). A survey of psychological test use patterns among forensic psychologists. *Journal of Personality Assessment, 87,* 84–94.

Ascione, F.R. (1998). Battered women's reports of their partners' and their children's cruelty to animals. *Journal of Emotional Abuse, 1,* 119–133.

Ascione, F.R., Weber, C.V., Thompson, T.M., Heath, J. Maruyama, M., & Hayashi, K. (2007) Battered pets and domestic violence: Animal abuse reported by women experiencing intimate violence and by nonabused women. *Violence Against Women, 13,* 354–373.

Ash, P., Slora, K.B., & Britton, C.F. (1990). Police agency officer selection practices. *Journal of Police Science and Administration, 17,* 258–269.

Atkinson, J.L. (1996). Female sex offenders: A literature review. *Forum on Corrections Research, 8,* 39–43.

Austin, J. (2006). How much risk can we take? The misuse of risk assessment in corrections. *Federal Probation, 70,* 58–63.

Azpiri, J. (2008, October 9). *Judge sentences hip-hop fan to listen to classical music.* Retrieved from http://www.nowpublic.com/strange/judge-sentences-hip-hop-fan-listen-classical-music

Babcock, J.C., Green, C.E., & Robie, C. (2004). Does batterers' treatment work? A meta-analytic review of domestic violence treatment. *Clinical Psychology Review, 23,* 1023–1053.

Babiak, P. (2000). Psychopathic manipulation at work. In C.B. Gacono (Ed.), *Clinical and forensic assessment of psychopathy: A practitioner's guide* (pp. 287–311). Mahwah, NJ: Lawrence Erlbaum Associates.

Babiak, P., Neumann, C.S., & Hare, R.D. (2010). Corporate psychopathy: Talking the walk. *Behavioral Sciences and the Law, 28,* 174–193.

Baca-Garcia, E., Perez-Rodriguez, M., Basurte-Villamor, I., Fernandez, d. M., Jimenez-Arriero, M., Gonzalez, d. R., & Oquendo, M. A. (2007). Diagnostic stability of psychiatric disorders in clinical practice. The British Journal of Psychiatry, 190, 210-216.

Baer, R.A., Wetter, M.W., & Berry, D.T.T. (1995). Sensitivity of MMP-2 validity scales to underreporting of symptoms. *Psychological Assessment, 7,* 419–423.

Bagby, R.M., Nicholson, R.A., Bacchiochi, J.R., Ryder, A.B., & Bury, A.S. (2002). The predictive capacity of MMPI-2 and PAI validity scales and indexes of coached and uncoached feigning. *Journal of Personality Assessment, 78,* 69–86.

Bandura, A. (1965). Influence of models' reinforcement contingencies on the acquisition of imitative responses. *Journal of Personality and Social Psychology, 1,* 589–595.

Bandura, A. (1973). *Aggression: A social learning analysis.* Englewood Cliffs, NJ: Prentice-Hall.

Banfield, A., Kunin, S., Dolak, K., & Ng, C. (2011). *Casey Anthony to be released from jail July 17.* Retrieved from http://abcnews.go.com/US/casey_anthony_trial/casey-anthony-released-jail-week/story?id=14015562#.T0UDz4dumSo

Banning, A. (1989). Mother–son incest: Confronting a prejudice. *Child Abuse and Neglect, 13,* 563–570.

Barbaree, H. (1997). Evaluating treatment efficacy with sexual offenders: The insensitivity of recidivism studies to treatment effects. *Journal of Research and Treatment, 9,* 111–128.

Barbaree, H.E. (1991). Denial and minimization among sex offenders: Assessment and treatment outcome. *Forum on Corrections Research, 3,* 300–333.

Barbaree, H.E., Seto, M.C., Langton, C.M., & Peacock, E.J. (2001). Evaluating the predictive accuracy of six risk assessment instruments for adult sex offenders. *Criminal Justice and Behavior, 28,* 490–521.

Barbaree, H.E., Seto, M.C., Serin, R., Amos, N., & Preston, D. (1994). Comparisons between sexual and nonsexual rapist subtypes: Sexual arousal to rape, offense precursors, and offense characteristics. *Criminal Justice and Behavior, 21,* 95–114.

Barille, L. (1984). Television and attitudes about crime: Do heavy views distort criminality and support retributive justice? In R. Surette (Ed.), *Justice and the media: Issues and research* (pp 141–158). Springfield, IL: Charles C. Thomas

Barkley, R.A. (1991). Attention deficit hyperactivity disorder. *Psychiatric Annals, 21,* 725–733.

Barkley, R.A. (1997). Attention-deficit/hyperactivity disorder. In E.J. Mash & L.G. Terdal (Eds.), *Assessment of childhood disorders* (pp. 71–129). New York, NY: Guilford Press.

Baron, R.A., & Bryne, D. (1991). *Social psychology: Understanding human interaction* (6th ed.). Toronto, ON: Allyn & Bacon.

Barthlow, B.D., Bushman, B.J., & Sestir, M.A. (2006). Chronic violent video game exposure and desensitization to violence: Behavioral and event-related brain potential data. *Journal of Experimental Social Psychology, 42,* 532–539.

Bartol, C.R., & Bartol, A.M. (1994). *Psychology and law* (2nd ed.). Pacific Grove, CA: Brooks/Cole Publishing Company.

Bartol, C.R., & Bartol, A.M. (2004). *Introduction to forensic psychology.* London, England: Sage Publications.

Bartol, C.R., & Bartol, A.M. (2006). History of forensic psychology. In I.B. Weiner & A. Hess (Eds.), *Handbook of forensic psychology* (3rd ed., pp. 3–27). New York, NY: John Wiley & Sons.

Bateman, A.L., & Salfati, C. G. (2007). An examination of behavioral consistency using individual behaviors or groups of behaviors in serial homicide. Behavioral Sciences & the Law, 25, 527-544.

Battin, S.R., Hill, K.G., Abbott, R.D., Catalano, R.F., and Hawkins, J.D. 1998. The contribution of gang membership to delinquency beyond delinquent friends. Criminology 36, 93–115.

Baum, K., Catalano S., Rand, M., & Rose, K. (2009). *Stalking victimization in the United States* (NCJ Publication No. 224527). Washington, DC: Bureau of Justice Statistics.

Beck, N.C., Menditto, A.A., Baldwin, L., Angelone, E., & Maddox, M. (1991). Reduced frequency of aggressive behavior in forensic patients in a social learning program. *Hospital and Community Psychiatry, 42,* 750–752.

Becker, H.S. (1963). *Outsiders: Studies in the sociology of deviance.* London, England: Macmillan.

Behrman, B.W., & Davey, S.L. (2001). Eyewitness identification in actual criminal cases: An archival analysis. *Law and Human Behavior, 25,* 475–491.

Bekerian, D.A., & Dennett, J.L. (1993). The cognitive interview technique: Reviving the issues. *Applied Cognitive Psychology, 7,* 275–298.

Benda, B.B. (2005). Gender differences in life-course theory of recidivism: A survival analysis. *International Journal of Offender Therapy and Comparative Criminology, 49,* 325–342.

Benjamin, L.T., & Crouse, E.M. (2002). The American Psychological Association's response to *Brown v. Board of Education*: The case of Kenneth B. Clark. *American Psychologist, 57,* 38–50.

Bennell, C., & Canter, D.V. (2002). Linking commercial burglaries by modus operandi: Tests using regression and ROC analysis. *Science & Justice, 42,* 153–164.

Bennell, C., & Jones, N.J. (2005). Between a ROC and a hard place: A method for linking serial burglaries using an offender's modus operandi. *Journal of Investigative Psychology and Offender Profiling, 2,* 23–41.

Bennell, C., Jones, N.J., Taylor, P.J., & Snook, B. (2006). Validities and abilities in criminal profiling: A critique of the studies conducted by Richard Kocsis and his colleagues. *International Journal of Offender Therapy and Comparative Criminology, 50,* 344–360.

Bennell, C., Taylor, P.J., & Snook, B. (2007). Clinical versus actuarial geographic profiling strategies: A review of the research. *Police Practice and Research, 8,* 335–345.

Bennett, L.W., Stoops, C., Call, C., & Flett, H. (2007). Program completion and re-arrest in a batterer intervention system. *Research on Social Work Practice, 17*(1), 42–54.

Ben-Porath, Y.S. (1994). The ethical dilemma of coached malingering research. *Psychological Assessment, 6,* 14–15.

Ben-Shakhar, G., & Elaad, E. (2003). The validity of psychophysiological detection of information with the guilty knowledge test: A meta-analytic review. *Journal of Applied Psychology, 88,* 131–151.

Ben-Shakhar, G., & Furedy, J. J. (1990). *Theories and applications in the detection of deception: Psychophysiological and cultural perspectives.* New York, NY: Springer-Verlag.

Benton, T., Ross, D.F., Bradshaw, E., Thomas, W., & Bradshaw, G. (2006). Eyewitness memory is still not common sense: Comparing jurors, judges, and law enforcement to eyewitness experts. *Applied Cognitive Psychology, 20,* 115–130.

Bergen, R. K. (2006). Marital rape: New research and directions. Retrieved May 21, 2012 from http://new.vawnet.org/Assoc_Files_VAWnet/AR_MaritalRapeRevised.pdf

Berk, R.A., Berk, S.F., Loseka, O.R., & Rauma, D. (1983). Mutual combat and other family violence myths. In D. Finkelhor, R.J. Gelles, G.T. Hotaling & M.A. Straus (Eds.), *The darker side of families: Current family violence research* (pp. 197–212). Beverly Hills, CA: Sage.

Binet, A. (1900). *La suggestibilité.* Paris, France: Schleicher Freres.

Bjerregaard, B. (2002). An empirical study of stalking victimization. In K.E. Davis, I.H. Frieze, & R.D. Maiuro (Eds.), *Stalking: Perspectives on victims and perpetrators* (pp. 112–137). New York, NY: Springer.

Blair, R.J.R. (2006a). The emergence of psychopathy: Implications for the neuropsychological approach to developmental disorders. *Cognition, 101,* 414–442.

Blair, R.J.R. (2006b). Subcortical brain systems in psychopathy: The amygdala and associated structures. In C.J. Patrick (Ed.), *Handbook of psychopathy* (pp. 296–312). New York, NY: Guilford Press.

Blair, R.J.R. (2008). The cognitive neuroscience of psychopathy and implications for judgments of responsibility. *Neuroethics, 1,* 149–157.

Blair, R.J.R., Budhani, S., Colledge, E., & Scott, S. (2005). Deafness to fear in boys with psychopathic tendencies. *Journal of Child Psychology and Psychiatry, 46,* 327–336.

Blanchette, K.D., & Brown, S.L. (2006). *The assessment and treatment of women offenders: An integrative perspective.* Chichester, England: John Wiley & Sons.

Bland, R.C., Newman, S.C., Dyck, R.J., & Orn, H. (1990). Prevalence of psychiatric disorders and suicide attempts in a prison population. The Canadian Journal of Psychiatry / La Revue Canadienne De Psychiatrie, 35(5), 407–413. Retrieved from http://search.proquest.com/docview/617787683?accountid=9894

Blonigen, D.M., Carlson, S.R., Krueger, R.F., & Patrick, C.J. (2003). A twin study of self reported psychopathic personality traits. *Personality and Individual Differences, 35,* 179–197.

Blonigen, D.M., Hicks, B.M., Krueger, R.F., Patrick, C.J., & Iacono, W.G. (2005). Psychopathic personality traits: Heritability and genetic overlap with internalizing and externalizing psychopathology. *Psychological Medicine, 35,* 637–648.

Blumstein, A., & Cohen, J. (1987). Characterizing criminal careers. *Science, 237,* 985–991.

Boccaccini, M.T., Murrie, D.C., Clark, J.W., & Cornell, D.G. (2008). Describing, diagnosing, and naming psychopathy: How do youth psychopathy labels influence jurors? *Behavioral Sciences and the Law, 26,* 487–510.

Boccaccini, M.T., Murrie, D.C., & Duncan, S.A. (2006). Screening for malingering in a criminal-forensic sample with the Personality Assessment Inventory. *Psychological Assessment, 18,* 415–423.

Bohner, G., Siebler, F., Sturm, S., Effler, D., Litters, M., Reinhard, M., & Rutz, S. (1998). Rape myth acceptance and accessibility of the gender category. *Group Processes and Intergroup Relations, 1,* 67–79.

Bonazzoli, M.J. (1998). Jury selection and bias: Debunking invidious stereotypes through science. *Quinnipiac Law Review, 18,* 247–305.

Bond, C.F., & DePaulo, B.M. (2006). Accuracy of deception judgments. *Personality and Social Psychology Review, 10,* 214–234.

Bond, C.F., & DePaulo, B.M. (2008). Individual differences in judging deception: Accuracy and bias. *Psychological Bulletin, 134,* 477–492.

Bonnie, R.J., & Grisso, T. (2000). Adjudicative competence and youthful offenders. In T. Grisso & R.G. Schwartz (Eds.), *Youth on trial: A developmental perspective on juvenile justice* (pp. 73–103). Chicago, IL: University of Chicago Press.

Bonta, J. (2002). Offender risk assessment: Guidelines for selection and use. *Criminal Justice and Behavior, 29,* 355–379.

Bonta, J.L., Law, M., & Hanson, R.K. (1998). The prediction of criminal and violent recidivism among mentally disordered offenders: A meta-analysis. *Psychological Bulletin, 123,* 123–142.

Boothby, J., & Clements, C.B. (2000). A national survey of correctional psychologists. *Criminal Justice and Behavior, 27,* 715–731.

Borum, R. (1996). Improving the clinical practice of violence risk assessment: Technology, guidelines and training. *American Psychologist, 51,* 945–956.

Borum, R., & Fulero, S.M. (1999). "Empirical research on the insanity defense and attempted reforms: Evidence toward informed policy": Erratum. Law and Human Behavior, 23(3), 375-394.

Borum, R., Cornell, D.G., Modzeleski, W., & Jimerson, S.R. (2010). What can be done about school shootings? A review of the evidence. Educational Researcher, 39(1), 27-37.

Borum, R., Otto, R., & Golding, S. (1993). Improving clinical judgment and decision making in forensic evaluation. *Journal of Psychiatry and Law, 21,* 35–76.

Bottoms, B.L., Davis, S.L., & Epstein, M.A. (2004). Effects of victim and defendant race on jurors' decisions in child sexual abuse cases. Journal of Applied Social Psychology, 34, 1-33.

Brodsky, S. (1991). Testifying in court: Guidelines and maxims for the expert witness. Washington, DC: American Psychological Association.

Brodsky, S. (1999). The expert witness: More maxims and guidelines for testifying in court. Washington, DC: American Psychological Association.

Brown v. Mississippi, 297 U.S. 278 (1936)

Bowden, D. (2011). *Casey Anthony's team used social media to shape its arguments*. Retrieved from http://latino.foxnews.com/latino/news/2011/07/20/casey-anthonys-team-used-social-media-to-shape-their-arguments

Bowen, E., & Gilchrist, E. (2006). Predicting dropout of court-mandated treatment in a British sample of domestic violence offenders. *Psychology, Crime and Law, 12,* 573–587.

Bowlby, J. (1944). Forty-four juvenile thieves. *International Journal of Psychoanalysis, 25,* 1–57.

Bradfield, A., & McQuiston, D. (2004). When does evidence of eyewitness confidence inflation affect judgments in a criminal trial? *Law and Human Behavior, 28,* 369–387.

Bradfield, A.L., Wells, G.L., & Olson, E.A. (2002). The damaging effect of confirming feedback on the relation between eyewitness certainty and identification accuracy. *Journal of Applied Psychology, 87,* 112–120.

Bradford, J.M., & Pawlak, A. (1993). Effects of cyproterone acetate on sexual arousal patterns of pedophiles. *Archives of Sexual Behavior, 22,* 629–641.

Bradshaw, W., & Roseborough, D. (2005). Restorative justice dialogue: The impact of mediation and conferencing on juvenile recidivism. *Federal Probation, 69,* 15–21.

Brainerd, C., & Reyna, V. (1996). Mere testing creates false memories in children. *Developmental Psychology, 32,* 467–476.

Brainerd, C.J., & Reyna, V.F. (2004). Fuzzy-trace theory and memory development. *Developmental Review, 24,* 396–439.

Brame, B., Nagin, D.S., & Tremblay, R.E. (2001). Developmental trajectories of physical aggression from school entry to late adolescence. *Journal of Child Psychology and Psychiatry, 42,* 503–512.

Brennan, S., & Taylor-Butts, A. (2008). *Sexual assaults in Canada: 2004 and 2007.* Ottawa, ON: Canadian Centre for Justice Statistics.

Breslin, N.A. (1992). Treatment of schizophrenia: Current practice and future promise. *Hospital and Community Psychiatry, 43,* 877–885.

Brewer, N., Potter, R., Fisher, R.P., Bond, N., & Luszcz (1999). Beliefs and data on the relationship between consistency and accuracy of eyewitness testimony. *Applied Cognitive Psychology, 13,* 297–313.

Brigham, J.C. (1999). What is forensic psychology, anyway? *Law and Human Behavior, 23,* 273–298.

Brodsky, S. (1991). *Testifying in court: Guidelines and maxims for the expert witness.* Washington, DC: American Psychological Association.

Brodsky, S. (1999). *The expert witness: More maxims and guidelines for testifying in court.* Washington, DC: American Psychological Association.

Brown, D., & Pipe, M-E. (2003). Variations on a technique: Enhancing children's recall using narrative elaboration training. *Applied Cognitive Psychology, 17,* 377–399.

Brown, D., Scheflin, A.W., & Hammond, D.C. (1998). *Memory, trauma treatment, and the law.* New York, NY: Norton.

Brown, G.R. (2004). Gender as a factor in the response of the law-enforcement systems to violence against partners. *Sexuality and Culture, 9,* 1–87.

Brown, J.M., & Campbell, E.A. (1994). *Stress and policing: Sources and strategies.* New York, NY: John Wiley & Sons.

Brown, S.L., & Forth, A.E. (1997). Psychopathy and sexual assault: Static risk factors, emotional precursors, and rapist subtypes. *Journal of Consulting and Clinical Psychology, 65,* 848–857.

Browne, A., & Finkelhor, D. (1986). Impact of child sexual abuse: A review of the research. *Psychological Bulletin, 99,* 66–77.

Bureau of Justice Statistics. (2009). Felony sentences in state courts, 2006 – statistical tables. Retrieved from http://bjs.ojp.usdoj.gov/content/pub/pdf/fssc06st.pdf

Buss, D.M., & Shackelford, T.K. (1997). Human aggression in evolutionary psychological perspective. Clinical Psychology Review, 17, 605-619.

Bruck, M., & Ceci, S.J. (1999). The suggestibility of children's memory. *Annual Review of Psychology, 50,* 419–439.

Buck, S.M., Warren, A.R., Betman, S., & Brigham, J.C. (2002). Age differences in Criteria-Based Content Analysis scores in typical child sexual abuse interviews. *Journal of Applied Developmental Psychology, 23,* 267–283.

Bull, R., & Clifford, B.R. (1984). Earwitness voice recognition accuracy. In G. Wells, & E. Loftus (Eds.), *Eyewitness testimony, psychological perspectives* (pp. 92–123). Cambridge, England: Cambridge University Press.

Bumby, K.M., & Hansen, D.J. (1997). Intimacy deficits, fear of intimacy, and loneliness among sexual offenders. *Criminal Justice and Behavior, 24,* 315–331.

Burgess, A.W., & Holmstrom, L.L. (1974). Rape trauma syndrome. *American Journal of Psychiatry, 131,* 981–986.

Burke, R.J. (1993). Work–family stress, conflict, coping, and burnout in police officers. *Stress Medicine, 9,* 171–180.

Burt, M.R. (1980). Cultural myths and supports for rape. *Journal of Personality and Social Psychology, 38,* 217–230.

Bushman, B.J., & Anderson, C.A. (2001). Media violence and the American public: Scientific facts versus media misinformation. *American Psychologist, 56,* 477–489.

Butcher, J.N., Dahlstrom, W.G., Graham, J.R., Tellegen, A., & Kaemmer, B. (1989). *MMPI-2: Manual for administration and scoring.* Minneapolis, MN: University of Minnesota Press.

Cadoret, R.J., & Cain, C. (1980). Sex differences in predictors of antisocial behavior in adoptees. *Archives of General Psychiatry, 37,* 1171–1175.

Caldwell, M.F., McCormick, D.J., Umstead, D., & Van Rybroek, G.J. (2007). Evidence of treatment progress and therapeutic outcomes among adolescents with psychopathic features. *Criminal Justice and Behavior, 34,* 573–587.

Caldwell, M.F., Skeem, J., Salekin, R., & Van Rybroek, G. (2006). Treatment response of adolescent offenders with psychopathy-like features. *Criminal Justice and Behavior, 33, 5,* 571–596.

Caldwell, R.M., Silverman, J., Lefforge, N., & Silver, N.C. (2004). Adjudicated Mexican American adolescents: The effects of familial emotional support on self-esteem, emotional well-being, and delinquency. *American Journal of Family Therapy, 32,* 55–69.

Campbell, C. (1976). Portrait of a mass killer. *Psychology Today, 9,* 110–119.

Campbell, J.C., Webster, D., & Koziol-McLain, J. (2003). Risk factors for femicide in abusive relationships: Results from a multisite case control study. *American Journal of Public Health, 93,* 1089–1097.

Campbell, M.A., French, S., & Gendreau, P. (2009). The prediction of violence in adult offenders: A meta-analytic comparison of instruments and methods of assessment. *Criminal Justice and Behavior, 36,* 567–590.

Campion, M.A., Palmer, D.K., & Campion, J.E. (1997). A review of structure in the selection interview. *Personnel Psychology, 50,* 655–702.

Campbell, M.A., Porter, S., & Santor, D. (2004). Psychopathic traits in adolescent offenders: An evaluation of criminal history, clinical, and psychosocial correlates. *Behavioral Sciences and the Law, 22,* 23–47.

Cannon, L. (1999). *Official negligence: How Rodney King and the riots changed Los Angeles and the LAPD.* Boulder, CO: Westview Press.

Canter, D.V. (1994). *Criminal shadows.* London, England: HarperCollins.

Canter, D.V. (2000). Offender profiling and criminal differentiation. *Legal and Criminological Psychology, 5,* 23–46.

Canter, D.V. (2005). Confusing operational predicaments and cognitive explorations: Comments on Rossmo and Snook et al. *Applied Cognitive Psychology, 19,* 663–668.

Canter, D.V., & Alison, L.J. (Eds.) (1999). *Interviewing and deception.* Aldershot, UK: Ashgate Publishing.

Canter, D.V. (2003). Mapping murder" The secrets of geographical profiling. London, UK: Virgin Books.

Canter, D.V. (2011). Resolving the offender "profiling equations" and the emergence of an investigative psychology. Current Directions in Psychological Science, 20, 5-10.

Canter, D.V., Alison, L.J., Wentink, N., & Alison, E. (2004). The organized/disorganized typology of serial murder: Myth or model? *Psychology, Public Policy, and Law, 10,* 293–320.

Canter, D.V., Coffey, T., Huntley, M., & Missen, C. (2000). Predicting serial killers' home base using a decision support system. *Journal of Quantitative Criminology, 16,* 457–478.

Canter, D.V., & Wentink, N. (2004). An empirical test of Holmes and Holmes's serial murder typology. *Criminal Justice and Behavior, 31,* 489–515.

Canter, D.V., & Youngs, D. (2009). *Investigative psychology: Offender profiling and the analysis of criminal action.* Chichester, England: Wiley.

Caprara, G.V., Barbaranelli, C., & Pastorelli, C. (2001). Facing guilt: Role of negative affectivity, need for reparation, and fear of punishment in leading to pro-social behaviour and aggression. *European Journal of Personality, 15,* 219–237.

Caputo, G.A. (2004). *Intermediate sanctions in corrections.* Denton, TX: University of North Texas Press.

Carich, M.S. (2007). *Interview with Ray Knight.* Retrieved from http://newsmanager.commpartners.com/atsa/issues/2007-03-15/3.html

Carney, M., Buttell, F., & Dutton, D. (2007). Women who perpetrate intimate partner violence: A review of the literature with recommendations for treatment. *Aggression and Violent Behavior, 12,* 108–115.

Cassell, P.G. (1998). Protecting the innocent from false confessions and lost confessions—and from Miranda. *Journal of Criminal Law and Criminology, 88,* 497–556.

Cattell, J.M. (1895). Measurements of the accuracy of recollection. *Science, 2,* 761–766.

Cavanaugh, M.M., & Gelles, R.J. (2005). The utility of male domestic violence offender typologies: New directions for research, policy, and practice. *Journal of Interpersonal Violence, 20,* 155–166.

Ceci, S.J., & Bruck, M. (1993). The suggestibility of the child witness: A historical review and synthesis. *Psychological Bulletin, 113,* 403–439.

Ceci, S.J. & Bruck, M. [1995]. Jeopardy in the courtroom: The scientific analysis of children's testimony. Washington, D.C.: American Psychological Association.

Ceci, S.J., & Liker, J.K. (1986) A day at the races: IQ, expertise and cognitive complexity. *Journal of Experimental Psychology: General, 115,* 255–266.

Cervone, D., & Shoda, Y. (Eds.) (1999). *The coherence of personality: Social-cognitive bases of consistency, variability and organization.* New York, NY: Guilford Press.

Chadee, D. (1996). Race, trial evidence and jury decision making. *Caribbean Journal of Criminology and Social Psychology, 1,* 59–86.

Chaiken, J.M., & Chaiken, M.R. (1983). Crime rates and the active offender. In J.Q. Wilson (Ed.), *Crime and public policy* (pp. 203–229). New Brunswick, OH: Transaction Books.

Chan, K.L., Strauss, M.R., Brownridge, D.A., Tiwari, A., & Leung, W.C. (2008). Prevalence of dating partner violence and suicidal ideation among male and female university students worldwide. *Journal of Midwifery & Women's Health, 53,* 529–537.

Chandler, R.K., Peters, R.H., Field, G., & Juliano-Bult, D. (2004). Challenges in implementing evidence-based treatment practices for co-occurring disorders in the criminal justice system. *Behavioral Science and the Law, 22,* 431–448.

Chapman, L.J., & Chapman, J.P. (1967). Genesis of popular but erroneous psychodiagnostic observations. *Journal of Abnormal Psychology, 74,* 193–204.

Cheung, P.T.K. (1986). Maternal filicide in Hong Kong. *Medicine, Science, and Law, 26,* 185–192.

Chibnall, J.T., & Detrick P. (2003). The NEO PI-R, Inwald Personality, Inventory, and MMPI-2 in the prediction of police academy performance: A case of incremental validity. *American Journal of Criminal Justice, 27,* 224–233.

Cirincione, C., Steadman, H.J., Clark-Robbins, P.C., & Monahan, J. (1992). Schizophrenia as a contingent risk factor for criminal violence. *International Journal of Law and Psychiatry, 15,* 347–358.

Cirincione, C., & Jacobs, C. (1999). Identifying insanity acquittals: Is it any easier? Law and Human Behavior, 23(4), 487–497.

City of Cincinnati Police Department. (2010). *City of Cincinnati police recruit selection process.* Retrieved from http://www.cincinnati-oh.gov/cityhr/downloads/cityhr_pdf7052.PDF

Clark, S.E. (2005). A re-examination of the effects of biased lineup instructions in eyewitness identification. *Law and Human Behavior, 29,* 575–604.

Cleckley, H.R. (1976). *The mask of sanity* (5th ed.). St. Louis, MO: Mosby.

Clifford, B.R. (1980). Voice identification by human listeners: On earwitness reliability. *Law and Human Behavior, 4,* 373–394.

CNN. (2006). *No DNA match, no JonBenet charges.* Retrieved from http://www.cnn.com/2006/LAW/08/28/ramsey.arrest

Cochrane, R.E., Tett, R.P., & Vandecreek, L. (2003). Psychological testing and the selection of police officers: A national survey. *Criminal Justice and Behavior, 30,* 511–537.

Cocozza, J.J., Melick, M.E., & Steadman, H.J. (1978). Trends in violent crime among ex-mental patients. *Criminology: An Interdisciplinary Journal, 16,* 317–334.

Cocozza, J.J., & Steadman, H.J. (1978). Prediction in psychiatry: An example of misplaced confidence in experts. *Social Problems, 25,* 265–276.

Cohen, A.J., Adler, N., Kaplan, S.J., Pelcovitz, D., & Mandel, F.G. (2002). Interactional effects of marital status and physical abuse on adolescent psychopathology. *Child Abuse and Neglect, 26,* 277–288.

Cohen, J., & Tonry, M.H. (1983). Sentencing reforms and their impacts. In A. Blumstein, J. Cohen, S.E. Martin, and M.H. Tonry (Eds.), *Research on sentencing: The search for reform* (pp. 305–459). Washington, DC: National Academy Press.

Cohn, E.S., Buccolo, D., Pride, M., & Sommers, S.R. (2009). Reducing white juror bias: The role of race salience and racial attitudes. *Journal of Applied Social Psychology, 39,* 1953–1973.

Coid, J., Yang, M., Ullrich, S., Roberts, A., & Hare, R.D. (2009). Prevalence and correlates of psychopathic traits in the household population of Great Britain. *International Journal of Law and Psychiatry, 32,* 65–73.

Coie, J.D., Belding, M., & Underwood, M. (1988). Aggression and peer rejection in childhood. In B.B. Lahey & A.E. Kazdin (Eds.), *Advances in clinical child psychology* (Vol. II, pp. 125–158). New York, NY: Plenum.

Coie, J.D., Lochman, J.E., Terry, R., & Hyman, C. (1992). Predicting early adolescent disorder from childhood aggression and peer rejection. *Journal of Consulting and Clinical Psychology, 60,* 783–792.

Cole, W.G., & Loftus, E.F. (1979). Incorporating new information into memory. *American Journal of Psychology, 92,* 413–425.

Conaway, L.P., & Hansen, D.J. (1989). Social behavior of physically abused and neglected children: A critical review. *Clinical Psychology Review, 9,* 627–652.

Conley, M. (2011). *Public irate over Casey Anthony verdict; social media sites explode with opinions.* Retrieved from http://abcnews.go.com/Health/casey-anthony-verdict-outrage-spills-online/story?id=14002257#.T0UFRIdumSo

Connolly, D.A., & Read, J.D. (2006). Delayed prosecutions of historic child sexual abuse: Analyses of 2064 Canadian criminal complaints. *Law and Human Behavior, 30,* 409–434.

Cook, S., & Wilding, J. (1997). Earwitness testimony 2: Voices, faces, and context. *Applied Cognitive Psychology, 11,* 527–541.

Cooke, D.J., & Michie, C. (2001). Refining the construct of psychopathy: Towards a hierarchical model. *Psychological Assessment, 13,* 171–188.

Copson, G. (1995). *Coals to Newcastle? Part 1: A study of offender profiling.* London, England: Home Office.

Corder, B.F., Ball, B.C., Haizlip, T.M., Rollins, R., & Beaumont, R. (1976). Adolescent parricide: A comparison with other adolescent murder. *American Journal of Psychiatry, 133,* 957–961.

Cornell, D.G., Benedek, E.P., & Benedek, D.M. (1987). Characteristics of adolescents charged with homicide: Review of 72 cases. *Behavioral Sciences and the Law, 5,* 11–23.

Cornell, D.G., & Hawk, G.L. (1989). Clinical presentation of malingerers diagnosed by experienced forensic psychologists. *Law and Human Behavior, 13,* 374–383.

Cornell, D.G., Warren, J., Hawk, G., Stafford, E., Oram, G., & Pine, D. (1996). Psychopathy in instrumental and reactive violent offenders. *Journal of Consulting and Clinical Psychology, 64,* 783–790.

Corrado, R.R., Vincent, G.M., Hart, S.D., & Cohen, I.M. (2004). Predictive validity of the Psychopathy Checklist: Youth Version for general and violent recidivism. *Behavioral Sciences and the Law, 22,* 5–22.

Cortina, J.M., Goldstein, N.B., Payne, S.C., Davison, H.K., & Gilliland, S.W. (2000). The incremental validity of interview scores over and above cognitive ability and conscientiousness scores. *Personnel Psychology, 53*, 325–351.

Cottle, C.C., Lee, R.J., & Heilbrun, K. (2001). The prediction of criminal recidivism in juveniles: A meta-analysis. *Criminal Justice and Behavior, 28*, 367–394.

Coy, E., Speltz, M.L., DeKlyen, M., & Jones, K. (2001). Social-cognitive processes in preschool boys with and without oppositional defiant disorder. *Journal of Abnormal Child Psychology, 29*, 107–119.

Crawford, M., & Gartner, R. (1992). *Women killing: Intimate femicide in Ontario, 1974–1990.* Women's Directorate, Ministry of Social Services, Toronto, ON.

Crick, N.R., & Dodge, K.A. (1994). A review and reformulation of social information-processing mechanisms in children's social adjustment. *Psychological Bulletin, 115*, 74–101.

Cross, J.F., Cross, J., & Daly, J. (1971). Sex, race, age, and beauty as factors in recognition of faces. *Perception and Psychophysics, 10*, 393–396.

Cross, T.P., & Saxe, L. (2001). Polygraph testing and sexual abuse: The lure of the magic lasso. *Child Maltreatment, 6*, 195–206.

Cullen, D. (1999). *Columbine killers thank gun providers on video.* Retrieved from http://www.salon.com/1999/11/12/videos

Cullen, F., & Gendreau, P. (2000). Assessing correctional rehabilitation: Policy, practice, and prospects. In J. Horney (Ed.), *NIJ criminal justice 2000: Changes in decision-making and discretion in the criminal justice system* (pp. 109–175). Washington, DC: U.S. National Institute of Justice.

Cullen, F.T. (2002). It's a wonderful life: Reflections on a career in progress. In G. Geis and M. Dodge (Eds.), *Lessons of criminology* (pp. 1–22). Cincinnati, OH: Anderson.

Cummings, E.M., Davies, P.T., & Campbell, S.B. (2000). *Developmental psychopathology and family process: Theory, research, and clinical implications.* New York, NY: Guilford Press.

Cutler, B.L., Fisher, R.P., & Chicvara, C.L. (1989). Eyewitness identification from live versus videotaped lineups. *Forensic Reports, 2*, 93–106.

Cutler, B.L., & Penrod, S.D. (1989a). Forensically relevant moderators of the relationship between eyewitness identification accuracy and confidence. *Journal of Applied Psychology, 74*, 650–652.

Cutler, B.L., & Penrod, S.D. (1989b). Moderators of the confidence-accuracy relation in face recognition: The role of information processing and base rates. *Applied Cognitive Psychology, 3*, 95–107.

Dahle, K.P. (2006). Strengths and limitations of actuarial prediction of criminal reoffence in a German prison sample: A comparative study of LSI-R, HCR-20 and PCL-R. *International Journal of Law and Psychiatry, 29*, 431–442.

Dalby, J.T. (2006). The case of Daniel McNaughton: Let's get the story straight. *American Journal of Forensic Psychiatry, 27*, 17–32.

Daly, K. (1989). Rethinking judicial paternalism: Gender, work–family relations, and sentencing. *Gender and Society, 3*, 9–36.

Daly, M., & Wilson, M.I. (1982). Homicide and kinship. *American Anthropologist, 84*, 372–378.

Daly, M., & Wilson, M. (1988). Evolutionary social psychology and family homicide. *Science, 242*, 519–524.

Daly, M., & Wilson, M.I. (1996). Violence against stepchildren. *Current Directions in Psychological Science, 5*, 77–81.

Dando, C., Wilcock, R., & Milne, R. (2009). The cognitive interview: The efficacy of a modified mental reinstatement of context procedure for frontline police investigators. *Applied Cognitive Psychology, 23*, 138–147.

Darby, P.J., Allan, W.D., Kashani, J.H., Hartke, K.L., & Reid, J.C. (1998). Analysis of 112 juveniles who committed homicide: Characteristics and a closer look at family abuse. *Journal of Family Violence, 13*, 365–375.

Davies, G., Tarrant, A., & Flin, R. (1989). Close encounters of the witness kind: Children's memory for a simulated health inspection. *British Journal of Psychology, 80*, 415–429.

Davies, G.M., Stevenson-Robb, Y., & Flin, R. (1988). Telling tales out of school: Children's memory for an unexpected event. In M. Gruneberg, P. Morris, & R. Sykes (Eds.), *Practical aspects of memory* (pp. 122–127). Chichester, England: John Wiley & Sons.

Davis, G.E., & Leitenberg, H. (1987). Adolescent sex offenders. *Psychological Bulletin, 101*, 417–427.

Davidson, W.S., & Redner, R. (1988). The prevention of juvenile delinquency: Diversion from the juvenile justice system. In R.H. Price, E.L. Cowen, R.P. Lorion, & J. Ramos-McKay (Eds.), Fourteen ounces of prevention: Theory, research, and prevention (pp. 123-137). New York: Pergamon.

Davis, K.E., & Frieze, I.H. (2000). Research on stalking: What do we know and where do we go? *Violence and Victims, 15,* 473–487.

De Vaney Olvey, C., Hogg, A., & Counts, W. (2002). Licensure requirements: Have we raised the bar too far? *Professional Psychology: Research and Practice, 33,* 323–329.

Death Penalty Information Center. (2011). *Sentencing for life: Americans embrace alternatives to the death penalty.* Retrieved from http://www.deathpenaltyinfo .org/sentencing-life-americans-embrace-alternatives-death-penalty

DeFronzo, J., Ditta, A., Hannon, L., & Prochnow, J. (2007). Male serial homicide: The influence of cultural and structural variables. *Homicide Studies: An Interdisciplinary & International Journal, 11,* 3–14.

DeGue, S., & DiLillo, D. (2009). Is animal cruelty a "red flag" for family violence? Investigating the co-occurring violence toward children, partners, and pets. *Journal of Interpersonal Violence, 24,* 1036–1056.

Deitz, S.R., Blackwell, K.T., Daley, P.C., & Bentley, B.J. (1982). Measurement of empathy toward rape victims and rapists. *Journal of Personality and Social Psychology, 43,* 372–384.

Dekovic, M. (1999). Risk and protective factors in the development of problem behavior during adolescence. *Journal of Youth and Adolescence, 28,* 667–685.

DeLisi, M. (2006). Zeroing in on early arrest onset: Results from a population of extreme career criminals. *Journal of Criminal Justice, 34,* 17–26.

DeLoache, J.S., & Marzolf, D.P. (1995). The use of dolls to interview young children: Issues of symbolic representation. *Journal of Experimental Child Psychology, 60,* 155–173.

DeMatteo, D., & Edens, J.F. (2006). The role and relevance of the Psychopathy Checklist-Revised in court: A case law survey of U.S. courts (1991–2004). *Psychology, Public Policy, and Law, 12,* 214–241.

DeMatteo, D., Heilbrun, K., & Marczyk, G. (2005). Psychopathy, risk of violence, and protective factors in a noninstitutionalized and noncriminal sample. *International Journal of Forensic Mental Health, 4,* 147–157.

Dempsey, J.L., & Pozzulo, J.D. (2008). Identification accuracy of eyewitnesses for a multiple perpetrator crime: Examining the simultaneous and elimination lineup procedures. *American Journal of Forensic Psychology, 26,* 67–81.

Denham, S., & Almeida, M. (1987). Children's social problem solving skills, behavioral adjustment, and interventions: A meta-analysis evaluating theory and practice. *Journal of Applied Developmental Psychology, 8,* 391–409.

Department of Juvenile Justice. (2010). *Restorative justice.* Retrieved from Health & Social Services, State of Alaska, website: http://www.hss.state.ak.us/djj/restorative .htm

DePaulo, B.M., Charlton, L., Cooper, H., Lindsay, J.J., & Muhlenbruck, L. (1997). The accuracy-confidence correlation in the detection of deception. *Personality and Social Psychology Review, 1,* 346–357.

DePaulo, B.M., Kashy, D.A., Kirkendol, S.E., Wyer, M.M., & Epstein, J.A. (1996). Lying in everyday life. *Journal of Personality and Social Psychology, 70,* 979–995.

DePaulo, B.M., & Kirkendol, S.E. (1989). The motivational impairment effect in the communication of deception. In Y.C. Yuille (Ed.), *Credibility assessment* (pp. 51–70). Dordrecht, The Netherlands: Kluwer.

DePaulo, B.M., Lassiter, G.D., & Stone, J.I. (1982). Attentional determinants of success at detecting deception and truth. *Personality and Social Psychology Bulletin, 8,* 273–279.

DePaulo, B.M., Lindsay, J.J., Malone, B.E., Muhlenbruck, L., Charlton, K., & Cooper, H. (2003). Cues to deception. *Psychological Bulletin, 129,* 74–118.

DePaulo, B.M., & Pfeifer, R.L. (1996). On-the-job experience and skill at detecting deception. *Journal of Applied Social Psychology, 16,* 249–267.

Deregowski, J.B., Ellis, HD., & Shepherd, J.W. (1975). Descriptions of White and Black faces by White and Black subjects. *International Journal of Psychology, 10,* 119–123.

Desmarais, S.L., Nicholls, T.L., Read, D., & Brink, J. (2010). Confidence and accuracy in assessments of short-term risks presented by forensic psychiatric patients. *Journal of Forensic Psychiatry & Psychology, 21,* 1–22.

Devine, D.J., Clayton, L.D., Dunford, B.B., Seying, R., & Pryce, J. (2001). Jury decision making: 45 years of empirical research on deliberating groups. *Psychology, Public Policy, and Law, 7,* 622–727.

Devlin, K., & Lorden, G. (2007). *The numbers behind numb3rs: Solving crime with mathematics.* New York, NY: Plume.

Diamond, S.A. (2008). Sympathy for the devil: What made her do it? Retrieved May 21, 2012 from http://www.psychologytoday.com/blog/evil-deeds/200805/sympathy-the-devil

Diamond, S.S., & Zeisel, H. (1975). Sentencing councils: A study of sentencing disparity and its reduction. *University of Chicago Law Review, 43,* 109–149.

Dickinson, J., Poole, D., & Bruck, M. (2005). Back to the future: A comment on the use of anatomical dolls in forensic interviews. *Journal of Forensic Psychology Practice, 5,* 63–74.

Dobash, R., & Dobash, R.E. (1979). *Violence against women.* New York, NY: Free Press.

Dodge, K.A. (1991). The structure and function of reactive and proactive aggression. In D. Pepler & K. Rubin (Eds.), *The development and treatment of childhood aggression* (pp. 201–218). Hillsdale, NJ: Earlbaum.

Dodge, K.A. (2000). Conduct disorder. In A.J. Sameroff, M. Lewis, & S.M. Miller (Eds.), *Handbook of developmental psychopathology* (2nd ed., pp. 447–463). New York, NY: Kluwer Academic/Plenum Publishers.

Dodge, K.A., Lochman, J.E., Harnish, J.D., Bates, J.E., & Pettit, G.S. (1997). Reactive and proactive aggression in school children and psychiatrically impaired chronically assaultive youth. *Journal of Abnormal Psychology, 106,* 37–51.

Doehring, D.G., & Ross, R.W. (1972). Voice recognition by matching the sample. *Journal of Psycholinguistic Research, 1,* 233–242.

Doerner, W.G. (1997). The utility of the oral interview board in selecting police academy admissions. *Policing: An International Journal of Police Strategies & Management, 20,* 777–785.

Dolan, M., & Völlm, B. (2009). Antisocial personality disorder and psychopathy in women: A literature review on the reliability and validity of assessment instruments. *International Journal of Law and Psychiatry, 32,* 2–9.

Douglas, J. (2010). *John Douglas.* Retrieved from http://www.johndouglasmindhunter.com/bio.php

Douglas, J.E., & Burgess, A.W. (1986). Criminal profiling: A viable investigative tool against violent crime. *FBI Law Enforcement Bulletin, 12,* 9–13.

Douglas, J.E., Burgess, A.W., Burgess, A.G., & Ressler, R.K. (1992). *Crime classification manual.* New York, NY: Lexington Books.

Douglas, J.E., & Olshaker, M. (1995). *Mindhunter: Inside the FBI's elite serial crime unit.* New York, NY: Charles Scribner's.

Douglas, J.E., Ressler, R.K., Burgess, A.W., & Hartman, C.R. (1986). Criminal profiling from crime scene analysis. *Behavioral Sciences and the Law, 4,* 401–421.

Douglas, K.S., Guy, L.S., & Hart, S.D. (2009). Psychosis as a risk factor for violence to others: A meta-analysis. *Psychological Bulletin, 135,* 679–706.

Douglas, K.S., & Skeem, J.L. (2005). Violence risk assessment: Getting specific about being dynamic. *Psychology, Public Policy, and Law, 11,* 347–383.

Douglas, K.S., Yeomans, M., & Boer, D.P. (2005). Comparative validity analysis of multiple measures of violence risk inn a sample of criminal offenders. *Criminal Justice and Behavior, 32,* 479–510.

Douglass, A.B., & Steblay, N. (2006). Memory distortion in eyewitnesses: A meta-analysis of the post-identification feedback effect. *Applied Cognitive Psychology, 20,* 859–869.

Dowden, C., & Brown, S.L. (2002). The role of substance abuse factors in predicting recidivism: A meta-analysis. *Psychology, Crime, and Law, 8,* 243–264.

Dowler, K. (2003). Media consumption and public attitudes toward crime and justice: The relationship between fear of crime, punitive attitudes, and perceived police effectiveness. *Journal of Criminal Justice and Popular Culture, 10,* 109–126.

Doyle, A. (2003). *Arresting images: Crime and policing in front of the television camera.* Toronto, ON: University of Toronto Press.

Dube, S.R., Anda, R.F., Whitfield, C.L., Brown, D.W., Felitti, V.J., Dong, M., & Giles, W. (2005). Long-term consequences of childhood sexual abuse by gender of victim. *American Journal of Preventive Medicine, 28,* 430–438.

Dutton, D.G. (1995). *The domestic assault of women: Psychological and criminal justice perspectives.* Vancouver, BC: University of British Columbia Press.

Dutton, D.G., & Corvo, K. (2006). Transforming a flawed policy: A call to revive psychology and science in domestic violence research and practice. *Aggression and Violent Behavior, 11,* 457–483.

Dysart, J.E., Lindsay, R.C.L., & Dupuis, P. (2006). Showups: The critical issue of clothing bias. *Applied Cognitive Psychology, 20,* 1009–1023.

Easterbrook, J.A. (1959). The effect of emotion on cue utilization and the organization of behavior. *Psychological Review, 66,* 183–201.

Eastwood, J., & Snook, B. (2010). Comprehending Canadian police cautions: Are the rights to silence and legal counsel understandable? *Behavioral Sciences and the Law, 28,* 366–377.

Ebata, A.T., Peterson, A.C., & Conger, J.J. (1990). The development of psychopathology in adolescence. In J. Rolf, A.S. Masten, D. Cicchetti, K. Nuechterlein, & S. Weintraub (Eds.), *Risk and protective factors in the development of psychopathology* (pp. 308–333). Cambridge, MA: Cambridge University Press.

Ebbesen, E.G., & Konecni, V.J. (1997). Eyewitness memory research: Probative versus prejudicial value. *Expert Evidence, 5,* 2–28.

Eberhardt, J.L., Davies, P.G., Purdie-Vaughns, V.J., & Johnson, S.L. (2006). Looking deathworthy: Perceived stereotypicality of black defendants predicts capital-sentencing outcomes. *Psychological Science, 17,* 383–386.

Edens, J.F., Colwell, L.H., Desforges, D.M., & Fernandez, K. (2005). The impact of mental health evidence on support for capital punishment: Are defendants labeled psychopathic considered more deserving of death. *Behavioral Sciences and the Law, 23,* 603–625.

Edens, J.F., Guy, L.S., & Fernandez, K. (2003). Psychopathic traits predict attitudes toward a juvenile capital murderer. *Behavioral Sciences & the Law, 21,* 807–828.

Edens, J.F., Petrila, J., & Buffington-Vollum, J.K. (2001). Psychopathy and the death penalty: Can the Psychopathy Checklist-Revised identify offenders who represent "a continuing threat to society"? *Journal of Psychiatry & Law, 29,* 433–481.

Edens, J.F., Poythress, N.G., & Watkins-Clay, M.M. (2007). Detection of malingering in psychiatric unit and general population prison inmates: A comparison of the PAI, SIMS, and SIRS. *Journal of Personality Assessment, 88,* 33–42.

Edens, J.F., Skeem, J.L., Cruise, K.R., & Cauffman, E. (2001). Assessment of "juvenile psychopathy" and its association with violence: A critical review. *Behavioral Sciences and the Law, 19,* 53–80.

Egeth, H.E. (1993). What do we not know about eyewitness identification. *American Psychologist, 48,* 577–580.

Egger, S.A. (1999). Psychological profiling: Past, present and future. *Journal of Contemporary Criminal Justice, 15,* 242–261.

Eisendrath, S.J. (1996). Current overview of physical factitious disorders. In M.D. Feldman & S.J. Eisendrath (Eds.), *The spectrum of factitious disorders* (pp. 21–36). Washington DC: American Psychiatric Association.

Ekman, P. (1992). *Telling lies: Clues to deceit in the marketplace, politics, and marriage.* New York, NY: W. W. Norton.

Ekman, P., & Friesen, W.V. (1974). Detecting deception from the body or face. *Journal of Personality and Social Psychology, 29,* 288–298.

Ekman, P., & O'Sullivan, M. (1991). Who can catch a liar? *American Psychologist, 46,* 913–920.

Ekman, P., & O'Sullivan, M., & Frank, M.G. (1999). A few can catch a liar. *Psychological Science, 10,* 263–266.

Elaad, E. (1990). Detection of guilty knowledge in real-life criminal applications. *Journal of Applied Psychology, 75,* 521–529.

Elaad, E., Ginton, A., & Jungman, N. (1992). Detection measures in real-life criminal guilty knowledge tests. *Journal of Applied Psychology, 77,* 757–767.

Elbogen, E.B. (2002). The process of violence risk assessment: A review of descriptive research. *Aggression and Violent Behavior, 7,* 591–604.

Elbogen, E.B., & Johnson, S.C. (2009). The intricate link between violence and mental disorder: Results from the national epidemiologic survey on alcohol and related conditions. Archives of General Psychiatry, 66, 152-161.

Esbensen, F.A. 2000. Preventing Adolescent Gang Involvement. Youth Gang Series. Washington, DC: U.S. Department of Justice, Office of Juvenile Justice and Delinquency Prevention.

Elkins, I.J., Iacono, W.G., Doyle, A.E., & McGue, M. (1997). Characteristics associated with the persistence of antisocial behavior: Results from recent longitudinal research. *Aggression and Violent Behavior, 2,* 102–124.

Elliott, D. (1994). Serious violent offenders: Onset, development course, and termination. The American Society of Criminology 1993 presidential address. *Criminology, 32,* 1–21.

Ellis, D. (1989). Male abuse of a married or cohabiting female partner: The application of sociological theory to research findings. *Violence and Victims, 4,* 235–255.

Ellis, H.D., Shepherd, J.W., & Davies, G.M. (1980). The deterioration of verbal descriptions of faces over different delay intervals. *Journal of Police Science and Administration, 8,* 101–106.

Ellsworth, P.C., & Mauro, R. (1998). Psychology and law. In D.T. Gilbert, S.T. Fiske, & G. Lindzey. *The handbook of social psychology* (pp. 684–732). New York, NY: Aronson.

Ennis, B. J., & Litwack, T.R. (1974). Psychiatry and the presumption of expertise: Flipping coins in the courtroom. *California Law Review, 62,* 693–752.

Epstein, J., & Langenbahn, S. (1994). *The criminal justice and community response to rape.* Washington, DC: U.S. Department of Justice.

Erickson, P.G., & Butters, J.E. (2006). *Youth, weapons, and violence in Toronto and Montreal.* Report prepared for Public Safety and Emergency Preparedness Canada, Ottawa.

Estroff, S.E., & Zimmer, C. (1994). Social networks, social support and violence. In J. Monahan & S. J. Steadman (Eds.), *Violence and mental disorder* (pp. 259–295). Chicago, IL: Chicago University Press.

Everly, Jr., G. S., & Boyle, S. H. (1999). Critical incident stress debriefing (CISD): A meta-analysis. *International Journal of Emergency Mental Health, 1,* 165–168.

Everly, Jr., G. S., Boyle, S. H., & Lating, J. (1999). The effectiveness of psychological debriefings in vicarious trauma: A meta-analysis. *Stress Medicine, 15,* 229–233

Everly, Jr., G. S., Flannery, Jr., R. B., & Mitchell, J. T. (2000). Critical incident stress management: A review of literature. *Aggression and Violent Behavior: A Review Journal, 5,* 23–40.

Ewing, C.P., & Aubrey, M. (1987). Battered woman and public opinion: Some realities about the myths. *Journal of Family Violence, 2,* 257–264.

Eysenck, H.J. (1964). *Crime and personality* (1st ed.). London, England: Methuen.

Fabricatore, J.M. (1979). Pre-entry assessment and training: Performance evaluation of police officers. In C.D. Speilberger (Ed.), *Police selection and evaluation: Issues and techniques* (pp. 77–86). New York, NY: Praeger Publishers.

Fagan, A.A. (2005). The relationship between adolescent physical abuse and criminal offending: Support for an enduring and generalized cycle of violence. *Journal of Family Violence, 20,* 279–290.

Fagot, B.I., & Kavanagh, K. (1990). The prediction of antisocial behavior from avoidant attachment classifications. *Child Development, 61,* 864–873.

Falkenberg, S., Gaines, L.K., & Cordner, G. (1991). An examination of the constructs underlying police performance appraisals. *Journal of Criminal Justice, 19,* 151–160.

Faller, K.C. (1987). Women who sexually abuse children. *Violence and Victims, 2,* 263–276.

Farkas, G.M., DeLeon, P.H., & Newman, R. (1997). Sanity examiner certification: An evolving national agenda. *Professional Psychology: Research and Practice, 28,* 73–76.

Farooque, R., & Ernst, F. A. (2003). Filicide: A review of eight years of clinical experience. *Journal of the National Medical Association, 95,* 90-94.

Farrington, D. (2006). Family background and psychopathy. In C.J. Patrick (Ed.), *Handbook of psychopathy* (pp. 229–250). New York, NY: Guilford Press.

Farrington, D.P. (1991). Psychological contributions to the explanation of offending. *Issues in Criminological and Legal Psychology, 1,* 7–19.

Farrington, D.P. (1995). The development of offending and antisocial behavior from childhood: Key findings from the Cambridge Study in Delinquent Development. *Journal of Child Psychology and Psychiatry, 36,* 929–964.

Farrington, D.P. (2007). Advancing knowledge about desistance. *Journal of Contemporary Criminal Justice, 23,* 125–134.

Farwell, L.A., & Donchin, E. (1991). The truth will out: Interrogative polygraphy ("lie detection") with event-related brain potentials. *Psychophysiology, 28,* 531–547.

Faulkner, S. (1991). *Action-response use of force continuum.* Unpublished manuscript. Ohio Peace Officers Training Academy.

Faver, C.A., & Strand, E.B. (2003). To leave or to stay? Battered women's concern for vulnerable pets. *Journal of Interpersonal Violence, 18,* 1367–1377.

Fazel, S., & Danesh, J. (2002). Serious mental disorder in 23,000 prisoners: A systematic review of 62 surveys. *Lancet, 359,* 545–550.

Federal Bureau of Investigation. (2008). *Serial murder: Multidisciplinary perspectives for investigators.* Washington, DC: U.S. Department of Justice.

Federal Bureau of Investigation. (2009). *Crime in the United States.* Retrieved from http://www2.fbi.gov/ucr/cius2009/offenses/violent_crime/index.html

Federoff, J.P., & Federoff, I.C. (1992). Buspirone and paraphilic sexual behavior. *Journal of Offender Rehabilitation, 18,* 89–108.

Feinman, S., & Entwisle, D.R. (1976). Children's ability to recognize other children's faces. *Child Development, 47,* 506–510.

Fergusson, D.M., & Horwood, L.J. (1996). The role of adolescent peer affiliations in the continuity between childhood behavioral adjustment and juvenile offending. *Journal of Abnormal Child Psychology, 24,* 205–221.

Fergusson, D.M., & Horwood, L.J. (1998). Early conduct problems and later life opportunities. *Journal of Child Psychology and Psychiatry, 39,* 1097–1108.

Fergusson, D.M., & Lynskey, M.T. (1997). Early reading difficulties and later conduct problems. *Journal of Child Psychology and Psychiatry, 38,* 899–907.

Fergusson, D.M., & Woodward, L.J. (2000). Educational, psychological, and sexual outcomes of girls with conduct problems in early adolescence. *Journal of Child Psychology and Psychiatry, 41,* 779–792.

Fiedler, K., & Walka, I. (1993). Training lie detectors to use nonverbal cues instead of global heuristics. *Human Communication Research, 20,* 199–223.

Finkel, N.J., Burke, J.E., & Chavez, L.J. (2000). Commonsense judgments of infanticide: Murder, manslaughter, madness, or miscellaneous? *Psychology, Public Policy, and Law, 6,* 1113–1137.

Finkelhor, D. (1984). *Child sexual abuse: New theory and research.* New York, NY: Free Press.

Finkelhor, D., Hotaling, G., Lewis, I.A., & Smith, C. (1990). Sexual abuse in a national survey of adult men and women: Prevalence, characteristics, and risk factors. *Child Abuse and Neglect, 14,* 19–28.

Finkelhor, D., Ormrod, R., Turner, H., & Hamby, S. (2005). The victimization of children and youth: A comprehensive, national survey. *Child Maltreatment, 10,* 5–25.

Finn, P., & Tomz, J.E. (1996). *Developing a law enforcement stress program for officers and their families.* Washington, DC: U.S. Department of Justice.

Firestone, P., Bradford, J.M., Greenberg, D.M., & Larose, M.R. (1998). Homicidal sex offenders: Psychological, phallometric, and diagnostic features. *Journal of the American Academy of Psychiatry and the Law, 26,* 537–552.

Fisher, B.S., Cullen, F.T., & Turner, M.G. (2002). Being pursued: Stalking victimization in a national study of college women. *Criminology and Public Policy, 1,* 257–308.

Fisher, R.P. (1995) Interviewing victims and witnesses of crime. *Psychology, Public Police, and Law, 1,* 732–764.

Fisher, R.P., & Geiselman, R.E. (1992). *Memory-enhancing techniques for investigative interviewing.* Springfield, IL: Charles C. Thomas.

Fisher, R.P., Geiselman, R.E., & Raymond, D.S. (1987). Critical analysis of police interviewing techniques. *Journal of Police Science and Administration, 15,* 177–185.

Fitzpatrick, K.M. (1997). Fighting among America's youth: A risk and protective factors approach. *Journal of Health and Social Behavior, 38,* 131–148.

Flannery, D.J., & Williams, L. (1999). Effective youth violence prevention. In T. Gullotta & S.J. McElhaney (Eds.), *Violence in homes and communities: Prevention, intervention, and treatment.* Thousand Oaks, CA: Sage.

Flight, J., & Forth, A.E. (2007). Instrumentally violent youth: The roles of psychopathic traits, empathy, and attachment. *Criminal Justice and Behavior, 34,* 721–738.

Flynn, C.P. (2000). Woman's best friend: Pet abuse and the role of companion animals in the lives of battered women. *Violence against Women, 6,* 162–177.

Foa, E.B., & Rothbaum, B.O. (1998). *Treating the trauma of rape: Cognitive-behavioral therapy for PTSD.* New York, NY: Guilford Press.

Fontaine, R.G., Burks, V.S., & Dodge, K.A. (2002). Response decision processes and externalizing behavior problems in adolescents. *Development and Psychopathology, 14,* 107–122.

Forero, C.G., Gallardo-Pujol, D., Maydeu-Olivares, A., Andres-Pueyo, A. (2009). A longitudinal model for predicting performance of police officers using personality and behavioral data. *Criminal Justice and Behavior, 36,* 591–606.

Forth, A.E., Hart, S.D., & Hare, R.D. (1990). Assessment of psychopathy in male young offenders. *Psychological Assessment, 2,* 342–344.

Forth, A.E., Kosson, D.S., & Hare, R.D. (2003). *The Psychopathy Checklist: Youth Version manual.* Toronto, ON: Multi-Health Systems.

Fox, J.A., & Levin, J. (2012). Extreme killing: Understanding serial and mass murder. Los Angeles, CA: Sage Publications, Inc.

Frank, M.G., & Ekman, P. (1997). The ability to detect deceit generalizes across different types of high-stake lies. *Journal of Personality and Social Psychology, 72,* 1429–1439.

Franke, W.D., Collins, S.A., & Hinz, P.N. (1998). Cardiovascular disease morbidity in an Iowa law enforcement cohort, compared with the general population. *Journal of Occupational and Environmental Medicine, 40,* 441–444.

Frederick, R.I., Crosby, R.D., & Wynkoop, T.F. (2000). Performance curve classification of invalid responding on the Validity Indicator Profile. *Archives of Clinical Neuropsychology, 15,* 281–300.

Fremouw, W.J., Westrup, D., & Pennypacker, J. (1997). Stalking on campus: The prevalence and strategies for coping with stalking. *Journal of Forensic Science, 42,* 666–669.

Frick, P.J. (1994). Family dysfunction and the disruptive disorders: A review of recent empirical findings. In T.H. Ollendick & Prinz, R.J. (Eds.), *Advances in clinical child psychology* (Vol. 16). New York, NY: Plenum Press.

Frick, P.J., Bodin, S.D., & Barry, C.T. (2000). Psychopathic traits and conduct problems in community and clinic-referred samples of children: Further development of the Psychopathy Screening Device. *Psychological Assessment, 12,* 382–393.

Frick, P.J., & Hare, R.D. (2001). *Antisocial Process Screening Device.* Toronto, ON: Multi-Health Systems.

Frick, P.J., Kimonis, E.R., Dandreaux, D.M., & Farell, J.M. (2003). The 4 year stability of psychopathic traits in non-referred youth. *Behavioral Sciences and the Law, 21,* 713–736.

Frick, P.J., Lahey, B.B., Loeber, R., Stouthamer, M., Christ, M.A.G., & Hanson, K. (1992). Familial risk factors to oppositional defiant disorder and conduct disorder: parental psychopathology and maternal parenting. *Journal of Consulting and Clinical Psychology, 60,* 49–55.

Friedrich, W.N., & Luecke, W.J. (1988). Young school-age sexually aggressive children. *Professional Psychology: Research and Practice, 19,* 155–164.

Fritz, G., Stoll, K., & Wagner, N. (1981). A comparison of males and females who were sexually molested as children. *Journal of Sex and Marital Therapy, 7,* 54–58.

Fulero, S.M., & Everington, C. (2004). Mental retardation, competency to waive Miranda rights, and false confessions. In G.D. Lassiter (Ed.), *Interrogations, confessions, and entrapment* (pp. 163–179). New York, NY: Kluwer Academic.

Furedy, J.J. (1996). The North American Polygraph and psychophysiology: Disinterested, uninterested, and interested perspectives. *International Journal of Psychophysiology, 21,*97–105.

Fyfe, J.J. (1979). Administrative interventions on police shooting discretion: An empirical examination. *Journal of Criminal Justice, 7,* 309–324.

Gallagher, C.A., Wilson, D.B., Hirschfield, P., Coggeshall, M.B., & MacKenzie, D.L. (1999). A quantitative review of the effects of sex offender treatment of sexual reoffending. *Corrections Management Quarterly, 3,* 19–29.

Gallup Poll. (1999). *Racial profiling is seen as widespread, particularly among young black men.* Princeton, NJ: Gallup Poll Organization.

Gamer, M., Rill, H.-G., Vossel, G., & Gödert, H.W. (2005). Psychophysiological and vocal measures in the detection of guilty knowledge. *International Journal of Psychophysiology, 60,* 76–87.

Ganis, G., Kosslyn, S.M., Stose, S., Thompson, W.L., & Yurgelun-Todd, D.A. (2003). Neural correlates of different types of deception: An fMRI investigation. *Cerebral Cortex, 13,* 830–836.

Garber, C. (1947). Eskimo infanticide. Scientific Monthly, 64, 98-102.

Gardner, J., Scogin, F., Vipperman, R., & Varela, J.G. (1998). The predictive validity of peer assessment in law enforcement: A 6-year follow-up. *Behavioral Sciences and the Law, 16,* 473–478.

Garmezy, N. (1985). Stress-resistant children: The search for protective factors. In J.E. Stevenson (Ed.), *Recent research in developmental psychopathology* (pp. 213–233). New York, NY: Pergamon.

Garmezy, N. (1991). Resilience in children's adaptation to negative life events and stressed environments. *Pediatric Annuals, 20,* 460–466.

Garner, J., & Maxwell, C. (2009). Prosecution and conviction rates for intimate partner violence. *Criminal Justice Review, 34,* 44–79.

Garven, S., Wood, J.M., Malpass, R.S., & Shaw III, J.S. (1998). More than suggestion: The effect of interviewing techniques from the McMartin Preschool case. Journal of Applied Psychology, 83, 347-359.

Gauce, A.M., Cormer, J.P., & Schwartz, D. (1987). Long term effects of a systems oriented school prevention program. *American Journal of Orthopsychiatry, 57,* 125–131.

Geberth, V.J. (1990). *Practical homicide investigation: Tactics, procedures, and forensic techniques* (2nd ed.). New York, NY: Elsevier.

Geiselman R.E., & Padilla J. (1988). Interviewing child witnesses with the cognitive interview. Journal

Geiselman R.E., & Padilla J. (1988). Interviewing child witnesses with the cognitive interview. Journal of Police Science and Administration, 16, 236–242.

Geiselman, R.E., Fisher, R.P., Firstenberg, I., Hutton, L.A., Sullivan, S., Avetissian, I., & Prosk, A. (1984). Enhancement of eyewitness memory: An empirical evaluation of the cognitive interview. *Journal of Police Science and Administration, 12,* 74–80.

Geiselman, R.E., Fisher, R.P., MacKinnon, D.P., & Holland, H.L. (1985). Eyewitness memory enhancement in the police interview: Cognitive retrieval mnemonics versus hypnosis. *Journal of Applied Psychology, 70,* 401–412.

Geller, W., & Scott, M.S. (1992). *Deadly force: What we know.* Washington, DC: Police Executive Forum.

Gendreau, P., Goggin, C., Cullen, F., & Andrews, D. (2001). The effects of community sanctions and incarceration of recidivism. In L. Motiuk and R. Serin (Eds.), *Compendium 2000 on effective correctional programming* (pp. 18–21). Ottawa, ON: Correctional Service Canada.

Gendreau, P., Little, T., & Goggin, C. (1996). A meta-analysis of the predictors of adult offender recidivism: What works! *Criminology, 34,* 575–607.

Gerbner, G., Gross, L., Morgan, M., & Signorielli, N. (1980). The "mainstreaming" of America: Violence profile no. 11. *Journal of Communication, 30,* 10–27.

Giancola, P.R., Parrott, D.J., & Roth, R.M. (2006). The influence of difficult temperament on alcohol-related aggression: Better accounted for by executive functioning? *Addictive Behaviors, 31,* 2169–2187.

Gibbs, J.L., Ellison, N.B., & Heino, R.D. (2006). Self-presentation in online personals: The role of anticipated future interaction, self-disclosure, and perceived success in Internet dating. *Communication Research, 33,* 1–25.

Glazebrook, S. (2010). Risky business: Predicting recidivism. *Psychiatry, Psychology, & Law, 17,* 88–120.

Glueck, S., & Glueck, E.T. (1968). *Delinquents and non-delinquents in perspective.* Cambridge, MA: Harvard University Press.

Golding, S.L. (1993). *Training manual: Interdisciplinary fitness interview revised.* Department of Psychology, University of Utah.

Golding, S.L., Roesch, R., & Schreiber, J. (1984). Assessment and conceptualization of competency to stand trial. Preliminary data on the interdisciplinary fitness interview. *Law and Human Behavior, 8,* 321–334.

Goldman, N. (1963). *The differential selection of juvenile offenders for court appearance.* New York, NY: National Research and Information Centre, National Council on Crime and Delinquency.

Goldstein, A.G. (1979). Race-related variation of facial features: Anthropometric data I. *Bulletin of the Psychonomic Society, 13,* 187–190.

Gondolf, E., & Fisher, E. (1988). *Battered women as survivors: An alternative to treating learned helplessness.* Lexington, MA: Lexington Books.

Gondolf, E.W. (1985). *Men who batter: An integrated approach for stopping wife abuse.* Holmes Beach, CA: Learning Publications.

Gondolf, E.W. (1988). Who are these guys? Towards a behavioral typology of batterers. *Violence and Victims, 3,* 187–202.

Gonzalez, R., Ellsworth, P., & Pembroke, M. (1993). Response biases in lineups and showups. *Journal of Personality and Social Psychology, 64,* 525–537.

Goodman, G.S., Pyle-Taub, E.P., Jones, D.P.H., England, P., Port, L.K., Rudy, L., & Prado, L. (1992). Testifying in court: The effects on child sexual assault victims. *Monographs of the Society for Research in Child Development, 57* (Serial No. 229), 1–163.

Goodman, G.S., Quas, J.A., Batterman-Faunce, J.M., Riddlesberger, M., & Kuhn, J. (1997). Children's reactions to and memory for a stressful event: Influences of age, anatomical dolls, knowledge, and parental attachment. *Applied Developmental Science, 1,* 54–75.

Gottfredson, M.R., & Hirschi, T. (1990). *A general theory of crime.* Palo Alto, CA: Stanford University Press.

Gowan, M.A., & Gatewood, R.D. (1995). Personnel selection. In N. Brewer & C. Wilson (Eds.), *Psychology and policing* (pp. 177–204). Hillsdale, NJ: Lawrence Erlbaum Associates.

Granger, C. (1996). *The criminal jury trial in Canada.* Toronto, ON: Carswell.

Grann, M., Belfrage, H., & Tengström, A. (2000). Actuarial assessment of risk for violence: Predictive validity of the VRAG and the historical part of the HCR-20. *Criminal Justice and Behavior, 27,* 97–114.

Greco, C.M., & Cornell, D.G. (1992). Rorschach object relations of adolescents who committed homicide. *Journal of Personality Assessment, 59,* 574–583.

Greene, E. (1990). Media effects on jurors. *Law and Human Behavior, 14,* 439–450.

Greene, E., Raitz, A., & Lindblad, H. (1989). Jurors' knowledge of battered women. *Journal of Family Violence, 4,* 105–125.

Gretton, H.M., Hare, R.D., & Catchpole, R.E.H. (2004). Psychopathy and offending from adolescence to adulthood: A 10-year follow-up. *Journal of Consulting and Clinical Psychology, 72,* 636–645.

Grisso, T. (1981). *Juveniles' waiver of rights: Legal and psychological competence.* New York, NY: Plenum.

Groscup, J., Penrod, S., Studebaker, C., Huss, M., & O'Neil, K. (2002). The effects of *Daubert v. Merrell Dow Pharmaceuticals* on the admissibility of expert testimony in state and federal criminal cases. *Psychology, Public Policy & Law, 8,* 339–372.

Grossman, F.K., Beinashowitz, J., Anderson, L., Sakurai, M., Finnin, L., & Flaherty, M. (1992). Risk and resilience in young adolescents. *Journal of Youth and Adolescence, 21,* 529–550.

Grossman, R. (2008, December 27). Psychiatric manual's update needs openness, critics say. *Chicago Tribune.*

Groth, A.N. (1979). *Men who rape: The psychology of the offender.* New York, NY: Plenum.

Groth, A.N., Burgess, A.W., & Holmstrom, L.L. (1977). Rape: Power, anger, and sexuality. *American Journal of Psychiatry, 134,* 1239–1243.

Groth, A.N., Hobson, W.F., & Gary, T.S. (1982). The child molester: Clinical observations. *Journal of Social Work and Human Sexuality, 1,* 129–144.

Grove, W., & Meehl, P (1996). Comparative efficiency of informal (subjective, impressionistic) and formal (mechanical, algorithmic) prediction procedures: The clinical-statistical controversy. *Psychology, Public Policy and Law, 2,* 293–323.

Grove, W.M., Zald, D.H., Lebow, B.S., Snitz, B.F., & Nelson, C. (2000). Clinical versus mechanical prediction: A metaanalysis. *Psychological Assessment, 12,* 19–30.

The Guardian. (1988, October 28). Police set up unit for stress crisis.

Gudjonsson, G.H. (1992). Interrogation and false confessions: Vulnerability factors. *British Journal of Hospital Medicine, 47,* 597–599.

Gudjonsson, G.H. (2003). *The psychology of interrogations, confessions, and testimony.* Chichester, England: John Wiley & Sons.

Gudjonsson, G.H., Clare, I.C.H., & Cross, P. (1992). The revised PACE "Notice to Detained Persons": How easy is it to understand? *Journal of the Forensic Science Society, 32,* 289–299.

Gudjonsson, G.H., & MacKeith, J.A.C. (1988). Retracted confessions: Legal, psychological and psychiatric aspects. *Medicine, Science, and the Law, 28,* 187–194.

Gudjonsson, G.H., & Sigurdsson, J.F. (1994). How frequently do false confessions occur? An empirical study among prison inmates. *Psychology, Crime and Law, 1,* 21–26.

Gureje, O., Simon, G.E., Ustun, T.B., & Goldberg, D.P. (1997). Somatization in cross-cultural perspective: A world health organization study in primary care. *American Journal of Psychiatry, 154,* 989–995.

Guy, L.S., Edens, J.F., Anthony, C., & Douglas, K.S. (2005). Does psychopathy predict institutional misconduct among adults? A meta-analytic investigation. *Journal of Consulting and Clinical Psychology, 73,* 1056–1064.

Guy, L.S., Kwartner, P.P., & Miller, H.A. (2006). Investigating the M-FAST: Psychometric properties and utility to detect diagnostic specific malingering. *Behavioral Sciences & the Law, 24,* 687–702.

Guy, L.S., & Miller, H.A. (2004). Screening for malingered psychopathology in a correctional setting: Utility of the Miller-Forensic Assessment of Symptoms Test (M-FAST). *Criminal Justice and Behavior, 31,* 695–716.

Gylys, J.A., & McNamara, J.R. (1996). Acceptance of rape myths among prosecuting attorneys. *Psychological Reports, 79,* 15–18.

Haggard, U., Gumpert, C.H., & Grann, M. (2001). Against all odds: A qualitative follow-up study of high-risk violent offenders who were not reconvicted. *Journal of Interpersonal Violence, 16,* 1048–1065.

Häkkänen-Nyholm, H., & Hare, R.D. (2009). Psychopathy, homicide, and the courts: Working the system. *Criminal Justice and Behavior, 36,* 761–777.

Hall, G.C.N., & Hirschman, R. (1992). Sexual aggression against children: A conceptual perspective of etiology. *Criminal Justice and Behavior, 19,* 8–23.

Halman, L. (2001). The European values study: A third wave (Sourcebook of the 1999/2000 European values study). Tilburg, NL: Tilburg University.

Haney, C. (1980). Psychology and legal change: On the limits of a factual jurisprudence. *Law and Human Behavior, 17,* 371–398.

Hans, V.P., & Doob, A.N. (1976). Section 12 of the Canada Evidence Act and the deliberation of simulated juries. *Criminal Law Quarterly, 18,* 235–253.

Hanson, K.R., & Bourgon-Morton, K.E. (2009). The accuracy of recidivisim risk assessments for sexual offenders: A metaanalysis of 118 prediction studies. *Psychological Assessment, 21,* 1–21.

Hanson, K.R., Helmus, L., & Bourgon, G. (2007). *The validity of risk assessment measures for intimate partner violence: A meta-analysis* (Public Safety Canada, 2007-07). Retrieved from http://www.publicsafety .gc.ca/res/cor/rep/vra_ipv_200707-eng.aspx

Hanson, R.K. (1990). The psychological impact of sexual assault on women and children: A review. *Annuals of Sex Research, 3,* 187–232.

Hanson, R.K., Broom, I., & Stephenson, M. (2004). Evaluating community sex offender treatment programs: A 12-year follow-up of 724 offenders. *Canadian Journal of Behavioural Sciences, 36,* 85–94.

Hanson, R.K., & Bussière, M.T. (1998). Predicting relapse: A meta-analysis of sexual offender recidivism studies. *Journal of Consulting and Clinical Psychology, 66,* 348–362.

Hanson, R.K., & Scott, H. (1995). Assessing perspective-taking among sexual offenders, nonsexual criminals, and offenders. *Sexual Abuse: Journal of Research and Treatment, 7,* 259–277.

Hanson, R.K., & Thornton, D. (1999). *Static-99: Improving actuarial risk assessment for sexual offenders.* Ottawa, ON: Department of Solicitor General.

Hanson, R.K., Gordon, A., Harris, A.J.R., Marques, J.K., Murphy, W., Quinsey, V.L., & Seto, M.C. (2002). First report of the collaborative outcome data project on the effectiveness of psychological treatment for sex offenders. Sexual Abuse: A Journal of Research and Treatment, 14, 169-194.

Hanson, R.K., & Thornton, D. (2000). Improving risk assessments for sex offenders: A comparison of three actuarial scales. *Law and Human Behavior, 24,* 119–136.

Hare, R.D. (1991). *The Hare Psychopathy Checklist–Revised.* Toronto, ON: Multi-Health Systems.

Hare, R.D. (1998). The Hare PCL-R: Some issues concerning its use and misuse. *Legal and Criminological Psychology, 3,* 99–119.

Hare, R.D. (2003). *The Hare Psychopathy Checklist–Revised* (2nd ed.). Toronto, ON: Multi-Health Systems.

Hare, R.D. (2007). Forty years aren't enough: Recollections, prognostications, and random musings. In H. Hervé & J.C. Yuille (Eds.), *The psychopath: Theory, research and practice* (pp. 3–28). Mahway, NJ: Lawrence Erlbaum Associates.

Hare, R.D., Clark, D., Grant, M., & Thornton, D. (2000). Psychopathy and the predictive validity of the PCL-R: An international perspective. *Behavioral Sciences and the Law, 18,* 623–645.

Hare, R.D., Forth, A.E., & Strachan, K.E. (1992). Psychopathy and crime across the life span.

In R.D. Peters & R.J. McMahon (Eds.), *Aggression and violence throughout the life span* (pp. 285–300). Thousand Oaks, CA: Sage.

Hare, R.D., Harpur, T.J., Hakstian, A.R., Forth, A.E., Hart, S.D., & Newman, J.P. (1990). The Revised Psychopathy Checklist: Reliability and factor structure. *Psychological Assessment: A Journal of Consulting and Clinical Psychology, 2,* 338–341.

Hare, R.D., & Neumann, C.S. (2008). Psychopathy as a clinical and empirical construct. *Annual Review of Clinical Psychology, 4,* 217–246.

Hargrave, G.E., & Hiatt, D. (1987). Law enforcement selection with the interview, MMPI, and CPI: A study of reliability and validity. *Journal of Police Science and Administration, 15,* 110–117.

Hart, J.L., O'Toole, S. K., Price-Sharps, J., & Shaffer, T. W. (2007). The risk and protective factors of violent juvenile offending: An examination of gender differences. Youth Violence and Juvenile Justice, 5(4), 367-384.

Harris, D. (1999a). *Driving while black: Racial profiling on our nation's highways.* Washington, DC: American Civil Liberties Union.

Harris, D. (1999b). The stories, the statistics, and the law: Why "driving while black" matters. *Minnesota Law Review, 84,* 265–326.

Harris, G.T., Rice, M.E., & Quinsey, V.L. (1993). Violent recidivism of mentally disordered offenders: The development of a statistical prediction instrument. *Criminal Justice and Behavior, 20,* 315–335.

Harrison, L.A., & Esqueda, C.W. (1999). Myths and stereotypes of actors involved in domestic violence: Implications for domestic violence culpability attributions. *Aggression and Violent Behavior, 4,* 129–138.

Harrison, S. (1993). *Diary of Jack the Ripper: The discovery, the investigation, the debate.* New York, NY: Hyperion.

Hart, S.D. (1998). The role of psychopathy in assessing risk for violence: Conceptual and methodological issues. *Legal and Criminological Psychology, 3,* 121–137.

Hart, S.D., Cox, D.N., & Hare, R.D. (1995). *Manual for the Psychopathy Checklist: Screening Version (PCL: SV).* Toronto, ON: Multi-Health Systems.

Hart, S.D., Michie, C., & Cooke, D. J. (2007). Precision of actuarial risk assessment instruments: Evaluating the 'margins of error' of group v. individual predictions of violence. *British Journal of Psychiatry, 190,* 60–65.

Hartley, J. (2002). Notetaking in non-academic settings: A review. *Applied Cognitive Psychology, 16,* 559–574.

Hartney, C., & Marchionna, S. (2009). Attitudes of U.S. voters toward nonserious offenders and alternatives to incarceration. Retrieved from http://www.sjra1.com/cjreports/2009%20FOCUS%20US%20attitudes%20on%20nonserious_offenders.pdf

Hastie, R. (Ed.). (1993). Inside the juror: *The psychology of juror decision making.* New York, NY: Cambridge University Press.

Hastie, R., Penrod, S.D., & Pennington, N. (1983). *Inside the jury.* Cambridge, MA: Harvard University Press.

Hazelwood, R.R., & Douglas, J.E. (1980). The lust murderer. *FBI Law Enforcement Bulletin, 50,* 18–22.

Heath, L., & Gilbert, K. (1996). Mass media and fear of crime. *American Behavioral Scientist, 39,* 379–386.

Heinrick, J. (2006, Fall). *Everyone's an expert: The CSI effect's negative impact on juries.* Arizona State University: The Triple Helix.

Helmus, L. Thornton, D., Hanson, K., & Babchishin, K. (in press). Improving the predictive accuracy of Static-99 and Static-2002 with older sex offenders: Revised age weights. *Sexual Abuse: A Journal of Research and Treatment.*

Hemphill, J.F., Hare, R.D., & Wong, S. (1998). Psychopathy and recidivism: A review. *Legal and Criminological Psychology, 3,* 139–170.

Henggeler, S.W., & Borduin, C.M. (1990). *Family therapy and beyond: A multisystemic approach to treating the behavior problems of children and adolescents.* Pacific Grove, CA: Brooks/Cole.

Henggeler, S.W., Rodick, D., Borduin, C., Hanson, C., & Watson, S. (1986). Multisystemic treatment of juvenile offenders: Effects on adolescent behavior and family interaction. Developmental Psychology, 22, 132-141.

Henggeler, S.W., Melton, G.B., & Smith, L.A. (1992). Family preservation using multisystemic therapy: An effective alternative to incarcerating serious juvenile offenders. *Journal of Consulting and Clinical Psychology, 60,* 953–961.

Henggeler, S.W., Schoenwald, S.K., Borduin, C.M., Rowland, M.D., & Cunningham, P.B. (1998).

Multisystemic treatment of antisocial behavior in children and adolescents. New York, NY: Guilford Press.

Henggeler, S.W., Schoenwald, S.K., & Pickrel, S.A.G. (1995). Multisystemic therapy: Bridging the gap between university and community baed treatment. *Journal of Consulting and Clinical Psychology, 63,* 709–717.

Hess, A.K. (1987). Dimensions of forensic psychology. In I.B. Weiner & A.K. Hess (Eds.), *The handbook of forensic psychology* (1st ed., pp. 22–49). New York, NY: John Wiley & Sons.

Hess, A.K. (1999). Defining forensic psychology. In A.K. Hess & I.B. Weiner (Eds.), *The handbook of forensic psychology* (2nd ed.) (pp. 24–47). New York, NY: John Wiley & Sons.

Heuer, L., & Penrod, S. (1994). Juror note taking and question asking during trials: A national field experiment. *Law and Human Behavior, 18,* 121–150.

Hickey, E.W. (2006). Serial murderers and their victims. Belmont, CA: Wadsworth.

Hickey, E.W. (2010). Serial murderers and their victims (5th edition). Belmont, CA: Wadsworth

Hicks, S.J., & Sales, B.D. (2006). *Criminal profiling: Developing an effective science and practice.* Washington, DC: American Psychological Association.

Hildebrand, M., de Ruiter, C., & de Vogel, V. (2004). Psychopathy and sexual deviance in treated rapists: Association with sexual and nonsexual recidivism. *Sexual Abuse: A Journal of Research and Treatment, 16,* 1–24.

Hillbrand, M. (1995). Aggression against self and aggression against others in violent psychiatric patients. *Journal of Consulting and Clinical Psychology, 63,* 668–671.

Hilton, N.Z., Carter, A.M., Harris, G.T., & Sharpe, A.J.B. (2008). Does use of nonnumerical terms to describe risk aid violence risk communication? Clinician agreement and decision making. *Journal of Interpersonal Violence, 23,* 171–188.

Hilton, N.Z., Harris, G.T., Rawson, K., & Beach, C.A. (2005). Communicating violence risk information to forensic decision makers. *Criminal Justice and Behavior, 32,* 97–116.

Hilton, N.Z., & Simmons, J.L. (2001). The influence of actuarial risk assessment in clinical judgments and

tribunal decisions about mentally disordered offenders in maximum security. *Law and Human Behavior, 25,* 393–408.

Hinshaw, S.P., Lahey, B.B., & Hart, E.L. (1993). Issues of taxonomy and comorbidity in the development of conduct disorder. *Development and Psychopathology, 5,* 31–49.

Hirschell, D., & Buzawa, E. (2002). Understanding the context of dual arrest with directions for future research. *Violence Against Women, 8,* 1449–1473.

Hirschell, D.J., Hutchison, I.W., & Dean, C.W. (1990). The failure of arrest to deter spouse abuse. *Journal of Research in Crime and Delinquency, 29,* 7–33.

Hirsh, H.R., Northrop, L.C., & Schmidt, F.L. (1986). Validity generalization for law enforcement occupations. *Personnel Psychology, 39,* 399–420.

Hoaken, P.N.S., & Stewart, S.H. (2003). Drugs of abuse and elicitation of human aggressive behavior. *Addictive Behaviors, 28,* 1533–1554.

Hodgins, S., Tengström, A., Eriksson, A., Österman, R., Kronstrand, R., Eaves, D., et al. (2007). A multisite study of community treatment programs for mentally ill offenders with major mental disorders: Design, measures, and the forensic sample. Criminal Justice and Behavior, 34(2), 211-228.

Hogarth, J. (1971). *Sentencing as a human process.* Toronto, ON: University of Toronto Press.

Hoge, R.D. (1999). *Assessing adolescents in educational, counselling, and other settings.* Mahwah, NJ: Lawrence Erlbaum Associates.

Hoge, R.D., Andrews, D.A., & Lescheid, A.W. (1996). An investigation of risk and protective factors in a sample of youthful offenders. *Journal of Child Psychology and Psychiatry and Allied Disciplines, 37,* 419–424.

Hoge, S.K., Bonnie, R.J., Poythress, N., & Monahan, J. (1992). Attorney–client decision-making in criminal cases: Client competence and participation as perceived by their attorneys. *Behavioral Sciences and the Law, 10,* 385–394.

Holliday, R.E., & Albon, A. (2004). Minimizing misinformation effects in young children with cognitive interview mnemonics. *Applied Cognitive Psychology, 18,* 263–281.

Holliday, R.E. (2003). Reducing misinformation effects in children with Cognitive interviews: Dissociating recollection and familiarity. Child Development, 74, 728-751.

Holmes, R.M., & Holmes, S.T. (1998). *Serial murder* (2nd ed.). Thousand Oaks, CA: Sage.

Holmes, R.M., & Holmes, S.T. (2002). *Profiling violent crimes: An investigative tool* (3rd ed.). Thousand Oaks, CA: Sage.

Holtzworth-Munroe, A., & Stuart, G.L. (1994). Typologies of male batterers: Three subtypes and the differences among them. *Psychological Bulletin, 116,* 476–497.

Homant, R.J., & Kennedy, D.B. (1998). Psychological aspects of crime scene profiling: Validity research. *Criminal Justice and Behavior, 25,* 319–343.

Honts, C.R., & Raskin, D.C. (1988). A field study of the validity of the directed lie control question. *Journal of Police Science and Administration, 16,* 56–61.

Honts, C.R., Raskin, D.C., & Kircher, J.C. (1994). Mental and physical countermeasures reduce the accuracy of polygraph tests. *Journal of Applied Social Psychology, 79,* 252–259.

Honts, C.R., & Schweinle, W. (2009). Information gain of psychophysiological detection of deception in forensic and screening settings. *Applied Psychophysiology Biofeedback, 34,* 161–172.

Horowitz, I.A., & Seguin, D.G. (1986). The effects of bifurcation and death qualification on assignment of penalty in capital crimes. *Journal of Applied Social Psychology, 16,* 165–185.

Horselenberg, R., Merckelbach, H., & Josephs, S. (2003). Individual differences and false confessions: A conceptual replication of Kassin and Kiechel (1996). *Psychology, Crime & Law, 9,* 1–8.

Howell, J.C. (1998). Promising programs for youth gang violence prevention and intervention. In Serious and Violent Juvenile Offenders: Risk Factors and Successful Interventions, edited by R. Loeber and D.P. Farrington. Thousand Oaks, CA: Sage Publications, pp. 284–312.

Howitt, D. (2002). Forensic and criminal psychology. London, UK: Prentice Hall.

Hubbard, K.L., Zapf, P.A., & Ronan, K.A. (2003). Competency restoration: An examination of the differences between defendants predicted restorable and not restorable to competency. *Law and Human Behavior, 27,* 127–139.

Huesmann, L.R., Eron, L.D., Lefkowitz, M.M., & Walder, L.O. (1984). Stability of aggression over time and generations. *Developmental Psychology, 20,* 1120–1134.

Huff, C.R., Rattner, A., & Sagarin, E. (1996). *Convicted but innocent: Wrongful conviction and public policy.* Thousand Oaks, CA: Sage.

Hughes, M., & Grieve, R. (1980). On asking children bizarre questions. *First Language, 1,* 149–160.

Humm, D.G., & Humm, K.A. (1950). Humm-Wadsworth temperament scale appraisals compared with criteria of job success in the Los Angeles Police Department. *Journal of Psychology, 30,* 63–57.

Iacono, W.G., Cerri, A.M., Patrick, C.J., & Fleming, J.A.E. (1992). Use of antianxiety drugs as countermeasures in the detection of guilty knowledge. *Journal of Applied Psychology, 77,* 60–64.

Iacono, W.G., & Patrick, C. J. (1988). Polygraphy techniques. In R. Rogers (Ed.), *Clinical assessment of malingering and deception* (2nd ed., pp. 252–281). New York, NY: Guilford Press.

Iacono, W.G., & Patrick, C.J. (1999). Polygraph ("lie detector") testing: The state of the art. In A.K. Hess & I.B. Weiner (Eds.), *The handbook of forensic psychology* (2nd ed., pp. 440–473). New York, NY: John Wiley & Sons.

Iacono, W.G., & Patrick, C.J. (2006). Polygraph ("lie detector") testing: Current status and emerging trends. In I.B. Weiner & A. Hess (Eds.), *Handbook of forensic psychology* (3rd ed., pp. 552–588). New York, NY: John Wiley & Sons.

Inbau, F.E., Reid, J.E., Buckley, J.P., & Jayne, B.C. (2004). *Criminal interrogation and confessions* (4th ed.). Boston, MA: Jones and Bartlett.

Inciardi, J.A. (1986). Getting busted for drugs. In G. Beschner & A.S. Friedman (Eds.), *Teen drug use* (pp. 63–83). Lexington, MA: Lexington Books.

Independent Commission on the Los Angeles Police Department (1991). *Report of the Independent Commission on the Los Angeles Police Department.* Retrieved from http://www.parc.info/client_files/Special%20Reports/1%20-%20Chistopher%20Commision.pdf

International Association of Chiefs of Police. (2010). *Social media for recruitment fact sheet.* Retrieved from http://theiacp.org/LinkClick.aspx?fileticket=4UAKKWP%2fz%2fw%3d&tabid=700

International Association for Identification (2012). Forensic disciplines. Retrieved May 17, 2012 from http://www.theiai.org/disciplines/

Inwald, R.E. (1992). *Inwald personality inventory technical manual* (Rev. ed.). Kew Gardens, NY: Hilson Research.

Inwald, R.E., & Shusman, E.J. (1984). The IPI and MMPI as predictors of academy performance for police recruits. *Journal of Police Science and Administration, 12,* 1–11.

Izzett, R.R., & Leginski, W. (1974). Group discussion and the influence of defendant characteristics in a simulated jury setting. *Journal of Social Psychology, 93,* 271–279.

Jackson, J.L., Sijlbing, R., & Thiecke, M.G. (1996). The role of human memory processes in witness reporting. *Expert Evidence, 5,* 98–105.

Jackson, J.L., van Koppen, P.J., & Herbrink, J. (1993). *An expert/novice approach to offender profiling.* Paper presented at the First NISCALE Workshop on Criminality and Law Enforcement, Leiden.

Jackson, R.L., Rogers, R., & Sewell, K.W. (2005). Forensic application of the Miller Forensic Assessment of Symptoms Test (MFAST): Screening for feigned disorders in competency to stand trial evaluations. *Law and Human Behavior, 29,* 199–210.

Jacobs, P.A., Brunton, M., Melville, M.M., Brittain, M.M., & McClemonts, W.F. (1965). Aggressive behaviour, mental subnormality, and the XYY male. *Nature, 208,* 351–352.

Jaffe, P., Hastings, E., Reitzel, D., & Austin, G. (1993). The impact of police laying charges. In Z. Hilton (Ed.) *Legal responses to wife assault: Current trends and evaluation* (pp. 62–95). Newbury Park, CA: Sage.

Janoff-Bulman, R. (1979). Characterological versus behavioral self-blame: Inquiries into depression and rape. *Journal of Personality and Social Psychology, 37,* 1798–1809.

Jarey, M.L., & Stewart, M.A. (1985). Psychiatric disorder in the parents of adopted children with aggressive conduct disorder. *Neuropsychobiology, 13,* 7–11.

Jayne, B.C. (1986). The psychological principles of criminal interrogation: An appendix. In F.E. Inbau, J.E. Reid, & J.P. Buckley (Eds.), *Criminal interrogation and confessions* (3rd ed., pp. 327–347). Baltimore, MD: Williams and Williams.

Jessor, R., Turbin, M.S., & Costa, F. (1998). Risk and protection in successful outcomes among disadvantaged adolescents. *Applied Developmental Science, 2,* 194–208.

Jokinen, A., Santilla, P., Ravaja, N., & Puttonen, S. (2006). Salience of guilty knowledge test items affects accuracy in realistic mock crimes. *International Journal of Psychophysiology, 62,* 175–184.

Jolliffe, D., & Farrington, D.P. (2007) *A systematic review of the national and international evidence on the effectiveness of interventions with violent offenders* (Research Series 16/07). Retrieved from Ministry of Justice website: http://www.justice.gov.uk/docs/review-evidence-violent.pdf

Jones, A.B., & Llewellyn, J. (1917). *Malingering.* London, England: Heinemann.

Jones, W.D. (1997). *Murder of justice: New Jersey's greatest shame.* New York, NY: Vantage Press.

Jordan, C., Logan, T.K., Walker, R., & Nigoff, A. (2003). Stalking: An examination of the criminal justice response. *Journal of Interpersonal Violence, 18,* 148–165.

Kahneman, D., & Tversky, A. (1982). Variants of uncertainty. *Cognition, 11,* 143–157.

Kalmuss, D.S. (1984). The intergenerational transmission of marital aggression. *Journal of Marriage and the Family, 46,* 11–19.

Kalvern, H., & Zeisel, H. (1966). *The American jury.* Boston, MA: Little, Brown.

Kanas, N., & Barr, M.A. (1984). Self-control of psychotic productions in schizophrenics (Letter to the editor). *Archives of General Psychiatry, 41,* 919–920.

Kask, K., Bull, R., & Davies, G. (2006). Trying to improve young adults' person descriptions. *Psychiatry, Psychology, and Law, 13,* 174–181.

Kassin, S.M. (1997). The psychology of confession evidence. *American Psychologist, 52,* 221–233.

Kassin, S.M. (1998). Eyewitness identification procedures: The fifth rule. *Law and Human Behavior, 22,* 649–653.

Kassin, S.M. (2008). False confessions: Causes, consequences, and implications for reform. *Current Directions in Psychological Science, 17,* 249–253.

Kassin, S.M., Drizin, S.A., Grisso, T., Gudjonsson, G.H., Leo, R., & Redlich, A. D. (2010). Police-induced confessions: Risk factors and recommendations. *Law and Human Behavior, 34,* 3–38.

Kassin, S.M., Ellsworth, P., & Smith, V.L. (1989). The "general acceptance" of psychological research on eyewitness testimony. *American Psychologist, 49,* 878–893.

Kassin, S.M., Goldstein, C.C., & Savitsky, K. (2003). Behavioral confirmation in the interrogation room: On the dangers of presuming guilt. *Law and Human Behavior, 27,* 187–203.

Kassin, S.M., & Gudjonsson, G.H. (2004). The psychology of confessions: A review of the literature and issues. *Psychological Science in the Public Interest, 5,* 33–67.

Kassin, S.M., & Kiechel, K.L. (1996). The social psychology of false confessions: Compliance, internalization, and confabulation. *Psychological Science, 7,* 125–128.

Kassin, S.M., Leo, R.A., Meissner, C.A., Richman, K.D., Colwell, L.H., Leach, A-M., & La Fon, D. (2007). Police interviewing and interrogation: A self-report survey of police practices and beliefs. *Law and Human Behavior, 31,* 381–400.

Kassin, S.M., & Sommers, S.R. (1997). Inadmissible testimony, instructions to disregard, and the jury: Substantive versus procedural considerations. *Personality and Social Psychology Bulletin, 23,* 1046–1054.

Kassin, S.M., & Sukel, H. (1997). Coerced confessions and the jury: An experimental test of the "harmless error" rule. *Law and Human Behavior, 21,* 27–46.

Kassin, S.M., Tubb, V., Hosch, H.M., & Memon, A. (2001). On the "general acceptance" of eyewitness testimony research. *American Psychologist, 56,* 405–416.

Kassin, S.M., & Wrightsman, L.S. (1985). Confession evidence. In S.M. Kassin & L.S. Wrightsman (Eds.), *The psychology of evidence and trial procedures* (pp. 67–94). London, England: Sage.

Kauder, N. B., & Ostrom, B. J. (2008). *State sentencing guidelines: Profiles and continuums.* Retrieved from http://www.ncsconline.org/csi/PEW-Profiles-v12-online.pdf

Kaufman, J., & Zigler, E. (1987). Do abused children become abusive parents? *American Journal of Orthopsychiatry, 57,* 186–192.

Kazdin, A.E. (1996). *Conduct disorders in childhood and adolescence* (2nd ed.). Thousand Oaks, CA: Sage.

Kebbell, M.R., & Wagstaff, G.F. (1998). Hypnotic interviewing: The best way to interview eyewitnesses. *Behavioural Sciences and the Law, 16,* 115–129.

Kendall-Tackett, K.A., Williams, L.M., & Finkelhor, D. (1993). Impact of sexual abuse in children: A review

and synthesis of recent empirical studies. *Psychological Bulletin, 113,* 164–180.

Kendell, R.E., Chalmers, J.C., & Platz, C.L. (1987). Epidemiology of puerperal psychoses. *British Journal of Psychiatry, 150,* 662–673.

Kendell, R., & Jablensky, A. (2003). Distinguishing between the validity and utility of psychiatric diagnoses. The American Journal of Psychiatry, 160, 4-12.

Keppel, R.D., & Walter, R. (1999). Profiling killers: A revised classification model for understanding sexual murder. *International Journal of Offender Therapy and Comparative Criminology, 43,* 417–437.

Kershner, R. (1996). Adolescent attitudes about rape. *Adolescence, 31,* 29–33.

Kerstholt, J.H., Jansen, N.J.M., Van Amelsvoort, A.G., & Broeders, A.P.A. (2006). Earwitnesses: Effects of accent, retention, and telephone. *Applied Cognitive Psychology, 20,* 187–197.

Kilpatrick, D.G. (2000). *Rape and sexual assault: An overview.* Charleston, SC: National Violence Against Women Prevention Research Center, Medical University of South Carolina.

Kilpatrick, D.G., Edwards, C.N., & Seymour, A.E. (1992). *Rape in America: A report to the nation.* Arlington, VA: National Crime Victims Center.

Kilpatrick, D.G., Saunders, B.E., Veronen, L.J., Best, C.L., & Von, J.M. (1987). Criminal victimization: Lifetime prevalence, reporting to police, and psychological impact. *Crime and Delinquency, 33,* 479–489.

Kim, Y.S., Barak, G., & Shelton, D.E. (2009). Examining the CSI-effect in the cases of circumstantial evidence and eyewitness testimony: Multivariate and path analyses. *Journal of Criminal Justice, 37,* 452–460.

Kind, S.S. (1987). Navigational ideas and the Yorkshire Ripper investigation. *Journal of Navigation, 40,* 385–393.

Kingsbury, S.J., Lambert, M.T., & Hendrickse, W. (1997). A two-factor model of aggression. *Psychiatry: Interpersonal and Biological Processes, 60,* 224–232.

Kirkman, C.A. (2005). From soap opera to science: Towards gaining access to the psychopaths who live amongst us. *Psychology and Psychotherapy: Theory, Research and Practice, 78,* 379–396.

Klassen, D., & O'Connor, W.A. (1989). Assessing the risk of violence in released mental patients: A cross-validation study. *Psychological Assessment, 1,* 75–81.

Klassen, D., & O'Connor, W.A. (1994). Demographic and case history variables in risk assessment. In J. Monahan & H.J. Steadman (Eds.), *Violence and mental disorder: Developments in risk assessment* (pp. 229–257). Chicago, IL: University of Chicago Press.

Kleinman, L., & Gordon, M. (1986). An examination of the relationship between police training and academy performance. *Journal of Police Science and Administration, 14,* 293–299.

Kleinmuntz, B., & Szucko, J.J. (1984). Lie detection in ancient and modern times: A call for contemporary scientific study. *American Psychologist, 39,* 766–776.

Knight, R.A. (1999). Validation of a typology for rapists. *Journal of Interpersonal Violence, 14,* 303–330.

Knight, R.A, & Guay, J.P. (2006). The role of psychopathy in sexual coercion against women. In C.J. Patrick (Ed.), *Handbook of psychopathy* (pp. 512–532). New York, NY: Guilford Press.

Knight, R.A., & Prentky, R.A. (1990). Classifying sexual offenders: The development and corroboration of taxonomic models. In W.L. Marshall & D.R. Laws (Eds.), *Handbook of sexual assault: Issues, theories, and treatment of the offender* (pp. 23–52). New York, NY: Plenum Press.

Knight, R.A., Prentky, R.A., & Cerce, D.D. (1994). The development, reliability, and validity of an inventory for the multidimensional assessment of sex and aggression. *Criminal Justice and Behavior, 21,* 72–94.

Knoll, C., & Sickmund, M. (June, 2010). Delinquency cases in Juvenile Court, 2007. Office of Juvenile Justice and Delinquency Prevention. Retrieved from https://ncjrs.gov/pdffiles1/ojjdp/230168.pdf, July 6, 2012.

Kocsis, R.N. (2003). Criminal psychological profiling: Validities and abilities. *International Journal of Offender Therapy and Comparative Criminology, 47,* 126–144.

Kocsis, R.N. Irwin, H.J., Hayes, A.F., & Nunn, R. (2000). Expertise in psychological profiling: A comparative assessment. *Journal of Interpersonal Violence, 15,* 311–331.

Köehnken, G. (1987). Training police officers to detect deceptive eyewitness statements. Does it work? *Social Behavior, 2,* 1–17.

Köehnken, G. (1995). Interviewing adults. In R. Bull and D. Carson (Eds.), *Handbook of psychology in legal contexts* (pp. 215–233). Toronto, ON: John Wiley & Sons.

Kohnken, G., Milne, R., Memon, A., & Bull, R. (1999). The cognitive interview: A meta-analysis. *Psychology, Crime, and Law, 5,* 3–28.

Konecni, V.J., & Ebbesen, E.B. (1984). The mythology of legal decision making. *International Journal of Law and Psychiatry, 7,* 5–18.

Koocher, G.P., Goodman, G.S., White, C.S., Friedrich, W.N., Sivan, A.B., & Reynolds, C.R. (1995). Psychological science and the use of anatomically detailed dolls in child sexual-abuse assessments. *Psychological Bulletin, 118,* 199–222.

Koss, M.P. (1993). Detecting the scope of rape: A review of the prevalence research methods. *Journal of Interpersonal Violence, 8,* 198–222.

Kosson, D.S., Cyterski, T.D., Steuerwald, B.L., Neumann, C.S., & Walker-Matthews, S. (2002). Reliability and validity of the Psychopathy Checklist: Youth Version (PCL:YV) in nonincarcerated adolescents males. *Psychological Assessment, 14,* 97–109.

Kozel, F.A., Johnson, K.A., Mu, Q., Grenesko, E.L., Laken, S.J., & George, M.S. (2005). Detecting deception using functional magnetic resonance imaging. *Biological Psychiatry, 58,* 605–613.

Kramer, J.H., & Lubitz, R. (1985). Pennsylvania's sentencing reform: The impact of commission-established guidelines. *Crime & Delinquency, 31,* 481–500.

Kroes, W.H., Margolis, B.L., & Hurrell, J.J. (1974). Job stress in policemen. *Journal of Police Science and Administration, 2,* 145–155.

Kropp, P.R., & Hart, S.D. (2000). The Spousal Assault Risk Assessment (SARA) Guide: Reliability and validity in adult male offenders. *Law and Human Behavior, 24,* 101–118.

Kropp, R., Hart, S., & Lyon, D. (2002). Risk assessment of stalkers: Some problems and potential solutions. *Criminal Justice and Behavior, 29,* 590–616.

Kropp, P.R., Hart, S., Webster, C., & Eaves, D. (1999). *Manual for the spousal assault risk assessment guide* (3rd ed.). Toronto, ON: Multi-Health Systems.

Kumpfer, K.L., & Alvarado, R. (2003). Family-strengthening approaches for the prevention of youth problem behaviors. *American Psychologist, 58,* 457–465.

Laboratory of Community Psychiatry, Harvard Medical School. (1973). *Competency to stand trial and mental fitness* (DHEW Pub. No. ADM-77-103). Rockville, MD: Department of Health, Education, and Welfare.

Lahey, B.B., Waldman, I.D., & McBurnett, K. (1989). The development of antisocial behavior: An integrative causal model. *Journal of Child Psychology and Psychiatry, 40,* 669–682.

Laird, R.D., Jordan, K.Y., Dodge, K.A., Petit, G.S., & Bates, J.E. (2001). Peer rejection in childhood, involvement with antisocial peers in early adolescence and the development of externalizing behavior problems. *Development and Psychopathology, 13,* 337–354.

Laliumière, M., Harris, G., Quinsey, V., & Rice, M. (2005). *The causes of rape: Understanding individual differences in male propensity for sexual aggression.* Washington, DC: American Psychological Association.

Lamb, M., Hershkowitz, I., Orbach, Y., & Esplin, P. (2008). *Tell me what happened: Structured investigative interviews of child victims and witnesses.* West Sussex, England: John Wiley and Sons.

Lamberth, J. (1999, August 16). Driving while black: A statistician proves that prejudice still rules the road. *Washington Post.*

Lamphear, V.S. (1985). The impact of maltreatment on children's psychosocial adjustment: A review of the research. *Child Abuse and Neglect, 9,* 251–263.

Langan, P. A., Schmitt, E. L., Durose, M. R., (2003). *Recidivism of sex offenders released from prison in 1994.* Washington, DC: U.S. Department of Justice.

Langevin, R. (1979). The effect of assertiveness training, Provera and sex of therapist in the treatment of genital exhibitionism. *Journal of Behavior Therapy and Experimental Psychiatry, 10,* 275–282.

Langevin, R., Handy, L., Paitich, D., & Russon, A. (1985). A new version of the Clarke Sex History Questionnaire for Males. In R. Langevin (Ed.), *Erotic preference, gender identity, and aggression in men: New research studies* (pp. 287–306). Hillsdale, NJ: Erlbaum.

Langleben, D.D., Loughead, J.W., Bilker, W.B., Ruparel, K., Childress, A.R., Busch, S.I., & Gur, R.C. (2005). Telling truth from lie in individual subjects with fast event-related fMRI. *Human Brain Mapping, 26,* 262–272.

Langleben, D.D., Schroeder, L., Maldjian, J.A., Gur, R.C., McDonald, S., Ragland, J.D., . . . Childress, A.R.

(2002). Brain activity during simulated deception: An event-related functional magnetic resonance study. *Neuroimage, 15,* 727–732.

Larsson, A. S., & Lamb, M.E. (2009). Making the most of information-gathering interviews with children. *Infant and Child Development, 18,* 1–16.

Larsson, H., Andershed, H., & Lichtenstein, P. (2006). A genetic factor explains most of the variation in the psychopathic personality. *Journal of Abnormal Psychology, 115,* 221–230.

Latessa, E. J., Cullen, F. T., Gendreau, P. (2002). Beyond correctional quackery: professionalism and the possibility of effective treatment. *Federal Probation, 66,* 43–49.

Leach, A.-M., Talwar, V., Lee, K., Bala, N., & Lindsay, R.C.L. (2004). "Intuitive" lie detection of children's deception by law enforcement officials and university students. *Law and Human Behavior, 28,* 661–685.

Leadbeater, B.J., Kuperminc, G.P., Blatt, S.J., & Hertzog, C. (1999). A multivariate model of gender differences in adolescents' internalizing and externalizing problems. *Developmental Psychology, 35,* 1268–1282.

Leblanc, M. (1993). Late adolescent deceleration of criminal activity and development of self- and social control. *Studies on Crime and Crime Prevention, 2,* 51–68.

Lee, M.Y., Uken, A., & Sebold, J. (2007). Role of self-determined goals in predicting recidivism in domestic violence offenders. *Research on Social Work Practice, 17,* 30–41.

Lees-Haley, P.R. (1997). MMPI-2 base rates for 492 personal injury plaintiffs: Implications and challenges for forensic assessment. *Journal of Clinical Psychology, 53,* 745–755.

Leichtman, M.D., & Ceci, S.J. (1995). The effects of stereotypes and suggestions on preschoolers' reports. *Developmental Psychology, 31,* 568–578.

Leinwand, D. (February 24, 2004). *Judges write creative sentences.* Retrieved from http://www.usatoday.com/news/nation/2004-02-24-oddsentences_x.htm

Leippe, M.R. (1995). The case for expert testimony about eyewitness memory. *Psychology, Public Policy, and Law, 1,* 909–959.

Leistico, A.R., Salekin, R.T., DeCoster, J., & Rogers, R. (2008). A large-scale meta-analysis relating the Hare measures of psychopathy to antisocial conduct. *Law and Human Behavior, 32,* 28–45.

Leiter, M. P., & Maslach, C. (2005). *Banishing burnout: Six strategies for improving your relationship with work*. San Francisco, CA: Jossey-Bass.

Lemmon, J.H. (2006). The effects of maltreatment recurrence and child welfare services on dimensions of delinquency. *Criminal Justice Review, 31,* 5–32.

Leo, R.A. (1992). From coercion to deception: The changing nature of police interrogation in America. *Crime, Law and Social Change, 18,* 35–39.

Leo, R.A., & Ofshe, R.J. (1998). The consequences of false confessions: Deprivations of liberty and miscarriages of justice in the age of psychological interrogation. *Journal of Criminal Law and Criminology, 88,* 429–496.

Levenson, M.R., Kiehl, K.A., & Fitzpatrick, C.M. (1995). Assessing psychopathic attributes in a noninstitutionalized population. *Journal of Personality and Social Psychology, 68,* 151–158.

Legal Information Institute. (2012a). 18. USC Chapter 109A - Sexual Abuse. Retrieved May 21, 2012 from http://www.law.cornell.edu/uscode/text/18/part-I/chapter-109A

Legal Information Institute. (2012b). 18. USC Chapter 51 - Homicide. Retrieved May 21, 2012 from http://www.law.cornell.edu/uscode/text/18/part-I/chapter-51

Levine, N. (2007). *CrimeStat: A spatial statistics program for the analysis of crime incident locations.* Washington, DC: National Institute of Justice.

Lieberman, J.D., & Sales, B.D. (1997). What social science teaches us about the jury instruction process. *Psychology, Public Policy, and Law, 3,* 589–644.

Lightfoot, L.O., & Barbaree, H.E. (1993). The relationship between substance use and abuse and sexual offending in adolescents. In H.E. Barbaree & W.L. Marshall (Eds.), *Juvenile sex offender* (pp. 203–224). New York, NY: Guilford Press.

Lilienfeld, S.O., & Andrews, B.P. (1996). Development and preliminary validation of a self-report measure of psychopathic personality traits in noncriminal populations. *Journal of Personality Assessment, 66,* 488–524.

Lindberg, M., Chapman, M.T., Samsock, D., Thomas, S.W., & Lindberg, A. (2003). Comparisons of three different investigative interview techniques with young children. *Journal of Genetic Psychology, 164,* 5–28.

Lindsay, D.S. (1994). Memory source monitoring and eyewitness testimony. In D.F. Ross, J.D. Read, & M.P. Toglia (Eds.), *Adult eyewitness testimony: Current trends and development* (pp. 27–55). New York, NY: Cambridge University Press.

Lindsay, D.S., & Read, J.D. (1995). "Memory work" and recovered memories of childhood sexual abuse: Scientific evidence and public, professional, and personal issues. *Psychology, Public Policy, and Law, 1,* 846–909.

Lindsay, R.C.L., Lea, J.A., & Fulford, J.A. (1991). Sequential lineup presentation: Technique matters. *Journal of Applied Psychology, 76,* 741–745.

Lindsay, R.C.L., Mansour, J.K., Beaudry, J.L., Leach, A., & Bertrand, M.I. (2009). Sequential lineup presentation: Patterns and policy. *Legal and Criminological Psychology, 14,* 13–24.

Lindsay, R.C.L., Martin, R., & Webber, L. (1994). Default values in eyewitness descriptions: A problem for the match-to-description lineup foil selection strategy. *Law and Human Behavior, 18,* 527–541.

Lindsay, R.C.L., Wallbridge, H., & Drennan, D. (1987). Do clothes make the man? An exploration of the effect of lineup attire on eyewitness identification accuracy. *Canadian Journal of Behavioural Science, 19,* 463–478.

Lindsay, R.C.L., & Wells, G.L. (1985). Improving eyewitness identification from lineups: Simultaneous versus sequential lineup presentations. *Journal of Applied Psychology, 70,* 556–564.

Lipsey, M.W. (1992). Juvenile delinquency treatment: A metaanalytic inquiry into the variability of effects. In T.D. Cook, H. Cooper, D.S. Corday, H. Hartmann, L.V. Hedges, R.J. Light, . . . F. Mosteller (Eds.), *Meta-analysis for explanation* (pp. 83–127). New York, NY: Sage.

Lipsey, M.W., & Derzon, J.H. (1998). Predictors of violent or serious delinquency in adolescence and early adulthood: A synthesis of longitudinal research. In R. Loeber & D.P. Farrington (Eds.), *Serious and violent juvenile offenders: Risk factors and successful interventions* (pp. 86–105). Thousand Oaks, CA: Sage Publications.

Lipsitt, P.D., Lelos, D., & McGarry, L. (1971). Competency to stand trial: A screening instrument. *American Journal of Psychiatry, 128,* 104–109.

Lisak, D., & Roth, S. (1988). Motivational factors in nonincarcerated sexually aggressive men. *Journal of Personality and Social Psychology, 55,* 795–802.

Liska, A. E., & Baccaglini, W. (1990). Feeling safe by comparison: Crime in the newspapers. *Social Problems, 37,* 360–274.

Lochman, J.E., Whidby, J.M., & Fitzgerald, D.P. (2000). Cognitive-behavioural assessment and treatment with aggressive children. In P. Kendall (Ed.), *Child and adolescent therapy: Cognitive behavioural procedures* (2nd ed., pp. 31–87). New York, NY: Guilford Press.

Loeber, R., & Farrington, D.P. (1998a). Never too early, never too late: Risk factors and successful interventions for serious and violent juvenile offenders. *Studies on Crime and Crime Prevention, 7,* 7–30.

Loeber, R., & Farrington, D.P. (1998b). *Serious and violent juvenile offenders: Risk factors and successful interventions.* Thousand Oaks, CA: Sage.

Loeber, R., & Stouthamer-Loeber, M. (1986). Family factors as correlates and predictors of juvenile conduct problems and delinquency. In M. Tonry and N. Morris (Eds.), Crime and justice: An annual review of research (Volume 7) (pp. 29-149). Chicago, IL: Chicago University Press.

Loeber, R., & Farrington, D.P. (2000). Young children who commit crime: Epidemiology, developmental origins, risk factors, early interventions, and policy implications. *Development and Psychopathology, 12,* 737–762.

Loeber, R., Keenan, K., Lahey, B.B., Green, S.M., & Thomas, C. (1993). Evidence for developmentally based diagnoses of Oppositional Defiant Disorder and Conduct Disorder. *Journal of Abnormal Psychology, 100,* 379–390.

Loftus, E., & Palmer, J.C. (1974). Reconstructions of automobile destruction: An example of the interaction between language and memory. *Journal of Verbal Learning and Verbal Behavior, 12,* 585–589.

Loftus, E.F. (1975). Leading questions and the eyewitness report. Cognitive Psychology, 7, 560–572.

Loftus, E.F. (1979a). Reactions to blatantly contradictory information. *Memory and Cognition, 7,* 368–374.

Loftus, E.F. (1979b). The malleability of human memory. *American Scientist, 67,* 312–320.

Loftus, E.F. (1983). Silence is not golden. *American Psychologist, 38,* 564–572.

Loftus, E.F., Altman, D., & Geballe, R. (1975). Effects of questioning upon a witness' later recollections. *Journal of Police Science and Administration, 3,* 162–165.

Loftus, E.G., Miller, D.G., & Burns, H.J. (1978). Semantic integration of verbal information into a visual memory. Journal of Experimental Psychology. *Human Learning and Memory, 4,* 19–31.

Loh, J. (1994, January 23). Keeping the job from becoming a killer: Counselors fight rising police suicide rate. *Fort Worth Star-Telegram*, p. A4.

Loo, R. (1994). Burnout among Canadian police managers. *The International Journal of Organizational Analysis, 2,* 406–417.

Loos, M.E., & Alexander, P.C. (1997). Differential effects associated with self-reported histories of abuse and neglect in a college sample. *Journal of Interpersonal Violence, 12,* 340–360.

Lösel, F., & Schmucker, M. (2005). The effectiveness of treatment for sexual offenders: A comprehensive meta-analysis. *Journal of Experimental Criminology, 1,* 117–146.

Lowry, P.E. (1996). A survey of the assessment center process in the public sector. *Public Personnel Management, 25,* 307–321.

Low, P.W., Jeffries, J.C., & Bonnie, R.J. (1986). The trial of John W. Hinckley, Jr. Mineola, NY: Foundation Press.

Luus, C.A.E., & Wells, G.L. (1991). Eyewitness identification and the selection of distractors for lineups. *Law and Human Behavior, 15,* 43–57.

Luus, C.A.E., & Wells, G.L. (1994). The malleability of eyewitness confidence: Co-witness and perseverance effects. *Journal of Applied Psychology, 79,* 714–723.

Lykken, D.L. (2006). Psychopathic personality: The scope of the problem. In C.J. Patrick (Ed.), *Handbook of psychopathy* (pp. 3–13). New York, NY: Guilford Press.

Lykken, D.T. (1960). The validity of the guilty knowledge technique: The effects of faking. *Journal of Applied Psychology, 44,* 258–262.

Lykken, D.T. (1998). *A tremor in the blood. Uses and abuses of the lie detector.* New York, NY: Plenum.

Lynam, D.R., Caspi, A., Moffitt, T.E., Loeber, R., & Stouthamer-Loeber, M. (2007). Longitudinal evidence that psychopathy scores in early adolescence predict adult psychopathy. *Journal of Abnormal Psychology, 116,* 155–165.

MacCoun, R.J., & Kerr, N.L. (1988). Asymmetric influence in mock deliberation: Jurors' bias for leniency.

Journal of Personality and Social Psychology, 54, 21–33.

MacDonald, J.M., Manz, P.W., Alpert, G.P., & Dunham, R.G. (2003). Police use of force: Examining the relationship between calls for service and the balance of police force and suspect resistance. *Journal of Criminal Justice, 31,* 119–127.

Malinosky-Rummell, R., & Hansen, D.J. (1993). Long-term consequences of childhood physical abuse. *Psychological Bulletin, 114,* 68–79.

Malpass, R.S., & Devine, P.G. (1981). Eyewitness identification: Lineup instructions and the absence of the offender. *Journal of Applied Psychology, 66,* 482–489.

Malpass, R.S., Tredoux, C.G., & McQuiston-Surrett, D. (2009). Response to Lindsay, Mansour, Beaudry, Leach, and Bertrand's sequential lineup presentation patterns and policy. *Legal and Criminological Psychology, 14,* 25–30.

Manchak, S.M., Skeem, J.L., Douglas, K.S., & Siranosian, M. (2009). Does gender moderate the predictive utility of the Level of Service Inventory-Revised (LSI-R) for serious violent offenders? *Criminal Justice and Behavior, 36,* 425–442.

Mann, C. (2011). *Casey Anthony trial update: Cindy Anthony attorney talks chloroform testimony on Today Show.* Retrieved from http://www.cbsnews.com/8301-504083_162-20074017-504083.html

Mann, S., Vrij, A., & Bull, R. (2004). Detecting true lies: Police officers' ability to detect suspects' lies. *Journal of Applied Psychology, 89,* 137–149.

Manson, A. (2006). Fitness to be sentenced: A historical, comparative and practical review. *International Journal of Law and Psychiatry, 29,* 262–280.

Manzoni, P., Brochu, S., Fischer, B., & Rehm, J. (2006). Determinants of property crime among illicit opiate users outside of treatment across Canada. *Deviant Behavior, 27,* 351–376.

Marcus, K.D., Lyons Jr., P.M., & Guyton, M.R. (2000). Studying perceptions of juror influence in vivo: A social relations analysis. *Law and Human Behavior, 24,* 173–186.

Mark, V.H., & Ervin, F.R. (1970). *Violence and the brain.* New York, NY: Harper and Row.

Marques, J.K. (1999). How to answer the questions "Does sexual offender treatment work?" *Journal of Interpersonal Violence, 14,* 437–451.

Marshall, W.L. (1999). Current status of North American assessment and treatment programs for sexual offenders. *Journal of Interpersonal Violence, 14,* 221–239.

Marshall, W.L., Anderson, D., & Champagne, F. (1997). Self-esteem and its relationship to sexual offending. *Psychology, Crime and Law, 3,* 161–186.

Marshall, W.L., & Barbaree, H.E. (1988). An outpatient treatment program for child molesters. *Annals of the New York Academy of Sciences, 528,* 205–214.

Marshall, W.L., & Barbaree, H.E. (1990). An integrated theory of the etiology of sexual offending. In W.L. Marshall & D.R. Laws (Eds.), *Handbook of sexual assault: Issues, theories, and treatment of the offender* (pp. 257–275). New York, NY: Plenum Press.

Marshall, W.L., Barbaree, H.E., & Fernandez, Y.M. (1995). Some aspects of social competence in sexual offenders. *Sexual Abuse: Journal of Research and Treatment, 7,* 113–127.

Marshall, W.L., & Fernandez, Y.M. (2003). Sexual preferences are they useful in the assessment and treatment of sexual offenders? *Aggression and Violent Behavior, 8,* 131–143.

Marshall, W.L., Eccles, A., & Barbaree, H.E. (1991). The treatment of exhibitionists: A focus on sexual deviance versus cognitive and relationship features. *Behavior Research and Therapy, 29,* 129–135.

Martin, M. (2007). *Men who solicited sex ordered to wear chicken suits: Judge orders 3 who solicited sex to don outfit, hold anti-brothel sign.* Retrieved from http://www.chron.com/news/bizarre/article/Men-who-solicited-sex-ordered-to-wear-chicken-1555834.php

Martinson, R. (1974). What works? Questions and answers about prison reform. *The Public Interest, 35,* 22–54.

Marlatt, G. A., & Gordon, J. R. (Eds.). (1985). Relapse prevention: Maintenance strategies in the treatment of addictive behaviors. New York, NY: Guilford Press.

Martin Daly & Margo Wilson (1997). Crime and conflict: Homicide in evolutionary psychological perspective. Crime & Justice, 22, 51-100.

Masten, A., & Coatsworth, J. (1998). The development of competence in favourable and unfavourable environments: Lessons from research on successful children. *American Psychologist, 53,* 205–220.

Masten, A.S., Best, K.M., & Garmezy, N. (1990). Resilience and development: Contributions from the study of children who overcome adversity. *Development and Psychopathology, 2,* 425–444.

Maume, M.O., Ousey, G.C., & Beaver, K. (2005). Cutting the grass: A reexamination of the link between marital attachment, delinquent peers and desistance from marijuana use. *Journal of Quantitative Criminology, 21,* 27–53.

McCann, J.T. (1998). A conceptual framework for identifying various types of confessions. *Behavioral Sciences and the Law, 16,* 441–453.

McCloskey, M., & Egeth, H. (1983). Eyewitness identification: What can a psychologist tell a jury? *American Psychologist, 38,* 550–563.

McLennan, F. (2006). Mental health and justice: The case of Andrea Yates. The Lancet, 368, 1951-1954.

McCloskey, M., & Zaragoza, M. (1985). Misleading post event information and memory for events: Arguments and evidence against memory impairment hypothesis. *Journal of Experimental Psychology: General, 114,* 1–16.

McCormick, C.T. (1972). *Handbook of the law of evidence* (2nd ed.). St. Paul, MN: West.

McCoy, S.P., & Aamodt, M.G. (2010). A comparison of law enforcement divorce rates with those of other occupations. *Journal of Police and Criminal Psychology, 25,* 1–16.

McCraty, R., Tomasino, D., Atkinson, M., & Sundram, J. (1999). *Impact of the HeartMath self-management skills program on physiological and psychological stress in police officers.* Boulder Creek, CA: HeartMath Research Center, Institute of HeartMath.

McDaniel, M.A., Whetzel, D.L., Schmidt, F.L., & Maurer, S.D. (1994). The validity of employment interviews: A comprehensive review and meta-analysis. *Journal of Applied Psychology, 79,* 599–616.

McFarlane, J., Campbell, J.C., & Watson, K. (2002). Intimate partner stalking and femicide: Urgent implications for women's safety. *Behavioral Sciences and the Law, 20,* 51–68.

McFatter, R.M. (1986). Sentencing disparity. *Journal of Applied Social Psychology, 16,* 150–164.

McKenna, P.F. (2002). *Police powers.* Toronto, ON: Prentice Hall.

McMahon, R.J. (1994). Diagnosis, assessment, and treatment of externalizing problems in children: The role of longitudinal data. *Journal of Consulting and Clinical Psychology, 62,* 901–917.

McNiel, D.E., Sandberg, D.A., & Binder, R.L. (1998). The relationship between confidence and accuracy in clinical assessment of psychiatric patients' potential for violence. *Law and Human Behavior, 22,* 655–669.

McQuiston-Surrett, D., Malpass, R.S., & Tredoux, C.G. (2006). Sequential vs. simultaneous lineups: A review of methods, data, and theory. *Psychology, Public Policy, and Law, 12,* 137–169.

Meadow, R. (1977). Munchausen syndrome by proxy: The hinterland of child abuse. *Lancet, 2,* 343–345.

Meehl, P.E. (1954). *Clinical vs. statistical prediction.* Minneapolis, MN: University of Minnesota Press.

Meissner, C.A., & Brigham, J.C. (2001). Thirty years of investigating the own-race bias in memory for faces: A metaanalytic review. *Psychology, Public Policy, and Law, 7,* 1–35.

Meissner, C.A., Brigham, J.C., & Pfeifer, J.E. (2003). Jury nullification: The influence of judicial instruction on the relationship between attitudes and juridic decision making. *Basic and Applied Social Psychology, 25,* 243–254.

Meissner, C.A., & Russano, M.B. (2003). The psychology of interrogations and false confessions: Research and recommendations. *The Canadian Journal of Police and Security Services: Practice, Policy and Management, 1,* 53–64.

Meissner, D. (2000, March 5). Reena Virk murder trial set to begin this week. *Canadian Press.* Retrieved from Canoe website: http://acmi.canoe.ca/CNEWSLaw0003/13_virk6.html

Melnyk, L., Crossman, A., & Scullin, M. (2006). The suggestibility of children's memory. In M. Toglia, J.D. Read, D. Ross, & R.C.L. Lindsay (Eds.), *The handbook of eyewitness psychology, Vol I: Memory for events* (pp. 401–427). Mahwah, NJ: Lawrence Erlbaum Associates.

Meloy, J.R. (1997). Predatory violence during mass murder. *Journal of Forensic Sciences, 42,* 326–329.

Melton, G.B. (1990). Realism in psychology and humanism in law: Psycholegal studies at Nebraska. *Nebraska Law Review, 69,* 251–277.

Melton, G., Petrila, J., Poythress, N.G., & Slobogin, C. (1997). Competency to stand trial. In *Psychological evaluations for the court: A handbook for mental health professionals and lawyers* (2nd ed., pp. 119–155). New York, NY: Guilford Press.

Melton, H.C. (1999). Police response to domestic violence. *Journal of Offender Rehabilitation, 29,* 1–21.

Memon, A., & Bull, R. (1991). The cognitive interview: Its origins, empirical support, evaluation and practical implications. *Journal of Community and Applied Social Psychology, 1,* 291–307.

Memon, A., & Gabbert, G. (2003). Improving the identification accuracy of senior witnesses: Do prelineup questions and sequential testing help? *Journal of Applied Psychology, 88,* 341–347.

Memon, A., Holliday, R., & Hill, C. (2006). Pre-event stereotypes and misinformation effects in young children. *Memory, 14,* 104–114.

Memon, A., Vrij, A., & Bull, R. (2003). *Psychology and law: Truthfulness, accuracy, and credibility.* London, England: Jossey-Bass.

Menard, S., & Huizinga, D. (1989). Age, period, and cohort size effects on self-reported alcohol, marijuana, and polydrug use: Results from the National Youth Survey. *Social Science Research, 18,* 174–194.

Merton, R.K. (1938). Social structure and anomie. *American Sociological Review, 3,* 672–682.

Messman-Moore, T.L., & Long, P.J. (2003). The role of childhood sexual abuse sequelae in the sexual revictimization of women: An empirical review and theoretical reformulation. *Clinical Psychology Review, 23,* 537–571.

Miethe, T.D., & Drass, K.A. (1999). Exploring the social context of instrumental and expressive homicides: An application of qualitative comparative analysis. *Journal of Quantitative Criminology, 15,* 1–21.

Michigan State University (2012). Frequently asked questions. Retrieved May 17, 2012 from http://www .forensic.msu.edu/frequentlyaskedquestions

Miller, M.K., Maskaly, J., Morgan, G., & Peoples, C.D. (2011). The effects of deliberations and religious identity on mock jurors' verdicts. Group Processes & Intergroup Relations, 14, 517-532.

Miranda v. Arizona, 384 U.S. 436 (1966).

Miller, H.A. (2001). M-FAST: *Miller Forensic Assessment of Symptoms Test and professional manual.* Odessa, FL: Psychological Assessment Resources.

Miller, H.A. (2005). The Miller-Forensic Assessment of Symptoms Test (M-FAST): Test generalizability

and utility across race, literacy, and clinical opinion. *Criminal Justice and Behaviour, 32,* 591–611.

Miller, M.K., & Hayward, R.D. (2008). Religious characteristics and the death penalty. *Law and Human Behavior, 32*(2), 113-123.

Millis, J.B., & Kornblith, P.R. (1992). Fragile beginnings: Identification and treatment of postpartum disorders. *Health and Social Work, 17,* 192–199.

Mills, J.F., & Kroner, D.G. (2006). The effect of baserate information on the perception of risk for reoffense. *American Journal of Forensic Psychology, 24,* 45–56.

Milne, R., & Bull, R. (1999). *Investigative interviewing: Psychology and practice.* Chichester, UK: Wiley.

Mischel, W. (1968). *Personality and assessment.* New York, NY: Lawrence Erlbaum Associates.

Mitchell, J.T. (1983). When disaster strikes . . . The critical incident stress debriefing process. *Journal of Emergency Medical Services, 8,* 36–39.

Mitchell, K.J., Finkelhor, D., & Wolak, J. (2001). Risk factors for and impact of online sexual solicitation of youth. *Journal of the American Medical Association, 285,* 3011–3014.

Mitchell, K.J., Livosky, M., & Mather, M. (1998). The weapon focus effect revisited: The role of novelty. *Legal and Criminological Psychology, 3,* 287–303.

Mitchell, T.L., Haw, R.M., Pfeifer, J.E., & Meissner, C.A. (2005). Racial bias in mock juror decision-making: A meta-analytic review of defendant treatment. *Law and Human Behavior, 29,* 621–637.

Mitte, K., Steil, R., & Nachtigall, C. (2005). Eine meta-analyse unter einsatz des random-effects-modells zur effektivität kurzfristiger psychologischer interventionen nach akuter traumatisierung. *Zeitschrift für Klinische Psychologie und Psychotherapie, 1,* 1–9.

Moffitt, T.E. (1993). Adolescence-limited and life-course persistent antisocial behaviour: A developmental taxonomy. *Psychological Review, 100,* 674–701.

Moffitt, T.E., Caspi, A., Harrington, H., & Milne, B.J. (2002). Males on the life-course persistent and adolescence limited antisocial pathways: Follow-up at age 26 years. *Development and Psychopathology, 14,* 179–207.

Moffitt, T.E., & Henry, B. (1989). Neurological assessment of executive functions in self-reported delinquents. *Developmental and Psychopathology, 1,* 105–118.

Mokros A, Alison LJ (2002) Is offender profiling possible? Testing the predicted homology of crime scene actions and background characteristics in a sample of rapists. Legal and Criminological Psychology, 7, 25-37

Mokros, A., Osterheider, M., Hucker, S.J., & Nitschke, J. (2010). Psychopathy and Sexual Sadism. *Law and Human Behavior.* Retrieved from http://www.springer-link.com/content/121631662p604u2u/fulltext.html

Monahan, J. (1981). *Predicting violent behavior: An assessment of clinical techniques.* Beverly Hills, CA: Sage.

Monahan, J., & Steadman, H.J. (1994). *Violence and mental disorder: Developments in risk assessment.* Chicago, IL: University of Chicago Press.

Monahan, J., Steadman, H.J., Robbins, P.C., Appelbaum, P., Banks, S., Grisso, T., . . . Silver, E. (2005). An actuarial model of violence risk assessment for persons with mental disorders. *Psychiatric Services, 56,* 810–815.

Moore, C.A., & Miethe, T.D. (1986). Regulated and unregulated sentencing decisions: An analysis of first-year practices under Minnesota's felony sentencing guidelines. *Law & Society Review, 20,* 253–277.

Moore, T.E., & Gagnier, K. (2008). "You can talk if you want to": Is the police caution on the "right to silence" understandable? *Criminal Reports, 51,* 233–249.

Moran, R. (1985). The modern foundation for the insanity defense: The cases of James Hadfield (1800) and Daniel M'Naughten (1843). *Annals of the American Academy of Political and Social Science, 477,* 31–42.

Mossman, D. (1994). Assessing predictions of violence: Being accurate about accuracy. *Journal of Consulting and Clinical Psychology, 62,* 783–792.

Motiuk, L.L., & Porporino, F.J. (1991). *The prevalence, nature, and severity of mental health problems among federal male inmates in Canadian penitentiaries* (Research Report No. 24). Ottawa, ON: Correctional Service of Canada.

Muffler, S.J. (Ed.) (2006). *Racial profiling: Issues, data and analyses.* New York, NY: Nova Science.

Mulvey, E. (2005). Risk assessment in juvenile justice policy and practice. In K. Heilbrun, N. Goldstein, & R. Redding (Eds.), *Juvenile delinquency: Prevention, assessment, and intervention* (pp. 209–231). New York, NY: Oxford University Press.

Mulvey, E.P., Arthur, M.W., & Reppucci, N.D. (1993). The prevention and treatment of juvenile delinquency: A review of the research. *Clinical Psychology Review, 13,* 133–167.

Munsterberg, H. (1908). *On the witness stand.* Garden City, New York, NY: Doubleday.

Murphy, J.M. (1976). Psychiatric labelling in cross-cultural perspective: Similar kinds of behaviour appear to be labelled abnormal in diverse cultures. *Science, 191,* 1019–1028.

Murrie, D.C., Boccaccini, M.T., Johnson, J.T., & Janke, C. (2008). Does interrater (dis)agreement on Psychopathy Checklist score in sexually violent predator trials suggest partisan allegiance in forensic evaluations? *Law and Human Behavior, 32,* 352–362.

Murrie, D.C., Boccaccini, M.T., McCoy, W., & Cornell, D.G. (2007). Diagnostic labels in juvenile court: How do descriptions of psychopathy and conduct disorder influence judges? *Journal of Clinical Child and Adolescent Psychology, 36,* 288–291.

Murrie, D.C., Cornell, D.G., Kaplan, S., McConville, D., & Levy-Elkon, A. (2004). Psychopathy scores and violence among juvenile offenders: A multi-measure study. *Behavioral Sciences and the Law, 22,* 49–67.

Murrie, D.C., Cornell, D.G., & McCoy, W. (2005). Psychopathy, conduct disorder, and stigma: Does diagnostic language affect juvenile probation officer recommendations. *Law and Human Behavior, 29,* 323–342.

Mustard, D.B. (2001). Racial, ethnic, and gender disparities in sentencing: Evidence from the U.S. federal courts. *Journal of Law and Economics, XLIV,* 285–314.

Narby, D.J., Cutler, B.L., & Moran, G. (1993). A meta-analysis of the association between authoritarianism and jurors' perceptions of defendant culpability. *Journal of Applied Psychology, 78,* 34–42.

Nathanson, C., Paulhus, D.L., & Williams, K.M. (2006). Predictors of a behavioral measure of scholastic cheating: Personality and competence but not demographics. *Contemporary Educational Psychology, 31,* 97–122.

National Crime Prevention Council. (1995). *Risk or threat to children.* Ottawa, ON: Author.

National Crime Prevention Council. (1997). *Preventing crime by investing in families and communities: Promoting positive outcomes in youth twelve-to eighteen-years-old.* Ottawa, ON: Author.

National District Attorneys Office. (2009). *Comfort items for child witnesses during criminal proceedings*. National Center for Prosecution of Child Abuse. Retrieved from http://www.ndaa.org/pdf/regarding_use_of_comfort_items_for_child_witnesses.pdf.

National Institute for Occupational Safety and Health. (2010). *Police and stress*. Retrieved from http://blogs.cdc.gov/niosh-science-blog/2008/06/police

National Research Council. (2003). *The polygraph and lie detection*. Washington, DC: National Academies Press.

Navon, D. (1990). How critical is the accuracy of eyewitness memory? Another look at the issue of lineup diagnosticity. *Journal of Applied Psychology, 75,* 506–510.

Nazroo, J. (1995). Uncovering gender differences in the use of marital violence: The effect of methodology. *Sociology, 29,* 475–494.

Nestle, M.E. (2008). Qualifying child witnesses to testify. *American Jurisprudence Proof of Facts, 35*(2D), 665.

Neumann, C.S., & Hare, R.D. (2008). Psychopathic traits in a large community sample: Links to violence, alcohol use, and intelligence. *Journal of Consulting and Clinical Psychology, 76,* 893–899.

New York Police Department. (2011). *Frequently asked questions*. Retrieved from http://www.nypdrecruit.com/faq

Newman, J.P., Brinkley, C.A., Lorenz, A.R., Hiatt, K.D., & MacCoon, D.G. (2007). Psychopathy as psychopathology: Beyond the clinical utility of the Psychopathy Checklist-Revised. In H. Hervé & J.C. Yuille (Eds.), *The psychopath: Theory, research and practice* (pp. 173–206). Mahway, NJ: Erlbaum.

Newman, J.P., Curtin, J.J., Bertsch, J.D., & Baskin-Sommers, A.R. (2010). Attention moderates the fearlessness of psychopathic offenders. *Biological Psychiatry, 67,* 66–70.

Ng, W., & Lindsay, R.C.L. (1994). Cross-race facial recognition: Failure of the contact hypothesis. *Journal of Cross-Cultural Psychology, 25,* 217–232.

Nicholls, T.L., Ogloff, J.R.P., & Douglas, K.S. (2004). Assessing risk for violence among male and female civil psychiatric patients: The HCR-20, PCL:SV, and VSC. *Behavioral Sciences and the Law, 22,* 127–158.

Nichols, T.R., Graber, J.A., Brooks-Gunn, J., & Botvin, G.J. (2006). Sex differences in overt aggression and delinquency among urban minority middle school students. *Applied Developmental Psychology, 27,* 78–91.

Nicholson, R.A., & Kugler, K. (1991). Competent and incompetent criminal defendants: A quantitative review of comparative research. *Psychological Bulletin, 109,* 355–370.

Nisbett, R.E., & Wilson, T.D. (1977). Telling more than we can know: Verbal reports on mental processes. *Psychological Review, 84,*231–259.

Note. (1953). Voluntary false confessions: A neglected area in criminal investigation. *Indiana Law Review, 28,* 374–392.

Nunes, K.L., Firestone, P., Wexler, A., Jensen, T.L., & Bradford, J.M. (2007). Incarceration and recidivism among sexual offenders. *Law and Human Behavior, 31,* 305–318.

Nunes, K.L., Hanson, K., Firestone, P., Moulden, H.M., Greenberg, D.M., & Bradford, J. M. (2007). Denial predicts recidivism for some sexual offenders. *Sexual Abuse: A Journal of Research and Treatment, 19,* 91–106.

Oberlander, L.B., & Goldstein, N.E. (2001). A review and update on the practice of evaluating Miranda comprehension. *Behavioral Sciences and the Law, 19,* 453–471.

Odeh, M.S., Zeiss, R.A., & Huss, M.T. (2006). Cues they use: Clinicians' endorsement of risk cues in predictions of dangerousness. *Behavioral Sciences and the Law, 24,* 147–156.

Odgers, C.L., & Moretti, M.M. (2002). Aggressive and antisocial girls: Research update and challenges. *International Journal of Forensic Mental Health, 1,* 103–119.

Odgers, C.L., Moretti, M.M., & Reppucci, N.D. (2005). Examining the science and practice of violence risk assessment with female adolescents. *Law and Human Behavior, 29,* 7–27.

Odgers, C.L., Reppucci, N.D., & Moretti, M.M. (2005). Nipping psychopathy in the bud: An examination of the convergent, predictive, and theoretical utility of the PCLYV among adolescent girls. *Behavioral Sciences and the Law, 23,* 743–763.

Office of Juvenile Justice and Delinquency (2000). Comprehensive responses to youth at risk: Interim findings from the Safefutures initiative. Retrieved from https://www.ncjrs.gov/pdffiles1/ojjdp/183841.pdf, July 6, 2012.

Offord, D.R., Lipman, E.L., & Duku, E.K. (2001). Epidemiology of problem behaviour up to age 12 years. In R. Loeber & D.P. Farrington (Eds.), *Child delinquents* (pp. 95–134). Thousand Oaks, CA: Sage.

Ofshe, R.J., & Leo, R.A. (1997). The social psychology of police interrogation: The theory and classification of true and false confessions. *Studies in Law, Politics, and Society, 16,* 189–251.

Ofshe, R.J., & Watters, E. (1994). *Making monsters: False memories, psychotherapy, and sexual hysteria.* New York, NY: Charles Scribner's.

Ogloff, J.R.P. (Ed.). (2002). *Taking psychology and law into the 21st century.* New York, NY: Kluwer Academic.

Ogloff, J.R.P., & Cronshaw, S.F. (2001). Expert psychological testimony: Assisting or misleading the trier of fact. *Canadian Psychology, 42,* 87–91.

Ogloff, J.R.P., Wallace, D.H., & Otto, R.K. (1991). Competencies in the criminal process. In D. K. Kagehiro & W.S. Laufer (Eds.), *Handbook of psychology and law* (pp. 343–360). New York, NY: Springer Verlag.

O'Hara, M.W. (1995). Childbearing. In M.W. O'Hara, R.C. Reiter, S.R. Johnson, A. Milburn, & J. Engeldinger (Eds.), *Psychological aspects of women's reproductive health* (pp. 26–48). New York, NY: Springer.

O'Keefe, M., & Schnell, M.J. (2007). Offenders with mental illness in the correctional system. *Mental Health Issues in the Criminal Justice System,* 81–104.

Olczak, P.V., Kaplan, M.F., & Penrod, S. (1991). Attorneys' lay psychology and its effectiveness in selecting jurors: Three empirical studies. *Journal of Social Behavior and Personality, 6,* 431–452.

Olio, K.A., & Cornell, W.F. (1998). The façade of scientific documentation: A case study of Richard Ofshe's analysis of the Paul Ingram case. *Psychology, Public Policy, and Law, 4,* 1182–1197.

Oliver, M. B., & Armstrong, B.G. (1995). Predictors of viewing and enjoyment of reality-based and fictional crime shows. *Journalism and Mass Communication Quarterly, 72,* 559–570.

Olver, M.E., & Wong, S.C.P. (2006). Psychopathy, sexual deviance, and recidivism among sex offenders. *Sexual Abuse: A Journal of Research and Treatment, 18,* 65–82.

O'Neill, M.L., Lidz, V., & Heilbrun, K. (2003). Adolescents with psychopathic characteristics in a substance abusing cohort: Treatment process and outcomes. *Law and Human Behavior, 27,* 299–313.

Orchard, T.L., & Yarmey, A.D. (1995). The effects of whispers, voice-sample duration, and voice distinctiveness on criminal speaker identification. *Applied Cognitive Psychology, 9,* 249–260.

O'Toole, M. (2007). Psychopathy as a behavior classification system for violent and serial crime scenes. In H. Hervé & J.C. Yuille (Eds.), *The psychopath: Theory, research and practice* (pp. 301–325). Mahway, NJ: Erlbaum.

Otto, R., & Heilbrun, K. (2002). The practice of forensic psychology: A look toward the future in light of the past. *American Psychologist, 57,* 5–19.

Paglia, A., & Schuller, R.A. (1998). Jurors' use of hearsay evidence: The effects of type and timing of instructions. *Law and Human Behavior, 22,* 501–518.

Paolucci, E., Genuis, M., & Violato, C. (2001). A meta-analysis of the published research on the effects of child sexual abuse. *Journal of Psychology, 135,* 17–36.

Park, J., Felix, K., & Lee, G. (2007). Implicit attitudes toward Arab-Muslims and the moderating effect of social information. *Basic and Applied Social Psychology, 29,* 35–45.

Parker, A.D., & Brown, J. (2000). Detection of deception: Statement Validity Analysis as a means of determining truthfulness or falsity of rape allegations. *Legal and Criminological Psychology, 5,* 237–259.

Parker, J. (1995). Age differences in source monitoring of performed and imagined actions. *Journal of Experimental Child Psychology, 60,* 84–101.

Parker, J.G., & Asher, S.R. (1987). Peer relations and later personal adjustment: Are low accepted children at risk? *Psychological Bulletin, 102,* 357–389.

Patrick, C.J., Bradley, M.M., & Lang, P.J. (1993). Emotion in the criminal psychopath: Startle reflex modulation. *Journal of Abnormal Psychology, 102,* 82–92.

Patrick, C.J., & Iacono, W.G. (1989). Psychopathy, threat, and polygraph test accuracy. *Journal of Applied Psychology, 74,* 347–355.

Patrick, C.J., & Iacono, W.G. (1991). Validity of the control question polygraph test: The problem of sampling bias. *Journal of Applied Social Psychology, 76,* 229–238.

Patrick, C.P. (2007). Getting to the heart of psychopathy. In H. Hervé & J.C. Yuille (Eds.), *The psychopath: Theory, research and practice* (pp. 207–252). Mahway, NJ: Erlbaum.

Patry, M.W. (2008). Attractive but guilty: Deliberation and the physical attractiveness bias. *Psychological Reports, 102,* 727–733.

Patterson, G.R., Reid, J.B., & Dishion, T.J. (1998). *Antisocial boys.* Eugene, OR: Castalia.

Paul, G.L., & Lentz, R.J. (1977). *Psychosocial treatment of chronic mental patients: Milieu versus social learning programs.* Cambridge, MA: Harvard University Press.

Paulhus, D.L., Williams, K.M., & Nathanson, C. (2002). *The Dark Triad revisited.* Paper presented at the 3rd annual meeting of the Society for Personality and Social Psychology, Savannah, GA.

Pavlidis, I., Eberhardt, N.L., & Levine, J.A. (2002). Seeing though the face of deception. *Nature, 415,* 35.

Pearson, F.S., Lipton, D.S., & Cleland, C.M. (1996, November 20). *Some preliminary findings from the CDATE project.* Paper presented at the Annual Meeting of the American Society of Criminology, Chicago, IL.

Pence, E., & Paymar, M. (1993). *Education groups for men who batter: The Duluth model.* New York, NY: Springer.

Pennington, N., & Hastie, R. (1986). Evidence evaluation in complex decision making. *Journal of Personality and Social Psychology, 51,* 242–258.

Pennington, N., & Hastie, R. (1988). Explanation-based decision making: Effects of memory structure on judgement. *Journal of Experimental Psychology: Learning, Memory, and Cognition, 14,* 521–533.

Penrod, S.D., & Cutler, B. (1995). Witness confidence and witness accuracy: Assessing their forensic relation. *Psychology, Public Policy, and Law, 1,* 817–845.

Penrod, S.D., & Heuer, L. (1997). Tweaking commonsense: Assessing aids to jury decision making. *Psychology, Public Policy, and Law, 3,* 259–284.

Perez, D.A., Hosch, H.M., Ponder, B., & Trejo, G.C. (1993). Ethnicity of defendants and jurors as influences on jury decisions. *Journal of Applied Social Psychology, 23,* 1249–1262.

Perfect, T., Wagstaff, Moore, D., Andrews, B., Cleveland, Newcombe, S., . . . Brown, L. (2008). How can we help witnesses to remember more? It's an (eyes) open and shut case. *Law and Human Behavior, 32,* 314–324.

Peterson, C., & Biggs, M. (1997). Interviewing children about trauma: Problems with "specific" questions. *Journal of Traumatic Stress, 10,* 279–290.

Pezdek, K., Morrow, A., Blandon-Gitlin, I., Goodman, G., Quas, J.A., Saywitz, K., . . . Brodie, L. (2004). Detecting deception in children: Event familiarity affects criterion-based content analysis ratings. *Journal of Applied Psychology, 89,* 119–126.

Phillips, H.K., Gray, N.S., MacCulloch, S.I., Taylor, J., Moore, S.C., Huckle, P., & MacCulloch, M.J. (2005). Risk assessment in offenders with mental disorders: Relative efficacy of personal demographic, criminal history and clinical variables. *Journal of Interpersonal Violence, 20,* 833–847.

Picard, A. (2003, July 22). Grieving mother's farewell: "Adieu, my little flower." *The Globe and Mail.* Retrieved from http://www.globeandmail.com

Pickel, K.L. (1998). Unusualness and threat as possible causes of weapon focus. *Memory, 6,* 277–295.

Pinizzotto, A. J. (1984). Forensic psychology: Criminal personality profiling. Journal of Police Science and

Pirelli, G., Gottdiener, W.H., & Zapf, P.A. (2011). A meta-analytic review of competency to stand trial research. Psychology, Public Policy, and Law, 17, 1-53.

Pickel, K.L., Karam, T.J., & Warner, T.C. (2009). Jurors' responses to unusual inadmissible evidence. *Criminal Justice and Behavior, 36,* 466–480.

Pinizzotto, A.J., & Davis, E.F. (1992). *Killed in the line of duty.* Washington, DC: Department of Justice, FBI Uniform Crime Reporting Program.

Pinizzotto, A.J., & Finkel, N.J. (1990). Criminal personality profiling: An outcome and process study. *Law and Human Behavior, 14,* 215–233.

Piquero, A.R., Blumstein, A., Brame, R., Haapanen, R., Mulvey, E.P., & Nagin, D.S. (2001). Assessing the impact of exposure time and incapacitation on longitudinal trajectories of criminal offending. *Journal of Adolescent Research, 16,* 54–74.

Piquero, A.R., & Chung, H.L. (2001). On the relationships between gender, early onset, and the seriousness of offending. *Journal of Criminal Justice, 29,* 189–206.

Pithers, W.D., Martin, G.R., & Cumming, G.F. (1989). Vermont Treatment Program for Sexual Aggressors. In R.D. Laws (Ed.), *Relapse prevention with sex offenders* (pp. 292–310). New York, NY: Guilford Press.

Platz, S.J., & Hosch, M. (1988). Cross-racial/ethnic eyewitness identification: A field study. *Journal of Applied Social Psychology, 18,* 972–984.

Polaschek, D.L.L., & Collie, R.M. (2004). Rehabilitating serious adult violent offenders: An empirical and theoretical stock-take. *Psychology, Crime & Law, 10,* 321–334.

Pope, H.G., Jonas, J.M., & Jones, B. (1982). Factitious psychosis: Phenomenology, family history, and long-term outcome of nine patients. *American Journal of Psychiatry, 139,* 1480–1483.

Porter, S., & Birt, A.R. (2001). Is traumatic memory special? A comparison of traumatic memory characteristics with memory for other emotional life experiences. *Applied Cognitive Psychology, 15,* S101–S117.

Porter, S., Birt, A., & Boer, D.P. (2001). Investigation of the criminal and conditional release profiles of Canadian federal offenders as a function of psychopathy and age. *Law and Human Behavior, 25,* 647–661.

Porter, S., Doucette, N.L., Woodworth, M., Earle, J., & MacNeil, B. (2008). "Halfe the world knows not how the other halfe lies": Investigation of verbal and nonverbal signs of deception exhibited by criminal offenders and non-offenders. *Legal and Criminological Psychology, 13,* 27–38.

Porter, S., Fairweather, D., Drugge, J., Herve, H., Birt, A., & Boer, D.P. (2000). Profiles of psychopathy in incarcerated sexual offenders. *Criminal Justice and Behavior, 27,* 216–233.

Porter, S., Juodis, M., ten Brinke, L., Klein, R., & Wilson, K. (2010). Evaluation of a brief deception detection training program. *Journal of Forensic Psychiatry & Psychology, 21,* 66–76.

Porter, S., ten Brinke, L., & Wilson, K. (2009). Crime profiles and conditional release performance of psychopathic and nonpsychopathic offenders. *Legal and Criminological Psychology, 14,* 109–118.

Porter, S., Woodworth, M., & Birt, A. (2000). Truth, lies, and videotape: An investigation of the ability of federal parole officers to detect deception. *Law and Human Behavior, 24,* 643–658.

Porter, S., Woodworth, M., Earle, J., Drugge, J., & Boer, D. (2003). Characteristics of sexual homicides committed by psychopathic and nonpsychopathic offenders. *Law and Human Behavior, 27,* 459–470.

Pozzulo, J.D., & Balfour, J. (2006). The impact of change in appearance on children's eyewitness identification accuracy: Comparing simultaneous and elimination lineup procedures. *Legal and Criminological Psychology, 11,* 25–34.

Pozzulo, J.D., Dempsey, J., Corey, S., Girardi, A., Lawandi, A., & Aston, C. (2008). Can a lineup procedure designed for child witnesses work for adults: Comparing simultaneous, sequential, and elimination lineup procedures. *Journal of Applied Social Psychology, 38,* 2195–2209.

Pozzulo, J.D., Dempsey, J., & Crescini, C. (2009). Preschoolers' person description and identification accuracy: A comparison of the simultaneous and elimination lineup procedures. *Journal of Applied Developmental Psychology, 30,* 667–676.

Pozzulo, J.D., & Lindsay, R.C.L. (1998). Identification accuracy of children versus adults: A meta-analysis. *Law and Human Behavior, 22,* 549–570.

Pozzulo, J.D., & Lindsay, R.C.L. (1999). Elimination lineups: An improved identification procedure for child eyewitnesses. *Journal of Applied Psychology, 84,* 167–176.

Pozzulo, J.D., Dempsey, J., Maeder, E., & Allen, L. (2010). The effects of victim gender, defendant gender, and defendant age on juror decision making. *Criminal Justice and Behavior, 37,* 47–63.

Pozzulo, J.D., & Warren, K.L. (2003). Descriptions and identifications of strangers by youth and adult eyewitnesses. *Journal of Applied Psychology, 88,* 315–323.

Prentky, R., Lee, A., Knight, R., & Cerce, D. (1997). Recidivism rates among child molesters and rapists: A methodological analysis. *Law and Human Behavior, 21,* 635–659.

Prentky, R.A., Knight, R.A., Lee, A.F.S., & Cerce, D.D. (1995). Predictive validity of lifestyle impulsivity for rapists. *Criminal Justice and Behavior, 22,* 106–128.

Pratt, T. C., & Cullen, F. T. (2000). The empirical status of Gottfredson and Hirschi's gender theory of crime: A meta-analysis. Criminology, 38, 931-964.

Pryke, S., Lindsay, R.C.L., Dysart, J.E., & Dupuis, P. (2004). Multiple independent identification decisions: A method of calibrating eyewitness identifications. *Journal of Applied Psychology, 89,* 73–84.

Pugh, G. (1985a). The California Psychological Inventory and police selection. *Journal of Police Science and Administration, 13,* 172–177.

Pugh, G. (1985b). Situation tests and police selection. *Journal of Police Science and Administration, 13,* 31–35.

Putnam, F.W. (2003). Ten-year research update review: Child sexual abuse. *Journal of the American Academy of Child Adolescent Psychiatry, 42,* 269–278.

Pynes, J., & Bernardin, H.J. (1992). Entry-level police selection: The assessment centre as an alternative. *Journal of Criminal Justice, 20,* 41–52.

Quas, J., Schaaf, J., Alexander, K., & Goodman, G. (2000). Do you really remember it happening or do you only remember being asked about it happening. Children's source monitoring in forensic contexts. In K.P. Roberts & M. Blades (Eds.), *Children's source monitoring* (pp. 197–226). Mahwah, NJ: Lawrence Erlbaum Associates.

Quayle, J. (2008). Interviewing a psychopathic suspect. *Journal of Investigative Psychology and Offender Profiling, 5,* 79–91.

Quinsey, V.L. (2002). Evolutionary theory and criminal behaviour. *Legal and Criminological Psychology, 7,* 1–13.

Quinsey, V.L., & Ambtman, R. (1979). Variables affecting psychiatrists' and teachers' assessments of the dangerousness of mentally ill offenders. *Journal of Consulting and Clinical Psychology, 47,* 353–362.

Quinsey, V.L., Chaplin, T.C., & Upfold, D. (1984). Sexual arousal to nonsexual violence and sadomasochistic themes among rapists and non-sex-offenders. *Journal of Consulting and Clinical Psychology, 52,* 651–657.

Quinsey, V.L., & Earls, C.M. (1990). The modification of sexual preferences. In W.L. Marshall & D.R. Laws, *Handbook of sexual assault: Issues, theories, and treatment of the offender* (pp. 279–295). New York, NY: Plenum Press.

Quinsey, V.L., Harris, G.T., Rice, M.E., & Cormier, C. (1998). *Violent offenders: Appraising and managing risk.* Washington, DC: American Psychological Association.

Quinsey, V.L., Harris, G.T., Rice, M.E., & Lalumière, M.L. (1993). Assessing the treatment efficacy in outcome studies of sex offenders. *Journal of Interpersonal Violence, 8,* 512–523.

Quinsey, V.L., Jones, G.B., Book, A.S., & Barr, K.N. (2006). They dynamic prediction of antisocial behavior among forensic psychiatric patients: A prospective field study. *Journal of Interpersonal Violence, 21,* 1539–1565.

Quinsey, V.L., Khanna, A., & Malcolm, P.B. (1998). A retrospective evaluation of the regional treatment centre sex offender treatment program. *Journal of Interpersonal Violence, 13,* 621–644.

Quinsey, V.L., & Lalumière, M. L. (1995). Evolutionary perspectives on sexual offending. *Sexual Abuse: Journal of Research and Treatment, 7,* 301–315.

Quinsey, V.L., & Maguire, A. (1983). Offenders remanded for a psychiatric examination: Perceived treatability and disposition. *International Journal of Law and Psychiatry, 6,* 193–205.

Quinsey, V.L., Rice, M.E., & Harris, G.T. (1995). Actuarial prediction of sexual recidivism. *Journal of Interpersonal Violence, 10,* 85–105.

Ragatz, L., Fremouw, W., Thomas, T., & McCoy, K. (2009). Vicious dogs: The antisocial behaviors and psychological characteristics of owners. *Journal of Forensic Science, 54,* 699–703.

Ramirez, D., McDevitt, J., & Farrell, A. (2000). A resource guide on racial profiling data collection systems: Promising practices and lessons learned. Washington, DC: U.S. Department of Justice.

Ramsland, K. (2011). *School killers.* Retrieved from http://www.trutv.com/library/crime/serial_killers/weird/kids1/index_1.html

Raphael, B., & Wilson, J. P. (Eds.). (2000). *Psychological debriefing: Theory, practice and evidence.* Cambridge, UK: Cambridge University Press.

Raskin, D.C., & Esplin, P.W. (1991). Statement validity assessment: Interview procedures and content analysis of children's statements of sexual abuse. *Behavioral Assessment, 12,* 265–291.

Raskin, D.C., Honts, C.R., & Kircher, J.C. (1997). The scientific status of research on polygraph techniques: The case for polygraph tests. In D.L. Faigman, D. Kaye, M.J. Saks, & J. Sanders (Eds.), *Modern scientific evidence: The law and science of expert testimony* (pp. 565–582). St. Paul, MN: West.

Rasmussen, L.A., Burton, J.E., & Christopherson, B.J. (1992). Precursors to offending and the trauma outcome process in sexually reactive children. *Journal of Child Sexual Abuse, 1,* 33–48.

Ratner, P.A. (1998). Modeling acts of aggression and dominance as wife abuse and exploring their adverse health effects. *Journal of Marriage and the Family, 60,* 453–465.

Read, J.D. (1999). The recovered/false memory debate: Three steps forward, two steps back? *Expert Evidence, 7,* 1–24.

Read, J.D., Connolly, D.A., & Welsh, A. (2006). An archival analysis of actual cases of historic child sexual abuse: A comparison of jury and bench trials. *Law and Human Behavior, 30,* 259–285.

Reifman, A., Gusick, S.M., & Ellsworth, P.C. (1992). Real jurors' understanding of the law in real cases. *Law and Human Behavior, 16,* 539–554.

Reinhart, M.A. (1987). Sexually abused boys. *Child Abuse and Neglect, 11,* 229–235.

Reiser, M. (1982). *Police psychology: Collected papers.* Los Angeles, CA: LEHI.

Reiser, M. (1989). Investigative hypnosis. In D. Raskin (Ed.), *Psychological methods in criminal investigation and evidence,* (pp. 151–190). New York, NY: Springer.

Resick, P.A. (1993). The psychological impact of rape. *Journal of Interpersonal Violence, 8,* 223–255.

Resnick, P.J. (1969). Child murder by parents: A psychiatric review of filicide. *American Journal of Psychiatry, 126,* 325–334.

Resnick, P.J. (1970). Murder of the newborn: A psychiatric review of neonaticide. *American Journal of Psychiatry, 126,* 1414–1420.

Resnick, P.J. (1997). Malingered psychosis. In R. Rogers (Ed.), *Clinical assessment of malingering and deception* (2nd ed., pp. 47–67). New York, NY: Guilford Press.

Reuter, R.P. (1995, July 25). Consider "9 days of deceit" prosecutors urge Smith jury. *Toronto Star,* p. A4.

Reuters. (2001, October 29). *U.S. judge sentences men to dress as women.* Retrieved from http://www.zipadeeday.com/story/103/u.s.-judge-sentences-men-to-dress-as-women/

Reuters. (2011). *Casey Anthony found not guilty of murder of daughter.* Retrieved from http://www.reuters.com/article/2011/07/05/us-crime-anthony-idUSTRE7620Y720110705

Rice, M.E., & Harris, G.T. (1997a). Cross validation and extension of the Violence Risk Appraisal Guide with child molesters and rapists. *Law and Human Behavior, 21,* 231–241.

Rice, M.E., & Harris, G.T. (1997b). The treatment of mentally disordered offenders. *Psychology, Public Policy, and Law, 3,* 126–183.

Rice, M.E., Harris, G.T., & Cormier, C.A. (1992). An evaluation of a maximum security therapeutic community for psychopaths and other mentally disordered offenders. *Law and Human Behaviour, 16,* 399–412.

Rice, M.E., Harris, G.T., Lang, C., & Cormier, C. (2006). Violent sex offenses: How are they best measured from official records? *Law and Human Behavior, 30,* 525–541.

Richards, H.J., Casey, J.O., & Lucente, S.W. (2003). Psychopathy and treatment response in response to incarcerated female substance abusers. *Criminal Justice and Behavior, 30,* 251–276.

Risin, L.I., & Koss, M.P. (1987). The sexual abuse of boys: Prevalence and descriptive characteristics of childhood victimizations. *Journal of Interpersonal Violence, 2,* 309–323.

Roberts, J. (2007). Public attitudes to sentencing in Canada: Exploring recent findings. *Canadian Journal of Criminology and Criminal Justice, 49,* 75–107.

Roberts, J.V. (1991). Sentencing reform: The lessons of psychology. *Canadian Psychology, 32,* 466–477.

Roberts, S., Zhang, J., and Truman, J. (2010). *Indicators of school crime and safety: 2010* (NCES 2011-002/NCJ 230812). Washington, DC: National Center for Education Statistics, U.S. Department of Education, and Bureau of Justice Statistics, Office of Justice Programs, U.S. Department of Justice.

Roesch, R., & Golding, S.L. (1980). Competency to stand trial. Urbana: University of Illinois Press.

Robins, L.N. (1986). The consequences of conduct disorder in girls. In D. Olweus, J. Block, & M. Radke-Yarrow (Eds.), *Development of antisocial and prosocial behavior* (pp. 385–408). New York, NY: Academic Press.

Rockett, J.L., Murrie, D.C., & Boccaccini, M.T. (2007). Diagnostic labeling in juvenile justice settings: Do psychopathy and conduct disorder findings influence clinicians? *Psychological Services, 4,* 107–122

Roebers, C.M., Bjorklund, D.F., Schneider, W., & Cassel, W.S. (2002). Differences and similarities in event recall and suggestibility between children and adults in Germany and the United States. *Experimental Psychology, 49,* 132–140.

Rogers, R. (1984). *Rogers Criminal Responsibility Assessment Scales.* Psychological Assessment Resources. Odessa, FL.

Rogers, R. (1986). *Conducting insanity evaluations.* New York, NY: Van Nostrand Reinhold.

Rogers, R. (1990). Models of feigned mental illness. *Professional Psychology, 21,* 182–188.

Rogers, R. (1997). Structured interviews and dissimulation. In R. Rogers (Ed.), *Clinical assessment of malingering and deception* (2nd ed., pp. 301–327). New York, NY: Guilford Press.

Rogers, R. (2008). *Clinical assessment of malingering and deception* (3rd ed.). New York, NY: Guilford Press.

Rogers, R., Bagby, R.M., & Dickens, S.E. (1992). *Structured Interview of Reported Symptoms (SIRS) and professional manual.* Odessa, FL: Psychological Assessment Resources.

Rogers, R., & Ewing, C.P. (1992). The measurement of insanity: Debating the merits of the R-CRAS and its alternatives. *International Journal of Law and Psychiatry, 15,* 113–123.

Rogers, R., Sewell, K.W., & Goldstein, A.M. (1994). Explanatory models of malingering: A prototypical analysis. *Law and Human Behavior, 18,* 543–552.

Rogers, R., Sewell, K.W., Martin, M.A., & Vitacco, J.J. (2003). Detection of feigned mental disorders: A meta-analysis of the MMPI-2 and malingering. *Assessment, 10,* 160–177.

Rogers, R., Ustad, K.L., & Salekin, R.T. (1998). Convergent validity of the Personality Assessment Inventory: A study of emergency referrals in a correctional setting. *Assessment, 5,* 3–12.

Rosenberg, D.A. (1987). A web of deceit: A literature review of Munchausen syndrome by proxy. *Child Abuse & Neglect, 11,* 547–563.

Rosenfeld, B. (2004). Violence risk factors in stalking and obsessional harassment: A review and preliminary metaanalysis. *Criminal Justice and Behavior, 31,* 9–36.

Rosenfeld, J.P., Angell, A., Johnson, M., & Qian, J. (1991). An ERP-based, control-question lie detector analog: Algorithms for discriminating effects within individuals' average waveforms. *Psychophysiology, 38,* 319–335.

Rosenfeld, J.P., Nasman, V.T., Whalen, R., Cantwell, B., & Mazzeri, L. (1987). Late vertex positivity in event-related potentials as a guilty knowledge indicator: A new method of lie detection. *Polygraph, 16,* 223–231.

Rosenfeld, J.P., Soskins, M., Bosh, G., & Ryan, A. (2004). Simple, effective countermeasures to P300-based tests of detection of concealed information. *Psychophysiology, 41,* 205–219.

Rosenhan, D.L. (1973). On being sane in insane places. *Science, 179,* 250–257.

Rossmo, D.K. (1995). Place, space and police investigations: Hunting serial violent criminals. In J.E. Eck & D. Weisburd (Eds.), *Crime and place* (pp. 217–235). Monsey, NY: Criminal Justice Press.

Rossmo, D.K. (2000). *Geographic profiling.* Boca Raton, FL: CRC Press.

Rossmo, D.K. (2005). Geographic heuristics or shortcuts to failure? A response to Snook et al. (2004). *Applied Cognitive Psychology, 19,* 651–654.

Rotenberg, K.J., Hewlet, M.G., & Siegwart, C.M. (1998). Principled moral reasoning and self-monitoring as predictors of jury functioning. *Basic and Applied Social Psychology, 20,* 167–173.

Rothbaum, B.O., Foa, E.B., Riggs, D., Murdock, T., & Walsh, W. (1992). A prospective examination of post-traumatic stress disorder in rape victims. *Journal of Traumatic Stress, 5,* 455–475.

Ruby, C.L., & Brigham, J.C. (1997). The usefulness of the criteria-based content analysis technique in distinguishing between truthful and fabricated allegations: A critical review. *Psychology, Public Policy, and Law, 3,* 705–727.

Ruback, R.B., Shaffer, J.N., & Clark, V.A. (2011) Easy Access to Firearms: Juveniles' Risks for Violent Offending and Violent Victimization. 26, 2111-2138.

Rudolph, K.D., & Asher, S.R. (2000). Adaptation and maladaptation in the peer system: Developmental processes and outcomes. In A.J. Sameroff, M. Lewis, & S.M. Miller (Eds.), *Handbook of developmental psychopathology* (2nd ed., pp. 157–175). New York, NY: Kluwer Academic/Plenum Publishers.

Russano, M.B., Meissner, C.A., Narchet, F.M., & Kassin, S.M. (2005). Investigating true and false confessions within a novel experimental paradigm. *Psychological Science, 16,* 481–486.

Rutherford, M.J., Alterman, A.I., Cacciola, J.S., & McKay, J.R. (1997). Validity of the psychopathy checklist-revised in male methadone patients. *Drug and Alcohol Dependence, 44,* 143–149.

Rutter, M. (1979). Protective factors in children's responses to stress and disadvantage. In M.W. Kent & J.E. Rolf (Eds.), *Primary Prevention of Psychopathology, Vol. 3: Social Competence in Children* (pp. 49–74). Hanover, NH: University Press of New England.

Rutter, M. (1988). Studies of psychosocial risk: The power of longitudinal data. Cambridge, MA: Cambridge University Press.

Rutter, M. (1990). Psychosocial resilience and protective mechanisms. In J. Rolf, A.S. Masten, D. Cicchetti, K. Nuechterlein, & S. Weintraub (Eds.), *Risk and protective factors in the development of psychopathology* (pp. 181–214). Cambridge, MA: Cambridge University Press.

Rutter, M. (Ed.). (1995). Psychosocial disturbances in young people: Challenges for prevention. Cambridge, MA: Press Syndicate of the University of Cambridge.

Ruva, C., McEvoy, C., & Bryant, B. (2007). Effects of pre-trial publicity and jury deliberation on juror bias and source memory errors. *Applied Cognitive Psychology, 21*, 45–67.

Ruva, C.L., & McEvoy, C. (2008). Negative and positive pretrial publicity affect juror memory and decision making. *Journal of Experimental Psychology: Applied, 14*, 226–235.

Ryan, G., Miyoshi, T.J., Metzner, J.L., Krugman, R.D., & Fryer, G.E. (1996). Trends in a national sample of sexually abusive youths. *Journal of the American Academy of Child and Adolescent Psychiatry, 35*, 17–25.

Saad, L. (2007). *Perceptions of crime problem remain curiously negative: More see crime worsening rather than improving.* Retrieved from http://www.gallup.com/poll/102262/perceptions-crime-problem-remain-curiously-negative.aspx

Saks, M.J., & Marti, M.W. (1997). A meta-analysis of the effects of jury size. *Law and Human Behavior, 21*, 451–466.

Salekin, R.T. (2002). Factor-analysis of the Millon Adolescent Clinical Inventory in a juvenile offender population: Implications for treatment. *Journal of Offender Rehabilitation, 34*, 15–29.

Salekin, R.T., Rogers, R., & Machin, D. (2001). Psychopathy in youth: Pursuing diagnostic clarity. *Journal of Youth and Adolescence, 30*, 173–195.

Sampson, R.J., & Laub, J.H. (2005). A life-course view of the development of crime. *Annals of the American Academy of Political and Social Science, 602*, 12–45.

Sanders, B.A. (2003). Maybe there's no such thing as a "good cop": Organizational challenges in selecting quality officers. *Policing: An International Journal of Police Strategies and Management, 26*, 313–328.

Sanders, B.A. (2008). Using personality traits to predict police officer performance. *Policing: An International Journal of Police Strategies and Management, 31*, 129–147.

Sandys, M., & Dillehay, R.C. (1995). First ballot votes, predeliberation dispositions and final verdicts in jury trials. *Law and Human Behavior, 19*, 175–195.

Saslove, H., & Yarmey, A.D. (1980). Long-term auditory memory: Speaker identification. *Journal of Applied Psychology, 65*, 111–116.

Saunders, D.G. (2002). Are physical assaults by wives and girlfriends a major social problem? A review of the literature. *Violence Against Women, 8*, 1424–1448.

Saywitz, K., Goodman, G.S., Nicholas, E., & Moan, S. (1991). Children's memories of physical examinations involving genital touch: Implications for reports of child sexual abuse. *Journal of Consulting and Clinical Psychology, 59*, 682–691.

Saywitz, K.J., & Snyder, L. (1996). Narrative elaboration: Test of a new procedure for interviewing children. *Journal of Consulting and Clinical Psychology, 64*, 1347–1357.

Scheck, B., Neufeld, P., & Dwyer, J. (2000). *Actual innocence.* Garden City, NY: Doubleday.

Schembri, A.J. (n.d.). *Scared straight programs: Jail and detention tours.* Retrieved from http://www.djj.state.fl.us/Research/Scared_Straight_Booklet_Version.pdf

Schmidt, F., McKinnon, L., Chattha, H.K., & Brownlee, K. (2006). Concurrent and predictive validity of the Psychopathy Checklist: Youth Version across gender and ethnicity. *Psychological Assessment, 18*, 393–401.

Schneider, R.D., Bloom, H., & Heerema, M. (2007). *Mental health courts: Decriminalizing the mentally ill.* Toronto, ON: Irwin Law.

Schuller, R.A. (1992). The impact of battered woman syndrome evidence on jury decision processes. *Law and Human Behavior, 16*, 597–620.

Schuller, R.A. (1995). Expert evidence and hearsay: The influence of "secondhand" information on jurors' decisions. *Law and Human Behavior, 19*, 345–362.

Schuller, R.A., & Hastings, P. (1996). Trials of battered women who kill: The impact of alternative forms of expert evidence. *Law and Human Behavior, 20*, 167–187.

Schuller, R.A., & Hastings, P.A. (2002). Complainant sexual history evidence: Its impact on mock jurors' decisions. *Psychology of Women Quarterly, 26*, 252–261.

Schuller, R.A., & Ogloff, J.R.P. (2001). *Introduction to psychology and law: Canadian perspectives.* Toronto, ON: University of Toronto Press.

Schuller, R.A., & Rzepa, S. (2002). Expert testimony pertaining to battered woman syndrome: Its impact on jurors' decisions. *Law and Human Behavior, 26,* 655–673.

Schuller, R.A., Smith, V.L., & Olson, J.M. (1994). Jurors' decisions in trials of battered women who kill: The role of prior beliefs and expert testimony. *Journal of Applied Social Psychology, 24,* 316–337.

Schuller, R.A., Terry, D., & McKimmie, B. (2005). The impact of expert testimony on jurors' decisions: Gender of the expert and testimony complexity. *Journal of Applied Social Psychology, 6,* 1266–1280.

Schwartz, D., Dodge, K.A., Coie, J.D., Hubbard, J.A., Cillessen, A.H.N., Lemerise, E.A., & Bateman, H. (1998). Social-cognitive and behavioral correlates of aggression and victimization in boys' play groups. *Journal of Abnormal Child Psychology, 26,* 431–440.

Scogin, F., Schumacher, J., Gardner, J., & Chaplin, W. (1995). Predictive validity of psychological testing in law enforcement settings. *Professional Psychology: Research and Practice, 26,* 68–71.

Seagrave, D., & Grisso, T. (2002). Adolescent development and the measurement of juvenile psychopathy. *Law and Human Behavior, 26,* 219–239.

Sear, L., & Williamson, T. (1999). British and American interrogation strategies. In D.V. Canter and L.J. Alison (Eds.), *Interviewing and deception* (pp. 67–81). Aldershot, England: Ashgate Publishing.

Seltzer, R. (2006). Scientific jury selection: Does it work? *Journal of Applied Social Psychology, 36,* 2417–2435.

Serin, R.C. (1991). Psychopathy and violence in criminals. *Journal of Interpersonal Violence, 6,* 423–431.

Serin, R.C., Gobeil, R., & Preston, D. (2009). Evaluation of the persistently violent offender treatment program. *International Journal of Offender Therapy and Comparative Criminology, 53,* 57–73.

Serin, R.C., & Lloyd, C. (2009). Examining the process of offender change: The transition to crime desistance. *Psychology, Crime, & Law, 15,* 347–364.

Serota, K.B., Levine, T.R., & Boster, F.J. (2010). The prevalence of lying in America: Three studies of self-reported lies. *Human Communication Research, 36,* 2–25.

Seto, M.C., & Barbaree, H.E. (1999). Psychopathy, treatment behavior, and sex offender recidivism. *Journal of Interpersonal Violence, 14,* 1235–1248.

Sevecke, K., Pukrop, R., Kosson, D.S., & Krischer, M.K. (2009). Factor structure of the Hare Psychopathy Checklist: Youth version in German female and male detainees and community adolescents. *Psychological Assessment, 21,* 45–56.

Shanks, L. (2010). *Evaluating children's competency to testify: Developing a rational method to assess a young child's capacity to offer reliable testimony in cases alleging child sex abuse* (Legal Studies Research Paper No. 32 of 2009–2010). Albany Law School. Retrieved from http://ssrn.com/abstract=1577228

Shaw, D.S., Keenan, K., & Vondra, J.I. (1994). Developmental precursors of externalizing behaviour: Ages 1 to 3. *Developmental Psychology, 30,* 355–364.

Shaw, J.S., III. (1996). Increases in eyewitness confidence resulting from postevent questioning. *Journal of Experimental Psychology: Applied, 12,* 126–146.

Shaw, J.S., III, & McClure, K.A. (1996). Repeated postevent questioning can lead to elevated levels of eyewitness confidence. *Law and Human Behavior, 20,* 629–654.

Shaw, M. (1994). Women in prison: A literature review. *Forum on Corrections Research, 6,* 13–18.

Sheehan, P.W., & Tilden, J. (1984). Real and simulated occurrences of memory distortion in hypnosis. *Journal of Abnormal Psychology, 93,* 47–57.

Sheehan, R., & Cordner, G.W. (1989). *Introduction to police administration* (2nd ed.). Cincinnati, OH: Anderson Publishing.

Sheldon, D.H., & Macleod, M.D. (1991). From normative to positive data: Expert psychological evidence re-examined. *Criminal Law Review,* 811–820.

Sheldon, W.H. (1949). *Varieties of delinquent youths: A psychology of constitutional differences.* New York, NY: Harper & Row.

Shepherd, J.W. (1981). Social factors in face recognition. In G. Davies, H. Ellis, & J. Shepherd (Eds.), *Perceiving and remembering faces* (pp. 55–79). London, England: Academic Press.

Shepherd, J.W., & Deregowski, J.B. (1981). Races and faces: A comparison of the responses of Africans and Europeans to faces of the same and different races. *British Journal of Social Psychology, 20,* 125–133.

Sheridan, M.S. (2003). The deceit continues: An updated literature review of Munchausen syndrome by proxy. *Child Abuse & Neglect, 27,* 431–451.

Sherman, L.W., & Berk, R.A. (1984). The specific deterrent effects of arrest for domestic assault. *American Sociological Review, 49,* 261–272.

Sherman, L.W., Schmidt, J.D., & Rogan, D.P. (1992). *Policing domestic violence: Experiments and dilemmas.* New York, NY: Free Press.

Shover, N., & Thompson, C.Y. (1992). Age differential expectations, and crime desistance. *Criminology, 30,* 89–104.

Siegal, L., & Senna, J. (1994). *Juvenile delinquency: Theory, practice and law* (5th ed.). St. Paul, MN: West.

Silver, E. (2006). Understanding the relationship between mental disorder and violence: The need for a criminological perspective. *Law and Human Behavior, 30,* 685–706.

Silver, E. (1995). Punishment or treatment? comparing the lengths of confinement of successful and unsuccessful insanity defendants. Law and Human Behavior, 19(4), 375-388.

Simourd, L., & Andrews, D.A. (1994). Correlates of delinquency: A look at gender differences. *Forum on Corrections Research, 6,* 26–31.

Skeem, J.L., Mulvey, E.P., Odgers, C., Schubert, C., Stowman, S., Gardner, W., & Lidz, C. (2005). What do clinicians expect? Comparing envisioned and reported violence for male and female patients. *Journal of Consulting and Clinical Psychology, 73,* 599–609.

Slone, A.E., Brigham, J.C., & Meissner, C.A. (2000). Social and cognitive factors affecting the own-race bias in Whites. *Basic and Applied Social Psychology, 22,* 71–84.

Slobogin, C. (1985). The guilty but mentally ill verdict. An idea whose time should not have come. George Washington Law Review, 53, 494-527.

Smith, C., & Thornberry, T.P. (1995). The relationship between childhood maltreatment and adolescent involvement in delinquency. *Criminology, 33,* 451–481.

Smith, C.A., Ireland, T.O., & Thornberry, T.P. (2005). Adolescent maltreatment and its impact on young adult antisocial behavior. *Child Abuse & Neglect, 29,* 1099–1119.

Smith, D.W., Letourneau, E.J., Saunders, B.E., Kilpatrick, D.G., Resnick, H.S., & Best, C.L. (2000). Delay in disclosure of childhood rape: Results from a national survey. *Child Abuse & Neglect, 24,* 273–287.

Smith, M.D. (1990). Patriarchal ideology and wife beating: A test of a feminist hypothesis. *Violence and Victims, 5,* 257–273.

Smith, P., Cullen, F.T., & Latessa, E.J. (2009). Can 14,373 women be wrong? A meta-analysis of the LSI-R and recidivism for female offenders. *Criminology and Public Policy, 8,*183–208.

Smith, S. M., Patry, M., & Stinson, V. (2008). Is the CSI effect real? If it is, what is it? In G. Bourgon, R.K. Hanson, J.D. Pozzulo, K.E. Morton Bourgon, & C.L. Tanasichuk (Eds.), *The proceedings of the 2007 North American Correctional & Criminal Justice Psychology Conference (user report).* Ottawa, ON: Public Safety Canada.

Snook, B., Eastwood, J., Gendreau, P, Goggin, C., & Cullen, R.M. (2007). Taking stock of criminal profiling: A narrative review and meta-analysis. *Criminal Justice and Behavior, 34,* 437–453.

Snook, B., Eastwood, J., Stinson, M., Tedeschini, J., & House, J.C. (2010). Reforming investigative interviewing in Canada. *Canadian Journal of Criminology and Criminal Justice, 52,*203–217.

Snook, B., Haines, A., Taylor, P.J., & Bennell, C. (2007). Criminal profiling belief and use: A survey of Canadian police officer opinion. *Canadian Journal of Police and Security Services, 5,* 169–179.

Snook, B., Taylor, P.J., & Bennell, C. (2004). Geographic profiling: The fast, frugal and accurate way. *Applied Cognitive Psychology, 18,* 105–121.

Snook, B., Taylor, P.J., & Bennell, C. (2005). Shortcuts to geographic profiling success: A reply to Rossmo. *Applied Cognitive Psychology, 19,*1–7.

Snook, B., Zito, M., Bennell, C., & Taylor, P.J. (2005). On the complexity and accuracy of geographic profiling strategies. *Journal of Quantitative Criminology, 21,* 1–26.

Söchting, I., Fairbrother, N., & Koch, W.J. (2004). Sexual assault of women: Prevention efforts and risk factors. *Violence Against Women, 10,* 73–93.

Sonkin, D.J., Martin, D., & Walker, I.E. (1985). *The male batterer: A treatment approach.* New York, NY: Springer.

Spanos, N.P., DuBreuil, S.C., & Gwynn, M.I. (1991–1992). The effects of expert testimony concerning rape on the verdicts and beliefs of mock jurors. *Imagination, Cognition, and Personality, 11,* 37–51.

Spitzberg, B.H., & Cupach, W.R. (2007). The state of the art of stalking: Taking stock of the emerging literature. *Aggression and Violent Behavior, 12,* 64–86.

Spohn, C. (2009). *How do judges decide? The search for fairness and justice in punishment* (2nd ed.). Thousand Oaks, CA: Sage.

Sporer, S.L. (1996). Psychological aspects of person descriptions. In S. Sporer, R. Malpass, & G. Köehnken (Eds.), *Psychological issues in eyewitness identification* (pp. 53–86). Mahwah, NJ: Lawrence Erlbaum Associates.

Sporer, S.L., Penrod, S.D., Read, D., & Cutler, B.L. (1995). Choosing confidence and accuracy: A meta-analysis of the confidence-accuracy relations in eyewitness identification studies. *Psychological Bulletin, 118,* 315–327.

Sporer, S.L., & Schwandt, B. (2006). Paraverbal indicators of deception: A meta-analytic synthesis. *Applied Cognitive Psychology, 20,* 421–446.

Sprott, J.B., & Doob, A. (1997). Fear, victimization, and attitudes to sentencing, the courts, and the police. *Canadian Journal of Criminology, 39,* 275–291.

Stanton, J., & Simpson, A. (2002). Filicide: A review. *International Journal of Law and Psychiatry, 25,* 1–14.

Steadman, H.J. (2000). From dangerousness to risk assessment of community violence: Taking stock at the turn of the century. *Journal of the American Academy of Psychiatry and the Law, 28,* 265–271.

Steadman, H.J., & Cocozza, J. (1974). *Careers of the criminally insane.* Lexington, MA: Lexington Books.

Steadman, H.J., Redlich, A., Callahan, L., Robbins, P.C., & Vesselinov, R. (2011). Effect of mental health courts on arrests and jail days: A multisite study. Archives of General Psychiatry, 68(2), 167-172.

Steadman, H.J., McGreevy, M.A., Morrissey, J.P., Callahan, L.A., Robbins, P.C., & Cirincione, C. (1993). *Before and after Hinckley: Evaluating insanity defense reform.* New York, NY: Guilford Press.

Steadman, H.J., Monahan, J., Appelbaum, P.S., Grisso, T., Mulvey, E.P., Roth, L.H., . . . D. Klassen. (1994). Designing a new generation of risk assessment research. In J. Monahan & H. J. Steadman (Eds.), Violence and mental disorder: Developments in risk assessment (297–318). Chicago, IL: University of Chicago Press.

Steadman, H.J., Mulvey, E.P., Monahan, J., Robbins, P.C., Appelbaum, P.S., Grisso, T., . . . Silver, E. (1998). Violence by people discharged from acute psychiatric inpatient facilities and by others in the same neighborhoods. *Archives of General Psychiatry, 55,* 393–401.

Steadman, H.J., Silver, E., Monahan, J., Appelbaum, P.S., Robbins, P.C., Mulvey, E.P., . . . Banks, S. (2000). A classification tree approach to the development of actuarial violence risk assessment tools. *Law and Human Behavior, 24,* 83–100.

Steblay, N.M. (1992). A meta-analytic review of the weapon focus effect. *Law and Human Behavior, 16,* 413–424.

Steblay, N.M. (1997). Social influence in eyewitness recall: A meta-analytic review of lineup instruction effects. *Law and Human Behavior, 21,* 283–298.

Steblay, N.M., Besirevic, J., Fulero, S.M., & Jimenez-Lorente, B. (1999). The effects of pretrial publicity on juror verdicts: A meta-analytic review. *Law and Human Behavior, 23,* 219–235.

Steblay, N.M., & Bothwell, R.B. (1994). Evidence for hypnotically refreshed testimony: The view from the laboratory. *Law and Human Behavior, 18,* 635–651.

Steblay, N.M., Dysart, J., Fulero, S., & Lindsay, R.C.L. (2001). Eyewitness accuracy rates in sequential and simultaneous lineup presentations: A meta-analytic comparison. *Law and Human Behavior, 25,* 459–474.

Steblay, N., Dysart, J.E., Fulero, S., & Lindsay, R.C.L. (2003). Eyewitness accuracy rates in police showup and lineup presentations: A meta-analytic comparison. *Law and Human Behavior, 27,* 523–540.

Steffensmeier, D., Ulmer, J., & Kramer, J. (1998). The interaction of race, gender, and age in criminal sentencing: The punishment cost of being young, black, and male. *Criminology, 36,* 763–798.

Stein, M., Koverola, C., Hanna, C., Torchia, M., & McClarry, B. (1997). Hippocampal volume in woman victimized by childhood sexual abuse. *Psychological Medicine, 27,* 951–959.

Steinberg, L. (2009). Adolescent development and juvenile justice. Annual Review of Clinical Psychology, 5, 459-485.

Stellar, M. (1989). Recent developments in statement analysis. In J.C. Yuille (Ed.), *Credibility assessment* (pp. 135–154). Dordrecht, The Netherlands: Kluwer.

Stellar, M., & Kohnken, G. (1989). Statement analysis: Credibility assessment of children's testimonies in sexual abuse cases. In D.C. Raskin (Ed.), *Psychological methods in criminal investigation and evidence* (pp. 217–245). New York: Springer.

Stern, W. (1910). Abstracts of lectures on the psychology of testimony and on the study of individuality. *American Journal of Psychology, 21,* 270–282.

Sternberg, K., Lamb, M., Esplin, P., Orbach, Y., & Hershkowitz, I. (2002). Using a structure interview protocol to improve the quality of investigative interviews. In M. Eisen, J. Quas, & G. Goodman (Eds.), *Memory and suggestibility in the forensic interview. Personality and clinical psychology series* (pp. 409–436). Mahwah, NJ: Lawrence Erlbaum Associates.

Stevens, D.J. (1994). Predatory rapists and victim selection techniques. Social Science Journal, 31, 421-433.

Stevenson, M., & Bottoms, B. (2009). Race shapes perceptions of juvenile offenders in criminal court. *Journal of Applied Social Psychology, 39,* 1660–1689.

Storm, J., & Graham, J.R. (2000). Detection of coached general malingering on the MMPI-2. *Psychological Assessment, 12,* 158–165.

Stouthamer-Loeber, M., Wei, E., Loeber, R., & Masten, A.S. (2004). Desistance from persistent serious delinquency in the transition to adulthood. *Development and Psychopathology, 16,* 897–918.

Strand, S., Belfrage, H., Fransson, G., & Levander, S. (1999). Clinical and risk management factors in risk prediction of mentally disordered offenders—more important than historical data? A retrospective study of 40 mentally disordered offenders assessed with the HCR-20 violence risk assessment scheme. *Legal and Criminological Psychology, 4,* 67–76.

Straus, M.A. (1977). Wife beating: How common and why? *Victimology, 2,* 443–458.

Straus, M.A. (1979). Measuring family conflict and violence: The Conflict Tactics Scale. *Journal of Marriage and the Family, 41,* 75–88.

Straus, M.A. (1990). Measuring intrafamily conflict and violence: The Conflict Tactics (CTS) Scales. In M. Straus & R. Gelles (Eds.), *Physical violence in American families: Risk factors and adaptations to violence in 8,145 families* (pp. 29–47). New Brunswick, NJ: Transaction.

Straus, M.A., Gelles, R.J., & Steinmetz, S. (1980). *Behind closed doors: Violence in the American family.* Garden City, NY: Anchor/Doubleday.

Straus, M.A., Hamby, S.L., Boney-McCoy, S., & Sugarman, D.B. (1996). The revised Conflict Tactics Scales (CTS2): Development and preliminary psychometric data. *Journal of Family Issues, 17,* 283–316.

Strier, F. (1999). Whither trial consulting? Issues and projections. *Law and Human Behavior, 23,* 93–115.

Strömwall, L.A., Hartwig, M., & Granhag, P.A. (2006). To act truthfully: Nonverbal behaviour and strategies during a police interrogation. *Psychology, Crime & Law, 12,* 207–219.

Sundby, S.E. (1997). The jury as critic: An empirical look at how capital juries perceive expert and lay testimony. *Virginia Law Review, 83,* 1109–1188.

Surette, R. (1990). *The media and criminal justice policy: Recent research and social effects.* Springfield, IL: Charles C. Thomas.

Sutherland, E.H. (1939). *Principles of criminology.* Philadelphia, PA: J.B. Lippincott Company.

Swanson, J.W. (1994). Mental disorder, substance abuse, and community violence: An epidemiological approach. In J. Monahan & H. J. Steadman (Eds.), *Violence and mental disorder: Developments in risk assessment* (101–137). Chicago, IL: University of Chicago Press.

Sykes, J.B. (Ed.). (1982). *The Concise Oxford Dictionary* (7th ed.). Oxford: Oxford University Press.

Szymanski, L.A., Devlin, A.S., Chrisler, J.C., & Vyse, S.A. (1993). Gender role and attitudes toward rape in male and female college students. *Sex Roles, 29,* 37–57.

Taylor, A., & Bennell, C. (2006). Operational and organizational police stress in an Ontario police department: A descriptive study. *Canadian Journal of Police and Security Services, 4,* 223–234.

Taylor, S.P., & Sears, J.D. (1988). The effects of alcohol and persuasive social pressure on human physical aggression. *Aggressive Behavior, 14,* 237–243.

Technical Working Group for Eyewitness Evidence. (1999). *Eyewitness evidence: A guide for law enforcement* (NCJ Publication No. 178240). Washington, DC: U.S. Department of Justice. Retrieved from http://www.ojp.usdoj.gov

Teplin, L.A. (1984). Criminalizing mental disorder: The comparative arrest rate of the mentally ill. *American Psychologist, 39,* 784–803.

Teplin, L.A. (2000, July). Keeping the peace: Police discretion and mentally ill persons. *National Institute of Justice Journal*, 8–15.

Teplin, L.A., Abram, K.M., & McClelland, G.M. (1994). Does psychiatric disorder predict violent crime among released jail detainees? *American Psychologist, 49*, 335–342.

Terman, L.M. (1917). A trial of mental and pedagogical tests in a civil service examination for policemen and firemen. *Journal of Applied Psychology, 1*, 17–29.

Territo, L., & Sewell, J.D. (2007). *Stress management in law enforcement* (2nd ed.). Durham, NC: Carolina Academic Press.

Test, M.A. (1992). Training in community living. In R.P. Liberman (Ed.), *Handbook of psychiatric rehabilitation* (pp. 153–170). New York, NY: Macmillan.

Thierry, K.L., Lamb, M.E., Orbach, Y., & Pipe, M. (2005). Developmental differences in the function and use of anatomical dolls during interviews with alleged sexual abuse victims. *Journal of Consulting and Clinical Psychology, 73*, 1125–1134.

Thornhill, R., & Palmer, C.T. (2000). *A natural history of rape: Biological bases of sexual coercion.* Cambridge, MA: MIT Press.

Timmons-Mitchell, J., Bender, M.B., Kishna, M.A., & Mitchell, C.C. (2006). An independent effectiveness trial of multisystemic therapy with juvenile justice youth. *Journal of Clinical Child & Adolescent Psychology, 35*, 227–236.

Tjaden, P., & Thoennes, N. (2006). *Extent, nature, and consequences of rape victimization: Findings from the national violence against women survey.* Washington, DC: National Institute of Justice and the Centers for Disease Control and Prevention.

Tjaden, P.G., & Thoennes, N. (2001). Coworker violence and gender: Findings from the National Violence Against Women Survey. *American Journal of Preventive Medicine, 20*, 85–89.

Tolan, P., & Thomas, P. (1995). The implications of age of onset for delinquency risk: II. Longitudinal data. *Journal of Abnormal Child Psychology, 23*, 157–181.

Tolman, R.M., & Weisz, A. (1995). Coordinated community intervention for domestic violence: The effects of arrest and prosecution on recidivism of woman abuse perpetrators. *Crime and Delinquency, 41*, 481–495.

Toma, C.L., Hancock, J.T., & Ellison, N.B. (2008). Separating fact from fiction: An examination of deceptive self-presentation in online dating profiles. *Personality and Social Bulletin, 34*, 1023–1036.

Toomey, J.A., Kucharski, L.T., & Duncan, S. (2009). The utility of the MMPI-2 Malingering Discriminant Function Index in the detection of malingering: A study of criminal defendants. *Assessment, 16*, 115–121.

Toppo, G. (2009, April 14). Usa today. Retrieved from http://www.usatoday.com/news/nation/2009-04-13-columbine-myths_N.htm

Townsend, M., Hunt, D., Kuck, S., Baxter, C. (2006). *Law enforcement response to emergency domestic violence calls for service.* Washington, DC: U.S. Department of Justice.

Trager, J., & Brewster, J. (2001). The effectiveness of psychological profiles. *Journal of Police and Criminal Psychology, 16*, 20–28.

Triplett, R.A., & Turner, E.M. (2009). Where is criminology?: The institutional placement of criminology within sociology and criminal justice. *Criminal Justice Review, 35*, 5–31.

Turtle, J.W., Lindsay, R.C.L., & Wells, G.L. (2003). Best practice recommendations for eyewitness evidence procedures: New ideas for the oldest way to solve a case. *The Canadian Journal of Police and Security Services, 1*, 5–18.

Turvey, B. (2002). *Criminal profiling: An introduction to behavioral evidence analysis* (2nd ed.). San Diego, CA: Academic Press.

Turvey, B. (2008). *Criminal profiling: An introduction to behavioral evidence analysis* (3rd ed.). London, UK: Elsevier Science.

Tversky, A., & Kahneman, D. (1981). The framing of decisions and the psychology of choice. *Science, 211*, 453–458.

Tweed, R.G., & Dutton, D.G. (1998). A comparison of impulsive and instrumental subgroups of batters. *Violence and Victims, 13*, 217–230.

Uggen, C. (1999). Ex-offenders and the conformist alternative: A job quality model of work and crime. *Social Problems, 46*, 127–151.

Ullman, S.E., & Knight, R.A. (1993). The efficacy of women's resistance strategies in rape situations. *Psychology of Women Quarterly, 17*, 23–38.

Ulmer, J.T. (1997). *Social worlds of sentencing: Court communities under sentencing guidelines.* Albany, NY: State University of New York Press.

Undeutsch, U. (1989). The development of statement reality analysis. In J.C. Yuille (Ed.), *Credibility assessment* (pp.101–121). Dordrecht, The Netherlands: Kluwer.

United States Courts. (2011a). *Understanding federal and state courts.* Retrieved from http://www.uscourts.gov/EducationalResources/FederalCourtBasics/CourtStructure/UnderstandingFederalAndStateCourts.aspx

United States Department of Justice. (2010). Correctional populations in the United States, 2009. Washington, DC: United States Department of Justice.

United States Courts. (2011b). *Jurisdiction of state and federal courts.* Retrieved from http://www.uscourts.gov/EducationalResources/FederalCourtBasics/CourtStructure/JurisdictionOfStateAndFederalCourts.aspx

University of Nebraska. (2010). *The department: Law/psychology.* Retrieved from http://www.unl.edu/psypage/grad/lawpsych.shtml

U.S. Bureau of Justice Statistics. (2005). *Contacts between police and the public: Findings from the 2002 national survey.* Washington, DC: U.S. Bureau of Statistics.

U.S. Bureau of Justice Statistics. (2011a). *Sourcebook of criminal justice statistics.* Retrieved from http://www.albany.edu/sourcebook

U.S. Department of Justice. (1999). *Homicide trends in the United States: Infanticide.* Washington, DC: Author.

U.S. Department of Justice. (2001). Internet crimes against children. *Office for Victims of Crime Bulletin.* Washington, DC: Author.

U.S. Department of Justice. (2011a). *Crime in the United States (table 1).* Retrieved from http://www2.fbi.gov/ucr/cius2009/data/table_01.html

U.S. Department of Justice. (2011b). *Expanded homicide data.* http://www2.fbi.gov/ucr/cius2009/offenses/expanded_information/homicide.html

U.S. Department of Justice. (2011c). *Expanded homicide data (table 2).* http://www2.fbi.gov/ucr/cius2009/offenses/expanded_information/data/shrtable_02.html

U.S. Department of Justice. (2011d). *Expanded homicide data (table 3).* http://www2.fbi.gov/ucr/cius2009/offenses/expanded_information/data/shrtable_03.html

U.S. Department of Justice. (2011e). *Expanded homicide data (table 10).* http://www2.fbi.gov/ucr/cius2009/offenses/expanded_information/data/shrtable_10.html

U.S. Sentencing Commission. (1989). *Guidelines manual (Section 3E1.1).* Washington, DC: Author.

U.S. Sentencing Commission. (2011a). *2011 federal sentencing guidelines manual.* Retrieved from http://www.ussc.gov/Guidelines/2011_Guidelines/Manual_PDF/2011_Guidelines_Manual_Full.pdf

U.S. Sentencing Commission. (2011b). *Sentencing table.* Retrieved from http://www.ussc.gov/Guidelines/2011_Guidelines/Manual_PDF/Sentencing_Table.pdf

van Emmerik, A.A.P., Kamphuis, J.H., Hulsbosch, A.M., Emmelkamp, P.M.G. (2002). Single session debriefing after psychological trauma: A meta-analysis. *The Lancet, 360,* 766–771.

Van Kesteren, J. (2009). Public attitudes and sentencing policies across the world. *European Journal of Criminal Policy and Research, 15,* 25–46.

Van Koppen, P.J., & Lochun, S.K. (1997). Portraying perpetrators: The validity of offender descriptions by witnesses. *Law and Human Behavior, 21,* 661–685.

Vance, J.P. (2001). Neurobiological mechanisms of psychosocial resiliency. In J.M. Richman & M.W. Fraser (Eds.), *The context of youth violence: Resilience, risk, & protection* (pp. 43–81). Westport, CN: Praeger.

Vandiver, D.M., & Teske, R.J. (2006). Juvenile female and male sex offenders: A comparison of offender, victim and judicial processing characteristics. *International Journal of Offender Therapy and Comparative Criminology, 50,* 148–165.

Varendonck, J. (1911). Les temoignages d'enfants dans un proces retentisaant. *Archives de Psycholgie, 11,* 129–171.

Viding, E., Blair, R.J., Moffitt, T.E., & Plomin, R. (2005). Evidence for substantial genetic risk for psychopathy in 7-year-olds. *Journal of Child Psychology and Psychiatry and Allied Disciplines, 46,* 592–597.

Viljoen, J.L., Roesch, R., Ogloff, J.R.P., & Zapf, P.A. (2003). The role of Canadian psychologists in conducting fitness and criminal responsibility evaluations. *Canadian Psychology, 44,* 369–381.

Vincent, G.M., Odgers, C.L., McCormick, A.V., & Corrado, R.R. (2008). The PCL:YV and recidivism in male and female juveniles: A follow-up into young adulthood. *International Journal of Law and Psychiatry, 31,* 287–296.

Vingoe, F.J. (1995). Beliefs of British law and medical students compared to expert criterion group on forensic hypnosis. *Contemporary Hypnosis, 12,* 173–187.

Violanti, J.M., Marshall, J.R., & Howe, B. (1985). Stress, coping and alcohol use: The police connection. *Journal of Police Science and Administration, 31,* 106–110.

Violanti, J.M., Vena, J.E., & Marshall, J.R. (1986). Disease risk and mortality among police officers: New evidence and contributing factors. *Journal of Police Science and Administration, 14,* 17–23.

Vitacco, M.J., Neumann, C.S., Caldwell, M.F., Leistico, A., & Van Rybroek, G.J. (2006). Testing four models of the Psychopathy Checklist: Youth Version and their association with instrumental aggression. *Journal of Personality Assessment, 87,* 74–83.

Vizard, E., & Trantor, M. (1988). Helping young children to describe experiences of child sexual abuse: General issue. In A. Bentovim, A., Elton, J. Hilderbrand, M. Tranter, & E. Vizard (Eds.), *Child sexual abuse within the family: Assessment and treatment* (pp. 84–104). Bristol, England: John Wright.

Vrij, A. (1995). Behavioural correlates of deception in simulated police interview. *Journal of Psychology: Interdisciplinary and Applied, 129,* 15–29.

Vrij, A. (1998). Nonverbal communication and credibility. In A. Memon, A. Vrij, & R. Bull (Eds.), *Psychology and law: Truthfulness, accuracy, and credibility* (pp. 32–58). London, England: McGraw-Hill.

Vrij, A. (2000). *Detecting lies and deceits: The psychology of lying and the implications for professional practice.* Chichester, England: John Wiley & Sons.

Vrij, A. (2005). Criteria-Based Content Analysis: A qualitative review of the first 37 studies. *Psychology, Public Policy, and Law, 11,* 3–41.

Vrij, A. (2008). *Detecting lies and deceit: Pitfalls and opportunities* (2nd ed.). Chichester, England: Wiley.

Vrij, A., Akenhurst, L., Soukara, S., & Bull, R. (2002). Will the truth come out?: The effect of deception, age, status, coaching, and social skills on CBCA scores. *Law and Human Behavior, 26,* 261–284.

Vrij, A., & Mann, S. (2001). Who killed my relative? Police officers' ability to detect real-life high-stake lies. *Psychology, Crime, and Law, 7,* 119–132.

Vronsky, P. (2007). Female serial killers: How and why women become monsters. New York, NY: Penguin Group, Inc.

Vrij, A., & Semin, G.R. (1996). Lie experts' beliefs about nonverbal indicators of deception. *Journal of Nonverbal Behavior, 20,* 65–80.

Wadsworth, M.E.J. (1976). Delinquency, pulse rates, and early emotional deprivation. *British Journal of Criminology, 16,* 245–256.

Wagstaff, G.F., MacVeigh, J., Boston, R., Scott, L., Brunas-Wagstaff, J., & Cole, J. (2003). Can laboratory findings on eyewitness testimony be generalized to the real world? An archival analysis of the influence of violence, weapon presence, and age on eyewitness accuracy. *Journal of Psychology, 137,* 17–28.

Waite, S., & Geddes, A. (2006). Malingered psychosis leading to involuntary psychiatric hospitalization. *Australian Psychiatry, 14,* 419–421.

Wakefield, H., & Underwager, R. (1998). Coerced or nonvoluntary confessions. *Behavioral Sciences and the Law, 16,* 423–440.

Walker, L. (1979). *The battered woman.* New York, NY: Harper Perennial.

Walma, M.W., & West. L. (2002). *Police powers and procedures.* Toronto, ON: Emond Montgomery Publications.

Walsh, T., & Walsh, Z. (2006). The evidentiary introduction of Psychopathy Checklist–Revised assessed psychopathy in U.S. courts: Extent and appropriateness. *Law and Human Behavior, 30,* 493–507.

Walsh, Z., Swogger, M.T., & Kosson, D.S. (2009). Psychopathy and instrumental violence: Facet level relationships. *Journal of Personality Disorders, 23,* 416–424.

Walters, M.L. (2011). Straighten up and act like a lady: A qualitative study of lesbian survivors of intimate partner violence. *Journal of Gay & Lesbian Social Services, 23,* 250–270.

Waltz, J., Babcock, J.C., Jacobson, N.S., & Gottman, J.M. (2000). Testing a typology of batterers. *Journal of Consulting and Clinical Psychology, 68,* 658–669.

Ward, T., & Siegert, R. (2002). Rape and evolutionary psychology: A critique of Thornhill and Palmer's theory. *Aggression and Violent Behavior, 7,* 145–168.

Warr, M. (2000). Fear of crime in the United States: Avenues for research and policy. *Criminal Justice, 4,* 451–489.

Warren, J.L., Burnette, M., South, C.S., Chauhan, P., Bale, R., & Friend, R. (2002). Personality disorders and violence among female prison inmates. *Journal of the American Academy of Psychiatry and the Law, 30,* 502–509.

Waschbusch, D.A. (2002). A meta-analytic examination of comorbid hyperactive-impulsive-attention problems and conduct problems. *Psychological Bulletin, 128,* 118–150.

Wasserman, G.A., & Saracini, A.M. (2001). Family risk factors and interventions. In R. Loeber, & D.P. Farrington (Eds.), *Child delinquents: Development, intervention, and service needs* (pp. 165–190). Thousand Oaks, CA: Sage.

Wasserman, G.A., Jensen, P.S., Ko, S.J., Cocozza, J., Trupin, E., Angold, A., & Grisso, T. (2003). Mental health assessments in juvenile justice: Report on the consensus conference. Journal of the American Academy of Child & Adolescent Psychiatry, 42(7), 751-761.

Waterman, A., Blades, M., & Spencer, C. (2004). Indicating when you do not know the answer: The effect of question format and interviewer knowledge on children's "don't know" response. *British Journal of Developmental Psychology, 22,* 135–148.

Weaver, J., & Wakshlag, J. (1986). Perceived vulnerability to crime, criminal victimization experience, and television viewing. *Journal of Broadcasting and Electronic Media, 30,* 141–158.

Webster, C.D., Douglas, K., Eaves, D., & Hart, S. (1997). *HCR 20: Assessing risk for violence, Version 2.* Burnaby, British Columbia: Simon Fraser University and Forensic Psychiatric Services Commission of British Columbia.

Webster, C.D., & Jackson, M.A. (Eds.). (1997). *Impulsivity: Theory, assessment, and treatment.* New York, NY: Guilford Press.

Webster-Stratton, C. (1992). *The incredible years: A trouble shooting guide for parents of children ages 3–8 years.* Toronto, ON: Umbrella Press.

Webster-Stratton, C., & Hammond, M. (1997). Treating children with early-onset conduct problems: A comparison of child and parenting training interventions. *Journal of Consulting and Clinical Psychology, 65,* 93–109.

Weiler, B.L., & Widom, C.S. (1996). Psychopathy and violent behaviour in abused and neglected young adults. *Criminal Behaviour and Mental Health, 6,* 253–271.

Wells, G.L. (1978). Applied eyewitness- testimony research: System variables and estimator variables. *Journal of Personality and Social Psychology, 12,* 1546–1557.

Wells, G.L. (1993). What do we know about eyewitness identification? *American Psychologist, 48,* 553–571.

Wells, G.L., & Bradfield, A.L. (1998). "Good, you identified the suspect": Feedback to eyewitnesses distorts their reports of the witnessing experience. *Journal of Applied Psychology, 83,* 366–376.

Wells, G.L., Leippe, M.R., & Ostrom, T.M. (1979). Guidelines for empirically assessing the fairness of a lineup. *Law and Human Behavior, 3,* 285–293.

Wells, G.L., Malpass, R.S., Lindsay, R.C.L., Turtle, J.W., & Fulero, S.M. (2000). From the lab to the police station: A successful application of eyewitness research. *American Psychologist, 55,* 581–598.

Wells, G.L., & Olson, E.A. (2003). Eyewitness testimony. *Annual Psychology Review, 54,* 277–295.

Wells, G.L., Rydell, S.M., & Seelau, E.P. (1993). On the selection of distractors for eyewitness lineups. *Journal of Applied Psychology, 78,* 835–844.

Wells, G.L., Small, M., Penrod, S., Malpass, R.S., Fulero, S.M., & Brimacombe, C.A.E. (1998). Eyewitness identification procedures: Recommendations for lineups and photo spreads. *Law and Human Behavior, 22,* 603–647.

Wells, G.L., & Turtle, J.W. (1986). Eyewitness identification: The importance of lineup models. *Psychological Bulletin, 99,* 320–329.

Werner, E.E., & Smith, R.S. (1992). *Overcoming the odds: High-risk children from birth to adulthood.* Ithaca, NY: Cornell University Press.

Wetter, M.W., & Corrigan, S.K. (1995). Providing information to clients about psychological tests: A survey of attorneys' and law students' attitudes. *Professional Psychology: Research and Practice, 26,* 474–477.

Wheeler, S., Book, A., & Costello, K. (2009). Psychopathic traits and perceptions of victim vulnerability. *Criminal Justice and Behavior, 36,* 635–648.

Whipple, G.M. (1909). The observer as reporter: A survey of "the psychology of testimony." *Psychological Bulletin, 6,* 153–170.

Whipple, G.M. (1910). Recent literature on the psychology of testimony. *Psychological Bulletin, 7,* 365–368.

Whipple, G.M. (1911). The psychology of testimony. *Psychological Bulletin, 8,* 307–309.

Whipple, G.M. (1912). The psychology of testimony and report. *Psychological Bulletin, 9,* 264–269.

White, M.D. (2001). Controlling police discretion to use deadly force: Re-examining the importance of administrative policy. *Crime and Delinquency, 47,* 131–151.

Whitman, D. (1993, May 31). The untold story of the LA riot. *U.S. News & World Report,* pp. 34–57.

Widom, C., & Ames, M. (1994). Criminal consequences of childhood sexual victimization. *Child Abuse and Neglect, 18,* 303–318.

Widom, C.S. (1989a). Does violence beget violence? A critical examination of the literature. *Psychological Bulletin, 106,* 2–28.

Widom, C.S. (1989b). The cycle of violence. *Science, 244,* 160–166.

Wigmore, J.H. (1909). Professor Munsterberg and the psychology of testimony. *Illinois Law Review, 3,* 399–434.

Wiley, T., & Bottoms, B. (2009). Effects of defendant sexual orientation on jurors' perceptions of child sexual assault. *Law and Human Behavior, 33,* 46–60.

Williams, S.L., & Frieze, I.H. (2005). Patterns of violent relationship, psychological distress, and marital satisfaction in national sample of men and women. *Sex Roles, 52,* 771–785.

Williamson, S., Hare, R.D., & Wong, S. (1987). Violence: Criminal psychopaths and their victims. *Canadian Journal of Behavioral Science, 19,* 454–462.

Williamson, S., Harpur, T., & Hare, R. (1991). Abnormal processing of affective words by psychopaths. *Psychophysiology, 28,* 260–273.

Wilson, M., & Daly, M. (1993). Spousal homicide risk and estrangement. *Violence and Victims, 8,* 3–16.

Wilson, M., Daly, M., & Daniele, A. (1995). Familicide: The killing of spouse and children. *Aggressive Behavior, 21,* 275–291.

Wilson, P., Lincoln, R., & Kocsis, R. (1997). Validity, utility and ethics of profiling for serial violent and sexual offenders. *Psychiatry, Psychology and Law, 4,* 1–12.

Wong, S.C.P., & Gordon, A. (2006). The validity and reliability of the violence risk scale: A treatment-friendly violence risk assessment tool. *Psychology, Public Policy, and Law, 12,* 279–309.

Woodworth, M., & Porter, S. (1999). Historical foundations and current applications of criminal profiling in violent crime investigations. *Expert Evidence, 7,* 241–264.

Woodworth, M., & Porter, S. (2002). In cold blood: Characteristics of criminal homicides as a function of psychopathy. *Journal of Abnormal Psychology, 111,* 436–445.

Wooldredge, J.D. (1988). Differentiating the effects of juvenile court sentences on eliminating recidivism. *Journal of Research in Crime and Delinquency, 25,* 264–300.

Worden, R. E., & Myers, S. M. (2001). *Police encounters with juvenile suspects.* Albany, NY: Criminal Justice Research Center and School of Criminal Justice, University of Albany.

Worling, J.R., & Curwen, T. (2000). Adolescent sexual offender recidivism: Success of specialized treatment and implications for risk prediction. *Child Abuse and Neglect, 24,* 965–982.

Wright, A.M., & Holliday, R.E. (2007). Enhancing the recall of young, young-old, and old-old adults with cognitive interviews. *Applied Cognitive Psychology, 21,* 19–43.

Wrightsman, L.S. (2001). *Forensic psychology.* Belmont, CA: Wadsworth.

Yarmey, A.D. (2001). Expert testimony: Does eyewitness memory research have probative value for the courts? *Canadian Psychology, 42,* 92–100.

Yarmey, A.D., Jacob, J., & Porter, A. (2002). Person recall in field settings. *Journal of Applied Social Psychology, 32,* 2354–2367.

Yarmey, A.D., Yarmey, M.J., & Yarmey, A.L. (1996). Accuracy of eyewitness identifications in showups and lineups. *Law and Human Behavior, 20,* 459–477.

Yardley, J. (March 16, 2002). Mother drowned 5 children in tub avoids and death sentence. Retrieved May 21,

2012 from http://www.nytimes.com/2002/03/16/us/mother-who-drowned-5-children-in-tub-avoids-a-death-sentence.html?pagewanted=all&src=pm

Yllo, K., & Straus, M. (1990). Patriarchy and violence against wives: The impact of structural and normative factors. In M. Straus & R. Gelles (Eds.), *Physical violence in American families* (pp. 383–399). New Brunswick, NJ: Transaction.

Yuille, J.C., Hunter, R., Joffe, R., & Zaparniuk, J. (1993). Interviewing children in sexual abuse cases. In G. Goodman & B. Bottoms (Eds.), *Child victims, child witnesses: Understanding and improving testimony* (pp. 95–115). New York, NY: Guilford Press.

Yurchesyn, K.A., Keith, A., & Renner, K.E. (1992). Contrasting perspectives on the nature of sexual assault provided by a service for sexual assault victims and by the law courts. *Canadian Journal of Behavioral Science, 24,* 71–85.

Zamble, E., & Quinsey, V.L. (1997). *The criminal recidivism process.* Cambridge, England: Cambridge University Press.

Zanis, D.A., Mulvaney, F., Coviello, D., Alterman, A.I., Savitz, B., & Thompson, W. (2003). The effectiveness of early parole to substance abuse treatment facilities on 24-month criminal recidivism. *Journal of Drug Issues, 33,* 223–236.

Zinger, I., & Forth, A. (1998). Psychopathy and Canadian criminal proceedings: The potential for human rights abuses. *Canadian Journal of Criminology, 40,* 237–276.

Zingraff, M.T., Leiter, J., Johnsen, M.C., & Myers, K.A. (1994). The mediating effect of good school performance on the maltreatment delinquency relationship. *Journal of Research in Crime and Delinquency, 31,* 62–91.

Zoucha-Jensen, J.M., & Coyne, A. (1993). The effects of resistance strategies on rape. *American Journal of Public Health, 83,* 1633–1634.

CREDITS

TEXT CREDITS

p. 3, *Arresting Images: Crime and Policing in Front of the Television Camera* by Aaron Doyle, University of Toronto Press (2003). **p. 4,** "The Practice of Forensic Psychology: A Look Toward the Future in Light of the Past" by Randy K. Otto and Kirk Heilbrun from *American Psychologist*, Vol. 57. Copyright © 2002 by The American Psychological Association. **p. 4,** "History of Forensic Psychology" by Anne M. and Curt R. Bartol from *Handbook of Forensic Psychology* by Irving B. Weiner and Allen K. Hess. Copyright © 2006 by John Wiley & Sons, Inc. Reprinted with permission. **p. 8,** "Forensic entomology: The use of insects in death investigations" by G. Anderson from *Forensic Disciplines*, International Association for Identification (2012). **p. 9,** "What Is Forensic Psychology Anyway?" by John C. Bringham from *Law and Human Behavior*, Vol. 23. Copyright © 1999 by The American Psychological Association. **p. 9,** Excerpt from "Specializes in Training Scholars Who Will be Able to Apply Psychology" . . . from University of Nebraska website. **p. 9,** *Psychology and Law* by Curt R. Bartol and Anne M. Bartol, Cengage Learning (1994). **p. 11,** "Some Important European and North American Developments in the History of Forensic Psychology", based on Bartol & Bartol, 2004; Brigham,1999. **p. 13,** "The Suggestibility of the Child Witness: A Historical Review and Synthesis" by Stephen J. Ceci and Maggie Bruck from *Psychological Bulletin*, Vol. 113. Copyright © 1993 by The American Psychological Association. **pp. 13, 14,** Excerpt from on *The Witness Stand* by Hugo Munsterberg, 1908. **p. 16,** Excerpt from Case: *State v. Driver*, 1921. **p. 16,** Excerpt from *Brown v. Board of Education of Topeka*, Opinion; May 17, 1954; Records of the Supreme Court of the United States; Record Group 267; National Archives. **p. 16,** "Psychology and the Law: Jenkins v. The United States." Copyright © 2007 by The American Psychological Association. **p. 20,** "From Normative to Positive Data: Expert Psychological Re-Examined" by D. H. Sheldon and Malcolm D. MacLeod from *The Criminal Law Review*, Thompson-Reuters (1991). **p. 20,** Excerpt from *Frye v. United States*, 293 F. 1013 (D.C.Cir.1923). **p. 26,** "What does a police officer's duties entail?" © New York City Police Department. All rights reserved. Used with permission of the New York City Police Department. **p. 28,** Based on data from "Psychological Testing and the Selection of Police Officers: A National Survey" by Robert E. Cochrane, Robert P. Tett, Leon Vandecreek, from *Criminal Justice and Behavior*, Vol. 30, Sage Publications (2003). **p. 32,** "The Utility of the Oral Interview Board in Selecting Police Academy Admissions" by William G. Doerner from *Policing: An International Journal of Police Strategies & Management*, Vol. 20, National Criminal Justice Reference Service (NCJRS), 1997. **p. 35,** Excerpt from *Police Powers* by Paul McKenna, Pearson Education (2002). **p. 36,** Excerpt from *Introduction to Police Administration* by Robert Sheehan and Gary W. Cordner, Elsevier Science, Inc. (1989). **p. 38,** "Keeping the peace: Police discretion and mentally ill persons" by Linda A. Teplin from *National Institute of Justice Journal*, National Criminal Justice Reference Service (2000). **p. 39,** "Award for Distinguished Contribution to Research in Psychology: Linda A. Teplin" from *American Psychologist*, Vol. 48. Copyright © 1993 by American Psychological Association. **p. 42,** "Police use of force: Examining the relationship between calls for service and the balance of police force and suspect resistance" by John MacDonald et al. from *Journal of Criminal Justice*, Elsevier Science, Inc. (2003). **p. 43,** *Police powers and procedures* by Mark W. Walma and Leigh West, Emond Montgomery Publications, (2002). **p. 43,** Based on data from "Police use of force and the cumulative force factor" from *Policing: An International Journal of Police Strategies & Management*, Vol. 32, Emerald Group Publishing, Ltd. (2009). **pp. 45, 46,** *Developing a law enforcement stress program for officers and their families* by Peter Finn and Julie E. Tomz, 1996. **p. 47,** National Institute for Occupational Safety and Health, 2010. **p. 47,** Table from "Possible consequences of police stress" adapted from *Stress and Policing: Sources and Strategies* by Jennifer M. Brown and Elizabeth A. Campbell. Copyright © 1994 by Jennifer M. Brown and Elizabeth A. Campbell. Published by John Wiley & Sons. Reprinted with permission of the author. **p. 49,** *Impact of the Heartmath Self-Management Skills Program on Physiological and Psychological Stress in Police Officers* by Rollin Mccraty et al., Institute of HeartMath® (2009). **p. 49,** Excerpt from "A conceptual model and implications for coping with stressful events in police work" by Mark H. Anshel from *Criminal Justice and Behavior*, Vol. 27, Sage Publications, (2000). **p. 53,** *Handbook of the Law of Evidence* by Charles T. McCormick, Thomson Learning Global Rights Group (1972). **p. 55,** *Criminal Interrogation and Confessions* by Fred E. Inbau, John E. Reid, Joseph P. Buckley, and Brian C. Jayne. Copyright © 2004 by Jones and Bartlett Learning. Reprinted with permission. **pp. 55, 56,** "The psychology of confession evidence" by Saul M. Kassin from *American Psychology*. Copyright © 1997 by The American Psychological

Association. **p. 59,** "Police-induced confessions: Risk factors and recommendations" by Saul M. Kassin et. al. from *Law and Human Behavior*, Springer (2010). **p. 61,** "Coerced confessions: The logic of seemingly irrational action" by Richard Ofshe from *Journal of Cultic Studies*, International Cultic Studies Association (1989). **p. 64,** Based on data from "The social psychology of false confessions: Compliance, internalization, and confabulation" by Saul M. Kassin and Katherine L. Kiechel from *Psychological Science*, Vol. 7, Sage Publications (1996). **p. 67,** Excerpt from "Criminal profiling from crime scene analysis" by John E. Douglas et al. from *Behavioral Sciences and the Law*. Copyright ©1986 by John Wiley and Sons, Inc. **p. 67,** Excerpt from "Psychological aspects of crime scene profiling: Validity research" by Robert J. Homant and Daniel B. Kennedy from *Criminal Justice and Behavior*, Vol. 25, Sage Publications (1998). **p. 69,** Excerpt from "Historical foundations and current applications of criminal profiling in violent crime investigations" by Mike Woodworth and Stephen Porter from *Expert Evidence*, Vol. 7, Kluwer Academic Publishers (1999). **p. 70,** Excerpt from "Criminal personality profiling: An outcome and process study" by Anthony J. Pinizzotto and Normal J. Finkel from *Law and Human Behavior*. Copyright © 1990 by The American Psychological Association. **p. 71,** Excerpt from "Offender profiling and criminal differentiation" by David Canter from *Legal and Criminological Psychology*, Vol. 5, John Wiley and Sons, Inc. (2000). **p. 71,** Excerpt from *Profiling Violent Crimes: An Investigative Tool* by Ronald M. Holmes and Stephen T. Holmes, Sage Publications, (2002). **p. 72,** Based on data from "Sexual killers and their victims: Identifying patterns through crime scene analysis" by Robert K. Pessler et al. from *Journal of Interpersonal Violence*, Vol. 1, Sage Publications (1986). **p. 75,** Based on data from "Expertise in psychological profiling: A comparative assessment" by Richard N. Kocsis from *Journal of Interpersonal Violence*, Vol. 15, Sage Publications (2000). **p. 76,** Excerpt from "Expertise in psychological profiling: A comparative assessment" by Richard N. Kocsis from *Journal of Interpersonal Violence*, Sage Publications (2000). **p. 86,** Based on data from "Physiological parameters and credibility; The polygraph" by A. Vrij from *Psychology and Law: Truthfulness, Accuracy, and Credibility*, ed. A. Memon, A. Vrij, and R. Bull, McGraw Hill (1998). **p. 87, 88,** Excerpt from *The Polygraph and lie detection*, National Academies Press (2003). **p. 88,** Excerpt from *United States v. Scheffer*, 523 U.S. 303 (1998). **p. 93,** Excerpt from "Separating fact from fiction: An examination of deceptive self-presentation in online dating profiles" by Catalina L. Toma, Jeffrey T. Hancock, and Nicole B. Ellison from *Personality and Social Bulletin*, Vol. 34, Sage Publications (2008). **p. 95,** Based on data from "Nonverbal communication and credibility" by A. Vrij from *Psychology and Law: Truthfulness, Accuracy, and Credibility*, ed. A. Memon, A. Vrij, and R. Bull, McGraw Hill (1998). **p. 96,** Excerpt from "Individual differences in judging deception: Accuracy and bias" by Charles F. Bond and Bella M. DePaulo from *Psychological Bulletin*. Copyright © 2008 by The American Psychological Association. **p. 96,** Excerpt from "Focus on Susan Smith's lies and a smile" by Rick Bragg from *The New York Times* (1995). **p. 98,** Excerpt from "Structured interviews and dissimulation" from *Clinical Assessment of Malingering Deception* by Richard Rogers, Guilford Press (1977). **p. 101,** Excerpt from "The ethical dilemma of coached malingering research" by Yossef S. Ben-Porath from *Psychological Assessment*. Copyright © 1994 by The American Psychological Association. **p. 102,** "Psychopathy, threat, and polygraph test accuracy" by Christopher J. Patrick and William G. Iacono from *Journal of Applied Psychology*, Vol. 74. Copyright © 1989 by The American Psychological Association. **pp. 103, 104,** Excerpt from "On being sane in insane places" by David L. Rosenham from *Science*, Vol. 179, American Association for the Advancement of Science (1973). **p. 104,** *Malingering* by A. Bassett Jones, 1917. **p. 104,** Table from "Malingered psychosis" by P. J. Resnick from *Clinical Assessment of Malingering and Deception* by Richard Rogers. Copyright © 1997 by Guilford Publications, Inc. Reprinted with permission. **p. 115,** Excerpt from Elizabeth Loftus. Reprinted with permission. **p. 118,** "Eyewitness responses to leading and misleading questions under the cognitive interview" by Edweard R. Geiselman et al. from *Journal of Police Science and Administration*, Vol. 14. Copyright © 1986 by The American Psychological Association. **p. 122,** Table from "What do we know about eyewitness identification?" by Gary L. Wells from *American Psychologist*. Copyright © 1993 by The American Psychological Association. **p. 122,** "Eyewitness identification: The importance of lineup models" by Gary L. Wells and John W. Turtle from *Psychological Bulletin*, Vol. 99. Copyright © 1986 by The American Psychological Association. **p. 127,** Figure from "'Good, you identified the suspect:' Feedback to eyewitnesses distorts their reports of the witnessing experience" by Gary L. Wells and Amy L. Bradfield from *Journal of Applied Psychology*. Copyright © 1998 by The American Psychiatric Association. **p. 130,** "What do we know about eyewitness identification?" by Gary L. Wells from *American Psychologist*, Vol. 48. Copyright © 1993 by The American Psychological Association. **p. 132,** From Innocence Project webpage: "Profiles," "Facts Sheet," and "Charles Chapman Case." Copyright © 2011 by *The Innocence Project*. Reprinted with permission. **pp. 132, 134,** Tables from Innocence Project webpage: "Profiles," "Facts Sheet," and "Charles Chapman Case." Copyright © 2011 by The Innocence Project. Reprinted with permission. **p. 133,** Excerpt from "Eyewitness ID: Not seeing eye to eye" by J. Smith, from *The Austin Chronicle*, April 10, 2009. **p. 134,** From Innocence

Project webpage: "Profiles," "Facts Sheet," and "Charles Chapman case." Copyright © 2011 by *The Innocence Project*. Reprinted with permission. **p. 142,** Reprinted with permission of Stephen J. Ceci. **p. 146,** Table: "Statement validity assessment: Interview procedures and content analysis of children's statements of sexual abuse" by David C. Raskin and Phillip W. Esplin from *Behavioral Assessment*. Copyright © 2012 by The American Psychological Association. **p. 147,** Table from "Interviewing children in sexual abuse cases" by J. C. Yuille, R. Hunter, R. Joffe, and J. Zaparniuk from *Child Victims, Child Witnesses: Understanding and Improving Testimony*, Ed. Gail S. Goodman and Bette L. Bottoms. Copyright © 1993 by Guilford Publications, Inc. Reprinted with permission. **p. 148,** Figure from "Narrative elaboration: Test of a new procedure for interviewing children" by Karen J. Saywitz and Lynn Snyder from *Journal of Consulting and Clinical Psychology*. Copyright © 1996 by The American Psychological Association. **p. 151,** "'Memory work' and recovered memories of childhood sexual abuse: Scientific evidence and public, professional, and personal issues" by Stephen D. Lindsey and Don J. Read from *Psychology, Public Policy, and Law*, Vol 1. Copyright © 1995 by The American Psychological Association. **p. 151,** Excerpt from "Delayed prosecutions of historic child sexual abuse: Analyses of 2064 canadian criminal complaints" by Deborah A. Connolly and J. Don Read from *Law and Human Behavior*, Springer (2006). **p. 156,** Excerpt from "Evaluating children's competency to testify: Developing a rational method to assess a young child's capacity to offer reliable testimony in cases alleging child sex abuse" by Laurie Shanks from *Cleveland State Law Review*, Vol. 58, Cleveland State Law Review (2010). **p. 159,** The Child Abuse Prevention and Treatment Act (CAPTA) (42 U.S.C.A. 5106) **p. 160,** Table from "Child maltreatment: What we know in the year 2000" by Harriet L. MacMillan from *Canadian Journal of Psychiatry*. Copyright ©2000 by the Canadian Psychiatric Association. Reprinted with permission. **p. 162,** Based on "Arvada cell phone salesman arrested over text messages teen reports messages to mother who contacts DA investigators" from TheDenverChannel.com, 2009. **p. 162,** Based on "NBC resolves lawsuit over 'to catch a predator' suicide" from *Los Angeles Times*, June 24, 2008. **p. 169,** Based on "The O. J. Simpson Trial: The jury" from http://law2.umkc.edu/. **p. 171,** Based on "Officers in bronx fire 41 shots, and an unarmed man is killed" by Michael Cooper, from *The New York Times*, February 5, 1999. **p. 172,** Based on "Homaidan al-turki, Colorado man who kept house keeper as slave, has appeal denied by supreme court," April 5, 2010. **p. 173,** Excerpt from "Jury nullification: The influence of judicial instruction on the relationship between attitudes and juridic decision making" by Christian A. Messiner, John C. Bringham, and Jeffrey F. Pfeifer from *Basic and Applied Psychology*, Vol. 25, Lawrence Erlbaum Associates, Inc. (2003). **p. 185,** Excerpt by Bette Bottoms. Reprinted with permission. **p. 190,** Excerpt from "Psychiatric manual's update needs openness, critics say" R. Grossman from *The Chicago Tribune* (2008). **p. 191,** *Dusky v. United States*, 362 U.S. 402 (1960). **p. 192, 200, 202,** "Competency to stand trial" by G. Melton et al. from *Psychological Evaluations for The Court: A Handbook for Mental Health Professionals and Lawyers*, Guilford Press (2007). **p. 196,** Based on "Ruling offers hope for jailing accused cop killer" by M. Durand, *The Daily Journal*, January 7, 2004, San Mateo County. **p. 200,** Based on "John du Pont Found Guilty, Mentally Ill" by D. Goldberg, Washington Post, February 26, 1997. **p. 201,** Excerpt from Henry Steadman. Reprinted with Permission. **p. 203,** "Prevalence of psychiatric disorders and suicide attempts in prison population" by R. C. Bland et al. from *The Canadian Journal of Psychiatry*, Canadian Psychiatric Association, (1990). **p. 205,** Based on "Are the mentally ill really violent?" by E. Mulvey and J. Fardella from *Psychology*, November 1, 2000. **p. 212,** Jurisdiction of state and federal courts, U.S. courts from administrative office of the U.S. courts on behalf of the federal judiciary. **p. 215,** Based on Azpiri, 2008; Leinwand, 2004; Martin, 2007; Reuters, 2001. **p. 216,** Excerpt from "Restorative justice dialogue: The impact of mediation and conferencing on juvenile recidivism" by William Bradshaw and David Roseborough from *Federal Probation*, Vol. 69, U.S. Courts Publishing (2005). **p. 216,** Excerpt from *Sentencing as a Human Process* by John Hogarth, The University of Toronto Press (1971). **p. 218,** Excerpt from "Sentencing disparity" by Robert M. McFatter from *Journal of Applied Psychology*, Vol. 16, John Wiley and Sons, Inc. (1986). **pp. 221, 222,** Tables from "Sentencing disparity" by Robert M. McFatter from *Journal of Applied Social Psychology*. Copyright © 1986 by John Wiley and Sons. Reprinted with permission. **p. 223,** Table from *The United States Ssentencing Commission Guidelines*, from http://www.ussc .gov/. **p. 226,** Table from "The effects of community sanctions and incarceration of recidivism" by Paul Gendreau, Paula Smith, and Claire Goggin from *Compendium 2000 on effective correctional programing* (p. 18–21). Copyright © 2001 by The Minister of Public Works and Government Services Canada. Reprinted with permission. **p. 227,** ABC News, 2011; Schembri, n.d. **p. 230,** Excerpt from "Fear, victimization, and attitudes to sentencing, the courts, and the police" by Jane B. Sprott and Anthony N. Doob from *Canadian Journal of Criminology*, Vol. 39, Canadian Criminal Justice Association, (1997). **p. 234,** "Improving the clinical practice of violence risk assessment: Technology, guidelines, and training" by Randy Borum from *American Psychologist*, Vol. 51. Copyright © 1996 by The American Psychological Association. **p. 234,** Excerpt from "Offender risk assessment: guidelines for selection and use" by James Bonta from *Criminal Justice and Behavior*, Vol. 29, Sage Publications, 2002. **p. 234,** "The role of psychopathy in assessing risk for violence: Conceptual and methodological issues" by Stephen D. Hart from *Legal and Criminological Psychology*, Vol. 3, John Wiley and Sons, Inc. (1998). **p. 239,** "Prediction in psychiatry: An example of misplaced confidence in experts" by Stephen Cocozza J. and Henry J. Steadman from *Social Issues*, Vol. 25. Copyright © 1978 by The American Psychological Association. **p. 239,** Excerpt from *Predicting Violent Behavior: An Assessment of Clinical Techniques* by John Monahan, Sage Publications (1981). **p. 240,** Excerpt from John Monahan. Reprinted with permission. **p. 243,** Tex Cr. Code Ann. § 37.072: Texas Statutes–Article 37.072: Procedure in repeat sex offender capital case. **p. 253,** Based on Campbell et al., 2009. **p. 254,** "Understanding the relationship between mental disorder and violence: The need for a criminological perspective" by Eric Silver from *Law and Human Behavior*, Vol. 30, Springer (2006). **p. 255,** Table from *The Criminal Recidivism Process* by Vernon L. Quinsey and Edward Zamble. Copyright © 1997 by Cambridge University Press. Reprinted with the permission of Cambridge University Press. **p. 260,** "Against all odds: A qualitative follow-up study of high risk violent offenders who were not re-convicted" by Clara H. Gumpert, Ulrika Haggard, and Martin Grann from *Journal of Interpersonal Violence*, Vol. 16, Sage Publications (2001). **p. 263,** "Psychological labeling in cross-cultural perspective: Similar kinds of behaviour appear to be labeled abnormal in diverse cultures" by J. M. Murphy from *Science*, Vol. 191, Sage Publications (1976). **p. 267,** DSM-IV "Antisocial personality disorder and PCL-R Psychopathy: Construct overlap in offenders", Copyright © 1994 by American Psychological Association. **p. 271,** Excerpts from "Fatal Sddiction: Ted Bundy's Final Interview" by James Dobson and Ted Bundy. Copyright © 1989 by *Focus on the Family*. Reprinted with permission. **p. 269,** Excerpt from *The Hare Psychopathy Checklist Revised* by Robert D. Hare. Copyright © 2003 by Multi-Health Systems, Inc. Reprinted with permission. **p. 272,** Excerpt from *Without Conscience: The Disturbing World of Psychopaths Amongst Us* by Robert D. Hare, Atria Books, (1996). **p. 275,** Excerpt from "Psychopathic traits predict attitudes toward a juvenile capital murderer" by Krissie Fernandez, John F. Edens, and Laura S. Guy from *Behavioral Sciences & The Law*, Vol. 21, John Wiley and Sons, Inc. (2003). **p. 275,** Table from "Psychopathic traits predict attitudes toward a juvenile capital murderer" by Krissie Fernandez, John F. Edens, and Laura S. Guy from *Behavioral Sciences & The Law*. Copyright © 2003 by John Wiley and Sons. Reprinted with permission. **p. 276,** Excerpt from "Psychopathy, conduct disorder, and stigma: Does diagnostic language affect juvenile probation officer recommendations" by Daniel C. Murrie, Dewey G. Cornell, and Wendy K. McCoy from *Law and Human Behavior*, Vol. 29, John Wiley and Sons, Inc. (2005). **p. 276,** Excerpt from "Assessment of 'juvenile psychopathy' and its association with violence: A critical review" by J. F. Edens et al. from *Behavioral Science & The Law*, Vol. 19, John Wiley and Sons, Inc. (2001). **p. 278,** Excerpt from "Psychopathy as a clinical empirical construct" by Robert D. Hare and C. S. Neumann from *Annual Review of Clinical Psychology*, Annual Reviews, Inc. (1998). **p. 279,** Excerpt from *Violent Offenders: Appraising and Managing Risk* by Vernon L. Quincey et al. Copyright © 1998 by The American Psychological Association. **p. 279,** Excerpt from "Psychopathy as a behavior classification system for violent and serial crime scenes" by M. O'Toole from *The psychopath: Theory, Research and Practice*, ed. Hugues Herve and John C. Yuille, Lawrence Erlbaum Associates, Inc. (2007). **p. 285,** Based on "High court: Juvenile death penalty unconstitutional slim majority cites 'evolving standards' in american society" by Bill Mears, from CNN Washington Bureau, March 1, 2005 and Graham v. Florida from http://www.scotusblog.com/. **p. 286,** http://www.nytimes .com/2002/04/02/us/youth-may-change-to-guilty-plea-in-dartmouthprofessors'-death; http://www.nytimes .com/2002/04/05/us/teenagers-are-sentenced-for-killing-two-professors; http://www.nytimes.com/2002/05/18/us/ youth-dreamed-ofadventure-but-settled-for-killing-a-couple". **p. 288,** Number of youth under 18 years arrested in the United States in 2010 (partial list) from FBI.gov. **p. 290,** Reprinted with permission of Rolf Loeber. **p. 292,** Based on: http://www.nytimes.com/1999/04/21/us/terror-littleton-overview-2-students-colorado-schoolsaid-gun-down-many-23- kill.html?ref5columbinehighschool; http://topics.nytimes.com/top/reference/timestopics/organizations/c/columbine_high_ school/index.html; http://www.nytimes.com/1999/04/22/us/terror-in-littleton-the-suspects-portrait-of-outcasts-seeking- tostand-out.html?ref5columbinehighschool. **p. 295,** Based on http://www.timesonline.co.uk/tol/news/world/us_and_ americas/article5512446.ece; http://www.cbsnews.com/8300-504083_162-504083.html?keyword5Daniel1Petric. **p. 297,** Excerpts from "Psychosocial resilience and protective mechanisms" by M. Rutter from *Risk and Protective Factors in the Development of Psychopathology*, ed. Jon Rolf et al, Cambridge University Press (1990). **p. 300,** SafeFutures, office of juvenile justice and delinquency prevention, 2000. **p. 307,** "Measuring intrafamily conflict and violence: The conflict tactics (CTS) scales" by Murray A. Strauss from *Physical Violence in American Families: Risk Factors and Adaptations to Violence in 8,145 Families*, ed. Murray A. Strauss and Richard J. Gelles, Transaction Publishers (1990). **p. 309,** Excerpt from "Mutual combat and other family violence myths" by R. A. Berk et al. from *The Darker Side of Families: Current Family Violence Research*, ed. David Finkelhor et al, Sage Publications (1983). **p. 309,** Excerpt from "Women who perpetrate intimate partner violence: A review of the literature with recommendations for treatment" by Michelle Carney, Fred Buttell, and Don Dutton from *Aggression and Violent Behavior*, Elsevier (2007). **p. 310,** Excerpt from *Violence Against Women* by

Russell P. Dobash and Rebecca E. Dobash, Sage Publications (1998). **p. 310,** Chan et al., 2008. **p. 314,** Based on *Lenore Walker's Cycle of Violence* by Walker, 1979. **p. 318,** Based on Sherman and Berk, 1984. **p. 320,** Excerpt from "Does batterers' treatment work? A meta-analytic review of domestic violence treatment" by Julia C. Babcock, Charles E. Green, and Chet Robie from *Clinical Psychology Review*, Vol. 23, Elsevier (2004). **p. 320,** Excerpt from "Developing guidelines for domestic violence offenders: What can we learn from related fields and current research?" by D. G. Saunders from *Domestic Violence Offenders: Current Interventions, Research, and Implications for Policies and Standards*, ed. Alan Rosenbaum and R. A. Geffner, Haworth Press (2001). **p. 321,** Excerpt from "The utility of male domestic offender typologies: New directions for research, policy, and practice" by Mary J. Cavanaugh and Richard J. Gelles from *Journal of Interpersonal Violence*, Vol. 20, Sage Publications (2005). **p. 322, 323,** "Stalking victimization in the United States" by Kristina Rose et al. from *Bureau of Justice Statistics*, 2009. **p. 323,** Based on Baum et al., 2009. **p. 330,** Excerpt from The *Criminal Justice and Community Response to Rape* by Joel Epstein and Stacia Langenbahn, DIANE Publishing Company (1994). **p. 334,** Based on "Interview with Ray Knight" by Mark S. Carich from *ATSA Forum*, Vol. 19, No. 2, Association for The Treatment of Sexual Abusers (2007). **p. 339,** Excerpt from "Evolutionary theory and criminal behavior" by Vernon L. Quinsey from *Legal and Criminological Psychology*, John Wiley and Sons, Inc. (2002). **p. 345,** Excerpt from "First report of the collaborative outcome data project on the effectiveness of psychological treatment for sex offenders" by R. Karl Hanson et al. from *Sexual Abuse: A Journal of Research and Treatment*, Vol. 14, Sage Publications (2002). **p. 349,** Based on Diamond, 2008; McLellan, 2006; Yardley, 2002. **p. 352,** Based on data from *Serial Murderers and Their Victims* by Eric W. Hickey, Cengage Learning (2006). **p. 356,** Table from "Human aggression" by Craig A. Anderson and Brad J. Bushman from *Annual Review of Psychology* Vol. 53. Copyright © 2002 by Annual Reviews. www.annual reviews.org. Reproduced with permission.

PHOTO CREDITS

p. 2, AF archive/Alamy **p. 5,** Curt Bartol **p. 17,** Gordon Parks/Library of Congress Prints and Photographs Division [LC-USZC4-4866] **p. 39,** Claire Pelliccia **p. 46,** Mikael Karlsson/Alamy **p. 54,** Spencer Grant/PhotoEdit **p. 57,** Dr. Saul Kassin, Distinguished Professor of Psychology, John Jay College of Criminal Justice **p. 81,** Spencer Grant/PhotoEdit **p. 100,** Angilee Wilkerson **p. 110,** Bill Aron / PhotoEdit **p. 115,** REUTERS/Jodi Hilton/Pool /Landov **p. 142,** Dr. Stephen Ceci, Cornell University **p. 144,** Eduard Kornienko/Reuters /Landov **p. 174,** Joanna Pozzulo **p. 179,** HANDOUT/Reuters /Landov **p. 185,** Courtesy of UIC Photo Services **p. 199,** Robert Tinker/First Light/Alamy **p. 201,** Dr. Henry J. Steadman/Policy Research Associates **p. 211,** Brandon Bourdages/Shutterstock.com **p. 224,** Dr. Francis T. Cullen **p. 240,** Ian Bradshaw/University of Virginia School of Law **p. 238,** MARK Leffingwell/AFP/Newscom **p. 268,** Michael Forster RothBart/University of Wisconsin-Madison **p. 289,** Nancy Honey/Glow Images, Inc. **p. 290,** Dr. Rolf Loeber, University of Pittsburgh **p. 305,** 4634093993/Shutterstock **p. 306,** Dr. Murray A. Straus **p. 334,** Courtesy of Dr. Raymond Knight **p. 341,** Mona Reeder/Dallas Morning News/MCT/Newscom Cover photo, SueC/Shutterstock

CASE INDEX

NAME INDEX

SUBJECT INDEX